The Jewish Apocalyptic Tradition and the Shaping of New Testament Thought

The Jewish Apocalyptic Tradition and the Shaping of New Testament Thought

Benjamin E. Reynolds and Loren T. Stuckenbruck, editors

Fortress Press
Minneapolis

THE JEWISH APOCALYPTIC TRADITION AND THE SHAPING OF NEW TESTAMENT THOUGHT

Cover image: Basrelief from old building depicting Archangel Gabriel ©Jurand/Shutterstock.
Cover design: Laurie Ingram

Hardcover ISBN: 978-1-4514-9266-8
Paperback ISBN: 978-1-5064-2342-5
eBook ISBN: 978-1-5064-2342-5

The paper used in this publication meets the minimum requirements of American National Standard for Information Sciences — Permanence of Paper for Printed Library Materials, ANSI Z329.48-1984.

Manufactured in the U.S.A.

This book was produced using Pressbooks.com, and PDF rendering was done by PrinceXML.

To
Adela Yarbro Collins
in recognition of her contribution to the understanding of early Christianity
in relation to the Jewish apocalyptic tradition

Contents

Preface xi

Abbreviations xiii

Introduction 1
Benjamin E. Reynolds and Loren T. Stuckenbruck

Part I. Jesus and the Gospels

1. Jesus the Revealer and the Revealed *15*
Leslie A. Baynes

2. Apocalypticism, Angels, and Matthew *31*
Kristian Bendoraitis

3. Apocalypse and the Gospel of Mark *53*
Grant Macaskill

4. Angels and Visions in Luke-Acts *79*
Kindalee Pfremmer De Long

5. Apocalyptic Revelation in the Gospel of John *109*
Revealed Cosmology, the Vision of God, and Visionary Showing
Benjamin E. Reynolds

Part II. Paul and the Pauline Letters

6. Paul as an Apocalyptist *131*
Christopher Rowland

7. The Apocalyptic Eschatology of Romans — 155
Creation, Judgment, Resurrection, and Glory
Karina Martin Hogan

8. The Mystery of God's Wisdom, the Parousia of a Messiah, and Visions of Heavenly Paradise — 175
1 and 2 Corinthians in the Context of Jewish Apocalypticism
Matthew Goff

9. A Comparison of Paul's Letter to the Galatians with the Epistle of Enoch — 193
James M. Scott

10. Apocalyptic Thought in the Epistles of Colossians and Ephesians — 219
Benjamin Wold

11. Apocalyptic Thought in Philippians — 233
Angela Standhartinger

12. Paul the Seer and the Apocalyptic Community at Thessalonica — 245
John Byron

13. Apocalypticism in the Pastoral Epistles — 259
Mark Harding

Part III. Hebrews, the Catholic Epistles, and Revelation

14. Heavenly Revelation in the Epistle to the Hebrews — 277
Eric F. Mason

15. James and Apocalyptic Wisdom — 293
Mariam Kamell Kovalishyn

16. Apocalypse and the Epistles of 1, 2 Peter and Jude — 307
Chad Pierce

17. Demonology and Eschatology in the Oppositional Language of the Johannine Epistles and Jewish Apocalyptic Texts — 327
Bennie H. Reynolds, III

18. The Book of Revelation as a Disclosure of Wisdom — 347
Loren T. Stuckenbruck

Contributors *361*
Index of Subjects and Key Terms *365*
Index of Modern Authors *369*

Preface

The present volume developed out of a concern that revelation or the disclosure of heavenly mysteries is rarely considered part of "apocalypticism" within New Testament studies. While New Testament scholars primarily use terms like *apocalypticism* and *apocalyptic* in reference to future eschatology, revelatory features and revealed content, such as cosmology and wisdom, are often neglected. Without making any attempt at a redefinition, we hope that this volume will broaden perspectives on what may be considered "apocalyptic." In addressing each document or series of documents in the New Testament, the contributions of this book consider the ways an essentially revelatory approach to Jewish apocalyptic tradition allows us to see how that tradition has influenced and shaped New Testament thought. In evaluating a number of ways writings in the New Testament reflect the revelatory nature of the "apocalyptic," the chapter authors open up new horizons for future study.

We would like to express our thanks to Neil Elliott for taking on this project, and particularly for his patience. In addition, we would like to thank the rest of team at Fortress Press for their excellent work bringing the volume through to its final stages.

Benjamin E. Reynolds and Loren T. Stuckenbruck

Abbreviations

AB	Anchor Bible
ABRL	Anchor Bible Reference Libary
AcT	*Acta Theologica*
AGJU	Arbeiten zur Geschichte des antiken Judentums und des Urchristentums
AnBib	Analecta biblica
BBR	*Bulletin for Biblical Research*
BECNT	Baker Exegetical Commentary on the New Testament
BETL	Bibliotheca Ephemeridum Theologicarum Lovaniensium
Bib	*Biblica*
BibInt	Biblical Interpretation
BNTC	Black's New Testament Commentary
BTS	Biblical Tools and Studies
BZAW	Beihefte zur Zeitschrift für die alttestamentliche Wissenschaft
BZNW	Beihefte zur Zeitschrift fur die neutestamentliche Wissenschaft
CBET	Contributions to Biblical Exegesis and Theology
CBQ	*Catholic Biblical Quarterly*
CEJL	Commentaries on Early Jewish Literature
CRINT	Compendia Rerum Iudaicarum ad Novum Testamentum
CSEL	Corpus Scriptorum Ecclesiasticorum Latinorum
CurBR	*Currents in Biblical Research*

DCLS	Deuterocanonical and Cognate Literature Studies
DSD	*Dead Sea Discoveries*
ECC	Eerdmans Critical Commentary
ECL	Early Christianity and Its Literature
EJL	Early Judaism and Its Literature
ExpTim	*Expository Times*
FAT	Forschungen zum Alten Testament
FBBS	Facet Books, Biblical Series
FRLANT	Forschungen zur Religion und Literatur des Alten und Neuen Testaments
HBT	*Horizons in Biblical Theology*
Hen	*Henoch*
HNT	Handbuch zum Neuen Testament
HR	*History of Religions*
HTR	*Harvard Theological Review*
HThKNT	Herders Theologischer Kommentar zum Neuen Testament
HTS	Harvard Theological Studies
HvTSt	*Hervormde teologiese studies*
IBC	Interpretation: A Bible Commentary for Teaching and Preaching
ICC	International Critical Commentary
Int	*Interpretation*
JAJSup	Journal of Ancient Judaism Supplements
JBL	*Journal of Biblical Literature*
JCTC	Jewish and Christian Texts in Context and Related Studies
JJS	*Journal of Jewish Studies*
JSJ	*Journal for the Study of Judaism in the Persian, Hellenistic, and Roman Periods*
JSJSup	Supplements to the Journal for the Study of Judaism
JSNT	*Journal for the Study of the New Testament*
JSNTSup	Journal for the Study of the New Testament Supplement Series
JSOTSup	Journal for the Study of the Old Testament Supplement Series
JSPL	*Journal for the Study of Paul and His Letters*
JSPSup	Journal for the Study of the Pseudepigrapha Supplement Series
JTS	*Journal of Theological Studies*

KEK Kritisch-exegetischer Kommentar über das Neue Testament (Meyer-Kommentar)

LCL Loeb Classical Library

LHBOTS Library of Hebrew Bible /Old Testament Studies

LNTS The Library of New Testament Studies

LSTS The Library of Second Temple Studies

MM Moulton, James H., and George Milligan. *The Vocabulary of the Greek Testament.* London, 1930. Repr. Peabody: Hendrickson, 1997

MNTC Moffat New Testament Commentary

NCB New Century Bible

NCT New Century Theology

NHMS Nag Hammadi and Manchiaean Studies

NICNT New International Commentary on the New Testament

NIGTC New International Greek Testament Commentary

NovT *Novum Testamentum*

NovTSup Supplements to Novum Testamentum

NRSV New Revised Standard Version

NTAbh Neutestamentliche Abhandlungen

NTL New Testament Library

NTOA Novum Testamentum et Orbis Antiquus

NTS *New Testament Studies*

ÖTK Ökumenischer Taschenbuch-Kommentar

OTL Old Testament Library

OTP *The Old Testament Pseudepigrapha.* Edited by James H. Charlesworth. 2 vols. New York: Doubleday, 1983, 1985

OtSt *Oudtestamentische Studiën*

Pillar Pillar New Testament Commentary

PSB *Princeton Seminary Bulletin*

RB *Révue biblique*

RBS Resources for Biblical Studies

RevQ *Révue de Qumrân*

RILP Roehampton Institute London Papers

RSB *Religious Studies Bulletin*

SBLDS Society of Biblical Literature Dissertation Series

SBLMS	Society of Biblical Literature Monograph Series
SBLSBS	Society of Biblical Literature Sources for Biblical Study
SBT	Studies in Biblical Theology
ScEs	*Science et Esprit*
SNT	Studien zum Neuen Testament
SNTSMS	Society for New Testament Studies Monograph Series
SP	Sacra Pagina
SR	*Studies in Religion*
SSU	Studia Semitica Upsaliensia
STAC	Studies and Texts in Antiquity and Christianity
StBiblLit	Studies in Biblical Literature
STDJ	Studies on the Texts of the Desert of Judah
SVTP	Studia in Veteris Testamenti Pseudepigrapha
SVTQ	*St. Vladimir's Theological Quarterly*
SymS	Symposium Series
TDNT	*Theological Dictionary of the New Testament.* Edited by Gerhard Kittel and Gerhard Friedrich. Translated by Geoffrey W. Bromiley. 10 vols. Grand Rapids: Eerdmans, 1964–1976
TGST	Testi Gregoriana, Serie Teologia
ThWAT	*Theologisches Wörterbuch zum Alten Testament.* Edited by G. Johannes Botterweck and Helmer Ringgren. Stuttgart: Kohlhammer, 1970–
TSAJ	Texte und Studien zum antiken Judentum
TynBul	*Tyndale Bulletin*
VTSup	Supplements to Vetus Testamentum
WBC	Word Biblical Commentary
WLAW	Wisdom Literature from the Ancient World
WMANT	Wissenschaftliche Monographien zum Alten und Neuen Testament
WUNT	Wissenschaftliche Untersuchungen zum Neuen Testament
ZBK	Zürcher Bibelkommentare
ZNW	*Zeitschrift für die neutestamenliche Wissenschaft und die Kunde der älteren Kirche*
ZTK	*Zeitschrift für Theologie und Kirche*

Introduction

Benjamin E. Reynolds and Loren T. Stuckenbruck

In a frequently repeated statement, Ernst Käsemann famously said that "Apocalyptic was the mother of all Christian theology."[1] Not as well-known is that two years later, Käsemann clarified what he actually meant by "apocalyptic": for him, it referred to "eschatology," or in his words, "the expectation of an imminent Parousia."[2] Similarly, Philipp Vielhauer contended that "the main interest" of apocalypses is "in eschatology. We may therefore designate Apocalyptic as a special expression of the Jewish eschatology. . . ."[3] More recently, in his award-winning and posthumously published monograph on *Apocalypticism and the Bible*, Frederick Murphy treats apocalypticism and eschatology as one and the same.[4] This future-oriented perspective on "apocalyptic" has dominated New Testament studies, and to a lesser extent the study of early Judaism. In this vein, the term "apocalyptic" continues to be used loosely by New Testament scholarship as a reference to future, cataclysmic judgment or to an imminent expectation of the end of time.[5]

1. Ernst Käsemann, "The Beginnings of Christian Theology," in *New Testament Questions of Today*, trans. W. J. Montague, NTL (London: SCM Press, 1969), 82–107 (102).
2. Ernst Käsemann, "On the Subject of Primitive Christian Apocalyptic," in *New Testament Questions of Today*, trans. W. J. Montague, NTL (London: SCM Press, 1969), 108–37 (108n1).
3. Philipp Vielhauer, "Introduction," in *New Testament Apocrypha*, ed. Wilhelm Schneemelcher, trans. R. McL. Wilson, vol. 2 (London: Lutterworth Press, 1965), 581–607 (587).
4. Frederick J. Murphy, *Apocalypticism in the Bible and Its World: A Comprehensive Introduction* (Grand Rapids: Baker Books, 2012). For example, when examining the Dead Sea Scrolls *pesharim*, Murphy states that he will "point out where something specifically eschatological and/or apocalyptic is foretold" (219). And in his discussion of the kingdom of God, Murphy contends: "The 'good news' . . . is that God's kingdom is near. This is an apocalyptic pronouncement. . . . It is not here, but it is close" (292).
5. Cf. Adela Yarbro Collins, "Apocalypticism and Christian Origins," in *The Oxford Handbook of Apocalyptic Literature*, ed. John J. Collins (Oxford: Oxford University Press, 2014), 326–39. In tracing the scholarly history of apocalypticism and Christian origins, Yarbro

Within Jesus scholarship, a continuous source of debate has been the question of whether or not Jesus was an apocalyptic prophet[6] or a non-apocalyptic figure.[7] At stake in this debate, whose language of "apocalyptic" is indebted to Albert Schweitzer,[8] has not so much been the broader Jewish apocalyptic tradition, but more narrowly whether Jesus's proclamation of the kingdom of God was concerned with apocalyptic eschatology. Was Jesus a prophetic figure who announced the coming judgment and end of the world complete with the imagery of fire, angelic beings, and God enthroned on the judgment seat with open books (cf. Dan 7:9–10)? If this was the essential mission of Jesus, then one can argue that he was "apocalyptic"; if not, he was "non-apocalyptic."[9] Similarly, within Pauline scholarship, the question of whether or not Paul proclaimed an "apocalyptic" gospel often centers on the future-oriented perspective of an already-and-not-yet eschatology evident in Paul's letters.[10] Accordingly, Paul's apparent emphasis on the divide between the two ages—the age before the Messiah and the age after his resurrection—has been described as "apocalyptic."[11] However, some scholars have used the term "apocalyptic" to describe Paul's theological perspective[12] or "God's expected eschatological activity" of salvation.[13]

Unsurprisingly, much of New Testament scholarship's understanding and use of "apocalyptic" tends to be uncritical,[14] and at the very least inconsistent,[15] often referring somewhat simplistically to a future-oriented expectation of end-time judgment. Since the books of Daniel and Revelation are the most familiar writings commonly called "apocalypses," a primarily future-

Collins highlights the frequent interchangeability of the terms eschatology and apocalyptic and has paraphrased Käsemann's statement as "apocalypticism is the mother of Christianity" (338).

6. E.g., Dale C. Allison, *Jesus of Nazareth: Millenarian Prophet* (Minneapolis: Fortress, 1998); Bart D. Ehrman, *Jesus: Apocalyptic Prophet of the New Millennium* (Oxford; New York: Oxford University Press, 1999).
7. As, for example, John Dominic Crossan, *The Historical Jesus: The Life of a Mediterranean Jewish Peasant* (San Francisco: HarperSanFrancisco, 1991).
8. Albert Schweitzer, *The Quest of the Historical Jesus: A Critical Study of Its Progress from Reimarus to Wrede*, trans. W. Montgomery (New York: Macmillan, 1964). German original, *Von Reimarus zu Wrede*, 1906.
9. For an extensive examination, see Jörg Frey, "Die Apokalyptik als Herausforderung der neutestamentlichen Wissenschaft. Zum Problem: Jesus und die Apokalyptik," in *Apokalyptik als Herausforderung neutestamentlicher Theologie*, ed. Michael Becker and Markus Öhler, WUNT II/214 (Tübingen: Mohr Siebeck, 2006), 23–94.
10. Martinus C. de Boer, "Paul and Apocalyptic Eschatology," in *The Encyclopedia of Apocalypticism, Volume 1: The Origins of Apocalypticism in Judaism and Christianity*, ed. John J. Collins (New York: Continuum, 1998), 345–83. See esp. James D. G. Dunn, *The Theology of St. Paul the Apostle* (Grand Rapids: Eerdmans, 1998), 461–98, esp. the section on "Eschatological Tension."
11. Cf. Loren T. Stuckenbruck, "Posturing 'Apocalyptic' in Pauline Theology: How much Contrast to Jewish Tradition?," in *The Myth of Rebellious Angels: Studies in Second Temple Judaism and New Testament Texts*, WUNT 335 (Tübingen: Mohr Siebeck, 2014), 240–56, for an overview and critique of this view.
12. J. Louis Martyn, *Galatians: A New Translation with Introduction and Commentary*, AB 33A (New York: Doubleday, 1997); Douglas A. Campbell, *The Deliverance of God: An Apocalyptic Rereading of Justification in Paul* (Grand Rapids: Eerdmans, 2009); Beverly Roberts Gaventa, "'Neither Height Nor Depth': Cosmos and Soteriology in Paul's Letter to the Romans," in *Apocalyptic and the Future of Theology*, ed. J. B. Davis and D. Harink (Eugene, OR: Wipf & Stock, 2012), 183–99.
13. De Boer, "Paul and Apocalyptic Eschatology," 354.
14. Lorenzo DiTommaso, "Apocalypses and Apocalypticism in Antiquity. (Part I)," *CurBR* 5, no. 2 (2007): 235–86 (244), observes that the uncritical use of "apocalyptic" terminology is "most acute among New Testament scholars."
15. For a recent collection that reflects a wide range of approaches, see *Paul and the Apocalyptic Imagination*, eds. Ben C. Blackwell, John K. Goodrich, and Jason Maston (Minneapolis: Fortress Press, 2016).

oriented eschatological understanding of the term "apocalyptic" is understandable. Both these writings describe signs, events, and historical timeframes that will precede the end of the world and final judgment. Daniel and John the seer experience visions and dreams that include events that take place in the near or ultimate future. Regarding one of Daniel's visions, the angel Gabriel tells Daniel, "Understand, O mortal, that the vision is for the time of the end" (8:17).[16] At the conclusion of Daniel's visions of the end, he is told to seal the book until "the time of the end" (12:4, 9). Similarly, in the book of Revelation, John receives the revelation of Jesus Christ, which was given "to show to his servants what must soon take place" (Rev 1:1; cf. 22:6 and 10). John's visions occur after he sees a door open in heaven and a voice says to him, "Come up here, and I will show you what must take place after this" (Rev 4:1). Both of these canonical works contain visions revealed to their human seers that include information about the events and signs that occur before the end. Those events are typically cataclysmic; they are expected to wreak destruction and havoc on humanity, and will result in the reward of those who remain faithful to God and in the judgment and in the punishment of wicked humanity, as well of demonic forms of evil (cf. Dan 8:2–14, 19–26; 9:24–27; 11:2–12:13; Rev 6:1–17; 8:6–9:21; 20:1–15).

Two other Jewish apocalypses generally known among New Testament scholars, 4 Ezra and 2 Baruch, may also perpetuate this future-oriented understanding of "apocalyptic." Fourth Ezra shares many parallels with the book of Revelation,[17] and both 4 Ezra and 2 Baruch make extensive use of Daniel and Danielic imagery.[18] In particular, 4 Ezra refers to Daniel and the vision of the fourth beast (4 Ezra 12:11–13; cf. Dan 7:7–8, 19–27). Moreover, both apocalypses relate events concerned with a coming Messiah (4 Ezra 7:28–29; 12:31–34; 2 Baruch 29:3–30:5; 39:7–40:3; 70:9–73:7)[19] and reinterpret Daniel's "one like a son of man" (Dan 7:13) as the very figure who will bring judgment for the wicked and prosperity for the righteous (4 Ezra 13; 2 Baruch 39:1–40:4; 72:1–6). In addition, 2 Baruch divides history into various periods leading to the final consummation of time in which heaven and earth will return to their state in the beginning, so that *Endzeit* corresponds to *Urzeit* (2 Baruch 54–74; cf. 1 Enoch 93:1–10; 91:11–17).[20]

If Daniel, Revelation, 4 Ezra, and 2 Baruch were the only extant Jewish apocalyptic texts, the use of the adjective "apocalyptic" in the main as a referent to future-oriented eschatology

16. All translations from the NRSV unless otherwise noted.

17. For a focus on such a comparison, see the still important study by Ulrich B. Müller, *Messias und Menschensohn in jüdischen Apokalypsen und in der Offenbarung des Johannes*, SNT 6 (Gütersloh: Gerd Mohn, 1972).

18. On the influence of Daniel on these texts, respectively, cf. Michael E. Stone, *4 Ezra*, Hermeneia (Minneapolis: Augsburg Fortress Press, 1990), 347–49 and 383–85, and Matthias Henze, *Jewish Apocalypticism in Late First Century Israel: Reading* Second Baruch *in Context*, TSAJ 142 (Tübingen: Mohr Siebeck, 2011), 175–76, 268–70, and 309–11.

19. For an overview, see Loren T. Stuckenbruck, "Messianic Ideas in the Apocalyptic and Related Literature of Early Judaism," in *The Messiah in the Old and New Testaments*, ed. Stanley E. Porter (Grand Rapids: Eerdmans, 2007), 90–113.

20. Cf. Matthias Henze, "Time Made Visible: Second Baruch's Eschatology," in *Jewish Apocalypticism in Late First Century Israel*, 253–320, for a nuanced discussion of this evidence.

would—though in need of considerable qualification[21]—be warranted. However, these works are not our only examples of apocalyptic literature, nor are apocalyptic texts, when taken as a whole, primarily concerned with future eschatology. More fundamentally, Christopher Rowland has argued that the heart of Jewish apocalyptic literature consists in the disclosure of hidden knowledge.[22] This essentialist description is rooted in the words "apocalypse" and "apocalyptic" and derives from the Greek word ἀποκάλυψις, which means "revelation" or "unveiling."[23] Rather than eschatology being the centerpiece of Jewish apocalypses, the point of departure, whether in relation to time or space, may have been a matter of hidden mysteries being revealed through mediator figures to human beings.

For example, compared to the writings mentioned above, some of the earliest apocalypses, the Book of the Watchers (1 Enoch 1–36) and the Book of the Luminaries (1 Enoch 72–82),[24] are not overwhelmed by a concern for eschatology.[25] Rather, it could be argued that these two works reflect a particular interest in the revelation of heavenly mysteries.[26] In the Book of the Watchers, Enoch ascends to the heavenly throne room of God (1 Enoch 14) and is also given tours of the cosmos by archangels (chs. 17–36). Most of the Book of the Luminaries is taken up with Enoch's learning of the movements of the sun, moon, and stars. This unveiling of heavenly secrets does not altogether do away with an interest in the end of time or the fate of the dead in the Book of the Watchers and the Book of the Luminaries, since they mention the gathering places of the dead (1 Enoch 22) and "the days of the sinners" (1 Enoch 80:2–8; cf. 72:1), respectively[27]; however, these two works suggest that eschatology is not necessarily a point of departure in apocalyptic writings and that the revelation of heavenly mysteries may, more broadly, be regarded as more central to their content.

The common equation of "apocalyptic" with eschatology often depends upon whether one

21. On 4 Ezra in this respect, see Karina Martin Hogan, *Theologies in Conflict in 4 Ezra: Wisdom, Debate, and Apocalyptic Solution*, JSJSup 130 (Leiden; Boston: Brill, 2008).

22. Christopher Rowland, *The Open Heaven: A Study of Apocalyptic in Judaism and Early Christianity* (London: SPCK, 1982; repr. Eugene, OR: Wipf & Stock, 2002), 14, 49–72; Christopher Rowland and Christopher R. A. Morray-Jones, *The Mystery of God: Early Jewish Mysticism and the New Testament*, CRINT 12 (Leiden; Boston: Brill, 2009), 13–27.

23. Morton Smith, "On the History of *Apocalyptō* and *Apocalypsis*," in *Apocalypticism in the Mediterranean World: Proceedings of the International Colloquium on Apocalypticism, Uppsala, August 12-17, 1979*, ed. David Hellholm (Tübingen: Mohr Siebeck, 1983), 9–20.

24. George W. E. Nickelsburg and James C. VanderKam, *1 Enoch 2: A Commentary on the Book of 1 Enoch, Chapters 37–82*, Hermeneia (Minneapolis: Fortress Press, 2012), 339–45.

25. This should not imply, however, that eschatology is neglected *per se*. Michael E. Stone, "Apocalyptic Literature," in *Jewish Writings of the Second Temple Period: Apocrypha, Pseudepigrapha, Qumran Sectarian Writings, Philo, Josephus*, ed. Michael E. Stone, CRINT 2 (Assen, Netherlands: Van Gorcum, 1984), 383–441, states: "The content and character of these oldest fragments of apocalyptic literature are far from exclusively or even predominantly eschatological" (391).

26. Michael E. Stone, "Lists of Revealed Things in the Apocalyptic Literature," in *Magnalia Dei: The Mighty Acts of God: Essays on the Bible and Archaeology in Memory of G. Ernest Wright*, ed. Frank Moore Cross, Werner E. Lemke, and Patrick D. Miller (Garden City, NY: Doubleday, 1976), 414–52; Rowland, *Open Heaven*, 23–48; Cf. DiTommaso, "Apocalypses and Apocalypticism in Antiquity. (Part I)"; Lorenzo DiTommaso, "Apocalypses and Apocalypticism in Antiquity. (Part II)," *CurBR* 5, no. 3 (2007): 367–432.

27. Nickelsburg and VanderKam, *1 Enoch 2*, 523–29. VanderKam states: "None of these topics figures elsewhere in the Book of the Luminaries" (529).

focuses on the form of apocalypses or on the content of what is revealed in them.[28] If one focuses on form or content, the semantic range of the adjective "apocalyptic" is extended, although in different directions. When scholars emphasize form, they tend to include mystical, mantic, and other revelatory literature.[29] When content is emphasized (i.e., eschatological content), various texts among the Dead Sea Scrolls and other eschatological compositions are described as "apocalyptic" despite the obvious differences of genre. Thus, in his emphasis on form, Rowland has claimed that eschatology is not a "constitutive feature" of apocalyptic literature or apocalypticism.[30] By contrast, Lorenzo DiTommaso, who takes the analysis of content as his starting point, contends that "eschatological matters are frequently the primary but by no means the exclusive subject of apocalypses."[31] Future events are revealed in some apocalyptic literature, but Rowland's critique has highlighted that eschatology need not be considered the main point of departure in the apocalypses, so that a casual equation of "apocalyptic" with "eschatology" cannot be upheld.[32]

One of the challenges to achieving any sort of consensus regarding the use of the term "apocalyptic" is that many New Testament scholars continue not to differentiate between apocalypses (apocalyptic genre), apocalypticism (apocalyptic worldview), and apocalyptic eschatology or regard each of the three as somehow eschatological.[33] Though the expression "apocalyptic eschatology" clearly refers to an eschatological outlook as it occurs in apocalypses, apocalyptic eschatology is primarily understood in New Testament scholarship through the eschatology of the "historical" apocalypses, especially Daniel, Revelation, and 4 Ezra. Apocalypticism as a term should reflect the worldview of the apocalypses in general, but it is almost entirely used as a reference to a worldview shaped by the eschatology of the historical apocalypses, as Klaus Koch's definition of "apocalypticism" has highlighted (dualism, end of the world, etc.).[34]

28. See, John J. Collins, "What Is Apocalyptic Literature?," in *The Oxford Handbook of Apocalyptic Literature*, ed. John J. Collins (Oxford; New York: Oxford University Press, 2014), 1–16 (1–6), who responds to recent criticisms regarding the use of form and content to define the literary genre "apocalypse."

29. See the breadth of material included in Rowland and Morray-Jones, *Mystery of God*; also note the focus on prophetic material in Lester L. Grabbe, "Prophetic and Apocalyptic: Time for New Definitions—and New Thinking," in *Knowing the End from the Beginning: The Prophetic, the Apocalyptic, and Their Relationship*, ed. Lester L. Grabbe and Robert D. Haak, JSPSup 46 (London; New York: T & T Clark International, 2003), 107–33.

30. Rowland, *Open Heaven*, 48.

31. DiTommaso, "Apocalypses and Apocalypticism in Antiquity. (Part I)," 241.

32. Rowland, *Open Heaven*, 71: "Any attempt, therefore, to use the term apocalyptic as a synonym of eschatology must be rejected." *Contra* Murphy, *Apocalypticism*, 7: "although apocalyptic literature demonstrates a wide range of interests, eschatology is always present in some form and is often central."

33. David E. Aune, "Understanding Jewish and Christian Apocalyptic," in *Apocalypticism, Prophecy, and Magic in Early Christianity* (Grand Rapids: Baker Academic, 2008), 1–12.

34. Klaus Koch, *The Rediscovery of Apocalyptic*, trans. Margaret Kohl, SBT 2.22 (London: SCM Press, 1972), 24–30; cf. Murphy, *Apocalypticism*, 8–14; cf. Stone, "Apocalyptic Literature," 393, who speaking of Koch's characteristics, states: "All these features bear upon eschatology."

In *Semeia* 14, John Collins presented the Society of Biblical Literature genre project's definition of the literary genre "apocalypse." This definition considered both form and content of apocalypses,[35] and it has served as a useful starting point for many definitional discussions.[36] According to the definition, apocalypses are narratives in which angelic beings reveal hidden mysteries to humans. The mediated revelation may include both temporal transcendence (i.e., eschatological salvation) and spatial transcendence (i.e., the existence of otherworldly beings and regions) without requiring the preeminence of either. The revelation of temporal transcendence has, more often than not, been emphasized at the expense of the revelation of spatial transcendence. The revealed temporal transcendence as it relates to the consummation of time is a contingent part of many apocalypses, yet it is worth noting that when the *Semeia* 14 definition of apocalypses mentions "eschatology," it does so in terms of "eschatological salvation" or what John Collins has referred to as the "transcendence of death."[37] In other words, the temporal transcendence of the Jewish apocalypses includes the fate of the dead, whether that is the punishment of the wicked or the vindication of the righteous. It answers the question: "What happens to the wicked and the righteous when they die?" Eschatological salvation does not require an end-of-the-world scenario; instead, it may describe the way that apocalyptic literature gives hope to the righteous by looking beyond death (cf. 1 Enoch 22:1–14; 94:6–104:8[38]). Such a temporal transcendence offers hope that the righteous will eventually be saved and their enemies will be punished. Eschatology is common to many apocalypses, but by fixating on Daniel, Revelation, and historical apocalypses, scholars have often inappropriately equated apocalyptic eschatology with the entirety of the Jewish apocalyptic tradition. As Michael Stone has aptly stated in his famous essay over forty years ago, "As long as we remember that by explaining 'apocalyptic eschatology' we have not explained the apocalypses, there is hope for the future of the discussion."[39]

The disclosure of spatial transcendence or "speculative material"[40] is just as relevant as tem-

35. John J. Collins, "Introduction: Toward the Morphology of a Genre," *Semeia* 14 (1979): 9–10. The question of function was intentionally left unmentioned, but it was addressed later by others. See especially, Adela Yarbro Collins, "Introduction: Early Christian Apocalypses," *Semeia* 36 (1986): 1–11.

36. Recent criticism of the definition has come from Carol A. Newsom, "Spying out the Land: A Report from Genology," in *Seeking Out the Wisdom of the Ancients: Essays Offered to Honor Michael V. Fox on the Occasion of His Sixty-Fifth Birthday*, ed. Ronald L. Troxel, Kelvin G. Friebel, and Dennis R. Magary (Winona Lake, IN: Eisenbrauns, 2005), 437–50; and Crispin Fletcher-Louis, "Jewish Apocalyptic and Apocalypticism," in *Handbook for the Study of the Historical Jesus*, vol. 2, 4 vols. (Leiden; Boston: Brill, 2011), 1569–1607; however, the definition remains an important starting point for discussions of "apocalyptic," see DiTommaso, "Apocalypses and Apocalypticism in Antiquity. (Part I)," 241; Todd R. Hanneken, *The Subversion of the Apocalypses in the Book of Jubilees*, EJL 34 (Atlanta: Society of Biblical Literature, 2012); Timothy Jay Johnson, *Now My Eye Sees You: Unveiling an Apocalyptic Job* (Sheffield: Sheffield Phoenix, 2009); Bennie H. Reynolds, III, *Between Symbolism and Realism: The Use of Symbolic and Non-Symbolic Language in Ancient Jewish Apocalypses 333–63 B.C.E.*, JAJSup 8 (Göttingen: Vandenhoeck & Ruprecht, 2011).

37. John J. Collins, "Apocalyptic Eschatology as the Transcendence of Death," *CBQ* 36, no. 1 (January 1, 1974): 21–43.

38. Of course, an end-time scenario is depicted in the Epistle of Enoch (cf. 1 Enoch 100:1–4), but this is not immediately connected with the discussion of the post-mortem existence of the righteous and the wicked (as in 102:1–103:8).

39. Stone, "Lists of Revealed Things," 443.

poral transcendence for understanding Jewish apocalyptic thought, and perhaps even more so.[41] The revelation of otherworldly beings and otherworldly regions draws attention to the revelatory form as well as the spatial content. Angelic beings either come from heaven to earth or they function as guides for humans who have entered heaven. These otherworldly beings reveal knowledge of the heavens and earth, the numbers and types of angels, even the throne room of God. Additional speculative material is included in the "lists of revealed things" found in a number of Jewish apocalypses.[42] The revelation of spatial transcendence is part of the revelation given to a human recipient and should be considered in understanding the Jewish apocalyptic tradition.

An evenly focused understanding of "apocalyptic" as revelation of temporal *and* spatial transcendence opens the possibility for considering the disclosure of the cosmos and of wisdom as "apocalyptic." Wisdom and the revelation of wisdom have long been recognized as contributing, in some way, to Jewish apocalyptic tradition.[43] In the Enochic literature, wisdom constitutes a portion of the revelation given to Enoch which he then passes on to his son Methuselah. In the Book of the Watchers, Enoch is shown the Tree of Wisdom from which the holy ones eat and learn wisdom (1 Enoch 32:1–6).[44] In the Book of the Luminaries, the angel Uriel tells Enoch, "Wisdom I have given to you and to your children and to those who will be our children so that they may give this wisdom which is beyond their thought to their children for generations" (82:2; cf. 5:8). As Randall Argall contends, "The phrase 'to give wisdom' is a technical expression for Enoch's revelation."[45] Enoch, who is referred to as the wisest of humans in the Aramaic Enoch texts (4QEng 1 ii 23; cf. 1 Enoch 92:1),[46] has wisdom revealed to him in all the various texts of 1 Enoch, and, in turn, he reveals that wisdom to others through his own writings (82:1; 83:1; 92:1).[47] In the book of Daniel, the prophet is presented as the recipient of wisdom, a kind of wisdom that is only revealed to the wise (9:22; 12:10).[48] Likewise, 4 Ezra's conclusion concern-

40. Stone, "Apocalyptic Literature," 393–94.

41. Fletcher-Louis, "Jewish Apocalyptic and Apocalypticism," 1578–79, states, "there remain swathes of material in the apocalypses which have nothing to do with eschatology, nor an obviously 'transcendent' kind of eschatology."

42. Stone, "Lists of Revealed Things," 414: "astronomy and meterology, uranography and cosmology, the secrets of nature and Wisdom as well as other aspects of esoterical lore not easily classified in accepted categories."

43. There is, however, less agreement about the nature of that contribution. See Gerhard von Rad, *Old Testament Theology*, 2 vols. (Louisville, KY: Westminster John Knox, 2001); Hans-Peter Müller, "Mantische Weisheit und Apokalyptik," in *Congress Volume: Uppsala 1971*, VTSup 22 (Leiden: Brill, 1972), 268–93; Jonathan Z. Smith, "Wisdom and Apocalyptic," in *Religious Syncretism in Antiquity: Essays in Conversation with Geo Widengren* (Missoula, MT: Scholars Press, 1975), 131–56; Benjamin G. Wright and Lawrence M. Wills, eds., *Conflicted Boundaries in Wisdom And Apocalypticism*, SymS 35 (Atlanta: Society of Biblical Literature, 2005).

44. Randal A. Argall, *1 Enoch and Sirach: A Comparative Literary and Conceptual Analysis of the Themes of Revelation, Creation, and Judgment*, EJL 8 (Atlanta: Scholars, 1995), 33–35.

45. Ibid., 20.

46. Michael A. Knibb, "The Book of Enoch in the Light of the Qumran Wisdom Literature," in *Essays on the Book of Enoch and other early Jewish Texts and Traditions*, SVTP 22 (Leiden; Boston: Brill, 2009), 94.

47. Alex P. Jassen, *Mediating the Divine Prophecy and Revelation in the Dead Sea Scrolls and Second Temple Judaism*, STDJ 68 (Leiden; Boston: Brill, 2007), 265, 268, 269.

48. Ibid., 274–75, notes that the wisdom revealed to Enoch and Daniel "relates to eschatological speculation."

ing the books Ezra is given to dictate suggests that their content is revealed wisdom since 70 of these 94 books are only intended for the wise (14:46).[49]

Revealed cosmology is closely related to wisdom. Information about nature is itself considered wisdom that is revealed (Job 38:1–4; Ps 19:1–2; Sir 1:3; Wis 7:17–21).[50] Stone draws attention to the historical apocalypses 2 Baruch 59 and 4 Ezra 4:5–8, which include speculation on the revelation of natural phenomena.[51] But this revelation of nature only scratches the surface of the revealed cosmologies in the Jewish apocalypses. Throughout the Jewish apocalypses, the movements of the celestial bodies, the realms of the earth, the levels of heaven,[52] the hierarchies of angels and their authorities, and other cosmological wonders are revealed.[53] In the Book of the Watchers, the opening chapters present creation as an example of consistency and describe how creation carries out God's work and obeys his word in contrast to humanity's sinfulness and lack of consistency (1 Enoch 2:1–5:4).[54] Enoch ascends to heaven and sees the heavenly temple (14), and he is taken on a journey and shown various aspects of earth and heaven (17–19[55]; 20–36). Enoch, Levi, and Baruch are figures who experience ascending to heaven and see the mysteries of the heavenly realm. Enoch and Levi even catch glimpses of God (1 Enoch 46–48, 62; Testament of Levi 4–5; 2 Enoch 1–9; 3 Baruch). In 2 Enoch and 3 Baruch, the revealed cosmologies include the levels of heaven and what is contained in them, such as various classes of angels and the rebellious Watchers. Often, as in the Book of the Watchers, naming the angels consists of describing the aspects of creation over which they have authority.[56] Even the symbolic use of numbers in the Jewish apocalypses reveals aspects of cosmology in their description of an ordered cosmos.[57]

If revealed wisdom and revealed cosmology are part of the revelation in the Jewish apocalyptic tradition alongside a revealed consummation of time, why are wisdom and cosmology not likewise considered "apocalyptic"? Since both temporal and spatial transcendence make up what is revealed in the Jewish apocalypses, is it worth considering how the Jewish apocalyptic tradition has shaped New Testament thought with regard to revealed wisdom, revealed

49. See Michael A. Knibb, "Apocalyptic and Wisdom in 4 Ezra," in *Essays on the Book of Enoch and Other Early Jewish Texts and Traditions*, SVTP 22 (Leiden; Boston: Brill, 2009), 271–88, especially 277–80.

50. Martha Himmelfarb, *Ascent to Heaven in Jewish and Christian Apocalypses* (New York; Oxford: Oxford University Press, 1993), 77–91.

51. Stone, "Lists of Revealed Things," 414–21.

52. Adela Yarbro Collins, *Cosmology and Eschatology in Jewish and Christian Apocalypticism*, JSJSup 50 (Leiden; New York: Brill, 1996).

53. See Martinus C. de Boer, *The Defeat of Death: Apocalyptic Eschatology in 1 Corinthians 15 and Romans 5*, JSNTSup 22 (Sheffield: JSOT, 1988), 182, who refers to "cosmological Jewish apocalyptic eschatology" in which the "two ages" are temporal and spatial since "the two ages are fundamentally two confrontational or conflicting spheres of power."

54. Himmelfarb, *Ascent to Heaven*, 77–78.

55. Kelley Coblentz Bautch, *A Study of the Geography of 1 Enoch 17–19: "No One Has Seen What I Have Seen,"* JSJSup 81 (Leiden; Boston: Brill, 2003).

56. Stone, "Lists of Revealed Things"; Himmelfarb, *Ascent to Heaven*, 80–93; Edward Adams, "Graeco-Roman and Ancient Jewish Cosmology," in *Cosmology and New Testament Theology*, ed. Jonathan T. Pennington and Sean M. McDonough, LNTS 355 (London: T & T Clark, 2008), 5–27, esp. 24–26.

57. Yarbro Collins, *Cosmology and Eschatology in Jewish and Christian Apocalypticism*, 110–11, 135.

cosmology, *and* revealed consummation of time? What happens when we reconsider the New Testament's relationship to the revelatory aspect of the Jewish apocalyptic tradition rather than solely apocalyptic eschatology? Might Jesus's statement, "for nothing is covered up (κεκαλυμμένον) that will not be uncovered (ἀποκαλυφθήσεται), and nothing secret that will not become known" (Matt 10:26) reflect the hidden and revelatory essence of Jewish apocalyptic thought? What of Paul's statement that he speaks the wisdom of God that has been hidden in mystery, which was not known to the rulers of this age but was revealed through the Spirit (1 Cor 2:6–10; ἀπεκάλυψεν, 2:7)? Or Paul's own experience of being caught up to the third heaven (2 Cor 12:2–6)? Is the reference to the gospel as "the mystery that has been hidden throughout the ages and generations but has now been revealed (ἐφανερώθη) to his saints" (Col 1:26) indicative of some shaping of early Christian tradition by Jewish apocalyptic thought? It is the placing of these and similar questions in conversation with Jewish apocalyptic writings to which the chapters of the present volume are devoted.

The contributors to this volume have been asked to address the question of whether a revelatory understanding of the Jewish apocalyptic tradition sheds any light on understanding the shaping of New Testament thought. Or said another way, was Käsemann more correct than he knew? Is Jewish apocalyptic thought the mother of early Christianity not merely regarding the resolution of time but also regarding hidden cosmology and wisdom that is revealed to the righteous? This volume's contributors approach the New Testament documents from one or more of three areas of exploration relevant to current scholarship on the Jewish apocalyptic tradition: (1) revealed wisdom, (2) revealed cosmology, and (3) revealed resolution of time. What is striking about the following contributions is the way that comparing New Testament texts with a revelatory understanding of Jewish apocalyptic thought brings new perspectives to light. Texts that have not been traditionally considered "apocalyptic" because they lack an apocalyptic eschatology indicate some shared motifs and features of Jewish apocalyptic thought (e.g., John, Hebrews, and James). On the other hand, texts previously considered "apocalyptic" because of their future-oriented eschatology point to other connections with Jewish apocalyptic tradition. For example, the so-called apocalyptic discourse in the Synoptic Gospels, Mark 13 in particular, is obviously evidence of apocalyptic eschatology, but Mark, Matthew, and Luke also include evidence of revelatory material—angelic appearances, teaching of hidden mysteries in the parables, and cosmological insights. The book of Revelation also intimates revealed wisdom apart from its description of the consummation of time, particularly since wisdom is needed to understand its message (13:18; 17:9). The chapters that follow clearly effect these connections and seek to reverse what has too often been a lopsided perspective in New Testament Studies.

The first set of chapters addresses Jesus and the Gospels. In the first essay on "Jesus the Revealer and the Revealed," Leslie Baynes highlights the concern of the Synoptic Gospels to present Jesus both as the content of revelation and as the revealer of content. Jesus receives heavenly revelation at his baptism and transfiguration, and yet, he also becomes the content of the revelation in these events. Baynes contends that Jesus's parables serve as evidence for his revealing and concealing of heavenly mysteries and that the Synoptic Gospels present Jesus in a way that can be compared to depictions of angelic mediators in the Jewish apocalypses.

Kristian Bendoraitis traces the scholarly discussion of "apocalyptic traits" in Matthew and demonstrates Matthew's interest in angels, as illustrated in the Matthean redaction of received tradition. Bendoraitis contends that Matthew's recognizable emphasis on angelology corresponds to the role of the Son of Man at the judgment, illustrates the presence of God's activity in Jesus's life, and reflects a certain diversity within Matthew's symbolic universe.

Concerning the Gospel of Mark, Grant Macaskill deftly draws attention to the significance of the revelation of heavenly mysteries in the opening narrative of Mark, Jesus's parables, and even the so-called apocalyptic discourse. Macaskill helpfully offers four isolated findings, one of which includes an understanding of Jesus in Mark as both revealer and revealed.

Kindalee Pfremmer De Long surveys the extensive role of angels in Luke-Acts, highlighting how the angels are depicted, including how they function as revealers and the content of what they disclose as divine agents. She also includes discussion of the angels' roles in cosmic warfare and the angelic praise of God. She concludes that the apocalyptic scenes in Luke-Acts not only anticipate eschatological restoration but also underscore a tension between apocalyptic glory and suffering.

Benjamin E. Reynolds maintains that, contrary to scholarly consensus, the Gospel of John should be recognized as representative of Jewish apocalyptic thought, particularly in the Gospel's revealed cosmology, its vision of God in the person of Jesus, and what he describes as "visionary showing."

Adding to his already prolific writing on the subject of Paul and Jewish apocalyptic thought, Christopher Rowland contends that Paul's own visionary experiences shaped the apocalyptic dimensions of his writing. Rowland presses the importance of the "apocalyptic element" in Paul and offers a valuable contribution to the discussion of the "apocalyptic Paul."

Karina Martin Hogan brings her expertise in Second Temple Judaism to Romans and argues that the concepts of creation, resurrection, judgment, and glory in Romans have "unexpected points of contact" with Jewish apocalyptic literature, especially 4 Ezra, 2 Baruch, and some texts from the Dead Sea Scrolls.

Matthew Goff discusses the scholarship on the "apocalyptic Paul" and draws attention to existing problems with this debate in light of contemporary research on Jewish apocalyptic thought. Goff skillfully makes the case that the Corinthian correspondence shares similarities with Jewish apocalyptic texts. Notably, Goff discusses the emphasis on the *parousia* in 1 Corinthians and Paul's ascent to the third heaven in 2 Corinthians.

Since Galatians is often at the heart of the "apocalyptic Paul" debates, James Scott makes a point of avoiding definitions. Instead, he provides an extensive textual comparison between Galatians and the Epistle of Enoch (1 Enoch 92–105) and argues that the resemblances between the texts allow for Galatians to be described as an "apocalyptic" writing.

Benjamin Wold moves beyond the myopic focus on eschatology in the "apocalyptic Paul" debates. Wold notes that Colossians opens with an emphasis on the revelation of mysteries, conflict expressed with dualities, otherworldly features, and future rewards and punishments. He asserts a relationship between the "Colossian heresy" and heavenly ascents. Regarding Ephesians, Wold highlights its evident Jewish apocalyptic thought, noting the apocalyptic themes it shares with Colossians (e.g., revelation and heavenly ascent) and addressing its cosmological portrayal of evil.

Angela Standhartinger maintains that apocalyptic motifs—transformation within the heavenly world, resurrection, and the heavenly book of life—are noticeable throughout Philippians, even though the epistle does not figure into many "apocalyptic Paul" discussions. In comparing Paul to a teacher of wisdom, she makes a case for understanding Paul as an apocalyptic prophet who reveals to the Philippians an apocalyptic hope of heavenly transformation.

John Byron reasons that confining discussions of apocalyptic thought in 1 Thessalonians to 4:13–17 and 5:3–11 (i.e., Paul's eschatology) is too limiting. He contends that in 1 Thessalonians, Paul functions as an apocalyptic seer who discloses to the Thessalonians aspects of heavenly mysteries which are relevant—not for a promised future paradise but for how the Thessalonians live in the present.

In his chapter on the Pastoral Epistles, Mark Harding provides an informative introduction to apocalyptic thought in the New Testament, and especially, in Paul. Harding, arguing against scholarly consensus, asserts that the Pastoral Epistles' revelation of apocalyptic eschatology, use of apocalyptic rhetoric, disclosure of the mystery of faith, and the epiphany of Jesus Christ serve as evidence of Jewish apocalyptic thought in 1 and 2 Timothy and Titus.

Eric F. Mason describes the speech of God in Hebrews as divine revelation. He addresses each place in Hebrews where God speaks. Then Mason concentrates on Hebrews 1:5–14 and maintains that God's proclamation in these verses resembles apocalyptic revelation found in Jewish apocalyptic literature.

Mariam Kamell Kovalishyn admits that while the Epistle of James indicates little evidence of Jewish apocalyptic thought, James does portray wisdom functioning as an intermediary between God and humanity. The epistle is also interested in the division between the righteous and the wicked. These observations contribute to Kovalishyn's argument that James offers an example of "apocalyptic wisdom."

Concerning 1–2 Peter and Jude, Chad Pierce examines the evidence of revealed consummation of time, emphasis on glory, and depiction of angels found in these epistles. He interprets 1 Peter 3:18–22 in relation to apocalyptic fallen angel traditions and contends that 3:18–22 "serves as the fulcrum for the apocalyptic elements of the epistle." With 2 Peter and Jude, Pierce notes the role of revelation in the respective defenses against opposing revelations offered by the false teachers.

Bennie H. Reynolds, III, centers on the manner in which the Johannine epistles use oppositional language to express their demonology and eschatology. He compares 1–3 John's binary rhetorical contrast of truth and lies with that of Jewish apocalyptic texts—1QS; 4QVisions of Amran; 4QCatena; Daniel; Epistles of Enoch. By doing so, Reynolds draws attention to these texts' shared apocalyptic worldview, particularly with respect to their articulation of eschatology and demonology.

Loren Stuckenbruck's contribution on the Book of Revelation takes the use and function of "wisdom" as a point of departure. Stuckenbruck argues that although the term occurs only four times in the work, a close reading of the contexts in which it is found opens up the way for larger portions of the book to be read not only as a disclosure of knowledge but also as a call to interactive discernment of the seer's visions among its recipients.

The findings in these chapters present new horizons in the study of the New Testament and Jewish apocalyptic tradition. The contributors push the boundaries of current discussions concerning the influence of Jewish apocalyptic tradition on the shaping of New Testament thought. As a whole, the contributions also underscore the significance of the fundamentally revelatory nature of the Jewish apocalyptic tradition—a tradition that could both lead to and embrace the rise of the Jesus movement, in all its diversity, during the first century.

PART I

Jesus and the Gospels

1

Jesus the Revealer and the Revealed

Leslie A. Baynes

John's Apocalypse begins with the words Ἀποκάλυψις Ἰησοῦ Χριστοῦ, "the revelation of Jesus Christ," an ambiguous grammatical construction in which Jesus could be either the subject or the object of the prepositional phrase, either the one who unveils or the one who is revealed. It may well be that the ambiguity is purposeful, presenting him simultaneously in both modes.[1] The last book of the New Testament is not the only one that makes Jesus implicitly both the subject and object of revelation, however. The Gospels portray the earthly figure of Jesus in the same way—simultaneously as the revealer and the revealed. From among the Jewish apocalypses, the Gospels quote only Daniel, but they use images and strategies that appear in many other apocalyptic texts in order to reveal the person of Jesus to their audiences.[2]

1. Cf. G. K. Beale, *The Book of Revelation: A Commentary on the Greek Text*, NIGTC (Grand Rapids: Eerdmans, 1999), 183–84.
2. Methodological challenges in the following work include the question of the historical Jesus and the dangers of painting a picture of Jesus from the Gospels as a whole rather than from each evangelist's individual portrait of him. This chapter will take a narrative-critical approach to the material, making little attempt to investigate questions of historicity, and it will restrict itself to the Synoptics, noting significant differences between each of them as they arise.

Jesus as the Recipient of Divine Revelation at His Baptism and Temptation

Apocalypses feature a heavenly figure, usually an angel, who provides access to supernatural phenomena and explains them to the human recipient of the revelation.[3] The Synoptic Gospels even in their most "apocalyptic" moments never become apocalypses in a formal generic sense,[4] but they nonetheless can be seen portraying Jesus as a revealer who takes on the role that the *angelus interpres* plays in an apocalypse, or, somewhat less frequently, as the content of the revelation itself. At the beginning of Jesus's ministry, he is portrayed both as the human recipient of revelation and as its content when, after his baptism, he sees the heavens split open (σχίζω, Mark 1:10).[5] Ezekiel in Ezekiel 1:1, Levi in the Testament of Levi 2, Baruch in 2 Baruch 22, and John in Revelation 4 are also granted such a sight, after which Ezekiel sees the heavenly throne room, Levi and John are invited to go up to heaven, and Baruch enters into conversation with the heavenly voice that speaks to him. Jesus does none of these things; instead, he hears God call him his beloved son, and thus, in addition to being the recipient of the vision,[6] he is, at the same time, its content. The scene bears some small resemblance to the final vision-audition of the Parables of Enoch, where the title character hears God tell him that he is the exalted Son of Man (1 Enoch 71).[7] Although Enoch's vision may be understood as a climax of the Book of Parables, Jesus's introduces his career. From the start, Jesus is presented as a man specially favored by God, on par with classical prophets such as Ezekiel and apocalyptic visionaries such as Levi and Enoch. The fact that he is deemed God's beloved son does not, by itself, greatly differentiate Jesus from other recipients of revelation. Levi, for example, also learns that he will be a son of God in Testament of Levi 4:2, and God calls Abraham "my beloved" in the Apocalypse of Abraham. The meaning of the phrase "son of God" in the Judaism of this time continues to be the topic of lively conversation, but scholars concur on several points: the baptismal

3. John J. Collins, "Introduction: Towards the Morphology of a Genre," *Semeia* 14 (1979): 1–20.

4. While a scholarly consensus has emerged in the last several decades concerning the definition of the literary genre "apocalypse" (cf. Collins, "Introduction"), similar agreement on the definition of the adjective "apocalyptic" remains elusive.

5. Mark uses this verb only one other time in his Gospel, at Jesus's death when the veil of the temple is torn apart. See Dorothy Lee, *Transfiguration*, NCT (London; New York: Continuum, 2004), 29. Matthew and Luke use the more neutral ἀνοίγω.

6. John Paul Heil rightly notes that "vision," "theophany," and "epiphany" are often used imprecisely. He argues that Jesus' baptism is a "vision," at least in Mark and Matthew, whereas the transfiguration scene (see below) is an "epiphany." John Paul Heil, *The Transfiguration of Jesus: Narrative Meaning and Function of Mark 9:2-8, Matt 17:1-8 and Luke 9:28-36*, AnBib 144 (Rome: Editrice Pontificio Istituto Biblico, 2000), 35–42.

7. For more on this passage, see J. C. VanderKam, "Righteous One, Messiah, Chosen One, and Son of Man in 1 Enoch 37–71," in *The Messiah: Documents in Earliest Judaism and Christianity*, ed. James H. Charlesworth (Minneapolis: Fortress, 1992), 169–91. Because the concept "Son of Man" has been exhaustively surveyed in relation to Jewish apocalypses and other literature, we will not expand upon it here. See Gabriele Boccaccini, ed., *Enoch and the Messiah Son of Man: Revisiting the Book of Parables* (Grand Rapids: Eerdmans), 2007.

announcement alludes to Psalm 2:7, where it describes the king; kings are considered sons of God, and by the first century CE, any good person, man or woman, may be a "son of God."[8]

After Jesus's baptism in the Synoptics, the spirit that descended on him like a dove drives him into the wilderness for forty days, where, at least in Q, he fasts before his temptation by Satan. In this period of fasting, he resembles several other human recipients of revelation, first among them Moses, who neither eats nor drinks for his forty days on the mountain with God (Exod 34:28). The apocalyptic Ezra, another Moses figure, fasts for seven days in preparation for his visions (4 Ezra 5:13, 6:31), and heads into the countryside to nourish himself on nothing but wildflowers for the same amount of time (9:23–27). Baruch also fasts in the wilderness for seven days, but unlike Jesus, he does not get hungry (2 Baruch 21:1, cf. 47:2). Perhaps the most notable of these apocalyptic fasting figures in light of Jesus's temptation by Satan is Abraham. Abraham's inaugural encounter with God in the eponymous apocalypse begins with God calling him "my beloved" (9:6).[9] God then asks him to fast for forty days before making his first major sacrifice (Apocalypse of Abraham 9:7, cf. 12:2). As he fasts on Mount Horeb with his sacrifices prepared, an unclean bird swoops down upon them, remarks pointedly on Abraham's hunger, and tries to persuade him to abandon his post before God's fire consumes him. Abraham's angelic companion, Yaoel, informs him that the bird is, in fact, Azazel, evidently assuming that Abraham knows Azazel is one of the chief fallen angels, and as such requires no further description. Yaoel denounces the adversarial demonic bird, exclaiming, "You have no permission to tempt all the righteous!" (Apocalypse of Abraham 13).[10]

Jesus as Revealer and Concealer of Mysteries in Parables

The occasions in the Gospels where Jesus plays the part of the human recipient of revelation are succeeded by his acting in a more commanding role as the supernatural revealer, functioning much like an *angelus interpres*. Following Mark's chronology of Jesus's ministry, we see this first in chapter 4. Jesus tells the parable of the sower and the seed to the crowds, but his puzzled disciples do not understand it and ask him what it means. He says, "To you has been given the secret (μυστήριον)[11] of the kingdom of God, but for those outside, everything is in parables"

8. Adela Yarbro Collins, "Mark and His Readers: The Son of God among Jews," *HTR* 92 (1999): 394–96. "Son of God" has different connotations in the Greco-Roman world; see eadem, "Mark and His Readers: The Son of God among Greeks and Romans," *HTR* 93 (2000): 85–100.

9. Translation of R. Rubinkiewicz, "The Apocalypse of Abraham," in *The Old Testament Pseudepigrapha*, ed. James H. Charlesworth, ABRL (New York: Doubleday, 1983), 1:693. Box prefers "friend" or "lover." G. H. Box, *The Apocalypse of Abraham*, Translations of Early Documents, Series I (London: SPCK, 1919).

10. For more on Azazel and fallen angels, see Annette Yoshiko Reed, *Fallen Angels and the History of Judaism and Christianity: The Reception of Enochic Literature* (Cambridge: Cambridge University Press, 2005); Andrei Orlov, *Dark Mirrors: Azazel and Satanael in Early Jewish Demonology* (Albany: State University of New York Press, 2011); idem, *Selected Studies in the Slavonic Pseudepigrapha* (Leiden/Boston: Brill, 2009), 47–50.

11. Matthew and Luke, "secrets." Raymond Brown, relying on the work of Cerfeaux, notes that the singular may reflect Paul's preferred

(Mark 4:11), and he proceeds to explain it to them allegorically. If the Synoptic evangelists are trustworthy on this point—and it seems likely that they are—Jesus delivered a great deal of his teaching in parables: "With many such parables he spoke the word to them, as they were able to hear it; he didn't speak to them except with a parable, but he explained everything privately (κατ᾽ ἰδίαν) to his own disciples" (Mark 4:33–34). Matthew adds, "This was to fulfill what was spoken by the prophet, 'I will open my mouth in parables; I will declare what has been hidden since the foundation of the world'" (Matt 13:35). "Declare" does not do justice to the connotations of the Greek ἐρεύγομαι, to belch, which suggests an uncontrollable physical urge to speak, an almost visceral compulsion on the part of Jesus to reveal heavenly secrets. These passages introduce several important concepts, including the use of parables both to reveal and conceal, the concept of secret/mystery, and the question of who delivers revelation, who receives it, and why.

Some modern followers of Jesus labor under the misconception that he spoke "everything in parables" because he was a gifted teacher, and he told quaint little stories for the easy edification of his audience. The reality is more complex. In Judaism, a parable is a "varied and capricious genre." Among other things, it can be a pithy saying, often called a "proverb" in English translation, and it can also be a longer, allegorical narrative.[12] Ezekiel 17 and Ezekiel 18:2–3, taken together, conveniently demonstrate these two ways of understanding מָשָׁל/παραβολή. Ezekiel 18:2–3, "The parents have eaten sour grapes, and the children's teeth are set on edge," is an example of a מָשָׁל as proverb. The מָשָׁל of Ezekiel 17, on the other hand, tells an allegorical tale of two eagles and a vine, the meaning of which God must explain to the prophet. It is no accident that Ezekiel 17, which closely resembles the apocalyptic parables we will consider below, places מָשָׁל in poetic parallelism with חִידָה, enigmatic saying or riddle (17:2).[13]

In the tradition of Ezekiel 17, several Jewish apocalypses, including 4 Ezra, 2 Baruch, and the Parables of Enoch, also employ parables as an integral part of their ostensibly revelatory process. For example, the angel Uriel volunteers to show Ezra "the interpretation of a parable,"

usage, while the plural may have been influenced by Qumran's predilection for the plural form of *raz*. See Raymond E. Brown, *The Semitic Background of the Term "Mystery" in the New Testament*, FBBS 21 (Philadelphia: Fortress Press, 1968), 33. For an examination of the extensive use of *raz* and related terms at Qumran, see Samuel I. Thomas, *The "Mysteries" of Qumran: Mystery, Secrecy, and Esotericism in the Dead Sea Scrolls*, EJL 25 (Atlanta: Society of Biblical Literature, 2009).

12. John Drury, "Parable," in *A Dictionary of Biblical Interpretation*, ed. R. J. Coggins and J. L. Houlden (London/Philadelphia: SCM/Fortress Press, 1990), 510.

13. Ezek 17:2, בֶּן־אָדָם חוּד חִידָה וּמְשֹׁל מָשָׁל; LXX Υἱὲ ἀνθρώπου, διήγησαι διήγημα καὶ εἰπὸν παραβολήν. See also Psalms 49 and 78 for the same juxtaposition of "parable" and "riddle." For an opposing view arguing for the clarity of Jesus's parables, see Charles Hedrick, *Many Things in Parables: Jesus and His Modern Critics* (Louisville, KY: Westminster John Knox, 2004), 35. In the Hebrew Scriptures, too, a מָשָׁל may be quite clear, as demonstrated by many proverbs. See Andreas Schüle, "Mashal (מָשָׁל) and the Prophetic 'Parables'," in *Hermeneutik der Gleichnisse Jesu: Methodische Neuansätze zum Verstehen urchristlicher Parabeltexte*, ed. Ruben Zimmermann and Gabi Kern, WUNT 231 (Tübingen: Mohr Siebeck, 2008), 205–16, and Drury, "Parable," 509–11. Adela Yarbro Collins surveys the problems and contradictions inherent in Mark 4's theory of the parables in "The Discourse in Parables in Mark 4," *Hermeneutik der Gleichnisse Jesu*, 521–22.

which is, in fact, a vision of smoke and flame, raindrops and rain (4 Ezra 4:47–50). Ezra does not understand it, so Uriel must explain how the parable illustrates the passing of time. Ezra, like Jesus's disciples who hear the parable of the sower and the seed, cannot grasp its underlying message on his own. He requires personal tutelage from the storyteller. In 4 Ezra 8:1–3, the angel again uses the word "parable," this time referring to a hypothetical conversation with the personified earth (cf. 7:54–56).[14] These examples illustrate the fact that defining the concept of "parable" is not straightforward, and suggest, in addition, that other narratives that do not bear the name may have been understood as parables.[15] A pertinent example of that category is 4 Ezra 8:41, not labeled as a parable in that book, although its counterpart in Mark 4:1–20 is: "For just as the farmer sows many seeds in the ground and plants a multitude of seedlings, and yet not all that have been sown will come up in due season, and not all that were planted will take root; so also those who have been sown in the world will not all be saved." Ezra shows more courage and critical acumen than the disciples of Jesus typically do when he challenges the angel on the implications of this parable:

> If the farmer's seed does not come up, because it has not received your rain in due season, or if it has been ruined by too much rain, it perishes. But people, who have been formed by your hands and are called your own image because they are made like you, and for whose sake you have formed all things—have you also made them like the farmer's seed? Surely not, O Lord above! But spare your people and have mercy on your inheritance, for you have mercy on your own creation (4 Ezra 8:43–45).

Like 4 Ezra 8:41, Baruch's vision of the vine, fountain, and cedar that God explains to him in 2 Baruch 36–39 is not called a parable, but it very likely could have been understood as one. That a vision may be designated as a parable is amply demonstrated in the Parables of Enoch, which is structured in three major sections explicitly called parables (Ge'ez *messālē*). The content of these sections looks much more like visions than the narrative parables that Jesus tells, and indeed the introductory sentence of the book describes what follows as a "vision of wisdom" (37:1).[16] Enoch, like Ezra, Baruch, and Jesus's disciples, cannot understand what he sees, and he requires explanation from a knowledgeable figure. In the Parables of Enoch, as in 4 Ezra, that figure is an angel. For example, after viewing a brief vision of lightning and stars and their names, Enoch asks his *angelus interpres* what these "hidden things" are. He replies, "The Lord of Spirits has shown you a parable concerning them; these are the names of the holy ones who

14. Michael E. Stone, *Fourth Ezra: A Commentary on the Book of Fourth Ezra*, Hermeneia (Minneapolis: Fortress Press, 1990), 261.
15. On the difficulties of defining "parable," especially in an apocalyptic context, see David Suter, "Māšāl in the Similitudes of Enoch," *JBL* 100 (1981): 193–212. Cf. Schüle, "Mashal (מָשָׁל) and the Prophetic 'Parables'," 205–16, and Amos N. Wilder, *The Language of the Gospel: Early Christian Rhetoric* (New York: Harper & Row, 1964), 80–81.
16. For more on the definition and use of "parable" in the context of the Parables of Enoch, see George W. E. Nickelsburg and James C. VanderKam, *1 Enoch 2: A Commentary on the Book of 1 Enoch, Chapters 37-82*, Hermeneia (Minneapolis: Fortress Press, 2012), 92–94.

dwell on the earth and believe in the name of the Lord of Spirits" (43:1–4). Parables and the hidden things of heaven appear together, hand in glove, in these Jewish apocalypses and the portrayal of Jesus's manner of teaching in Mark 4. Even when parables are presented as revelation, as in 4 Ezra and 1 Enoch, they usually require explanation and interpretation.

In the Jewish apocalypses discussed above, the word "parable" emerges only from the mouths of heavenly beings, but in the Synoptic Gospels, it belongs to Jesus. Jesus corresponds to the apocalyptic heavenly figure who narrates and explains parables, and the disciples play the role of the privileged inner circle of human recipients, who in turn act as proxies for the readers of the revelatory text. However revelatory the text may be, Jesus uses parables not only to reveal but also to conceal his message, especially from outsiders, at least as Mark 4 articulates their purpose. As Maxime Hermaniuk writes, "the Christ preaching in parables appears as one who reveals mysteries, and not as one who instructs the multitudes."[17] Mysteries by definition are not easy to understand, and parables, dark and puzzling, require skilled interpretation. Only the wise person "penetrates the subtleties of parables . . . seeks out the hidden meanings of proverbs, and is at home with the obscurities of parables," Ben Sira notes (Sir 39:2–3). The parable is the hard outward shell that protects the kernel within, setting up an ever-present "dialectic of revelation and secrecy."[18] Outsiders hear parables with no explanation and consequently without understanding. Jesus's parables are potentially kerygmatic only to his inner circle, who, he claims, receive the mystery of the kingdom of heaven.[19]

The word *μυστήριον*, mystery or secret, is attributed to Jesus only once in the canonical Gospels, in Mark 4:11 and its parallels.[20] In those passages, the mystery concerns the kingdom of God, the very essence of Jesus's message (cf. Mark 1:15). The Parables of Enoch also links the concepts of mystery and kingdom: "I saw all the secrets (*ḫebu'āt*) of the heavens and how the kingdom is divided" (41:1), but within the larger context of the Parables, the "kingdom" here most likely does not belong to God, but rather to the author's antagonists, the oppressive kings and mighty.[21] In 1 Enoch 52, however, the title character asks the angel about the "hidden things of heaven" that he had seen "in secret," and the angel replies that "All these things that you have seen will be for the authority of his messiah, so that he may be powerful and mighty

17. Maxime Hermaniuk, *La parabole évangélique* (Louvain, 1947), 287–88, as quoted by Wilder, *The Language of the Gospel*, 80n1.

18. Adela Yarbro Collins, "Response to Israel Knohl, Messiahs and Resurrection in 'The Gabriel Revelation,'" in *Hazon Gabriel: New Readings of the Gabriel Revelation*, ed. Matthias Henze, EJL 29 (Atlanta: SBL, 2011), 97.

19. Werner H. Kelber, "Narrative and Disclosure: Mechanisms of Concealing, Revealing, and Reveiling," *Semeia* 43 (1988): 1–20; Robert M. Arida, "Hearing, Receiving and Entering ΤΟ ΜΥΣΤΗΡΙΟΝ/ΤΑ ΜΥΣΤΗΡΙΑ: Patristic Insights Unveiling the *Crux Interpretum* (Isaiah 6:9–10) of the Sower Parable," *SVTQ* 38 (1994): 211–34, esp. 212–15.

20. Outside the Pauline corpus, the word appears in the New Testament only here and in the Apocalypse of John. See Brown, *Semitic Background*, 36–38.

21. Brown, *Semitic Background*, 34, writes that 1 Enoch 41:1 is "a reference to God's kingdom as a mystery, in a context dealing with judgment on man's deeds." George Nickelsburg, on the contrary, compares the usage of "kingdom" in 41:1 to its other two occurrences in 1 Enoch 46:5 and 63:7, both of which refer it to the kings and the mighty (*1 Enoch 2*, 137).

on the earth. . . . Wait a little while, and all the hidden things that surround the Lord of Spirits will be revealed to you" (52:1–5).[22] Jesus echoes this idea when he says that "there is nothing hidden, except to be exposed, and nothing secret, except that it may be revealed" (Mark 4:22). Although Jesus tells his disciples that they have received the secret of the kingdom of God, in fact, they never learn exactly what it is. In their ignorance, the disciples in the first century, and Jesus's followers to this day, could be the "we" of Robert Frost's tiny two-line poem "The Secret Sits:"

> We dance round in a ring and suppose
> But the Secret sits in the middle and knows.

Revelation of secrets or mysteries is the heart of the apocalyptic endeavor, and typically they are divulged only to those deemed wise.[23] Wisdom is elusive; it must be sought; it is a gift from God, and only a few will receive it.[24] As 2 Baruch 48:3 notes, "You do not reveal your secrets to many,"[25] but according to the Wisdom of Solomon, personified Wisdom promises to those who love and seek her, "I will hide no secrets (μυστήρια) from you" (Wis 6:22). In 4 Ezra, the title character learns that only he among humanity is worthy to learn the secrets of the Most High, which he is to write in a book and hide, but is also to teach to the wise of his people, those who are able to keep secrets (12:36–38). In 4 Ezra 14, the wise among Ezra's people are permitted to read the 70 secret books out of the 94 that he received via heavenly inspiration. Those who lack wisdom should not attempt to strive after it. As Ben Sira advises, "Neither seek what is too difficult for you, nor investigate what is beyond your power. Reflect upon what you have been commanded, for what is hidden is not your concern" (3:21–22), an exhortation that may well be a verbal strike against those who read apocalyptic literature such as the Enochic booklets.[26] Daniel thanks the Lord that "he gives wisdom to the wise and knowledge to those who have understanding," so that God may reveal "deep and hidden things" to them (Dan 2:21–22). Daniel's self-deprecating remark about his lack of extraordinary wisdom to King Nebuchadnezzar in Daniel 2:30 also manifests the trope that one must be wise in order to merit special revelation.

22. The concept of being hidden or secret appears in the Parables of Enoch 47 times. Nickelsburg, *1 Enoch 2*, 41.
23. William Adler, "Introduction," in *The Jewish Apocalyptic Heritage in Early Christianity*; ed. William Adler and J. C. VanderKam, CRINT 4 (Assen: Van Gorcum; Minneapolis: Fortress Press, 1996), 13.
24. Markus N. A. Bockmuehl, *Revelation and Mystery in Ancient Judaism and Pauline Christianity*, WUNT II/36 (Tübingen: Mohr Seibeck, 1990), 60–61, 66.
25. Cf. 4 Ezra 5:9–10; 1 Enoch 42. For more about the role of wisdom in 2 Baruch, see Liv Ingebord Lied, "Those Who Know and Those Who Don't: Mystery, Instruction, and Knowledge in *2 Baruch*," in *Mystery and Secrecy in the Nag Hammadi Collection and Other Ancient Literature: Ideas and Practices*, ed. Christian H. Bull, Liv Ingebord Lied, and John D. Turner, NHMS 76 (Leiden: Brill, 2012), 427–46.
26. Benjamin G. Wright III, "Putting the Puzzle Together: Some Suggestions Concerning the Social Location of the Wisdom of Ben Sira," in *Conflicted Boundaries in Wisdom and Apocalypticism*, ed. Lawrence M. Wills and Benjamin G. Wright III, SymS 35 (Atlanta: Scholars, 2005), 100–103.

By way of contrast, in the Synoptic Gospels, Jesus explicitly thwarts the expectation that revelation belongs only to the wise, the worthy, or those who earn the privilege. Instead, it is given to his all too unwise followers, who are likened to infants:

> At that same hour Jesus rejoiced in the Holy Spirit and said, "I thank you, Father, Lord of heaven and earth, because you have hidden (ἀπέκρυψας) these things from the wise and the intelligent and have revealed (ἀπεκάλυψας) them to infants; yes, Father, for such was your gracious will. All things have been handed over to me by my Father; and no one knows who the Son is except the Father, or who the Father is except the Son and anyone to whom the Son chooses to reveal (ἀποκαλύψαι) him" (Luke 10:21–22; cf. Matt 11:25–27).

Verse 21 employs wordplay that defies translation into English: ἀπέκρυψας ταῦτα ἀπὸ σοφῶν καὶ συνετῶν καὶ ἀπεκάλυψας αὐτὰ νηπίοις, further emphasizing the ongoing dialectic dance between "hiding" and "revealing." Here, most importantly, Jesus is the one who reveals the father, an idea that the evangelist John places at the center of his Christology.[27]

This Q passage is both clearer and more apocalyptic when read in its Lukan than in its Matthean context, both in the material that precedes it and that which follows it. In Luke's preceding material, 10:17–20, Jesus welcomes back the seventy disciples who have just returned from their mission of exorcism. They report that even the demons have obeyed them, and Jesus responds, "I saw Satan fall from heaven like lightning . . . but do not rejoice in this, that the spirits submit themselves to you, but rather rejoice that your names are written in heaven." In material unique to this Gospel, Luke's Jesus draws back the curtain on supernatural scenes previously known only to him: first, a vision of the fall of Satan illuminated by the simile of a lightning flash, and then, an allusion to the seventy's names written on the book of life. Heavenly books are a common motif in apocalypses, where they typically are shown to the privileged human recipient of revelation by his *angelus interpres*. Here, Jesus takes on that angelic role, acting as the purveyor of the heavenly books. Luke is the only evangelist of the four to employ this motif.[28]

In the material that follows the Lukan version of the pericope, 10:23–24, Jesus emphasizes its revelatory nature, using forms of the verb "to see" five times, and "to hear" three times: "Blessed are the eyes that see what you see! For I tell you that many prophets and kings desired to see what you see, but did not see it, and to hear what you hear, but did not hear it." It is noteworthy that Jesus says these things to his disciples "privately" (κατ' ἰδίαν), another example of the ongoing tension between secrecy and revelation in the Synoptic Gospels. A slightly different version of this saying appears in Matthew 13:16–17, placed after the quotation of Isaiah on

27. Cf. Benjamin Reynolds, "Apocalypticism in the Gospel of John's Written Revelation of Heavenly Things," *Early Christianity* 4 (2013): 64–95.

28. Leslie Baynes, *The Heavenly Book Motif in Judeo-Christian Apocalypses, 200 B.C.E.–200 C.E.*, JSJSup 152 (Leiden; Boston: Brill, 2012), 138–39.

outsiders' neither seeing nor hearing the meaning of the parables. There, it functions to reiterate the disciples' status as privileged insiders ("blessed are *your* eyes, that they see, and *your* ears, that they hear"), as opposed to Luke's use of it to congratulate them on their part in the fall of Satan. In both Matthean and Lukan contexts, the saying is revelatory, but the latter, by virtue of the inclusion of demons and heavenly writing, is more conventionally apocalyptic.

It is well known that Matthew and Luke often attempted to soften the perceived harshness of Mark's messianic secret by modifying their source material. Many later readers of the Gospels followed suit by devising explanations according to their own lights.[29] By putting Jesus's use of parables and other strategies of revelation and concealment into conversation with early Jewish apocalypses, however, we can observe that Jesus was not unique in sharing enigmatic parables with a small, specially chosen, and usually befuddled audience. Neither was he alone in giving parables allegorical explanations. At the beginning of critical parable study, Adolf Jülicher and his followers argued that those allegorical explanations were constructions of the early church.[30] Doubtless some of them are not original to Jesus, and careful argument on a case-by-case basis would be necessary to demonstrate that others are, but our work here suggests that it would be the most natural thing in the world for a first-century Jewish wisdom teacher with a flair for eschatology to tell parables and interpret them allegorically. Although the way Jesus uses parables in the Gospels may be a literary construction, it is not a construction ex nihilo, but rather one that finds good company in Jewish apocalyptic texts.

Jesus as Revealer and Revealed in the Transfiguration

Jesus offers his followers other glimpses behind the veil, as when he admonishes them, "Take care that you do not despise one of these little ones; for I tell you, in heaven their angels continually see the face of my Father in heaven" (Matt 18:10).[31] Most importantly, however, what Jesus reveals in the Gospels is himself. The premier example of this in the Synoptics is the transfiguration, which Markus Bockmuehl calls an "apocalyptic preview for the saints."[32] In repeating the divine words that proclaim Jesus "my beloved son," the transfiguration hearkens back to Jesus's baptism, and its vision of Jesus's shining face and white garments alludes to traditions long associated with the resurrection and angelic glory.

This most visually arresting appearance of Jesus in the Gospels occurs shortly after Peter proclaims him messiah.[33] In Matthew, Jesus says that flesh and blood have not revealed this fact

29. Cf. Arida, "Hearing, Receiving and Entering ΤΟ ΜΥΣΤΗΡΙΟΝ/ΤΑ ΜΥΣΤΗΡΙΑ," 211–34.

30. Adolf Jülicher, *Die Gleichnisreden Jesu*, 2 vols. (Tübingen: Mohr Siebeck), 1888, 1899.

31. This saying is unique to Matthew.

32. Bockmuehl, *Revelation and Mystery*, 39.

33. In Mark and Matthew, after six days, the amount of time Moses waited before speaking with God on the mountain in Exod 24:16. Luke reads "about eight."

to Peter, but rather his father in heaven (Matt 16:16–17). In all three Gospels, Jesus affirms his messianic identity, swears the disciples to secrecy about it, and gives the first prediction of his passion and resurrection, a disclosure that Werner Kelber argues is the most profound of them all.[34] In describing himself as the suffering Son of Man, Jesus's passion prediction confounds his disciples' understanding of messiahship.[35] Howard Clark Kee writes, "Why suffering is necessary is never explained, but *that* it is necessary to the working-out of God's plan is assumed, as it is generally in apocalyptic literature." As an example, Kee cites the first few chapters of Daniel, where Daniel and his companions' sufferings "are *necessary* to prove their moral merit and demonstrate their fidelity" to God.[36] One might add to this the persecution that precedes the resurrection of the wise in Daniel 12:1–3, who will shine like the sun, the oppression of the elect in the Parables of Enoch 62, who will be clothed in "garments of glory" at the messianic banquet, and the misery of the righteous poor in the Epistle of Enoch 104:1–4, who will enjoy an afterlife shining like stars. Of course, that the concept of resurrection developed in Second Temple Judaism at all was in response to the unavenged persecution of the righteous during their mortal lives, so from a historical rather than a theological or narrative standpoint, the direction of cause and effect is somewhat different than how Kee explains it.[37] Nonetheless, like hiddenness and revelation, the suffering and consequent resurrection and glorification of the righteous go hand in hand in Jewish apocalypses and in the Gospels. Hence a prediction of suffering is followed by a preview of glorification. Only after he predicts the worst, his crucifixion, may Jesus invite his disciples, or at least the privileged trio of Peter, James, and John, to see him at his best on the mount of transfiguration—a paradoxically "secret epiphany"[38] that they must keep to themselves until after he is raised from the dead (Mark 9:9).[39]

The symbolism of mountains was universally well known in the ancient world. Rooted in the

34. Kelber, "Narrative and Disclosure," 13.

35. Jesus's self-designation as Messiah and Son of Man can be illuminated by careful readings of several Jewish apocalypses and other literature, including the Dead Sea Scrolls, the book of Daniel, the Parables of Enoch, the Testament of Levi, the Psalms of Solomon, 4 Ezra, and 2 Baruch. The bibliography that does so is enormous, and for that reason, we will not take on the topic in this chapter, which aims rather to highlight material that has not received quite as much attention in its relation to Jewish apocalyptic texts. Valuable resources that summarize the continuing debate and move the conversation forward include Gabriele Boccaccini, ed., *Enoch and the Messiah Son of Man* (Grand Rapids: Eerdmans), 2007, and Adela Yarbro Collins and John J. Collins, *King and Messiah as Son of God: Divine, Human, and Angelic Figures in Biblical and Related Literature* (Grand Rapids: Eerdmans), 2008.

36. Howard Clark Kee, "The Transfiguration in Mark: Epiphany or Apocalyptic Vision?" in *Understanding the Sacred Text: Essays in Honor of Morton S. Enslin on the Hebrew Bible and Christian Beginnings,* ed. John Reumann (Valley Forge, PA: Judson, 1972), 141, emphasis original.

37. George W. E. Nickelsburg, Jr., *Resurrection, Immortality, and Eternal Life in Intertestamental Judaism,* expanded ed., HTS 56 (Cambridge, MA: Harvard University Press), 2006; Claudia Setzer, *Resurrection of the Body in Early Judaism and Early Christianity: Doctrine, Community, and Self-Definition* (Boston: Brill), 2004.

38. In the words of Martin Dibelius, reported by Rudolf Bultmann in *The Theology of New Testament* (New York: Charles Scribner's Sons, 1951), 1.32.

39. In Mark 9:9 and its parallel passage in Matthew, Jesus charges them not to say anything about the transfiguration until after his resurrection, which verse becomes the *locus classicus* for Wrede's theory of the messianic secret. See Wilhelm Wrede, *The Messianic Secret* (Greenwood, SC: Attic, 1971), 67–68. In Luke 9:36, the narrator suggests that the disciples kept the secret of their own accord. Jesus does not ask them to do so, and there is no mention of the resurrection.

earth, they touch the heavens, and thus they serve as locations par excellence for bridging the gap between humanity and the gods. Levi is on a mountain when he sees the heavens split open and then ascends (Testament of Levi 2:6), and Abraham lays out his sacrifice on a mountain (Apocalypse of Abraham 9:8). The geographic locale of Jesus's transfiguration is not specified, but it brings to mind Mount Sinai in Exodus 24, where Moses received the law, Mount Horeb in 1 Kings 19, where Elijah met God as a still, small voice, and Mount Hermon in 1 Enoch, where the Watchers made landfall, and from which Enoch launched his tour of heaven (1 Enoch 6:5–6; 13:7). Mounts Sinai and Horeb are connected to the transfiguration scene via the presence of Moses and Elijah there, but Enoch is never mentioned, so the connection of the mount of transfiguration to Mount Hermon is more subtle, while no less important. In Matthew and Mark, the last named location before the transfiguration is Caesarea Philippi, where Peter confesses Jesus as messiah (Mark 8:27; Matt 16:13).[40] Caesarea Philippi is nestled on the south side of Mount Hermon, and the area had been known for centuries as a hotspot of divine activity, making it a perfect candidate for the site of Jesus's self-revelation.[41]

Once on the mountain, the disciples see Jesus's appearance change. In all of the Gospels, his clothing becomes bright white, but each one describes it differently:

Mark 9:3 – τὰ ἱμάτια αὐτοῦ ἐγένετο στίλβοντα λευκὰ λίαν οἷα γναφεὺς ἐπὶ τῆς γῆς οὐ δύναται οὕτως λευκᾶναι, his clothes were glistening, very white, such as no fuller on earth could bleach them

Matthew 17:2 – τὰ δὲ ἱμάτια αὐτοῦ ἐγένετο λευκὰ ὡς τὸ φῶς, his clothes became white as light

Luke 9:29 – ὁ ἱματισμὸς αὐτοῦ λευκὸς ἐξαστράπτων,[42] his clothing was flashing white

In addition to his clothes, Matthew and Luke, but not Mark, describe Jesus's face, which Matthew says "shone like the sun." Luke writes that his face "became different," and Luke alone notes that the disciples saw his glory (9:32; cf. John 2:11; 12:28–30). Matthew's version alludes to the face of Moses after he descended from Mount Sinai with the tablets of the law: "Moses did not know that the skin of his face shone because he had been talking with God. When Aaron and all the Israelites saw Moses, the skin of his face was shining, and they were afraid to come near him" (Exod 34:29–30). This Exodus passage is also echoed at Qumran: "I give you thanks, Lord, because you have lightened my face for your covenant. . . . Like perfect dawn you have revealed yourself to me with per[fect] light. . . . Those who walk on the path of your heart have listened

40. Mark places Peter's confession "on the way" to Caesarea Philippi, while Matthew sets it squarely "in the district of Caesarea Philippi." For more on mountain symbolism throughout Matthew, see Simon S. Lee, *Jesus' Transfiguration and the Believers' Transformation: A Study of the Transfiguration and Its Development in Early Christian Writings*, WUNT II/265; Tübingen: Mohr Siebeck, 2009), 41–46. Luke does not set Peter's confession on a mountain (Luke 9:18), but he does place the transfiguration on one.

41. Lee, *Jesus' Transfiguration*, 19n38; George W. Nickelsburg, "Enoch, Levi, and Peter: Recipients of Revelation in Upper Galilee," *JBL* 100 (1981): 582–84; 590–91.

42. The root of this word denotes lightning, an important image in Luke, Matthew, and the Jewish apocalypses.

to me. . . . Through me you have enlightened the face of the Many . . . for you have shown me your wondrous mysteries" (1QH^{a} 12[4]:5–6, 24, 27).[43]

Like "mountain," "light" is a universally recognized symbol. Shining faces and/or white clothing appear frequently in Jewish apocalyptic literature, where they characterize three orders of being: (1) God, (2) angels or other exalted/heavenly figures, or (3) happily resurrected humanity, as opposed to those who are raised to "shame and everlasting contempt (Dan 12:2).[44] Brilliant faces and bright clothing appear together often in these texts, with more imagery added besides—stars, snow, lightning, and glory—that paint the same portrait of glowing or flashing radiance.[45] It is helpful to gather these texts together in one place:

God

- Psalm 104:1–2 The Lord is "clothed with honor and majesty, wrapped in light as with a garment."[46]
- Daniel 7:9 The Ancient of Days' clothes are "white as snow."
- 1 Enoch 14:20–21 God's "raiment was like the appearance of the sun and whiter than much snow, and no angel could enter into his house or behold his face because of the splendor and glory, and no flesh could behold him."

Angels or other exalted figures

- Daniel 10:6 The face of the man in linen is "like lightning."
- Testament of Levi 8:2 In a vision, Levi sees seven men in white clothing.
- Testament of Levi 18:4, 6–7 The eschatological priest will "shine forth like the sun in the earth. . . . The heavens will be opened, and from the temple of glory sanctification will come upon him . . . and the glory of the most High shall burst forth upon him."
- 1 Enoch 87:2, 90:31 Three "white men" lead Enoch in a vision.
- 1 Enoch 71:1 "I saw the sons of the holy angels, and they were stepping on flames of fire; and their garments were white, as were their tunics, and the light of their faces was like snow."
- 1 Enoch 106:2 Newborn Noah's eyes light up his house like the sun, and Lamech is concerned that Noah's father is actually an angel.
- Mark 16:5 The young man next to Jesus's tomb is wearing a white robe.
- Matthew 28:3 The appearance of the angel of the Lord next to Jesus's tomb is "like lightning, and his clothing white as snow."

43. Joel Marcus, *Mark 8–16*, AB 27A (New Haven: Yale University Press, 2009), 634–35.

44. John Collins notes that dualistic ideas of bodily resurrection vs. immortality of the soul are not entirely applicable to this material, and that many philosophers believed souls to consist of some sort of "stuff." John J. Collins, "The Angelic Life," in *Metamorphoses: Resurrection, Body and Transformative Practices in Early Christianity*, ed. Turid Karlsen Seim and Jorunn Økland, Ekstasis 1 (Berlin: Walter de Gruyter, 2009), 291–92.

45. Collins, "Angelic Life," 291–93.

46. Reference cited in Daniel Olson, *Enoch: A New Translation* (N. Richland Hills, TX: Bibal, 2004), 47.

- Luke 24:4 The clothing of the two men next to Jesus's tomb flashes like lightning.
- John 20:11 Two angels in white sit in Jesus's tomb.
- Acts 1:10 Two men in white appear after Jesus's ascension.
- Revelation 1:14–16 One like a son of man with hair and head as white as wool and snow, whose face shines like the sun at full force.
- Revelation 10:1 Another mighty angel with a face like the sun.
- Revelation 19:14 The heavenly cavalry on white horses is dressed in white linen.
- Apocalypse of Zephaniah 6:11 The angel Eremiel's face shines "like the rays of the sun in its glory."
- 4 Ezra 10:25 The woman's face "shone and flashed like lightning" before she turned into a city.

Resurrected humanity

- Daniel 12:2–3 "Many of those who sleep in the dust of the earth shall awake, some to everlasting life, and some to shame and everlasting contempt. Those who are wise shall shine like the brightness of the sky, and those who lead many to righteousness, like the stars forever and ever."
- 1 Enoch 39:7 "All the righteous and chosen were mighty before [the Lord of Spirits] like fiery lights."
- 1 Enoch 62:15–16 "And the righteous and chosen will have arisen from the earth, and have ceased to cast down their faces, and have put on the garment of glory. And this will be your garment, the garment of life from the Lord of Spirits; and your garments will not wear out, and your glory will not fade in the presence of the Lord of Spirits."
- 1 Enoch 104:2 "Take courage, then, for formerly you were worn out by evils and tribulations, but now you will shine like the luminaries of heaven; you will shine and appear, and the portals of heaven will be opened for you."
- 1 Enoch 108:12–15 "Indeed, I will bring forth in shining light those who loved my holy name, and I will seat each one on the throne of his honor, and they will shine for times without number. For righteous is the judgment of God, and to the faithful he shows faithfulness, because they abide in the paths of truth. And the righteous, as they shine, will see those who were born in darkness cast into darkness; and the sinners will cry out and see them shining; and they, for their part, will depart to where the days and times are written for them."
- Matthew 13:43 "The righteous will shine like the sun in the kingdom of their Father."
- Revelation 4:4 The twenty-four elders around the throne are dressed in white robes.
- Revelation 6:11 The souls under the heavenly altar are given white robes.
- Revelation 7:9 The innumerable multitude is dressed in white.
- 4 Ezra 2:39–40 "Those who have departed from the shadow of this age have received glorious garments from the Lord. Take again your full number, O Zion, and close the list of your people who are clothed in white, who have fulfilled the law of the Lord."
- 4 Ezra 7:55, 125 "The faces of those who practiced self-control shall shine more than the stars, but our faces shall be blacker than darkness?"

- 4 Ezra 7:88–91, 97 "Now this is the order of those who have kept the ways of the Most High, when they shall be separated from their mortal body. During the time that they lived in it, they laboriously served the Most High, and withstood danger every hour so that they might keep the law of the Lawgiver perfectly. Therefore this is the teaching concerning them: First of all, they shall see with great joy the glory of him who receives them, for they shall have rest in seven orders. . . . The sixth order, when it is shown them how their face is to shine like the sun, and how they are to be made like the light of the stars, being incorruptible from then on."
- 2 Baruch 51:3, 5, 10 "For the glory of those who proved to be righteous on account of my law, those who possessed intelligence in their life, and those who planted the root of wisdom in their heart—their splendor will then be glorified by transformations, and the shape of their face will be changed into the light of their beauty so that they may acquire and receive the undying world which is promised to them. . . . When [the unrighteous] see that those over whom they are exalted now will be more exalted and glorified than they, then both these and those will be changed, these into the splendor of angels and those into startling visions and horrible shapes. . . . And time will no longer make them older. For they will live in the heights of that world and they will be like the angels and be equal to the stars. And they will be changed into any shape which they wished, from beauty to loveliness, and from light to the splendor of glory."[47]

Most of the references on this list come from Jewish apocalyptic literature. Although the Synoptic evangelists need not have known anything more than Psalm 104, Exodus 24, and Daniel 7 to describe Jesus as they did in the transfiguration, they may also have been aware of some of the traditions represented in the above works, if not the works themselves. Certainly our awareness of these texts opens up new insights on the scene. To observe a small point, Mark's description of Jesus's clothes as "whiter than any fuller on earth could bleach them" stands out as fresh and creative in contrast to the vocabulary the above texts employ. Evidently Matthew and Luke were not amused, however, as both of them rejected his idiosyncratic comparison and reverted to language typical of their predecessors.

Through the list, we can see that the preponderance of references to white clothes and shining faces in early Jewish and Christian literature describes angelic figures and resurrected humanity. Many scholars in the first half of the twentieth century, following Wellhausen, believed that the transfiguration was a misplaced resurrection story[48]—a view that has been rightly and decisively refuted.[49] While rejecting Wellhausen, some later scholars have inter-

47. For more on this passage, see Liv Ingebord Lied, "Recognizing the Righteous Remnant? Resurrection, Recognition, and Eschatological Reversals in *2 Baruch* 47–52," in *Metamorphoses: Resurrection, Body and Transformative Practices in Early Christianity*, ed. Turid Karlsen Seim and Jorunn Økland, Ekstasis 1 (Berlin: Walter de Gruyter, 2009), 313–35, and Eugen J. Pentiuc, "The Nature of Resurrected Bodies: *2 Baruch* and the New Testament," in *Fourth Ezra and Second Baruch: Reconstruction after the Fall*, ed. Matthias Henze and Gabriele Boccaccini, JSJSup 164 (Leiden: Brill, 2013), 309–34.

48. Rudolf Bultmann, for example, takes this idea as a given. Bultmann, *The History of the Synoptic Tradition*, trans. John Marsh, rev. ed. (New York: Harper & Row, 1963), 259–61.

49. C. H. Dodd, "The Appearance of the Risen Christ: An Essay in Form Criticism of the Gospels," in *Studies in the Gospels: Essays in Memory of R. H. Lightfoot*, ed. D. E. Nineham (Oxford: Basil Blackwell, 1955), 9–35; Robert H. Stein, "Is the Transfiguration (Mark 9:2–8) a Misplaced Resurrection Account?" *JBL* 95 (1976): 79–96; Adela Yarbro Collins, *Mark: A Commentary*, Hermeneia (Minneapolis: Fortress Press, 2007), 414–16.

preted it as a proleptic intimation of a resurrection scene, an idea "that is related to, but logically distinct from, the assertion that the story *originated*" as such.[50] Joel Marcus, for example, writes that it is "the first breaker of that eschatological tsunami, Jesus' resurrection," and suggests as evidence for this position the presence of Elijah, who was taken up to heaven and was expected to return at the end of time, and Moses, about whom several ancient authors wrote interesting afterlife tales.[51] In addition, Marcus cites Jesus's command to say nothing about what they have seen until after he is raised from the dead.[52] However, when Jesus actually is raised from the dead, in every Gospel it is the angels next to his empty tomb who are clothed in brilliant white, not he himself. Nor does his face shine. Sometimes his friends do not recognize him in his resurrected state, but this does not seem to be due to any change in his looks.[53] In fact, in all of the canonical Gospels, his risen appearance is altogether ordinary.[54] The transfiguration probably anticipates the general resurrection of the dead, particularly in Matthew (cf. "the righteous will shine like the sun in the kingdom of their father," 13:43), but it may be somewhat less likely to prefigure Jesus's own, since it shares nothing in common with any rendition of it.[55] Alternatively, one may conjecture that the clothes and faces of resurrected humanity (a group to which Jesus belongs, even under Nicene definitions) can shine only in the eschaton, while those of the angels can shine here and now (Mark 16:5, Matt 28:3, Luke 24:4). Although the Kingdom of God is breaking into the world through Jesus's ministry and his passion and resurrection from the dead, the final consummation of the age has not yet arrived.

What, then, is the transfiguration, and what does it reveal about Jesus? In Matthew, Jesus calls it a τὸ ὅραμα, a vision (17:9). But it is not just a vision; it is also an audition that repeats the words heard at Jesus's baptism: "This is my beloved son, with whom I am well pleased; listen to him!" (Matt 17:5).[56] When the disciples in Matthew hear this, they fall on their faces. Jesus touches them, telling them to get up and not to be afraid (cf. Exod 34:30). Here again, Jesus fulfills a function typical of the *angelus interpres*, comforting or reviving the fearful human

50. Marcus, *Mark 8–16*, 637.
51. For a convenient summary of these traditions on Elijah and Moses, see Heil, *The Transfiguration of Jesus*, 100–113.
52. Marcus, *Mark 8–16*, 637.
53. On a related topic, how did Peter recognize Elijah and Moses in an age largely without pictorial representations, especially in the Jewish world? As R. D. Miller writes, "Even on its own terms, the story does not seem plausible" in this regard (as quoted by Lee, *Transfiguration*, 3). In LAB 62:9, Jonathan tells David that their respective souls will know one another after they die, but those two men were friends in their lifetimes, unlike Peter, Elijah, and Moses. The Apocalypse of Peter solves the problem by having Jesus explicitly inform Peter who Elijah and Moses are. More recently, one interpreter writes that they were mutually recognizable because "the saints know each other." Archimandrite Athanasios Mitilinaios, *Revelation: The Seven Seals*, trans. Constantine Zalalas, Vol. 2 (Dunlap, CA: Zoe, 2014), 15.
54. We must separate his resurrected visual appearance from the peculiar properties of his resurrected body, which can both eat solid food and move through solid objects (Luke 24:36–43).
55. Stein, "Is the Transfiguration (Mark 9:2–8) a Misplaced Resurrection Account?" does a particularly fine job laying out the differences between the two narratives.
56. With the exception of "listen to him," Matthew's Greek exactly matches the words spoken at the baptism. The other two Gospels differ from Matthew, each other, and the baptism, Luke more so than Mark.

recipients of a vision, which is often a theophany or angelophany (cf. Dan 8:15–18; 10:1–19; 1 Enoch 60:4; Matt 28:1–5; Luke 1:26–30; 4 Ezra 5:14–15).[57] The closest parallel to this aspect of the Matthean transfiguration is Revelation 1:9–20's picture of Jesus as "one like a son of man"—whose face shines like the sun at full force. John, the human recipient of the vision, falls down before him, and Jesus picks him up, urging him not to be afraid. Loren Stuckenbruck's work has demonstrated how much the Jesus in this scene is portrayed in the manner of an angel.[58] What we have observed in our reading of the transfiguration suggests that Jesus is not only a beloved son of God, but that he may also have been understood as possessing some of the characteristics of an apocalyptic angel, especially in the Gospel of Matthew.

Conclusion

By examining the figure of Jesus in the Synoptic Gospels in light of the Jewish apocalyptic tradition, we see that he appears first as a human recipient of revelation at his baptism and temptation in the wilderness. He then takes on several significant attributes of an *angelus interpres*: he delivers heavenly mysteries to his disciples in parables, and he explains them allegorically; he is the purveyor of heavenly books, a task almost always given to an angel; he appears in a radiant vision dressed in white; in Matthew, his face shines,[59] and he comforts the recipients of the vision by charging them not to be afraid. While several of these angelic characteristics appear in all the Synoptics, a few are unique to certain Gospels, such as Jesus's knowledge of heavenly books in Luke and his comforting of the disciples after the epiphany in Matthew. Finally, in the baptism and transfiguration, he is the content of the revelation, with the latter scene bearing some resemblance to an angelophany. This is not to say that the evangelists believed Jesus was an angel, or that they set about, purposely and with forethought, to present him as such. Jesus is angelomorphic in the Synoptic Gospels, possessing some of the attributes and functions associated with angels in the first century, without ever being explicitly identified as one.[60] Reading the Gospels of Matthew, Mark, and Luke in conjunction with Jewish apocalyptic literature uncovers the fact that the Revelation of John is not the only book of the New Testament to portray Jesus as both revealer and revealed.

57. John J. Collins, *Daniel: A Commentary*, Hermeneia (Minneapolis: Fortress Press, 1993), 375.

58. Loren T. Stuckenbruck, *Angel Veneration and Christology: A Study in Early Judaism and in the Christology of the Apocalypse of John*, WUNT II/70 (Tübingen: Mohr Siebeck, 1995), 209–32.

59. Darrell D. Hannah, *Michael and Christ: Michael Traditions and Angel Christology in Early Christianity*, WUNT II/109 (Tübingen: Mohr Siebeck, 1999), 152, rightly notes that the imagery of "brightness" is not specific to angels; as we have seen, it may apply to God, to other exalted figures who are not angels, and to resurrected humanity.

60. See the definition of Charles A. Gieschen, *Angelomorphic Christology: Antecedents and Early Evidence*, AGJU 42 (Leiden: Brill, 1998), 28.

2

Apocalypticism, Angels, and Matthew

Kristian Bendoraitis

Introduction

Among the canonical Gospels, the book of Matthew is unique in its frequent display of apocalyptic elements. As a result, Matthew has been called both "the apocalyptic gospel" and "the most apocalyptic of all the evangelists."[1] Consequently, this chapter will highlight some of the studies that have contributed to furthering the understanding of apocalypticism in Matthew as well as invite one to see a broader perspective of apocalyptic elements and apocalypticism in the Gospel's narrative. The topic of angels in Matthew will be surveyed as an illustration of the value of apocalypticism for interpretation. The hope is that another voice will be added to the chorus of scholars championing the value of viewing apocalypticism in the New Testament as well as generating further interest in reading this perspective in the Gospel of Matthew.

1. Respectively, Donald A. Hagner, "Apocalyptic Motifs in the Gospel of Matthew: Continuity and Discontinuity," *HBT* 7 (1985): 53–82 (60); and Leopold Sabourin, "Apocalyptic Traits in Matthew's Gospel," *RSB* 3, no. 1 (1983): 19–36 (19); orig. "Traits Apocalyptiques dans L'evangile de Matthieu," *ScEs* 33 (1981): 357–72.

Apocalypses and Apocalypticism

There is occasionally confusion surrounding the terms "apocalyptic" and "apocalypticism" as they evoke thoughts of end-times and modern film depictions of global disasters of epic proportion, likely as a result of the events described in Revelation and Daniel. The concept of an apocalypse as a great and cosmic calamity has the potential to muddle a biblical understanding, yet there is greater depth to what has been called "apocalyptic" that can be found in the study of ancient apocalyptic texts and its related literature. To understand how to discuss apocalypticism and how it relates to Matthew, it is helpful to first clarify some terminology, and then, explain these terms in a little more detail.[2] For this chapter, the noun "apocalypse" refers to a literary work in a specific genre, "apocalypticism" is a worldview, and "apocalyptic" is an adjective that describes elements of an apocalypse, such as its imagery, language, symbols, or eschatology.[3] It will not be argued that Matthew is an apocalypse (even when considering Matthew 24–25), but rather reflects or refracts certain characteristics of the pattern of apocalypticism. Yet, before discussing elements of apocalypticism in the Gospel, a bit more explanation is needed on the definition of an apocalypse and apocalypticism.

One of the significant milestones in the study of apocalypses was the 1979 publication of the findings of the SBL group on apocalypses.[4] Their task was to identify and define the literary genre "apocalypse."[5] Collectively, the members created a working definition of an "apocalypse" by analyzing a determined cluster of characteristics that distinguished apocalypses from other works.[6] While there was a not a clear and unified body of traits or structure that showed up in every apocalypse (or even a perfect example that possessed every trait), they created a genre framework, a "common core" of features that were phenomenologically similar (as opposed to historically related).[7] The core of traits formed their definition of an apocalypse: "a genre of revelatory literature with a narrative framework, in which a revelation is mediated by an otherworldly being to a human recipient, disclosing a transcendent reality which is both temporal, insofar as it envisages eschatological salvation, and spatial insofar as it involves another, supernatural world."[8]

2. Being that this topic will have been introduced in more detail in a previous chapter, only a brief summary will be provided here. Outside this, see John J. Collins, *The Apocalpytic Imagination: An Introduction to Jewish Apocalyptic Literature*, 2nd ed. (Grand Rapids: Eerdmans, 1998), 1–42; Frederick J. Murphy, *Apocalypticism in the Bible and Its World: A Comprehensive Introduction* (Grand Rapids: Baker Academic, 2012), 1–26; Lorenzo DiTommaso, "Apocalpyses and Apocalypticism in Antiquity (Part I)," *CurBR* 5, no. 2 (2007): 235–86; "Apocalpyses and Apocalypticism in Antiquity (Part II)," *CurBR* 5, no. 3 (2007): 367–432.
3. Murphy, *Apocalypticism*, 4–5.
4. John J. Collins, ed., *Apocalypse: The Morphology of a Genre*, *Semeia* 14 (Missoula, MT: Scholars, 1979).
5. John J. Collins, "Introduction: Towards the Morphology of a Genre," *Semeia* 14 (1979): 1–20.
6. Collins, *Apocalyptic Imagination*, 4.
7. Collins, "Morphology," 1; idem, *Apocalyptic Imagination*, 5.
8. Collins, "Morphology," 9. The work of the SBL group is instrumental in advancing the definition of the genre, yet there has been some debate on their definition. DiTommaso, "Apocalpyses I," 242–47; Collins, *Apocalyptic Imagination*, 12–14, 28; Stefan Beyerle,

While a definition of the apocalyptic genre advanced the study of apocalypses, there are texts that possess some of the characteristics and elements of the apocalypses, such as their structure and language, while also differing significantly in other aspects. These differences are enough to place them outside the definition of an apocalypse but also closely enough that warrants examining their family resemblance. More than displaying a similar content to apocalypses, these texts reflect an analogous relationship to apocalypses through their worldview.[9] This perspective, called "apocalypticism," can be understood as the symbolic universe that forms the basis for an apocalyptic movement's interpretation of reality.[10] However, this is more challenging to define than the genre since attested elements are not present in every text and creating an exhaustive list would cast too wide a net, losing focus and meaning to an understanding of apocalypticism. Nevertheless, a list of common elements present may include characteristics such as the unseen spiritual world (including demonology and angelology), the future, divine sovereignty, dualism, dissatisfaction with the present, eschatology, and apocalyptic language. While this list is by no means complete, it gives a means to see the diversity and analogy to the apocalyptic genre.

One element in particular—apocalyptic eschatology—is worth expanding. In the same way that an apocalyptic worldview has been identified in texts that are not considered apocalypses, so too has apocalyptic eschatology. This raises the question of how to define the kind of eschatology found in apocalypses. The end of history is a distinctive of the "historical" type of apocalypse, but apocalyptic eschatology is not identified with the "historical" type only.[11] Moreover, eschatological elements, such as the judgment of the dead or the end of history, are not peculiar only to apocalypses. Thus, the application of apocalyptic eschatology to a text should be reserved for the eschatology found in apocalypses or when it is recognizably similar.[12] While the boundaries of a definition of apocalypticism could be considered nebulous at times, one must take caution not to limit it to its close association with eschatology and perspectives of the end of time.[13] Christopher Rowland's approach to apocalypticism even seeks to move the emphasis from eschatology to an attempt to explain the human condition in a present reality, highlighting the importance of the relationship between heavenly mysteries and contempo-

"Angelic Revelation in Jewish Apocalyptic Literature," in *Angels: The Concept of Celestial Beings - Origins, Development and Reception*, ed. Friedrich V. Reiterer, Tobias Nicklas, and Karin Schöpflin, DCLS (Berlin: Walter de Gruyter, 2007), 205–7.

9. Collins points out the challenges of determining when a movement can suitably be called apocalyptic and that the degree to which apocalypticism is related to apocalypse varies. Collins, *Apocalyptic Imagination*, 13.

10. Ibid.

11. Ibid., 11–12.

12. Collins, "Morphology," 4.

13. Benjamin Reynolds reflects this concern in his article on John. Benjamin E. Reynolds, "Apocalypticism in the Gospel of John's Written Revelation of Heavenly Things," *Early Christianity* 4 (2013): 64–95, esp. 65–66. See also Daniel M. Gurtner, "Interpreting Apocalyptic Symbolism in the Gospel of Matthew," *BBR* 22, no. 4 (2012): 530–31; Christopher Rowland, *The Open Heaven: A Study of Apocalyptic in Judaism and Early Christianity* (London: SPCK, 1982), 71; Murphy, *Apocalypticism*, 8–14.

rary persons and events. Similarly, he argues that the distinguishing feature of apocalypticism is a belief in a direct revelation from God through a dream, vision, or divine intermediary.[14] This does not mean that a broad understanding of apocalypticism is devoid of eschatology, but it does mean that apocalypticism is not always associated with eschatology.[15] In this manner, when examining apocalyptic motifs or elements in a particular book, such as in this case with Matthew, observations need not always give a view toward the eschaton.

Apocalypticism and Matthew

The presence of apocalypticism in the New Testament has not gone unnoticed in the study of Matthew. Each inquiry into the relationship Matthew has with apocalypticism has illustrated that the Gospel of Matthew exhibits a debt to apocalyptic literature and its symbolic universe.[16] Not unlike apocalyptic texts, which use apocalyptic language, symbols, and metaphors to communicate their own ideas, Matthew has customized his language and symbols to fit the needs of his theological narrative within the context of a gospel, a different genre from the apocalypse.[17] The attempts to try and understand and interpret the merging of Matthew and apocalypticism have been the interest of some recent research. Some of the more significant works that highlight this relationship will be reviewed before the discussion continues with specific examples in Matthew.[18]

Prior to the SBL group's publication, P. Hadfield, in a short article published in 1959, argues that Matthew has emphasized apocalyptic teaching in his Gospel. Hadfield's brief survey examines Matthew's editing of his sources (Mark, Q, and his own unique material) and shows how Matthew not only belonged to an apocalyptic school of thought, but also, in some cases, added new apocalyptic meaning to his source material.[19] While Hadfield did not clarify what he meant by an apocalyptic school of thought, he explained that this includes elements of apocalypticism (the belief in angels and rewards for the righteousness) as well as eschatology. Later, in

14. Rowland, *Open Heaven*, 2, 21.
15. Rowland even questions if there can be a particular type of apocalyptic eschatology. Ibid., 28–29; Collins, *Apocalyptic Imagination*, 12.
16. Hagner, "Apocalyptic," 54–57.
17. Ibid., 73; P. Hadfield, "Matthew the Apocalyptic Editor," *London Quarterly and Holborn Review* 184 (1959): 128–32. Examinations of other elements in Matthew's Gospel often incorporate an apocalyptic aspect. For example, Powell's analysis of the plot of Matthew and its portrayal of a cosmic conflict implicitly reflects an apocalyptic perspective. Mark Allan Powell, "The Plot and Subplots of Matthew's Gospel," *NTS* 38 (1992): 198–203. Similarly, Syreeni sees the significance of some of Matthew's language of heaven and earth as indicative of a symbolic universe (one that echoes apocalyptic ideals). Kari Syreeni, "Between Heaven and Earth: On the Structure of Matthew's Symbolic Universe," *JSNT* 40 (1990): 3–13.
18. Due to the limited scope of this study, other important studies on apocalypticism and Matthew are not discussed in detail. These include David E. Orton, *The Understanding Scribe: Matthew and the Apocalyptic Ideal*, JSNTSup 25 (Sheffield: Sheffield Academic, 1989); O. Lamar Cope, "'To the Close of the Age': The Role of Apocalyptic Thought in the Gospel of Matthew," in *Apocalyptic and the New Testament: Essays in Honor of J. Louis Martyn*, ed. Joel Marcus and Marion L. Soards, JSNTSup 24 (Sheffield: Sheffield Academic, 1989); and Günther Bornkamm, "End-Expectation and Church in Matthew," in *Tradition and Interpretation in Matthew*, ed. Günther Bornkamm, Gerhard Barth, and Heinz Joachim Held (Philadelphia: Westminster Press, 1963).
19. Hadfield, "Editor," 128–32.

1981, Leopold Sabourin addressed the apocalyptic elements in Matthew's Gospel, concentrating his focus on evidence of the apocalyptic genre in specifically Matthean material.[20] Sabourin's approach to apocalypticism places the interpretation of history at the center, with the course of history nearing its end and the intervention of God as imminent. As such, Sabourin frequently identifies elements of eschatology within Matthew's apocalypticism. In his analysis, he succinctly examines individual Matthean verses, citing possible related apocalyptic literature. Here, he creates a significant list of references for the study and understanding of an apocalyptic influence.[21] In addition, Sabourin suggests Matthew does not necessarily follow all the patterns of apocalypticism. Citing Jesus's refusal to grant a sign from heaven (Matt 12:38–42; 16:1–4) as an example of transforming apocalyptic ideas, Sabourin argues one should "reread apocalyptic in light of Jesus," not simply interpret Jesus's teachings through the lens of apocalypticism.[22] Similarly, when Jesus announces the kingdom of Heaven is at hand, the focus shifts to Jesus's life and teachings and away from a spectacular display of eschatological events.[23] This transformation of apocalypticism in Matthew, he posits, has consequences for Matthew's delayed expectation of the *parousia* of the Son of Man (which, he argues, Matthew separates from the destruction of Jerusalem), the expected persecution of the church, and the reassurance offered through the portrayal of the Son of Man as universal judge and one who suffers.[24]

A few years later, Donald Hagner offered a more developed analysis of Matthew's apocalyptic motifs, seeking to read them in a "biblical-theological way" within the whole of the Gospel.[25] Noting the developing interest in the sociological basis of the study of apocalypticism, Hagner presents a comparison of Matthew and apocalyptic perspectives with a view toward developing a better understanding of Matthew's sociological setting. Hagner begins with defining how to understand apocalypticism, referring to the distinctions between an apocalypse, apocalyptic eschatology, and apocalypticism. He then proceeds to advocate for an "apocalyptic viewpoint" in Matthew, which, according to Hagner, is a "complex mixture of traits" similar to characteristics of an apocalypse and apocalypticism, but mostly that of apocalyptic eschatology.[26] Hagner's examination of Matthew and the life-setting of its readers is divided into two parts, based on whether the material looks toward the past or the future.[27] After addressing the apocalyptic-like material describing the past in the narrative sections of the Gospel, Hagner examines the

20. Sabourin, "Traits Apocalyptiques"; revised English translation: "Apocalyptic Traits."
21. Afterward, he concludes that 'the apocalyptic interest of Matthew seems to be amply demonstrated.' Sabourin, "Traits," 32.
22. Ibid., 21.
23. Ibid., 32.
24. Ibid., 32–33.
25. He also concludes that in Matthew, "the apocalyptic perspective holds a much more prominent place than in any of the other Gospels." Hagner, "Apocalyptic," 53.
26. Ibid., 56–57.
27. Ibid., 57–60.

"apocalyptic view of the future," concentrating on the words of Jesus in the five discourses.[28] Within his review of the apocalyptic elements, Hagner notices that Matthew not only heightens the apocalyptic language (compared to Mark and Luke),[29] but also expresses both a continuity with apocalypticism, and, as a result of a "newness brought by Christ," a discontinuity as well. Thus, he considers Matthew's apocalypticism an "altered apocalyptic," where Matthew has creatively integrated elements of apocalypticism into his text and portrait of Jesus.[30] As a conclusion, Hagner applies the apocalyptic viewpoint to the Gospel and suggests that it assists in the Gospel's presentation of instruction, endurance in suffering, the faithful state of preparedness, and its exhortation for righteous moral conduct in light of a final reckoning.[31]

David Sim's monograph, *Apocalyptic Eschatology in the Gospel of Matthew,* explores the sociological concept of apocalypticism and offers a comprehensive analysis of apocalyptic eschatology and Matthew in order to understand further the concerns and community of Matthew's Gospel. With this as his objective, he explores why Matthew might have adopted this particular apocalyptic eschatology and suggests Matthew's community was in a time of crisis and used this scheme to aid unity and assurance in the midst of hostile and opposing forces.[32] He begins this endeavor by clearly defining his framework of apocalyptic eschatology in terms of dualism and determinism,[33] and then, examining the nature and extent of apocalyptic eschatology in Matthew.[34] While his focus is on apocalyptic eschatology primarily, Sim's research is valuable in that it demonstrates a developed examination of apocalyptic elements in Matthew.

In a more recent article, Daniel Gurtner examines apocalyptic symbolism in the Gospel of Matthew. Gurtner expresses dissatisfaction with the repeated emphasis on eschatology in research into the apocalyptic elements in Matthew.[35] Instead, he refers to a broader definition of apocalypticism and appeals for greater clarity in analyzing apocalyptic elements in Matthew. With this in mind, Gurtner suggests that a more fruitful way to interpret the apocalyptic elements in Matthew would be through examining apocalyptic "symbolism." By looking at symbols, Gurtner capitalizes on the nature of apocalypticism to use images and descriptive visions in order to relay the heavenly or spiritual aspect of an earthly event.[36] Drawing from research

28. Although his article comments on the discourses, Hagner admits that an apocalyptic viewpoint is not limited to them. Ibid., 68.
29. Ibid., 53–59; Sabourin, "Traits," 22.
30. This is a result of understanding that the coming of the Messiah has changed the present order without also bringing the final consummation. Hagner, "Apocalyptic," 54, 69–73.
31. Ibid., 57–60.
32. David C. Sim, *Apocalyptic Eschatology in the Gospel of Matthew*, SNTSMS 88 (Cambridge: Cambridge University Press, 1996), 181–243; see also Hagner, "Apocalyptic," 57–59.
33. Under this framework, Sim is able to discuss the other characteristics of apocalyptic—namely, the eschatological woes, arrival of a savior, judgment (as well as the fate of righteous and wicked), and the imminence of the end. Sim, *Apocalyptic*, 88, 31–53.
34. Ibid., 75–177.
35. Gurtner, "Symbolism," 528–31.
36. Ibid., 531. David Aune adds "apocalyptic imagery" as a fourth category to the subdivisions in the definition of apocalypticism. David

on Revelation as a guide to identifying apocalyptic symbols, Gurtner is able to successfully show how this method can be helpful to interpret similar types of symbols in Matthew.[37] As an example, Gurtner draws from his research on the rending of the temple veil,[38] demonstrating that the tearing of the veil in Matthew 27:51 is an apocalyptic symbol of the opening of heaven.[39] The virtue of Gurtner's way of linking Matthew and apocalypticism is that it provides a sound methodology for interpretation. He even suggests a number of other texts in Matthew that would together "help contribute to a composite picture of apocalyptic symbolism in Matthew."[40] While Gurtner's focus is on the tearing of the veil, he aptly raises the concept of a composite picture, a proposal that would also have relevance for multiple references to apocalyptic elements within the Gospel traditions. Furthermore, the metaphor displays the complex and blended nature of apocalypticism and the Gospels. To further explore and interpret this relationship, the next section will discuss the apocalyptic presence of angels in Matthew's narrative.

Angels in Matthew

The topic of angels in Matthew is both significant and relevant for two reasons: angels were a common tradition and element in the cosmology of apocalypticism, and second, Matthew demonstrates an elevated interest in angels, as illustrated in the handling and editing of his sources.

Angels as Elements in Apocalypticism and Matthew

When traditions of apocalypticism and its revelation of heavenly mysteries burgeoned in the Second Temple period, they also showed an expansion of a seer's ability to gaze into the heavens and partake of God's glory, his throne room, and heavenly denizens. As heaven's descriptions began to include various levels and elaborate geography, the angelologies in the apocalypses and related literature blossomed.[41] Some have suggested that the development of angelologies is the result of an increasing sense of God's transcendence.[42] Alternatively (or con-

E. Aune, *The New Testament in Its Literary Environment* (Philadelphia: Westminster, 1987), 227. See also Rowland, *Open Heaven*, 58–61; Murphy, *Apocalypticism*, 11–14; and Collins, *Apocalyptic Imagination*, 17–19.

37. Gurtner, "Symbolism," 544.
38. Gurtner, *The Torn Veil: Matthew's Exposition of the Death of Jesus*, SNTSMS 139 (Cambridge: Cambridge University Press, 2007).
39. Gurtner, "Symbolism," 539.
40. In this list, Gurtner includes the transfiguration (Matt 17:1–7), Matthew 24–25, and the four references to "revelation" (Matt 10:26; 11:25, 27; 16:17). Ibid., 535.
41. Rowland, *Open Heaven*, 78–82; see also Harold Barnes Kuhn, "The Angelology of the Non-Canonical Jewish Apocalypses," *JBL* 67, no. 3 (1948); Darrell D. Hannah, *Michael and Christ: Michael Traditions and Angel Christology in Early Christianity*, WUNT II/109 (Tübingen: Mohr Siebeck, 1999), 28–31; and Murphy, *Apocalypticism*, 11.
42. Wilhelm Bousset and Hugo Gressmann, *Die Religion Des Judentums Im Späthellenistischen Zeitalter*, 3rd ed., HNT (Tübingen: Mohr,

currently), the myriad of angels in these traditions may demonstrate the complete control of God and the relativizing of earthly structures to the heavenly realm.[43] In apocalyptic literature, a more developed hierarchy of angels often supplants the council or celestial court in which God was surrounded by heavenly beings (Job 1:6–12; 25:3; Zech 3:1–7; cf. Ps 82).[44] For example, in Daniel and 1 Enoch, multitudes of angels are described as ministering before the Lord (Dan 7:10; 1 Enoch 1:9; 40:1; 60:1–2; 71:7–8; cf. 2 Baruch 59:11; Jude 14; Rev 5:11).[45] Jubilees describes various angels and their functions as being created in what appears to be three categories: angels of the presence, angels of sanctification, and angels over natural phenomena (Jubilees 2:2, cf. 30:18; 1 Enoch 60:16–21; 2 Enoch 14:3, 19:4–5).[46] In addition, angels are one of the mediums through which the disclosure of divine secrets is mediated.[47] Collins even states that the presence of an angel as an interpreter of visions or guide on otherworldly journeys is one of the constant elements in the narrative framework of an apocalypse.[48] For example, an angel can also serve as a guide in an ascent through the heavens (2 Enoch 1:3–10; Testament of Abraham 10–15A, 8–12B; Apocalypse of Abraham 15–18), direct one to untraveled places (1 Enoch 17–36), or explain the significance of dreams and visions (Zech 1–6, Dan 7:16–18; 8:15–16; 4 Ezra).[49] While angels rarely take center stage, they are often considered part of the apocalyptic worldview and cosmology.[50]

With regard to the Gospel, the frequency and consistency with which Matthew has incorporated angels from his sources reveal he is interested in these traditions. For example, Matthew does not omit a single reference to angels from Mark's Gospel,[51] and while there are comparatively few references to angels in the material that appears only in Matthew and Luke (Luke 4:10; cf. further 1:8–2:21), Matthew includes these references (Matt 4:6; cf. also 1:18–2:23)[52] with

1926), 320–31. Russell also includes the influence of foreign thought, including Hellenism and Persian beliefs, upon the developing angelologies. D. S. Russell, *The Method and Message of Jewish Apocalyptic, 200 BC - AD 100*, OTL (London: SCM, 1964), 235, 57–62; ibid., 235; see also Gerhard von Rad, *Old Testament Theology*, 2 vols. (Edinburgh: Oliver and Boyd, 1962), 81.

43. Hurtado is specifically criticizing the claims of Bousset. Larry W. Hurtado, *One God, One Lord: Early Christian Devotion and Ancient Jewish Monotheism* (Philadelphia: Fortress Press, 1988), 24–26.

44. E. Theodore Mullen, *The Divine Council in Canaanite and Early Hebrew Literature* (Chico, CA: Scholars, 1980), 277. Mullen also calls attention to the developing character of Satan in the council texts.

45. Ibid., 275–76. In the Hebrew Bible, there is no evidence of an attempt to systematize a doctrine of angels. Kuhn, "Angelology," 218–19.

46. Russell, *Method*, 241; Hannah, *Michael*, 29. A fourth category of Watchers is added in 1 Enoch (cf. Dan. 4:10, 14, 20). This includes both guardian angels over the nations and fallen angels. Rowland, *Open Heaven*, 90–94.

47. Whereas, in the Hebrew Bible, the prophets speak of the hope of God rising out of the present and working through history, the apocalyptic writers describe the future breaking into the present with divine intervention. It is likely that the visions of prophets in the Hebrew Bible became the raw material for later accounts of visions and heavenly ascents (1 Kgs 22:19–23; Isa 6:1–13; Ezekiel 1). See Rowland, *Open Heaven*, 14, 20, 21.

48. Collins, *Apocalyptic Imagination*, 5.

49. Hannah, *Michael*, 31.

50. It also has been said that angelic beings and their activity 'are one of the most prominent and specific features' within apocalypticism. Beyerle, "Angelic," 205.

51. Mark 1:13; 8:38; 12:25; 13:27, 32; cf. Mark 16:5; and the parallels, respectively, in Matt 4:11; 16:27; 22:30; 24:30; 24:36; cf. Matt 28:2–3.

52. While the Lukan and Matthean infancy narratives do not share a high degree of same level or written similarity, the common ele-

only one exception (Matt 10:32–33).[53] Furthermore, Matthew does more than simply copy these references to angels into his Gospel. Nearly all of Mark's references to angels are adapted by Matthew to reflect his own narrative and theological interests,[54] and on more than one occasion, Matthew introduces additional references to angels that are unique to his Gospel (Matt 13:41, 49; 18:10; 25:31–46; 26:53; 28:2–10). If, after the previous discussion, Matthew's penchant for an "altered apocalyptic" is presumed, it is likely that Matthew not only preserves angel traditions represented in apocalyptic texts, but also adapts them, in order to illustrate the portrait of Jesus, who, as will be suggested, has a place in the cosmological hierarchy. This portrait will be more clearly revealed through examining the references to angels in three categories: the Son of Man and angels, God at work in Jesus's life, and Matthew's cosmology. These three categories also show the collective diversity of apocalyptic references to angels. Not only are there eschatological references, but there is also evidence of a worldview where God's activity regarding Jesus is demonstrated through divine revelation and instruction mediated through angels. While the following references have been categorized for this discussion, they also must be read together within the narrative of Matthew and its expression of the full dimensions of Matthew's altered apocalypticism.

Son of Man and Angels in Matthew

When the references to angels in Matthew are examined, some patterns begin to emerge. One of the more recognizable is Matthew's editing of the relationship between the Son of Man and the angels at the *parousia* and judgment.[55] At the end of the age, the angels that appear with the Son of Man are described as "his," underlining his authority and role as eschatological judge. Moreover, Matthew alone demonstrates this concept like no other Gospel writer.[56] The more readily observed redactional changes to the Son of Man and angels do not suggest that any of the other patterns are less important. All of the apocalyptic threads woven throughout the Gospel are crucial, even if certain characteristics are more clearly visible. Even so, one must start somewhere, and so, the discussion begins with the five passages in which Matthew combines the Son of Man and angels (Matt 13:41, 49; 16:27; 24:30; 25:31).

ments between the birth stories of Matthew and Luke may suggest a common source. Raymond E. Brown, *The Birth of the Messiah: A Commentary on the Infancy Narratives in Matthew and Luke* (New York: Doubleday, 1977), 34–37.

53. In light of the portrait of the Son of Man over the angels, it is likely that Matthew had good reason to change Matt 10:32–33 to portray Jesus standing before the Father in heaven than have his text indicate it was the Son of Man before angels of God (Luke 12:8–9).

54. The only reference to angels that remains significantly unedited is Matt 22:30.

55. For a developed discussion of the Son of Man, see Delbert Burkett, *The Son of Man Debate: A History and Evaluation*, SNTSMS 107 (Cambridge: Cambridge University Press, 1999); Ulrich Luz, "The Son of Man in Matthew: Heavenly Judge or Human Christ," *JSNT* 48 (1992): 3–21.

56. Outside of the Gospels, the same language of Jesus with his angels at the *parousia* appears only in 2 Thessalonians 1:7. In Revelation 1:1 and 22:16, the angel that reveals the revelation to John is referred to as Jesus's angel.

The first references to the angels and the Son of Man are in two uniquely Matthean parables, the Parable of the Weeds (Matt 13:24–30, 36–43) and the Parable of the Net (Matt 13:47–50).[57] In the first of these two parables, Matthew paints a portrait of two fates, with the Son of Man sending his angels to gather up out of his kingdom all causes of sin and evildoers (Matt 13:41).[58] The wicked are bound and tossed into a furnace of fire while the righteous shine as the sun in the kingdom of their father (Matt 13:42–43). In the final parable in the discourse, the Parable of the Net (Matt 13:47–50), angels are portrayed in a similar role, gathering and separating the good (τὰ καλά) and the bad (τὰ σαπρά)[59] caught in a drag-net (Matt 13:48–49).[60] The Parable of the Net echoes the more comprehensive description in the Parable of the Weeds, exhibiting the angels' activity at the judgment as an additional illustration of the consequences of decisions in the present.

In these two parables, the apocalyptic influence seems to be quite bold. The development of apocalypticism and delayed divine retribution reveals a variety of traditions in which angels are depicted as gathering, separating, and punishing. For example, the Book of Watchers (1 Enoch 1–36) illustrates a world under divine control portrayed through the agency of angels, obediently gathering and binding the wicked (1 Enoch 1:9; 10:4–20; cf. also 1 Enoch 38; 45; 53:3–4; 54:2; 56; 88; 90:21–24; 1QS 4:12–13; CD 2:5–6; Testament of Abraham A 12:1–18; 13:9–14). In the same manner, the Epistle of Enoch, in reference to the final judgment, describes angels descending "to the hidden places to gather into one place all those who have given aid to sin," (1 Enoch 100:4).[61] Angels are also pictured in apocalyptic visions of the judgment, acting as recorders and those exacting punishments, guaranteeing that the sins of the wicked will not go unpunished (1 Enoch 41:1; 61:8; 89:59–63; 90:20; 99:3; 100:10; Apocalypse of Zephaniah).[62] In the dramatic event portrayed in the parables' explanations, the image of the Son of Man sending

57. While there are similarities with the Gospel of Thomas (Gos. Thom. 8, 57; cf. Wis 4:3; 4 Ezra 4:28–32; 2 Baruch 70:2; Mark 4:26–29), it has also been argued that these parables are the creation of Matthew. David C. Sim, "Angels of Eschatological Punishment in the Jewish and Christian Apocalyptic Traditions and in the Gospel of Matthew," *HvTSt* 55 (1999): 693–718 (710); W. D. Davies and Dale C. Allison, *The Gospel According to Saint Matthew*, 3 vols., ICC (Edinburgh: T&T Clark, 1988), 2:426–27; Daniel J. Harrington, S.J., *The Gospel of Matthew*, SP (Collegeville, MN: Liturgical Press, 1991), 206–7; Robert H. Gundry, *Matthew: A Commentary on His Literary and Theological Art* (Grand Rapids: Eerdmans, 1982), 271–74, 79–80. Skeptical of this conclusion, Hagner argues that it could be derived from Matthew's own source or own creative composition. Donald A. Hagner, *Matthew*, 2 vols., WBC 33A, 33B (Waco: Word, 1993), 1:392.

58. There are other apocalyptic elements in the explanation of the Parables of the Weeds, including the element of the furnace of fire (LXX Dan 3:6; cf. Isa 66:24; Ezek 38:22; Mal 4:1; 1 Enoch 10:6; 18:15; 21:3–6,7–10; cf. 1 Enoch 90:24–25; 91:9; 108:3–5; 54:1–2, 6; Judith 16:17; Sir 21:9; Jubilees 9:15; 1QpHab x 5,13; 1QS 2:8–9, 15; Psalms Solomon 15:4–5; Sibylline Oracles 2.303–5; 3.53–54; 672–674; 4.159–161; 4 Ezra 7:35–38; 13:10–11; 2 Baruch 44:15; 48:39; 59:2; 3 Baruch 4:16), the Matthean catchphrase, "weeping and gnashing of teeth," (Matt 13:42, 50; 22:13; 24:51; 25:30; cf. 1 Enoch 98:3; 102:1; 103:8; 108:5–6), and the righteous, shining like the sun (Dan 12:3; cf. 1 Enoch 104). Loren T. Stuckenbruck, *1 Enoch 91-108*, CEJL (Berlin: Walter de Gruyter, 2007), 453.

59. "Fish" are never mentioned, only implied by use of the net.

60. The Son of Man is not explicitly mentioned, only implied.

61. Stuckenbruck, *1 Enoch*, 434.

62. In Revelation 7:1–4, the angels put God's seal on the mark of the righteous to protect them, and in Revelation 9:1–6, angels torture all those without the seal. Although there is no mention of angels at the judgment, Revelation 14 describes "one like a son of man" with a sickle, who harvests the earth. And yet, the binding of Satan with a great chain is performed by one of God's angels.

(ἀποστέλλω) his angels on this task into his kingdom portrays the Son of Man as the eschatological judge supported by his angels at the final judgment, who gather and execute punishment at the direction of the Son of Man. In this manner, the use of the pronoun "his" is not so much about possession, but about command.[63]

Unlike the two parables in Matthew 13, the angelic activity mentioned in Jesus's teaching following Peter's confession at Caesarea is described with less detail (Matt 16:27). Nevertheless, when one considers the individual references to angels within the larger framework, the "image" created with these references contributes to the greater picture and reveals a more cohesive portrait. Thus, in a way, Matthew 16:24–27 explains more of the expectations placed on the disciples in the parables in Matthew 13—namely, self-denial and discipleship are tested when the Son of Man comes in the glory of his Father with his angels, rendering to each according to how they have lived their lives (Matt 16:27). Matthew's redactional hand in this Markan passage (Mark 8:34–38) elevates the emphasis on the coming of the Son of Man and his role as judge. Not only does Matthew's text indicate the angels are the Son of Man's,[64] but his editing underlines the eschatological element of discipleship in this passages which focuses on the suffering of the disciples as they follow Jesus (Matt 16:24–26) and the repayment of one's deeds (Matt 16:27).[65] Evocative of the missionary discourse in Matthew 10 and the eschatological discourse in Matthew 24–25, Matthew describes suffering, persecution, and sacrifice as a result of choosing to follow Jesus. Here, Matthew illumines the eschatological values and reversal through his portrait of the coming of the Son of Man. Situated between the first passion prediction and the transfiguration's foreshadowing of Jesus's future glory (Matt 16:21; 17:1–8), Matthew indicates that a disciple's own suffering and glory is bound to Jesus, the Son of Man. The very one who suffers on the cross and whom the disciples are asked to follow (Matt 16:24) is also the one who commands an accompanying heavenly host at the close of the age (Matt 16:27; 13:41, 49; 24:30; 25:31–46). This is significant for Matthew 16:13–28 because Matthew draws together both the suffering and the exaltation of the Son of Man.[66] The exaltation of

63. Daniel Marguerat, *Le Jugement Dans L'evangile De Matthieu*, 2nd ed., Le Monde de la Bible (Geneva: Labor et Fides, 1995), 80.

64. This is in contrast to Mark's description of the Son of Man coming, "in the glory of his Father with the holy angels" (Mark 8:38; cf. Luke 9:26).

65. Ulrich Luz, *Matthew 8–20: A Commentary*, Hermeneia (Minneapolis: Fortress Press, 2001), 380–81; David Hill, *The Gospel of Matthew*, NCB (London: Oliphants, 1972), 265; Hagner, *Matthew*, 1:484. Consider also Gundry's comments, "In quick succession the first evangelist has written about the Father of the Son of Man, the angels of the Son of Man, and the kingdom of the Son of Man—a Christological emphasis is hard to overestimate." Gundry, *Matthew*, 340–41.

66. Often, the different sayings regarding the Son of Man are divided into three separate groups: those that refer to Jesus's present ministry, to his suffering, and to his future eschatological state. Rudolf Bultmann, *Theology of the New Testament*, 2 vols. (London: SCM, 1952), 1:30. Chrys C. Caragounis, *The Son of Man: Vision and Interpretation*, WUNT 38 (Tübingen: Mohr Siebeck, 1986), 145–47. Hooker notes that the final category also demonstrates most development between the Gospels. Morna D. Hooker, "The Son of Man and the Synoptic Problem," in *The Four Gospels: 1992 Festschrift Frans Neirynck*, 2 vols., ed. F. Van Segbroeck, et al., BETL 100 (Leuven: Leuven University Press, 1992), 1:195. In contrast, Maddox questions these categories and suggests that a better approach is to investigate what the evangelists meant, rather than what Jesus might have said. He then proceeds to explain every Son of Man passage through the lens of the Son of Man as eschatological judge. Robert Maddox, "The Function of the Son of Man According to

the Son of Man with angels seems to place an emphasis on the resurrected Jesus that can be read back into an understanding of the earthly Jesus. As a result, the two—the resurrected and earthly Jesus—need not be held in tension chronologically since Matthew's understanding of the earthly Jesus can be seen through the lens of the post-Easter Jesus. Thus, Matthew holds the suffering in tension with the exaltation so that the glorified Christ is in view on the cross and in a disciple's choice to follow Jesus.[67] This is all the more clear when the whole Gospel narrative is considered.

In the eschatological discourse (Matt 24:3–25:46), Matthew paints a picture of the arrival of the Son of Man at the end of the age. For Matthew, there is no mistaking his arrival. The sun will be darkened, the stars will fall from heaven, and the sign of the Son of Man will appear in heaven (Matt 24:29–31). Then, everyone will see the Son of Man coming on clouds of heaven with power and great glory (Matt 24:30). The fanfare will be accompanied by the sending out of his angels with a loud trumpet call to gather the elect.[68] The portrayal of the Son of Man and the angels is very much like what has been seen in the previous references (Matt 13:41, 49; 16:27)—namely, the angels are again described uniquely as "his angels" (unlike Mark 13:27 and Luke 21:27). Once more, Matthew has decided to demonstrate the authority of the Son of Man with his entourage of angels. Furthermore, the angels are commanded by the Son of Man and as such are sent out to collect the righteous. In the midst of the latter's trials and suffering, the coming of the Son of Man is a sign of rescue. Similar to Matthew 16:24–28, one's present relationship to Jesus, the Son of Man, is one that has eschatological consequences (cf. Matt 10:32–33).

Finally, at the end of the eschatological discourse, the portrait of the Son of Man and angels reaches its zenith in the Matthean description of the final judgment, sometimes referred to as the Parable of the Sheep and the Goats (Matt 25:31–46).[69] This scene is introduced with more majesty and celestial pomp than any of the other preceding passages: "When the Son of Man comes in *his* glory, and *all* the angels with him, then he will sit on *his* glorious throne" (Matt 25:31).[70] It is as if Matthew had built up this motif throughout his narrative so that at this point, he could describe the entire population of heaven attending to and being commanded by the Son of Man as he sits on his throne. Now, in this final passage before the passion narrative, the

the Synoptic Gospels," *NTS* 15 (1968): 46–47. Luz takes a similar approach, but argues the categories relate to each other, emphasizing the contrast between a suffering and exalted Son of Man. Luz, "Judge."

67. Luz, "Judge," 9.

68. Matthew once again describes the angels as those of the Son of Man ("his") and adds the reference to the trumpet, a signal traditionally associated with holy war, a theophany, or the close of the age (Joel 2:1; Zeph 1:16; Isa 27:13; 4 Ezra 6:23; 1 Thess 4:16; 1 Cor 15:52; Rev 8:2; LAE 22:1). See Gerhard Friedrich, "σάλπιγξ," in *Theological Dictionary of the New Testament*, ed. Gerhard Kittel, Geoffrey William Bromiley, and Gerhard Friedrich (Grand Rapids: Eerdmans, 1964), 7:78–84.

69. Snodgrass argues that this is a misnomer, being that it is not a parable. Klyne Snodgrass, *Stories with Intent: A Comprehensive Guide to the Parables of Jesus* (Grand Rapids: Eerdmans, 2008), 543.

70. Emphasis added.

glory of Jesus sits in tangible tension with the suffering and darkness that accompanies Jesus's death.[71] Moreover, Matthew gives the reader heavenly and future insight into the present situation. Not only does it give a revelatory context to the arrest, trial, and crucifixion, but it suggests that the suffering expected of the disciples also is experienced by a suffering messiah (Matt 16:24–27).

More than simply using apocalyptic judgment to offer hope to the righteous, Matthew uses the final assize to direct the behavior of the disciples. In light of this, Lamar Cope states, "The author is far more concerned with the coming judgment as a testing point of the followers of Jesus than he is with it as punishment for enemies or as punishment for unbelievers."[72] Matthew also encourages discipleship built not only upon the awareness of an eschatological judgment, but also upon other foundational elements such as forgiveness (Matt 18; 22:34–40), faith (Matt 8:10–13; 9:2, 22; 15:28; 17:20; 21:21–22; 23:23; 24:45), mercy (Matt 9:15–17; 12:1–8, cf. 23:23), self-denial (Matt 10:32–33; 16:27–29), and love (Matt 22:37–40). The life that is lived and the actions that represent it flow and grow out of one's character.[73] Throughout his Gospel, Matthew emphasizes Jesus's teaching the disciples to be distinct in their fruitful faithfulness (Matt 12:33–37; 13:23; 25:14–30). For example, consider how Matthew speaks about fruit and the type of tree from which it hangs. Good fruit is born by good trees, and a tree is known by its fruit (Matt 12:33–34; cf. 3:8). And yet, judgment lies in this metaphor also, "Even now the ax is lying at the root of the trees; every tree therefore that does not bear good fruit is cut down and thrown into the fire" (Matt 3:10). One's actions are the manifestation of what is already outpouring from the heart. In this manner, it is not surprising that the "sheep" in the last judgment in Matthew 25:31–46 are those that were not aware of their compassion. However, character does not simply occur naturally, but how someone is trained in the ways of righteousness. One must learn ways to live faithfully, but do so connected with the community and not merely as an individual.[74] In other words, discipleship is not only about the individual and their own virtues, but also about how the believer connects into the *ecclesia*. But, as the previous discussion shows, no matter how it is shaped, the idea of judgment remains in the picture, and for Matthew, this includes angel traditions to communicate the vividness of the kingdom message and the eschatological arrival of God's ultimate victory (cf. Matt 24:30–31; 25:30). Moreover, the angels highlight the role of the Son of Man as judge. In light of this, Matthew, by portraying Jesus as the eschatological Son of Man, also reveals that the judge is one whom the disciples

71. If this evidence is enough to connote a pattern of angels at the eschatological judgment, more could be considered of passages like Matt 18:23–35 and 22:1–14. In this regard, Sim, "Angels," argues that the ones that do the punishing should be regarded as "angels."

72. Cope, "Apocalyptic," 118.

73. Richard B. Hays, *The Moral Vision of the New Testament: Community, Cross, New Creation: A Contemporary Introduction to New Testament Ethics* (Edinburgh: T. & T. Clark, 1997), 98.

74. Ibid., 99.

know and trust.[75] The one whom the disciples have accompanied and whose teaching they have heard, the one who will suffer and die on the cross, is the same one that will sit in glory judging the world (Matt 25:31–46; 28:18).

God at Work in Jesus's Life

As of yet, the discussion has focused primarily on the eschatological picture of the Son of Man and his angels in Matthew's Gospel. While this group could be considered a more unified body of references that represent an apocalyptic interest in Matthew, it captures neither the full breadth of apocalypticism introduced earlier nor the entire picture of apocalypticism in the Gospel. Consequently, the survey of angels in Matthew continues with a view toward examining God's presence in Jesus's life and ministry as illustrated by these angelic intermediaries through their appearances and revelatory messages. Matthew, as noted by David Kupp, has an established interest in the way God's presence is demonstrated in the Gospel. For Kupp, this has great significance for understanding Jesus as God's presence manifested (Matt 1:23; 28:20).[76] While the presence of God can be detected throughout the Gospel, the interest of this survey lies primarily in the references to angels as evidence of God at work in Jesus's life through their divine messages or through their appearances (or lack thereof).

In the birth narratives (Matt 1:18–2:23), Matthew draws on the traditions of an angelic mediator to reveal God's plan in Jesus's early life. Being placed between the spheres of heaven and earth, angels often function as a revelatory medium in apocalyptic literature.[77] For example, the angel Gabriel comes to Daniel to interpret his visions (Dan 8:15–16; cf. also 10:12–14) and Uriel visits Ezra (4 Ezra 4:1–11) and Enoch (1 Enoch 21:5; 27:2; 33:3; 72:1; 74:2; 75:3–4; 78:10; 79:6–80:1; 82:7). In Matthew, an angel of the Lord visits Joseph in his dreams, a unique and important angel in the Hebrew Bible and Second Temple literature.[78] Unlike Luke, no name is given to the angel in Matthew, both here and at the resurrection (e.g. Gabriel in Luke 1:19, 26; cf. Dan 8:16; 9:21; 10:13, 21; 12:1; 1 Enoch 9:1; 40:9; 54:6; 71:8; Apocalypse of Abraham 10). Combined with the obedient responses and Hebrew Bible fulfillment, this suggests that for Matthew, the emphasis is on the message, not the appearance itself.[79] Three times, the angel of

75. Matthew's portrayal of the Son of Man also indicts those who oppose Jesus and his teachings.

76. While Kupp thoroughly analyzes the significance of God's presence in key verses (Matt 1:23; 18:20; 28:16–20), he also traces Matthew's incorporation of the presence of God throughout the whole of the Gospel's narrative. David D. Kupp, *Matthew's Emmanuel: Divine Presence and God's People in the First Gospel*, SNTSMS 90 (Cambridge: Cambridge University Press, 1996), 52–108.

77. Beyerle, "Angelic," 206–7.

78. von Rad, *Theology*, 1:285–86. See also Walther Eichrodt, *Theology of the Old Testament*, trans. John Baker, 5th ed., 2 vols., OTL (London: SCM Press, 1967), 2:23; Charles A. Gieschen, *Angelomorphic Christology: Antecedents and Early Evidence*, AGJU 42 (Leiden: Brill, 1998), 57–67. See also R. M. M. Tuschling, *Angels and Orthodoxy: A Study in Their Development in Syria and Palestine from the Qumran Texts to Ephrem the Syrian*, STAC 40 (Tübingen: Mohr Siebeck, 2007), 93–107. Tuschling specifically differentiates the angel of the Lord from principal angels and archangels, who are distinct from God in a way that the angel of the Lord is not (102).

79. Ulrich Luz, *Matthew 1-7: A Commentary*, trans. Wilhelm C. Linss, Hermeneia (Minneapolis: Augsburg, 1989), 120. See also Saul M

the Lord appears to Joseph in a dream and gives him instructions (Matt 1:20–21; 2:13, 19–20).[80] Each dream is followed by a prompt and faithful reaction to the angel's instruction, which, in turn, is instrumental in the fulfillment of a Hebrew Bible text (Matt 1:22–23; 2:15, 23). Matthew reflects angel of the Lord traditions and angelic mediators to communicate the authority and origin of the messages to Joseph.[81] As a result, these messages carry significance for Matthew as they reveal the hand of God at work in Jesus's life, announcing the significance of Jesus's life through his name, "you are to name him Jesus, for he will save his people from their sins" (Matt 1:21), and guiding him and his family away from danger on a journey that paralleled Israel's own (out of Egypt and to the land of Israel). The result of Matthew's portrayal of the angel's presence communicates God's activity and interest in the life of Jesus very early in his Gospel's narrative. In his own style, Matthew takes the traditions of the angelic mediator, angel of the Lord, and angelophanic birth announcements to foreshadow the importance and unique identity of this child as the Son of God.

Between the birth narrative (Matt 1:18–2:21) and Jesus's temptation (Matt 4:1–11), both of which include angel references, Matthew describes Jesus's baptism (Matt 3:1–17), complete with its own unveiling of apocalyptic elements: the heavens split open, the spirit comes down as a dove, and a voice calls from heaven (Matt 3:16–17).[82] The significance of this event is brought to the forefront in the testing that immediately follows the baptism. Jesus is led into the wilderness by the Spirit and is tempted by the devil (Matt 4:1).[83] After forty days, Jesus is tested three times. In the second temptation, Jesus is taken to the top of the temple and challenged, "Since you are the Son of God, throw yourself down; for it is written, 'He will command his angels concerning you,' and 'On their hands they will bear you up, so that you will not dash your foot against a stone'" (Matt 4:6; Ps 91:11).[84] The devil taunts Jesus with Psalm 91's promise of angelic assistance in the time of need. Here, in Matthew 4, it is not the military might of angels that are intimated (as will be in Matthew 26), but a picture of angels coming to one's aid. Outside Psalm 91's picture of celestial help, angels act as personal guides and protectors (Gen 24:7; Dan 3:28; 6:22; Tob 5:17, 22; Acts 12:11; cf. Testament of Simeon 2:8; 4 Baruch 6:22), deliver

Olyan, *A Thousand Thousands Served Him: Exegesis and the Naming of Angels in Ancient Judaism*, TSAJ 36 (Tübingen: Mohr, 1993), 14–18; Rowland, *Open Heaven*, 94–95.

80. The angel as a guide is a constant element in apocalypticism. Collins, *Apocalyptic Imagination*, 5; Beyerle, "Angelic," 206–7.

81. Perhaps the magi as well are visited by the angel (Matt 2:12). In the Hebrew Bible, when the angel of the Lord appears, he delivers a specific message from the Lord himself. At times, the differentiation between the angel and the Lord speaking all but disappears (Exod 3:2–4; 23:20–23; see also Gen 16:7–13; 21:17; 22:9–17; Judg 6:11–14; 13:19–24; 1 Kgs 19:5–7; Zech 1:11–12; 3:1–6). In Numbers 22, the angel of the Lord delivers a message and threatens Balaam's life. See also Brown, *Birth*, who looks at Hebrew Bible birth narratives (Gen 16:7–13; 17:21; 18:1–15; Judg 13:3–23), which often include angelic revelation, for their influence on the New Testament birth stories. Brown, *Birth*.

82. Rowland, *Open Heaven*, 358–65.

83. This contributes to the picture of a cosmic conflict being played out on earth in Jesus's life. See Powell, "Plot."

84. It is unclear whether Jesus was taken there physically or in a visionary experience. Davies and Allison, *Matthew*, 1:364–65. For the purpose of the narrative, this distinction is not significant.

Lot out of Sodom (Genesis 19), and accompany the Israelites out of Egypt, "my angel shall go in front of you" (Exod 32:34; cf. also 23:23).[85] Compared to the angel in Matthew 1–2, whose actions and words guide the narrative, the angels in Matthew 4 represent a different scenario concerning God's presence and Jesus's understanding of the heavenly words spoken at his baptism. This time, the presence is much more hands-off (without being absent). Despite the promise of an angelic "safety-net," Matthew defines Jesus's identity as rooted in obedience to the will of the Father, and not dependent upon angelic assistance. And yet, once the testing is over, as if in response to Jesus's faithfulness throughout the testing, angels come (προσέρχομαι) and serve (διακονέω) Jesus (Matt 4:11). If considered on its own, the angels' activity could be seen simply as tending to the physical needs of Jesus's forty-day fast.[86] However, it is likely part of a larger picture of angels and apocalyptic cosmology in Matthew's Gospel. In other words, Matthew's understanding of Jesus's cosmological identity and the confirmation of God's activity and presence in Jesus's life are revealed through the presentation of angels under the command of Jesus the Son of Man at the final judgment (as discussed above), and Matthew's editing of the text to show the angels coming (προσέρχομαι) to Jesus.[87]

Near the end of the Gospel, when the Last Supper is completed and Jesus and the disciples are in the Garden of Gethsemane, Jesus is tested again in a similar fashion to the temptation narrative. After Jesus has gone off three times to pray, asking God if the cup may pass from before him and declaring his obedience, Judas approaches with a large, armed crowd (Matt 26:36–46). When Jesus is seized, one of the disciples in the garden reacts impulsively, cutting off the ear of the high priest's servant. Jesus, turning to his disciple, says, "Put your sword back into its place; for all who take the sword will perish by the sword. Do you think that I cannot appeal to my Father, and he will at once send me more than twelve legions of angels?" (Matt 26:53). While reflecting traditions of protecting angels evidenced in the temptation narrative, Matthew also capitalizes on traditions that portray angels as warriors at God's command. For example, there are traditions of angels participating in an apocalyptic holy war (1QM 10:3–5; 12:7–9; 13:10; Rev 12:7) and 2 Baruch 51:11 speaks of the army of angels ready at the Lord's command (cf. Zech

85. See also Enoch's preservation by angels in 2 Enoch (2 Enoch 33:11–12; 36:2) and the allusion to an angelic protective hedge (4Q434 f1 i:11–12).

86. This is the common understanding; for example, see the commentaries of Gundry, Nolland, and Davies and Allison. However, others are not satisfied with it, for example, Birger Gerhardsson, *The Testing of God's Son (Matt. 4:1-11 & Par.): An Analysis of an Early Christian Midrash* (Lund: C.W.K. Gleerup, 1966), 69; and Ernest Best, *The Temptation and the Passion: The Markan Soteriology*, SNTSMS 2 (Cambridge: Cambridge University Press, 1965), 9–10.

87. The frequent use of προσέρχομαι in Matthew may appear to be a stylistic element, but Davies and Allison have suggested that Matthew's addition of προσέρχομαι is more than stylistic. When προσέρχομαι is connected with "worship" (προσκυνέω) in Matthew (8:2; 9:18; 20:20; 28:9), the cult in Judaism, and with drawing near to royalty and their courts (Lev 9:5; Num 18:4; Deut 25:1; Jer 7:16; Heb 10:1; 1 Pet 2:4; Josephus, *Ant.* 12.19), the verb carries with it the undertone of an approach with reverence. Davies and Allison, *Matthew*, 1:360. See also Jeffery B. Gibson, "Jesus' Wilderness Temptation According to Mark," *JSNT* 53 (1994): 19–33; H. W. Beyer, "διακονέω," in *Theological Dictionary of the New Testament*, ed. Gerhard Kittel, Geoffrey William Bromiley, and Gerhard Friedrich (Grand Rapids: Eerdmans, 1964), 2:81.

14:5). In addition, one must not forget descriptions of the angel that destroyed 185,000 Assyrians single-handedly (2 Kgs 19:35; 2 Chron 32:21; Isa 37:36; cf. Pss 34:7; 35:5–6). This is recounted vividly in 2 Baruch 63:5–11, where Hezekiah prays to the Mighty One for relief from the attacks of Sennacherib. The Mighty One sends Ramael (2 Baruch 55:3), who destroys the army for the glory of God (burning their insides, leaving their weapons and clothes).[88] If one merges the traditions of the power of one angel in a battle and the understanding that a legion was about 6,000 troops, then the angelic force that Matthew is describing to rescue Jesus would be close to 72,000 angels![89] Yet, Matthew suggests that had Jesus's arrest and death not been part of God's plan, then the overwhelming resource of angelic strength would have certainly quelled the arresting crowd (Matt 26:47).[90] Drawing from apocalyptic elements of angels as mediators, divine servants, and celestial warriors, Matthew creates a unique and dramatic illustration of Jesus's obedient journey to the cross. Moreover, he goes without direct divine intervention or assistance, for he alone will save his people from their sins (Matt 1:21). At the same time, God is not far from Jesus, for Matthew portrays Jesus admitting that angels would be at the Father's behest, should he appeal to him (Matt 26:53).

Matthew's handling of angels in this passage and Matthew 4:6 may offer some insight into the Gospel's apocalyptic characteristics and angels assisting Jesus. In both occasions, Matthew portrays Jesus at a point where his decisions reveal his identity as an obedient Son of God. While one can say that what Jesus does and says defines him, it cannot be ignored that what Jesus does not do communicates something as well. In this way, it is possible that Matthew's narrative could be commenting implicitly on the expectation of a dramatic appearance of divine assistance accompanying the inauguration of the Messianic rule. Rather, the fact that God's victory is not initiated in this way may contribute to correcting "military-like" apocalyptic expectations of God's intervention while also presenting a Matthean understanding of apocalypticism based on faithfulness to God and divine intervention in the person of Jesus.[91]

88. See also, Deut 20:3–4; 1 Sam 17:46–47; 2 Kgs 6:15–19; cf. LAB 61:5–9; 2 Baruch 7:1–8:2; 2 Macc 11:6–15; 3 Macc 6:18–19; 4 Macc 4:10–11.

89. Hagner, *Matthew*, 2:789.

90. There is some debate regarding whether or not Jesus had command of the angels at this point. So far, all descriptions of the angels at the ready of the Son of Man have been eschatological portraits (in Matt 4:11, the angels come to Jesus, but their arrival is not due to an appeal or command by Jesus). Nevertheless, many think Jesus had this power. Douglas R. A. Hare, *Matthew*, IBC (Louisville: John Knox, 1993), 304; Harrington, *Matthew*, 375; Davies and Allison, *Matthew*, 3:513; Donald Senior, *The Passion Narrative According to Matthew: A Redactional Study*, BETL 39 (Louvain: Leuven University Press, 1975), 141; Hagner, *Matthew*, 2:789–90; Theodore Robinson, *The Gospel of Matthew*, MNTC (Harper & Brothers, 1939), 220. On the contrary, both Morris and Patte agree with the point this discussion is making, namely, Jesus would have to appeal for the angels to come. Leon Morris, *The Gospel According to Matthew*, Pillar (Grand Rapids: Eerdmans, 1992), 676; Daniel Patte, *The Gospel According to Matthew: A Structural Commentary on Matthew's Faith* (Philadelphia: Fortress Press, 1987), 370. Whether or not Jesus had command of the angels at this point, Matthew is not commenting directly on Jesus's power, but shows Jesus himself as living out his own teaching, turning the other cheek, loving one's enemy, pursuing righteousness, loving God, and remaining obedient.

91. Sabourin, "Traits," 21. Perhaps the rebuke by Peter or the reply to John's disciples can be included as a similar kind of misunderstanding of Jesus (Matt 11:2–6; 16:22). This may also fit into Hagner's idea of the suffering messiah as "a kind of turning apocalyptic on its head." Hagner, "Apocalyptic," 72.

If the arrest scene hints at God's activity behind the scenes, then the curtain is pulled back in the depiction of the death and resurrection of Jesus in Matthew.[92] At Jesus's death, darkness envelops the land, the earth shakes, tombs are split open, the temple veil is torn, and the righteous dead are raised so that they may go into the holy city after Jesus's resurrection, bearing witness of his raising (Matt 27:45–53).[93] Later, at the tomb, the apocalyptic language continues: an angel of the Lord descends from heaven, shakes the earth, rolls back the stone that blocked the entrance to the tomb, and sits upon the stone triumphantly in resplendent attire (Matt 28:2–3).[94] While the apocalyptic symbols at Jesus's death inspires the centurion's confession (Matt 27:54; cf. Mark 15:39), the spectacular nature of the angel's appearance and activity at the tomb causes the guards at the tomb to faint out of fear (Matt 28:4).[95] The angel's description suggests that he comes from the realm of the Lord's glory and is acting for and in the power of God.[96] Like the infancy narratives, the angel brings a message concerning Jesus (Matt 28:5–7). Yet, instead of appearing in a dream (Matt 1:20; 2:13, 19), the description of the angel in dramatic apocalyptic imagery evokes the concept of the inbreaking of God into history and communicates the significance and cosmic victory of the resurrection.[97] As with Joseph in the infancy narratives, Matthew describes the women responding obediently to the angel's message, embracing the content of the revelation with "great joy and fear" (Matt 28:8; cf. 2:10).[98] In both the infancy and resurrection narratives, Matthew has chosen a mediator to convey the divine origin and significance of this message (cf. Matt 16:17), worthy of all the apocalyptic color intimated with his other references to angels.

92. In a way similar to the infancy narratives, the activity of God is revealed with the use of angels and other apocalyptic and eschatological elements. Matthew incorporates much of Mark in his passion and resurrection narratives, but quenches any doubts about these events having divine importance.

93. For more, see the discussions in Gurtner, *Veil*, 144–51; Kenneth L. Waters, Sr., "Matthew 27:52–53 as Apocalyptic Apostrophe: Temporal-Spatial Collapse in the Gospel of Matthew," *JBL* 122, no. 3 (2003): 489–91. Tobias Nicklas, "Angels in Early Christian Narratives on the Resurrection of Jesus: Canonical and Apocryphal Texts," in *Angels: The Concept of Celestial Beings - Origins, Development and Reception*, ed. Friedrich V. Reiterer, Tobias Nicklas, and Karin Schöpflin, DCLS (Berlin: Walter de Gruyter, 2007), 298–300.

94. In 1 Enoch 14:20, the Lord's garment is described as "shining more brightly than the sun, it was whiter than any snow," and at the end, the author of the Parable of Enoch describes the clothing of the angels as white and the "light of their faces was like snow," (1 Enoch 71:1; see also Ezek 10:4; Dan 10:5–6; cf. Dan 12:6–7; Rev 15:6; 19:14; LAB 9:10.) In Exod 34:29–35, Moses's face is described as bright after his encounters with the presence of the Lord and in Dan. 12:3, the righteous will shine in the resurrection (cf. 4 Ezra 7:97; 2 Baruch 51:3; cf. Matt 13:43).

95. Gurtner, "Symbolism," 540–43. After reading Matthew, the appearance of a "young man" in the tomb in Mark 16:5 seems comparatively tame. For fear as a response to angels, see Loren T. Stuckenbruck, *Angel Veneration and Christology: A Study in Early Judaism and in the Christology of the Apocalypse of John*, WUNT II/70 (Tübingen: Mohr Siebeck, 1995), 75–103. For more on apocalyptic symbols, see Gurtner, "Symbolism."

96. Nicklas, "Resurrection," 300.

97. Here also, Matthew seems to hint at his descriptions of the Son of Man with full angelic entourage.

98. For a list of sources that compare Matthew 1–2 with Matthew 27–28, see Kupp, *Emmanuel*, 111.

Matthew's Cosmology

Even though an attempt has been made to categorize Matthew's reference to angels, not every piece needs to fit neatly into a systematic approach. For example, the diversity of the remaining references suggests Matthew was comfortable with a cosmology that reflected angels and related apocalyptic elements in his Gospel narrative. Moreover, their interpretation is part of the larger picture of Matthew's display and interest in angels, and thus, invites an understanding of the whole portrait. Of the four following references, two are uniquely Matthean (Matt 18:10; 25:41), while the remaining two are adapted from Mark with a very light editorial hand (Matt 22:30; 24:36; par. Mark 12:25; 13:32).

In a chapter that discusses the importance of forgiveness and reconciliation, Matthew uniquely introduces the Parable of the Sheep (Matt 18:12–14, par. Luke 15:3–7) with a command to not look down on "one of the little ones" for "in heaven their angels continually see the face of my Father in heaven" (Matt 18:10). The appearance and activity of angels in the Father's presence is the explanation for avoiding treating the "little ones" with contempt. Traditions that refer to angels of the nations (Deut 32:8–9; Dan 12:1; Sir. 17:17; cf. Job 15:30), interceding angels (1 Enoch 89:76; 100:4–5; Jubilees 35:16–17; cf. LAB 15:5), and angels of the presence (Rev 8:2; Jubilees 2:2, 18; Tob 12:12–15; 1 Enoch 40:9–10; 4Q400 1 i:4; 1QH[a] 14:16) suggest that the "little ones" had great value to the Father because of their own heavenly representative and that angel's proximity to God.[99] While this, with the preceding references, continues to demonstrate a Matthean apocalyptic cosmology, it also aptly introduces the parable of the loving care of the shepherd for his "sheep" (Matt 18:11–14) because it accents God's heavenly care of his earthly people (1 Enoch 8:4).

Within a series of challenges to Jesus's authority in Matthew 21–22, Matthew narrates the Sadducees' riddle concerning the law of levirate marriage.[100] Jesus responds by turning the Sadducees' question to him on its head and compares the state of the resurrected to that of the angels, "You are wrong, because you know neither the Scriptures nor the power of God. For in the resurrection they neither marry nor are given in marriage, but are like angels in heaven" (Matt 22:29–30). The verse reflects the significance of angels' heavenly origin and traditions of their immortality,[101] suggesting the understanding that angels represent a heavenly life differ-

99. See also Darrell D. Hannah, "Guardian Angels and Angelic National Patrons in Second Temple Judaism and Early Christianity," in *Angels: The Concept of Celestial Beings – Origins, Development and Reception*, ed. Friedrich V. Reiterer, Tobias Nicklas, and Karin Schöpflin, DCLS (Berlin: Walter de Gruyter, 2007).

100. This is the only passage Matthew does not significantly redact Mark. Nevertheless, this does not mean that Matthew did not express interest in his portrayal of angels. Since Matthew has redacted all of the other references to angels, his lack of editing suggests that this passage was important to Matthew as it was received.

101. Linked to the idea of immortality is also that sex and marriage were for procreation and the protection of life (1 Enoch 15:6–7). Dale C. Allison, "Divorce, Celibacy and Joseph (Matthew 1.18-25 and 19.1-12)," JSNT 15, no. 3 (1993): 6–10. Similarly, angels are rarely

ent from that found on earth. Earthly concerns, such as those of the Sadducees (and that of marriage), will not be important compared to life in the resurrection.

In the eschatological discourse (Matt 24:3–25:46), Matthew answers the question of when Jesus will return (Matt 24:3) by indicating the coming of the Son of Man will be both sudden and unpredictable. Without giving any explicit chronological clues, the discourse invites the disciples to live a faithful life, expecting paradoxically both a long wait and an immediate return. Moreover, Matthew explains "about that day and hour no one knows, neither the angels of heaven, nor the Son, but only the Father" (Matt 24:53).[102] Matthew deviates from traditions that have angels possess special heavenly knowledge (e.g. Prov 30:2–3; cf. Greek Apocalypse of Ezra 1:5), while at the same time using rhetoric that highlights the superiority of a certain piece of knowledge by angelic ignorance (11Q5 26:12; 2 Enoch 40:3 and 24:3: "For not even to my angels have I explained my secrets, nor related to them their origin, nor my endlessness. . ."). The understanding that angels would be among the group with "inside" information helps establish that the Father alone knows the time.

For the final reference to angels in this survey, the discussion returns to the portrayal of the final judgment in which the Son of Man is with all the angels (Matt 25:31–46). From his glorious throne, the Son of Man separates the righteous and the wicked, pronouncing judgment (Matt 25:34).[103] The righteous are given eternal life and their inheritance in the kingdom, but the wicked are sent away "into the eternal fire prepared for the devil and his angels" (Matt 25:41). By referring to the angels of the devil, Matthew causally displays evidence of the cosmic conflict centered on Jesus.[104] At the same time, the narrative implies that the Son of Man is in a position of authority over the devil and his angels.

In summary, if the portrait of angels at the judgment (Matt 13:41; 49; 16:27; 24:30–31; 25:31; cf. 25:41) is included with the references to angels that demonstrate God's presence, revelation, and Matthew's cosmology, it can be argued that Matthew is using apocalyptic ideas as a means of revealing more of Jesus's heavenly identity as well as orienting a disciple's life toward righteous obedience.[105] Luz calls Matthew a special kind of apocalypticist—one whose views serve, in the most part, to advance the idea of judgment rather than strengthen the identity of an apocalyptic group.[106] Thus, Matthew could be attempting to shape behavior with a cosmology

depicted as eating, a necessity for mortal humans (Testament of Abraham 4:9; Tob 12:19). Thus, being like the angels (Matt 22:30) would suggest indirectly there would be no need for marriage. Furthermore, there are some traditions that suggest the resurrected righteous become like angels (2 Baruch 51:3–10; 1 Enoch 104:4–6; 4 Ezra 7:97–8; LAB 33:5).

102. The emphasis on the Father in Matt 24:36 is further illustrated by Matthew's addition of μόνος so that it is clear that the Father alone knows the time.

103. Although the narrative says "king," it seems that Matthew has the Son of Man in mind.

104. While the conflict between God and the devil is clear in the temptation narrative, the opposition to Jesus in the bulk of Matthew's narrative is manifested through a different set of opponents—namely, the Jewish leaders, and sometimes, Jesus's disciples (cf. Matt 16:21–23). Powell, "Plot," 199–203. See also the previous discussion of an apocalyptic holy war.

105. Ulrich Luz, *Matthew 21-28: A Commentary*, Hermeneia (Minneapolis: Fortress Press, 2005). See also Hagner, "Apocalyptic," 73–77.

that reflects angels and other apocalyptic elements. If this is true, then Matthew 18:10 rises to the top of the list, for in the instruction to the disciples, Jesus explains that their behavior must take into account the heavenly reality of angels. The assumption is that Matthew's readers would share both this belief and reaction to its portrayal of reality. Without the acceptance of angels and a worldview that supports their participation, verses such as Matthew 18:10 have little value.[107] In addition, the portrait of Jesus in Matthew is developed by the bestowal of heavenly imagery concerning of the Son of Man and the revelation of the availability of angelic assistance in Jesus's time of need. This special information regarding Jesus influences a reader's understanding of who he is according to Matthew, a feature that is indebted to apocalypticism.

Conclusion

In the proceeding discussion, it was argued that apocalypticism was displayed in Matthew's deliberate portrayal of angels in his Gospel narrative. Moreover, the survey facilitated the explanation of how the angels and their place in a Matthean cosmology reflect Jewish apocalyptic thought in more than just its eschatological understanding. This was demonstrated through an explanation of Matthean references to angels separated into three categories, each contributing parts to the portrait of Jesus and life of discipleship Matthew was trying to portray. In particular, the picture Matthew created through this aspect of apocalypticism elevated the role of the Son of Man at the judgment, illustrated the presence of God's activity in Jesus's life, and elaborated on the apocalyptic diversity within Matthew's symbolic universe. As was mentioned earlier, angels are but one element in a larger picture of apocalypticism in Matthew. The breadth of Jewish apocalyptic thought offers more opportunities to explore how this tradition has influenced the Gospels and the rest of the New Testament.

106. Luz, *Matthew 21-28*, 3:295. On the contrary, Sim sees Matthew's church as an apocalyptic community, unified and strengthened in the midst of crisis by its acceptance of the apocalyptic eschatology and alternative symbolic universe. Sim, *Apocalyptic*, 88, 243.

107. While these references advance the place of angels in Matthew's worldview, they are not alone in communicating the cosmological dimension of the Gospel. The Gospel contains numerous references to demons and Jesus's exorcisms and healings. Jesus's healings themselves are an attack on the spiritual world itself. For Powell, these are evidence of the cosmological conflict that dominates the plot and subplots of Matthew. Powell, "Plot," 198–203. In addition, Pennington also places a similar value on Matthew's symbolic universe in his research on "heaven" and "earth" in Matthew, arguing that the use of "heaven" is more than a reverential circumlocution. Jonathan T. Pennington, *Heaven and Earth in the Gospel of Matthew* (Grand Rapids: Baker Academic, 2009), 331–36.

3

Apocalypse and the Gospel of Mark

Grant Macaskill

An examination of the apocalyptic features or elements of Mark's Gospel requires a methodological awareness of the complex nature of our object of study. It is a work that integrates stories about Jesus and accounts of his teaching into a form that is today generally considered to be coherent and carefully constructed. As such, discussions must be sensitive to the traditional questions of historical criticism—those concerning redaction, sources, form, and so on—and also, to the questions central to more recent methodologies, such as narrative criticism or performance criticism. Much of the discussion of "apocalyptic" in Mark (notably concerning Mark 13) has been dominated by a source critical agenda that is itself shaped by received scholarly accounts of apocalyptic thought. Hence, the task of the scholar is to examine the eschatology of Mark, or the stages of tradition that he inherited, in the light of an assumed apocalyptic preoccupation with eschatology and an assumed apocalyptic configuration of the phenomenon. Such conversations should not be bypassed, and we will engage with them later in this chapter, but they require to be challenged by developments in research into the apocalyptic texts typically used as background or context. They must also be prevented from emphasizing the issue of eschatology to an extent that displaces the theme of *disclosure* or *revelation* that is at the heart of this particular volume of studies. By and large, that theme has been handled more fully by those works that have utilized narrative critical methodologies, which have been sensitive to the ways in which the revealing of wisdom and its reception are represented in the narrative of the Gospel, often using subtle literary devices. Even here, though, the account of "apocalyptic" that underpins such studies is often based on older scholarship or on assumptions about which texts should be admitted to the canon of apocalyptic literature; one has a sense that the apocalyptic texts or the genre apocalypse are referred to only in generalized terms.

My approach within this chapter will then be methodologically eclectic: I will make use of standard historical-critical scholarship and discussions of source or tradition, but I will also make use of narrative and performance critical scholarship. Because our focus is particularly on themes of disclosure, rather than eschatology, I will pass over some of the blocks of material in the Gospel that may normally feature in discussions of Mark and the apocalyptic, concentrating instead on those blocks that reflect distinctive concepts of revelation. I will devote a significant part of the chapter to an examination of the opening of the Gospel, since this will allow us to engage with some of the key elements in the discussion of Markan apocalypticism. After that, I will examine the "parable theory" discussed in Mark 4, the Transfiguration, and the eschatological discourse of Mark 13.

The Opening of Mark's Narrative

The opening chapter of Mark contains a collection of stories that swiftly introduce us to key themes subsequently developed in the narrative; it has a distinctive importance to the reader's understanding of the whole account, and it is appropriate that we begin our study here.

The Prophetic Quotation and the Identity of the Baptist

The Gospel opens with a statement about its subject matter: it is the "good news" about Jesus Christ.[1] While the term εὐαγγέλιον has a particular significance in Christian tradition, and its use here undoubtedly reflects the currency it already possessed when the Gospel was written,[2] it is quite striking that it occurs in close proximity to a quotation from Isaiah that is contextu-

1. Some manuscripts further identify Jesus at this point as the Son of God, but there is good reason to consider this particular addition as secondary. See Adela Yarbro Collins, "Establishing the Text: Mark 1:1," in *Texts and Contexts: The Function of Biblical Texts in their Textual and Situational Contexts*, ed. Todd Fornberg and David Hellholm (Oslo: Scandinavian University Press, 1995), 111–27. See also the discussion of Mark 1 in her commentary: Adela Yarbro Collins, *Mark: A Commentary*, Hermeneia. (Minneapolis: Augsburg Fortress Press, 2007), 130. Yarbro Collins's commentary provides an excellent access point to the vast secondary literature on Mark. For this reason, I will frequently refer to it in my notes, with a view to directing the reader most economically to scholarly discussions.
2. There is, of course, a significant issue of genre here, related to the question of how the Gospels relate to the genre of Graeco-Roman *bioi*. The classic study of this is Richard Burridge, *What are the Gospels? A Comparison with Graeco-Roman Biography* (Cambridge: Cambridge University Press, 1992).

ally associated with the related term ὁ εὐαγγελιζόμενος ("herald of good news", occurring twice in Isa 40:9). The quotation bears some closer examination, for two reasons: first, it is the only explicit quotation in the whole of Mark, and second, it is a characteristic feature of apocalyptic texts that their revelatory elements are developed by means of the reinterpretation of older texts and traditions.[3]

It is, in fact, a composite quotation, bringing together Malachi 3:1 and Isaiah 40:3, but ascribed exclusively to Isaiah.

> Mark 1.2 ἰδοὺ ἀποστέλλω τὸν ἄγγελόν μου πρὸ προσώπου σου, ὃς κατασκευάσει τὴν ὁδόν σου. (Mal 3:1)
> Mark 1.3 φωνὴ βοῶντος ἐν τῇ ἐρήμῳ· ἑτοιμάσατε τὴν ὁδὸν κυρίου, εὐθείας ποιεῖτε τὰς τρίβους αὐτοῦ. (Isa 40:3)

The identification of the first half of the conflated quotation as Malachi 3:1 is not straightforward. The text does not correspond to any Greek version of this particular verse. LXX reads: ἰδοὺ ἐγὼ ἐξαποστέλλω τὸν ἄγγελόν μου, καὶ ἐπιβλέψεται ὁδὸν πρὸ προσώπου μου. There is a significant correspondence here, but it is not perfect: πρὸ προσώπου σου is located at the end of the sentence, and the word for "prepare" is different. A case could be made that the Greek of Exodus 23:20 is, in fact, the source of the quotation:

> Καὶ ἰδοὺ ἐγὼ ἀποστέλλω τὸν ἄγγελόν μου πρὸ προσώπου σου, ἵνα φυλάξῃ σε ἐν τῇ ὁδῷ, ὅπως εἰσαγάγῃ σε εἰς τὴν γῆν, ἣν ἡτοίμασά σοι.

Here, the word order of the opening clause is identical to that found in Mark, but the second clause, despite sharing the term ὁδός, departs dramatically from it. It is likely that, in fact, the two texts (Exod 23:20 and Mal 3:1) have been hybridized because of their overlapping vocabulary, read together by the practice of what would come to be labeled as *gezerah shewa* in the Middoth.[4] The same principle provides the warrant for combining Malachi 3:1 with Isaiah 40:3, but interestingly, only on the basis of the Hebrew text: both use the verb פנה for "prepare." The Greek term used in Mark 1:2 (κατασκευάσει) is found in all of the Synoptic quotations of this verse, but not in LXX, where ἐπιβλέψεται is found; neither Greek word corresponds to the vocabulary of Isaiah 40:3, but the Hebrew does.

While all of the synoptic Gospels contain both of these quotations, Mark alone presents

3. On this point, see Eibert Tigchelaar, *Prophets of Old and the Day of the End: Zechariah, the Book of the Watchers and Apocalyptic*, OtSt 35 (Leiden: Brill, 1996) 243–47. In my view, Tigchelaar's study has been badly neglected by New Testament scholars. The observation concerning reinterpretation demands that New Testament scholars familiarize themselves with the discussions concerning "inner biblical exegesis." An excellent starting point for those interested is William Tooman, *Gog and Magog: Reuse of Scripture and Compositional Technique in Ezekiel 38–39*, FAT II/52 (Tübingen: Mohr Siebeck, 2011).
4. In fact, the Malachi text may itself reflect the creative uptake of Exod 23:20. See David L. Petersen, *Zechariah 9–14 and Malachi: A Commentary* (Louisville: Westminster John Knox, 1995), 210.

them in this conflated form. In Matthew and Luke, the Malachi 3:1/Exodus 23:20 quotations are located in later passages that refer to John the Baptist (Matt 11:10 and Luke 7:27, respectively). Either, then, Mark has himself conflated the quotations because of their common concern with preparing the way, in order to embed John's ministry within the story of salvation suggested by Isaiah, or he has inherited a composite text reflecting a conflation on the basis of *gezerah shewa* that is now masked by the Greek. Regardless of this, readers are directed back to two passages in the Hebrew Bible that evoke a common hope: the coming of God himself to his people.

The immediate contexts of both Isaiah and Malachi speak of the coming of Yahweh himself (cf. Isa 40:10, Mal 3:1) and in both cases, the "way" that is to be "prepared" is Yahweh's own. In the case of Malachi, that context also speaks of purification, with the famous image of the refiner and his fire (3:2–4).[5] The wider context in Malachi represents this coming as the "day of the Lord" and speaks of the sending of Elijah in anticipation of that day (Mal 4:5), allowing the messenger of 3:1 to be identified with the prophetic figure of Elijah.

All of this forms the background to the arrival of John the Baptist in Mark's narrative. John's appearance is evocative of Elijah's (cf. Mark 1:6 with 2 Kgs 1:8) and his activity revolves around a ritual of cleansing and repentance that is intended as preparatory for the one who will come after him, who will baptize with the Holy Spirit (1:7). All then points to John's eschatological identity as the one by whom the way of the Lord will be prepared and to the story that follows as concerning the day of the Lord's visitation. It is important to note, though, that this eschatology can hardly be labeled as distinctively "apocalyptic" since it channels the hopes and expectations associated more broadly with the "day of the Lord" traditions in the prophets, as they are represented in Malachi. This, indeed, is Rowland's objection to the emphasis placed on eschatology in many discussions: that the eschatological expectations are hardly distinctive to the apocalypses.[6] What *is* apocalyptic is the revelatory application of these verses to John: the Baptist's true identity and significance is revealed to readers by the reinterpretation of older traditions and their application to him. While this is a significant move for the identification of John himself, it has further significance for the identification of Jesus as the one who comes after him, who must then be identified in some sense with the coming of God.

While the Malachi text is crucial to the particular identification of John, the labeling of the conflated quotation with the name of Isaiah ensures that this prophet is seen to constitute the base text. As such, the Gospel as a whole is introduced with reference to the hopes articulated within that particular prophecy, particularly the block of material from Isaiah 40 onwards, in

5. In fact, this image of purification is also encountered in Exod 23:20–24, where the idols and altars of the people of Canaan are to be destroyed and not tolerated, furthering the likelihood that the quotation incorporates an allusion to Exodus 23.

6. See Christopher Rowland and Christopher Morray-Jones, *The Mystery of God: Early Jewish Mysticism and the New Testament*, CRINT 12 (Leiden: Brill, 2009), 15.

which the motif of the "prepared way" recurs several times (twice in 57:14 and once in 62:10, in addition to the occurrence in 40:3). The "new exodus" that is represented in this section of Isaiah has been considered to serve as a key motif in Mark's own narrative.[7] Again, what is striking is that this tradition becomes the interpretive context in which the surface level tragedy of the story of Jesus is revalorized to become a story of victory. As we will see, this is reflected in the narrative strategies employed in the Gospel.

It is worth noting that a comparable interpretation of Isaiah 40:3 is seen in the Rule of the Community at 1QS 8:12–16 (developed further in 1QS 9:17–20). The comparison is interesting: there, the verse is understood as a description of the wilderness community itself, which has withdrawn to prepare the way for God. That preparation is then specified to be constituted by "the study of the Law which he commanded by the hand of Moses," understood in relation to the prophets who have revealed God's will "by the Holy Spirit." Again, it is tempting to see the apocalyptic dimension of this as being constituted by eschatology, but the eschatology, and indeed, the ethics of the community are specified to be those of the Law and the prophets. What is distinctive is the identification of the community as the subject matter of the scriptural tradition: the apocalyptic character of the community is constituted rather more by its self-identity as the wilderness community to which wisdom has been revealed than by anything distinctive in its eschatology.

The Description and Baptism of Jesus

The description of John leads into the account of the baptism of Jesus. John's description of Jesus is worthy of some attention. Jesus is "the one stronger than I" (ὁ ἰσχυρότερός μου), a title that Adela Yarbro Collins rightly considers to evoke connotations of the divine warrior.[8] The statement that John is unworthy to untie his sandals further develops Jesus's superior status to the Baptist.

The subsequent description of Jesus as baptizing with the Holy Spirit where John baptized with water is generally considered to be derived from Ezekiel 36:25–27.

> [25]I will sprinkle clean water upon you, and you shall be clean from all your uncleannesses, and from all your idols I will cleanse you. [26]A new heart I will give you, and a new spirit I will put within you; and I will remove from your body the heart of stone and give you a heart of flesh. [27]I will put my spirit within you, and make you follow my statutes and be careful to observe my ordinances.

Interestingly, this passage combines the idea of the giving of the spirit with that of purification

7. See Rikki Watts, *Isaiah's New Exodus and Mark*, WUNT II/88 (Tübingen: Mohr Siebeck, 1997).
8. Yarbro Collins, *Mark*, 146.

with water, both actions being performed by God. It is taken up also in 1QS 4:18–23 with the same combination of purification and the pouring out of the Spirit as part of a single act realized in the community, to which "all the glory of Adam/Man" is given in the eternal covenant. Elsewhere in the New Testament, Ezekiel 36:25–27 seems to lie behind the new birth imagery of John 3 ("no-one can enter the kingdom of God without being born of water and of the spirit").

Immediately after the baptism, the heavens are described as being "split open." The word is interesting: where Luke and Matthew use ἀνοίγω,[9] Mark uses σχίζω, the same verb that is used in the synoptic tradition of the tearing of the curtain in the temple when Jesus dies (cf Mark 15:38). The distinctive choice of verb[10] ties these two passages together and achieves something important in the baptism account: while all of the synoptic accounts represent this as a moment when the heavenly realm is opened, and represent the Spirit descending from the heavenly realm to the earthly one, Mark distinctively represents this access to heaven in a way that, for the returning reader or hearer, evokes the temple.[11] This close identification of the earthly temple and heaven is common in the apocalyptic texts and often provides the conceptual framework for the revelatory content of these: a seer ascends into the heavenly temple and is given privileged access to the secrets of that realm.[12] The intrinsic holiness of the heavenly temple means that such visionary experience is limited to an elite few, whose visions are then transmitted to the elect community, and carries risks for those inadequately prepared. Here, the opening of the heavenly temple facilitates not *ascent* but *descent*, as the Spirit comes to rest on Jesus; it is, nevertheless, a moment of disclosure, as the true identity of Jesus as God's Son is revealed to him, and thence, to the readers of the Gospel by an event that bridges heavenly realities and earthly ones.[13]

There may be a further significance to the use of σχίζω here, but it is one that I suggest cautiously. The same verb is used in LXX of Isaiah 48:21 to describe God's action of splitting open rocks to provide water for his people. Within the New Testament, that action is taken by Paul in 1 Corinthians 10:1–5 to anticipate (and in some sense, participate in) the "spiritual" (πνευματικός) reality of life in Christ. The frequency with which the adjective "spiritual" is used in that passage and the importance of the Spirit to the wider context of 1 Corinthians 10–12 combine to suggest that the water is itself identified with the presence of the Spirit. The use

9. The same verb is generally used in apocalyptic texts for the opening of the heavens. For examples, see Yarbro Collins, *Mark*, 148n80.
10. There is only one other parallel to the use of the word for the opening of heaven, in *Jos. Asen.* 14:1–3. The Greek of Isa 64:1, which is obviously parallel in concept to this, nevertheless uses ἀνοίγω.
11. If the veil in question is the outer veil, then Josephus's observation that this was embroidered with imagery of the heavens is interesting (*Bell.* 5.5.4).
12. See Martha Himmelfarb, *Ascent to Heaven in Jewish and Christian Apocalypses* (Oxford: Oxford University Press, 1993).
13. For a recent discussion of the narrative significance of the tearing of the veil, with good coverage of the secondary literature, see Robin Griffith-Jones, "Going Back to Galilee to See the Son of Man: Mark's Gospel as an Upside Down Apocalypse," in *Between Author and Audience in Mark: Narration, Characterization, Interpretation*, ed. Elizabeth Struthers Malbon (Sheffield: Sheffield Phoenix, 2009), 82–102, esp. 92–94.

of σχίζω here in Mark 1:10, where it denotes a splitting that opens the way for the Spirit to be present on earth, may evoke a similar such typology.

Regardless of whether this speculation is correct, the opening reference to Isaiah in Mark 1:2 invites the reader to consider the descent of the Spirit against the background of that particular prophecy. There, the Spirit is closely linked to the figure of the Servant (Isa 42:1; 61:1), so that Jesus is emphatically identified with that figure and his narrative. In fact, the description of his kingdom proclamation in 1:14–15 seems to be governed by Isaiah 52:7:

> How beautiful upon the mountains are the feet of the messenger who announces peace, who brings good news, who announces salvation, who says to Zion, "Your God reigns."

It is worth noting that this same cluster of texts and expectations shapes the representation of the Son of Man figure in the Parables of Enoch, a work now generally considered to be of early Jewish origin, and of course, a representative of the genre apocalypse. There, too, the figure of the Isaianic Servant plays a crucial generative role in the depiction of the central agent of redemption,[14] and there too, a particular emphasis is placed on the empowering of this individual by the Spirit:

> The elect one stands before the Lord of Spirits; his glory is for ever and ever and his power is unto all generations. In him dwells the Spirit of wisdom, the Spirit that gives thoughtfulness, the Spirit of knowledge and strength and the Spirit of those who have fallen asleep in righteousness (1 Enoch 49:2b–3).

That both works draw upon the Isaianic imagery is important, calling further attention to the fact that what is distinctively apocalyptic in each is not the eschatology, which is drawn from Isaiah, but rather the identification of the Servant and his representation as a glorious heavenly being.

The identification of Jesus with the Servant is elaborated by the voice from heaven that addresses him as "My beloved Son" (ὁ υἱός μου ὁ ἀγαπητός). This introduces a pattern that will characterize Mark's narrative of representing Jesus as the Messianic Son of God,[15] a pattern that will reach its ironic climax with the centurion's proclamation in 15:39. There is a widely acknowledged allusion here to Psalm 2:7:

> I will tell of the decree of the LORD: He said to me, "You are my son; today I have begotten you."

14. See my "Matthew and the Parables," in *Parables of Enoch: A Paradigm Shift*, ed. Darrell Bock and James Charlesworth, JCTC 11 (New York: Bloomsbury T&T Clark, 2013), 218–30.

15. See Robert D. Rowe, *God's Kingdom and God's Son: The Background to Mark's Christology from Concepts of Kingship in the Psalms*, AGJU 50 (Leiden: Brill, 2002), 232. Rowe, referring to the extensive scholarly literature on this point, notes the importance of the title "Son of God" and its apposition to the word "Christ."

The psalm is generally read in the New Testament in relation to 2 Samuel 7:12–16[16] and there may be a further echo of Isaiah 42:1 in the apposed term ὁ ἀγαπητός.[17] There is, of course, a long history of scholarly conversation about whether these verses came to be applied to Jesus only after the resurrection.[18] Those conversations, however, pertain to the development of early Christian theology and not to the theology of Mark as a composition. The latter, in common with the other Synoptics, ensures that the true identity of Jesus is disclosed, *within* the narrative to Jesus himself and *through* the narrative to the Gospel's readers, in terms of a complex of textual traditions.[19] He is the Servant, the Messianic Son.

Satan and the Evil Spirits

Once this identification is made, it is important that the narrative then represents the Spirit as compelling Jesus to go into the wilderness, where he will be tempted for forty days by the Satan. As we have seen already, Isaiah 40:3 is treated as programmatic by the New Testament authors and by the Qumran community, with the wilderness specified as the place in which the way of God's coming will be prepared. That Jesus's conflict with Satan takes place in the desert is, then, important. The description is brief by comparison with the other Synoptics and lacks the detail of the temptations themselves. In its brevity, however, it calls greater attention to the duration of the wilderness sojourn: forty days. The obvious parallel with the forty years of wandering in the wilderness that Israel was forced to undertake is well established, but its significance must not be passed over too quickly: it means that the story of Jesus is told in a way that evokes the story of Israel, rather than being told in a way that marginalizes or bypasses that story. In the context of broader discussions of New Testament (notably, Pauline) apocalypticism, where the apocalyptic dimension is often considered to displace the story of Israel, that detail is important.

The identity of the antagonist, Satan, is deeply embedded in the New Testament traditions. The conspicuous presence of this figure at key points in the narrative is important evidence for some that Mark should be taken to be an apocalyptic work.[20] There is a valid and important point to that observation: it is a feature of texts displaying apocalyptic thought that reality is rendered in terms of forces and powers that cannot be perceived directly by the senses, but

16. See Rowe, *God's Kingdom and God's Son,* 246–47.
17. See Yarbro Collins, *Mark,* 150.
18. The position is developed forcefully in W. Schmithals, *Das Evangelium nach Markus*, 2 vols., ÖTK (Würzburg: Gütersloh and Echter, 1979), 1:84–89. Other representatives of the position are listed there.
19. The possibility that this reflects a genuine visionary experience of Jesus is considered by Joel Marcus, "Jesus' Baptismal Vision," *NTS* 41 (1995): 512–21.
20. For example, Elizabeth Shively, *Apocalyptic Imagination in the Gospel of Mark: The Literary and Theological Role of Mark 3:22-30*, BZNW 189 (Berlin: Walter de Gruyter, 2012).

that shape the outworking of earthly events.[21] Earthly events and powers are thus valorized and relativized: those powers that seem terrifyingly dominant, such as Rome, are set within a framework that consoles the reader by means of the revealed truth of God's sovereignty. The reuse of biblical traditions, such as those of Daniel or Zechariah, is an important part of this imaginative reconstrual of the significance of such powers. Within the context of Mark's Gospel, Shively rightly points to the importance of 3:22–30, in which Satan is represented as ruler of an undivided kingdom, to the narrative as a whole: Jesus's own purpose is cast in terms of the binding of this figure and his exorcisms are part of this work.[22]

New Testament scholars have largely neglected, however, the fact that the antagonist is so consistently and singularly identified in the New Testament as Satan. In the context of our demonstrably early Jewish texts, such as the Qumran Scrolls, the component texts of 1 Enoch, and Jubilees, we find a range of figures and titles: notably, Mastema, Belial,[23] Aza(z)el, Shemihazah,[24] with the title Satan used more occasionally for one of the leading antagonists. The predominance of Satan as the identified enemy is, in fact, a conspicuous feature only of the biblical texts (including the Hebrew Bible books of Job and Zechariah) and pseudepigraphical texts whose date and provenance are rather more debatable, such as The Life of Adam and Eve and 2 Enoch.[25] There is, though, an interesting parallel in Jubilees, where Satan seems to be identified with Mastema, and where the eschatological hope of Israel is connected to Satan's end and the purification of the world:

> And jubilees will pass until Israel is purified from all the sin of fornication, and defilement, and uncleanness, and sin and error. And they will dwell in confidence in all the land. And then it will not have any Satan or any evil (one). And the land will be purified from that time and forever (50:3, drawing on 23:29–30).[26]

In fact, this text provides an interesting background to the link that emerges in Mark between exorcism and purification. It is worth noting that the designation "unclean spirit" (e.g., 1:23)

21. This is not unconnected to belief in demonic beings, but the latter takes on a broader popular influence beyond the apocalyptic literature. The best current overview is Archie Wright, *The Origin of Evil Spirits: The Reception of Genesis 6:1-4*, WUNT II/198 (Tübingen: Mohr Siebeck, 2005), which traces the development of Jewish demonology in the Second Temple Period from readings of Gen 6:1–4 through the Enochic literature. See also his "Evil Spirits in Second Temple Judaism: The Watcher Tradition as a Background to the Demonic Pericopes in the Gospels," *Hen* 28 (2006): 141–59.
22. Shively, *Apocalyptic Imagination in the Gospel of Mark, in toto.*
23. The figures of Mastema and Belial appear frequently in the Dead Sea Scrolls and in Jubilees. The title Satan also occurs in the latter work, but only incidentally (e.g., in Jubilees 10:11).
24. These two figures are the chief antagonists in the Book of the Watchers.
25. On the possible Christian origin of the Adam and Eve books, see M. de Jonge, "The Christian Origins of the *Greek Life of Adam and Eve*," in *Literature on Adam and Eve: Collected Essays*, ed. Gary A. Anderson, Michael E. Stone, and Johannes Tromp, STVP 15 (Leiden; Boston: Brill, 2000), 347–63. The sections of text in which Satan is found in 2 Enoch belong only to one recension of the text and are likely to have been added to the original. See my discussion in *The Slavonic Texts of 2 Enoch*, Studia Judeoslavica 6 (Boston; Leiden: Brill, 2013), 23–25.
26. Translation, O. S. Wintermute, "Jubilees," in *The Old Testament Pseudepigrapha*, ed. James H. Charlesworth, 2 vols. (New York: Doubleday, 1983), 2:142.

is unusual in the literature of the time, but consistent with those apocalyptic texts connected to the Enochic traditions, in which the sins of the Watchers are represented as uncleanness (notably in 1 Enoch 15:3–4) and the demonic offspring they generate as being unclean demons (Jubilees 10:1). The connection between demonic evil and uncleanness, and hence, between exorcism and purification is important. Tigchelaar, in fact, notes the extent to which the removal of evil is represented precisely as purification in the apocalyptic texts.[27]

The representation of Jesus's role as set in opposition to the power of Satan is thus naturally connected to the place that exorcisms occupy in the Gospel narratives. Following the calling of the first disciples—a section of the text that I will pass over for the sake of space—the narrative describes one such exorcism that takes place on a Sabbath, in the synagogue in Capernaum. Several features require some closer attention.

First, while scholars often point to widespread contemporary evidence for Jewish belief in (and practice of) exorcism, reflecting also widespread belief in the existence of evil spirits,[28] they also generally acknowledge that the Gospel exorcisms are unusual in the absence of any ritual or spell.[29] In other words, there is nothing unique in the fact that Jesus is represented in the narratives as casting out demons, but the fact that he does so on the basis of simple command is quite distinctive. The second point follows from this: this evidence of authority over the demons is taken to validate the authority of his teaching (1:27). The emphasis falls, then, on the function of the exorcisms as validations of Jesus's status as a revealer of the true wisdom of God, a status that is connected to the presence of the Spirit. Taking this together with what we have seen already about the baptism narrative in 1:9–11, it is clear that Jesus is represented as both the revealer and the thing that is revealed. Third, there is a clear overlap of vocabulary between this scene and the calming of the storm in 4:35–41. There, in 4:39, Jesus employs the same verb in his command to the waves to be still that he uses to silence the evil spirit (φιμόω); while the forms are slightly different, reflecting predictable uses of tense, the root is the same and the occurrences beg to be read together. The narrative effect is strong: the same authority by which Jesus casts out demons with a simple command allows him also to control the forces of nature, again with a simple command. The two events are merely different enactments of the same authority. The subsequent description of the disciple's response is highly suggestive: they "fear with great fear" (a response associated with divine presence) and ask who Jesus is. Their question—"Who is this that even the wind and the waves obey him?"—is one that invites an identification to be made with the God who is alone considered sovereign over nature.

27. Tigchelaar, *Prophets of Old*, 255–57.
28. We have noted already Archie Wright, *Origin of Evil Spirits*. See, too, Chilton et al., *Comparative Handbook to the Gospel of Mark*, 83–89.
29. Yarbro Collins, *Mark*, 173.

The Messianic Secret

The exorcism also introduces us to one of the major discussions in Markan scholarship, concerning the "Messianic Secret." The evil spirit discloses the identity of Jesus as "the Holy One of God" and is immediately commanded to be silent before being cast out (1:25–26). It is one example of set of texts that was classically understood by Wrede to reflect the Markan doctrine of the "Messianic Secret."[30] Wrede proposed this idea as an explanation for the presence of a range of features in Mark that suggest that Jesus did not wish his identity as the Messiah or Son of God to be known. The silencing of demons is one example of this (a second instance of this is found in 1:34, "he would not let the demons speak, because they knew who he was"); another is exemplified later in the chapter when the man healed of leprosy is commanded to tell no one (1:44); a further key example is the stated purpose of the use of parables as being to obscure the truths of Jesus's teaching to "those outside" (ἐκείνοις δὲ τοῖς ἔξω 4:11). Wrede considered that the Messianic Secret was retrojected into the Gospel following the ascription of Messianic status to Jesus after the resurrection. Once his identity as the Messianic Son of God was incorporated into the narrative (in passages such as the baptism account), an explanation also had to be given for why this detail had been neglected in the traditions about Jesus's life. Wrede's solution was to argue that Mark presented Jesus as deliberately seeking to keep his identity a secret.

Wrede's thesis reflected a particular view of the development of Christology, with the secrecy motif having no basis in the historical Jesus traditions themselves. That view has been subject to criticism, though is still a matter of debate.[31] For our purposes here, a more important line of criticism concerns whether the various categories that Wrede brought together ought to be seen as serving a single purpose or as comprising a single theme. Much recent scholarship has argued against this, maintaining that there are various distinct themes of secrecy or hiddenness,[32] and that the *hiddenness* represented by the parable theory should be considered in quite different terms to the *secrecy* commanded of the demons and the disciples. The hiddenness of the meaning of the parables seems to be related to the different capacities of the insiders and the outsiders to understand the wisdom of Jesus, as we shall see: it is hid-

30. William Wrede, *Das Messiasgeheimnis in den Evangelien: zugleich ein Beitrag zum Verständnis des Markusevangeliums* (Göttingen: Vandenhoeck & Ruprecht, 1901).

31. For an excellent overview of the discussion, see Adela Yarbro Collins, "Messianic Secret and the Gospel of Mark: Secrecy in Jewish Apocalypticism, the Hellenistic Mystery Religions and Magic," in *Rending the Veil: Concealment and Secrecy in the History of Religions*, ed. Elliott R. Wolfson (New York: Seven Bridges, 1999), 11–30. Much of the article is reproduced in her *Mark* commentary.

32. See, e.g., Heikki Räisänen, *The Messianic Secret in Mark*, trans. Christopher Tuckett (Edinburgh: T&T Clark, 1990). Yarbro Collins, "Messianic Secret," 23–24, agrees with Wrede that the various hiddenness/secrecy motifs do share a common purpose, but disagrees with Wrede's explanation for this. She argues that the various themes work together to communicate the importance of the teaching about Jesus. In my view, however, she does not address the basic distinction between capacity to understand and permission to communicate.

den only to those incapable of comprehension. Secrecy, by contrast, is a matter of those who are capable of knowing the truth being prohibited from publicizing it. If we simply conflate the hiddenness motif with it, we will overlook an important marker of apocalyptic thought—specifically, the subjective capacity to receive revealed wisdom.[33]

The Stated Purpose of Jesus

One last point must be noted before we move on from the opening chapter of Mark, since it is an important (but easily overlooked) detail. In 1:38, Jesus indicates that his purpose is one of proclamation:

> ἄγωμεν ἀλλαχοῦ εἰς τὰς ἐχομένας κωμοπόλεις, ἵνα καὶ ἐκεῖ κηρύξω· εἰς τοῦτο γὰρ ἐξῆλθον.

The verse represents the role of Jesus, particularly in terms of "preaching," with the emphasis that it places on the verb *κηρύσσω*. That potentially reflects the continued programmatic significance of the Isaianic Servant for Mark's representation of Jesus (or indeed, for the conscious self-identification of Jesus himself): in Isaiah 61:1–3, this figure endowed with "the Spirit of wisdom and understanding" is represented as coming "to proclaim liberty to the captives and release to the prisoners," with the last clause altered in the LXX to "recovery of sight for the blind" (κηρύξαι αἰχμαλώτοις ἄφεσιν καὶ τυφλοῖς ἀνάβλεψιν). The healing and liberation spoken of in these verses has been enacted in the miracles that Jesus has already begun to perform at this stage in the narrative, and the identification of Jesus's purpose as one of preaching is at least suggestive of the figure of the Servant. Regardless of whether this is indeed the background of 1:38, the statement emphasizes the centrality of revelation to Jesus's role: he has come to *announce*. It is, I think, noteworthy that his proclamation in the synagogues of Galilee is accompanied by exorcism: his proclamation of the kingdom of God (1:15) is linked to the overturning of Satan's imperial reign, maintaining the Isaianic resonances noted above of liberation.

The Parables

As we have noted already, discussions of the Messianic Secret have typically linked the secrecy commanded of both demons and disciples to the statement of Mark 3:11–12, concerning the use of parables to hide the message of Jesus. All of this is taken together to reflect the idea that Jesus's life and ministry were considered non-messianic during his lifetime because the truth of his identity was deliberately protected. I have already suggested that we should distinguish

33. This is a pervasive theme in my *Received Wisdom and Inaugurated Eschatology in Ancient Judaism and Early Christianity*, JSJSup 115 (Leiden: Brill, 2007).

secrecy from hiddenness and some further discussion of the parables, or "parable theory," is now required in order to demonstrate this point more conclusively. In doing so, we will ensure that the apocalyptic character of the parables is not overlooked because of the concept of the messianic secret.

Jesus's teaching on his use of parables appears in the context of what is commonly labeled "The Parable of the Sower" (Mark 4:1–8), although it might also be labeled "The Parable of the Seed and Soils,"[34] since the emphasis falls not on the person of the Sower, but on the varying productivity of the seed, depending on which soil it reaches. This parable is told in public (4:1), with Jesus teaching "the crowd" from a boat upon the lake, but it is only to the disciples that Jesus gives the interpretation of the parable itself, accompanied by an explanation of why he uses parables. That explanation begins with the statement that the disciples have been given the mystery of the kingdom of God (ὑμῖν τὸ μυστήριον δέδοται τῆς βασιλείας τοῦ θεοῦ). A number of scholars rightly point to the parallels between the use of the word μυστήριον here and that of the Persian loanword *rāz*, which occurs widely in Daniel and in the Dead Sea Scrolls.[35] That word is used, particularly in the Scrolls, in ways that point to a body of wisdom that has been revealed specifically to the community and that is constitutive of their special identity as "the wise." While that body of wisdom is also to be kept within the community (in a way that is reminiscent of the Messianic Secret),[36] it is also clear that the capacity to receive and to understand the *rāz* is a special property of the community, given to it by God. Joel Marcus sees a clear parallel to this in the phrase "He who has ears to hear, let him hear."

> Only the one who, in the terms of the parable of the sower, is good soil will be addressable, will be able to hear, only the one to whom God has given ears can hear. Compare with this 1QH 1:21, where the author thanks God for unstopping his ears. With regard to Mark 4:24, "take heed what you hear," it should be noticed that this warning is framed by 4:23 and 4:25, both of which imply that "hearing" is not something that one can simply *decide* to do.[37]

In fact, for Marcus, this a crucial distinction between apocalyptic and gnostic notions of knowledge:

> [A]ll the emphasis is on God's action in the present which *creates* perception or, in this case, blinding. As opposed to the dynamism of apocalyptic epistemology, gnostic epistemology emphasizes the hearer's capacity to perceive as a given.[38]

34. See, Rikki E. Watts, "Mark," in *Commentary on the New Testament Use of the Old Testament*, ed. G. K. Beale and D. A. Carson (Grand Rapids: Baker Academic, 2007), 150.
35. For specimen texts, see Chilton *et al.*, *Comparative Handbook to the Gospel of Mark*, 161–64.
36. 1QS 8:2–4.
37. Joel Marcus, "Mark 4:10–12 and Markan Epistemology," *JBL* 103 (1984): 562.
38. Marcus, "Mark 4:10–12," 561.

This observation stems from Jeremias's recognition that three words in Mark 4:11–12 are circumlocutions for the activity of God, even though he is not explicitly identified as the agent: δέδοται, γίνεται and ἀφεθῇ.[39] Without the agency of God in giving access to wisdom, hearers remain deaf, which is why the author of the Hodayot thanks God for unstopping his ears (1QH[a] 1:21).[40] Interestingly, Matthew and Luke (Matt 13:11; Luke 8:10) agree in having the further word γνῶναι: "to you it has been given *to know* the mystery, etc." This makes more explicit that the gift is not simply the body of wisdom, but the capacity to comprehend it. But does the absence of this word in Mark indicate that the emphasis on the divine enabling of comprehension is less developed in this Gospel? Such a conclusion would overlook Mark's distinctively negative portrayal of the disciples. Mark represents these privileged recipients of the mystery as incapable of understanding it: hence the questions in 4:13 with which Jesus introduces his interpretation, "Don't you understand this parable? How, then, will you understand any parable?" In fact, this strategy reinforces the necessity of divine enabling: at this point in the narrative, the disciples are as bewildered as "those outside," but the same disciples will be directed at the end of the Gospel to go to Galilee where they will *see* the risen Jesus, when their sense will be capable of comprehension. By that point, of course, the identity of Jesus will have been grasped properly by the centurion (15:39).

All three versions of this parable in the Synoptic Gospels include quotations of Isaiah 6:9–10 in their explanation of the parable. In the case of Mark and Luke, the quotation is partial, omitting much of the original to the extent that the alternative term "allusion" may be justified.[41] There are modest differences between the Synoptics that need not detain us, but one feature common to Mark and Luke requires comment: both introduce the Isaianic material with the word ἵνα, indicating that the parables are intended to bring about incomprehension. Some have balked at this, considering it absurd and proposing that Mark mistranslated the Aramaic tradition of Jesus's words, an error maintained by Luke.[42] Most, though, recognizing the literary and rhetorical strategies at work in Mark, take the word seriously and grapple with its force. For Snodgrass, the original sense (in context) of Isaiah 6:9–10 is the crucial element: those verses speak of the blindness and hard-heartedness of Israel.

> The function of this language is both a warning of what is happening—that judgment is inevitable, that the people have not responded and will not—and also a challenge and an invitation not to remain in such insensitivity, but to hear the word and repent.[43]

39. J. Jeremias, *The Parables of Jesus*, 2nd ed. (New York: Scribner, 1972), 15–16.
40. The parallel is noted by Marcus, "Mark 4:10–12," 562.
41. Yarbro Collins, *Mark*, 249.
42. So T. W. Manson, *The Teaching of Jesus* (Oxford: Clarendon, 1939), 75–80.
43. Klyne Snodgrass, *Stories with Intent: A Comprehensive Guide to the Parables of Jesus* (Grand Rapids: Eerdmans, 2008), 160.

Once this background is taken into account, for Snodgrass, we are prompted to read Mark 4:10–12 in a less "crassly literalistic"[44] way. The whole quotation or allusion presents Jesus as a prophet, whose ministry corresponds to that of Isaiah or Jeremiah and elicits a similar response: one largely of hard-heartedness, but with a remnant who hear and respond. The purpose that is indicated by the use of ἵνα is this deliberate correspondence with the prophetic tradition.

Perhaps, though, Snodgrass neglects the extent to which traditions can be reread or reinterpreted in apocalyptic thought and his rejection of "crassly literalistic" readings of the verses minimizes their force. If we allow that ἵνα points to purpose, then the use of parables can be seen to operate intentionally to demarcate insider from outsider. Such an approach, with its parallels to the apocalyptic texts from Qumran noted above, allows us to see the parables not as code that requires decoding, and therefore inaccessible to the outsider—only the Parable of the Sower is explained, after all—but rather as a form of communication that is meaningful to those with the "ears to hear" but baffling to those without such capacities. Functionally, it reinforces the readers' perceptions of themselves as belonging to the community enlightened by divine transformation.[45] Crucially, it directs faith and gratitude to the God whose revelatory activity lies behind this and explains the failure of most to respond to the Gospel. Such an explanation makes good sense of the use of the label "those outside," reflecting the narrative development of a social identity based on revealed wisdom.

The Transfiguration of the Son of God and the Suffering of the Son of Man

The account of Jesus's transfiguration is one of the blocks of Markan text that connects most obviously with the apocalypses, reflecting a pattern of texts in which humans are transformed in some way as part of their experience of heavenly realities. In fact, comparison with those other texts is highly instructive, revealing some significant distinctives within the biblical account of transfiguration.

Before we examine these, however, it is important to note that this account also has links with other passages within the Gospel that we have identified as having apocalyptic significance. Most striking in this regard is the repetition of the words spoken by the voice from heaven, which are now directed not to Jesus, but to the disciples: οὗτός ἐστιν ὁ υἱός μου ὁ

44. Ibid., 158.
45. On this, see Maxine Grossman, "Cultivating Identity: Textual Virtuosity and 'Insider' Status," and Carol A. Newsom, "Constructing 'We, You and the Others' through Non-Polemical Discourse," both in *Defining Identities: We, You, and the Other in the Dead Sea Scrolls: Proceedings of the Fifth Meeting of the IOQS in Gröningen*, ed. Florentino García Martínez and Mladen Popović, STDJ 70 (Leiden: Brill, 2008), 1–12 and 13–22, respectively.

ἀγαπητός, ἀκούετε αὐτοῦ (Mark 9:7, cf. 1:11). At the risk of belaboring a point that we have now made several times, it is worth noting that these words call attention to Jesus's unique authority as an agent of instruction: the proper acknowledgement of his sonly identity, the response that is commanded of the witnesses, is to "listen to him."[46] Alongside this explicit recapitulation of the baptismal address, there are less obvious (but still important) echoes of the opening chapter, and particularly, the baptism narrative. The presence of Elijah and Moses (9:4–6) is one of these. Elijah, of course, provides the template for the representation of John the Baptist (1:6), a fact that lies in the background of the discussion in 9:11–13, in which John is identified as the promised Elijah *redivivus*. This takes us back to a point that was made earlier in this study—namely, that John's ministry is identified with the eschatological scenario described in Malachi 3:1–6, that of the day of the Lord. Clearly, then, we are dealing with debates over eschatology, but these are the outworking of prophetic expectations and do not themselves constitute anything distinctively apocalyptic. Similarly, the presence of Moses evokes the theme of new exodus, with its Isaianic overtones, that is widely acknowledged to characterize Mark's narrative.[47]

Both of these figures, of course, are also associated with acts of divine self-disclosure and human vision (Exodus 24, 33–34; 1 Kings 19), each of which takes place upon a mountain. That biblical tradition provides an important background to this scene, one that is arguably more relevant than some of the apocalyptic parallels that may be adduced and that is specifically evoked by the mountaintop context. In fact, the evoking of those narratives casts the representation of Jesus in a different light. Both Moses and Elijah encountered the glory of God on mountaintops. Here, both of these men are again represented as being in the presence of glory, but now that glory is a property of Jesus.

This is an important point to tease out further. Much of the scholarly literature on the Transfiguration uses the adjective "angelic" of Jesus's glory, paralleling a tendency in some research on apocalyptic texts to speak of transformed human beings in similar terms; their glory is sometimes designated as "angelomorphic." Whether the latter term is defensible need not preoccupy us;[48] our concern, instead, is with Mark's specific representation of the glory of Jesus and whether this is best understood as angelic or as parallel to the transformation of humans, whether in the eschaton,[49] in ascent to heaven,[50] or in earthly participation in heavenly liturgy.[51] I would suggest not, and that, instead, the glory is to be identified as that of God himself. I have already mentioned one reason for understanding the passage in this way,

46. There may be a deliberate allusion to Deut 18:15 and the response expected to the prophet spoken of there.
47. See Watts, *Isaiah's New Exodus*, details in note 7, above.
48. See my *Union with Christ in the New Testament* (Oxford: Oxford University Press, 2013), 119–21.
49. Cf. 2 Baruch 51:3–5.
50. Cf. 2 Enoch 22.

the narrative evocation of previous encounters with divine glory, but others emerge on closer examination.

As Rowland notes, the Transfiguration resembles apocalyptic theophany scenes, particularly Daniel 10 and Revelation 1:13–16, both of which are connected to the throne-theophany of Ezekiel 1, from which they derive their imagery and language.

> Here alone of all the Synoptic texts . . . we come closest to the glorious heavenly appearance of the angelic figure.[52]

Rowland, however, proceeds to note the similarities with 1 Enoch 14:20–21 (and its wider context):

> And the Great Glory sat upon it [the throne];
> His raiment was like the appearance of the sun;
> And whiter than much snow.
> And no angel could enter into this house and behold his face because of the splendor and glory;
> and no flesh could behold him.[53]

The similarity is striking indeed, with some shared vocabulary: "sun," "face," and "clothing." In fact, Matthew and Luke both have variant readings that incorporate the word "snow," possibly reflecting awareness of the Enochic theophany traditions.[54] The key point, of course, is that this is a description of God himself, not angelic beings and the parallel texts in Daniel 10 and Revelation 1 allow for the possibility that the heavenly figure encountered is, in fact, this same God. Rowland presents this scene as the removal of a veil from the identity of Jesus.

> [H]e is beheld in communion with those who were his "natural" companions—the exalted Elijah and Moses—a mystery which has hitherto only been recognized by the demons.[55]

This, though, is to understate the uniqueness of Jesus in the scene, particularly in Mark's version. For Elijah and Moses are not described as transfigured beings; only Jesus is represented in such terms (cf. Luke 9:31). Only one of the three figures on the mountain is presented as embodied glory; there remains a qualitative distinction between Jesus and the other two figures.

Other details confirm that we are dealing, here at least, not with the disclosure of heavenly identity, but with the disclosure of properly divine identity. The appearance of the cloud is

51. Carol Newsom, *Songs of the Sabbath Sacrifice: A Critical Edition* (Atlanta: Scholars, 1985), highlights the pervasive presence of such ideas.
52. Rowland and Morray-Jones, *Mystery of God*, 106.
53. Translation from George W. E. Nickelsburg, *1 Enoch 1: A Commentary on the Book of 1 Enoch, Chapters 1-36; 81-108*, Hermeneia (Minneapolis: Fortress, 2001), 257.
54. For these lexical connections and discussions of variants, see Rowland and Morray-Jones, *Mystery of God*, 106.
55. Rowland and Morray-Jones, *Mystery of God*, 107.

one such detail. This is a feature typically associated with divine manifestation (cf. Exod 34:5). While here, it could be identified with the voice that proclaims Jesus's identity as Son—and hence disconnected from the glory of Jesus himself—this would overlook the broader significance of the detail as evoking theophany. The comparison with the glory of Moses in Exodus 34:29–30 is now particularly instructive: there, merely the face of Moses is radiant, while here, Jesus is thoroughly resplendent. As Adela Yarbro Collins notes, there are also some strong parallels between such imagery and Hellenistic theophanies,[56] and these point in the direction of an identification of Jesus as a divine, not just a heavenly being.

One apocalyptic text perhaps deserves special mention here, since it provides a description of an exalted human that corresponds closely to the description of Jesus. Second Enoch 22 belongs to the Enochic tradition that considers the patriarch to have been taken to heaven and transformed. It is a difficult text to date and to locate and may not really provide much by way of background or context to this passage.[57] Even if this is allowed, for the sake of argument, the differences are important. Enoch's transfiguration occurs in the heavenly throne room, after a lengthy and detailed ascent narrative. It involves ritual elements, as Enoch is stripped and re-dressed and then anointed with oil that alters his form (2 Enoch 22:8–9). Most importantly, this is done in order to allow Enoch to endure a position of proximity to the glory of the Lord (22:6; 24:1; cf. also ch. 39). By contrast, here in Mark, we have a simple and sparse description of transfiguration that merely describes Jesus using words traditionally associated with the glory of God.

In keeping with his negative representation of the disciples at this stage in the narrative, Mark represents this moment of revelation as one that brings only confusion for Peter and the disciples (Mark 9:6). We must bear in mind as we read this that Mark's narrative will close with the disciples being directed to return to Galilee, where they will again "see" Jesus; some of the theories that have absolutized the ignorance of the disciples in the Gospel fail to recognize this important point and overlook the pivotal significance of the cross for the comprehension of Jesus's identity.

That point is significant here, for the account of the Transfiguration is also linked with the representation of Jesus as the suffering Son of Man. In all of the Synoptic accounts, the descent from the mountain involves Jesus instructing the disciples to keep what they have seen secret—a command that is not confined to Mark—and further instructing them concerning the suffering of the Son of Man. It is, perhaps, a surprising move, given the glorification that has just been witnessed. The obvious parallels that we would note are with the representations of

56. Yarbro Collins, *Mark*, 418–19.
57. See my discussion in *The Slavonic Texts of Enoch*, Studia Judaeoslavica 6 (Leiden; Boston: Brill, 2013).

the glorious Son of Man figure in the Parables of Enoch or the "one like a son of man" in Daniel 7. These parallels are real and striking and we can see here the traditions of the Son of Man that they reflect dovetailing with Mark's dominant presentation of Jesus as the Son of God (Mark 9:7).

But, by contrast to the figure in the Parables, the Son of Man in Mark is destined to suffer. That is the point made in 9:12, with reference to what has been "written" of this figure. All scholars recognize that there is some combination of traditions at work here: there are no texts that provide any direct background to the idea that the Son of Man, specifically, must suffer. Isaiah 53 is often noted as a potential source for the language, with its representation of the suffering Servant, but it does not use the term Son of Man. Similarly, the lexical connection of ἐξουδενηθῇ (Mark 9:12) with Psalm 22:7 (21:7 LXX) has led some scholars to see this psalm as lying in the background, but with the same problem: there is no mention of the Son of Man.

The crucial piece of evidence may lie in the Parables of Enoch. There is nothing there to present the Son of Man as a figure who suffers, but there is evidence for a tradition that identified the Danielic Son of Man with the Isaianic Servant: the depiction of the Son of Man is a complex one that clearly draws upon, and is fundamentally determined by, that of Isaiah's Servant passages.[58] Once this is recognized as an interpretative tradition within Judaism, the further move to identifying the Son of Man with the suffering individual in Isaiah 53 is less difficult to explain.

Whether or not this is correct, an important analogy is established between John's experience of suffering as the returning Elijah—"they have done to him everything they wished"—and that of the Son of Man. Even with this testimony, however, the disciples are incapable of understanding the revelation of Jesus, and the place that suffering must take within it, until after the crucifixion. The following story, in which the disciples fail to exorcise an evil spirit (9:14–29), is followed by a block of private instruction (9:30–31) providing further detail on the death and resurrection of the Son of Man. Again, however, the disciples fail to understand (9:31–32).

Mark 13

The final major block of the Gospel that we must examine is that of Mark 13, often inappropriately labeled as the "little apocalypse" and paralleled in the other Synoptics with some variation. This discourse has received extensive scholarly attention over the years, with particular attention paid to issues of source and redaction. The detail of these scholarly debates is impor-

58. See my discussion in "Matthew and the Parables" (n. 14 above).

tant, but will be impossible to explore in any meaningful depth in the context of this chapter.[59] Instead, we will focus on a small number of key issues in the text, noting the broader point that the reworking and reinterpretation of older traditions is a standard feature of apocalyptic texts: Mark undoubtedly draws upon older traditions that themselves reinterpret biblical texts. Similarly, scholarly discussions about the eschatology reflected in the passage are extensive and there is little point in discussing these in detail here, except for a small number that we will examine more closely. While source critical and eschatological issues have been examined at length by scholarship, less has, however, been written on the themes of disclosure and revelation of wisdom in the passage. It is on these that we shall concentrate in the discussion that follows.

The Temple and the True Messiah

The discourse is introduced with reference to the fate of the temple: the disciples' misplaced wonder at the magnificence of the temple buildings, and the stones of which they are built, prompts Jesus to speak of their future destruction (13:2), using language that probably intentionally inverts Haggai's prophecy of the building of the temple (Haggai 2:15–16).[60] Where Haggai prophesies of stone being placed upon stone, Jesus prophesies that no stone will be left upon stone. The expectation of a new temple being built in place of the Second Temple is an important feature of some Jewish literature that may be categorized as apocalyptic,[61] and is associated with the work of the Messiah.[62] Here, though, the promise of the temple's destruction is not followed be any expectation that it will be rebuilt. In the context of Mark's narrative, as distinct from pre-Markan traditions,[63] this detail must be related by the reader to the moment of Jesus's death, when the veil is torn. The temple's destiny and role are, hence, inextricably linked to the destiny and role of Jesus himself.

It is interesting that Jesus's response to the question that his statement provokes—"When will this be, and what will be the sign that all these things are about to be accomplished?" (13:4)—is introduced with a warning about false prophets and claimants of his identity: "Beware that no one leads you astray. Many will come in my name and say, 'I am he!' and they will lead many astray" (13:5–6). It is easy to pass too quickly over this point in our rush to

59. See the discussion in Yarbro Collins, *Mark*, 594–600.

60. See Rudolf Pesch, *Das Markusevangelium II: Kommentar zu Kap. 8.27–16.20*, HThKNT 2:2 (Freiburg: Herder, 1977), 271.

61. E.g., 11Q19 29:6–10. So, too, Jubilees 1:17, 27.

62. Cf. Zech 6:12–13.

63. Yarbro Collins, *Mark*, 601, argues that the original saying must have included a reference to the rebuilding of the temple; this, though, neglects the possibility that Jesus himself may have taught some species of the "eschatological community as temple" concept that seems to run through the wider New Testament and that can be traced back to its earliest strata. See my discussion in *Union with Christ*, 147–71.

reach what follows: this is not simply a warning about one element in an eschatological scenario (the emergence of false prophets), but rather a basic concern that Jesus's disciples—and Mark's readers—know the truth and are not deceived by false revelation. That false claimants to the title of Christ are also listed highlights that at the core of this battle between truth and falsehood is the proper identification of Jesus himself as the true Messiah (13:6). This theme continues through the chapter, occurring again in 13:21–23.

> 21And if anyone says to you at that time, "Look! Here is the Messiah!" or "Look! There he is!"—do not believe it. 22False messiahs and false prophets will appear and produce signs and omens, to lead astray, if possible, the elect. 23But be alert; I have already told you everything.

Again, the concern that is articulated concerns proper knowledge of the truth that Jesus has revealed, including his own identity as Messiah. It is expected that the ideal disciple or reader will be capable of identifying falsehood by means of this disclosure.[64] The recipients of that teaching must be alert and watchful, both for falsehood and for the return of the "master of the house" (13:34–36), whose identity we will discuss below.

Catastrophe, Truth, and Martyrdom

Jesus predicts a catastrophic situation, with wars, earthquakes, and famines constituting the "beginning of birth pains" (ἀρχὴ ὠδίνων, 13:8). This language and imagery is clearly eschatological in character. While some of the imagery may be connected to events that lay in the past at the point when the Gospel was written, prompting suspicions of *ex eventu* prophecy, it can also be traced back to biblical images, particularly in the prophetic writings. There is nothing necessarily distinctive in itself about the *use* of such imagery here, though it is obviously *configured* in a particular way and there are significant parallels with properly designated apocalypses. What is most distinctive is the emphasis on the protracted duration of the period that precedes the appearance of the Son of Man in the clouds and on the dangers that face believers during such a time of eschatological fervor, namely, that they will be misled by false prophets and false Christs (13:21–23). Instead of looking for such figures in the midst of catastrophe, the followers of Jesus should wait ever more expectantly for the arrival of the true Messiah, the Son of Man who is at the gates (13:26, 29). As those to whom the identity of this one has now been disclosed, they are expected to recognize the falsehood of other claimants.

In fact, this emphasis on *whom* the followers of Jesus are rightly to expect rather displaces the question of *when* they are to expect him, slicing through the eschatological schema. While

64. Related to this, there has been much discussion of the significance of the expression, "Let the reader understand," in 13:14. See Yarbro Collins, *Mark*, 596–98. For the sake of space, I will not engage with this expression: while it may have apocalyptic significance, a case can also be made that it is a help for readers to deal with the awkward syntax of the Daniel quotation.

they are told to interpret the catastrophic events as signs that indicate the Son of Man will come soon (13:28–29), they are also warned that neither the angels nor the Son know the hour at which this will happen (13:32), but only the Father. This is an important contribution to the depiction of Jesus as revealer, since it represents his capacity to reveal as having limits and as being subordinated to the knowledge of the Father. It also means that those who have received Jesus's revelation are fully aware, in the midst of eschatological fervor and schematization, that it has not been given them to know when the Son of Man will come, but rather to know who that one is.

Those who know the truth of Jesus are also expected to testify publicly to it (13:9–13). The description of this activity is inextricably linked to the representation of Jesus throughout the Gospel. Like him, they will stand trial before the authorities (13:9; cf. 14:53–15:15), before whom their witness will constitute the proclamation of the εὐαγγέλιον to the nations (13:10; cf. 1:1, 1:14–15); like him, they will be beaten (13:9; cf. 14:65, 15:16–20). Crucially, too, they will share in his capacity to proclaim and reveal the good news because of the Holy Spirit, who will speak through them. The description of Jesus's followers, then, represents them not just as the recipients of revealed wisdom, but as revealers participating in his work of proclamation. This is related both to the opening of the Gospel, with the descent of the Spirit and the heralding of the good news, and to the trial of Jesus that will follow in the next chapter.

The Son of Man Coming with the Clouds

The links between Mark 13:9–13 and the trial narrative are important to any discussion of Mark 13:26–27, since the same quotation from Daniel is repeated by Jesus before the Sanhedrin (14:62), immediately after his public acknowledgement that he is "the Messiah, the Son of the Blessed One" (14:61). The narrative effect is to ensure that Jesus, specifically, is identified as the Danielic Son of Man, who is, in turn, identified as the Messianic Son of God. It is worth noting the cues in the text that require the ideal reader of Mark to identify Jesus with God himself.

> 62 ὁ δὲ Ἰησοῦς εἶπεν· ἐγώ εἰμι, καὶ ὄψεσθε τὸν υἱὸν τοῦ ἀνθρώπου ἐκ δεξιῶν καθήμενον τῆς δυνάμεως καὶ ἐρχόμενον μετὰ τῶν νεφελῶν τοῦ οὐρανοῦ. 63 ὁ δὲ ἀρχιερεὺς διαρρήξας τοὺς χιτῶνας αὐτοῦ λέγει· τί ἔτι χρείαν ἔχομεν μαρτύρων;

The opening words, ἐγώ εἰμι, evoke the same texts as the Johannine "I am" sayings, particularly Deuteronomy 32:39, Isaiah 43:25 and 48:12, and possibly also Exodus 3:14.[65] It is not inappropriate to consider the words to constitute such an allusion to those items of divine speech, since the high priest immediately thereafter accuses Jesus of blasphemy. A distinction is maintained,

65. See my discussion in *Union with Christ*, 257–59.

of course, by the fact that the Son of Man is seated at the right hand of the power (ἐκ δεξιῶν καθήμενον τῆς δυνάμεως), but we are clearly in the territory of a high, even proto-Trinitarian, Christology.

All of this is important to how we understand Mark 13:26–27 in relation to its wider context, and particularly, to the image of the returning master (13:34–36). While it is not my intention to discuss in any depth the eschatology of these verses, it is important that we reflect on the identification of the Son of Man, and how this identification relates to Daniel 7:13–14. In recent years, some have argued that Daniel's image would have been understood by Jesus and his contemporaries as a symbolic corporate representation of the vindication of God's people, rather than as a description of the physical arrival of a heavenly being.[66] The cosmic imagery that surrounds the quotation, likewise, would be taken as symbolic and not literal. As such, this would not necessarily be an "end of the world" event, but rather a symbolic representation of some historical event that would constitute such a vindication. For N.T. Wright, this is the destruction of the temple, so that the Son of Man saying is part of a discourse that, from beginning to end, describes the destruction of Jerusalem and the temple in 70 CE. While this is attractive, and would allow us to consider the account as a whole to be more integrated and focused than scholars have sometimes believed it to be, there are problems. Most importantly, there is little clear evidence that such interpretations of Daniel 7 existed until much later, in the writings of Ibn Ezra. This reflects structural elements within the text of Daniel 7 itself that resist a corporate identification.[67] Moreover, there is good evidence for contemporary belief in real cosmic catastrophes within eschatological scenarios, so that the claim that these elements are *necessarily* symbolic here must also be considered problematic.[68]

What this means is that the more traditional interpretation of the verses as describing the anticipated *parousia* of Jesus, as a creative reinterpretation of Daniel 7, is to be preferred, even if it raises problems for the integrity of the discourse as a whole. Jesus is thus identified with the Danielic Son of Man, and hence, revealed to be a heavenly being, a revelation that will be disclosed at the point of his return to the whole world (13:23–26). If that claim appears hollow in the light of Jesus's impending death, the narrative will challenge the reader still further: since it is at the very point of that death that the identity of Jesus as the Son of God will finally be recognized (15:39).

66. The best-known example of this position is N.T. Wright, *Jesus and the Victory of God* (London: SPCK, 1996), 339–67.
67. See the discussion of Daniel 7 in John J. Collins, *A Commentary on the Book of Daniel*, Hermeneia. (Minneapolis: Fortress Press, 1993).
68. Edward Adams, *The Stars Will Fall From Heaven: 'Cosmic Catastrophe' in the New Testament and its World*, LNTS 347 (London: T&T Clark, 2007).

Conclusions: The Conclusion of the Gospel

By considering apocalyptic thought as principally about revelation, we have been able to take a distinctive approach to Mark's apocalyptic elements, highlighting elements generally overlooked. Rather than simply rehearsing our observations, I want to close this essay by isolating some of our key findings and noting how these are worked into the Gospel's own conclusion.

The Earthly Jesus as Revealer and Revealed

From the opening of the narrative, it is clear that Jesus is represented as the one proclaiming the good news, revealing the truth, but also as the one whose true identity is revealed to his followers. The disclosure of that identity involves moments of apocalyptic unveiling, such as the baptism and transfiguration narratives, but also involves the uptake and transformation of biblical texts and traditions, particularly those of Isaiah, which serve to integrate the range of biblical texts to which allusions are made. As Robin Griffith-Jones notes, though, these texts are applied precisely to the earthly Jesus of the Gospel narrative; the closing of the Gospel hence directs the reader to go back to the Galilee where the stories of this Jesus take place, to return to the beginning of the Gospel and reread the account with open eyes, in order to "see" him truly (16:7).[69]

The Death of Jesus as Revelatory Event

Those whom Jesus directs in this way within the narrative are the disciples, who have thus far been consistently unable to understand Jesus's teaching or penetrate his identity as the Messianic Son of God who will suffer as the Son of Man. The turning point in the narrative is the death of Jesus itself. While the disciples are not represented as being enlightened at this point, the centurion's moment of insight is clearly of greater significance than just his own capacity to perceive. It is connected to the rending of the veil that prevents access to the temple (15:38–39), lexically parallel to the opening of the heavens at the baptism of Jesus, and paves the way for the promise of 16:7 that the disciples will now see Jesus. Why the death of Jesus has such revelatory significance is not made clear in the Gospel, only the fact that it is pivotal.

Epistemic Incapacity and Divine Power

The parallel of 1:10 and 15:39 in Mark has an important narrative function that contributes to our understanding of revealed wisdom in the Gospel. There, as here, the tearing is associated

69. Griffith-Jones, "Going Back to Galilee," 82–83.

with a revelation of the true identity of Jesus as the Son of God: the statement of the centurion echoes the words of the voice from heaven in 1:10. In the latter, however, the statement is one of human (not divine) acknowledgement, and it is associated with the death of Jesus. In terms of the narrative, it represents an interesting outworking of the idea that revealed wisdom involves both an objective truth that is disclosed and the subjective realization of this by humans. Hence, as the narrative progresses, we move from "You are my Son" (1:10) to "This is my Son," (9:7) to "Truly this man was the Son of God" (15:39), and in the process, the reader is faced with the incongruity of the event that triggers the subjective recognition. This means that the surface-level tragedy of the cross is narratively reconfigured as the redemptive outworking of the baptism event. This recognition of a *real* significance that is contrary to the *natural* or *sensory* significance of an event is a strikingly apocalyptic feature. To return to the comment in the previous section: it is not made clear why the death of Jesus has such apocalyptic significance, but the key may lie in the programmatic significance of the Isaianic Servant, and particularly, the play in the Fourth Servant song on the contrast between human estimation and divine purpose (Isa 53:3–6).

Eschatology Subordinated to Revealed Identity

The last point to note is that, while the narrative of the Gospel is eschatological, representing the events of Jesus's life and death as the outworking of Scriptural hopes, what is prioritized throughout is the identification of those hopes with the person of Jesus. Again, the *denouement* of the eschatological drama that centers on the death of Jesus is the centurion's acknowledgement of the identity of Jesus (15:39). The centrality of this revealed identity to the work of salvation is reflected in Mark 13, with its warnings about false Christs and the dangers of false teaching in the midst of the eschatological woes.

4

Angels and Visions in Luke-Acts

Kindalee Pfremmer De Long

The issue of the apocalyptic nature of Luke-Acts has been a subject of much discussion since Hans Conzelmann's groundbreaking study. However, most studies investigating apocalyptic aspects of the two-volume work have followed Conzelmann in equating the words "apocalyptic" and "eschatological." From the fuller view of apocalyptic laid out in the introduction to this volume, an apocalyptic scene or discourse in Luke-Acts may be defined as the direct unveiling or disclosure of divine secrets to a human being. The word "direct" in this definition refers to visions, dreams, or pronouncements by a heavenly intermediary. In content, this revelation may be eschatological, laying out the divine plan for future of the universe, but it may also reveal the present or the past. Some revealed secrets may be purely heavenly in nature, such as a glimpse of God's glory, but often, revealed heavenly realities have a correlative component or effect on earth. Apocalypticism then is not extra-historical or a-historical but seeks to understand history in light of the divine plan.

From this perspective, Luke-Acts, a two-volume historiographical narrative, includes many apocalyptic moments of direct revelation, including appearances by angels, visionary experiences, and direction by the Holy Spirit. Scenes of interaction with demons or Satan, while not precisely revelatory, have affinities with apocalyptic literature as well. Since Luke depicts Jesus as light from on high (e.g., Luke 1:78; 2:32), any special revelation by the earthly Jesus to his followers might also be considered apocalyptic. Because the length of this chapter precludes investigation of all this material, I have chosen to focus on moments in the narrative in which characters experience revelation by means of heavenly figures or phenomena. The most obvious instances are the appearance of angels, so the analysis begins there. It then turns to overview scenes that do not involve angels but are identified in the narrative as visions or visionary experiences.

Angelic Revelation

Angels enter the story with some regularity in Luke-Acts. They appear three times in the infancy narrative, providing revelation and interpretation foundational to Luke's story, but after that, they disappear as active participants in the story until after Jesus's death, when two angelic men interpret the empty tomb and ascension (Luke 24:23; Acts 1:10).[1] After Pentecost, angels provide revelation, help, instruction, and encouragement as the Gospel moves outward from Jerusalem (Acts 5:19; 8:26; 10:3, 7, 22; 11:13; 12:7–15; 27:23–26) and an angel punishes Herod (Agrippa I) when he accepts praise due to God (Acts 12:23). Most often, the angel appears alone; exceptions are the heavenly host in Luke 2 and the scenes of the empty tomb, where two angelic men appear together. After Gabriel's first two appearances, angels are not named, but for scenes involving only one angel, the most natural reading envisions the same angel appearing successively rather than a series of different angelic beings. If so, it would be reasonable to assume that Gabriel reappears in each scene, although commentators on Luke do not generally hold this view. Beyond their active role in the narrative, angels also appear in the discourse or thoughts of other characters.[2] While this material provides fertile ground for investigation of apocalyptic aspects of Luke-Acts, due to limits of space, the analysis below focuses on scenes in which angels participate as characters in the story.

Luke's narrative depiction of angels mirrors the way angels appear in biblical narrative. The "angel of the Lord"—or the angel who stands in the presence of the Lord—appears period-

1. In some manuscripts, Jesus receives the help of angels as he prays in the garden of Gethsemane (Luke 22:43). For arguments for and against originality, respectively, see Claire Clivaz, "The Angel and the Sweat Like 'Drops of Blood' (Lk 22:43–44): P69 and F13," *HTR* 98 (2005): 419–40; Bart D. Ehrman and Mark A. Plunkett, "The Angel and the Agony: The Textual Problem of Luke 22:43–44," *CBQ* 45 (1983): 401–16. Because of the textual issue, I have not included this verse in the analysis below.

2. The devil states that angels will intervene to protect Jesus (Luke 4:10). Jesus speaks about the role and nature of angels in heaven (Luke 9:26; 12:8–9; 15:10; 16:22; 20:36) and seems to view Satan as an angel (Luke 10:18). The opponents of Stephen perceive that his face was like that of angel (Acts 6:15), and when he tells the story of the exodus, he includes the details that Moses was sent to his people by an angel (Acts 7:30, 35) and received the law through angelic revelation (7:38, 53). The people in Mary's house wonder whether it is actually Peter's angel who stands outside their door knocking (Acts 12:15). Paul states that Pharisees acknowledge angels but Sadducees do not (Acts 23:8–9).

ically in Scripture to provide help and revelation for the sake of Israel as a whole.[3] Biblical writers so closely associate this angel with God that the two sometimes become indistinguishable: less a distinct being, and more a way of describing how God interacts with humans.[4] This lays the foundation for the narrative function of the angel to "maintain the tension between divine transcendence and divine immanence without sacrificing either half of the paradox. The angel is a face of the infinite God that is suited to our limitations as finite beings."[5] Similarly, Luke often identifies angels with the biblical phrases "angel of the Lord" (ἄγγελος κυρίου) (Luke 1:11; 2:9; Acts 5:19; 8:26; 12:7, 23) or angel of God (Acts 10:3; 27:23). As in the Hebrew Bible, angels function to foreground divine intervention and initiative, establishing that God directs the events of the story.[6]

Because angels reveal God, they are, by definition, an apocalyptic aspect of biblical narrative. But in portions of Ezekiel, Daniel, and Zechariah, as well as later apocalyptic texts, their revelatory nature becomes more pronounced. Possessing names and distinct identities, they often reveal cosmological or eschatological mysteries, sometimes by means of a vision of heaven or heavenly ascent. These texts also offer glimpses of the cosmological role of angels, who fight a spiritual battle against evil, and serve as heavenly priests, praising God in the heavenly temple. In Luke-Acts, angels reflect some of this more strongly apocalyptic character. In Luke, they reveal Jesus's birth as beginning eschatological restoration and interpret his death as a necessary part of the divine plan, leading to the resurrection. In Acts, they work against powers opposed to God, while directing the mission West toward the center of the Roman Empire.

Angels in the Infancy Narrative

Angels figure prominently in three of Luke's opening scenes. In Luke 1:11–20, Gabriel, an "angel of the Lord," appears to Zechariah in the temple announcing that the priest's prayer has been heard, and his wife will give birth to a son. In 1:26–28, Gabriel appears again to Mary, revealing her future miraculous pregnancy. And in 2:9–12, an "angel of the Lord" appears to shepherds, again revealing divine activity and interpreting it. Immediately thereafter, a "heavenly host" joins this angel, praising God (2:13–14). Angels in these scenes are apocalyptic aspects of Luke's story because they reveal eschatological mysteries, provide two glimpses of the divine presence, suggest the spiritual conflict underlying the narrative, and respond to divine initiative with praise, encouraging humans to recognize God's salvation and respond likewise.

3. Susan R. Garrett, *No Ordinary Angel: Celestial Spirits and Christian Claims About Jesus* (New Haven: Yale University Press, 2008), 30.
4. As James Vanderkam observes, the "presence and the Lord himself are nearly identical," "The Angel of the Presence in the Book of Jubilees," *DSD* 7 (2000): 378–93 at 387.
5. Garrett, *No Ordinary Angel*, 29.
6. John T. Squires, *The Plan of God in Luke-Acts*, SNTSMS 76 (Cambridge: Cambridge University Press, 1993), 27–31.

Revelation and Interpretation

The single angel (perhaps Gabriel in all three cases) offers revelation and acts as *angelus interpres*. To Zechariah, the angel provides the name of child, reveals John's future mission, and discloses his own identity as Gabriel (1:13–17, 19). In addition, through allusion to LXX Malachi 3:1, 22–23 (and perhaps to Sir 48:10 also), the angel interprets John's birth as an eschatological event: the appearance of Elijah before the glorious day of Israel's restoration (Luke 1:16–17).

Revelation of eschatological events becomes more specifically messianic in Gabriel's words to Mary: Jesus will be great, holy, and Son of the Most High/God; will receive the throne of David; and will reign over the house of Jacob in an everlasting kingdom (1:32–33, 35).[7] The angel also discloses to Mary two secrets: her virginal conception through the Holy Spirit (1:35) and the hidden fact that Mary's previously barren cousin is sixth months pregnant (1:36).[8] Both secrets disclose the power of God (1:37).

An "angel of the Lord" (possibly Gabriel again) returns to proclaim to a group of shepherds good news for all the people of Israel (Luke 2:9–11). As in the previous two scenes, the angel interprets events as the inauguration of eschatological salvation. A child, whom the shepherds will find swaddled in a manger, is actually savior, Messiah, and Lord. The angel's description of the infant in the manger as a "sign" provides a clue to the need for an *angelus interpres*. In apocalypses, seers require angelic interpretation to understand the esoteric signs of visions, but Luke's characters need such interpretation because the surprising sign of salvation arrives in the midst of mundane circumstances.

The revelatory and interpretive function of Gabriel in Luke corresponds to some extent with Gabriel's role in other early Jewish texts. The scene with Zechariah in Luke 1 echoes Daniel. In both texts, Gabriel responds to a petition (δέησις) (Dan 9:17, 23; Luke 1:13); appears during prayer at the time of the incense offering (Dan 9:3, 21; Luke 1:10);[9] engenders the visionary's fear and silence (σιωπάω), albeit for different reasons (Dan 10:7–12, 15; Luke 1:12–13, 20); and is described as a "vision" (ὀπτασία) (Dan 9:23 Θ; Luke 1:21).[10] In Daniel, Gabriel twice reveals

7. John Nolland, *Luke 1–9:20*, WBC 35a (Waco: Word, 1989), 19. Curiously, Hans Klein states conversely that while Gabriel's speech to Mary heralds the "dawn of salvation," it does not "interpret eschatological events," "The Angel Gabriel According to Luke 1," in *Angels: The Concept of Celestial Beings—Origins, Development and Reception*, ed. Friedrich V. Reiterer, Tobias Nicklas, and Karin Schöpflin, DCLS (Berlin: Walter de Gruyter, 2007), 313–24 (320).

8. The narrator previously describes Elizabeth's pregnancy as hidden (περικρύβω) (Luke 1:24).

9. The incense offering occurred once in the morning and once in the evening. For Darrell Bock, the presence of a crowd of people suggests the evening offering, in which case, the parallel with Daniel is more pronounced, Darrell L. Bock, *Luke 1:1—9:50*, BECNT 3a (Grand Rapids: Baker, 1994), 79–80.

10. The word ὀπτασία is rare in biblical literature. In the Septuagint, besides the angel who appears to Daniel to interpret his eschatological visions (Θ Dan 9:23; 10:1, 7, 8, 16), ὀπτασία describes a vision only in LXX Mal 3:2, which anticipates an appearance or vision of the Lord, accompanied by a messenger/angel or two such figures. These figures may be heavenly beings (angels) or human figures (messengers), an ambiguity that invites multiple interpretations. In Luke, both the human messenger who prepares the way for the Lord (John) and the heavenly messenger/angel who appears suddenly in the temple (Gabriel) resonate with Mal 3:1. Since

the meaning of Daniel's vision of four kingdoms leading to the eschatological restoration (Dan 8:21–26; 9:21–25).[11] In Luke, Gabriel is both vision and interpreter of the same restoration, now being initiated by God.

In Luke, Gabriel refers to himself as one who "stands in the presence of God" (παρεστηκὼς ἐνώπιον τοῦ θεοῦ) (1:19). This language identifies him as one of the angels of the presence, who do not appear in the Hebrew Bible but play roles in later apocalyptic texts. In the Parables of Enoch, Enoch sees thousands of angelic beings "standing in the presence of the glory of the Lord of Spirits."[12] Amidst them stand a distinct a group of four named angels, the highest ranking "angels of the Lord of Spirits," assigned special duties by God, including Gabriel.[13] In *Jubilees*, a single unnamed "angel of the presence," identified as the same angel who accompanies and helps the Hebrews in the exodus, dictates from celestial sources almost the entire contents of the book of *Jubilees* and appears "at the key junctures in the book" to provide divine mediation, including help and revelation.[14] Although the Ethiopic version of *Jubilees* never names this angel of the presence, a Byzantine chronographer's introduction to a Greek fragment of Jubilees identifies him as Gabriel.[15]

Glimpses of the Divine Presence

Two of the angelic visits in Luke 1–2 also include moments of more direct revelation, in which characters glimpse the divine presence. Gabriel tells Mary her future pregnancy will happen through the Holy Spirit, which he describes as a power of the Most High that will overshadow her (δύναμις ὑψίστου ἐπισκιάσει σοι) (1:35). His explanation combines the eschatological expectation of a renewing Spirit (Isa 32:15; 44:3–4) with the apocalyptic image of God's glory (δόξα) overshadowing (ἐπισκιάζω) and filling the tabernacle in the form of a cloud (Exod 40:35).[16] This linguistic correspondence suggests that just as the divine presence overshadowed the tabernacle in Israel's past, so it will now overshadow Mary in the eschatological present of a miracu-

the scene of Gabriel with Zechariah alludes to both Daniel 9–10 and Malachi 3 in other ways, it is possible that the word ὀπτασία has served as link word, for Luke or his source, joining these passages hermeneutically.

11. In 4Q529, Gabriel similarly reveals divine information by providing an eschatological vision about a city to be built, although he gives this vision not to a human but to the archangel Michael.

12. 1 Enoch 40:1–10.

13. Gabriel also appears in a slightly different list of four named angels in 1 Enoch 9:1 and of seven named archangels in 20:1–8. The scrolls also depict groups of seven angels, Maxwell J. Davidson, *Angels at Qumran: A Comparative Study of 1 Enoch 1-36, 72-108 and Sectarian Writings from Qumran*, JSPSup 11 (Sheffield: JSOT Press, 1992), 238–39.

14. Jubilees 1:27, 29; 2:1, 2, 18; 6:19, 22, 35, 38; 12:22–24, 25–27; 15:27, 33; 16:5; 18:9–11; 30:12, 17, 21; 48:4, 13; 50:1–2, 6, 13; VanderKam, "Angel," 381. In Hebrew, the phrase is literally "angel of the face" (מלאכי פנים). VanderKam argues that this phrase, which does not appear in the Hebrew Bible, developed exegetically from descriptions of the angel of Exodus.

15. Georgius Cedrenus, *Comp. Hist.*, 1.87.3. This identification suggests that at least one ancient Christian linked Gabriel in Luke with the angel of the presence in *Jubilees*.

16. Numerous other Second Temple texts view the brightness (כבוד)/ δόξα) of God's presence as residing (שכן/σκιάζω) in the earthly sanctuary, just as it does in the heavenly sanctuary. Later Jewish texts refer to the presence as the Shekinah (שכנה).

lous conception. However, in comparison with Jewish apocalypses, Luke mutes the revelatory nature of this event by announcing it but not narrating it, so that the conception occurs "off screen."

By contrast, Luke directly narrates the appearance of divine glory in the third angelic visit at the time of Jesus's birth. When the angel appears, the shepherds see the glory (δόξα) of the Lord shine around them (Luke 2:9). Apocalyptic texts commonly connect angels with glory. In Exodus, the glory of the Lord, present in the cloud that guides the Hebrews, descends upon Sinai, visible as a fire (Exod 16:10; 24:16–17).[17] Because Exodus, in turn, closely associates this cloud with the angel of the presence (Exod 14:19), readers might naturally link the angel with God's glory. The throne-room vision of Isaiah makes this connection explicit, describing the sanctuary as filled with God's glory and populated with angelic beings (Isa 6:1–13; Ezek 1:4–28). Similarly, in Ezekiel, the prophet sees a vision of God's presence as a cloud with flashes of lightning and the divine throne-chariot surrounded by four angelic creatures who also shine with fire like lightning (Ezek 1:4, 13). The glory of the Lord moves along with these angelic beings (Ezek 1:28; 9:3; 10:18–22; 11:22–23).

In the Book of the Watchers, when Enoch ascends to heaven, he sees the "great glory" upon the throne, which may be approached by the holy watchers (but not humans or other angels).[18] So too in Revelation, when John sees the heavenly temple, seven linen-clad angels emerge from the presence of God's glory (15:5–8).[19] The sectarian texts from Qumran similarly place angels in the presence of divine glory.[20] Despite this close association of angels with God's glory, however, none of these texts describe the angels themselves as possessing glory or being glorious in nature; rather, their radiance results from their nearness to the divine presence.[21]

In the same way, Luke identifies the radiance seen by the shepherds as "the glory of the Lord" (Luke 2:9). This detail of divine glory (i.e., the presence of God) accompanying the angel correlates with Luke's previous description of Gabriel as one who "stands in the presence of God," a parallel that suggests Gabriel as the identity of the unnamed angel. More importantly, it moves the scene beyond angelic words to provide a moment of direct revelation of divine glory by means of a presumed (but not explicitly narrated) open heaven.[22] Given Luke's interest

17. The verb שכן is translated ἐπισκιάζω in LXX Exod 40:35. See also Exod 24:16, where the cloud and glory reside (שכן/καταβαίνω) on Mount Sinai. שכן is sometimes also translated σκιάζω (e.g., Num 9:22).

18. 1 Enoch 14:13–23.

19. See also Tob. 12:15, where Gabriel is one of seven angels who stands ready to enter before the glory of the Lord.

20. Davidson, *Angels at Qumran*, 290–93.

21. I have found only two texts that associate glory directly with angels: LXX Esther 5:2 and 1 Enoch 106:5. Interestingly, neither example is a narrative or visionary account of an actual angel. Both texts use the presumed glory of an angel as a metaphor to describe the glorious appearance of a human being (King Ahasuerus and the newborn Noah, respectively).

22. Bovon comments, "the glory of God . . . streams down to the shepherds; God incorporates the glory into a movement toward human beings." François Bovon, *Luke 1: A Commentary on the Gospel of Luke 1:1-9:50*, trans. Christine M. Thomas, 2 vols., Hermeneia (Minneapolis: Fortress, 2002), 1.90.

in the poor, it is surely significant that heaven opens not for a select seer—as in many apocalypses—but for shepherds, who represent the common people of Israel. In addition, by equating the luminosity accompanying a heavenly being with the glory of God, the scene establishes the narrative expectation that later appearances of such radiance also connote the presence of God's glory.

Together, these two moments of direct divine revelation—the anticipated overshadowing of Mary and the narrated vision of God's glory—bookend the Messiah's entry into the world with strikingly apocalyptic imagery. They also foreshadow the transfiguration, when Jesus will possess glory and be overshadowed by the cloud of the divine presence (9:32–35).

Cosmic Battle

For a reader familiar with apocalyptic texts, the name Gabriel—meaning something like "strong man of God" or "warrior of God"—suggests spiritual conflict. Moreover, Luke's intertextual links with Daniel call to mind not only Gabriel in Daniel 8–9, but the unnamed angelic being in Daniel 10:1–12:3, whom readers tend to identify as Gabriel.[23] This figure acts not only as an *angelus interpres*—offering the third, decisive interpretation of Daniel's vision—but also as cosmic warrior, engaged in battle with the princes of Persia and Greece, angelic beings opposed to God (Dan 10:20).[24] In Jubilees, a group of unnamed angels of the presence similarly fight as warriors for their king/emperor, God.[25] So too, the single angel of the presence, who narrates Jubilees, battles Mastema, the leader of the demons and the evil force behind the Pharaoh's oppression and obstinacy.[26] In Enochic literature, God specifically commissions Gabriel with destroying the half-human children of the watchers.[27] He is also given "charge of every power," a military role.[28] At the end time, Gabriel and two other angels will throw the servants of Satan into a furnace of burning fire.[29] In the War Scroll, Gabriel plays a part in the last great battle, in which God will finally triumph over oppression and evil.[30] And in the Testament of Solomon, he has the power to imprison a demon who causes headaches.[31]

23. Modern scholars are divided on this point.
24. The idea that particular heavenly beings ruled nations was common in the ancient world. For example, the Animal Apocalypse depicts the angels or gods of the nations as seventy shepherds, into whose power Israel is given (1 Enoch 89:59); John J. Collins, *Daniel: A Commentary on the Book of Daniel*, Hermeneia (Minneapolis: Fortress, 1993), 374.
25. VanderKam, "Angel," 385; Aleksander R. Michalak, *Angels as Warriors in Late Second Temple Jewish Literature*, WUNT II/330 (Tübingen: Mohr Siebeck, 2012), 83–85.
26. Jubilees 48:4, 13.
27. 1 Enoch 10:9–10. Gabriel is also in charge of "paradise and serpents and cherubim" (1 Enoch 20:7), although this is not a combative role, George W. E. Nickelsburg, *1 Enoch: A Commentary on the Book of 1 Enoch*, Hermeneia (Minneapolis: Fortress Press, 2001), 296.
28. 1 Enoch 40:1, 9; Michalak, *Angels as Warriors*, 126.
29. 1 Enoch 54:6.
30. 1QM 9:15–16. Four angelic names, including Gabriel's, are inscribed on the shields within the battle.
31. Testament of Solomon (A) 18.6.

The combative role ascribed to the angel of the presence and to Gabriel in these texts resonates with Luke's theme of eschatological conflict, woven through the infancy narrative. In response to Gabriel, Mary sings a hymn that praises God for showing "strength with his arm (βραχίων) and bringing down the powerful from their thrones" (1:51–52). As a scriptural metaphor for God's power, the word βραχίων appears in narratives about God's strength raised against Egypt or Pharaoh (Exod 6:1, 6; 15:16; Acts 13:17) and occurs in eschatological expectations about divine conflict with enemies or evil (Isa 51:9; 59:16; 63:15) or the nations' recognition of God's power (Isa 52:10). Mary's speech about the promise to Abraham alludes to Micah 7:20, which concludes a passage anticipating God's eschatological mercy envisioned as a conflict with sin personified as chaos.[32]

Similarly, when Zechariah regains his ability to speak, he sings of a savior who delivers God's people from their enemies (Luke 1:69–71), and the angel who appears to the shepherds also calls Jesus savior, echoing this military theme.[33] Zechariah also describes Jesus as a dawn or morning star (ἀνατολή) visiting from on high and giving light to those who sit in darkness and deathly shadow (Luke 1:78).[34] This language alludes to LXX Micah 4:2, which occurs in the midst of a prophetic description of eschatological conflict between the Lord and lawless beings (LXX Mic 4:1–3). Zechariah's description of Jesus as ἀνατολή also epitomizes the apocalyptic character of Luke's description of the birth of Jesus: he is a light shining not from earth but directly from heaven (ἐξ ὕψους).[35]

The appearance of a host or army (στρατιά) of heaven reinforces the martial tone established in these apocalyptic aspects of the infancy narrative. In some apocalyptic passages in the Hebrew Bible, the host of heaven (צבא השמים) refers to heavenly beings with an implied military sense (1 Kgs 22:19; par. 2 Chron 18:17; Dan 8:10).[36] Later texts depict the host of heaven more clearly as warriors. In an apocalyptic scene in 4 Maccabees, the host of heaven ride in on horseback with lightning-like weapons to battle Apollonius in defense of the temple (4 Macc 4:10–11). By contrast, in the scrolls, the host of heaven battles not humans but evil spiritual forces, especially the agents of Belial, albeit with disastrous effects on earth.[37]

32. "He will sink our injustices and cast all our iniquities into the depths of the sea" (Mic 7:19).

33. Bock, *Luke*, 216.

34. Bovon, *Luke 1*, 76.

35. Simon Gathercole, "The Heavenly ἀνατολή (Luke 1:78–79)," *JTS* 56 (2005): 471–88, argues that the phrase "a rising from on high" (ἀνατολὴ ἐξ ὕψους), particularly in combination with the idea of the divine visitation (ἐπισκέπτομαι), suggests the advent of the Messiah from the heavens, a being who "comes not from within the world but from outside it" (475–78).

36. More often, the phrase refers to the heavenly bodies, especially stars, created by God and wrongly worshipped by humans.

37. 1QM 11:17–12:1; 1QH[a] 11:36. One passage also anticipates that the host of heaven, like the presence and glory of God, will be in Jerusalem when God restores the city, 4Q434 2 8.

Angelic Praise

While Luke's description of a host of heaven in chapter 2 carries an implicit sense of spiritual conflict, explicitly, the host praises God (πλῆθος στρατιᾶς οὐρανίου αἰνούντων τὸν θεὸν) (Luke 2:13). The concept of angelic praise, closely related to praise offered by the heavens generally, appears occasionally in the Hebrew Bible/Septuagint.[38] Two of these texts (Neh 9:6; Pr Man 1:15) parallel Luke, in that the hosts of heaven specifically praise the Lord.[39] The host of heaven praise God in one text from Qumran and in 1 Enoch 61:10–12.[40]

Angelic praise in general appears frequently in Enochic literature and in apocalyptic portions of other early Jewish texts.[41] The Songs of the Sabbath Sacrifice from Qumran depict the praise of the angelic priesthood in the heavenly temple. These songs consist mostly of declarative praise, but sometimes express descriptive praise, as in Luke, lauding not divine attributes but divine actions.[42] The fifth song brings angelic praise together with the idea of cosmic battle: it praises God in anticipation of a host of angelic beings waging a victorious war against God's enemies among the clouds of heaven.[43] Closely related is the joy that angels and humans will share in the eschaton.[44]

The content of the angel's praise in Luke 2:14 depends, to some extent, on famously difficult grammar. I prefer an interpretation of this verse that balances the two lines of the angels' speech, understanding εὐδοκίας as a subjective genitive of origin modifying the verb εἰμί assumed in the sentence:[45]

δόξα ἐν ὑψίστοις θεῷ
καὶ ἐπὶ γῆς εἰρήνη ἐν ἀνθρώποις εὐδοκίας
[There is] glory on high to God
And upon earth peace among people by divine good pleasure

In this way of reading the couplet, εὐδοκία refers to the divine initiative that has led to Jesus's birth.[46] Just as angels (and shortly after them, the human shepherds) give glory to God on high

38. Deut 32:43; Neh 9:6; Pss 103:20; 148:2; Pr Azar 1:36–37; Pr Man 1:15. In Deut 32:43, the heavens rejoice and the angels worship (προσκυνέω), implying their praise. Praise is also implicit in Neh 9:6, which has the verb προσκυνέω. Pr Man 1:15 uses the verb ὑμνέω, which refers to the singing of a song that may and often does include praise. In this case, the context strongly suggests a hymn of praise. See also passages in which the heavens praise God or are called to do so, Pss 69:34 [LXX 69:35]; 89:6 [LXX 89:5].

39. For the host of heaven, Neh 9:6 uses the language αἱ στρατιαὶ τῶν οὐρανῶν while Pr Man 1:15 has πᾶσα ἡ δύναμις τῶν οὐρανῶν.

40. 1QM 12:1. In 1 Enoch 61, the host of heaven praise God, along with people on earth, upon the enthronement of the Chosen One.

41. 1 Enoch 36:4; 40:3; 41:7; 47:2; 61:12; 2 Enoch 19:3; 20:4; Testament of Levi 3:5–8; Life of Adam and Eve 28:1–2; 33:2.

42. Carol A. Newsom, *Angelic Liturgy: Songs of the Sabbath Sacrifice*, PTSDSSP 4b (Tübingen: Mohr Siebeck, 1999), 6.

43. 4Q402 4 5–10. The word "host" is reconstructed. Cf. Mas1k 1 1–6 (*ShirShab*).

44. 1 Enoch 51:3–5; 104:5; Testament of Joseph 19:9. On eschatological human joy in Luke-Acts, see Nolland, *Luke 1–9:20*, 30.

45. In the Septuagint, Ps 144:16 and Sir 15:15 offer analogies for such a translation, Kindalee Pfremmer De Long, *Surprised by God: Praise Responses in the Narrative of Luke-Acts* , BZNW 166 (New York: Walter de Gruyter, 2009), 163.

46. Divine initiative is an important theme in Luke-Acts, Squires, *Plan*, passim. Biblical texts associate the word εὐδοκία with eschatological redemption, De Long, *Surprised by God*, 163.

because of divine beneficence in providing a savior, this same beneficence now brings to earth long-awaited eschatological peace, a further reason for praise.[47] In other words, like the fifth of the *Songs of the Sabbath Sacrifice*, Luke presents an apocalyptic scene of angelic, declarative praise for God's eschatological intervention.

But in Luke, this divine activity occurs today (σήμερον; Luke 2:11). In 2:9, the shepherds see a glimpse of glory that comes from heaven, but in 2:14, they hear angelic praise that acknowledges God's activity *on earth*. As John Nolland puts it, this scene does not "reflect the timeless praise of God in heaven to which there is momentary privileged access (as Isaiah 6). It is God's new initiative which is here praised." Despite the common Christmas-pageant image of angels singing in the clouds above the shepherds, Luke describes the location for neither the appearance of the "angel of the Lord" nor the angelic praise that follows. The adjective "heavenly" (οὐράνιος) could mean either "in heaven" or "from heaven." Luke's use of it to describe Paul's Damascus road vision in Acts 26:19—which occurs on earth—suggests the latter. Moreover, after the angels sing their hymn, they "return to heaven" (Luke 2:15).

In contrast with the angel in 2:9–10, who reveals the glory of the Lord, the angelic song represents a moment neither of an open heaven nor a glimpse of praise in the heavenly sanctuary, but heavenly praise heard on earth.[48] As with the arrival of salvation in a manger, the hymn surprises—in two ways. First, characters hear this angelic praise not in the Jerusalem temple, as might be expected, but in a sheep pasture outside the city. Second, the heavenly army sings not of war on earth but of peace, foreshadowing the Lukan theme that God's arm will, for the most part, not be raised not against human enemies but spiritual ones.

This angelic praise ought also be understood within the larger context of praise in Luke-Acts, where spontaneous speech of joyous praise holds a central place. As Christopher Rowland and Christopher Morray-Jones observe, the motif of joyous praise situates "these stories within the general ambiance of the world of apocalypticism."[49] Joy first appears in Gabriel's speech to Zechariah. In this scene, an angel whom contemporary texts depict as a priest in the heavenly temple anticipates joy and gladness for a human priest in the earthly temple.[50] Eventually,

47. Conversely, later in the narrative, peace and glory in heaven will be the source of praise on earth (Luke 19:37–38). Peace is a key term for Luke. On peace as an eschatological expectation, see Acts 10:36, which draws on such passages as Isa 52:7.

48. Nolland, *Luke 1–9:20*, 108; Christopher Rowland and Christopher R. A. Morray-Jones, *The Mystery of God: Early Jewish Mysticism and the New Testament*, CRINT 12 (Boston: Brill, 2009), 100.

49. Rowland and Morray-Jones, *Mystery of God*, 100. The authors do not offer evidence in defense of this remark, but they must refer to praise in response to visions of heaven and other revelations, a common motif in apocalypses. Praise also responds to revelatory moments in early Jewish narratives, especially Tobit, *Joseph and Aseneth*, and Luke-Acts, De Long, *Surprised by God*, 75–250. As in Luke, the angel in Tobit responds to prayer (Tob 3:15), announces joy (Tob 5:10), and calls people to praise (12:6, 18). On parallels between the praise in Tobit and 1 Enoch, see George W. E. Nickelsburg, "Tobit and Enoch: Distant Cousins with a Recognizable Resemblance," in *George W. E. Nickelsburg in Perspective: An Ongoing Dialogue of Learning*, ed. Jacob Neusner and Alan J. Avery-Peck, JSJSup 80 (Boston: Brill, 2003), 217–39 (234).

50. On Gabriel's role as a priest in the earthly temple, see Newsom, *Angelic Liturgy*, 7.

Zechariah fulfills this expectation by speaking a hymn of praise.[51] In fact, all three times the angels appear, they announce or exhort joy (1:14, 28; 2:10); the human characters respond with joy, or more often, joyous praise (1:41,44, 46–55; 58, 64, 68–79; 2:20, 28, 30–32, 38), and then, a heavenly host joins in (2:14, 20).[52] This pattern of angelic announcement of joy followed by human responses of joyous praise suggests the correspondence between heavenly and earthly worshippers, which is evident in some Second Temple texts, the Qedushah of the synagogue liturgy, and Merkabah and Hekhalot traditions.[53] In Luke, joyous praise is eschatological, fulfilling expectations of joy and praise in the day of the Lord, expressed in the infancy narrative by those characters who recognize the salvation of God.[54] Because the motif of praise continues throughout the two volumes, these scenes of eschatological joy and praise sets an apocalyptic tone that continues throughout the whole story.[55]

Conclusion to Angels in the Infancy Narrative

A reader familiar with apocalyptic literature would recognize the significance of Gabriel's appearance and words, as well as the appearance of the angelic host. Revelation by one of heaven's highest ranking angels, who stands in the very presence of God's glory, with an anticipated role in the final eschatological battle, signals the advent of a divine salvation that will defeat the evil forces that oppress Israel and the Gentiles.[56] As the narrative proceeds, Jesus and those who follow him wage a cosmic struggle against demonic evil that unfolds on an anthropological level, its primary locus being earth, not heaven.[57] In particular, this spiritual battle plays out when Jesus heals people of both illnesses and demon possession, categories that tend to merge in Luke-Acts. In chapter 4, Jesus, drawing on restoration traditions in Isaiah (35:5–6; 58:6; 61:1–2), defines salvation not in terms of triumph over human powers but over oppression: the Spirit has anointed Jesus to bring good news to the poor, to proclaim release to the captives and recovery of sight to the blind, to let the oppressed go free, to proclaim the year

51. Joy and praise are closely linked in Jewish tradition.

52. De Long, *Surprised by God*, 135–52. For example, the narrator describes the angelic host as praising God (αἰνέω), and then they say "Glory (δόξα) to God" (Luke 2:14). So too, the narrator describes the shepherds as glorifying (δοξάζω) and praising (αἰνέω) God (Luke 2:20).

53. Newsom, *Angelic Liturgy*, 10.

54. Ironically, it is the priest in the earthly temple who does not immediately respond with joy and praise, but he eventually does.

55. Eschatological praise responds to healings, the revelation of Jesus's identity, and the inclusion of Gentiles in the restored people of Israel, De Long, *Surprised by God*, 95–103, 155–56, 262–63 and passim.

56. By contrast, Hans Klein, "The Angel Gabriel According to Luke 1," 315, argues that these texts "do not suit as parallels" and the name Gabriel "could be seen as pure coincidence." He interprets Gabriel's standing in the presence of the Lord as referring to his commissioning rather than describing his angelic nature. In Klein's view, Luke has significantly modified the early Jewish apocalyptic traditions about Gabriel (318).

57. For much evidence of the spiritual conflict in Luke-Acts between the devil and Jesus, taken up also by his followers, see Susan R. Garrett, *The Demise of the Devil: Magic and the Demonic in Luke's Writings* (Minneapolis: Fortress Press, 1989), passim. She also argues that Luke depicts the death/resurrection/ascension of Jesus as the decisive, eschatological defeat of Satan, a debatable point.

of the Lord's favor (Luke 4:18–19). In chapter 7, he links the same kind of activity to the arrival of the kingdom. Elsewhere, Luke makes clear that when Jesus heals and exorcises demons, he sets free those oppressed by Satan (Luke 13:16; Acts 10:38).[58] In his *Commentary on Daniel*, Jerome recognizes a correspondence in Luke between Gabriel's identity as warrior and Jesus's conflict with evil and oppression. After describing the meaning of the angel's name and his traditional role in having charge over battles, he writes, "And so at that time also when the Lord was about to be born and to declare war against the demons and to triumph over the world, Gabriel came to Zacharias and to Mary (Luke 1)."[59]

Accompanying the angelic revelation of Jesus's birth, the glory of God shines out from heaven, fulfilling an anticipated aspect of the restoration of Israel (Isa 42:8; 43:6–7; 48:10–11; 58:8; 60:1–3).[60] Moreover, the characters' praise of God links this heavenly radiance with Jesus: Zechariah's hymn describes Jesus as a dawning light (ἀνατολή) from on high (1:78), while Simeon's praise refers to Jesus as a light (φῶς) of salvation that will shine on both the gentiles and the people of Israel (Luke 2:32). The first group will experience this light as an apocalypse or unveiling (ἀποκάλυψις), and the second, as a receipt of divine glory (δόξα). Simeon's praise anticipates for the reader apocalyptic moments later in the narrative that will further reveal Jesus's heavenly glory, as discussed below.

In some apocalypses, angels bring the seer to heaven; in others, the seer remains on earth, getting a glimpse of what is happening or will happen in heaven, often with earthly consequences. The apocalyptic aspects of the infancy narrative are of the latter type, with the important difference that with the arrival of divine glory on earth in the person of the Messiah, the anticipated future has now become the eschatological present.

Angels at Jesus's Resurrection and Ascension (Luke 24:4–7, 43; Acts 1:10–11)

The appearance of two angelic men in shining clothes continue the theme of apocalyptic revelation. At the end of the Gospel, two men (ἄνδρες δύο) in "clothing dazzling like lightning" (ἐν ἐσθῆτι ἀστραπτούσῃ) (Luke 24:4), later identified as angels (24:43), interpret the empty tomb to the women disciples. In Acts 1:10, after Jesus's ascension, two men (ἄνδρες δύο) "in white clothing" (ἐν ἐσθήσεσι λευκαῖς) interpret Jesus's ascension to the eleven.

On the one hand, the angels' clothing, flashing like lightning (ἀστράπτω), reflects descrip-

58. Six times, characters acknowledge these moments of release from oppression by expressing praise of God, continuing the pattern of praise established by the apocalyptic scenes of the infancy narrative, De Long, *Surprised by God*, 181–212.

59. Jerome, *Comm. Dan*, 8:16. Translation is from *Commentary on Daniel*, trans. Gleason L. Archer (Grand Rapids: Baker, 1958).

60. J. E. Fossum, "Glory," in *Dictionary of Deities and Demons in the Bible*, ed. K. van der Toorn, Bob Becking, and Pieter Willem van der Horst (Grand Rapids: Eerdmans, 1999), 352.

tions of God's white or shining clothing in Jewish visions of the divine.[61] Poetic texts depict God as clothed in honor/glory and majesty, with "light like a garment" (φῶς ὡς ἱμάτιον) (Ps 104:1–2 [LXX 103:1–2]; Job 40:10). The scene of Enoch's ascent into heaven describes God as the Great Glory on the throne, wearing garments appearing like the sun and whiter than snow (1 Enoch 14:20), while comparing the ceiling of the heavenly sanctuary to flashes of lightning (ἀστραπή) (14:11, 17).[62]

On the other hand, the preceding examples depict the shining garments of God, not angels: there is no precise precedent for Luke's depiction of brilliant angelic clothing, especially clothing that flashes like lightning.[63] While luminosity is characteristic of angels, due to their proximity to divine glory, it is not associated in particular with their clothing. In 4 Maccabees, lightning flashes (περιαστράπτω) from the weapons of angels (4:10). Radiance streams from the body (but not the clothes) of the angel in Joseph and Aseneth, including his face, which "was 'like lightning'" (ὡς ἀστραπή) (14:9). Similarly, in Daniel, the heavenly man, clothed in linen and girded in gold, has a face in appearance like lightning (Dan 10:5–6). This description places a description of an angel's garments alongside a description of his radiance, coming close to portraying the radiant garments of a heavenly being other than God. By contrast, in later translations of Daniel, corresponding more closely with Luke's portrayal, both the faces and the garments of this figure shine with glory or light.[64]

In Luke, the splendor of the two angelic men recalls the transfiguration scene, also discussed in the section on visions below, which features both the glory of two men (ἄνδρες δύο) and the glory of Jesus, whose "clothes are white, flashing like lightning" (ὁ ἱματισμὸς αὐτοῦ λευκὸς ἐξαστράπτων, Luke 9:29–32). The word "glory," in turn, reminds the audience of the "glory of the Lord" seen by the shepherds. Together, these four scenes—Jesus's birth, transfiguration, resurrection, and ascension—constitute apocalyptic moments in the story, unveilings of the glory of God's presence.[65] From a narrative perspective, this revelation serves to punctuate four key events in the Gospel, and later, another glimpse of the divine presence will highlight the transformative moment when the restored community first welcomes the Gentiles (Acts 10:30).

The Gospel also links the transfiguration, resurrection, and ascension through the interpre-

61. John Paul Heil, *The Transfiguration of Jesus: Narrative Meaning and Function of Mark 9:2–8, Matt 17:1–8 and Luke 9:28–36*, AnBib 144 (Roma: Editrice Pontificio Istituto Biblico, 2000), 84–90.

62. Pieter G.R. de Villiers, "The Resurrection as Christ's Entry into His Glory (Lk. 24:26)," *AcT* 31, suppl. 15 (2011): 101–31.

63. Kevin P. Sullivan, *Wrestling with Angels: A Study of the Relationship between Angels and Humans in Ancient Jewish Literature and the New Testament*, AGJU 55 (Boston: Brill, 2004), 30–32.

64. Where the MT has the phrase "there was a man clothed in linen and his loins were girded with gold from Uphaz" (איש־אחד לבוש בדים ומתניו חגרים בכתם אופז), the OG has τὴν ὀσφὺν περιεζωσμένος βυσσίνῳ καὶ ἐκ μέσου αὐτοῦ φῶς. It appears that "Uphaz" has become φῶς. Similarly, the Peshitta has "magnificent raiment" instead of "linen" and "in glorious honor" instead of "gold from Uphaz," Richard A. Taylor, *The Peshitta of Daniel*, Monographs of the Peshitta Institute 7 (New York: Brill, 1994), 251, 259, 261.

65. The fragmentary Gospel of Peter, which seems to rely at least partially on Luke, states explicitly that the heavens open and two men descend, shining with great light, to retrieve Jesus from the tomb (Gos. Pet. 1:36).

tations about Jesus's death spoken by the heavenly figures. Just as the two glorious men on the mountain speak about Jesus's departure (ἔξοδος) (Luke 9:31), which is his death, so the later appearances of two men in shining clothes interpret Jesus's death as a necessary part of the divine plan, leading to his resurrection (Luke 24:7) and ascension into heaven, which, in turn, presages his return in glory from heaven (Acts 1:11). Elsewhere, Luke similarly identifies Jesus's departure and anticipated return as his glory, glimpsed previously in the transfiguration (Luke 9:26; 21:27; 24:26; Acts 7:55). But again, as in the infancy narrative, Luke adapts apocalyptic imagery. Instead of presenting only their own interpretation of these events, the two angelic men refer the disciples back to Jesus's own words, for in Luke, Jesus is the ultimate interpreter of his departure to glory.[66]

Angels after Pentecost

After Pentecost, as the Gospel moves outward from Jerusalem, on six occasions, an angel appears to rescue or instruct characters or to enact divine justice. The analysis below groups these stories into two sets, based on the primary activity of the angel. Three stories involve conflict, in which angels intervene directly in the physical world to oppose forces arrayed against God (Acts 5:15–20; 12:7–15, 20–23). Three other scenes depict angelic revelation that serves to move the good news to the center of the Roman Empire (Acts 8:26–39; 10:1–7, 22; 11:13–14; 27:21–26).

Rescue and Judgment

In the three stories of conflict, an angel twice sets free imprisoned apostles and visits divine justice upon Herod (Agrippa I). In the first story (Acts 5:15–20), the narrator sets a tone of spiritual conflict. Continuing the Gospel's theme of healing and exorcism as conflict, the scene opens with Peter freeing a great number of people from oppression by disease and unclean spirits (Acts 5:15–16). The authorities, however, interrupt this work of God by arresting the apostles (Acts 5:17–18). This act places them on the wrong side of the conflict in Luke-Acts, a point that Luke emphasizes by contrasting them with the apostles. While the authorities rise up against the apostles (5:17), employ military forces (5:26), and issue commands (5:28), the apostles obey the commands of God (5:29, 32).[67] The authorities are filled with jealousy (5:17), leading to an intense anger and desire to kill (5:33), whereas the apostles receive the Holy Spirit from God.[68]

66. John Nolland, *Luke 18:34-24:53*, WBC 35c (Waco: Word, 1993), 1190. Visions of the risen Jesus are discussed in more detail below.
67. In addition to the word στρατηγός, the words ἀνίστημι and παραγγέλλω/παραγγελία can also have a military sense.
68. In 5:17, the passive of the verb πίμπλημιmay very subtly suggest demonic influence.

In other words, to appropriate Gamaliel's language from the end of the chapter, the authorities fight against God (θεομάχος) (5:39).

Within this context, the appearance of an angel of the Lord shows that human militancy is no match for the power of heaven, revealing again that the earthly conflict involves spiritual forces far greater than the human players.[69] After accomplishing the apostles' release, the angel commands them to go preach about "this life" (5:20). By situating the victories of chapter five within the larger reality of life in Christ, the angel's instruction shows that defeat of evil forces—whether illness, demons, or military force—is not an end in itself. Rather, its goal is life for human beings. However, as with Jesus, access to angelic power does not ultimately prevent suffering: in the end, the apostles are apprehended again and beaten (Acts 5:40). As Robert Tannehill observes, divine victory over opposition has an unexpected twist: God succeeds by letting the opponents win and "then transforming the expected result."[70]

The second scene of angelic jailbreak, despite its many comic elements, concludes the narrative's serious theme of conflict in Jerusalem (chs. 4–12).[71] Conflict begins in the scene when Agrippa executes James, one of the twelve, and after recognizing the political expediency of this move, arrests Peter as well, which bodes the apostle's death (Acts 12:1–4; cf. 12:19). Luke's narration of this scene emphasizes a highly secure military environment by depicting Peter as bound together with two soldiers, while two others guard the door (12:6).[72] Peter will later refer to this power as the "hand of Herod" (12:11).[73]

The angel plays a more developed role in the story. As in the appearance to Zechariah, he comes suddenly in response to prayer (12:5–7). Like the angel who addresses the shepherds and like the "two men" of the transfiguration, resurrection, and ascension, the angel reflects the glory of God, implicit in the description of the light shining (φῶς ἔλαμψεν) with him (12:7). The story makes clear that despite the military security, the king's authority is nothing to the angel, who removes Peter without even waking the guards (Acts 12:7, 18). Through the experience, Peter remains in a dream-like state, believing that he experiences a vision (ὅραμα) and not a

69. By contrast, Joseph Fitzmyer sees the presence of the angel as incidental. It shows the protection of God but "plays no part in the rest of the account, being almost passed over," *The Acts of the Apostles*, AB 31 (New York: Doubleday, 1998), 333. The context of spiritual conflict suggests otherwise. Additionally, the angel's action in resistance to the Sadducees introduces a touch of ironic humor, as the Sadducees do not believe in the existence of angels, Mikeal Carl Parsons, *Acts*, Paideia (Grand Rapids: Baker Academic, 2008), 77.

70. Robert C. Tannehill, *The Narrative Unity of Luke-Acts: A Literary Interpretation,* The Acts of the Apostles, Vol. 2 (Philadelphia: Fortress Press, 1990), 73.

71. However, the narrative associates the opponents in this story more closely with Roman imperial power. For example, Agrippa follows Roman practice in using four squads of soldiers (12:4), Ben Witherington, III, *The Acts of the Apostles: A Socio-Rhetorical Commentary* (Grand Rapids: Eerdmans, 1998), 386. Readers familiar with Agrippa's history would also be aware that he was raised in Rome, a close friend of both Caligula and Claudius.

72. The latter half of Acts 12:6 contains five words that connote military opposition.

73. The narrative emphasizes that Pilate and Herod Antipas, Agrippa's father, band together against the plan of God but offer no real threat, Luke 23:12; Acts 4:27.

real release from prison (12:9).[74] Only after the angel leaves does he return to himself, recognizing that the Lord sent his angel to deliver him (12:11).

In the third scene of angelic intervention, the idea of angel as warrior comes to the fore. The king makes a speech, dressed in royal robes (ἐνδυσάμενος ἐσθῆτα βασιλικὴν), and the crowd acclaims him as a god, not a man (Acts 12:21–22). An angel of the Lord appears suddenly again, striking him down, so that he is eaten by worms and dies (12:23). Luke uses the same word (πατάσσω) to describe both this strike and the angel's blow to wake Peter in the prison, narratively linking the two scenes: Herod "meets the fate he intended for Peter."[75]

The king's death at the hand of the angel concludes a conflict between Agrippa and the power of heaven that has been ongoing throughout the narrative. In particular, the detail about Herod's royal clothing recalls the bright clothing placed mockingly by the king's father around Jesus (περιβαλὼν ἐσθῆτα λαμπρὰν) (Luke 23:11), as well as the genuinely luminous clothing of Jesus (Luke 9:29) and the angelic beings (Luke 24:4; Acts 1:20; 10:30).[76] The contrast could not be starker between true glory and one who, because he seeks his own glory, does not give glory to God. In the battle between life and death in Luke-Acts, Agrippa chooses the side of death one time too many.

An Angel Directs the Divine Plan through Revelation and Command

In three other stories of angels after Pentecost, angelic revelation makes clear God's continuing plan to take eschatological salvation in surprising directions: to the margins of the people of Israel, to the Gentiles, and to the very heart of the empire. In the first of these stories (Acts 8:26–39), an "angel of the Lord" reveals the Gaza road location of a traveler from Ethiopia, described primarily as a eunuch (Acts 8:27, 34, 36, 38, 39), and instructs him to go there. The rest of the story makes clear the content of this angelic revelation: God intends that the good news reach a deeply pious person at the margins of the people of Israel.[77] After the man responds with baptism, the Holy Spirit physically transports Philip to Azotus. Angelic revelation in this

74. Some view the angel's instruction to Peter to don certain clothing as humorous, but it may be less so when compared with angelically inspired wardrobing in other early Jewish texts.

75. Parsons, *Acts*, 178.

76. While Luke describes Herod's clothing as royal, Josephus describes it as luminous. In fact, in his account of this event, the crowd responds not to the king's words but to his silvery clothes, which reflect the sun so as to shine brightly (καταυγάζω) and flash (μαρμαίρω) in a supernatural manner. Josephus, *Ant.* 19.344.

77. The man is "going on a pilgrimage, reading the prophet, eager to understand its meaning, responsive to the message about Jesus," Luke Timothy Johnson, *The Acts of the Apostles*, Sacra Pagina 5 (Collegeville, MN: Liturgical, 1992), 160. Many recent interpreters view the Ethiopian not as a Gentile but as a Jew, which makes most sense, from a narrative perspective. Johnson, 159, observes, "The enormous effort Luke put into the Cornelius sequence (chs. 10–15) would make no sense at all if Cornelius did not represent a fundamentally new step."

story—part of a section that focuses the expansion of the restored community to included marginalized Jews (Samaritans and this eunuch) and Gentiles (chs. 8–15)—not only shows that God initiates this expansion but also implies that God sees and hears the worship and actions of these people as individuals.

This implication becomes explicit in the story of angelic revelation to Cornelius, when an "angel of God" intervenes to take the good news in another new direction (Acts 10:1–7, 22; 11:13–14). The Septuagintal phrase "angel of God" appears less frequently than "angel of the Lord." In Luke-Acts, however, it occurs elsewhere in a scene during Paul's sea voyage (Acts 27:23) and in two Gospel passages of teaching by Jesus, both of which suggest the universal acceptance of those who acknowledge God or repent (Luke 12:8–9; 15:10). In turn, the Son of Man will acknowledge these people before the angels of God or their repentance will cause the angels of God to rejoice. In the story of Cornelius, an "angel of God" intervenes to ensure that the restored community accepts a devout man who fears God and who has repented (Acts 10:4; 11:18).

The angel reveals to Cornelius that the centurion's prayer and acts of mercy have ascended into the divine presence (10:4) and have been heard by God (10:31), implying that God has sent the angel in response.[78] The angel also reveals the location of Peter, instructing Cornelius to summon him, which, in turn, sets in motion events that lead to belief in Jesus Christ, receipt of the Holy Spirit, baptism, and salvation for Cornelius and other Gentiles. Like the coming of the Holy Spirit in Cornelius's house, the angel's involvement—emphasized by three retellings (10:22; 10:30; 11:13)—confirms that God has ordained this surprising acceptance of the Gentiles.

In Tobit, the prayers of Sarah and Tobit and acts of mercy by Tobit are similarly "heard in the presence of the glory of God" and responded to by an angel sent by God (Tob [GII] 3:16; cf. 12:12). Commenting on these verses in Tobit, Carey Moore writes that they draw upon a "mental picture of the divine throne room of God, complete with angels interceding for mortals and being sent to execute the Lord's commands, as presented in 1 Enoch."[79] Except for the point about angelic intercession in heaven, not suggested in the Cornelius story, the same comment could hold true for Acts 10. Cornelius later reflects this idea when he says that Peter speaks to the gathering in his house in the presence of God (Acts 10:33). Having learned from the angel that his prayers ascended into God's presence, he now asserts that the meeting also occurs in the divine presence. This statement may describe the assembly as liturgical in nature.[80] Indeed, the household greets angelic intervention on its behalf with praise of God (Acts 10:46), in keep-

78. In Acts 12:11, Peter interprets the angel who breaks him out of prison as having been sent by God.

79. Carey A. Moore, *Tobit: A New Translation with Introduction and Commentary*, AB 40a (New York: Doubleday, 1996), 157, citing 1 En 8:4–10:22; 40:1–10; 47:1–4; 97:5; 99:3; 104:4. See also Nickelsburg, "Tobit and Enoch," 234.

80. Witherington, *Acts*, 354.

ing with other praise responses to revelatory events in the narrative.[81] This pattern supports the initial impression in the infancy narrative of a parallel between earthly and heavenly joy and praise, as in apocalyptic texts. However, it should be observed that in Luke-Acts, human joy and praise do not respond directly to mystical experience (the appearance of angels) but to what this experience signifies: eschatological salvation unfolding within history.

The story of Cornelius also echoes stories of previous angelic appearances in other ways. As in Zechariah's story, the angel comes as a vision (ὅραμα) in response to prayer, which Cornelius—unlike Peter in chapter 12—sees clearly (φανερῶς) (10:3–4). Cornelius receives angelic intervention because of his piety (10:4, 31), a point implied in the eunuch's story. Like the shining men at the empty tomb and ascension, as well as the angel who takes Peter from jail, the angel appears in luminescent clothing (ἐν ἐσθῆτι λαμπρᾷ) (10:30). Thus, the reader understands that Cornelius sees the divine glory previously revealed only in relation to Jesus's birth or to Jesus's disciples, underscoring the significance of this scene. As in Acts 5, where an angel physically relocates the apostles from prison so that they might proclaim "this life" in the temple, so now, an angel (along with accompanying visions to Peter) intervenes so that one of these apostles will physically enter Cornelius' household, that those gathered in it may receive repentance leading to life (τὴν μετάνοιαν εἰς ζωὴν) (Acts 11:18). These intratextual resonances communicate that while the angel reveals but does not physically intervene, the effect of this revelation is as boundary-breaking as in the scenes of rescue from prison: it relocates Peter and other believers in Jerusalem out of their preconceptions (Acts 10:34; 11:18) into a full recognition of God's impartiality so that they might welcome Cornelius, along with other Gentiles, into the restored community.

In the third story (Acts 27:21–26), an angel of God appears to Paul on board a ship headed to Rome. The angel reveals that the passengers will survive, but the ship will be lost. More specifically, he again discloses the divine plan: God intends for Paul to stand before the emperor in Rome. As in the two other scenes discussed in this section, this revelation directs proclamation in a surprising direction: the core of the empire. Paul's reaction of active belief in the angel's words recalls the response of Mary to Gabriel:

> πιστεύω γὰρ τῷ θεῷ ὅτι οὕτως ἔσται καθ' ὃν τρόπον λελάληταί μοι (Acts 27:25)[82]
> ἡ πιστεύσασα ὅτι ἔσται τελείωσις τοῖς λελαλημένοις αὐτῇ (Luke 1:45)

As we have seen above, Luke's interwoven stories of angelic intervention are mutually inter-

81. Characters praise God in response to angelic revelation in the infancy narrative (Luke 1:46–55, 64, 68–78; 2:13–14, 20, 28–33, 38), as well as to revelation by Jesus during his ministry (Luke 9:16; 10:21; 19:37–40) and after his resurrection (Luke 24:50–53). In Acts 8, the eunuch rejoices in response to angelic revelation (via Philip), and joy is closely related to praise in Luke-Acts.

82. This response is similar in kind (although not as linguistically linked) with the response of Cornelius, who immediately sends for Peter, ready to hear all that is commanded to Peter by the Lord (ἀκοῦσαι πάντα τὰ προστεταγμένα σοι ὑπὸ τοῦ κυρίου, Acts 10:33).

pretive. Here, he sets Paul in parallel with Mary, who—like Paul—serves the divine plan, ready to face potentially frightening and dangerous events. Paul will stand before the emperor, aided by an angel who stands in the glorious presence of God, and more importantly, by Jesus Christ, who now stands on the right hand of God's glory. Mary also sang of God bringing down the mighty from their thrones, in order to help Israel. Angelic revelation in Acts shows, on the one hand, that the mighty power of God's arm indeed rescues the restored community and brings down the mighty who oppose God (i.e., Herod Agrippa). But on the other hand, this revelation also discloses that the real enemy is Satan, not Rome, so that God's mercy extends to Gentiles, even those who represent Roman power (i.e., Cornelius, Julius, Agrippa II).

Visionary Revelation

As observed occasionally above, angels and visions overlap in Luke-Acts because Luke labels five angelic appearances as "visions" (Luke 1:11; 22:43; Acts 7:30; 10:3; 12:9). In addition to these five scenes, Luke's narrative includes fifteen other scenes of visionary revelation. As space does not permit a complete investigation of this material, this section examines Luke's vocabulary of visions, compares the visual and auditory components of the visionary scenes, and provides a general analysis of the revealed wisdom within them. Together, these scenes function in the narrative to disclose Jesus's identity and glory, along with its results, particularly the mission to the Gentiles.

Vocabulary of Visions

Most often, Luke narrates visions with the passive verb *ὁράω* and the related nouns *ὅραμα* and *ὅρασις*. While these words can simply mean something seen, Luke uses them almost exclusively in reference to mystical experiences.[83] The passive verb describes the appearance of angels (Luke 1:11; 22:43; Acts 7:30), tongues like fire (Acts 2:3), the risen Christ (Luke 24:34; Acts 13:31), Christ from heaven (Acts 26:16), the man from Macedonia (Acts 16:9, 10), and God to Abraham in Mesopotamia (Acts 7:2). The related noun *ὅραμα*, Luke's particular word for visions in Acts, occurs eleven times in that text but nowhere else in the New Testament. Stephen uses it to recount Moses's vision of the burning bush (7:30–31). In the second jailbreak scene, Peter thinks he's seeing a vision, but in fact, the angel is really leading him from jail (Acts 12:9). The word repeatedly narrates the two sets of double visions related to the turn of the gospel toward the Gentiles (Acts 9:10, 12; 10:3, 17, 19; 11:5), and describes two visions of Paul (Acts 16:9–10;

83. The sole exception is Acts 7:26, Bock, *Luke*, 80. However, it should be noted that not only Luke but the New Testament in general uses this vocabulary in this particular way; Mark 9:4; par. Matt 17:3; 1 Cor 15:5–8; Titus 3:16; Heb 9:28; Rev 4:3; 9:17; 11:19; 12:1, 3.

Acts 18:9). The second noun ὅρασις appears only in Peter's quotation of Joel in Acts 2, where it describes eschatological visions (Acts 2:17; Joel 2:28).

Luke's use of this word family is Septuagintal. In the LXX, the passive verb and related nouns frequently describe the appearance of God to the patriarchs, the sound of God's voice, characters' interaction with angels, revelatory dreams, and prophetic and apocalyptic visions, including the visions of Isaiah, Ezekiel, and Daniel. Some Greek-language Second Temple Jewish literature reflects similar usage of the word family.[84] In the Testament of Abraham, the passive verb ὁράω describes a particularly apocalyptic vision of the open heavens and a man descending from heaven, bearing light that flashes like lightning greater than seven suns.[85]

By contrast, Philo and Josephus use the nouns φαντασία or ὄψις for visions from God, which do not have this meaning in the LXX or NT. Luke's favorite words for visions (ὁράω in the passive and ὅραμα) appear nowhere in the works of Josephus or Philo, with the exception of two quotations of Numbers 12:6 by Philo, which have ὅραμα. Neither do these authors use the word ὅρασις, common in the Septuagint, but which Luke avoids. (It appears only in Peter's quotation of Joel 2:28.) Luke's primary vocabulary for visions also does not appear in the Jewish apocalypses preserved in Greek, with the exception of one occurrence of the noun ὅραμα, to describe false visions that will lead people astray.[86] Rather, 1 Enoch repeatedly uses the other Septuagintal word ὅρασις in the narration of Enoch's visions.[87]

By comparison then with Philo and Josephus, Luke's language is highly Septuagintal, yet he uses only two of the three common Septuagintal words (ὁράω in the passive and ὅραμα) while appearing studiously to avoid using the third (ὅρασις), which happens to be the most frequent term for visions in Enochic literature. Luke's avoidance of this word is all the more striking because of its use in Joel 2:28, the key text he uses to interpret the arrival of the Spirit in Acts 2. These observations raise the question of whether Luke's selection of vocabulary in contrast to Enochic literature was coincidental, whether it reflects his involvement with a group using different vocabulary, or whether he selected these words intentionally to distance his narration of visions from those of the more mystical traditions emerging within Judaism.[88]

Luke also uses the noun ὀπτασία for visions three times. As observed in the section on the

84. The passive verb refers to revelatory visions in Sibylline Oracles 1.200; Testament of Issachar 2:1; Testament of Naphtali 5:8; 8:3; Ezekiel the Tragedian 1.235. Two additional instances refer to general revelation without a narrated mystical component, 1:2; 2:11. The noun ὅραμα similarly refers to revelatory visions from God in Testament of Levi 9:3; 11:5; Testament of Abraham A 4:8; *Ord. Levi* 1:64; it once describes the appearance of an angel, Testament of Judah 3:10. The noun ὅρασις more often simply means something seen, but it is twice used for visions of angels: Levi's vision of seven heavenly men in white clothing (Testament of Levi 8:2; 9:2) and Abraham's vision of the angel Michael (Testament of Abraham A 3:9; 4:3).

85. Testament of Abraham 4:8, 11; 7:3.

86. 1 Enoch 99:8.

87. 1 Enoch 1:2; 13:8, 10; 14:1, 4, 8, 14; 21:8.

88. However, both Luke and 1 Enoch use the word θεωρέω, 1 Enoch 1:2; 10:5; 14:14, 18; 89:47; 98:7.

infancy narrative above, the Lukan narrator, from the perspective of people outside the temple, describes Zechariah's interaction with the angel as a vision (ὀπτασία) (1:22). Similarly, the two disciples on the road to Emmaus refer to the appearance of two men at the empty tomb—seen by the women disciples—as a "vision of angels" (ὀπτασία ἀγγέλων) (24:23). In both cases, the word describes one set of characters' perspective on what other characters have seen, and in the latter case, the disciples do not necessarily believe the women's story (Luke 24:11). From these two examples, one might speculate that the word ὀπτασία (as opposed to ὅραμα) functions to set apart these third-person descriptions as less reliable. But in Acts 26:19, Paul refers to his interaction with Christ on the road to Damascus as a vision from heaven (τῇ οὐρανίῳ ὀπτασίᾳ), so it is more likely that the two words are interchangeable in Luke-Acts.[89]

Another word used for visions in Luke-Acts, θεωρέω, has received much attention because in Luke 10:18, Jesus uses it to report a first-hand account of a vision: "I saw Satan fall like lightning from heaven." Debate has centered on whether the imperfect tense in this verse suggests when Jesus's vision may have occurred, a point of debate. However, since the aorist form is rare, interpretation should rely not too heavily on tense. Observing that the imperfect tense of this verb frequently describes visions in Daniel, scholars have also argued this verbal form may have become associated with visionary experiences.[90] In Acts, the word describes two visions of the open heaven: Stephen's sight of the heavens opened and the Son of Man standing on the right hand of God (Acts 7:56) and Peter's vision of the heavens opening and a large sheet descending (Acts 10:11). It also refers to the apostles' perception that they saw a ghost instead of the resurrected Jesus (Luke 24:37) and the inability of the men with Paul to see the vision on the road to Damascus (Acts 9:7).[91] Finally, ἔκστασις describes Peter's state as the linen sheet descends from an open heaven (Acts 10:11; 11:5) and Paul's visionary experience in the Jerusalem temple (Acts 22:17).

89. In 1 Cor 12:1–2, Paul uses this word to describe the man caught up to the third heaven.

90. Dan. [OG/Θ] 4:13; 7:2, 4, 6, 7, 9, 11, 13; [Θ only] 2:31, 34; 4:10; 5:5; 7:21. Similarly, the imperfect describes visions of angels in Judg 13:19–20 and Tob 12:19. However, the aorist also refers to heavenly visions in Wis 19:7 and Rev 11:12, so this point should not be pressed too hard.

91. On the ship headed to Rome, Paul states that he sees (θεωρέω, in the present tense) the voyage ending in disaster (Acts 27:10). Several days later, he gives more specific information, stating that the previous evening, an angel stood before him, giving information about the ship's fate (27:24). While the angelic appearance might suggest that the "seeing" in 27:10 was also a vision, the fact of its inaccuracy indicates instead that the word refers simply to Paul's human perception, F. F. Bruce, *The Acts of the Apostles: The Greek Text with Introduction and Commentary* (Chicago: InterVarsity Christian Fellowship, 1952), 516.

Visionary Experiences in Luke-Acts

The above analysis of the words ὁράω (passive), ὅραμα, ὅρασις, ὀπτασία, θεωρέω, or ἔκστασις yields a list of thirteen scenes explicitly identified as visions (but not involving an angel). We may add to this list two additional visionary scenes—Jesus's baptism and transfiguration—which do not feature this vocabulary but are clearly visionary in nature. In both, characters hear a voice from heaven. The baptism scene features an open heaven and bodily descent of the Holy Spirit, while the transfiguration involves heavenly glory, a cloud that echoes the cloud of the Exodus, and the seeing (ὁράω) of the apostles, although the verb appears in the active rather than the passive voice more typical of Luke's vision scenes. Table One below lists these fifteen vision scenes with their visual and auditory components.

Table One: Visionary Experiences in Luke-Acts

	Passage	Recipient(s)	Visual Element(s)	Auditory Element(s)
1	Luke 3:21–22	Jesus	Heaven opening; dove descending	The voice of God
2	Luke 9:28–36	Jesus then Peter, James, John	Jesus's transformed appearance; Moses and Elijah in glory; a cloud	Speech by Moses & Elijah; the voice of God
3	Luke 10:18	Jesus	Satan falling like lightning from heaven	Speech by Jesus[92]
4	Luke 24:13–35	Two disciples	Jesus interacting and eating (they do not recognize him until they eat together)	Speech by Jesus
5	Luke 24:36–49	The eleven and other disciples	Jesus appearing in a room and eating (they first think he is a ghost); touch Jesus's body	Speech by Jesus
6	Luke 24:50–53	The eleven and other disciples	Jesus carried up into heaven	Speech by Jesus
7	Acts 1:3–9	Apostles	Jesus alive with many proofs; Jesus's ascension; a cloud	Speech by Jesus

92. Jesus' speech interprets the vision.

8	Acts 2:2–4	The eleven, female disciples, Jesus's brothers[93]	Tongues like a fire	Sound like a violent wind from heaven; foreign languages
9	Acts 7:55–60	Stephen	Heavens opened; Son of Man standing at God's right hand	None
10	Acts 9:3–9; 22:6–10, 14–15; 26:13–19	Paul	A light from heaven; risen Jesus, the "Righteous One"	The voice of Jesus
11	Acts 9:10–16	Ananias	None narrated	Speech by Jesus
12	Acts 10:9–16	Peter	Heaven opening; something descending like a linen sheet with all kinds of creatures in it (three times); the return of the sheet to heaven	The voice of Jesus[94]
13	Acts 16:9–10	Paul	A Macedonian man	Speech by the man
14	Acts 18:9–10	Paul	None narrated	Speech by the Lord
15	Acts 22:17–21	Paul	Unidentified figure referred to by Paul as "Lord"	Speech by the Lord

The recipients of visions in Luke-Acts change over the course of the narrative, beginning with Jesus and transitioning to his disciples. In the scene of the baptism, Jesus is the visionary. While Luke does not explicitly identify him as such, God's voice speaks directly to him (σὺ εἶ ὁ υἱός μου), implying that the vision is intended for him, rather than others who may have been present (Luke 3:21–22). So too, in the transfiguration story, Jesus is transformed while praying—an experience common to apocalyptic seers—and Moses and Elijah speak directly to him (Luke 9:29–31). Thus, although the narrator again does not explicitly describe him as seeing or hearing anything, he is the vision's implied recipient. But in the next verse, the narration shifts to focus on the experience of the three apostles, who have been weighed down with sleep (βεβαρημένοι ὕπνῳ) but then awaken fully. At this point, they see (ὁράω) Jesus's glory, as well as Moses and Elijah and the overshadowing cloud (9:32–34). God's voice also provides evidence of this narrative shift, addressing not Jesus, as in the baptism scene, but Peter, James, and John. The transfiguration thus represents a transitional scene in a shift of seers from Jesus to his disciples. This transition is also evident in the vision of Satan falling, the only first-hand visionary

93. Presumed from Acts 1:13–14.

94. Peter addresses the unidentified voice as Lord, but because the speaker refers to God in the third person, the voice presumably belongs to Jesus.

report in the Gospels. While Jesus is clearly its recipient (Luke 10:18), the narrative focuses less on Jesus's visionary experience—much to the consternation of interpreters, as will be discussed below—and more on Jesus's interpretation of its meaning for the apostles (Luke 10:19–24). From this point on in the narrative, the remaining recipients of visions are Jesus's disciples (visions #4–15).

Almost all visions in Luke-Acts contain narrated visual components, with the exception of visions #11 and #14. The idea of a vision (something seen) without a visual element seems odd, but a solution lies in an examination of Paul's experience on the road to Damascus (#10) and his vision in the Jerusalem temple (#15). When Luke and Paul narrate the Damascus road experience, Paul appears only to see a bright light, not Jesus himself. However, the narrator mentions that the men with Paul hear the voice but see no one (μηδένα) (Acts 9:7), a word that in a non-neuter person refers to people, not things. This implies that, by contrast, Paul *did* see Jesus, which Paul confirms when he retells Ananias's summary of the vision: Paul was chosen to see (ὁράω) the Righteous One as well as to receive a command from his mouth (Acts 22:14). This network of texts show that when Jesus says he appeared (ὁράω) to Paul to tell him something (Acts 26:16) or when Paul refers to Jesus's instruction as a "heavenly vision" (οὐράνιος ὀπτασία) (Acts 26:19), their language means that Paul not only hears Jesus's words but sees him speak them. These examples explain the somewhat strange turn of phrase in Paul's Jerusalem vision, that Paul "saw the Lord saying to him" (ἰδεῖν αὐτὸν λέγοντά μοι) (Acts 22:18). In other words, whenever figures in visions speak, the visionary also sees them. Thus, in visions #11 and #14, it should be assumed that Ananias and Paul see Jesus as well as hear him speak.[95] Jesus is the visual subject of almost every vision after #3 (except #8 and 13).

The open heaven is a visual motif common in apocalyptic literature, encapsulating its authors' interest in direct revelation.[96] In Jewish apocalypses, seers experience the open heaven either through a journey into the heavens or disclosure by an angel. In accord with these texts, as argued in the section on angelic revelation, the two interactions with angels that bracket Jesus's birth imply an open heaven in descriptions of God's overshadowing presence and glory. Vision scenes of an explicitly open heaven occur three times in Luke-Acts (visions #1, 9, and 12), but they involve neither angels nor heavenly journeys. Rather, they center on Jesus. At Jesus's baptism, the heaven is opened (ἀνεῳχθῆναι τὸν οὐρανὸν), the Holy Spirit descends in the form of a dove, and a voice from heaven says, "You are my Son, the Beloved; with you I am well pleased" (Luke 3:21–22). Right before Stephen dies in Acts, he sees the heavens opening completely (τοὺς

95. On this point, see also John B. F. Miller, *"Convinced That God Had Called Us": Dreams, Visions, and the Perception of God's Will in Luke-Acts*, BibInt 85 (Boston: Brill, 2007), 11–13. He observes that auditory-only visions were not uncommon in the Greco-Roman world. Even so, in Luke's narrative world, visions almost always include a narrated visual component.

96. Christopher Rowland, *The Open Heaven: A Study of Apocalyptic in Judaism and Early Christianity* (London: SPCK, 1982; repr. Eugene, OR: Wipf and Stock, 2002), 113.

οὐρανοὺς διηνοιγμένους) and the Son of Man standing at God's right hand (Acts 7:56). In Joppa, Peter sees the heaven opening (τὸν οὐρανὸν ἀνεῳγμένον) and a linen sheet descending to earth, initiating his vision of all kinds of animals and dialogue with the exalted Jesus (Acts 10:11).

As Rowland observes about the baptism scene, "a vision marked the decisive moment" in Jesus's life, confirming his identity as the one to inaugurate the kingdom."[97] All three Gospels include the open heaven at Jesus's baptism, but Luke's version—by describing the descent of Holy Spirit as in the bodily form of a dove—narrates the vision as more clearly outside the mind of Jesus.[98] Luke also connects prayer with these three scenes of the open heaven. The heavens open for Jesus as he prays (Luke 3:22); Stephen prays to Jesus immediately after seeing the exalted Son of Man (Acts 7:59–60); and Peter's vision comes when he goes up on the roof to pray (Acts 10:9). Five other vision scenes suggest an open heaven, or at the very least, a glimpse of heaven, as each involves something that comes from or goes to (a presumably open) heaven. These include the cloud that descends on the mountain of transfiguration (#2), Satan falling from heaven (#3), Jesus's ascension to heaven in association with a cloud (#6, 7), tongues of fire associated with a sound that comes from heaven (#8), and Jesus appearing to Paul as a light from heaven (#10).

The auditory element of visions follows a consistent pattern, with Jesus's role moving from seer to interpreter to heavenly revealer. In the first two visions, God speaks directly to Jesus, and in the latter of these, God reveals Jesus's glory and commands the disciples to "listen to him." After this point, almost all visions feature the voice of Jesus.[99] With the resurrection appearances, Jesus's voice interprets events by revealing the meaning of Scripture to the disciples.[100] These scenes (along with their summary in Acts 1:3–8) serve as a transition into later visions of the exalted Jesus: the Holy Spirit comes with the sound of a rushing wind; Stephen sees the Son of Man standing at God's right hand but hears nothing; then five visions feature the voice of the exalted Jesus offering direct revelation to characters, with Jesus's words to Paul on the Damascus road experience retold two additional times.

Overall, the content of revealed wisdom in the visions focuses on the identity of Jesus and the mission to spread the good news from Jerusalem outward to the ends of the earth, with a particular emphasis on the revelation to Gentiles. With regard to Jesus's identity, visions disclose that he is God's beloved, pleasing, chosen Son, who, in turn, reveals the Father (#1, 2, 3).

97. Ibid., 363.

98. Matthew's version has a similar sense, in that the dove alights on Jesus (3:16).

99. Exceptions are the arrival of the Holy Spirit in Acts 2, the angelic vision to Cornelius, and the vision of the Macedonian man.

100. I have included the appearances of Jesus in Luke 24:13–49 as visions because of the narrator's use of ὁράω in the passive voice. Moreover, Jesus, while in bodily form, is clearly of a supernatural quality, unrecognizable to his friends until they receive special knowledge and appearing in closed rooms. In addition, Jesus's words interpret his death and resurrection in a way that suggests the *angelus interpres* of apocalyptic texts. However, the resurrection appearances are distinctive from most other visionary scenes in Luke-Acts because Jesus's words center on interpretation of Scripture.

As such, he is the one to whom God has revealed hidden knowledge and to whom the disciples should listen (#1, 2, 3). The visions also interpret the significance and meaning of Jesus's death and resurrection. The risen Jesus is not a ghost but is physical, and it was necessary for the Messiah to suffer, as an exodus to his glory and so that the message might be proclaimed to all nations (#2, 4, 5). After his resurrection, he is worthy of worship and stands alongside God in the divine throne room (#6, 9). A vision of Jesus corrects Paul's wrong direction, while also revealing that the risen Jesus so closely identifies with his followers that persecution of them equals persecution of him (#10).

Visions also reveal the earthly results of Jesus's identity and glory, particularly related to the mission to the Gentiles. The seventy have authority over the enemy (#3), while Paul's mission accomplishes God's rescue of the Gentiles from the power of darkness and of Satan through the mission to the Gentiles (#10; Acts 26:18). These two visions correspond particularly closely because the story of the seventy foreshadows the Gentile mission. Similarly, other visions reveal the receipt of the power of the Holy Spirit in order to accomplish this witness, beginning from Jerusalem and going outward (#5, 7, 8, 11); the selection and future suffering of Paul to spread the good news, particularly to the Gentiles (#10, 11, 15); God's impartiality and intention to welcome the Gentiles (#12); and divine protection from assault and mistreatment because Jesus has many people in Corinth (#14). Recalling God's command at the transfiguration, visions later in Acts specifically direct the mission as it extends into the Gentile world. Ananias should go to Paul and heal him (#11) and Peter should not call profane what God has made clean (#12). Similarly, Paul should wait for instruction in Damascus (#10), leave Jerusalem (#15), preach the good news in Macedonia (#13), and speak boldly in Corinth (#14).

The revelatory content of Jesus's vision in Luke 10:17–24 deserves particular consideration, because it is both particularly apocalyptic and controversial. When Jesus states that he saw (or was seeing) Satan fall, like lightning from heaven, these words are best understood as a first-person report of direct revelation via a vision of heavenly realities.[101] Because of the brevity of this vision report, interpreters of Luke have struggled to understand the temporal issue of when this fall of Satan occurs and the closely related spatial issue of what the vision reveals about heaven and/or earth.

For assistance, scholars turn to comparisons of Jesus's vision with similar content in apocalyptic texts. Some point to affinities with depictions of the primeval fall of Satan, around the time of creation, which brings evil to the earth.[102] Others note that the Testament of Solomon

101. Alternatively, a cogent argument has been made for understanding ἐθεώρουν as a third-person plural: Jesus asserts that the *demons* saw Satan fall, Julian Victor Hills, "Luke 10:18—Who Saw Satan Fall?," *JSNT* 46 (1992): 25–40.

102. This interpretation relies on Isa 14:12 (and in some cases Ezek 28:11) in combination with Life of Adam and Eve 14:3–15:3, depicts the devil being cast onto the earth shortly after the creation of humanity. In 2 Enoch 29:4–6, an archangel (named as Satanail in

describes the fall of demons as occasional and ongoing; whenever they tire from flying constantly around the heavens, they fall like stars, resulting in fiery destruction on earth.[103] An alternative approach examines similarities with texts that depict the ultimate binding or defeat of Satan (or other evil angels) by the angels of God in the eschaton.[104] The various affinities between Luke 10:18 and these texts[105] constitute strong evidence that the words of the Lukan Jesus are not simply metaphorical but recount his actual experience of an apocalyptic vision of divine conflict with Satan, resulting in his fall from heaven.[106]

However, caution must be exercised in using these texts to determine the precise meaning of the vision in Luke, because they might include Christian interpolations. Moreover, each of the options presents difficulties, in narrative context. For example, we might ask: when would Jesus have seen the primeval fall of Satan, and why would he refer to it upon the return of the seventy? Or, if Jesus has seen a vision of the eschatological defeat of Satan, does he equate this defeat with the current situation (the mission of the seventy) or does this triumph occur at some other point in (or beyond) narrative time? If it occurs within the narrative, then why does Satan continue to have power in the story?

It is beyond the scope of this chapter to fully address these questions, but from a narrative perspective, it should be observed that the Lukan Jesus follows this vision report with an interpretation highlighting a tension (Luke 10:19–24). The disciples have been given eschatological authority over demonic oppression on earth ("authority to tread on snakes and scorpions, and over all the power of the enemy"). However, they should rejoice not in this authority, but rather that their names are written in heaven (10:19–20).[107] In other words, they should rejoice not in their own power (on earth) but in their connection to the power of God (in heaven). Jesus's interpretation draws out the theme of spiritual conflict inherent in the apocalyptic scenes in Luke-Acts: the real battle is being fought and won by God, the appropriate source of their joy. Jesus then expresses his own eschatological (ἐν αὐτῇ τῇ ὥρᾳ) joy and praise to God that the disciples have received revealed (ἀποκαλύπτω), esoteric (ἀποκρύπτω) knowl-

P's chapter headings) has a similar experience of being thrown from heaven due to arrogance, except that his fall occurs earlier, before the creation of the earth. The primordial interpretation of Luke 10:18 was common among patristic interpreters.

103. Testament of Solomon 20:12–13. Demons also may simply come to earth for evil purposes—destruction, fire, the sword, or mishap—without falling, Testament of Solomon 20:15, 17. The word "mishap" (σύμπτωμα) could also mean disease, and demons are responsible for disease elsewhere in Testament of Solomon. This link between demons and illness is another affinity with the Gospel of Luke.

104. Some of these texts are explored in the section on angelic warriors above. Others include Testament of Levi 18:12, which anticipates the coming of an eschatological priest who will bind Beliar and give his own children the power to tread upon evil spirits; Testament of Judah 25:3, in which God frees Israel from a spirit of error because Beliar will have been "cast into the fire forever"; and Testament of Simeon 6:5–6, which expects the spirits of deceit to be trodden under foot and humans to rule over wicked spirits.

105. In Luke, Jesus's statement about giving the disciples authority to tread on snakes and scorpions and over all the power of the enemy (Luke 10:19) resembles these texts, while his words in the following chapter about attacking and conquering the strong man, Satan or Beelzebul, bear affinity with the depictions of Beliar's eschatological fall (Luke 11:15–22).

106. By contrast, some interpreters have seen Jesus's statement as simply a symbolic way of praising the disciples.

107. This reference to a heavenly book constitutes another apocalyptic element of this passage.

edge. He emphasizes, however, that this revelation has come not to those in earthly positions of authority or status (prophets or kings) but—by God's good pleasure—to those in the position of blessed infants, connected to the Father through the Son (10:21–24).

Jesus thus interprets the vision as a reminder that the real eschatological struggle is a conflict between God and Satan. In this context, they are simultaneously blessed (authority over demons, names written in heaven, recipients of the revelation of the Father) and mere infants. The vision encourages both spiritual confidence with respect to divine power and humility with respect to the disciples' role within it. It well suits the larger narrative context that leads up to it. Jesus has indeed revealed mysterious (παρακαλύπτω) knowledge of his coming death and resurrection (9:22, 27, 44–45), but the disciples are focused on human prestige, authority, and honor (9:46–50, 52–56). In this section, the disciples seem especially caught up in the spiritual power that they are receiving from Jesus, while Jesus is oriented (both in intent and physical journey) toward his coming suffering. The kingdom involves access to spiritual power, creating a danger with regard to the human response as this power breaks into the world. Jesus's report of his vision reminds the disciples that they that they are not in control. They are not casting out demons; rather, Satan is falling from *heaven*. They are not wise and intelligent, but infants who have received revelation. From this perspective of humility, perhaps it is not necessary to choose a specific moment that the vision of the fall of Satan reveals, for in all options, the point is that the all-powerful God enacts his fall. Perhaps even the primordial option—the preferred interpretation by the church fathers but generally rejected by modern scholars—can be instructive, for it reminds Jesus's audience that even a powerful angel such as Satan himself, endowed with the highest spiritual power of God, when he became enamored of this power and forgot his place, fell.

Conclusion

Apocalyptic scenes play a significant role in Luke-Acts and develop two key tensions in the narrative. First, they reveal that eschatological restoration—the visitation of God—has begun, bringing the light of glory and revelation, but in unexpected ways: through an infant in a manger; by suffering and resurrection; and open to all, even marginal Jews, Gentiles, and those associated with the power of Rome. In keeping with Mary's hymn, apocalyptic scenes show that the mighty are indeed falling—brought down by the saving, strong arm of God—but these scenes also redefine God's enemies: Satan and his demons, not Rome, are the true sources of evil and oppression. Second, as highlighted in Jesus's vision of Satan's fall and scenes of mission in Acts, Luke holds apocalyptic glory in tension with Messianic suffering. Jesus possesses the glory of the Father and the angels (Luke 9:26), but as Messiah, he suffers and dies. When heaven and earth meet in Jesus, power meets humility. In the same way, his disciples receive heavenly power and authority; yet, they too are called to take up their cross (Luke 9:23). This tension continues in Acts, where the disciples suffer even as the narrative's apocalyptic scenes reveal God's eschatological redemption moving powerfully across the Mediterranean world, triumphing over evil.

5

Apocalyptic Revelation in the Gospel of John

Revealed Cosmology, the Vision of God, and Visionary Showing

Benjamin E. Reynolds

New Testament scholarship has long seen little connection between the Gospel of John and Jewish apocalyptic thought. The reasons for such an understanding are fairly obvious as the Gospel of John is known for its realized eschatology in contrast to the primarily future eschatology of the Synoptic Gospels. Since New Testament scholars have considered Jewish apocalyptic thought primarily as apocalyptic (future) eschatology,[1] John's Gospel has been considered to have little or no connection with it.[2]

Yet, as is being argued in this volume, Jewish apocalyptic tradition includes more than apocalyptic eschatology. In fact, the Jewish apocalypses have more to do with revelation of hidden mysteries than with an expectation of the end, even though the resolution of time is sometimes the content of what is revealed. If Jewish apocalyptic thought centers on disclosure of

1. Philipp Vielhauer, "Introduction," in *New Testament Apocrypha. Volume 2: Writing Related to the Apostles, Apocalypses and Related Subjects*, ed. W. Schneemelcher, trans. R. McL. Wilson (London: Lutterworth, 1965), 581–607; and Ernst Käsemann, "On The Subject of Primitive Christian Apocalyptic," *New Testament Questions of* Today, trans. W. J. Montague, (London: SCM, 1969), 108–37.
2. Frederick J. Murphy, *Apocalypticism in the Bible and Its World: A Comprehensive Introduction* (Grand Rapids: Baker Books, 2012), 275–79; and Klaus Koch, *The Rediscovery of Apocalyptic*, trans. Margaret Kohl, SBT 2.22 (London: SCM Press, 1972), 66–67, on Rudolf Bultmann. Most recently, in her response essay to the volume *The Gospel of John and Intimations of Apocalyptic*, Adela Yarbro Collins focuses almost entirely on John's eschatology ("Epilogue," in *John's Gospel and Intimations of Apocalyptic*, ed. Catrin Williams and Christopher Rowland (London; New York: Bloomsbury T&T Clark, 2013), 300–307.

things hidden, then could the Gospel of John be considered "apocalyptic"? Rudolf Bultmann did argue that the Gospel's *Grundkonzeption* is revelation, but for Bultmann, the background of the Gospel's revelation was to be found in gnostic documents and the "Gnostic Redeemer myth," not Jewish apocalypticism.[3] Considering that Bultmann argued for a gnostic background before the discovery of the Dead Sea Scrolls and the resulting explosion of interest in early Judaism, his argument was plausible. In his evaluation of Bultmann's thesis, John Ashton agreed that revelation is the central concept in John's Gospel, but Ashton argued for Jewish apocalyptic thought as the proper background for this revelation.[4] Even though Ashton revised his arguments for an apocalyptic background, and quite possibly undermined them,[5] viewing the Johannine revelation in the context of revelation within Jewish apocalyptic thought makes much more sense with present understandings of Second Temple Judaism and, especially, the Jewish apocalyptic tradition.

The challenge of viewing the Gospel of John apocalyptically is to think beyond apocalyptic eschatology to recognize that Jewish apocalyptic thought also includes the revelation or unveiling of heavenly mysteries, whether they include cosmology or wisdom.[6] Since "apocalyptic" is often assumed by New Testament scholars to be equivalent with eschatology, I will focus on other revelatory aspects of John's Gospel—specifically, its revelation of cosmology. In this chapter, I will discuss the Gospel's revealed cosmology, its vision of God as revealed in and by the Son, and the Gospel's language of revelation and visionary showing, in particular, the word used to speak of Jesus's showing of the Father (δείκνυμι).[7]

Revealed Cosmology in John

One of the features of an apocalypse as defined in *Semeia* 14 by the Society of Biblical Literature genre project is that the revelation made known by an otherworldly being "discloses a transcendent reality which is . . . spatial insofar as it envisages another supernatural world."[8] John Collins speaks of this spatial aspect as including information about otherworldly regions and

3. Rudolf Bultmann, "Die Bedeutung Der Neuerschlossenen Mandäischen Und Manichäischen Quellen Für Das Verständnis Des Johannesevangeliums," *ZNW* 24 (1925): 100–146.

4. John Ashton, *Understanding the Fourth Gospel*, 2nd ed. (New York; Oxford: Oxford University Press, 2007), 307–29.

5. John Ashton, *The Gospel of John and Christian Origins* (Minneapolis: Fortress Press, 2014), ch. 6.

6. See Christopher C. Rowland and Christopher R. A. Morray-Jones, *The Mystery of God: Early Jewish Mysticism and the New Testament*, CRINT 12 (Leiden; Boston: Brill, 2009), 123. At the same time, the Gospel is not absent of an eschatology with its references to present judgment (John 3:18; 9:39–41; etc.), "the last day" (6:39, 40, 44, 54), and the resurrection of the righteous and the wicked (5:28–29). See Jörg Frey, *Die johanneische Eschatologie. Bände 1-3*, WUNT 96, 110, 117 (Tübingen: Mohr Siebeck, 1997, 1998, 2000).

7. This chapter is not an attempt to solve Bultmann's conundrum of the empty content of the Gospel of John's revelation—that all Jesus reveals is that he is the Revealer (Rudolf Bultmann, *Theology of the New Testament*, trans. Kendrick Grobel [New York: Scribner, 1951], 2:66). There are implications for answering that conundrum when John's Gospel is compared with Jewish apocalyptic thought, but anyone seeking a complete response to Bultmann will only find the beginnings of one here.

8. Collins, *Apocalyptic Imagination*, 5. While this definition has been critiqued on numerous occasions, it does serve as a useful starting point for defining what is and is not "apocalyptic."

otherworldly beings.[9] Throughout the Jewish apocalypses, this spatial aspect of the transcendent reality is often indicated by appearance of an otherworldly mediator who descends to earth from heaven, a human recipient who ascends and is given a tour of heaven, or some combination of both.

For example, in 4 Ezra, the angel Uriel is sent from heaven to answer Ezra's questions directed to the Lord. In the Book of the Watchers (1 Enoch 14), Enoch enters into heaven, sees "the Great Glory" seated on the throne (1 Enoch 14:19, 24; see also Testament of Levi 3–5), and is later led on a tour by the archangels (1 Enoch 17–19; 21–36). In the Book of the Luminaries (1 Enoch 72–82), Enoch recounts what he has been shown by the angel Uriel regarding the sun, moon, stars and their movements. Although the apocalypse is not overly specific concerning Enoch's journey, the content of the Book of the Luminaries reveals a cosmological perspective of the heavens and earth.[10] In Apocalypse of Abraham, the supernatural world is disclosed through the descent of Yahoel and his escorting of Abraham to heaven. There, in heaven, Abraham worships the Lord, and the Lord himself shows Abraham the heavens, earth, the abyss, and many other things. Testament of Abraham tells of the multiple descents of Michael the archangel from heaven and of Abraham's ascent and tour of the earth with Michael as his guide. In 3 Baruch, Baruch is led through five levels of heaven by Phanuel, and some of what he sees includes aspects of cosmology. All of these apocalypses reveal the existence of heaven and earth and of heavenly beings. Human beings are from the created realm of the earth, but heaven is another realm where the celestial bodies travel, and where God and his angelic messengers dwell.

"Otherworldly Regions" and Jesus as "Otherworldly Being" in the Gospel of John

The Gospel of John, like the Jewish apocalypses, reveals a spatial transcendence. The above and below language that appears overly mysterious when the Gospel of John is compared with the Synoptic Gospels seems less mysterious and quite apocalyptically revealing when laid side by side with the Jewish apocalypses.[11] The contents of the narrative of John and the narratives of the Jewish apocalypses are all clearly different, but the Gospel of John similarly discloses a cosmological portrait of heaven and earth.

9. John J. Collins, "Introduction: Toward the Morphology of a Genre," *Semeia* 14 (1979): 1–20 (7).

10. Cf. Kelley Coblentz Bautch, *A Study of the Geography of 1 Enoch 17-19: 'No One Has Seen What I Have Seen"*, JSJSup 81 (Leiden; Boston: Brill, 2003), 199–205.

11. Cf. Edward W. Klink III, "Light of the World: Cosmology and the Johannine Literature," in *Cosmology and New Testament Theology*, ed. Jonathan T. Pennington and Sean M. McDonough, LNTS 355 (London: T & T Clark, 2008), 74–89, who focuses on cosmic dualism and cosmic drama with no indication of similarities with Jewish apocalyptic thought.

The opening section of the Gospel reveals a primordial sense of time in which the Word was with the Father. The Word's involvement in the creation suggests a cosmological sense in that the Word is separate from what has come into being.[12] In 1:9, the Gospel writer states that the true light has come into the world. The implication is that a realm separate from the world exists and it is that realm from which the light comes. This realm becomes more explicit in 1:32 when John the Baptist states that he has seen the Spirit descending out of heaven like a dove. And again, more spectacularly, in 1:51, Jesus tells Nathanael that he will see heaven opened and the angels of God ascending and descending on the Son of Man. The opening of heaven has obvious connections to Jewish apocalyptic thought in the multiple instances of the opening of heaven in the Jewish apocalypses (e.g., 2 Baruch 22:1; Apocalypse of Abraham 19:4; Testament of Levi 2:6). In the Gospel of John, the opening of heaven makes possible the vision of Jesus as the one who unites heaven and earth, the light coming into the world, and it indicates the Gospel's revelation of the spatial axis of a transcendent reality.[13]

The revelation of cosmology occurs again in John 3, where Jesus tells Nicodemus that to enter the kingdom, one must be born above (ἄνωθεν; 3:3; cf. 3:7). Similarly, in 3:13, Jesus states that he has descended from heaven, and as such, is able to reveal the things of heaven (3:12). That this statement is made in the negative highlights Jesus's exclusive claim to ascent, but more importantly, his superiority of origin in that he did not ascend first to descend with heavenly mysteries.[14] Rather, "his true home is in heaven,"[15] and thus he only needed to descend to earth. His heavenly origin gives him more authority to disclose revelation (cf. Abraham, Moses, Isaiah, Elijah, etc.). At the least, the passage indicates the cosmological reality of heaven and earth, the existence of earthly things (τὰ ἐπίγεια) and heavenly things (τὰ ἐπουράνια), and that Jesus is a heavenly figure who has descended from heaven. John 3:31–36 summarizes the mission of Jesus, the one who is from above (ἄνωθεν) and is above all (ἐπάνω πάντων, 3:31). Jesus is from heaven, has been sent from heaven by God, and speaks the words of God. The phrase ἐκ τῆς γῆς (from the earth) which is repeated three times in 3:31 contrasts sharply with Jesus's origin from heaven (ὁ ἐκ τοῦ οὐρανοῦ ἐρχόμενος).

Another cosmological indication comes in Jesus's dispute with the Pharisees in 8:12–30. In 8:23, in response to their question about where he is going that they cannot go, Jesus states,

12. Ashton, *Christian Origins*, 145–55, argues that John 1:3 does not refer to creation.

13. For further details, see Benjamin Reynolds, "Apocalypticism in the Gospel of John's Written Revelation of Heavenly Things," *Early Christianity* 4, no. 1 (2013): 64–95.

14. Contra J.-A. Bühner, *Der Gesandte und sein Weg im 4. Evangelium: Die kultur- und religionsgeschichtlichen Grundlagen der johanneischen Sendungschristologie sowie ihre traditionsgeschichtliche Entwicklung*, WUNT II/2 (Tübingen: Mohr Siebeck, 1977), 374–99, and others. See Madison N. Pierce and Benjamin E. Reynolds, "The Perfect Tense-form and the Son of Man in John 3:13: Developments in Greek Grammar as a Viable Solution to the Ascent and Descent," *NTS* 60, no. 1 (2014): 149–55.

15. J. Louis Martyn, *History and Theology in the Fourth Gospel*, 3rd ed., NTL (Westminster John Knox, 2003), 131–32; Ashton, *Understanding*, 240.

"You are from below (ἐκ τῶν κάτω), and I am from above (ἐκ τῶν ἄνω). You are from this world, and I am not from this world (ἐγὼ οὐκ εἰμι ἐκ τοῦ κόσμου τούτου)." The statement clearly reveals a transcendent reality; Jesus is not from earth but from heaven. Again, in 8:42, he says that he has come from God (ἐκ τοῦ θεοῦ; cf. παρὰ θεοῦ, 9:33). The revealed cosmology of the Gospel is obvious in Jesus's statements in the last discourse, where he claims to have come from the Father (13:3; 16:27–30; 17:8). Further evidence of the Johannine revelation of a transcendent spatial reality is noticeable in Jesus's trial with Pilate. Implying that Pilate is correct that Jesus is a king, Jesus tells Pilate that his kingdom is not of this world (οὐκ ἔστιν ἐκ τοῦ κόσμου τούτου, 18:36). Pilate himself only has authority, Jesus says, because it has been given to him from above (ἄνωθεν, 19:11).

Jesus is not only a heavenly figure who is not from this world, but he will also return to heaven from this world (cf. Wisdom in 1 Enoch 42). Hints of this return are noticeable in his ascent mentioned in 3:13, and again, in 6:62 and 20:17. As the Gospel progresses, Jesus speaks about his going away, which is the same as his returning to the Father in heaven, the one who sent him (7:33; 8:14, 21–22; 13:3, 33, 36; 14:4–5; 14:28; 16:5, 10, 17; cf. 3:8 of the Spirit). "The Jew's" and Jesus's own disciples' lack of knowledge about where he is from (πόθεν) contrasts his heavenly origin with those from this world (7:27–28; 8:14, 22; 9:29–30; 14:5; 19:9).[16]

While the Gospel of John does not unveil levels of heaven or astronomical details, it does reveal a spatial transcendence. Heaven does exist and Jesus is from heaven and is returning to heaven. Similar to the Jewish apocalypses, John's Gospel reveals that Jesus is an otherworldly being from an otherworldly region.

"Otherworldly Beings" in the Gospel of John

While the Gospel discloses the existence of heaven and earth ("otherworldly regions") and of Jesus as an otherworldly being, the Gospel also indicates the existence of more otherworldly beings. Although angels make little appearance in the Gospel, they are depicted as ascending and descending on the Son of Man (1:51), and two angels are seen by Mary when she looks into the tomb after Peter and John depart (20:12–13). The appearance and description of these two angels is only briefly mentioned, but such brevity is typical of most depictions of otherworldly figures in Jewish apocalypses (1 Enoch 20:1–8; 4 Ezra 4:1; 5;14; 10:30; 2 Baruch 55:3).

Another otherworldly figure in John's Gospel is the "ruler of this world" (ὁ ἄρχων τοῦ κόσμου τουτοῦ, 12:31; 14:30; 16:11). This figure is also called Satan (ὁ σατανᾶς, 13:27), the devil (ὁ διάβολος, 8:44; 13:2; cf. 6:70), and the evil one (ὁ πονηρός, 17:15), yet as both Jutta Leonhardt-

16. Ashton, *Understanding*, 493, comments that πόθεν has an important revelatory function in the Gospel.

Balzer and Loren Stuckenbruck note, he acts through people and not on his own.[17] The contrast between the devil and God is set forth explicitly by Jesus in 8:42–44. Here, Jesus states that his opponents do not have God as their Father, but rather the devil is their Father because they do not accept Jesus, the one who is from God. While Jesus's kingdom is not of this world (18:36), the devil is the ruler of this world. Jesus's glorification and exaltation bring about the casting out of this ruler. And ironically, it is the devil who brings about his own demise when he enters into Judas and begins the betrayal of Jesus, which leads to Jesus's glorification through the crucifixion.[18] The Jewish apocalypses are full of evil figures—from Asael and Shemihazah in the Book of the Watchers, Azazel in the Apocalypse of Abraham, and Mastema in Jubilees. Similarly, John's Gospel reveals the existence of otherworldly beings, but as with the Gospel's revelation of heaven and earth, little more is said of these beings.

Although the above discussion has merely scratched the surface of the revealed cosmology of John's Gospel, what is clear is that the Gospel of John's revelation unveils a transcendent spatial reality that bears similarities with the spatial revelation of the Jewish apocalypses. The Fourth Gospel does so more than the Synoptic Gospels in that John's Gospel reveals a figure who comes from heaven to earth, and who will return to heaven. In contrast to the Synoptic Gospels, the Johannine Jesus speaks of heaven and earth and uses the language of above and below. He discloses things of heaven to those on earth and reveals the existence of angels and the devil. His death and resurrection are part of the cosmic struggle, and they result in the casting out of the devil from his place of rulership (12:32). It is in this revealed cosmology that the Gospel of John indicates at least one similarity with Jewish apocalyptic thought; however, as Bultmann has noted, the Gospel reveals no details of the heavenly world.[19] Unlike the revelation of various levels of heaven, the places of the dead, or God seated on the heavenly throne as depicted in Jewish apocalypses, the Gospel of John tells us nothing about heaven except that Jesus is from heaven, unites heaven and earth, and is returning to heaven. The concern of John's Gospel is not cosmological speculation but information about the one who came from heaven. The Gospel clearly reveals a cosmology that is in tune with the world of Jewish apocalyptic thought, but the portrait remains distinctly Johannine in that Jesus is the one from above who has been sent from the Father, has come into this world and returns from this world to the Father.[20]

17. See Jutta Leonhardt-Balzer, "The Ruler of the World, Antichrists and Pseudo-Prophets: Johannine Variations on an Apocalyptic Theme," in *John's Gospel and Intimations of Apocalyptic*, ed. Catrin H. Williams and Christopher Rowland (London; New York: Bloomsbury T&T Clark, 2013), 180–99; Loren T. Stuckenbruck, "Evil in Johannine and Apocalyptic Perspective: Petition for Protection in John 17," in *John's Gospel and Intimations of Apocalyptic*, ed. Catrin H. Williams and Christopher Rowland (London; New York: Bloomsbury T&T Clark, 2013), 200–232.

18. Judith L. Kovacs, "'Now Shall the Ruler of This World Be Driven Out': Jesus' Death as Cosmic Battle in John 12:20-36," *JBL* 114, no. 2 (1995): 227–47.

19. Bultmann, *Theology of the New Testament*, 2:62.

20. For a discussion of the use of *κόσμος* in the Gospel of John, see N. H. Cassem, "A Grammatical and Contextual Inventory of the Use

The Vision of God in the Jewish Apocalypses and John

The Gospel of John's emphasis on the vision of God in the person of Jesus also forms part of its revealed cosmology. God is in heaven, and thus otherworldly, but Jesus makes possible the vision of God. This vision of God forms another example of the Gospel's similarity with Jewish apocalyptic thought. For, as Christopher Rowland states, "The vision of God, the heart of the calling experiences of Isaiah and Ezekiel and the goal of the heavenly ascents of the apocalyptic seers and rabbinic mystics, is in the Fourth Gospel related to the revelation of God in Jesus."[21]

As the quote from Rowland implies, the Jewish apocalyptic visions of God have their beginning in Hebrew Bible visions. For example, Moses sees God on Mount Sinai (Exodus 24) and is shown God's glory (Exod 33:18). Elijah, also on Mount Sinai, has an experience of meeting the Lord (1 Kgs 19:9–18). Neither one of them sees God's face, since Elijah wraps his face in his mantle before going out to speak with the Lord (1 Kgs 19:13) and Moses only sees the Lord's back. Micaiah prophesies that he sees the divine council (1 Kings 22). But Isaiah's and Ezekiel's visions of the Lord became the most influential in shaping the depictions of heavenly ascents in the Jewish apocalypses.[22]

By the time the Jewish apocalypses were written, heavenly speculation seems to have increased to the extent that in order to describe God, an ascent to God's throne in heaven was practically a requirement.[23] In the Book of the Watchers, Enoch takes the plea of the Watchers to the Lord and he is taken up into heaven. He enters through the house of fire, then into the house of ice, before he finally comes to the place where God is seated on a throne. Enoch says that he does not see God's face (1 Enoch 14:19) and that he is on his face prostrate (14:24), but enigmatically, he is able to describe the throne and the Great Glory sitting upon it (14:18–20). God speaks with him and tells him what to say to the Watchers (14:24–16:4). The ascent to heaven makes possible Enoch's vision of God, even if in this instance, Enoch and the angels (14:21) are unable to see the Lord.[24]

Similarly, Enoch has a vision of God in the Parables of Enoch (1 Enoch 46–48, 62, 71) and also in 2 Enoch 22. In both of these texts, there is little or no reticence about God being seen by Enoch. Levi also sees "the Holy Most High" seated on a throne (Testament of Levi 5:1), as does Daniel who sees the Ancient of Days take his seat (Dan 7:9–10). In Apocalypse of Abraham,

of Κόσμος in the Johannine Corpus with Some Implications for a Johannine Cosmic Theology," *NTS* 19 (1972): 81–91; Klink, "Light of the World."

21. Rowland and Morray-Jones, *Mystery of God*, 124–25; idem, Rowland, *Open Heaven*, 84.
22. Martha Himmelfarb, *Ascent to Heaven in Jewish and Christian Apocalypses* (Oxford: Oxford University Press, 1993), 9–28; Rowland, *Open Heaven*, 78–80.
23. Rowland, *Open Heaven*, 80.
24. George W. E. Nickelsburg, *1 Enoch 1: A Commentary on the Book of 1 Enoch, Chapters 1-36; 81-108*, Hermeneia (Minneapolis: Fortress Press, 2001), 265, points out that some angels are able to approach the Lord.

Abraham has a vision of the heavenly throne and the fire encircling it (Apocalypse of Abraham 18), yet his angelic guide Yahoel tells him: "You will not look at him himself" (16:3).[25] Baruch in 3 Baruch is told that he will see the glory of God (3 Baruch 4:2 Slavonic; 6:12; 7:2; 11:2; 16:6 Slavonic), but he is turned back when he reaches fifth heaven (17:1; 17:1–4).[26] Not to mention John the seer who has a vision of the Lord on his throne in Revelation 4.[27]

In comparison with these Jewish apocalypses of heavenly ascent, the Gospel of John's statements that no one has seen the Father and no one has heard the Father apart from the Son are quite striking. Jesus, the one who is from heaven, is the one who has seen the Father and reveals the Father. No one else has seen the Father (1:18; 6:46), and no one else ascends to heaven (3:13). Most scholars have noted the polemical nature of these claims.[28] It may be claimed that Abraham, Jacob, Moses, Elijah, Isaiah, and Ezekiel have seen God or even have ascended to heaven, as well as Enoch, Baruch, Levi, and others in Jewish apocalyptic tradition. While visions of God are possible in Jewish apocalypses through ascents to heaven in the attendance of an otherworldly mediator, in the Gospel of John, Jesus, an otherworldly being, is the vision of God.[29]

One of the most significant passages regarding visionary experience in the Gospel of John is the reference to Isaiah's vision. In 12:41, as the Gospel moves from the narration of Jesus's life to his passion, the evangelist states that Isaiah did not see the Lord's glory, but Jesus's glory. This statement follows right on the heels of two citations of Isaiah: Isaiah 53:1 in John 12:38 and Isaiah 6:10 in John 12:40. The latter citation comes from the Lord's speech to Isaiah during his visionary calling. In Isaiah 6:1–5, Isaiah saw the Lord seated on his throne and the six-winged angels surrounding the throne. Isaiah responds to the vision by saying "Woe is me! I am lost, for I am a man of unclean lips, and I live among a people of unclean lips; yet my eyes have seen the King, the Lord of hosts!" (NRSV, 6:5).

For the Gospel of John, Isaiah's vision of the Lord is truly a vision of Jesus.[30] Herman Ridderbos states, "the glory of God as the prophet foresaw in his vision was no other than that which the Son of God had with the Father before the world was . . . (17:4; 1:14, 18)."[31] This explanation

25. Andrei A. Orlov, *Heavenly Priesthood in the Apocalypse of Abraham* (Cambridge; New York: Cambridge University Press, 2013), 46–53, has highlighted the "anti-anthropomorphic tendencies" of the Apocalypse of Abraham.

26. Alexander Kulik, *3 Baruch: Greek-Slavonic Apocalypse of Baruch*, CEJL (Berlin; New York: De Gruyter, 2010), 179. Kulik notes here that the "glory of God" may refer not to God specifically but "to a disclosure of his works," which is of interest considering Jesus's revelation of the Father's works in the Gospel of John.

27. Cf. 4 Ezra and 2 Baruch which have no vision of God. 4 Ezra 8:20–21 seems to reject heavenly speculation.

28. Hugo Odeberg, *The Fourth Gospel: Interpreted in Its Relation to Contemporaneous Religious Currents in Palestine and the Hellenistic-Oriental World* (Uppsala: Almqvist & Wiksells Boktryckeri, 1929), 72; more recently, James H. Charlesworth, "Did the Fourth Evangelist Know the Enoch Tradition?," in *Testimony and Interpretation: Early Christology in Its Judeo-Hellenistic Milieu. Studies in Honour of Peter Pokorný*, ed. J. Mrazek and J. Roskovec (London: T & T Clark, 2004), 223–39; Reynolds, "Apocalypticism in the Gospel of John's Written Revelation of Heavenly Things," 76–78.

29. Rowland and Morray-Jones, *Mystery of God*, 128, 131; Jey J. Kanagaraj, *'Mysticism' in the Gospel of John: An Inquiry into Its Background*, JSNTSup 158 (Sheffield, England: Sheffield Academic, 1998), 214–47.

30. Raymond E. Brown, *The Gospel According to John (I-XII): Introduction, Translation, and Notes*, AB 29 (Garden City, NY: Doubleday, 1966), 487, connects Isaiah's vision of Jesus with John 8:56 when Jesus says that Abraham saw his day and rejoiced.

of Isaiah's vision furthers the Gospel's claim that no one can see God except the Son. Isaiah saw Jesus's glory and not the Lord's, yet it is possible for God to be seen. John 12:38 has just asked the question from Isaiah 53:1: "To whom has the arm of the Lord been revealed (ἀπεκαλύφθη)?"[32] The implied answer to that question is that all who have seen the works and signs of Jesus have seen the Lord's glory, just as Isaiah did (12:37; cf. 1:14; 2:11; 12:23).[33] The vision of God which is the heart of Jewish apocalyptic ascent is possible in the person of Jesus who has descended from the Father.

In John 14:6, Jesus states that he is the way and no one comes to the Father except through him. This statement is another exception, like those in 1:18; 3:13; and 6:44. Jesus is the only one who has seen the Father, only he comes from the Father, and he is also the only one through whom people can come to the Father.[34] In response to Jesus's claim to be the only way to the Father, Philip asks Jesus to show the disciples the Father. Jesus says that if the disciples have seen him, they have seen the Father (14:8–9).[35] To see Jesus is to see the Father (see 12:45; cf. 5:19–30; 8:23–30; 17:6–8).[36] There is no need for heavenly ascent because the revelation or vision of God has taken place on earth. It is this inversion which is one of the primary reasons Ashton has claimed that the Gospel of John is "an apocalypse—in reverse, upside down, inside out."[37]

All that Jesus as the otherworldly mediator speaks, does, makes known, etc. reveals the Father. Bultmann has noted that there is no esoteric knowledge or mysteries that are communicated in this revelation,[38] which is why Bultmann claims that the revelation indicates only that Jesus is the Revealer and no more.[39] Saeed Hamid-Khani disagrees with Bultmann, arguing that there is content to the revelation. He asserts that Bultmann's claim goes against the message of the Gospel and contends that the incarnation, including the crucifixion and resurrection, sums up the Johannine revelation.[40]

31. Herman Ridderbos, *The Gospel of John: A Theological Commentary* (Grand Rapids: Eerdmans, 1997), 445.
32. This is the only use of the verb ἀποκαλύπτω in John's Gospel.
33. Catrin H. Williams, "Seeing the Glory: The Reception of Isaiah's Call-Vision in Jn 12.41," in *Judaism, Jewish Identity and Gospel Tradition*, ed. James G. Crossley (London; Oakville, CT: Equinox, 2010), 186–206 (198). This is an excellent study of the reception Isaiah 6 in Jewish apocalyptic literature and particularly John.
34. See C. K. Barrett, *The Gospel according to St. John: An Introduction with Commentary and Notes on the Greek Text*, 2nd ed. (Philadelphia: Westminster, 1978), 459.
35. See further discussion of this passage below.
36. See Craig R. Koester, "Jesus as the Way to the Father in Johannine Theology (John 14,6)," in *Theology and Christology in the Fourth Gospel: Essays by Members of the SNTS Johannine Writings Seminar*, ed. Gilbert Van Belle, J. G. Van der Watt, and P. Maritz, BETL 184 (Leuven: Leuven University Press, 2005), 117–33.
37. Ashton, *Understanding*, 328–29.
38. Bultmann, *Theology of the New Testament*, 2:62; Rudolf Bultmann, *The Gospel of John: A Commentary*, trans. G. R. Beasley-Murray, R. W. N. Hoare, and J. K. Riches (Philadelphia: Westminster, 1971), 254.
39. Bultmann, *Theology of the New Testament*, 2:66.
40. Saeed Hamid-Khani, *Revelation and Concealment of Christ: Theological Inquiry into the Elusive Language of the Fourth Gospel*, WUNT II/120 (Tübingen: Mohr Siebeck, 2000), 351–52; also Sjef Van Tilborg, "Cosmological Implications of Johannine Christology," in *Theology and Christology in the Fourth Gospel: Essays by Members of the SNTS Johannine Writings Seminar*, ed. Gilbert Van Belle, J. G. Van der Watt, and P. Maritz, BETL 184 (Leuven: Leuven University Press, 2005), 483–502. See Ashton, *Understanding*, 528–29.; Cf. Gail R. O'Day, *Revelation in the Fourth Gospel: Narrative Mode and Theological Claim* (Philadelphia: Fortress Press, 1986), 92.

The enigma of the Johannine revelation cannot be solved in a short essay directed in multiple directions, but the world of the Jewish apocalypses offers a much more promising comparison than that of Gnosticism and its redeemer myths.[41] Granted there is no list of revealed things in John's Gospel, but in agreement with Hamid-Khani, something is revealed. The heavens open and a connection is made between earth and heaven. God's glory is made visible, but in the human being, Jesus. To see Jesus, the Messiah, Son of God, and Son of Man, is to see God the Father.[42] Unlike otherworldly mediators who speak for God, Jesus speaks and acts for God. Jesus is able to give life and judge in the same way God is because God has granted him the authority to do so (5:20–27). His words, which are the words of God, are words of life (8:28–30; 12:48–50).

Language of Revelation: Visionary Showing

One final connection with Jewish apocalyptic thought concerns the Gospel's language of revelation. Ashton has pointed out how an examination of the theme of revelation in the Gospel of John is made difficult by its language. First, the noun ἀποκαλύπσις is not used in the Gospel, although, by comparison, there are multiple instances of the word in the Pauline literature (1 Cor 1:7; 2 Cor 12:7; Gal 1:12; 2 Thess 1:7; etc.).[43] The verb ἀποκαλύπω is used only once in John's Gospel and that is in the citation of Isaiah 53:1 in 12:38 mentioned above. Other verbs generally synonymous with ἀποκαλύπω include: φανερόω, γνωρίζω, ἐξεγέομαι, ἐμφανίζω, and ἀναγγέλω, but Ashton says that these words "are not sufficiently prominent and do not carry sufficient weight to merit an extended treatment."[44] The second difficulty, he notes, is the "sheer ubiquity" of the concept of revelation in John. If Jesus is the revealer as Bultmann argued and most scholars agree, then any action or speech by Jesus becomes revelation. To quote Ashton: "*Every major motif in the Gospel of John is linked to the concept of revelation.*"[45] Ashton lists the vocabulary of those motifs related to revelation in the Gospel of John, and this list is quite extensive, which, as he perceptively notes, makes more difficult any examination of revelation in John. His list includes: λόγος, δόξα, ἀλήθεια, ῥήματα, σημεῖα, μαρτυρία, μαρτυρέω, λαλέω, λέγω, κράζω, διδάσκω, ὑπομιμινήσκω, πιστεύω, ἀκούω, οἶδα, γινώσκω, to name a few.[46] All of this vocabulary indicates the pervasiveness of the theme of revelation in the Gospel of John, and also, the challenge of attempting to explain it.

41. Francis J. Moloney, "The Parables of Enoch and the Johannine Son of Man," in *Parables of Enoch: A Paradigm Shift*, ed. Darrell L. Bock and James H. Charlesworth, JCT 11 (London; New York: Bloomsbury T&T Clark, 2013), 293n87.
42. Rowland and Morray-Jones, *Mystery of God*, 131. Rowland states: "Heavenly visions are not what is on offer in the Fourth Gospel, for claims to see God must be regarded as claims to see Jesus."
43. See Matthew Goff's essay on 1 and 2 Corinthians in this volume.
44. Ashton, *Understanding*, 491.
45. Ibid., 491–92 (emphasis original).
46. Ibid., 492.

One word that I would argue should be included in Ashton's list and is worth an extended treatment is the word δείκνυμι.[47] The BDAG lexicon defines δείκνυμι as "to exhibit something that can be apprehended by one or more of the senses, *point out, show, make known*" or "to prove or make clear by evidence or reasoning, *explain, prove*."[48] While δείκνυμι is used six times in the Gospel of John, it is worthy of attention due to the implications it has for visionary claims, particularly in John 5 and John 14. Before addressing the context and use of δείκνυμι in the Gospel of John, a brief examination will be made of the word's use in the Septuagint and in Greek versions of Second Temple Jewish apocalyptic texts. These texts indicate the connection that the word—and more broadly, the concept of visionary showing—has within Jewish apocalyptic thought.

Δείκνυμι in the Septuagint

In the LXX, the word δείκνυμι is used in a number of different settings, but it is also found in some significant visionary experiences. For example, in Genesis 41:25, 28, Joseph tells Pharaoh that God has shown (ἔδειξεν) Pharaoh in his dream what God is about to do (41:25 41:28 הִגִּיד הֶרְאָה;). In response, Pharaoh says that God has shown Joseph "all these things" (41:39, הוֹדִיעַ). While Moses is on Mount Sinai, God is said to show Moses the tabernacle (Exod 25:9, 40; 26:30). And more suggestively for our concern with John's Gospel, Moses asks God to show him his glory (Exod 33:18: δεῖξόν μοι τὴν σεαυτοῦ δόξαν; הַרְאֵנִי). God does show Moses his glory, but only after telling Moses that he cannot see his face (Exod 33:20). When Balaam gives his prophecy in Numbers 24, he prophesies that the one truly seeing (ὁ ἄνθρωπος ὁ ἀληθινῶς ὁρῶν), hearing God's words (ἀκούων λόγια θεοῦ), understanding the understanding of the Most High (ἐπιστάμενος ἐπιστήμην παρὰ ὑψίστου), and seeing a vision of God (καὶ ὅρασιν θεοῦ ἰδὼν) is the one whom God will show (Num 24:17: δείξω αὐτῷ; אֶרְאֶנּוּ). Once this statement is made, Balaam continues with the well-known prophecy that was interpreted messianically in Second Temple Judaism concerning the star that will come out of Jacob and the scepter that will rise out of Israel (24:15–17; cf. 23:3). In Deuteronomy, Moses shows the people God's righteous deeds and judgment (Deut

47. He also does not list ἀπαγγέλω or σημαίω. The latter is used in relation to Jesus's death on three occasions (2:33; 18:32; 21:19; cf. Rev 1:1) and is the verbal cognate of the noun σημεῖα. For an examination of ἀναγγέλω in Theodotion Daniel in relation to the Gospel of John, see Catrin H. Williams, "Unveiling Revelation: The Spirit-Paraclete and Apocalyptic Disclosure in the Gospel of John," in *John's Gospel and Intimations of Apocalyptic*, ed. Catrin H. Williams and Christopher Rowland (London; New York: Bloomsbury T&T Clark, 2013), 104–27.

48. Walter Bauer and Frederick William Danker, eds., *A Greek-English Lexicon of the New Testament and Other Early Christian Literature*, 3rd ed. (Chicago: University of Chicago Press, 2001), s.v. "δείκνυμι" (emphasis original); cf. the Septuagint definitions in T. Muraoka, ed., *A Greek-English Lexicon of the Septuagint* (Louvain; Walpole, MA: Peeters, 2010): "to cause to be seen," "to point to," "to act in such a way as to show evidence of," and "to show by way of instruction"; and Johan Lust, Erik Eynikel, and Katrin Hauspie, eds., *Greek-English Lexicon of the Septuagint*, rev. ed. (Stuttgart: Deutsche Bibelgesellschaft, 2003): "to bring to light, to show, to point out; to make known, to explain; to display." Muraoka also draws attention to the article on ἀνα~, ἀπο~, παρα~, (ὑπο)δείκνυμι, ἀποκαλύπτω, γνωρίζω, σημαίω by Schlier in *TDNT* 2:25–30.

4:5: δέδειχα, לִמַּדְתִּי), and Moses reminds the people that God has shown them his glory (Deut 5:24: ἔδειξεν, הֶרְאָנוּ).

In Ezekiel, Zechariah, and Daniel, δείκνυμι functions primarily in relation to showing within visionary contexts. Ezekiel states in 11:25 that he told the exiles all the words that the Lord had showed him (καὶ ἐλάλησα πρὸς τὴν αἰχμαλωσίαν πάντας τοὺς λόγους τοῦ κυρίου οὓς ἔδειξέν μοι). The things he has been shown seem to refer at the least to Ezekiel's visionary experiences in chapters 8–11. The word δείκνυμι is used two times in Ezekiel 40:4 to describe the angel showing Ezekiel his vision of the temple (Heb: מַרְאֶה; הַרְאוֹתְכָה).[49] In Zechariah, when the angel who speaks with Zechariah says that he will answer Zechariah's questions about his vision, the word δείκνυμι functions to reflect that visionary showing (1:9;וַיַּרְאֵנִי ; also 1:20 [Heb 2:3], ,3:1 ;אַרְאֶךָּ וַיַּרְאֵנִי).[50]

Further Greek evidence of δείκνυμι may be found in the Old Greek (OG) of Daniel 10:1 which states that the decree was shown (πρόσταγμα ἐδείχθη; Hebrew דָּבָר נִגְלָה) to Daniel. The verse continues by stating that the vision and the decree are true (ἀληθὲς τὸ ὅραμα καὶ τὸ πρόσταγμα). And later in Daniel 10, we read that the angel Gabriel is the one who shows Daniel these decrees (τὰ προστάγματα, 10:15). The verb used for "showing" in 10:14, however, is not δείκνυμι but ὑποδείκνυμι, yet the context and content of Daniel's vision suggests that the terms are used interchangeably.

The word ὑποδείκνυμι occurs more frequently in the Old Greek of Daniel than δείκνυμι.[51] There are multiple instances where ὑποδείκνυμι indicates one human being "showing" or "explaining" a visionary experience to another human being (Dan 2:17; 4:18; 5:7, 9, 12, 16; cf. 4:37). For example, in OG Daniel 4:18, Nebuchadnezzar relates his dream to Daniel and Daniel shows (ὑπέδειξέ) him its interpretation. In OG Daniel 5, the verb is used often in reference to "showing" the interpretation of the writing on the wall.[52] First, Belshazzar (Baltasar) issues a decree proclaiming that anyone who "shows" (ὑποδείξῃ) the meaning of the writing will be rewarded (5:7). After no one can interpret the meaning, the queen comes and Belshazzar "shows" (ὑπέδειξεν) how large the writing is and that no one can explain it (5:9). She responds by telling Belshazzar that Daniel was able to show (ὑπέδειξε) such things to his father (5:12). In 5:16, the king asks Daniel if he is able "to show" (ὑποδεῖξαι) the interpretation of the writing. In each of these instances, one human being shows another an interpretation. The implication is that Daniel can or will do the showing.

49. δείκνυμι is used a third time in the same verse to speak of Ezekiel's showing of these things to the people.

50. Cf. Sirach's use of δείκνυμι with regard to Isaiah: "[Isaiah] showed the things being until the end of the age and the hidden things before they happened" (Sirach 48:25). Also with regard to Samuel (46:20).

51. Neither δείκνυμι nor ὑποδείκνυμι are found in Theodotion.

52. T. J. Meadowcroft, *Aramaic Daniel and Greek Daniel: A Literary Comparison*, JSOTSup 198 (Sheffield: Sheffield Academic, 1995), 82–83, notes the link in the use of ὑποδείκνυμι in OG Daniel 4 and OG Daniel 5.

In five other instances in the OG of Daniel, ὑποδείκνυμι is used to refer to an angelic figure "showing" a human being some heavenly mystery (9:22, 23; 10:14, 21; 11:2).[53] Gabriel says that he comes to Daniel to "show" or "explain" the meaning of his visions (ἦλθον ὑποδεῖξαί σοι, 9:22, 23; 10:14).[54] Again, in 10:21, Gabriel tells Daniel that he will show him the first things in the book of truth (ὑποδείξω σοι τὰ πρῶτα ἐν ἀπογραφῇ ἀληθείας). OG Daniel 11:2 continues this idea, with Gabriel stating: "I have come to show you the truth" (καὶ νῦν ἦλθον τὴν ἀλήθειαν ὑποδεῖξαί σοι). This "truth" includes the coming of kings in Persia, Greece, and Egypt.

In these LXX examples, δείκνυμι and ὑποδείκνυμι are used in revelatory contexts, often involving visions that require interpretation or "showing."[55] This is much more obvious in Ezekiel and Zechariah, and specifically, in the Jewish apocalypse of Daniel. In the later parts of the Old Greek of Daniel, δείκνυμι and ὑποδείκνυμι indicate the revelation of heavenly mysteries by an angelic being to Daniel. The usage is not so much the showing of a vision as it may be an explanation of a vision; however, the use is clearly within an apocalyptic visionary context where heavenly mysteries are revealed.

Δείκνυμι in the Jewish Apocalypses

A key aspect of the heavenly journeys in Jewish apocalypses is that apocalyptic seers are often shown visions or various aspects of heaven or earth while on heavenly tours. In Hebrew and Ethiopic, the same root often does double duty for what is seen and what is shown (ראה; *re'ya*).[56] The traditions surrounding Enoch reflect this visionary showing and make use of the Greek word δείκνυμι in a few instances, similar to what we have seen, particularly in Ezekiel, Zechariah, and Daniel.[57] In the extant Greek version of the Book of the Watchers, we find δείκνυμι in the opening lines: "He showed (it) to me, and the holy ones speaking holy things I heard; and when I heard everything from them, I understood as I looked"[58] (1 Enoch 1:2). The Ethiopic of that section is translated: "which the angels showed to me. And I heard everything from them, and I understood what I saw. . . ."[59] In both versions, Enoch's vision is described as having been shown to him. This same idea of angelic visionary showing, with the use of δείκνυμι, is found elsewhere in the Greek version of the Book of the Watchers (1 Enoch 14:4,

53. The Theodotion version of 9:23; 10:21; 11:2 uses ἀναγγέλω. See Williams, "Unveiling Revelation," on the use of ἀναγγέλω.

54. The Hebrew word used in 9:23; 10:21; 11:2 is נגד.

55. δείκνυμι most commonly translates the Hebrew verb ראה, although not exclusively. See above.

56. Nickelsburg and VanderKam, *1 Enoch* 2, 41, also 25, 251. The qal form of ראה is used for active seeing, and the hiphil form is used for passive seeing, i.e., when something is shown.

57. This examination cannot be as thorough considering that many of the extant versions of the Jewish apocalypses are not in Greek.

58. Translation from Michael A. Knibb, *The Ethiopic Book of Enoch: A New Edition in the Light of the Aramaic Dead Sea Fragments*, 2 Vols. (Oxford: Clarendon, 1978), 2:57.

59. George W. E. Nickelsburg and James K. VanderKam, *1 Enoch: The Hermeneia Translation* (Minneapolis: Fortress Press, 2012), 19.

8; 22:1; 24:1; 33:3–4; cf. ὑποδείκνυμι, 8:1). The word δείκνυμι is even used of the Watcher Asael showing unrighteous deeds to humanity (13:2; note the use of ὑποδείκνυμι also in this verse). While there are various ways in which revelation takes place in the Book of the Watchers, the showing of visions by an angelic being to Enoch is described on a number of occasions with the Greek word δείκνυμι.[60]

Further Greek evidence of visionary showing is found in the Birth of Noah: "For I know the mysteries that the holy ones have shown (ὑπέδειξέν) and revealed to me" (1 Enoch 106:19). Loren Stuckenbruck lists the Ethiopic as *'ar'ayani* and the Aramaic in 4Q Enc 5 ii 26 as ואחזיוני.[61] The Ethiopic root is the same root as that used at the beginning of the Apocalypse of Weeks (1 Enoch 93:2, *'astar'ayani*)[62] where Enoch says a vision of heaven was shown to him, along with hearing the words of the Watchers, and reading and understanding the heavenly tablets. Nickelsburg notes that this same Ethiopic verb occurs in 1 Enoch 104:8 where it has "revelatory connotations" and the Greek verb is ὑποδείκνυμι.[63]

Although there is incomplete Greek evidence for all of 1 Enoch, the concept of an angelic or otherworldly being showing Enoch heavenly mysteries is prevalent throughout. In the Book of the Luminaries, Enoch describes the angel Uriel as the one who showed him the heavenly luminaries and their movements. The phrase "Uriel . . . showed me" is so common in the Book of the Luminaries that James VanderKam refers to the phrase as a "set expression" (1 Enoch 72:1; 74:2; 75:3–4; 78:10; 79:6 [5x]; cf. 82:7).[64] Uriel also speaks in the first person, telling Enoch that he has shown him (80:1), and Uriel tells Enoch to show Methuselah what he has been shown (81:5). Similarly, the angel of peace who accompanies Enoch in the Parables of Enoch is constantly referred to as "the angel who showed me" (1 Enoch 40:2, 8; 43:3; 46:2; 52:3, 5; 53:4; 54:4; 56:2; 60:24; 64:2).[65]

In the Greek version of 3 Baruch, both δείκνυμι and ὑποδείκνυμι are found extensively and are used almost interchangeably. Throughout Baruch's heavenly tour, Phanuel "shows" Baruch various aspects of the first and second levels of heaven (δείκνυμι: 3 Baruch 2:2, 7; 3:3; 4:1 [twice], 3, 8; 5:3; 6:2; 7:2; 9:2; ὑποδείκνυμι: 1:4, 6, 7, 8; 2:3, 6; 3:1).[66] The showing is primarily visionary since what is shown includes mysteries, the doors of heaven, a plain and a serpent, the tree

60. Loren Stuckenbruck pointed out to me the intriguing fact that in the Greek versions of the Book of the Watchers (and also the Ethiopic versions, which were most likely translated from the Greek) δείκνυμι is in the active voice (Enoch is the indirect object, i.e, the one to whom the angels shows something). Likewise, the Gospel of John uses δείκνυμι in the active voice. However, in Hebrew, Aramaic, and OG Daniel, we find the verbs in the passive voice (divine passive; see use of δείκνυμι in OG Dan 10:1).

61. Loren T. Stuckenbruck, *1 Enoch 91-108*, CEJL (Berlin; New York: de Gruyter, 2007), 680; also Nickelsburg, *1 Enoch 1*, 539.

62. Stuckenbruck, *1 Enoch*, 66.

63. Nickelsburg, *1 Enoch 1*, 411; Stuckenbruck, *1 Enoch*, 580.

64. Nickelsburg and VanderKam, *1 Enoch 2*, 522.

65. Ibid., 41. Nickelsburg refers to 60:24 as an interpolation.

66. Kulik, *3 Baruch: Greek-Slavonic Apocalypse of Baruch*, 105, notes that "'Show' (ὑποδείξῃς/. . .) without an object corresponds to the biblical usage of הראה without *acc. rei* (cf. Ezek. 40:3; Esth. 4:8). . . ."

Adam ate from, and a fiery chariot. Testament of Abraham has multiple uses of δείκνυμι in both recensions. In Recension A at 15:12, at the conclusion of Abraham's heavenly tour, the angel Michael reports back to the Lord that he has shown Abraham the Lord's power, the entire earth and the sea, as well as God's judgment. The majority of uses of δείκνυμι indicate Death showing Abraham his various features, such as seven fiery heads of dragons and fourteen faces (A 17:9, 15, 16, 17; 19:7, 8, 9, 10, 11, 12, 13, 14 [twice], 16; B 14:1). R. H. Charles notes that Testament of Levi 3:1 uses δείκνυμι to speak of Levi's vision of heaven (δειχθέντων [Charles' version α]; also 9:6, ἐδειξέ).[67] Relatedly, in the extant Greek fragment of 2 Baruch, Baruch says that the Lord has shown him the ordered times (ἀποδείκνυμι, 14:1).[68]

While there are no Greek versions for the following texts, both indicate similar instances where the seer has a vision and is "shown" a mystery by an angelic being or God. In 2 Baruch 4:4, Adam, Abraham, and Moses are said to have been shown the renewed temple to which Baruch now gains insight. In Apocalypse of Abraham (9:8, 9; 28:1, 2), Abraham is shown heavenly mysteries by God.

The concept of showing is evidently important within visionary experiences in the "proto-apocalyptic" LXX texts of Ezekiel, Zechariah, and Daniel, the various sections of 1 Enoch, Testament of Abraham, Testament of Levi, Apocalypse of Abraham, and 2 Baruch. As with the formula in the Parables of Enoch and the Book of the Luminaries, an angel shows a human recipient something, and in the texts with Greek versions, the "showing" is usually indicated by the word δείκνυμι, or a similar word, such as ὑποδείκνυμι. While δείκνυμι is used in this way in the places noted above, it cannot be argued that the verb functions as a technical term; however, its consistent use in these settings indicates that visionary showing was often described with this verb.

Δείκνυμι and Visionary Showing in the Gospel of John

The Gospel of John has obvious connections to Jewish apocalyptic thought, no less so in its central focus on revelation. As Ashton has noted, the Gospel makes use of wide-ranging vocabulary related to the theme of revelation, and the word δείκνυμι should be considered part of that vocabulary. We have noted above that in the LXX and Jewish apocalypses the word is often found in contexts of revelation, and particularly, visionary showing. This usage highlights similarities between the Gospel of John and Jewish apocalyptic thought.

In the Gospel of John, the word δείκνυμι is used in five contexts (John 2:18; 5:20; 10:32; 14:8–9;

67. R. H. Charles, *The Greek Versions of the Testaments of the Twelve Patriarchs: Edited from Nine MSS. Together with the Variants of the Armenian and Slavonic Versions and Some Hebrew Fragments* (Oxford: Clarendon, 1908), 32, 46.

68. Note 1 Enoch 104:8 above.

20:20).[69] Perhaps unsurprisingly, each instance indicates something which can be shown, and thus seen, which is why English translations typically translate δείκνυμι as "to show." What was noticeable particularly in the Old Greek of Daniel, also takes place in the Gospel of John. Daniel functions as the one who "shows" or "explains" interpretations in the earlier part of Daniel, and in the latter part, Daniel "is shown" visions and explanations of visions (9:22, 23; 10:1, 14; 10:21–11:2). In John's Gospel, Jesus is shown things by the Father, and he also shows these things of the Father to his disciples and others.

The single instance of Jesus being shown something is found in John 5:19–20. Following the healing of the lame man and the ensuing Sabbath conflict, the tension in the narrative is heightened because "the Jews" are seeking to kill Jesus because he broke the Sabbath and claims equality with God (5:18). In response, Jesus says that he does nothing on his own, but only what he sees his Father doing. "For the Father loves the Son and shows (δείκνυσιν) him what he does, and [the Father] will show (δείξει) him greater works than these so that you might be amazed" (5:20). Scholars have found the meaning of the language of showing to be unclear and have sought various backgrounds for the Father's showing the Son. The starting point for many of the discussions of the Father's showing is often C. H. Dodd's well-known suggestion that John 5:19–20 is an example of a hidden parable in John's Gospel, a parable about how a son is apprenticed to his father. Dodd argues from Hellenistic, Hermetic, and Palestinian evidence that it was a father's responsibility to teach his son a trade. The son would watch his father at his work and learn to do just as his father does.[70] Dodd argued that the Evangelist drew from a parable based on this cultural background, especially considering that in the Synoptic tradition, Jesus was known to have told parables and to have grown up as the son of a τέκτων.[71]

Multiple commentators have echoed Dodd's suggestion about a hidden parable or parabolic language in 5:20.[72] Others who have not agreed that 5:20 reflects a parable see at least an apprenticeship model that would have been recognizable to the average hearer or reader.[73] Herman Ridderbos notes that there are "significant objections" against seeing a parable in the background of Jesus's statement.[74] The first being the difficulty of moving from a generic, parabolic reference of "a father" and "a son" to "the Father" and "the Son" without any indication of such a transition. Second, Ridderbos points out that this is not the only place where Jesus

69. ὑποδείκνυμι is not found in the Gospel of John. Cf. Matt 3:7; Luke 3:7, 6:47; 12:5; Acts 9:16; 20:35.

70. C. H. Dodd, *More New Testament Studies* (Grand Rapids: Eerdmans, 1968), 30–40.

71. Ibid., 40.

72. J. Ramsey Michaels, *The Gospel of John*, NICNT (Grand Rapids: Eerdmans, 2010), 308–9; Andrew T. Lincoln, *The Gospel according to St John*, BNTC (London; New York: Continuum, 2005), 202; Hartwig Thyen, *Das Johannesevangelium*, HNT (Tübingen: Mohr Siebeck, 2005), 311.

73. Ernst Haenchen, *John: A Commentary on the Gospel of John*, trans. Robert Walter Funk, 2 Vols., Hermeneia (Philadelphia: Fortress Press, 1984), 250. See Urban C. Von Wahlde, *The Gospel and Letters of John: Commentary on the Gospel of John*, 3 Vols., ECC (Grand Rapids: Eerdmans, 2010), 2:230, following Bühner, *Der Gesandte*.

74. Ridderbos, *Gospel of John*, 192.

acts on what he sees or hears the Father doing and saying, and rightly notes that there are no parables lurking in the background of those instances (3:32; 8:26, 40; 15:15). Thus, he concludes, "There is no reason to interpret 5:19ff. differently."[75]

If the background of the Father showing the Son is not an apprenticeship example or parable, what background might be evident? Writing before Dodd suggested a hidden parable, Bultmann saw elements of the Gnostic Redeemer myth in the Father's showing the Son.[76] Bultmann drew attention to the prophets of the Hebrew Bible as messengers of God in order to highlight the way in which they and Jesus speak the words of God. However, the difference between these prophets and Jesus is the unity between Jesus and the Father. Regarding this unity, Bultmann argued that the Gnostic Redeemer myth serves as the background since it speaks of the sending of a preexistent being who brings revelation in his unity with God, yet, even while he saw a parallel in the myth, he contended that the Son did not entirely fit the myth. Bultmann states: "John of course frees himself from this mythology, but at the same time he retains its terminology."[77] For C. K. Barrett, the Son's "godlikeness" is not dependent on the myth but on the "historical fact" of the person of Jesus, which is why he argued that Bultmann and Dodd's views were neither one "entirely satisfactory."[78]

Thus, other possibilities are open, not least because most scholars have rejected the Gnostic Redeemer myth as a possible background. Considering the use of δείκνυμι in LXX visionary passages and in the Jewish apocalypses, another plausible background more at home in Second Temple Judaism is visionary showing or "showing" within a visionary context. The showing by the Father to Jesus has some similarities with that of God showing heavenly mysteries to an angelic mediator or seer. Ridderbos's objections are nonexistent here since we are not moving from generic to specific and since a Jewish apocalyptic background explains more than just this instance. Jesus can be understood to function similarly throughout the Gospel of John as a heavenly mediator sent from heaven who speaks and acts for God before returning to heaven.[79]

The connection between Jewish apocalypticism and John 5:19–20 is not a new suggestion. Hugo Odeberg noted similarities between the showing in John 5:19–20 and 3 Enoch 11 in 1929. Odeberg states, "The Holy One *shows* (הראה), teaches (הורה), and reveals (גלה) to Metatron all secrets (רוים) and all *works* (מעשים). . . . Metatron watches intently 'to behold' what the Holy One shows him: *3 En 11.2*. . . ."[80] In 3 Enoch, Metatron is an angelic figure who is similar to God, shar-

75. Ibid., 192.
76. Bultmann, "Die Bedeutung," 103–4, and passim.
77. Bultmann, *Gospel of John*, 250–51.
78. Barrett, *Gospel*, 259–60; see also Rudolf Schnackenburg, *The Gospel According to St. John*, 3 Vols. (Tunbridge Wells: Burns & Oates, 1967), 2:104.
79. Cf. esp. Uriel in 4 Ezra.
80. Odeberg, *Fourth Gospel*, 204 (emphasis original).

ing similar garments and functions in certain traditions.[81] The Hebrew word translated "show" in 3 Enoch 11:2 (ראה) is the same verb that is often translated by δείκνυμι in the LXX. Also, ראה is related to the Ethiopic root used in 1 Enoch.

But the connection between John 5:19–20 and Jewish apocalyptic thought is broader than 3 Enoch. Metatron is not the only figure to have a visionary experience of being shown something. As pointed out above, Gabriel shows Daniel aspects of his visions. Enoch is shown mysteries by the archangels in the Book of the Watchers, by Uriel in the Book of the Luminaries and the Epistle of Enoch, and by the "angel of peace" in the Parables of Enoch. Baruch in 2 Baruch is shown aspects of heaven, as is Levi in Testament of Levi. In Apocalypse of Abraham, it is God who shows heavenly mysteries to Abraham (cf. 2 Baruch 4:3–5), yet in Testament of Abraham, it is the archangel Michael. Visionary showing is a significant part of Jewish apocalypses, and the Father showing the Son what he does in John 5:20 reflects similarities with these visionary experiences in the ascent apocalypses.[82]

At the same time, Jesus is not only shown heavenly mysteries in John's Gospel. He himself reveals them as well. In John 2:18, we have an example of Jesus as the subject of the verbal action of δείκνυμι. The content of what is shown in both instances is the signs and works that Jesus does. In 2:18, after Jesus has cast out the moneychangers and sellers of livestock from the temple, "the Jews" ask him, τί σημεῖον δεικνύεις ἡμῖν ὅτι ταῦτα ποιεῖς ("What sign will you show us that you [are allowed to] do these things?"). Jesus continues by telling them to tear down the temple and he will rebuild it in three days. The sign Jesus will show that provides the reason for his authority to disrupt the temple activities is his death and resurrection (2:22).

After the resurrection, Jesus entered the room in which his disciples were hiding and said, "Peace to you." Then, he showed (ἔδειξεν) them his hands and his side (20:20). The showing of Jesus's hands and side are the visible proof of his death and resurrection and may be understood as an answer to the question in 2:18: "What sign will you show us . . . ?" The resurrection, which was hinted at in 2:22, becomes the sign, the completion of the Father's work (cf. 4:34; 19:28, 30). Neither instance of δείκνυμι in 2:18 and 20:20 is particularly visionary when compared to the ascent apocalypses, Ezekiel, or Daniel. However, Jesus's appearance in the midst of his disciples, while the doors are locked, has elements of the visionary about it (20:19–20). What Jesus shows them is physical, yet it is visionary in that what is shown must be seen.

The use of δείκνυμι in 10:32 is similar to 2:18 in that Jesus again shows his works and signs.

81. Andrei A. Orlov, "Metatron," ed. John J. Collins and Daniel C. Harlow, *The Eerdmans Dictionary of Early Judaism* (Grand Rapids: Eerdmans, 2010), 942–43.

82. However, Bultmann, *Gospel of John*, 250, was correct to point out that there are also similarities with Hebrew Bible prophetic patterns. See Hindy Najman, "The Inheritance of Prophecy in Apocalypse," in *The Oxford Handbook of Apocalyptic Literature*, ed. John J. Collins (Oxford: Oxford University Press, 2014), 36–51.

After "the Jews" grab stones in order to stone Jesus, he responds by saying, "I have shown (ἔδειξα) you many good works from my Father. For which of them are you stoning me?" Since the works that Jesus does are the Father's works (5:36), the showing of these works points to Jesus's identity with the Father (10:36–38) and should lead to belief in him (10:37–38; cf. 6:29). John Ashton states, "But since, for John, it is Jesus who is commissioned to perform these works on God's behalf, acting as his agent, it is only a small step to concluding that in the Fourth Gospel the term ["works"] refers to God's self-revelation in Jesus."[83] The Father is shown by Jesus in his actions as well as in his speech.

That the content of what Jesus shows is the Father is much more explicit in John 14:8–10. During the last discourse, Jesus tells the disciples that if they know him, then they know the Father (14:7). Philip responds, "Show (δεῖξον) us the Father and it is enough" (14:8). Jesus says that if they have seen him, they have seen the Father, so there is no reason for them to be shown the Father: "How can you say, 'Show (δεῖξον) us the Father'?" (14:9). Jesus continues and speaks of his unity with the Father and again connects the theme of showing to belief and the works which are the Father's works (14:10–12; cf. 10:32; 10:30, 37–38). As has been argued above, God is visible in the person of Jesus (12:41). Similar to the Jewish apocalypses, the vision of God is possible, but in a much different way. In John 14:8–10, the content of the visionary showing is a vision of God in the person of Jesus.

The language of revelation is clearly prevalent throughout John's Gospel. The verb δείκνυμι, while being only one example of this revelatory vocabulary, highlights the Gospel's similarities with Jewish apocalyptic thought. The verb is used in visionary showing contexts both in the Septuagint and in the Jewish apocalypses. A heavenly figure usually "shows" a heavenly mystery to a human figure, whether God showing Moses his glory or the angel Uriel showing Enoch the astronomical spheres and their movements. In John's Gospel, Jesus similarly shows and makes known heavenly things. As Jesus is shown the activity of the Father, he, in turn, does what the Father does, and thus shows his disciples the Father in himself. The vision of God that is typical of the Jewish ascent apocalypses takes place on earth in the person of Jesus, the Word made flesh. This, of course, raises questions about whether Jesus is more like an otherworldly mediator or an apocalyptic seer. Ashton claims that in Jesus, angel and seer merge,[84] but I am inclined to see Jesus as more similar to an otherworldly mediator because he is from above.[85]

83. Ashton, *Understanding*, 497.
84. Ibid., 258.
85. On this topic, I plan to give more detail in a forthcoming book.

Conclusion

Three aspects of Jewish apocalyptic thought have been argued to be found in John's "non-apocalyptic" Gospel. Similarly to Jewish apocalypses, the Fourth Gospel presents a spatial transcendence in its portrayal of "otherworldly regions" (heaven and earth) and "otherworldly beings" (Jesus the one from above, the Father, angels, and the devil). Almost no details of the cosmological reality are revealed, apart from the fact of their existence and their directing attention to Jesus, the one descended from heaven, the revealer of God who will return to heaven.

The Gospel of John also relates a vision of God. Visions of God are typical in Jewish apocalypses, but the vision in John's Gospel is dissimilar in that heavenly ascent is not necessary to see God. In fact, heavenly ascent is impossible, apart from Jesus who uniquely knows and makes known the Father and is the vision of God.

Part of the multifaceted revelation of the Father by Jesus includes his "showing" of the Father in his works and signs. What Jesus does (and says) are the Father's works (and words). He himself has been shown the actions of judging and giving life by the Father. Although recognizably different, Jesus's showing of the Father in himself reflects similarities with the showing of heavenly mysteries by otherworldly mediators in Jewish apocalypses.

Much more could be said about the relationship between the Gospel of John and Jewish apocalyptic thought, especially when the latter is understood as the disclosing of heavenly mysteries and not merely as apocalyptic eschatology. The revelatory nature of John's Gospel is right at home in the world of Jewish apocalypticism. The heavens are opened, and Jesus, uniting heaven and earth, reveals an apocalyptic vision of the Father.

PART II

Paul and the Pauline Letters

6

Paul as an Apocalyptist

Christopher Rowland

When Ed Sanders's epoch-making book on Paul came out in 1977,[1] I recall being struck by a passing reference to ecstatic mysticism and thinking that there was a dimension of Pauline thought which was relegated to relative insignificance. Indeed, I gave a response to Ed's book when it was discussed at the New Testament seminar in the early 1980s. It was an issue that mattered to me, particularly at that time, as I had devoted the previous decade trying to explore the implications of apocalyptic/mysticism for the New Testament. Perhaps I was over optimistic in hoping that this doyen of the relationship of ancient Judaism to the New Testament might have seen what I had seen. Sanders knew Scholem's work as well as I did, but it was as refracted through Ephraim Urbach's view of the rabbinic material that counted.[2] That meant that the Scholem line on the importance of the mystical, in the sense of an experiential dimension, in ancient Judaism was downplayed. A theologically orientated view of Paul, which plays down the apocalyptic dimension and stresses continuity with Jewish traditions, omits

1. E. P. Sanders, *Paul and Palestinian Judaism: A Comparison of Patterns of Religion* (London: SCM, 1977), 220.
2. E. E. Urbach, "The Tradition about Merkabah Mysticism in the Tannaitic Period" (in Hebrew), in *Studies in Mysticism and Religion Presented to Gershom Scholem on his Seventieth Birthday by Pupils, Colleagues and Friends*, ed. E. E. Urbach, R. J. Zwi Werblowski, and Ch. Wirszubski (Jerusalem: Magnes, 1967), 1–30; and further, David J. Halperin, *The Faces of the Chariot: Early Jewish responses to Ezekiel's Vision*, TSAJ 16 (Tübingen: J. C. B. Mohr [Paul Siebeck]), 1988.

something crucial from the understanding of the Pauline corpus. Reading Paul in the light of "normal mysticism," or Urbach's entirely plausible construal of the rabbinic traditions about the *merkabah,* or, for that matter, Peter Schäfer's,[3] reduces the significance of the "apocalyptic Paul" who subordinated human traditions and convention to "the apocalypse of Jesus Christ" (Gal 1:16) and lived with the consequences for himself and those whom he influenced by his testimony. It is not that Paul is far removed from the rabbis. In many ways, his writing resembles their sentiments with regard to the management of the ecstatic and revelatory very closely. But that similarity was born in a situation where the ecstatic, the revelatory, the disruptive threatened to wreak havoc and something else was needed which would bring some kind of order to what seemed like an apocalyptic chaos, the divisiveness of whose power politics, rightly or wrongly, had alarmed Paul in Corinth. In the case of the rabbis, it was immersion in the tradition; that was true to some extent in Paul's case too (cf. 1 Cor 14:33–34) but there was also appeal to the authority of one who had seen the Lord (1 Cor 9:1) and carried in his body Jesus Christ (2 Cor 4:10; cf. Gal 2:20) to demand submission to his words.

"The apocalyptic Paul" is now a popular construal, but in a way different from what I then understood—and still understand. J. C. Beker and J. Louis Martyn, inspired by Ernst Käsemann, have trodden in Schweitzer's footsteps, as did Sanders to some extent in following Schweitzer in his advocacy of "participationist eschatology," in arguing for an "apocalyptic" Paul.[4] But apocalyptic in this context meant the cataclysmic disruptive eschatology, which Käsemann believed was typical of apocalyptic. When "apocalyptic" and "eschatological" are merged and have similar meanings, both lose their heuristic value for understanding the intellectual history of early Christianity, and Paul's thought, in particular.

On the margins of Pauline scholarship, there have been dissenting voices, many of which have, in recent years, been linked with the religious experience seminar at the Society of Biblical Literature. The late Alan Segal, in particular—and in a parallel but more overtly history of religions mode, John Ashton—argued for locating Paul in mystical and apocalyptic traditions.[5] As far as I am concerned, apocalyptic as eschatology, and apocalyptic as mysticism are not an either/or, as the eschatological Paul is every bit as crucial as the apocalyptic/mystical Paul. But, *in nuce,* I find it as impossible to understand Paul's activity without his belief in the breaking in of a new age as I do to understand that conviction without recourse to the life-changing vision which brought it about. As Martyn has pointed out, the epistemology of "the turn of the

3. Peter Schäfer, *The Origins of Jewish Mysticism* (Tübingen: Mohr Siebeck, 2009).
4. J. C. Beker, *Paul the Apostle: The Triumph of God in Life and Thought*, 2nd ed. (Edinburgh: T&T Clark, 1989); J. L. Martyn, *Galatians: A New Translation with Introduction and Commentary*, AB 33A (New York: Doubleday, 1997); E. Käsemann, "The Beginnings of Christian Theology," and "On the Subject of Primitive Christian Apocalyptic," in *New Testament Questions of Today* (London: SCM, 1969).
5. A. F. Segal, *Paul the Convert: The Apostolate and Apostasy of Saul the Pharisee* (New Haven: Yale University Press, 1990); John Ashton, *The Religion of Paul the Apostle* (New Haven: Yale University Press, 2000).

ages" is crucial for understanding.[6] That epistemology is intimately linked with the "apocalyptic." Apocalyptic epistemology—in the sense of the ways in which claim to visionary experience has consequences for the way in which one lives—may confirm prejudices or overturn them, for visions offer a mode of knowing which can either complement received wisdom or turn it on its head, and Gershom Scholem suggested that "the most radical of revolutionary mystics are those who not only reinterpret and transform a religious authority, but aspire to establish a new authority based on their own experience." According to Scholem, Paul is "the most outstanding example known to us of a revolutionary Jewish mystic."[7]

This chapter is about the importance of the apocalyptic element in understanding the writings and life of Paul. The consideration begins with a short survey of the change in the understanding of "apocalypse" and "apocalyptic" in writing over the last forty years before moving to consideration of "apocalypse" in Pauline texts. Particular consideration will be given to 1 Corinthians where the clash between the apocalyptic and community cohesion is particularly sharp and Paul's own apocalyptic authority comes into conflict with others who could make similar claims to be "taught by God" (cf. 1 Thess 4:9; John 6:45). The chapter concludes with a hermeneutical perspective informed by Samuel Taylor Coleridge's discussion of different types of mysticism and its possible implications for the study of Jewish apocalyptic in the thought of Paul the Apostle. This is not an exercise which seeks to explain the totality of Paul's thought by reference to apocalyptic but more an attempt to show that without attention to the "apocalyptic" in addition to the eschatological, we shall not understand what Paul writes, whether in terms of his positive assertions about the importance of the apocalypse of Jesus Christ for his own authority or the effects of apocalypse on the nascent Christian communities which had come together as a result of his activity as one who believed himself called by God to be the apostle to the gentiles. The Paul of the extant letters does not come across as an interpreter of apocalyptic or prophetic oracles with a divinely given wisdom so much as a figure whose authority in this phase of his life owes everything to an apocalyptic conviction. Such a claim seems to have puzzled his contemporaries (Acts 26:24) and inspired their claims and continued to inspire individuals down the centuries—for example, Mani.[8]

The focus of this discussion is on Galatians and 1 Corinthians, but letters attributed to Paul, such as Colossians and Ephesians should be taken into account in any discussion of "the apocalyptic Paul." The apocalyptic background of the cosmology of Ephesians was recognized long ago, and apocalyptic issues pervade the Letter to the Colossians with concern for the activities

6. J. L. Martyn, "Epistemology at the Turn of the ages: 2 Corinthians 5.16," in *Christian History and Interpretation: Studies Presented to John Knox*, ed. W. R. Farmer, C. F. D. Moule and R. R. Niebuhr (Cambridge: Cambridge University Press, 1967), 269–87.

7. G. Scholem, *On the Kabbalah and its Symbolism* (London: Routledge and Kegan Paul, 1965), 11, 14.

8. R. Cameron and A.J. Dewey, *The Cologne Mani codex (P. Colon. inv. nr. 4780): Concerning the Origin of his Body*, SBLTTS 15 (Missoula, MT: Scholars, 1979), 47–49.

of the angels and the emulating of them (Col 2:16–18; cf. 2:21).[9] We know from the apocalypses and later Jewish mystical material that strict preparation was a necessary prerequisite for the receipt of visions. In the Dead Sea Scrolls, just as the angels in heaven have their allotted place in the heavenly liturgy (4Q405 23 i; cf. 2 Enoch 20:3–21:1), so the earthly community is given a position corresponding to God's everlasting purpose (1QS 2:22–26; 5:23–24; 6:8–10). It is possible that the problem addressed had two components: the ritual preparations and the visions themselves and an unhealthy concentration on other, lesser, heavenly beings, rather than Christ. In the light of this, the remarkable words in Colossians 1:15–20 and 2:9 become comprehensible. Passages such as Justin, *Dialogue* 114, where Christ is identified with the human figure on the throne of glory, suggest that Christ as the image of the invisible God is the concrete expression of God, the divine *kabod* (cf. John 12:42; and 1:18; cf. 2 Cor 4:6; 1 Cor 15:49). He took the form of a slave who had put on a heavenly, glorious body (Phil 2:6; cf. 3:21).[10]

Apocalyptic as Revelation and the New Testament

In 1976, Michael Stone published a landmark contribution to the debate about apocalypticism.[11] The apocalyptic writings had to be seen not simply in a stream of tradition that flowed from the prophets; they bore some of the characteristics of Jewish wisdom literature. Stone argued that, if we take the opening chapters of 1 Enoch seriously, and particularly, the introductory miscellany preceding the story of the seduction of the women by the Watchers, the wisdom elements parallel lists of revealed things in other apocalyptic texts. The legends and the cosmography, which we also find in the opening chapters of 1 Enoch, might give us pause for thought before we emphasize eschatology as the interpretative key of "apocalyptic." His definition of apocalypticism began not with Daniel, but with 1 Enoch. That is, so-called apocalyptic eschatology and its prophetic roots could no longer be privileged in discussions and definitions of apocalypticism. Moreover, with the early dating of parts of 1 Enoch, one had to completely rethink the shape of Jewish religious and intellectual life in the third century BCE.

In the report of the Apocalypse Group of the SBL Genres Project, with references to apoca-

9. See the collection in Fred O. Francis and Wayne A. Meeks, *Conflict at Colossae: A Problem in the Interpretation of Early Christianity, Illustrated by Selected Modern Studies* (Missoula, MT: Scholars, 1975); Christopher C. Rowland and Christopher R. A. Morray-Jones, *The Mystery of God: Early Jewish Mysticism and the New Testament*, CRINT 12 (Leiden; Boston: Brill, 2009), 156–66.

10. Rowland and Morray-Jones, *Mystery of God*, 156–66; Jarl E. Fossum, *The Image of the Invisible God: Essays on the Influence of Jewish Mysticism on Early Christology*, NTOA 30 (Freiburg: Universitätsverlag, 1995); Markus *Bockmuehl*, "'The *Form of God*' (Phil 2:6): Variations on a Theme of Jewish Mysticism," *JTS* 48 (1997): 1–23; G. Scholem, *On the Mystical Shape of the Godhead: Basic Concepts in the* Kabbalah, trans. Joachim Neugroschel (New York: Schocken, 1991), 278n19; and G. Stroumsa, "Forms of God: Some Notes on Metatron and Christ," *HTR* 76 (1983): 269–88.

11. Michael E. Stone, "Lists of Revealed Things in the Apocalyptic Literature," in *Magnalia Dei: The Mighty Acts of God: Essays on the Bible and Archaeology in Memory of G. Ernest Wright*, ed. F. M. Cross, W. E. Lemke, and P. D. Miller (Garden City, NY: Doubleday, 1976), 414–52; also, "A Reconsideration of Apocalyptic Visions," *HTR* 96 (2003): 167–80.

lypses in antiquity, which included works of Jewish, Early Christian, Gnostic, Greek and Latin, Rabbinic and Mystical, and Persian origin, it offered the following definition:

> An apocalypse is a genre of revelatory literature with a narrative framework, in which a revelation is mediated by an otherworldly being to a human recipient, disclosing a transcendent reality which is both temporal, insofar as it envisages eschatological salvation, and spatial insofar as it involves another, supernatural world.[12]

This definition is the basis for a scholarly consensus. The only thing from which I would possibly dissent is the lack of clarity concerning the phrase "transcendent reality." While it is true that the revelation offered of salvation is at the time it is revealed—whether through vision or angelic mediation—a transcendent reality, that "transcendent reality" would be realized on earth, not in heaven or some transcendent world. I wonder if there is here still too much of a residue of the legacy of the influence of neat definitions of "Apokalyptik" in this otherwise acceptable definition.

The strength of the SBL project is the more "emic" approach to what constitutes apocalyptic. The same issue applies with mysticism. Bernard McGinn's definition in *The Foundations of Mysticism* arises out of a detailed historical study not only of the texts but also the terminological discussion. He summarizes his view under three headings: " a part or element of religion . . . a process or way of life . . . an attempt to express a direct consciousness of the presence of God."[13] He rightly argues that mysticism should not be hived off into a separate category but should be part and parcel of the fabric of religion, a particular dimension of its theological claim, which is encapsulated by his words "direction consciousness of the presence of God by whatever means, vision, a sense of being caught up into the divine or some other immediate apprehension of divinity."

Paul and Jewish Mysticism

It is the name of Albert Schweitzer that is linked with the discussion of Paul and mysticism.[14] Indeed, his study includes reference to eschatological texts in the apocalypses, but I want to begin this section by referring to an important study by John Bowker, which offered a detailed analysis of the different versions of Eleazar ben Arak's exposition of the *merkabah* chapter of Ezekiel before his teacher Rabban Yohanan ben Zakkai. Bowker suggests that Paul in the "perfectly ordinary process of *merkabah* contemplation reflected the voice of commission to Ezekiel

12. John J. Collins, "Introduction: Toward the Morphology of a Genre," *Semeia* 14 (1979): 1–20 (9).
13. B. McGinn, *The Foundations of Mysticism* (London: SCM 1992), xv–xvi.
14. A. Schweitzer, *The Mysticism of Paul the Apostle*, trans. William Montgomery (London: Black 1931). See further now Grant Macaskill, *Union with Christ in the New Testament* (Oxford: Oxford University Press, 2013).

in Ezekiel 2."[15] Whereas Ezekiel was told to go not to strangers but the house of Israel, Paul became convinced that it was not the Christians who were the rebellious people but the Jews who had commissioned him.[16] What may have happened is that Ezekiel 1–2 offered a coherent context for the sudden reversal of his beliefs. Ezekiel 2 took on a dramatic new meaning. Bowker notes that Ezekiel 2:1, 3 is quoted in part in Acts 26:16. The lack of explicit reference to the *merkabah* in the testimonies about Paul is the result of the fact that Saul's occupation at the time of the vision paled into insignificance compared with the transformative effects of the vision itself. Though visions were often regarded with suspicion, these were part of rabbinic orthodoxy, a form of "higher education," to be undertaken only by the very well trained (as stated in the Mishnah). The engagement with the *merkabah* chapter was exegetical as much as it was visionary, but "the attempt to understand the meaning of the passages (particularly the "chariot" chapters) might lead the exegete to 'see again' the vision of the original prophet: in a sense, the vision is the meaning of the passage. Hence the 'seeing again' of the vision might well arise from contemplation on the "chariot" chapters, but it did not necessarily do so on every occasion that the chapters were contemplated; . . . the answer to uncontrolled and privately inventive apocalyptic was apocalypse which arose from a *total* exegesis of Scripture, with the part remaining a part, and not becoming an independent end in itself."[17]

Ulrich Luz protests against the consequences of dialectical theology and Reformation suspicion of mysticism and enthusiasm and points us to the "etic" character of the word "mysticism."[18] He argues that it is a phenomenon that only since the eighteenth century has come to be seen as an independent form of piety (more of that anon). "Mysticism," he suggests, is a modern term and he sees in its emergence what he calls "the fate of modernity in the field of intellectual history: the concept of 'mysticism' arose as a result of a particular type of piety's gaining independence from *theologia*." For Luz, mysticism signifies the overcoming of distance between human and divine. He is opposed to the narrowing down of the discussion of Pauline mysticism to the ecstatic phenomena of 1 Corinthians 12–14 and insists that the discussion of Pauline mysticism embraces the gift of the Spirit which he considers, Schweitzer-like, to be the experiential basis of Pauline Christ-mysticism. Another passage to which he draws attention is Galatians 2:19–20, where in Luz's view, Paul applies his own path to Christ to all Christians. Luz sums up his point in the words: "All Christians are mystics!" Baptism is fundamental, and the identification with the suffering of Christ becomes an epiphany of Christ in the present. "If

15. J. Bowker, "'Merkabah' Visions and the Visions of Paul," *JSS* 16 (1971): 157–73; Dale Allison Jr., "Acts 9:1–9, 22:6–11, 26:12–18: Paul and Ezekiel," *JBL* 135 (2016): 807–26.
16. Bowker, "'Merkabah' Visions," 172.
17. Ibid., 158 (emphasis added).
18. U. Luz, "Paul as a Mystic," in *The Holy Spirit and Christian Origins: Essays in Honor of James D. G. Dunn*, ed. Graham N. Stanton, Bruce W. Longenecker and Stephen C. Barton (Grand Rapids: Eerdmans, 2004), 131–43.

we understand by mysticism, the significance and cultivation of particular experiences of the absolute, then Paul is certainly a mystic."[19]

Like Luz, Colleen Shantz considers discussions of Pauline mysticism and the ways in which Paul has been seen as an opponent of the ecstatic.[20] She outlines how ecstatic experiences are a key part of Paul's public discourse, and the way in which his claims about the gospel enable the crucified messiah to be a transformative force in Paul's own life and in the lives of those to whom he writes. Shantz has put her finger on a tension in much Pauline scholarship. In the way in which most of us write about the Pauline corpus, there is readily evident a tension between that sense of dealing with a person, Paul, while all we have are his words. It is the preoccupation with the latter, and the profound unease with the quest for the man, and even more what might have going on in his head and his heart which Shantz gets us to reconsider in a welcome contribution to the study of the religion of Paul and of the widespread phenomena of visionary and ecstatic experience in antiquity.

Paul and the Apocalypse of Jesus Christ

According to Galatians 1:16, Saul now understood that the glorious human figure seated on the throne was Jesus.[21] There is an affinity of Paul's views with those known in rabbinic sources, where a second power is given authority alongside God (e.g. bḤagigah 15a; 3 Enoch 16).[22] These were exactly the views which were typical of the early Christians, including Paul, who on the basis of Psalm 110 ("The Lord said to my Lord, 'Sit at my right hand'") gave the exalted Christ a position of prominence and divine authority, albeit derived from God the Father (1 Cor 15:24–28; cf. Matt 22:44). The problem posed for his contemporaries by Paul, was that he seemed to have engaged in what might have appeared as an "undisciplined" apocalyptic exegesis, whose christological consequences were at odds with the total exegesis of the Scripture he inherited from his Pharisaic teachers. Thus, for Paul, the Law of Moses and the culture in which he had been brought up took a subordinate place to the exalted messiah whom he had met in an apocalyptic vision. However much Paul may have protested, as the accounts in Acts suggest that he did, the basic challenge he posed was that it was not the tradition handed down from Moses through the elders and teachers to the ancient "fathers" which mattered, but the exercise of "apocalyptic imagination" which authenticated that tradition. That was the decisive move: first experience, and only then, the tradition. The problems of apocalyptic thought are

19. Ibid., 132.
20. Colleen Shantz, *Paul in Ecstasy: The Neurobiology of the Apostle's Life and Thought* (Cambridge; New York: Cambridge University Press, 2009).
21. Seyoon Kim, *The Origin of Paul's Gospel*, 2nd ed., WUNT II/4 (Tübingen: Mohr, 1984), esp. 242–53.
22. Christopher Rowland, *The Open Heaven: A Study of Apocalyptic in Judaism and Christianity* (London: SPCK, 1982), 331–40.

arguably as central to our understanding of the apocalyptic Paul as their positive contribution. In 1 Corinthians, especially, we find passages, which expound the revelatory, but in such a way that it is managed or qualified, and the attempt is made to impose the authority of the apostle on a community whose own apocalyptic ethos made acknowledgement of heteronomy problematic. Arguably, 1 Corinthians is all about the hegemony of the apocalyptic and the attempt to confine its impact. Despite the fact Paul was himself a visionary, he sought to circumscribe the power of the apocalyptic, by stressing his own authority at the expense of the apocalyptic freedom of the Corinthians.

Apart from Galatians 1:12–16, the most obvious link with the Jewish mystical tradition is the experience recorded in 2 Corinthians 12:2–4.[23] While Paul speaks of the ineffable words he heard on that occasion, the experience appears to differ from the Damascus Road experience in not having that peculiar life-changing quality about it, or if it did, Paul has chosen not to divulge it. If Acts is to be believed, it was not the only such experience that Paul had (Acts 22:17; 27:23). The experience in 2 Corinthians is obviously a highly stylized, fragmentary, account. Several explanations of it are possible. Paul may describe in two different ways the same experience, or two different events, or two stages of the same experience, or even two attempts to reach heaven with differing results on the same occasion. It is possible that the experience was embarrassing to Paul as it is linked to his weakness. It could be a "failed," mystical ascent.[24] Such a failure to achieve the climax of the mystical ascent would indeed have been an admission of weakness and would have few parallels in the extant texts. Normally, the climactic moment of the vision is reached when the seer beholds the glory of God in the highest heaven. That Paul is using traditional language and the style of Jewish apocalyptic is apparent from the cosmological language and rapture. His use of the Greek ἁρπάζω is particularly pertinent. It is a word used elsewhere in the New Testament to speak of the mysterious rapture of individuals whether to heaven (1 Thess 4:17; Rev 12:5 cf. Wis 4:11; LXX Gen 5:24), or from one place on earth to another. In 2 Corinthians 12, the mystical raptures are not the qualifications on which the apostle grounds his authority but his suffering and humiliation.

Another important apocalyptic theme is divine secrets and hidden wisdom. In 1 Corinthians 15:51, for example, he explains in climactic style the problem of the resurrection by resorting to the revelation of a mystery about eschatological transformation. Even more importantly, as a steward of the divine mysteries (1 Cor 4:1), he lets his Roman readers into the eschatological mystery of Israel's strange destiny in Romans 11:25. Such mysteries are hidden from the rulers of the present age (1 Cor 2:6–8). In Colossians 1:26 (cf. Rom 16:27; Eph 3:3), for example,

23. Rowland, and Morray-Jones, *Mystery of God*, 137–42, 341–420.
24. Paula R. Gooder, *Only the Third Heaven? 2 Corinthians 12.1-10 and Heavenly Ascent*, LNTS 313 (London; New York: T&T Clark, 2006).

God's plan for the salvation of the Gentiles is portrayed as an apocalyptic mystery which Paul has been privileged to receive and which forms the basis for the apostolic ministry in which he is engaged. It is an enterprise on a truly cosmic scale (1 Cor 4:10, cf. Rev 14:6) as God's fellow workers (1 Cor 3:9). Indeed, Paul sees himself as an architect working according to a divine master plan, parallel to Moses himself (Exod 25:9, 40; cf. 2 Cor 3; 1 Chron 28:18). The foundation of the divine mystery is *the* revelatory event (Rom 1:17–18). In Romans 3:22, this apocalyptic event was heralded by the Law and the Prophets, but is essentially a fresh and definitive revelation from God. The revelation of that divine wisdom to which the true apostle has access is a mystery taught by the Spirit, and can only be understood by others who themselves have the Spirit (1 Cor 2:10). The divine mysteries, knowledge of which is the goal of the mystical ascent, are available now through the Spirit and in the proclamation of the cross.

Second Corinthians 3–4 give us a glimpse of beliefs about the present transformation which takes place not through heavenly ascent to the angelic realm but through identification with the pattern of Christ whose path to glory involved affliction and death. The mystery hidden from before the foundation of the world is one that is now revealed, but this apocalypse is of the crucified Christ, a stumbling block to many. The divine is revealed in the world of flesh, not through heavenly ascent but in the cross of Christ and the lives of his followers, especially his apostle, whose path involves affliction and death. The revelation remains a mystery to those on the way to perdition (2 Cor 2:16).[25]

The goal of salvation is to become like the resurrected Christ (Phil 3:20). Paul's apocalyptic vision had devastating effects on his conventional assumptions and practice, which led him to advocate a new covenant, not merely a reaffirmation of what had gone before. As the one who outshone Moses in his *diakonia* (2 Corinthians 3), Paul had access to greater mysteries than were received by Moses but which rendered those obsolescent (hence, the repeated καταργουμένον) even if they were seen to be a herald of that greater glory. Second Corinthians 3, as a contrast between Moses and Paul, ends up as an assertion about the *present* transformative glory which belongs to those who are ministers of the new covenant. These ministers do not need their faces veiled, for they have nothing to hide, as the apostolic ministers reflect the divine glory. There is uncertainty about the precise meaning of κατοπτριζόμενοι in 3:18. Its middle form suggests the translation "reflect," but there could be ideas here that those reflecting the divine glory do so as a result of beholding it (cf. 2 Enoch 22) where the seer beholds the glory of God, and this results in his reflecting the glory which he had been privileged to see. Paul is both a steward of the divine mysteries (1 Cor 4:1) and the one who bears the glory of the crucified Jesus. As such, he is both a beholder, and a reflector, of the divine glory.

25. Rowland and Morray-Jones, *The Mystery of God*, 150–56.

The pattern of the transformation of which Paul speaks in 2 Cor 3:18 is the divine image, and the means by which it takes place is the Lord who is the Spirit. The phrase "from glory to glory" suggests a progressive transformation. It is the kind of pattern of development described in the Ascension of Isaiah, for example, where there are different levels of glory in the different heavens. Isaiah's ascent to the heavenly world brings about a transformation of his own body as he approaches the seventh heaven. In 2 Corinthians 3–4, Paul gives us a glimpse of beliefs about the present transformation which takes place not through heavenly ascent but through identification with the pattern of Christ whose path to glory involved affliction and death.

The visionary perspective of messianism and apocalyptic, prompting as it does the freedom of the Spirit in both Galatians and in Romans, sits uneasily with a different ethic evident in the Pauline corpus. But even there, the challenge to conventional religion, supported by an appeal to mysticism, sets these texts apart from the merely predictable and conformist and may explain something of their innovativeness and continuing effects. It is no coincidence that the author of Romans and Galatians should have been deemed an antinomian by his opponents (a fact that he is compelled to deny in Rom 3:8; 6:1; cf. Acts 21:17–26). The heart of his religion has ceased to be the Torah, and its place has been taken by "the revelation of Jesus Christ," with all that came to mean for belief about God and halakah, (though the Torah is not abandoned so much as seen in a new—perhaps one should say, mystical—light). That point is affirmed in the climax of his argument in the opening chapters of Romans, where he contends that "without the Law God's righteousness has been revealed." Apocalypticism explains Paul's new reading of inherited traditions. Of course, visions and revelations may only have confirmed accepted patterns of belief and practice, and need have offered no threat to conventional wisdom about the character of the covenant. The subversive element in early Christianity owes much to that apocalyptic inheritance.

The Consequences of Apocalypse: "Apocalyptic Faith Consummated in Active Life"

There is a dramatic moment in the trial of Anne Hutchinson in New England in 1637 when she explains to her interrogator the priority she gives to "speaking what in my conscience I know to be truth" and that the Lord "hath let me see which was the clear ministry and which the wrong" by "an immediate revelation." She appeals to Genesis 22 and Abraham's conviction that it was "an immediate voice" that bid him offer his son. This, she took as an analogy to the way in which "an immediate revelation," "By the voice of [God's] own spirit to my soul," a crucial matter was settled for her. In the opinion of those judging her, this clear enunciation of her convictions, at the climax of what had hitherto been a very measured response, condemned her.

So, John Winthrop, in his summing-up, thanked divine providence for making Hutchinson "lay open her self and the ground of all these disturbances to be by revelation."[26] The 1630s' Antinomian Controversy in New England is the tip of the iceberg of a network of beliefs, influenced in part by Paul's letters and biblical apocalyptic passages and claims to direct experience of the divine, which reverberated around New (and Old) England for a century or so. It is strange to describe this controversy as "antinomian," because at its heart is "apocalyptic," the appeal of God's own spirit to my soul, a reference which echoes 1 Corinthians 2:10–11, a passage to the consideration of which we now turn.

A. 1 Corinthians

One of the most apocalyptic passages in the Pauline corpus is found in 1 Corinthians 2. It deserves to take its place alongside the Book of Revelation as one of *the* apocalyptic passages in the New Testament. It is chock full of language about revelation (2:10), of mystery (2:1), of things hidden and things revealed (cf. 2:7), and at the heart of this apocalypse is the Spirit of God, enabling humans to understand the deep things of God (2:10). Paul comes to the Corinthians engaged in making an announcement which filled him with the fear and trembling which often accompanied accounts of apocalyptic moments (cf. Rev 1:16–17; 1 Enoch 14:9, 24; Apocalypse of Abraham 10). This is the Pauline chapter to which early Christian writers turned more than any other when they used Paul. It encapsulated for them the nature of the gospel and the truth to which they too had been privileged to see.[27]

The language in 1 Corinthians 2:2 about "mystery" echoes apocalyptic elements such as we find in Daniel 2:28 (and elsewhere in the New Testament, e.g., Mark 4:11; Rom 16:25; Eph 1:9; 3:3; Col 1:26; 1 Tim 3:16). In 2:7, we have the sharing of secrets, reminiscent of the kind of apocalyptic hermeneutical mediation claimed by the Teacher of Righteousness in 1QpHab 7 "to whom God made known all the mysteries of the words of his servants the prophets" (1 Cor 14:2; 15:51; cf. Matt 11:25–27; 13:35; Col 1:26; Rom 8:30; 16:25; Eph 1:4; 3:1–13; 1 Pet 1:20; Rev 13:8). Elsewhere in 1 Corinthians, Paul too is a broker of divine mysteries (1 Cor 4:1). The exploration of the "deep things of God" (1 Cor 2:10) once again takes us back to the paradigmatic apocalyptic chapter, (and its "deep mysteries," Dan 2:22). Possibly, it is a parody of this theme in either Daniel 2 or 1 Corinthians that the Son of Man alludes to in the reference to the "depths of Satan" (Rev 2:24). The context is the critique of the woman, Jezebel, who calls herself a prophet

26. David D. Hall, *The Antinomian Controversy, 1636–1638: A Documentary History*, 2nd ed. (Durham, N.C; London: Duke University Press, 1990), 337, 341; and Amy Schrager Lang, *Prophetic Woman: Anne Hutchinson and the Problem of Dissent in the Literature of New England* (Berkeley: University of California Press 1987), esp. 27.
27. Jennifer R. Strawbridge, "A Community of Interpretation: The Use of 1 Corinthians 2:6–16 by Early Christians," *Studia Patristica, Vol. LXIII: Papers Presented at the Sixteenth International Conference on Patristic Studies held in Oxford 2011* (Leuven: Peeters, 2013) 69–80; idem, *"According to the Wisdom Given to Him": The Use of Pauline Epistles by Early Christian Writers before Nicaea*, DPhil Oxford 2014.

(2:20) and is "teaching and beguiling my servants to practise fornication and to eat food sacrificed to idols." It may be the Pauline ethos in 1 Corinthians 8 which is implicitly criticized in Revelation 2, notwithstanding that the advice comes from one who regarded himself as a steward of the divine mysteries. Paul would probably have fallen foul of the visionary condemnation of the prophet of Patmos for calling himself an apostle of Christ, and yet, teaching people to eat food sacrificed to idols (cf. Rev 2:20).

First Corinthians 2 is, in part, an insistence on the contrast between human and divine wisdom, and the content of the supreme divine mystery being that which the Sprit reveals, the cross of Christ. This section outlines a very different epistemology which is based on divine knowledge, divine language, and judgment, and which contrasts with human wisdom (2:5), which led the obsolescent rulers of this age to crucify the lord of glory. The consistency of theme and the distinctiveness of the apocalyptic pneumatology, not only fits Paul's argument in the opening chapters of 1 Corinthians but is of a piece with his assertion of the contrast between human and apocalyptic authority (Gal 1:1–16) and the role of the Spirit of God in Romans 8:5, 16. Apocalyptic enthusiasm pervades the passage, whether Paul is echoing the language of his Corinthian opponents or adapting it for his own ends. In Paul's view, human and divine wisdom have been confused by the Corinthians and what they need to understand is that the criterion of the true divine mystery is a crucified messiah. This is the mystery hidden from the foundation of the world and which Paul now asserts as the heart of his preaching (2:1–6). The revelation of this mystery is the hallmark of the action of the divine Spirit.

The Corinthians were possibly excluded from the privilege of access to the divine mystery in verse 6, but by 2:10, the ἡμῖν does seem to include them, who after all have responded—however inadequately in Paul's view—to the "things God has revealed to us through the Spirit." What follows about life in the Spirit in 2:10–16, therefore, applies to them too, even if the wider context of 1 Corinthians suggests that in Paul's estimation, the Corinthians have not exemplified this in the lives that they have lived, and in particular, in the divisions that exist among them. In 2:16, possessing the mind of Christ, but here, the first person means that it probably applies only to the apostles, over against the majority of the Corinthians, who are still "babes" (3:1). These verses in which Paul begins to set up a hierarchy about imitation of Christ to which he returns later in the letter (1 Cor 11:1; cf. Rom 15:5; Phil 2:5) encapsulate the problem posed by apocalyptic epistemology. Claim to visions or the knowledge of God through the Spirit is all well and good when it affirms that which is conventional and already received. The problem comes, as it probably had for Paul in his dealings with the Corinthians when the recipients of his letter claimed that knowledge too, and Paul seeks to work out some criteria for deciding who did—and who did not—possess such knowledge. But this is the problem Paul himself posed, not only to those who were followers of Christ before him but also to his erstwhile companions as Pharisees as a result of "the apocalypse of Jesus Christ" (Gal 1:12). Paul's own position epitomizes the problem of giving priority to the heavenly call and the subordination of other authorities which may result. In 1 Corinthians 2, the tables are reversed as Paul seeks to counter those who claimed apocalyptic knowledge. It is one thing to be like Eliphaz in Job 4:17, whose vision confirmed his previous theological position; it is altogether different when the apocalyptic vision not only turned one's world upside down but inherited patterns of belief and practice and led to promoting different ways of living on the basis of such apocalyptic authority, however much such ethical advice may be related to received wisdom. The famous story of Elisha ben Abuyah (alias *Aher)* told in bḤagigah 15a demonstrates the catastrophic effects of a heavenly vision on received wisdom and its hegemony.[28]

As Margaret Mitchell has shown with regard to one example from the early reception of these verses, they indicate the importance of this crucial additional channel of interpretative insight rooted in the work of the apocalypticism indwelling Spirit, and not dependent on the Bible and tradition. In the following passage, Origen (Commentary on John, 13:5–6) appeals to 1 Corinthians 2 to make his point:

> If we say that someone knows "that which is beyond what which stands written" (*to hyper ha gegraptai*) (1 Cor 4:6), we are not saying that these things can be known by the many (*gnôsta tois pollois einai dynatai*) . . . but the things which Paul learned, the "unspeakable words" (*arrêta rhêmata*) (2 Cor 12:4) "beyond what stands written" (*to hyper ta gegraptai*) (1 Cor 4:6), if indeed human beings have spoken the things that stand written (*ei ge ta gegrammena anthrôpoi lelalêkasin*). And "what the eye has not seen" (*ha ophthalmos ouk eiden*) (1 Cor 2:9) is beyond what is written (*hyper ha gegrammena*), and "what the ear has not heard" (*ha ous ouk êkousen*) (1 Cor 2:9) is not able to be written (*graphênai ou dynatai*). And the things "that have not arisen in the heart of a human being" (*ta epi kardian de anthrôpou mê anabebêkota*) (1 Cor 2:9) are greater than the well of Jacob (*meizona estin tês tou Iakôb pêgês*) [John 4:11]. This is because from the well of water springing up to eternal life [John 4:13] they are made manifest to those who no longer have a human heart (*phaneroumena tois ouketi kardian anthrôpou echousin*), but who are able to say, "We possess the mind of Christ" (*hêmeis de noun Christou echomen*) (1 Cor 2:16) "so that we may know the things that have been given to us by God" (*hina eidômen ta hypo tou theou charisthenta hêmin*) (1 Cor 2:12) which also speak, "not in teachings of human wisdom but in teachings of the spirit" (*ha kai laloumen ouk en didaktois anthrôpinês sophias logios all' en didaktois pneumatos*) (1 Cor 2:13).[29]

Hermeneutics here is not solely, or even primarily, about engagement with what is written on the page of Scripture, but that which comes to the believer independent of what is found in Scripture. "The things that have been given to us by God which also speak not in teachings

28. Rowland, *Open Heaven*, 331–40.
29. Translation in Margaret Mitchell, *Paul, the Corinthians, and the Birth of Christian Hermeneutics* (Cambridge; New York: Cambridge University Press, 2010), 37–38.

of human wisdom but in teachings of the spirit" underlines the limited character of what was written, and the reference to necessary additional fructifying of the life-giving water of the Spirit (cf. John 7:37) indicates that the great biblical scholar, Origen, did not allow himself to be confined to what the words of the Bible said in order to understand the ways of God's Spirit.

What is most extraordinary about 1 Corinthians 2, however, is how it fits with the rest of 1 Corinthians, especially 1 Corinthians 5. Indeed, one might ask why do those who are taught by the Spirit require any one to teach them as they are themselves subject to no one else's scrutiny? Why does Paul write eloquently about the guidance of the Spirit, and out of the blue, offer his stern advice about how to treat one whom he believes to be a wrongdoer? As far as one can ascertain, the problem mentioned in 1 Corinthians 5:1–5 does not seem to have been a problem for the Corinthians who have asked Paul's advice (this may have come from Chloe's people or the household of Stephanas, cf. 7:1). In this chapter, I believe that Paul betrays his continuing Jewish theological and cultural assumptions as he questions the spiritual character of the Corinthians (3:1). Leviticus 18:8 is alluded to in 5:1 ("You shall not uncover the nakedness of your father's wife; it is the nakedness of your father") and Deuteronomy is alluded to at the end of the chapter.

Paul, vehemently opposed circumcision as an entry requirement into the Christian community, and like Jeremiah before him, was quite capable of interpreting it of the moral life (Col 2:2–11). When it came to sexual *mores* as in 1 Corinthians 5–6, the Gentile Church in Corinth was treated to full-blown levitical religion without so much as a word of explanation, other than the assertion of the authority of the apostle whose presence brooked no dissent (1 Cor 5:3–5). The sexual impurity had to be rooted out of their midst, just as it had to be out of the midst of the people of God. Paul was intent on creating a holy temple (1 Cor 3:16; 6:19; 2 Cor 6:14–7:1)—a purified space, an extension of the temple in Jerusalem—in the Corinthian community.[30] Linking the believer's body with a temple, which must be kept holy, means linking to purity laws. Grave sins, including sexual sins, defile the temple. If these sins are not expunged, God's presence will depart. The injunction to be holy is a central concern of the purity codes (Lev 10:10; 20:26). *Porneia* both defiles the land and the Temple as well as the offender, so believers, as the temple of God, the locus of the *Holy* Spirit, had to stay pure. Biblical holiness was now on the ethical agenda,

The "quotation" (if that is the right way of describing it) of Deuteronomy at the end of 1 Corinthians 5:13 has become part of Paul's rhetorical exposition and not, at least in the first instance, an authoritative proof. This is a remarkable phenomenon and significant for the

30. Cf. also the way in which communion with heaven is found in the life of the Christian community, similar to what we find in some of the Dead Sea Scrolls and in Eph 2:6; 3:10. See Rowland and Morray-Jones, *Mystery of God*, 173–77.

nature of biblical hermeneutics, it seems to me, in that the words of the Bible are part of an act of persuasion and not in themselves, directly, a source of authority or a court of appeal. I can see that Paul's giving voice to the Deuteronomy quotation here (as elsewhere) may, in addition to being part of the power of rhetorical appeal, reinforce his authority, for those with ears to hear an echo of Scripture in Paul's words. Paul does not solve the problem here by appealing to the Bible as an authority even if it pervades the answer he gives. It is an example of what Ed Sanders has pointed out, namely, that when it came to how converts *stayed* in the nascent Christian community (rather than getting into it), the Law of Moses had its (albeit severely constricted ethical) part to play.

If there *is* any Scripture to which he appeals, it is his own words and the proper exegesis of them:

> I wrote to you in my letter not to associate with sexually immoral persons—not at all meaning the immoral of this world, or the greedy and robbers, or idolaters, since you would then need to go out of the world. But now I am writing to you not to associate with anyone who bears the name of brother or sister who is sexually immoral.

What seems most important is to get the correct meaning of Paul's words rather than the right interpretation of the Bible! While Paul the Christian halakist is a little more lenient than letter of law, the fact is that he sets himself up as a teacher when he has said that those who have the Spirit need no one to teach them.

What we have in the opening verses of 1 Corinthians 5 is Paul uttering things that would be ethical commonplace for Hellenistic Judaism, apparently assuming that the recipients of his letter would have shared his Jewish assumptions, and expressing shock that they do not. Paul seems to press the panic button of his cultural prejudices. How this relates to his powerful evocation of life in the Spirit in 1 Corinthians 2, which he nowhere denies that the Corinthians share, is not made clear.

B. Wrestling with the Primacy of Apocalypse

Debates about antinomianism have a long history[31] but became an explicit part of theological vocabulary with the dispute between Luther and Johannes Agricola in the 1530s. Milton, while speaking dismissively of the "sort of men who follow Anabaptism, Familism, Antinomianism, and other fanatic dreams" goes on to make the perceptive point that this kind of approach to ethics, all this "proceed not partly, if not chiefly, from the restraint of some lawful liberty

31. Moisés Mayordomo, et al., "Antinomianism," *Encyclopedia of the Bible and its Reception*, ed. Hans-Josef Klauck, et al., Vol. 2 (Berlin: de Gruyter 2009), 233–46.

which ought to be given Men, and is deny'd them" (On Divorce, 14). The significant antinomian tradition in Judaism prompted by the life of Sabbatai Sevi (1626–76), has prompted comparisons with early Christianity. W. D. Davies, among New Testament scholars, and Jacob Taubes have noticed the antinomian parallels with early Christianity, but there has been little significant exploration of its impact, whether historically or in terms of the potential in the New Testament texts themselves.[32] The reception of the Pauline corpus has been responsible for the emergence of antinomianism at various points in Christian history.[33] The Pauline texts are themselves complex and seemingly contradictory, and while there are many warnings against antinomianism in the New Testament, including the Pauline corpus (Matt 7:23; 13:41; 23:28; 24:12; Rom 3:5–7; 6:1; 2 Cor 6:14; 2 Thess 2:3–8; 1 John 3:4), there is also rhetoric against law, and alongside it, assertions about the response to internal prompting rather than obedience to an external guide to behavior, echoing Jeremiah 31:33. So, for example, Paul seems concerned to show how "the just requirement of the law might be fulfilled" (Rom 8:3–4).

The issue was raised forty years ago and is now largely forgotten but deserves to be more than a footnote in the history of modern New Testament scholarship. It raised historical and hermeneutical problems, with regard to the interpretation of New Testament ethics and the emergence of Christianity. John Knox juxtaposed the ethic of Jesus and that of Paul, and found the latter wanting because of the lack of the dynamic of repentance and forgiveness, and what he considered was the inadequate theoretical structure of the theology underpinning Paul's doctrine of justification by faith, which failed to offer a coherent theological response to antinomianism.[34] Knox's challenge received a response in the Festschrift which was presented to him, including essays by Paul Schubert and C. F. D. Moule.[35] The latter analyzed Paul's understanding of identification with Christ and showed convincingly that even if Paul did not use the language of repentance and forgiveness, the Pauline language of submission to another lordship—say, in Romans 6—had an implicit notion of the dynamic of repentance and forgiveness, which paralleled that which Knox had identified in the Jesus tradition. That was the major concern of the Knox essay. What Moule failed to answer adequately, however, was the subsidiary point that there is inherent in the Pauline position a theological tendency which may lead to antinomianism. Even if the New Testament cannot in any overall sense be regarded as antin-

32. W. D. Davies, "From *Schweitzer to Scholem*: Reflections on Sabbatai Svi," *JBL* 95, no. 4 (1976): 529–58 repr. in *Jewish and Pauline Studies*, London: SPCK, 1984; Gershom Scholem, *Sabbatai Sevi: The Mystical Messiah, 1626-1676* (London: Routledge & Kegan Paul, 1973); J. Taubes, "The Price of Messianism," *JJS*, 33 (1982): 595–600; repr. in *Essential Papers on Messianic Movements and Personalities in Jewish History*, ed. Marc Saperstein (New York: New York University Press, 1992).

33. See D. Como, *Blown by the Spirit: Puritanism and the Emergence of an Antinomian Underground in Pre-Civil War England* (Stanford: Stanford University Press 2004), 104–12, for a concise statement of the problem; also Christopher Rowland, *Blake and the Bible* (London: Yale University Press, 2010), 203–7.

34. J. Knox, *The Ethic of Jesus and the Teaching of the Church: Its Authority and Relevance* (London: Epworth, 1962).

35. C. F. D. Moule, "Obligation in the Ethic of Paul," in *Christian History and Interpretation: Studies Presented to John Knox*, ed. W. R. Farmer, C. F. D. Moule, and R. R. Niebuhr (Cambridge: Cambridge University Press, 1967), 389–406.

omian, the later reception of Pauline texts suggest that there are very strong elements in the New Testament which push in that direction.

Paul's textual legacy is ambiguous.[36] On the one hand, at some points, Paul could suggest that followers of Christ were free from the Law (Rom 7:6). On the other hand, he made statements that even if believers were free from the Law, they were not free from moral duty to God. So, his letters are full of instructions to avoid the works of the flesh (e.g., 1 Thess 4:3–8). Paul's most morally didactic statements were handed down to the community in Corinth, where certain renegade teachers (very probably Paul's own converts) appeared to have deployed the rhetoric of Christian freedom to claim that Christians were free to determine how they lived. To counter this threat, Paul referred his readers to commands of the Lord (e.g., 1 Cor 7:10) and lists of vices as a warning (e.g., 1 Cor 6:9–10 cf. Rom 1:29–30; Gal 5:19–21). There is a tension, perhaps even an outright contradiction; Christ may have been the end of the Law (cf. Rom 10:4), but that did not mean the end of any kind of moral rectitude. Paul's favorite self-designation is the agent, or apostle, of Jesus Christ. As the peculiarly called agent of the Christ, he subordinates all human tradition to that. But he is not only an agent, for he is the one who imitated Christ (1 Cor 11:1). Rarely, he uses language about Christ indwelling (e.g., Gal 2:20), and can occasionally include fellow Christians also (Rom 8:3–9), though Galatians 2:20 is an unusual passage and contrasts with the more inclusive "Christ in us," which we find in passages such as Romans 8:20 and Colossians 1:27.

First Corinthians 2 encapsulates Paul's apocalyptic Gospel. The understanding of the divine will, and indeed knowledge of God, are not primarily dependent on obedience to a written code, but on the apocalypse of Jesus Christ. Nevertheless, Paul expounds the way in which Christ is formed in people through a subtle blend of being taught by God (1 Thess 4:9), imitating the apostolic example (1 Cor 11:1), altruistic concern for brothers and sisters in Christ—a prominent theme in 1 Corinthians as we shall see (cf. 1 Cor 13; 8:9–13) and obedience to injunctions inherited from the Mosaic Law (1 Cor 5:1, 13). So, 1 Corinthians is testimony to the way Paul qualifies the revelatory potential of the indwelling spirit, as he outlines a pattern of life for "the temple of the Holy Spirit" (1 Cor 6:19), which, understandably enough, reflects Jewish attitudes to holiness, including the avoidance of idolatry (1 Cor 10:14).

The theological dynamic of Paul's apocalyptic theology prioritized being indwelt by the divine (cf. Gal 2:20) or inspiration comes from the Spirit within, not from obedience to any external authority (1 Cor 2:10–16; cf. Rom 8:1–14). This theological epistemology is characterized by action "from impulse not from rules" as the English apocalyptic writer William Blake

36. See the interesting discussion of the positive contribution antinomian elements in the Pauline letters by the distinguished legal and political theorist Jeremy Waldron, in "'Dead to the Law': Paul's Antinomianism," *Cardozo Law Review 28* (2003): 301–32.

put it with regard to Jesus (*The Marriage of Heaven and Hell* 23–24, E43). The mature Paul came to link the evidence of the indwelling presence of the divine with the life of righteousness set out in the commandments of God (Rom 8:3), echoing the "new covenant", found in passages such as Ezekiel 36:25–27 and Jeremiah 31:31–4 (cf. 2 Cor 3:3).

First Corinthians 2:10–16 has, for long, been a favorite with the Christian radicals.[37] In 1 Corinthians 2, the knowledge of God comes through possession of the divine spirit. Those who are taught by the Spirit do not require any human teacher, nor for that matter any Scripture, and are subject to no one else's scrutiny (1 Cor 2:15). The beneficiaries of divine wisdom in the Spirit, however, possess the power of knowing God and the things of God and possess a discrimination that transcends the requirement of any human teacher. It is in a chapter such as 1 Corinthians 2 that we see the ways in which the "apocalyptic" and the "gnostic" overlap, and we begin to understand the New Testament Apocalypse as a revelation of the deepest structures of cosmos. We need to recall the mystical, gnostic, dimension of this which may help to explain the emergence of a "vertical" relationship with the divine world, which may compensate for the historical disappointment, once the synergism of human and divine in realizing apocalypse does not come about.

In his first letter to the Corinthians, Paul is confronted with groups who regarded themselves as elite because of their heavenly or angelic language. In 1 Corinthians 13, he explicitly contrasts a community of language, which ends up fragmenting and alienating, with the practice of charity: Paul deals with the issue by underlining the way in which the practice of human relating is the ultimate test of community, and the Babel whose currency is words can never match a basic human instinct of altruism and concern. Language—and that includes theology—must be shaped by the practice of love. Paul contrasts words and action, the "tongues of angels," typically private rather than public theology, with prophecy and the action of charity. Prophecy is to be preferred, so that if "an unbeliever or outsider enters, he is convicted by all, he is called to account by all, the secrets of his heart are disclosed" (1 Cor 14:25). Prophecy is for edification and encouragement. The need to be understood is paramount so the hermeneutical responsibility is essential (1 Cor 14:5, 13). Thus, Paul demands that the Corinthians attend to life in the public sphere, in the meat market, for example, and the ancient places of idolatry (1 Cor 8 and 10) away from the comfort of the holy huddle, and see that not only the esotericism of their language but also their behavior demand critical scrutiny. There is nothing to be gained from a language that provides no hard currency to purchase engagement with the wider public (cf. 1 Cor 1:23–25). In the final analysis, it is not the quality of theology that counts but love, as the most famous passage in the New Testament makes clear (1 Cor 13).

37. E.g. A. C. Thiselton, *The First Epistle to the Corinthians*, NIGTC (Carlisle: Paternoster, 2000), 276–86; Rowland, *Blake and the Bible*, 157–80.

First Corinthians is a letter which is full of authoritative advice (e.g. 7:10; 11:2; 14:37) from one who rather disarmingly describes himself as "one who by the Lord's mercy is trustworthy" (7:25), and includes apostolic pronouncements (7:6, 8, 12; 11:33; 16:1) and references to Paul's example (4:16; 9:1–23; 11:1). It is a curious mix of the pragmatic, the rhetorical, and the apologetic, apparently so far removed from apocalyptic writings. At the time Paul was writing 1 Corinthians, he was seeking to challenge a way of life which may be mystically sublime but not ethical enough. Paul offers himself as a role model, in a way like the stories that are offered in Jewish texts, like the tractates Ḥagigah in the Mishnah and Tosefta, with the further explications of the themes in the *talmudim* where Yohanan ben Zakkai gives his seal of approval to Eleazar ben Arak for his ability to expound well and perform well. The problem with the Corinthians, to paraphrase the encomium of Eleazar ben Arak, is that exposition and ethical performance did not coincide. High-flown angelic words, for example, are not matched by deeds. What is needed is following the example of the apostle/teacher who imitates Christ, accepting his authority and the halakah-like instructions he offered. So Paul states clearly who is disqualified from inheriting the kingdom of God (1 Cor 6:9), and outlines the holiness necessary for the life of those who would be part of the temple of the Holy Spirit. Paul lays out clear guidance expected of those who had access to the divine world in their midst and the measures needed to ensure that this holiness was not compromised. Peter Tomson's words perfectly sum up the Paul of 1 Corinthians, "truly Jewish and Pharisaic, Paul's apocalyptic faith is consummated in active life."[38]

Concluding Comments

In his *Aids to Reflection,* S. T. Coleridge discusses the nature of mysticism. Coleridge tries to make a distinction between what Douglas Hedley describes as *disciplined* speculative form of thought aimed at the vision of God and *self-indulgent* visionary enthusiasm, from which Coleridge wants to dissociate himself.[39] Coleridge was suspicious of any attempt on the part of the mystic to persuade others to enjoy similar experiences. What Coleridge prefers is the harmless mystic who is able to discern the difference between fantasy and reality and is able to distinguish a dream of truth, whereas "in the bewildered tale of the former there is truth mingled with the dream." Coleridge's words written about Jacob Boehme, of whose mysticism he was suspicious, could equally well apply to Paul:

38. Peter J. Tomson, *Paul and the Jewish Law: Halakha in the Letters of Paul*, CRINT 1 (Assen: Van Gorcum; Minneapolis: Fortress Press, 1990), 80.
39. Douglas Hedley, *Coleridge, Philosophy, and Religion: Aids to Reflection and the Mirror of the Spirit* (Cambridge: Cambridge University Press, 2000), 282.

> the craving for sympathy, strong in proportion to the intensity of his convictions, impels him to unbosom himself to abstract auditors; and the poor quietist becomes a penman, and, all too poorly stocked for the writer's trade, he borrows his phrases and figures from the only writings to which he has had access, the sacred books of his religion.

Coleridge's suspicion is anticipated by Festus in his comment to Paul: "Too much learning is driving you insane"—an interesting comment on Paul's account of his "heavenly vision" to which he "was not disobedient" (Acts 26:19–24; cf. Gal 1:12–16).

Even though Paul's extant writings are epistles, not accounts of ecstatic apocalyptic experiences, 2 Corinthians 12:2–4 excepted, there is implicit throughout an apocalyptic claim to authority. Alongside it are an ethical pragmatism and a rhetoric of persuasion linked with an exposition of, and apologia for, his authority. For Paul, the mystery of the divine economy in the crucified messiah is manifest for all even if it remains hidden from those on the way to perdition (2 Cor 2:16); it is not esoteric, therefore, even if it is enigmatic, and to some, it remains foolishness (1 Cor 1:18). Like the Lamb in the midst of the throne in Revelations 5:6, the mystery of the crucified messiah stands at the fulcrum of the ages and is the eschatological key which unlocks the meaning of history. Of this mystery as far as it affects the nations, Paul is mediator (1 Cor 4:1). Similar to the Teacher of Righteousness, who could make sense of the enigmas of the prophetic word (1QpHab), Paul is not only the steward of the divine mystery but also himself the interpreter of its meaning and agent of its eschatological fulfillment.

We are only offered glimpses of the ecstatic and mysterious, in passages such as 2 Corinthians 12:2–4.[40] The veil hides the precise moments of mystical ascent or visionary insight from us. What Paul chooses to reveal in his written words, however, is directed largely to the maintenance of community and his authority, as the apostle of Jesus Christ rather than the chain of tradition which went back to the Fathers (mAboth 1:1). In this respect, Paul maintains the pattern of religion which is evident in the tannaitic sources when it comes to the mystical: present revelation is subordinate to ensuring that the demand for the stable conformity to "traditional" patterns and habits of life (cf. 1 Cor 14:33–34) are maintained. The "routinization of charisma" is nowhere better exemplified than elsewhere in 1 Corinthians 14, where the ecstatic words of the spirit are subordinated to the rational communication of the comprehensible words of prophecy, or interpreted glossolalia, which have the effect of building up the community. Paul nowhere denies the force of that religious power which had turned his world upside down, but at least in the Corinthian correspondence, we find repeated attempts to contain the effects of the kind of disturbance in a community's common life which had previously caused the personal upheaval in his life. Obedience to the apostolic behest, and above all else,

40. Rowland and Morray-Jones, *Mystery of God*, 341–420; Shantz, *Paul in Ecstasy*.

mutual charity, take precedence over the individual moments of ecstasy or other exercises of spiritual power.

I started with Ed Sanders's brief reference to ecstatic mysticism, and I end with his succinct description of Pauline understanding of religion: when it came to how converts stayed in the nascent Christian community (rather than getting into it), the Law of Moses had its part to play.[41] These words, which are widely accepted, contain the seeds of the problem posed by the Pauline writings for his contemporaries and are germane to our thesis. Ed Sanders picked up on a fundamental tension in the Pauline corpus which is never resolved, between what Sanders terms "participationist eschatology" on the one hand, which has little to do with Law, "although the Law and the prophets bear witness to it" (Rom 3:22) and "covenantal nomism", or, more accurately, the Pauline version of it, on the other. The revelatory moment, which points to participation in the messianic life, is not dependent on Law, even if its novelty and its unpredictable outcomes required managing. Like any rabbi, Paul showed himself capable of making new rules relevant for a new situation, but he did it by virtue of an authority which had come to him "neither by human commission nor from human authorities, but through Jesus Christ and God the Father" (Gal 1:1), and what applied to him applied, at least in principle, to those who shared this messianic life. He acted (to quote Blake's memorable words about Jesus) "from impulse not from rules" (*The Marriage of Heaven and Hell* 23–24, E43). But what we find in his letters is a qualification of Blake's words with regard to those whom he influenced. In the letters, the bottom line was the ordering of the nascent community in the spirit of mutuality, with individual claims to apocalyptic knowledge subordinate to mutual concern, and most importantly, to the admonitions of the authoritative inspired apostle who was himself indwelt by the Messiah (Gal 2:19–20). That is the basis for his authority. His admonitions do not appeal to the tradition of the fathers, or rarely even the Bible, however influenced they might have been by both. Rather, central to Paul's position is an apocalyptic religion and communion with the divine through the Spirit. The ambiguities, even contradictions, in his thought owe much to it. Whence he derived his position on the place of gentiles in the messianic age, for example, we shall never know, but his advocacy of his rule for gentiles "getting in" to the community of the new age was at odds with much of what was prevalent in mainstream Judaism and typifies the radical break he encouraged and which accelerated the separation for Second Temple Judaism.

It may be thought that social cohesion and the needs of the community eclipse messianism, but it is not quite as simple as that. It may appear from the Pauline corpus that changing society

41. Sanders, *Paul and Palestinian Judaism*, 424; on "participationist eschatology," 453–63; also Schweitzer, *Mysticism*; Macaskill, *Union with Christ*; and earlier C. F. D. Moule, *The Origin of Christology* (Cambridge: Cambridge University Press, 1977), 54–69.

is not necessary because the imminent eschatological crisis is at hand: "in view of the impending crisis, it is well for you to remain as you are . . . the appointed time has grown short . . . for the present form of this world is passing away" (1 Cor 7:26–31). The "impending crisis", however, does not mean that there should be no change; far from it, as the rest of 1 Corinthians (and elsewhere) indicates. This is not being an ordinary member of society while inwardly living as if part of the age to come, as was the case with some later Christians.[42] Like Jews, there was a degree of distance and nonconformity in belief and practice, which Paul explores in 1 Corinthians 8–10. Messianic life, according to Paul, seems to be socially conservative, but that initial assessment conceals the complex mix of negotiating the time waiting for the impending crisis, which required the implementation of certain patterns of life to characterize life as "the temple of the Holy Spirit" (1 Cor 6:19). The messianic, the apocalyptic tradition, and community cohesion are in constant tension in the Pauline letters. The eventual priority of the community is unsurprising, given the perhaps inevitable investment that Paul had in the "success" of the communities he had established to maintain some kind of credible identity. By the time that Paul writes Romans, the criterion of the work of the messianic spirit is that "the just requirement of the law might be fulfilled in us, who walk not according to the flesh but according to the Spirit" (Rom 8:4). A certain ethical standard, in large part determined by the Law of Moses, becomes critical. "Staying in" for the Paul of the extant letters requires a form of pattern of adherence based on the Torah, even if somewhat less demanding than that laid down in the Torah as a whole. The impetus for the Pauline injunctions is intimately linked with the messianic dynamic and how that works itself out in lives lived in the midst of a world passing away. Being in the world means inhabiting the present age; not being of the world indicates that "our citizenship is in heaven, and it is from there that we are expecting a Saviour" (Phil 3:20).

The apocalyptic vision offered the seer communion with eternity. The presence of God and communion with the angels enabled the transcendence of time.[43] While we cannot know for certain what the position of the Corinthians is on this matter, we do know from 1 Corinthians that Paul accepts the centrality of the apocalyptic knowledge of God through the Spirit in 1 Corinthians 2, he insists that it must be informed by attention to life in time and space. That historical perspective is one that, in different ways, pervades what Paul writes. Not only does he draw attention to the ethical but also in his discussion of the resurrection, the injection of a necessary temporal perspective demands that the communion with eternity must be set in the context of time, a dimension the importance of which Loren Stuckenbruck has drawn to

42. Diarmaid MacCulloch, *Silence: A Christian History* (London: Penguin, 2013).

43. Rowland, *Open Heaven*, 113–20, Rowland and Morray-Jones, *Mystery of God*, 167–77, 303–40; Andrew T. Lincoln, *Paradise Now and Not Yet: Studies in the Role of the Heavenly Dimension in Paul's Thought with Special Reference to his Eschatology*, SNTSMS 43 (Cambridge: Cambridge University Press, 1981).

our attention.[44] There can be no escape from history, therefore. The Paul of the extant letters insists on an eschatology which still looks forward to the coming of the messianic age (1 Cor 15: 20–28).

I do not think that one can understand the fabric of Christian theology and ethics unless one grasps the significant role that antinomian elements linked with apocalyptic thought play in both the New Testament writings and in the history of Christianity. The antinomian, the apocalyptic, and the eschatological together are key to comprehending the structure motor of Paul's thought. They help us to see why Paul relativized the place of the Bible and tradition in the light of his apocalyptic and eschatological convictions; and the possibilities and problems they engendered are part of the account we must give of Paul's theology. In sum, the resistance to adherence to an external theological and moral code, and the conviction that it was possible to be taught by God through revelation, do not get the consideration they deserve.

44. Loren T. Stuckenbruck, "Posturing 'Apocalyptic' in Pauline Theology: How Much Contrast with Jewish Tradition?" in *The Myth of Rebellious Angels: Studies in Second Temple Judaism and New Testament Texts*, WUNT 335 (Tübingen: Mohr Siebeck, 2014), 240–56.

7

The Apocalyptic Eschatology of Romans

Creation, Judgment, Resurrection, and Glory

Karina Martin Hogan

Introduction

Since the early twentieth century, New Testament scholars who focus on Paul have had a love-hate relationship with Jewish apocalyptic literature. On the one hand, they have acknowledged, at least since the pioneering work of Albert Schweitzer,[1] that it is impossible to understand Paul without understanding the importance of apocalyptic thought within Judaism during Paul's lifetime. Ernst Käsemann went so far as to claim that "apocalyptic was the mother of all Christian theology."[2] On the other hand, New Testament scholars have striven to differentiate the apostle from his Jewish apocalyptic milieu, either by emphasizing other influences on Paul, such as Hellenistic philosophy, or by asserting the "uniqueness" of Paul's apocalypticism vis-à-vis his Jewish "background." In an earlier era, an embrace of Paul's apocalypticism could go hand-in-hand with an attempt to distance him from "Judaism," especially rabbinic Judaism; this, at least, was the case for Schweitzer.[3] Even Käsemann, who understood Paul's interpreta-

1. Albert Schweitzer, *The Mysticism of Paul the Apostle* (New York: H. Holt and Co, 1931).
2. Ernst Käsemann, "The Beginnings of Christian Theology," in *New Testament Questions of Today*, trans. W. J. Montague (Philadelphia: Fortress Press, 1969), 82–107 (102).

tion of the death and resurrection of Christ to be fundamentally apocalyptic, frequently contrasts Paul's theology with the dualism and exclusivism of Jewish apocalyptic thought.[4]

Post-Holocaust, and especially since the rise of the "New Perspective" on Paul, there has been much progress toward understanding Paul within the context of the rich diversity of Judaism in the Second Temple period.[5] In recent decades, the scholarly understanding of apocalypticism, and ancient Jewish apocalypticism in particular, has also changed and grown tremendously, in no small part due to the publication of the Qumran scrolls. New Testament scholars have begun to appreciate the complexity of Jewish apocalypticism and have become more hesitant to draw sweeping contrasts between Paul's thought and apocalyptic Judaism. One of the first scholars to bring a more sophisticated understanding of Jewish apocalypticism to bear on the interpretation of Paul was J. Christiaan Beker.[6]

Scholars of Paul still tend to see a fundamental difference in the way in which Paul and the Jewish apocalyptic authors conceptualize time and eschatology. Jewish apocalyptic eschatology is assumed to have a uniform doctrine of two ages, and the apocalypses anticipate the end of the present age and the inauguration of the age to come in the near or more distant future, while for Paul, the Christ-event has already inaugurated the eschatological age.[7] For Beker, the crucifixion and resurrection of Christ, an event without parallel in the Jewish apocalypses, represents to Paul "the apocalyptic turning point of history."[8] Yet, Beker acknowledges that the contrast between the Pauline already-not-yet eschatology and the Jewish apocalyptic two-age doctrine has been overstated by Käsemann and others, pointing to the Qumran sectarians as having a similar partially realized eschatology.[9] More than Käsemann, Beker focuses on the orientation of Paul's eschatology toward the future "triumph of God" that will accompany the *parousia.* The present chapter, while acknowledging the central place of the Christ-event in Paul's eschatology, will explore four themes in the eschatology of Romans that can be illuminated through a comparison with Jewish apocalyptic literature.

The Epistle to the Romans has historically been considered a summary or synthesis of Pauline doctrine, but more recent scholarship has tended to view it as a rhetorical work written

3. Dale Martin, "Paul and the Judaism/Hellenism Dichotomy: Toward a Social History of the Question," in *Paul Beyond the Judaism/Hellenism Divide*, ed. Troels Engberg-Pedersen (Louisville: Westminster John Knox, 2001), 29–61, esp. 35–38.
4. Ernst Käsemann, *Commentary on Romans*, trans. Geoffrey W. Bromiley (Grand Rapids: Eerdmans, 1980).
5. Scholars today generally point to E. P. Sanders' *Paul and Palestinian Judaism* (Philadelphia: Fortress Press, 1977) as inaugurating the New Perspective, although the term was coined in a 1983 lecture by James Dunn.
6. See, especially, his *Paul the Apostle: The Triumph of God in Life and Thought* (Philadelphia: Fortress Press, 1980).
7. See Loren T. Stuckenbruck, "Posturing 'Apocalyptic' in Pauline Theology: How Much Contrast to Jewish Tradition?" in *The Myth of Rebellious Angels: Studies in Second Temple Judaism and New Testament Texts,* WUNT 335 (Tübingen: Mohr Siebeck, 2014), 240–56.
8. Beker, *Paul the Apostle,* 205.
9. Beker, *Paul the Apostle,* 149–50. Loren T. Stuckenbruck develops this point much further in his essay "Overlapping Ages at Qumran and 'Apocalyptic' in Pauline Theology," in *The Dead Sea Scrolls and Pauline Literature,* ed. J.-S. Rey, STDJ 102 (Leiden: Brill, 2014), 309–26.

for a particular audience and situation, even though the occasion for writing is more difficult to discern than in Paul's other letters.[10] Joseph Fitzmyer observes, "some characteristic Pauline tenets are missing from Romans: his teaching on the church, the eucharist, or eschatology (save for some fleeting remarks)."[11] While I would not dispute the general point that Romans is not an exhaustive compendium of Paul's teaching, I think it is a rich source for understanding Paul's revealed eschatology, despite the lack of a sustained discussion of the *parousia*. I have chosen four recurring themes in Romans that are informed by Jewish apocalyptic eschatology: creation, resurrection, judgment, and glory.

The one that perhaps needs some justification as an *eschatological* theme is creation (κτίσις), which Paul uses in two senses: the beginning of the present world or age (1:20) or the world itself, which is awaiting redemption at the end of the present age (8:19–23). It is a common apocalyptic belief that the *Endzeit* will correspond to the *Urzeit*,[12] but even more fundamental to Jewish apocalyptic theology is the belief that the world is a divine creation and therefore good, but at the same time, corrupt and in need of eschatological redemption.[13] Resurrection is an obvious eschatological theme, but I argue that Paul's beliefs about resurrection are rooted in his beliefs about creation and have more in common with Jewish apocalyptic understandings of resurrection than is often recognized. In many Jewish apocalypses, the resurrection is for the sake of judgment; Paul understands the relationship between resurrection and judgment somewhat differently, but they are nevertheless associated with one another in Romans. Finally, glory follows from judgment as the reward of the righteous in many apocalyptic texts. These four apocalyptic themes (creation, resurrection, judgment, and glory) all come together in Romans 8, but they occur individually or in pairs throughout the letter. The present chapter considers how these themes function in Romans in the context of Jewish apocalyptic literature, with particular attention to two major apocalypses of the late first century CE, 4 Ezra and 2 Baruch.

Creation

The concept of a divinely created world is fundamental to apocalyptic eschatology, and Paul in Romans certainly shares that assumption. At the same time, Jewish apocalyptic texts differ

10. Robert Jewett, *Romans, A Commentary*, Hermeneia (Minneapolis: Fortress Press, 2007), 23–46.
11. Joseph A. Fitzmyer, S.J., *Romans: A New Translation with Introduction and Commentary*, AB 33 (New York: Doubleday, 1993), 103.
12. As demonstrated by Hermann Gunkel in *Schöpfung und Chaos in Urzeit und Endzeit* (Göttingen: Vandenhoeck und Ruprecht, 1895); for a more recent discussion, see Lutz Doering, "*Urzeit-Endzeit* Correlation in the Dead Sea Scrolls and Pseudepigrapha," in *Eschatologie-Eschatology: The Sixth Durham-Tübingen Research Symposium: Eschatology in the Old Testament, Ancient Judaism and Early Christianity (Tübingen, September, 2009)*, ed. H.-J. Eckstein, C. Landmesser, and H. Lichtenberger, WUNT 272 (Tübingen: Mohr Siebeck, 2011), 19–58.
13. See Harry A. Hahne, *The Corruption and Redemption of Creation: Nature in Romans 8:19–22 and Jewish Apocalyptic Literature* (London: T&T Clark, 2006).

widely in their assessment of the nonhuman creation and the role of human beings in relation to it. Specifically, although the creation is generally assumed to have been "very good" (Gen 1:31) when God first created it, apocalyptic texts differ on both the extent to which creation has become corrupted, and the extent to which human beings are to blame for its corruption.[14] Paul's apocalyptic understanding of these matters is expressed most clearly in two related passages in Romans, 1:18–25 and 8:18–23. These passages are related in that they share certain key terms: forms of *ἀποκαλύπτω* in 1:18 and 8:18; forms of *κτίσις* in 1:20, 25 and 8:19, 20, 21, 22; forms of *δόξα*, *δοξάζω* in 1:21, 23 and 8:18, 21 (cf. 8:30); *ἀφθάρτου*, *φθαρτοῦ* in 1:23 and *φθορᾶς* in 8:21; *ἐματαιώθησαν* in 1:21 and *ματαιότητι* in 8:20; *τὰ σώματα αὐτῶν* in 1:24 and *τοῦ σώματος ἡμῶν* in 8:23.[15]

The first passage, 1:18–25, is part of a larger argument in 1:18–32, but for present purposes, Paul's now problematic remarks about "unnatural" sexual unions in 1:26–27 and his judgment on various forms of wrongdoing in 1:28–32 are not as pertinent as the beliefs about creation expressed in the first part of the passage.[16] Here, Paul expresses an assumption about the natural order that is found in a number of Jewish apocalyptic as well as wisdom texts: that it serves a pedagogical function in relation to human beings.[17] Some of these texts focus on the responsibility of human beings to infer the existence and goodness of the Creator from the goodness of the creation. Wisdom of Solomon 13:1–9 vacillates on whether or not people who fail to perceive the Creator behind the creation are "without excuse," to use Paul's phrase in Romans 1:20.[18] The Testament of Naphtali (3:1–5) suggests that by discerning "in the firmament, in the earth, and in the sea, and in all the products of his workmanship . . . the Lord who made all things," the addressees will avoid falling into the sins of idolatry and "depart[ing] from the order of nature" through sexual deviancy, a similar train of thought to Paul's here (and cf. Wis 14:12, 22–27).[19] Other apocalyptic texts (e.g., 1 Enoch 2–5, 2 Baruch 54:17–18) contrast the order of the natural world with the disorderly conduct of human beings.[20] Paul presupposes this com-

14. See Hahne, *Corruption and Redemption*, 7–165 (Part I).
15. Most of these parallels are noted by Preston Sprinkle, "The Afterlife in Romans: Understanding Paul's Glory Motif in Light of the Apocalypse of Moses and 2 Baruch," in *Lebendige Hoffnung, ewiger Tod?!: Jenseitsvorstellungen im Hellenismus, Judentum und Christentum*, ed. M. Labahn and M. Lang (Leipzig: Evangelische Verlaganstalt, 2007), 201–33 (221).
16. On the Hellenistic Jewish background of Paul's condemnation of same-sex relations in 1:26–27, see Brendan Byrne, S.J., *Romans*, SP (Collegeville, MN: Liturgical, 1996), 64–79.
17. See Michael Stone, "The Parabolic Use of Natural Order in Judaism of the Second Temple Age," in *Selected Studies in Pseudepigrapha and Apocrypha, with Special Reference to the Armenian Tradition*, SVTP 9 (Leiden: Brill, 1991), 457–67.
18. Although they are frequently compared, there are of course important differences between the way Paul and the author of the Wisdom of Solomon conceptualize the knowledge of God and its relation to idolatry and immorality. See Alec J. Lucas, "Distinct Portraits and Parallel Developments of the Knowledge of God in Romans 1:18–32 and Wisdom of Solomon 13–15," in *Christian Body, Christian Self: Concepts of Early Christian Personhood*, ed. C. K. Rothschild and T. W. Thompson, WUNT 284 (Tübingen: Mohr Siebeck, 2011), 61–82.
19. Translation by H. C. Kee in *OTP* 1:812.
20. See George W. E. Nickelsburg, *1 Enoch 1: A Commentary on the Book of 1 Enoch, Chapters 1-36; 81-108*, Hermeneia (Minneapolis: Fortress Press, 2001), 152–55.

mon sapiential-apocalyptic technique of contrasting the orderliness of nature with human misconduct in his argument in Romans 1:18–32.

It is significant that Paul introduces his argument with the claim that "the wrath of God is revealed (ἀποκαλύπτεται γὰρ ὀργὴ θεοῦ) from heaven against all ungodliness and wickedness of those who by their wickedness suppress the truth (τῶν τὴν ἀλήθειαν ἐν ἀδικίᾳ κατεχόντων)" (1:18).[21] The present tense of "is [being] revealed," which echoes 1:17, points to the new eschatological situation that was initiated by the Christ-event; what previously was hidden is now being revealed.[22] In the context of the present revelation of God's wrath, Paul makes a universal claim about human beings: that they are "without excuse (ἀναπολογήτους)" because they failed to honor the Creator, about whom it is possible to know something (taking τὸ γνωστὸν τοῦ θεοῦ to mean "what is knowable about God") by observing the works of creation, which God manifested to them (1:19–20).[23] Their failure to acknowledge God leads to folly (1:21–22), which is demonstrated, on the one hand by their idolatry, and on the other by their immorality. Paul presents these sins as punishments in themselves; three times, he states that God "gave them up" or "handed them over" (παρέδωκεν; 1:24, 26, 28) to idolatry (1:25), "degrading passions" (1:26–27) and "every kind of wickedness" (1:29–31).[24] This way of explaining human sinfulness resembles a principle articulated in the Wisdom of Solomon that was fairly widespread in apocalyptic texts: "one is punished by the very things by which one sins" (Wis 11:16; cf. Testament of Gad 5:10; Jubilees 4:32).

Paul's argument about the culpability of all human beings resembles the universal claims made by the angel Uriel in 4 Ezra 7:21–23:

> [21]For the Lord strictly commanded those who came into the world, when they came, what they should do to live, and what they should observe to avoid punishment. [22]Nevertheless they were not obedient, and spoke against him; they devised for themselves vain thoughts, [23]and proposed to themselves wicked frauds; they even declared that the Most High does not exist, and they ignored his ways.[25]

Similarly, 2 Baruch condemns all humankind for failing to acknowledge God's law: "Because

21. NRSV. Unless otherwise noted, translations from Romans follow the NRSV.
22. Käsemann, *Commentary on Romans,* 35; Jewett, *Romans,* 150; Bruce W. Longenecker, *Eschatology and the Covenant: A Comparison of Fourth Ezra and Romans 1-11,* JSNTSup 57 (Sheffield: JSOT Press, 1991), 169–70.
23. Käsemann, *Commentary on Romans,* 38, writes: "To the intensity of the judgment corresponds the totality of the world which stands under it, so that the statement about the Gentiles applies to the heathen nature of mankind as such, and hence implies the guilty Jew as well."
24. Cf. Acts 7:41–43, where Stephen says that God "handed over" the Israelites to astral worship as punishment for the Golden Calf incident, which Paul alludes to in Rom 1:23.
25. Translation by Michael E. Stone, in Michael E. Stone and Matthias Henze, *4 Ezra and 2 Baruch: Translations, Introductions and Notes* (Minneapolis: Fortress Press, 2013). Translations of 4 Ezra and 2 Baruch will follow Stone and Henze, respectively.

every one of the inhabitants of the earth knew when he acted unjustly, but my Torah they did not know because of their pride" (48:40; cf. 4 Ezra 7:72).

The classic biblical example of what Paul is claiming is a universal human tendency to "suppress the truth" (1:18) is the Golden Calf incident (which stands for idolatry generally), evoked by Paul's allusion in 1:23 to Psalm 106:20 (LXX), "They exchanged their glory for the image of a calf that eats grass" (cf. Jer 2:11). Paul's formulation introduces the concept of the corruption of creation: "They exchanged the glory of the immortal (or incorruptible: ἄφθαρτος) God for images resembling a mortal (or corruptible: φθαρτός) human being or birds or four-footed animals or reptiles" (1:23).[26] The contrast between the incorruptible God and the corruptible creation points to a paradox within the apocalyptic view of creation: how can "what is knowable about God" be inferred from a creation that differs from God so fundamentally? And what does the present corrupt creation have to do with the eschatological "new creation"?

Nowhere is this problem explored at such length as in 4 Ezra, in which Uriel rebukes Ezra for trying to understand his people's fate as follows: "You cannot understand the things with which you have grown up; how then can your vessel comprehend the way of the Most High? For the way of the Most High is created immeasurable. And how can one who is corrupt in the corrupt world understand the way of the incorruptible?" (4:10–11). Yet, Uriel goes on to instruct Ezra about the ways of God, and especially about eschatology, using numerous parables and analogies to the "corrupt" world.[27] The ways of this corrupt world do not correspond exactly to the ways of the Most High, but human beings can still learn something about God from observing the workings of creation. Although the parabolic or pedagogical use of the natural order is not as obvious in Romans 1:18–25 as it is in 4 Ezra and some other apocalyptic texts, this passage is illuminated by reading it in light of that common apocalyptic theme.

Romans 8:18–23 brings Paul's views on the corruption of creation and the hope of a new creation into sharper focus. Whereas in 1:18–25, Paul speaks from the perspective of the "eschatological present"—"the wrath of God is [now being] revealed" (1:18) in light of the Christ-event—in 8:18–23, Paul is contrasting the sufferings of the present moment (τοῦ νῦν καιροῦ) with "the glory about to be revealed to us" (τὴν μέλλουσαν δόξαν ἀποκαλυφθῆναι εἰς ἡμᾶς) in the *parousia* (8:18). The present creation is characterized by corruption (φθορά, 8:21), the future creation by glory (8:18; cf. the contrast of these terms in 1:23). Instead of contrasting the order of creation with disorderly human conduct, Paul now emphasizes the common condition of humanity and the nonhuman creation.[28] He imagines the whole creation (πᾶσα ἡ

26. Cf. Wis 11:15, which caricatures the Egyptian worship of animals prior to asserting the principle cited above about people being punished by the very things by which they sin.

27. Stone discusses these parables and analogies in "Parabolic Use of the Natural Order," 463–66, and see my discussion of them in *Theologies in Conflict in 4 Ezra: Wisdom Debate and Apocalyptic Solution*, JSJSup 130 (Leiden: Brill, 2008), 105–8, 120–26.

κτίσις) groaning together as a pregnant woman in labor (συστενάζει καὶ συνωδίνει), just as Paul's addressees groan inwardly as they await the redemption of their bodies (8:22–23).

Jewett points out that Paul's maternal personification of creation may have been influenced by Roman depictions of Mother Earth—for example, on the Ara Pacis in Rome—although he contrasts her relaxed posture there with the mood of "eager expectation" (ἀποκαραδοκία) that Paul attributes to creation (8:19).[29] He also mentions as parallel the personification of the earth in the Book of the Watchers, where the earth cries out to heaven on behalf of her inhabitants, who are being devoured by the giants (1 Enoch 7:6, 9:2).[30] Joseph R. Dodson compares the personification of creation in Romans with that in the Wisdom of Solomon, but he finds that the personified creation behaves in quite different ways in the two works.[31] These comparisons are helpful, but much more illuminating parallels can be found in 4 Ezra. Some of the aforementioned analogies by which Uriel explains eschatological matters to Ezra compare the earth to a pregnant woman.[32] For example, in response to a question from Ezra about a possible delay of the final judgment, Uriel answers, "Go and ask a woman who is with child if, when her nine months have been completed, her womb can keep the child within her any longer" (4:40). After Ezra answers that it cannot, Uriel draws out the analogy: "The underworld and the treasuries of the souls are like the womb. For just as a woman who is in travail makes haste to escape the pangs of birth, so also do these [places] hasten to give back those things that were committed to them from the beginning" (4:41–42; cf. 1 Enoch 51:1; 2 Baruch 30:2, 50:2).

The maternal metaphor is extended from the earth to the creation as a whole in a later series of analogies in 4 Ezra. After establishing that a woman's womb cannot produce ten children at one time, Uriel concludes: "Even so I have made the earth a womb for those who from time to time come forth on it. For as an infant does not bring forth, and a woman who has become old does not bring forth any longer, so I have organized the world that I created" (5:48–49). Ezra then inquires if "our mother" is approaching old age (5:50). Uriel answers that just as "those born in the strength of youth are different from those born in the time of old age, when the womb is failing" (5:53), Ezra should consider that he and his contemporaries are smaller than people in the past, "and those who come after you will be smaller than you, as if born of a cre-

28. Jewett (*Romans*, 511) defends the view that ἡ κτίσις in 8:19 refers primarily to the nonhuman creation, even though in 1:25 it clearly referred to all created things, including human beings. Byrne (*Romans*, 255–56) concurs, as does Hahne (*Corruption and Redemption of Creation*, 176–81).

29. Jewett, *Romans*, 511.

30. See Karina Martin Hogan, "The Mortal Body and the Earth in Ben Sira and the Book of the Watchers," in *Christian Body, Christian Self: Concepts of Early Christian Personhood*, ed. C. K. Rothschild and T. W. Thompson, WUNT 284 (Tübingen: Mohr Siebeck, 2011), 21–39 (28).

31. Joseph R. Dodson, *The "Powers" of Personification: Rhetorical Purpose in the* Book of Wisdom *and the Letter to the Romans*, BZNW 161 (Berlin: de Gruyter, 2008), 194–201, and see also the separate discussions of personified creation in Wisdom (69–81) and Romans (162–77).

32. See Karina Martin Hogan, "Mother Earth as a Conceptual Metaphor in *4 Ezra*," *CBQ* 73 (2011): 72–91, esp. 78–82.

ation that already is aging and passing the strength of youth" (5:55). A similar formulation is found in 2 Baruch 85:10, "For the youth of the world has passed, and the strength of creation is already consumed." In 4 Ezra, however, the decay or corruptibility of creation is likened not simply to the human life cycle, but specifically to declining female reproductive potential.

Thus, when Paul imagines the creation as a woman in labor, it is not surprising that he should also describe it as "subjected to futility" (Rom 8:20) and hoping to be set free from its "slavery to corruption" (8:21, my translation). Many scholars see an allusion to Genesis 3:17–19 in Paul's remark that creation was subjected to futility "not of its own will, but by [the will of] the one who subjected it" (οὐχ ἑκοῦσα ἀλλὰ διὰ τὸν ὑποτάξαντα, 8:20). The most common interpretation is that this verse refers to God's curse upon the earth as a result of Adam's sin.[33] A frequently cited parallel is 4 Ezra 7:11–12: "For I made the world for [Israel's] sake and when Adam transgressed my statutes, what had been made was judged. And so the entrances of this world were made narrow and sorrowful and toilsome." The author of 4 Ezra seems to be extending the consequences of Adam's sin to creation as a whole, as many scholars believe Paul is doing in Romans 8:20.

If Paul is alluding in Romans 8:20 to Genesis 3:17–19, it is possible that his choice of the metaphor "groaning and laboring in pain" (8:22, my translation) to describe the present state of creation is also informed by the curse of Eve in Genesis 3:16. In the Second Temple period, the curse on the earth for Adam's sake (Gen 3:17) and the curse on Eve (Gen 3:16), both of which entail painful labor/toil (עצבון), were easily assimilated, as seen most clearly in the transfer of Eve's epithet "mother of all the living" (Gen 3:20) to the earth in Sirach 40:1 (NAB): "A great anxiety has God allotted, and a heavy yoke, to the sons of men; from the day one leaves his mother's womb to the day he returns to the mother of all the living." Since "sons of men" here translates בני אדם, and Adam is the only person who literally returns to the dust from which he was formed, Ben Sira is clearly reflecting on Genesis 3:17–19 in this verse. At the same time, Genesis 3:20 is the source of the title "mother of all the living" (אם כל חי) for Eve, which Ben Sira rightly perceived to be more aptly ascribed to the earth.[34] Hence, Eve is drawn into the association between the earth, toil, and mortality or corruption.

Finally, it seems possible to me that the "groaning and laboring in pain" metaphor in 8:22 also alludes to the concept of the messianic woes, or "birth pangs of the messiah," even though that idea is not attested earlier than Paul. Although the phrase "birth pangs of the messiah"

33. For a summary of the range of scholarly opinions on this verse, see Hahne, *Corruption and Redemption of Creation*, 186–90. There is disagreement about whether "the one who subjected it" refers to God, Adam or Satan. On my reading, the implied subject is God, who actually curses the earth, although Adam is ultimately to blame for the earth's subjection.

34. See my discussion of Sir 40:1 in "The Human Body and the Earth," 36–37. There, I cite Claus Westermann's opinion that a title originally belonging to the earth has been transferred to Eve in Gen 3:20, in his *Genesis 1-11: A Commentary*, trans. John R. Scullion (Minneapolis: Augsburg, 1984), 268.

(חבלו של משיח/חבלי משיח) occurs for the first time in rabbinic literature,[35] already in the Markan apocalypse, the "signs of the end" are designated "the beginning of the birth pangs" (ἀρχὴ ὠδίνων, Mark 13:8//Matt 24:8). Similarly, John 16:21–22 compares the disciples' pain while awaiting the *parousia* to a woman's childbirth pangs, and childbirth pain is a metaphor for eschatological crisis in 1 Enoch 62:4 and 1QH^{a} 11:7–18.[36] The "until now" (ἄχρι τοῦ νῦν) of 8:22 refers back to the eschatological "present moment" (τοῦ νῦν καιροῦ) of 8:18; in other words, the metaphor of "groaning in labor" describes a moment of crisis immediately preceding the turning point of the eschatological drama—in this case, the *parousia.*[37]

Resurrection

The first maternal metaphor concerning the earth in 4 Ezra, 4:40–42 is associated with the resurrection of the dead. The language in those verses of "giving back" the dead is also found in the description of the resurrection in 4 Ezra 7:32: "And the earth shall give back those who are asleep in it, and the dust those who rest in it, and the treasuries shall give up the souls which have been committed to them." As Richard Bauckham has shown, the language of the earth or underworld "giving back" or "returning" (*n-t-l* G-stem or *p-n-y* C-stem in the Syriac of 4 Ezra and 2 Baruch) the dead is quite widespread in Jewish apocalyptic literature, as well as in later Christian and Jewish texts.[38] He suggests that the tradition originated from an interpretation of the end of Isaiah 26:19, וארץ רפאים תפיל, understood to mean "the earth will give birth to the shades" (cf. the usage of נפל in Isa 26:18). Nevertheless, most of the examples he cites do not use birth imagery, but rather a legal metaphor of the earth returning something entrusted to it, perhaps based on a different understanding of Isaiah 26:19.[39] The common element in most of the examples is that the dead are "received" and held in trust by the earth until such time as

35. *Mek.* Vayassa' VI (ed. Lauterbach, 245); *b. Sanh.* 98b; *b. Šabb.* 118a; *b. Pesaḥ.* 118a; *b. Ket.* 111a. I am grateful to my colleague Sarit Kattan Gribetz for these references.
36. See Claudia D. Bergmann, *Childbirth as a Metaphor for Crisis: Evidence from the Ancient Near East, the Hebrew Bible, and 1QH XI, 1–18* (Berlin: de Gruyter, 2008).
37. Käsemann, *Commentary on Romans*, 236.
38. Richard Bauckham, "Resurrection as Giving Back the Dead" in *The Fate of the Dead: Studies on the Jewish and Christian Apocalypses* (Leiden: Brill, 1998), 269–89. He includes the following instances of the motif: 1 Enoch 51:1; 4 Ezra 7:32 (and 4:40–42); Rev 20:13; 2 Baruch 21:23, 42:8 and 50:2; LAB 3:10 and 33:3; Apoc. Pet. 4:3–4, 10–12; Tertullian, *Res.* 32:1; Midr. Psalms 1:20; Song Rab. 2:1:2; Pirqe R. El. 34; Pesiq. Rab. 21:4; b. Sanh. 92a.
39. Bauckham,"Resurrection as Giving Back the Dead," 277–78. The only one of his examples, besides 4 Ezra 4:40–42, that represents the earth "giving back" the dead as analogous to giving birth is the tradition found in b. Sanh. 92a (and also in b. Ber. 15b): "R. Tabi said in R. Josia's name: What is meant by: [*Three things are never satisfied . . .*] *Sheol and the barren womb [and the earth that is not filled by water]* (Prov. 30:16)—what connection has Sheol with the womb? [The verse is meant] to teach you: just as the womb receives and brings forth, so Sheol too receives and brings forth (כניס ומוציאם). Now, does this not furnish us with an argument a fortiori? If the womb, which receives in silence (בחושאי), brings forth amid cries (בקולות), then Sheol, which receives the dead amid cries, will much more so bring them forth amid great cries (בקולי קולות). This refutes those who maintain that resurrection does not appear in the Torah (אין תחית המיתים מן התורה)." Translation by Ishay Rosen-Zvi, in *Demonic Desires:* Yetzer Ha-Ra *and the Problem of Evil in Late Antiquity* (Philadelphia: University of Pennsylvania Press, 2011), 93.

God requires them back. That is, the earth (or Sheol) is the secondary agent of the resurrection, subject to the will of God, while the dead (whether conceived of as unitary or as separated bodies and souls being reunited in the resurrection) are the passive objects "received" and "given back" by the earth.

Thus, in light of the association of the earth with toil and mortality/corruption (based on Gen 3:17–19), I read "the redemption of our bodies" (ἀπολύτρωσις τοῦ σώματος ἡμῶν) in 8:23 as a reference to future bodily resurrection (which Paul mentions in 8:11), alluding to the motif of God's reclaiming of the dead from the earth. The noun ἀπολύτρωσις and verb ἀπολυτρόω are most often used of the manumission or redemption (in the sense of buying back) of slaves and prisoners in the Greco-Roman world; the verb occurs once in that meaning in the LXX (Exod 21:8) and the noun once, for the release of King Nebuchadnezzar from his madness (Dan 4:34).[40] Rather than understanding this phrase to mean "redemption *from* the body," as some have, I understand Paul to be anticipating the emancipation of the whole "body" of creation, human and non-human, from "slavery to corruption" (8:21).[41] The earth is both the symbol and the implied agent of the "slavery to corruption" from which our bodies will be redeemed (8:23). Although Paul understands resurrection somewhat differently from the Jewish sources that employ the legal metaphor of the earth receiving and giving back the dead, I think his choice of the word "redemption" in 8:23 is informed by that metaphor.

A related understanding of resurrection, not discussed by Bauckham, is found in Targum Neofiti's rendering of Genesis 3:19: "By the sweat of (before) your face you shall eat bread until you return to the earth(עד מחזרך לארעא) , for out of it you were created(ארום מנה אתברית) . For you are dust and to dust you shall return (ארום עפר את ולעפרא את עתיד חזר) and from the dust you shall return and rise and give account and reckoning for all that you have done (ומן עפרא את עתיד חזר וקאם ויהב דין וחושבן על כל מה דעבדת)."[42] Here, extrapolating from the concept of death as a return to the earth in Genesis 3:19, resurrection is conceptualized as a simple reversal of burial, without any active involvement of the earth. Just as "returning to dust" is an inherent property of human bodies, the Targum presents "returning from the dust" on judgment day as natural and inevitable. This is clearly an apocalyptic reinterpretation of Genesis 3:19, in the sense that it roots an important feature of apocalyptic eschatology in protology. Paul makes a

40. Fitzmyer, *Romans*, 122. He points out that the simple forms λύτρον, λύτρωσις and λυτρόω are much more common in the LXX to translate the nominal and verbal forms of גאל, which basically means to buy back.

41. This is Beker's understanding of the phrase (*Paul the Apostle*, 181), which many recent commentaries support (e.g., Jewett, *Romans*, 519; Byrne, *Romans*, 263). But none of them explain the use of the term "redemption" in light of the motif of the earth holding bodies in trust for God.

42. The Targum Pseudo-Jonathan is similar, but adds at the end: "on the Day of the Great Judgment." See Harry Sysling, *Tehiyyat Ha-Metim: The Resurrection of the Dead in the Palestinian Targums of the Pentateuch and Parallel Traditions in Classical Rabbinic Literature*, TSAJ 57 (Tübingen: Mohr Siebeck, 1996), 68–70.

similar argument for the inevitability of resurrection in Romans 6:1–11, although for him, its inevitability is rooted in the Christ-event.

In Romans 6, Paul interprets baptism—being submerged under water and brought back up to the air—as symbolic of death and resurrection. He argues first that those who have been baptized into Christ were baptized into his death (6:3) and buried with him (6:4). The first implication of this understanding of baptism is that the baptized must consider themselves dead to sin (6:2), since their "old self" has been crucified with Christ (6:6). The life that the baptized are now living is a "new life" in Christ (6:4). The second implication is that since Christ rose from the dead, the baptized must also share in his resurrection (6:5). Just as they must inevitably come up from under the water in baptism, participation in Christ's death and burial through baptism inevitably implies participation in his resurrection. Paul's understanding of baptism is a perfect example of his already-not yet eschatology, since while the life of the baptized is radically changed by being freed from sin (6:6–7), the fulfillment of the promise of sharing in Christ's resurrection is still in the future: "But if we have died with Christ, we believe (πιστεύομεν) that we will also live with him (συζήσομεν αὐτῳ)" (6:8). Although the future tense does not necessarily point to the eschatological future, the verb πιστεύομεν indicates something Paul and his audience must have faith in, because it belongs to the eschatological future (cf. 1 Thess 4:14).[43]

Whereas Paul seems to be speaking in Romans 6 about resurrection as an eschatological reward in itself, in the Jewish apocalypses, resurrection is always preliminary to the final judgment. The assumption is that dead are raised in order to be judged, and subsequently rewarded or punished. Elsewhere in Romans, Paul hints at a similar association of resurrection with the final judgment, but without the same uncertainty about the outcome of the judgment. For example, in 5:8–9, Paul argues that because Christ "died for us while we were still sinners," now that the believers have been justified by his death, they will all the more certainly be saved through him "from the wrath." "The wrath" refers to the eschatological judgment (see next section), and the association with resurrection comes in the next verse: "For if as enemies we were reconciled to God through the death of his son, how much more, having been reconciled, will we be saved in (or by) his life (σωθησόμεθα ἐν τῇ ζωῇ αὐτοῦ)" (5:10, my translation). The fact that "his life" is associated with a future verb while his death is clearly in the past suggests that it refers to his resurrection (cf. 2 Cor 4:10–12), which although already in the past for Christ, holds the promise of future salvation for those who believe in him.[44] Similarly, in Romans 14:9, Paul refers to Christ's resurrection and the future general resurrection: "For to this end

43. Jewett, *Romans*, 406. As Käsemann (*Commentary on Romans*, 169) puts it, "We have yet to participate in the resurrection even though its power already rules us and sets us in the new walk."
44. Käsemann, *Commentary on Romans*, 139.

Christ died and lived [again] (ἀπέθανεν καὶ ἔζησεν), that he might be Lord (κυριεύσῃ) of both the dead and the living." In the very next verse, he returns to the main topic of 14:1–13, judgment, announcing "For we will all stand before the judgment seat of God" (14:10). Hence, there appears to be a residual association between resurrection and the final judgment in Romans, even though Paul sometimes presents resurrection as a reward in itself.

Judgment

The concept of divine judgment is complex in Romans. When Paul is looking backward, he traces the origin of divine judgment to Adam's sin (5:12–21) and sees the suffering and futility of the present world as the result of divine judgment (8:20). From the perspective of Paul's "eschatological present," however, the death and resurrection of Christ have already put an end to the power of sin and death. On the contrary, the Christ-event revealed "the wrath of God" (1:18), so judgment is ongoing in the eschatological present. Paul still looks forward to a final judgment that will bring to completion the cosmic "triumph of God."[45] The function of "the law" in divine judgment is one of the most vexed questions in the interpretation of Romans (and of Paul's thought in general).

Jewish apocalyptic literature is far from uniform in its thinking about the origins of human sin and divine judgment. The Enochic literature, which takes the Flood as its paradigm for divine judgment, lays a good deal of the blame for the sin and corruption that the Flood was intended to wipe away on the Watchers and their offspring, the giants. Although human beings certainly share the responsibility for evil in the world in the Enochic tradition, the story of Adam and Eve, although known (1 Enoch 32:6), is not used to reflect on the problem of human sin and divine judgment. In this respect, Paul is more similar to 4 Ezra and 2 Baruch, both of which place a great deal of emphasis on the sin of Adam, though they draw different conclusions from it. As noted above, the judgment of creation appears to be linked to the sin of Adam in 4 Ezra 7:11–12, similar to Romans 8:20. Paul's claim in Romans 5:12 that "sin came into the world through one man, and death came through sin, and so death spread to all because all have sinned" finds its closest parallels in 4 Ezra and 2 Baruch. Both of these apocalypses consider death, both Adam's own and that of his descendants, to be punishment for Adam's sin (4 Ezra 3:7, 21; 2 Baruch 17:2–3, 54:15). Both use the same expostulation, "Oh Adam, what have you done?" (4 Ezra 7:118; 2 Baruch 48:42) to comment on the consequences for all humanity of Adam's sin.[46]

45. I borrow the phrase "the triumph of God" from J. Christiaan Beker.

46. Matthias Henze explains the close verbal parallels between 2 Baruch and 4 Ezra as the result of interaction between the authors at the earliest stage of their composition, quite possibly an oral phase. See his *Jewish Apocalypticism in Late First Century Israel: Rereading*

Neither of these apocalypses anticipates the Christian doctrine of original sin, however. Second Baruch is clear that Adam's sin did not cause anyone else to sin (2 Baruch 54:15, 19):

> [15]For even though Adam was first to sin and brought death upon all who were not in his time but rather [upon all] those who were born of him, each one of them has prepared for himself the torment to come, and furthermore, each of them has chosen for himself the praises to come. . . . [19]Adam is therefore not the cause, except for himself, but each of us has become our own Adam.

Some scholars have read this statement in 2 Baruch as a rejoinder to 4 Ezra, which seems, at times, to pin the blame on Adam for Israel's inability to keep the commandments (4 Ezra 3:20–22; cf. 7:118):

> [20]Yet thou didst not take away from them their evil heart, so that thy Torah might bring forth fruit in them. [21]For the first Adam, burdened with an evil heart, transgressed and was overcome, as were also all who were descended from him. [22]Thus the disease became permanent; the Torah was in the people's heart along with the evil root, but what was good departed, and the evil remained.

What Ezra is actually arguing here is that God is responsible for the failure of his people to keep the commandments, because God created Adam (representative of humankind) with an "evil heart." Uriel does not dispute that a tendency to evil is inherent in the human heart (4:30), but he argues people are nevertheless responsible for their own failures (7:72–73):

> [72]For this reason, therefore, those who dwell on earth shall be tormented, because though they had understanding they committed iniquity, and though they received the commandments they did not keep them, and though they obtained the law, they dealt unfaithfully with what they received. [73]What, then, will they have to say in judgment, or how will they answer in the last times?

Uriel simply universalizes the experience of Israel here, treating "receiving the law" as equivalent to "having understanding" about what is right and wrong.

For Paul, the inevitable cycle of sin, judgment, and death that was inaugurated by Adam has been broken by the death and resurrection of Christ (Rom 5:15–21). Nevertheless, judgment still has an important role in Paul's eschatology in Romans. Divine judgment in both the past and future senses is closely related to the "wrath of God" that is being revealed in the present, according to 1:18. This becomes clear in the opening verses of chapter 2, which turn the tables on the implied reader or imaginary interlocutor, who might have assumed that the condemnation in 1:18–32 applied only to Gentiles. Now, it is the presumably Jewish interlocutor who is "without excuse" (cf. 1:20), because "in judging another you condemn yourself" (2:1, my translation). The climax of this diatribe is 2:5: "In your hardness and impenitence of heart, you are

Second Baruch in Context, TSAJ 142 (Tübingen: Mohr Siebeck, 2011), 148–86, esp. 166–70 on the "Oh Adam, what have you done?" parallel.

storing up wrath for yourself on the day of wrath and of the revelation of God's righteous judgment (ἐν ἡμέρᾳ ὀργῆς καὶ ἀποκαλύψεως δικαιοκρισίας τοῦ θεοῦ, my translation). Once again, we have an already-not-yet situation regarding the revelation of God's wrath; it has already been revealed in the light of the death and resurrection of Christ, but it will be more fully revealed on the Day of Judgment.

Paul's subsequent description of the final judgment starts out with a noncontroversial sapiential aphorism: "For [God] will repay according to each one's deeds . . ." (2:6; cf. Prov 24:12b; LXX Ps 61:13b).[47] The way in which he elaborates this idea in the next several verses (2:7–11) has a much more apocalyptic flavor to it, however. The specific emphasis on the universal scope, individualism, and impartiality of divine judgment recalls Uriel's arguments in the dialogues of 4 Ezra; like Uriel, Paul has removed "the principle of judgment by works from its native covenantal context."[48] That is, he insists that Jews and Gentiles alike will be judged as individuals, based on their good or evil deeds, "for God shows no partiality" (Rom 2:9–11). He denies that possession of the Torah confers any advantage on Israel (2:12–16). Similarly, Uriel, in the third dialogue of 4 Ezra, takes a hard line on the final judgment, repeatedly denying Ezra's appeals for divine mercy on Israel.[49] Instead, he universalizes Moses's exhortation to Israel in Deuteronomy 30:19 (4 Ezra 7:127–29):

> 127This is the meaning of the contest which every man who is born on earth wages, 128that if he is defeated he shall suffer what you have said, but if he is victorious he shall receive what I have said. 129For this is the way of which Moses, while he was alive, spoke to the people, saying, "Choose for yourself life, that you may live!

The question of Paul's understanding of the law in Romans, especially Romans 7, is too large and disputed to address adequately here. But in 2:12–16, Paul struggles with one aspect of the question, which can perhaps be illuminated by a comparison with the apocalypses I have been focusing on—4 Ezra and 2 Baruch. Paul's initial question here is: will the Jewish people, as "hearers of the law," have any advantage over gentiles in the final judgment, because of their covenantal relationship with God? His answer is an unequivocal "no"; only "doers of the law will be justified" (2:13). But that answer raises a more difficult question: on what basis can gentiles be justified, given that they have not received the Torah? Paul's answer in 2:14, that some gentiles do "matters of the law" (τὰ τοῦ νόμου) "by nature" (φύσει) and hence "are a law unto themselves" (ἑαυτοῖς εἰσιν νόμος) has given rise to a debate about whether Paul has a theory of natural law.[50] Even if he does not have a fully worked out theory, he has a more developed

47. Jewett, *Romans*, 204.
48. Longenecker, *Eschatology and the Covenant*, 184–85.
49. E.g., 4 Ezra 7:33–34, 112–15; 8:1–3, 37–41. See my discussion of the issue of divine justice and mercy in *Theologies in Conflict*, 143–50.
50. For the positions of various scholars on this question, see Fitzmyer, *Romans*, 306.

answer to the question of the justification of non-Jews than can be found in any of the Jewish apocalypses: the consciences of gentiles bear witness to "the work of the law written on their hearts" (τὸ ἔργον τοῦ νόμου γραπτὸν ἐν ταῖς καρδίαις αὐτῶν), as will apparently be revealed on the Day of Judgment (2:15–16, my translation).[51]

Nevertheless, it is worth noting that Ezra does raise the possibility of observance of the commandments by non-Jews in the opening speech of the first dialogue in 4 Ezra: "When have the inhabitants of the earth not sinned in thy sight? Or what nation has kept thy commandments so well [as Israel]? Thou mayest indeed find individual men who have kept thy commandments, but nations thou wilt not find" (3:35–36). Ezra is not truly concerned with the question of how a non-Jew can keep the commandments or be saved, but rather with what he perceives as an impossible standard by which his own people have been judged by God. Some of Uriel's responses, quoted above, have implications for the question of how gentiles will fare in the final judgment, however. In 4 Ezra 7:127–29, he extends Moses's challenge to the Israelites to "Choose life!" to "every man who is born on earth." In 7:72–73, he implies that anyone who "had understanding" and committed iniquity is like someone who received the commandments and did not keep them. Second Baruch similarly equates receiving the Torah and having understanding: "It is right that man would not understand my judgment, had he not received the Torah and had I not instructed him in understanding. Now, however, since he transgressed knowingly, therefore he will also be tormented knowingly" (2 Baruch 15:5–6; cf. 48:40). All the descendants of Adam are also responsible for their own fates in the judgment in 2 Baruch 54:15. Both 4 Ezra and 2 Baruch are speaking from the perspective of someone who has received the Torah, whereas Paul in Romans 2:14–16 is putting himself in the shoes of someone who has not received the Torah, but still knows what it requires, thanks to conscience. Despite their different perspectives, these authors are all struggling with the idea of a universal final judgment based on a divine law to which not all people have equal access.

Glory

The final eschatological theme to be examined in this chapter is glory (δόξα), which is something of a *Leitwort* in Romans.[52] This term occurs in several different senses in Romans (and in Paul's letters in general), a diversity of usage which mirrors that of early Jewish literature in general. Two of the most common uses are not immediately pertinent to eschatology. First, there is the formulaic usage "the Lord/God of glory" and similarly "the throne of his glory"

51. I am less inclined than I once was to see Uriel's concept of Torah as including something similar to a theory of natural law, as I argued in "The Meanings of *tôrâ* in *4 Ezra*," *JSJ* 38 (2007): 330–52, esp. 542–44.

52. See Sprinkle, "Afterlife in Romans," 212nn41–42, for a list of all occurrences and an attempt at defining the different senses in which Paul uses the term.

(found especially in the Parables of Enoch), where glory is more or less synonymous with divinity, or the visible manifestation of divinity, the בוד יהוה of the Priestly source and Ezekiel. This is probably the sense of "glory" in its first occurrence in Romans, "They exchanged the glory of the immortal God for images resembling a mortal human being or birds or four-footed animals or reptiles" (1:23).[53] A second and related use of glory is as a divine attribute that people ascribe to God in the context of praise, as in "to him be the glory forever. Amen" (Rom 11:36; cf. 4:20), or for the sake of which they behave in a manner pleasing to God, as in "Welcome one another, therefore, just as Christ has welcomed you, for the glory of God" (Rom 15:7). Neither of these usages will be explored here, beyond noting the obvious—that glory is first and foremost a divine quality, not a human one.

Nevertheless, many Jewish apocalyptic texts hold out the promise of sharing in the divine glory, or at least the glory of the angels, as an eschatological reward. For the Qumran sectarians, participating in angelic glory was possible for the righteous not only as a reward after the final judgment, but even to a certain extent in the present, through liturgy.[54] This partially realized eschatology at Qumran was founded on a theological anthropology that held up "all the glory of Adam" as a reward that was attainable by "the perfect of way."[55] According to 4Q504 8 4, "Adam our father" was created "in the likeness of [God's] glory," and elsewhere in the same text, Israel is said to have been created "for [God's] glory" (4Q504 1–2 iii 2–4). Since the Qumran community identified themselves as the true Israel, Crispin Fletcher-Louis thinks that they believed "that it was their vocation to fulfill the responsibility originally given to Adam to embody God's own Glory."[56]

Paul's eschatological use of "glory" in Romans differs significantly from the Qumran usage examined by Fletcher-Louis. Nowhere does he mention angels in connection with glory, nor is Adam associated with glory. On the contrary, Adam stands for sin, death, and corruption (especially in Rom 5:12–21), while glory is associated with divine immortality (1:23).[57] Although some have seen an allusion to the fall of Adam in Romans 3:23, "for all have sinned and fall short of the glory of God," it is eisegetical to introduce the notion of the "glory of Adam" into that verse.[58] Rather, Paul is commenting on the present condition of all humanity as lacking a share in God's glory, without explicitly attributing this situation to the fall of Adam, and certainly

53. Fitzmyer, *Romans,* 283.

54. See Crispin H. T. Fletcher-Louis, *All the Glory of Adam: Liturgical Anthropology in the Dead Sea Scrolls*, STDJ 42 (Leiden: Brill, 2002).

55. 1QS 4:22–23. The phrase "all the glory of Adam" is also found in $1QH^a$ 4:14–15 and CD 3:19–20; the phrase "all the inheritance of Adam" is used in a similar way in 4Q171 3:1–2. See Fletcher-Louis, *All the Glory of Adam,* 88–135.

56. Fletcher-Louis, *All the Glory of Adam,* 97.

57. Sprinkle, "Afterlife in Romans," 231–32.

58. Fitzmyer, *Romans,* 347. Sprinkle believes that the Qumranic phrase "all the glory of Adam" "would have been foreign to Paul's theological vocabulary" ("Afterlife in Romans," 232n105.) Byrne (*Romans,* 130–31), by contrast, sees an allusion here to the "motif of loss of the primeval glory in the Jewish apocalyptic tradition."

without claiming that Adam possessed God's glory before his fall. Instead, Paul holds out the eschatological promise of partaking in the glory of the resurrected Christ at the time of the *parousia*.

This idea is introduced in Romans 8:17b, "if we now suffer with him in order also to be glorified with him (εἴπερ συμπάσχομεν ἵνα καὶ συνδοξασθῶμεν)." The next few verses, 8:18–23, twice use "glory" in an eschatological sense, illuminating what Paul means by being "glorified with" Christ. "The glory about to be revealed to us" in 8:18 probably refers to the glory of Christ, which will be revealed at the *parousia,* as will the "children (lit., sons) of God" (8:19).[59] That these children of God, the believers, will at that time come to share Christ's glory is confirmed in 8:21b, "the freedom of the glory of the children of God." The mechanism for this acquisition of glory is spelled out in 8:23, which equates "adoption as sons" (υἱοθεσία) with "the redemption of our bodies," which, I argued above, is a reference to resurrection. Although the word "glory" is not used in 8:29, it also helps to explicate the connection between being children of God and sharing in Christ's glory: "For those whom he foreknew he also predestined to be conformed to the image of his Son (συμμόρφους τῆς εἰκόνος τοῦ υἱοῦ αὐτοῦ), in order that he might be the firstborn within a large family (lit., among many brothers)."[60] The following verse (8:30) connects the idea of predestination, via a *sorites,* with glorification: "And those whom he predestined he also called; and those whom he called he also justified; and those whom he justified he also glorified." All of these verses taken together suggest that at the *parousia,* believers will be physically transformed into images of the glory of Christ (cf. 1 Cor 15:49, 51–52).[61] That God will ultimately "glorify" (δοξάζω, 8:30) human beings in Christ's image is an ironic reversal of the human refusal to glorify God (1:21) and their willingness to exchange God's glory for images of mortal creatures (1:23).[62]

The above interpretation of Romans 8:17 as introducing a description of a transformation of the children of God at the time of the *parousia* in 8:18–30 is supported by the use of "glory" in eschatological contexts in 4 Ezra and 2 Baruch. In the description of the experiences of the souls of the ungodly and the righteous after death in 4 Ezra 7:78–101, the term "glory" appears five times. As soon as the soul of a person leaves his or her body, it "adores the glory of the Most High" (7:78). Those who have not kept the laws of the Most High "wither with fear since they see the glory of the Most High, before whom they sinned now while they were alive, and before whom they are to be judged in the last times" (7:87), while those who have kept his laws "see with great joy the glory of him who receives them, for they shall have rest in seven orders"

59. Sprinkle, "Afterlife in Romans," 216–18.
60. See Brendan Byrne, *"Sons of God"—"Seed of Abraham": A Study of the Idea of the Sonship of God of All Christians in Paul against the Jewish Background,* AnBib 83 (Rome: Biblical Institute, 1979), 111–27.
61. Sprinkle, "Afterlife in Romans," 215.
62. Byrne, *Romans,* 263.

(7:91). While the first three mentions of glory in this passage establish it as a divine attribute, the latter part of the description of the "seven orders" of rest for the righteous looks forward to "the glory which awaits them in the last days" (7:95). The sixth order is "when it is shown to them how their face is to shine like the sun, and how they are to be made like the light of the stars, being incorruptible from then on" (7:97), and the seventh is confident joy, "for they hasten to behold the face of him whom they served in life and from whom they are to receive their reward when glorified" (7:98). Thus, although "glory" remains primarily a divine quality in 4 Ezra, this passage on the afterlife reveals that the righteous will partake in it in the last days.

Similarly, in 2 Baruch, "glory" is primarily ascribed to God, and once to Zion (11:1), but there is a lengthy description of the general resurrection (50:1–52:7) in which the terms "glory" and "glorify" are extended to the righteous.[63] Interestingly, in 2 Baruch, the resurrection of the righteous and their glorification are not simultaneous, but rather the earth will return the dead "while not changing anything in their form" (50:2), in order that they may be recognized, by one another and by the living (50:3–4). After the judgment day has passed, "the pride of those who are guilty will be changed, and also the glory of those who are righteous" (51:1). The nature of this "change" in the righteous is expounded in 51:3:

> Also, as for the glory of those who are now righteous in my Torah, those who have had understanding in their lives, and those who have planted in their heart the root of wisdom—then their splendor will be glorified through transformations: the shape of their faces will be turned into the light of their beauty, so that they will be able to acquire and receive the world that does not die, which was then promised to them.

A little further on, the glorification of the righteous is described further: "For on the summits of that world they will live, and they will be like the angels, and they will be deemed equal to the stars. They will change themselves into any shape they wish, from comeliness into beauty and from light into glorious splendor" (51:10). Significantly, 2 Baruch does not say that the righteous will be transformed into angels; rather, they will be "more excellent than the angels" (52:12). Further, although Paradise "will be spread out before them" (51:11), there is no mention of the righteous regaining the "glory of Adam." In 2 Baruch and in 4 Ezra, as in Romans, Adam is associated with sin, corruption, and death, not with glory.

In 2 Baruch 50–51, the sequence of eschatological events is very clear: first resurrection (50:2–3), then judgment (50:4), then glorification of the righteous (51:1–3). In 4 Ezra, it is less clear, because glorification is discussed in a separate context from the main description of the

63. There is one other passage in 2 Baruch associating the righteous with glory: in 2 Baruch 15:7–8, contrasting the present world with the world to come, the world to come is said to be for the sake of the righteous, for whom it will be "a crown in great glory."

resurrection and final judgment, in 7:26–44. The only glory that is mentioned there is "the glory of the Most High, by which all shall see what has been determined for them" (7:42). Similarly, in Romans, glorification is discussed most clearly in 8:18–30, where there is an implication of resurrection in 8:23 but no mention of judgment.

The main discussion of judgment in Romans 2 contains two mentions of glory, however, both referring to the eschatological reward of the righteous. In 2:7, those who do good are said to strive for "glory and honor and immortality" (*δόξαν καὶ τιμὴν καὶ ἀφθαρσίαν*); since their reward is simply "eternal life" (*ζωὴν αἰώνιον*), the three goals should probably not be distinguished from one another. Rather, they collectively refer to salvation, the goal of Christian existence, as does the similar trio "glory and honor and peace" in 2:10.[64] Similarly, in 5:2, "we boast in our hope of sharing the glory of God" probably means nothing more specific than the hope of salvation (cf. 5:10–11). It is not until chapter 8 that Paul develops his particular understanding of eschatological glory as being "conformed to the image of his Son" (8:29–30). The one eschatological usage of "glory" subsequent to chapter 8, occurring twice in 9:23, probably has the more specific connotation of transformation into the image of Christ, since the description of the recipients of "the riches of his glory" as "objects (lit., vessels) of mercy whom he has prepared beforehand (*προητοίμασεν*) for glory" recalls the emphasis on predestination in 8:29–30.[65]

Paul's usage of "glory" in Romans thus builds upon a Jewish apocalyptic usage seen in 2 Baruch and 4 Ezra, which does not include the concept of "the glory of Adam" or understand the reward of the righteous as a return to a primal perfection of humankind before the Fall. Rather, "glory" in 2 Baruch and 4 Ezra entails a physical transformation that will render the righteous unrecognizable as themselves. They will resemble the "splendor of the angels" (2 Baruch 51:5) or the sun and the stars (4 Ezra 7:97, 125; cf. 2 Baruch 51:10). Paul, in Romans 8, adapts this Jewish apocalyptic notion of glorification to his Christology by imagining a transformation of believers at the *parousia* into images of the glory of the resurrected Christ.

Conclusion

Because of the centrality of the Christ-event to Paul's theology, it is easy to overlook the numerous ways in which Paul's revealed eschatology in Romans builds upon Jewish apocalyptic concepts. Although Romans lacks an extended description of the *parousia*, much of Paul's teaching in Romans has an eschatological orientation. The ultimate "triumph of God" is still in the future for Paul, even though the turning point of history has already come, with the death and resurrection of Christ. A comparison of Paul's treatment of four key themes of apocalyp-

64. Byrne, *Romans*, 86; Fitzmyer, *Romans*, 302–3.
65. Fitzmyer, *Romans*, 570; Sprinkle, "Afterlife in Romans," 228.

tic eschatology—creation, resurrection, judgment, and glory—shows some unexpected points of contact with Jewish apocalyptic literature, especially with the first-century CE apocalypses 4 Ezra and 2 Baruch. For example, the memorable image of "the whole creation . . . groaning and laboring in pain together until now" (Rom 8:22) draws on the *topos* of the maternal earth, which takes various forms in early Jewish texts, but is a central metaphor in 4 Ezra, where it is extended to the entire created world (5:48–55). The earth is associated with corruption and mortality in many early Jewish texts that interpret Genesis 3:17–19 (or Gen 3:16–20, since Eve is sometimes drawn into this association), but the earth nevertheless plays an active role in many depictions of the general resurrection. I argued that Paul's interpretation of baptism as burial and resurrection with Christ (Rom 6:1–11) and also his description of resurrection as "the redemption of our body" (8:23) are informed by Jewish apocalyptic understandings of the role of the earth in the resurrection. I showed that Paul's reflections on divine judgment, both as a past response to human sinfulness beginning with Adam and as an eschatological reckoning with the divine law, share many preoccupations with 4 Ezra and 2 Baruch, despite the crucial difference that the Christ-event makes for Paul. Finally, the eschatological sense of "glory" in Romans, especially in Romans 8, is apparently informed by Jewish apocalyptic expectations of the "glorification" of the righteous following the final judgment, even though for Paul, this glorification takes the particular form of being "conformed to the image" of the resurrected Christ (8:29–30).

While it would be a mistake to minimize the differences between Paul's revealed eschatology and that of even those Jewish apocalypses with which Romans has the most in common, 4 Ezra and 2 Baruch, it is important to recognize that Paul developed his distinctive theology and eschatology within a Jewish apocalyptic framework. A critical comparison of Romans to Jewish apocalyptic literature can therefore shed light on striking but puzzling images such as the whole creation groaning in labor (Rom 8:22), or complicate our understanding of a familiar phrase such as "the redemption of our body" (8:23), or a common term such as "glory." The interpreter's appreciation for the richness and complexity of Romans can only be deepened by extending a similarly receptive reading to Jewish apocalyptic literature.

8

The Mystery of God's Wisdom, the Parousia of a Messiah, and Visions of Heavenly Paradise

1 and 2 Corinthians in the Context of Jewish Apocalypticism

Matthew Goff

Introduction

The study of apocalypticism in the Pauline Epistles has been a major topic of New Testament scholarship for over one hundred years. While this scholarship is rich and varied, one recurring theme in this tradition is that apocalypticism in Paul centers on his proclamation of the *parousia* of the resurrected Christ as an unique and epoch-changing event, signaling God's ultimate victory over sin and death.[1] This act is itself understood as "apocalyptic."[2] A key problem is how Paul's apocalypticism should be understood in relation to the Jewish apocalyptic tradition. There is a *Tendenz* among scholars who specialize on Paul to compare his writings to Jewish apocalyptic literature to emphasize the difference between them. Judaism is conceptualized as

1. See, for example, J. Christiaan Beker, *Paul the Apostle: The Triumph of God in Life and Thought* (Philadelphia: Fortress Press, 1984), 204–8; idem, *Paul's Apocalyptic Gospel: The Coming Triumph of God* (Philadelphia: Fortress Press, 1982). Consult also J. Louis Martyn, "Epistemology at the Turn of the Ages: 2 Corinthians 5:16," in *Theological Issues in the Letters of Paul* (Edinburgh: T&T Clark, 1997), 87–110; R. Barry Matlock, *Unveiling the Apocalyptic Paul: Paul's Interpreters and the Rhetoric of Criticism*, JSNTSup 127 (Sheffield: Sheffield Academic Press, 1996).
2. Beker, *Paul the Apostle*, 205: "The cross, then, is the apocalyptic turning point of history."

having false dichotomies that Paul transcends. Beker, for example, understands Jewish apocalypticism as centered on a doctrine of two ages, an eschatological dualism that radically distinguishes the present age from the world to come—for Beker, the cross is the fulcrum point between the two epochs that also blurs the distinction between them, since the crucifixion took place in the past but anticipates the coming *parousia*.[3] However, as Stuckenbruck hon 1984as demonstrated, it is not clear that Judaism should be characterized as having a "two ages" doctrine.[4] The eschatological defeat of evil is often characterized not as a sharp break with history, but rather as one element of a larger divine plan that guides the unfolding of history, from creation to judgment, as in, for example, the Apocalypse of Weeks and the Animal Apocalypse.

De Boer's characterization of Jewish apocalypticism relies upon a distinction between two types of apocalyptic eschatology—a cosmological mode, in which the present is under the dominion of evil, supernatural powers that will be overthrown at the eschaton, and a "forensic" type in which the emphasis is not on evil cosmological powers but the individual and his personal struggle with sin.[5] Again, the Jewish context provides a dichotomy that Paul collapses.[6] This distinction is grounded in traditional debates about Paul, with Bultmann understanding Paul's eschatology as "forensic," while for Käsemann, it is "cosmological."[7] De Boer acknowledges that his two types of apocalyptic eschatology blend together in the Dead Sea Scrolls. This is especially clear in the Treatise on the Two Spirits (1QS 3:13–4:26), which situates the individual's struggle with sin against a cosmological struggle between light and darkness.[8] I do not think that de Boer perceives the full significance of his observation—his understanding of Paul's apocalypticism is rooted in scholarship that was written long before the scrolls were fully published. The scrolls problematized existing paradigms in Pauline scholarship but they nevertheless persist. Perhaps the emphasis on the return of Christ as a unique event hinders comparative analysis.

These realizations underscore the importance of interpreting Paul in the context of Jewish apocalypticism. This article does so, focusing on 1 and 2 Corinthians. The writings of Paul, a Diaspora Jew familiar with both Judaism and the broader Hellenistic world, are complex and betray the influence of various cultural and literary traditions. These include not only Jewish apocalypticism, but also the wisdom tradition, exegetical traditions, and Stoic philosophy.

3. Ibid., 211.
4. Loren T. Stuckenbruck, "Overlapping Ages at Qumran and 'Apocalyptic' in Pauline Theology," in, *The Dead Sea Scrolls and Pauline Literature*, ed. J.-S. Rey, STDJ 102 (Leiden: Brill, 2014), 309–26.
5. He points to Testament of Moses 10 as an example of the former and 2 Baruch and 4 Ezra as examples of the latter type. See Martinus C. De Boer, "Paul and Apocalyptic Eschatology," in *The Encyclopedia of Apocalypticism*, ed. J. J. Collins; B. McGinn, and S. Stein, 3 vols. (New York: Continuum, 2000), 1.345–83 (359). Consult also idem, "Paul and Jewish Apocalyptic Eschatology," in *Apocalyptic and the New Testament: Essays in Honor of J. Louis Martyn*, eds. J. Marcus and M. L. Soards, JSNTSup 24 (Sheffield: JSOT, 1989), 169–90.
6. So also Leander E. Keck, "Paul and Apocalyptic Theology," *Int* 38 (1984): 229–41 (235).
7. De Boer, "Paul and Apocalyptic Eschatology," 361.
8. Ibid., 360.

When the focus is placed on 1 and 2 Corinthians in relation to Jewish apocalyptic literature, the overall impression is not one of Paul's radical break from this tradition but his continuity with it. This is evident in terms of the centrality of the motif of receiving and transmitting supernatural revelation, described with "mystery" terminology (1 Corinthians 1–4), the arrival of a messiah who ushers in the resurrection of the faithful (1 Corinthians 15), and the apostle's claims of a visionary ascent to the heavens (2 Corinthians 12). The fact that Paul understood the messiah to have already arrived and been crucified certainly changes the eschatological timetable when compared to Jewish writings, but the basic scenario, in which a messianic figure inaugurates the eschatological defeat of evil and the bestowal of eternal life to the righteous, is found in both Paul and Jewish apocalypticism. The parallels are even stronger, not surprisingly, when the apostle is examined in relation to Jewish apocalypses that are virtually contemporary, especially 2 Baruch (late-first century CE).

Jewish Apocalypticism

Our understanding of ancient Jewish apocalypticism has improved considerably over the past generation. This is true with regard to both primary and secondary sources. In terms of primary sources, many texts of the Dead Sea Scrolls were not published until the 1990s or even later. This horde brought to light the oldest available manuscripts of Jewish apocalypses, spurring extensive interest in this material.[9] This also led to renewed appreciation of numerous other Jewish apocalyptic texts that date roughly to this period that were already available, including 2 Baruch, the Apocalypse of Abraham, and the Parables of Enoch (1 Enoch 37–71). These developments have made it easier to discern the prominence of apocalyptic elements in the letters of Paul and the New Testament in general. Because of the Dead Sea Scrolls, the Judaism at the turn of the common era can be re-envisioned as a religion in which apocalypticism was dominant in diverse and significant ways.

With regard to secondary sources, John Collins's *The Apocalyptic Imagination* has exerted enormous influence since its publication in 1984 on how people understand apocalyptic literature, and continues to do so.[10] He proposes a form-critical approach to the genre apocalypse, with texts identified as apocalypses because they attest an assemblage of various literary features, including but not limited to pseudepigraphic authorship, an *angelus interpres* (an angel who

9. These include 4Q201 and 4Q208, Aramaic manuscripts, respectively, of the Book of the Watchers (1 Enoch 1–36) and the Astronomical Book (1 Enoch 72–82). These compositions are dated to the third century BCE. See Józef T. Milik, *The Books of Enoch: Aramaic Fragments of Qumrân Cave 4* (Oxford: Clarendon, 1976).

10. John J. Collins, *The Apocalyptic Imagination: An Introduction to Jewish Apocalyptic Literature*, 2nd ed. (Grand Rapids: Eerdmans, 1998). See also Lorenzo DiTommaso, "Apocalypses and Apocalypticism in Antiquity. (Part I)," *CurBR* 5, no. 2 (2007): 235–86; "Apocalypses and Apocalypticism in Antiquity. (Part II)," *CurBR* 5, no. 3 (2007): 367–432.

interprets the vision received by the visionary), the eschatological destruction of the wicked, and resurrection.[11]

Collins stresses that at the core of the apocalypses is a claim of divine revelation.[12] According to his well-known definition of the genre apocalypse, it constitutes a type of "revelatory literature with a narrative framework."[13] A person purports to have received knowledge from a heavenly source, such as a vision or interaction with angelic beings. The word "apocalypse" itself stresses this theme, derived from the Greek ἀποκαλύπτω, which literally means "to uncover."

While the apocalypses often are eschatological, this is not always the case. The earliest representatives of this genre, the Book of the Watchers and the Astronomical Book of 1 Enoch (third century BCE), are not primarily eschatological.[14] While these works have eschatological elements (e.g., 1 Enoch 10, 80), their main focus is the dissemination of knowledge about, respectively, the nature of the world at the time of the flood and the regular motion of the moon and sun. Moreover, highly eschatological apocalypses, such as Daniel and Revelation, illustrate the importance of the theme of revelation, since their eschatological content is revealed to a visionary by a heavenly source.

1 Corinthians: Worldly Strife and Heavenly Mysteries

First Corinthians is a lengthy example of broader exchange of correspondence between Paul and a community of Corinth. He probably wrote 1 Corinthians in the mid-50s CE in the city of Ephesus (16:8).[15] According to 1 Corinthians 1:11, Paul wrote this missive because he learned of a report from "Chloe's people" that described the Corinthian community as beset with divisions and quarrels (cf. 5:1). Paul seeks for this group to be "united in the same mind and the same purpose" in their devotion to Christ (1:10).

Paul claims to have himself received some form of divine revelation, presumably a vision of the resurrected Christ (15:3–8; cf. Acts 9:1–9). He uses forms of the word ἀποκαλύπτω when describing what was disclosed to him (1 Cor 1:7; Gal 1:12; 2 Thess 1:7). He, in turn, transmits these disclosures to his students. Paul encourages the Corinthians to move beyond the human or worldly issues that divide them and be united in their comprehension of the spiritual truth

11. Collins, *Apocalyptic Imagination*, 7.
12. So also Christopher Rowland, *The Open Heaven: A Study of Apocalyptic in Judaism and Early* Christianity (New York: Crossroad, 1982), 70.
13. Collins, *Apocalyptic Imagination*, 5.
14. There are also numerous texts that are eschatological but not apocalypses, such as the post-exilic prophetic writings of Joel or Isaiah 24–27.
15. Hans Conzelmann, *First Corinthians: A Commentary on the First Epistle to the Corinthians*, Hermeneia (Minneapolis: Fortress Press, 1988), 4.

that he has disclosed to them (e.g., 3:3–8; 6:12–20). He claims to give them a "mystery."[16] This is particularly evident in chapters 1–4. Paul offers to them "God's wisdom, secret and hidden (literally 'wisdom hidden in mystery'), which God decreed before the ages for our glory" (2:7). He also writes that one should "think of us in this way, as servants of Christ and stewards of God's mysteries" (οἰκονόμους μυστηρίων θεοῦ; 4:1). The "mystery" is a supernatural, transcendent reality that Paul has made known to the Corinthians. He conveys to them knowledge of God's wisdom, a comprehensive, deterministic divine scheme which guides the unfolding of history and creation, presented as a revealed "mystery" (2:1; 3:19).

Paul's focus on understanding mysteries at the beginning of 1 Corinthians helps establish the theological horizon against which the rest of the letter should be understood. Such language is also significant at the end of the letter: "Listen I will tell you a mystery! We will not all die but we will all be changed" (15:51).[17] Mystery language in a sense forms an *inclusio* for 1 Corinthians as a whole.

Pedagogical Mysteries in 1 Corinthians and the Dead Sea Scrolls

It used to be commonplace to understand the mystery language in Paul in terms of Hellenistic mystery cults.[18] Raymond Brown argued in the late 1960s that Qumran texts demonstrate that Paul's mystery terminology reflects his "Semitic background" and should be primarily interpreted in terms of Second Temple Judaism.[19] This perspective makes sense. The term רז (*rāz*) is employed frequently in the Dead Sea Scrolls to signify revealed knowledge, much like *mysterion* in Paul. The *Habakkuk Pesher*, for example, claims that God has revealed to the Teacher of Righteousness, a leading figure for the Qumran sect, "all the mysteries of the words of his servants, the prophets" (1QpHab 7:5; cf. 1QH[a] 9:21; 10:13; CD 3:18). The Qumran scrolls also establish that the term "mystery" signifies supernatural revelation in the apocalypses. The Aramaic version of 1 Enoch 106:19, for example, reads: "I know the mysteries of (רזי) <of the Lord> that the holy ones have revealed and shown to me" (4Q204 5 ii 26–27).[20] The Aramaic section of Daniel (chs. 2–7) employs this term extensively to denote supernatural knowledge. In Daniel 2, the word signifies God's revelation to Daniel of Nebuchadnezzar's dream and its interpretation (2:18–19,

16. Compare Eph 3:3–4, in which Paul claims to have received a mystery through revelation and in turn attempts to give the Ephesians an understanding of the "mystery of Christ." See also Rom 11:25; 16:25; Eph 6:19; Col 1:26–27; 2:2; 4:3. Consult Markus N. A. Bockmuehl, *Revelation and Mystery in Ancient Judaism and Pauline Christianity*, WUNT II/36 (Tübingen: J. C. B. Mohr [Paul Siebeck], 1990), 158–63.

17. First Corinthians 15 is discussed below. In 1 Cor 14:2, he describes speaking in tongues as speaking in mysteries (cf. 13:2).

18. For the history of scholarship on this issue, see Benjamin Gladd, *Revealing the Mysterion: The Use of Mystery in Daniel and Second Temple Judaism with its Bearing on First Corinthians*, BZNW 160 (Berlin: Walter de Gruyter, 2008), 8–16.

19. Raymond E. Brown, *The Semitic Background of the Term "Mystery" in the New Testament*, FBBS 21 (Philadelphia: Fortress Press, 1968).

20. For this reconstruction, see George W. E. Nickelsburg, *1 Enoch: A Commentary on the Book of 1 Enoch, Chapters 1-36, 81-108*, Hermeneia (Minneapolis: Fortress Press, 2001), 537. Cf. 4QEn[a] 1 iv 5 (1 Enoch 8:3).

27–30, 47 [2x]; 4:6). In the apocalypses Daniel and 1 Enoch, "mystery" (*rāz*) denotes esoteric knowledge from heaven to which a privileged visionary has access. Paul uses the Greek *mysterion* in a similar way.

The mystery language of Paul can be better understood through the publication of a Qumran text published in 1999 entitled 4QInstruction (1Q26; 4Q415–418, 423).[21] This work was written in Hebrew by a teacher to his students, called *mebinim* ("the ones who understand"), during the second century BCE. The *mebin* (typically addressed in the singular) has a form of elect status (4Q418 81 4–5). He is repeatedly asked to study the רז נהיה. This is an enigmatic phrase that can be translated "the mystery that is to be." The "mystery" was revealed previously to the student (4Q416 2 iii 18; 4Q418 123 ii 4). He can learn knowledge on many topics through the contemplation of this mystery, such as the knowledge of good and evil and the fates of people during the eschatological judgment (4Q417 1 i 8; 4Q417 2 i 10–11). The mystery that is to be is associated with the nature of history.[22] God created the world by means of this mystery (4Q417 1 i 8–9). The mystery that is to be signifies a divine deterministic plan, according to which history and creation are orchestrated.

The use of mystery terminology and the theme of revelation are somewhat different in 4QInstruction from what one typically finds in the apocalypses. The *rāz* in this Qumran text is not associated with the revelation of one particular issue, as in Daniel 2 (the disclosure of the king's dream). The רז נהיה constitutes a more comprehensive revelation about the nature of reality, as created by God. The mystery that is to be is also inextricably mingled with the pedagogy of 4QInstruction. The heavenly revelation does not itself provide knowledge; this comes, as the teacher incessantly reminds the student, from reflection and contemplation of the mystery that is to be. This is quite different from the apocalypses, in which a seer receives a cryptic vision that is then explained to him by an angel (e.g., Daniel 7; 4 Ezra 11–12). The *mebin* of 4QInstruction has no *angelus interpres* to guide him; he has to figure out the meaning of the mystery that is to be himself. The text likely represents a strand of the sapiential tradition that is characterized by extensive influence from the apocalyptic tradition.[23] This would help explain 4QInstruction's distinctive focus on the study of supernatural revelation.

The mystery that is to be in 4QInstruction offers an instructive parallel to the *mysterion* language of 1 Corinthians. The Corinthians, like the *mebin* of 4QInstruction, have mysteries revealed to them. Also, like this Qumran text, the *mysterion* they are given constitutes not a revelation regarding one particular issue, but rather a more general insight into God's dominion

21. Matthew J. Goff, *4QInstruction*, WLAW 2 (Atlanta: Society of Biblical Literature, 2013).

22. In 4Q417 1 i 3–4, for example, the mystery that is to be is linked to the past, present and future: "what exists, what has existed" and "what will be" (cf. 4Q418 123 ii 3–4). See Goff, *4QInstruction*, 144–47.

23. Goff, *4QInstruction*, 22.

over history and creation. First Corinthians includes neither a symbolic vision nor *angelus interpres*, in contrast to the apocalypses. Like the *mebin* of 4QInstruction, the Corinthians are students whose spiritual progress depends upon their comprehension of the mysteries conveyed to them by their teacher Paul. Understanding such mysteries requires his guidance. He compares the Corinthians to "fleshly" (i.e., worldly) infants to whom he feeds milk so that they may become "spiritual" (heavenly) adults (1 Cor 3:1–2; cf. 4:20). Both 4QInstruction and 1 Corinthians attest an engaging combination of pedagogy and the revelation of heavenly knowledge. Scholars have observed that 1 Corinthians 1–4, in which mystery terminology is most prominent in the letter, may have been influenced by the wisdom tradition.[24] The apostle may have drawn from a strand of the sapiential tradition best represented by 4QInstruction.[25]

The *Parousia* of a Messiah: 1 Corinthians 15 in the Context of Second Temple Judaism

Paul believed that cataclysmic changes would soon take place that would transform the world. His first sustained discussion in 1 Corinthians of this topic is in chapter 7 (cf. 3:13; 4:5). The Corinthians wrote to the apostle for guidance on matters regarding sex and marriage (7:1). Paul wants them to put these "worldly" topics in their proper context, as part of a form of existence that will come to an end:

> I think that, in view of the impending crisis (τὴν ἐνεστῶσαν ἀνάγκην), it is well for you to remain as you are. Are you bound to a wife? Do not seek to be free. Are you free from a wife? Do not seek a wife . . . I mean, brothers, the appointed time has grown short; from now on, let even those who have wives be as though they had none. . . . For the present form of this world is passing away (7:26–31; cf. 10:11).

Paul provides a more extensive discussion of the issue in chapter 15. He envisions a final, dramatic moment: "We will not all die, but we will all be changed, in a moment, in the twinkling of an eye, at the last trumpet. For the trumpet will sound and we will be changed" (15:51; cf. 16:22; 1 Thess 4:16; 2 Cor 5:1–5).[26] Paul shows relatively little interest in the life of Jesus or his teachings. For Paul, the central issue is the death and resurrection of Christ. This, he argues, has inaugurated a transformation of the natural order, the unfolding of the full and unfettered

24. The word σοφία occurs sixteen times in this unit, but only three times elsewhere in Paul (Rom 11:23; 1 Cor 12:8; 2 Cor 1:12). See Hermann von Lips, *Weisheitliche Traditionen im Neuen Testament*, WMANT 64 (Neukirchen-Vluyn: Neukirchener, 1990), 318–55. Consult also Sigurd Grindheim, "Wisdom for the Perfect: Paul's Challenge to the Corinthian Church (1 Cor 2:6–16)," *JBL* 121 (2002): 689–709.
25. Both texts may also draw on common exegetical traditions regarding Genesis 1–3. See Matthew J. Goff, "Being Fleshly or Spiritual: Anthropological Reflection and Exegesis of Genesis 1–3 in 4QInstruction and 1 Corinthians," in *Christian Body, Christian Self: Concepts of Early Christian Personhood*, ed. C. Rothschild and T. Thompson, WUNT 284 (Tübingen: Mohr Siebeck, 2011), 41–59.
26. The trumpet he expects to hear is likely played by an angel (Matt 24:31; Rev 8:2–9:14; 11:5; 1QM 2:16–3:11).

sovereignty of God, unblemished by any evil power. Christ is "the first fruits of those who have died," utilizing an agricultural metaphor that evokes the initial produce gathered at the harvest (1 Cor 15:20, 23). The resurrection of Christ is the beginning of a paradigm—the resurrection of the faithful will replicate his own experience of resurrection (cf. Rom 6:4–11). Paul uses an Adam/Christ typology to make this point: "For since death came through a human being, the resurrection of the dead has also come through a human being" (15:21; cf. vv. 43–49; Rom 5:12–21).[27] Whereas God introduced death through Adam, he has established (eternal) life through Christ.

Christ is resurrected, "then at his coming (ἐν τῇ παρουσίᾳ αὐτοῦ) those who belong to Christ" (1 Cor 15:23). The *parousia* signifies the return of the resurrected Christ, who will inaugurate the resurrection of the faithful.[28] As Paul explains in 15:35–55, they are to lose their perishable bodies and receive imperishable ones. After this, "then comes the end (τὸ τέλος), when (ὅταν) he hands over the kingdom to God the Father, after (ὅταν) he has destroyed every ruler and every authority and power" (v. 24).[29] At some point before he returns control of the kingdom to God, Christ defeats the worldly rulers. While Paul's language denotes kings and potentates, the apostle envisions a more comprehensive overthrow of wickedness, sin, and even death (15:26, 54–55; cf. Rom 8:38; Eph 1:21). When exactly this overthrow is to take place is not stated in the letter. It was perhaps thought to take place at the *parousia* of Christ. This is suggested, for example, by 2 Thessalonians 2:8 (see further below).[30]

There are three stages to Paul's eschatological proclamation in 1 Corinthians 15. The first for him had already occurred, the resurrection of Christ. The second is his *parousia*, which includes the resurrection of the faithful and the defeat of the worldly powers. The third is the *telos*, the fulfillment of God's plan, the transmission of divine rule back from Christ to God, submitting himself to the deity's rule (15:28). Paul does not fill out the details, but at some point, Christ receives control over God's kingdom.[31] This means, although this is not stated explicitly in the letter, that the resurrected Christ becomes a king or at least some sort of representative of the heavenly kingdom (cf. Rev 20:4–6). First Corinthians does not assert clearly when Christ is to assume this exalted status. It may take place at his resurrection or his *parousia*.[32] After

27. Goff, "Being Fleshly or Spiritual," 52–58; Stephen Hultgren, "The Origin of Paul's Doctrine of The Two Adams in 1 Corinthians 15.45–49," *JSNT* 25 (2003): 343–70.

28. For the *parousia* and its delay, see Jörg Frey, "New Testament Eschatology—an Introduction: Classical Issues, Disputed Themes, and Current Perspectives," in *Eschatology of the New Testament and Some Related Documents*, ed. J. G. van der Watt, WUNT II/315 (Tübingen: Mohr Siebeck, 2011), 3–32 (25–26).

29. In this verse, the second ὅταν class is subordinate to the first and thus translated "after." See Conzelmann, *First Corinthians*, 271.

30. "And then the lawless one will be revealed, whom the Lord will destroy with the breath of this mouth, annihilating him by the manifestation of his coming (τῆς παρουσίας αὐτοῦ)" (cf. 2:1; 1 Thess 4:15).

31. The kingdom of God is a prominent trope elsewhere in Paul: 1 Cor 4:20; 6:9–10; 15:50; Rom 14:17; Gal 5:21; Eph 5:15; 1 Thess 2:12.

32. See further below. De Boer, "Paul and Apocalyptic Eschatology," 377–78, engages the same problem.

Christ returns the kingdom to God, the dominion of his heavenly kingdom is exerted fully in the world.

The eschatological scenario in 1 Corinthians 15 is profitably interpreted in terms of Jewish apocalypses that are roughly contemporary with Paul—the Parables of Enoch, 4 Ezra and 2 Baruch, all of which are dated to the late-first century CE. The Parables is an important witness to Danielic traditions in this period. In Daniel 7, the ferocious fourth beast, who is explicitly identified as a worldly kingdom (the Seleucid Empire), is judged and destroyed by God, who sits on his heavenly throne attended by myriads of angels (vv. 25–27). Then "one like a son of man" descends from the clouds to earth, where he is given kingship. The sovereignty of the kingdom of heaven is reestablished on earth, with the one who descended understood as a heavenly representative of God's rule.[33]

In the Parables of Enoch, eschatological judgment is not implemented by God in heaven but by the Son of Man, understood as the title of a messianic figure, unlike Daniel 7 itself, who sits on a throne on earth (1 Enoch 46:2–3; cf. 61:8; 69:29). According to 1 Enoch 62:2, he will implement the eschatological destruction of the wicked: "And the word of his mouth will slay all the sinners, and all the unrighteous will perish from his presence" (cf. 46:4; 48:8). The Son of Man will overthrow kings and worldly powers: "all the kings and the mighty and the exalted and those who rule the land will fall on their faces in his presence" (62:9). The scenario inaugurated by this figure includes a cataclysmic transformation of the earth, in which the "mountains will leap like rams" and there will be a resurrection of the dead (51:1, 4). Those saved are called the righteous and chosen, establishing a correspondence between them and the messianic Son of Man, who is also called the Righteous and Chosen One.[34] The iteration of Danielic traditions in the Parables is closer to 1 Corinthians 15 than Daniel 7. In the Pauline text, like in the Parables, the messianic figure exerts divine dominion on earth. In both, the messiah overthrows the worldly powers, which represent not simply actual kings but wickedness more generally, as an obstacle to God's unfettered dominion over the earth.

There may be a reflex of Danielic tradition, as in the Parables, in the apostle's use of the term *parousia* in 1 Corinthians 15:23.[35] This is not explicit in this verse or elsewhere in the letter. However, elsewhere in the New Testament, this term has an explicitly Danielic resonance. Matthew 24:27 reads: "For as the lightning comes from the east and flashes as far to the west, so will be the coming of the Son of Man (ἡ παρουσία τοῦ υἱοῦ τοῦ ἀνθρώπου)" (cf. vv. 3, 37,

33. This was probably originally a reference to the archangel Michael. See John J. Collins, *Daniel: A Commentary on the Book of Daniel*, Hermeneia (Minneapolis: Fortress Press, 1993), 310.

34. George W. E. Nickelsburg, *1 Enoch 2: A Commentary on the Book of 1 Enoch, Chapters 37–82*, Hermeneia. (Minneapolis: Fortress Press, 2012), 44. See also John J. Collins, *The Scepter and the Star: Messianism in Light of the Dead Sea Scrolls*, 2nd ed. (Grand Rapids: Eerdmans, 2010), 196–205.

35. Maurice Casey, *Son of Man: The Interpretation and Influence of Daniel 7* (London: SPCK, 1979), 152.

39). This terminology patently relies upon Daniel 7, as does this figure's descent to earth on clouds.[36] This transformative moment is punctuated with a trumpet blast, not unlike 1 Corinthians 15:51.

Interpreting the *parousia* of Christ envisioned in 1 Corinthians 15 as the descent of the Son of Man (an expression admittedly never found in the letters of Paul), understood as a messianic figure who implements God's judgment, would help explain why Paul presents the resurrected Christ as the descent of a heavenly being who overthrows earthly kings. This would also make intelligible why 1 Corinthians describes Christ as a representative of God's kingdom. This may also suggest an answer to an issue left unclear in 1 Corinthians itself—when Christ assumed control of the kingdom that he returns to God in 15:24: not when he was resurrected, but rather when the resurrected Christ descends from heaven to judge, as does the Son of Man in the Parables.

In 4 Ezra, the emergence of a messianic figure also inaugurates an eschatological scenario.[37] According to chapter 7, a city shall appear, most likely a reference to the heavenly Jerusalem (v. 26). This shall happen when the messiah is revealed, a statement that implies he is preexistent and hidden, to emerge at a certain point, a theme expressed more clearly elsewhere in the book (12:32; 13:26, 52). Four hundred years afterwards, he is to die, although this may be a later Christian addition to the text (7:29), and then, after seven days of primeval silence, "the world that is not yet awake shall be roused and that which is corruptible shall perish. The earth shall give up those who are asleep in it and the dust those who rest there in silence. . . . The Most High shall be revealed on the seat of judgment" (4 Ezra 7:31–33).[38]

Both 4 Ezra and 1 Corinthians 15 assert that a major cataclysm will end the present form of this world. The righteous shall be resurrected and the wicked shall be destroyed. In both texts, the advent of a messiah signals that these events are to unfold, but what the messiah actually does during this cataclysmic period is unclear, at least in 4 Ezra 7. There, God, not a messiah, judges humankind from his throne, although a messiah carries out this function in 12:32–33. First Corinthians 15, likewise, states that a messianic figure destroys the wicked, as do other early Jewish texts (e.g., 4Q174 1 i 7–8; 11Q13 2 13).

Second Baruch, a work closely related to 4 Ezra, envisages a scenario that is even closer to that of 1 Corinthians 15.[39] This work includes an exposition on the nature of the coming tribu-

36. Adela Yarbro Collins, "The Influence of Daniel on the New Testament," in Collins, *Daniel*, 90–99.

37. For the messianism of 4 Ezra, see Michael E. Stone, *Fourth Ezra: A Commentary on the Book of Fourth Ezra*, Hermeneia (Minneapolis: Fortress Press, 1990), 207–13.

38. Collins, *Apocalyptic Imagination*, 203.

39. Ibid., 212–25; Matthias Henze, "'Then the Messiah will begin to be revealed': Resurrection and the Apocalyptic Drama in 1 Corinthians 15 and Second Baruch 29–30, 49–51," in *Anthropologie und Ethik im Frühjudentum und im Neuen Testament. Wechselseitige Wahrnehmungen. Internationales Symposium in Verbindung mit dem Projekt Corpus Judaeo-Hellenisticum Novi Testamenti (CJNHT) 17.–20. Mai 2012, Heidelberg*, ed. M. Konradt and E. Schläpfer, WUNT 322 (Tübingen: Mohr Siebeck, 2014), 441–62. In this volume, also see

lation (2 Baruch 26–30). The coming cataclysm, which is periodized into twelve units (ch. 27), will signal the advent of the messiah:

> That which will happen at that time bears upon the whole earth. Therefore, all who live will notice it. For at that time I shall only protect those found in this land at this time. And it will happen that when all that which should come to pass in these parts has been accomplished, the Anointed One will begin to be revealed (29:1–3).

The earth will become incredibly bountiful in terms of agricultural produce, a yield only enjoyed by the righteous of Israel. Everyone else has been destroyed. In 2 Baruch 29, the arrival of a messiah triggers these events but he himself appears to play a passive role. The expression "will begin to be revealed" suggests he existed prior to this moment, to emerge at the beginning of the eschatological scenario.

The importance of the messiah becomes clearer in chapter 30: "And it will happen after these things when the time of the appearance of the anointed one has been fulfilled and he returns with glory that then all who sleep in hope of him will rise" (v. 1; cf. 50:1). The term for "appearance" is *mʾtytʾ*. This term corresponds in the Syriac New Testament to the Greek *parousia*.[40] Second Baruch proclaims the *parousia* of a messiah. The phrase "the appearance of the anointed one has been fulfilled" is likely in parallelism with the one that follows, "he returns with glory"—two different ways of saying that the messiah, after he initially appeared shall reemerge upon the earth in a new and powerful way.[41] The return of the messiah is associated not with a universal resurrection of the dead, but rather only of those who had "hope in him." The most immediate antecedent of this last pronoun ("him") is not God but the anointed one. Elsewhere, the text discusses the physical transformation of the righteous at this moment.[42]

Second Baruch lays out a form of messianic expectation that is strikingly similar to that of 1 Corinthians 15. In both texts, the eschatological scenario begins with an initial phase associated with the appearance of a messiah. This is then followed by a second stage defined by his *parousia*, at which the resurrection shall take place, for those who had some sort of devotion to this figure. Also, both texts envision not simply a physical resurrection but present this as the ultimate exaltation of the righteous, who assume a heavenly, eternal form of existence. First Corinthians 15 is, however, more explicit than 2 Baruch 29–30 that the messiah shall assume a

Samuel Vollenwieder, "Auferstehung als Verwandlung. Die paulinische Eschatologie von 1Kor 15 im Vergleich mit der syrischen Baruchapokalypse (2Bar)," 463–90. Consult also Matthias Henze, *Jewish Apocalypticism in Late First Century Israel: Reading Second Baruch in Context*, TSAJ 142 (Tübingen: Mohr Siebeck, 2011), 324–39.

40. Henze, "Then the Messiah will begin to be revealed," 451.

41. It is not fully clear in the text where the messiah went, to return to this world. See Henze, ibid., 452.

42. 2 Baruch 51:3: "the glory of those who proved to be righteous on account of my law . . . their splendor will then be glorified by transformations, and the shape of their face will be changed into the light of their beauty so that they may acquire and receive the undying world which is promised to them."

form of heavenly kingship on earth, at which time he vanquishes the wicked. Elsewhere, however, 2 Baruch claims that the messiah is to have dominion on earth and defeat powerful rulers, not unlike 1 Corinthians 15:25 (39:7–40:1).

Comparison with 2 Baruch, 4 Ezra, and the Parables of Enoch helps clarify the oft made claim that 1 Corinthians 15 should be understood in terms of Jewish apocalypticism. The Jewish texts do not establish a false dichotomy that Paul transforms. It is primarily not an issue of Paul's Jewish "heritage" or "background." Rather, apocalypticism was, during Paul's life, a vibrant and creative complex of traditions that numerous Jews appropriated when composing apocalyptic writings. Paul did not transcend this cultural process. He was a participant in it. He turned to contemporary Jewish apocalyptic traditions to understand the death of Jesus. Jewish apocalypses of the first century CE, especially 2 Baruch, help explain why Paul, like other followers of Jesus, thought that the resurrected Christ would return in glory to resurrect the righteous and give them eternal life.

Was Paul Wary of Lustful Angels? 1 Corinthians 11:10 and the Watchers Myth

In terms of understanding 1 Corinthians vis-à-vis Jewish apocalypticism, one other issue merits discussion. It is often thought that chapter 11 alludes to the watchers myth of the Book of the Watchers.[43] In 11:2–16, Paul offers a much debated discussion of proper head coverings for the men and women of the Corinthian community. The key verse is 1 Corinthians 11:10: "For this reason a woman ought to have a symbol of authority on her head because of the angels (διὰ τοὺς ἀγγέλους)." The authority to which this verse refers denotes some sort of head covering. Paul asserts that a woman should cover her head when praying or prophesying, and that a veil or growing the hair long would suffice (11:6, 15). Whose authority is signified by the woman's covering is unclear.[44] It could refer to the authority that she demonstrates when taking part in worship, or it may denote that of the man over the woman.[45] The authority at issue is related to the social hierarchy of the genders. This is evident in the initial phrase "For this reason" of 1 Corinthians 11:10, which refers to what it immediately precedes: "Neither was man created for the sake of woman but woman for the sake of man" (v. 9), alluding to the creation of Eve

43. For an overview of the critical issues and scholarly discussion of this passage, see Loren T. Stuckenbruck, "Why Should Women Cover Their Heads Because of the Angels? (1 Corinthians 11:10)," in *The Myth of Rebellious Angels: Studies in Second Temple Judaism and New Testament Texts*, WUNT 335 (Tübingen: Mohr Siebeck, 2014). See also Scott M. Lewis, "'Because of the Angels': Paul and the Enochic Traditions," in *The Watchers in Jewish and Christian Traditions*, eds. A. Kim Harkins, K. Coblentz Bautch and J. C. Endres (Minneapolis: Fortress Press, 2014), 81–90; Jason D. DeBuhn, "'Because of the Angels': Unveiling Paul's Anthropology in 1 Corinthians 11," *JBL* 118 (1999): 295–320.

44. The precise meaning of "authority" in this verse is much debated. For an overview of common critical interpretations, see Stuckenbruck, "Why Should Women Cover Their Heads," 214–15.

45. Lewis, "Because of the Angels," 83.

for Adam in Genesis 2:18–24. While 1 Corinthians 11:10 is ambiguous, the woman's wearing of a head covering prevents her from being disgraced and ensures that her participation in worship is in harmony with the social order.

The members of the Dead Sea sect understood themselves to be in fellowship with the angels in the context of worship, praying, as it were, shoulder to shoulder with them (e.g., $1QH^a$ 11:21–23).[46] As Fitzmyer observed in the 1950s, the claim in 1 Corinthians 11:10 that a woman should cover her head "because of the angels" appears to likewise understand worship as taking place with angels (cf. 4:9).[47] First Corinthians 11:3 homologizes a gender hierarchy with a theological one: "Christ is the head of every man, and the husband (man; ἀνήρ) is the head of his wife (woman; γυναικός), and God is the head of Christ" (cf. 14:34–35). The social hierarchy of the genders (man over woman) is reinforced by superiority of God. This suggests that in 1 Corinthians 11:10, how women should pray amidst the angels is to reflect the overarching gender hierarchy advocated by Paul. This is quite in contrast to Galatians 3:28, which claims that participation in Christ transcends gender. First Corinthians 11:10 presents the female gender as somehow threatening or disturbing the community's liturgical communion with the angels, and her head covering mitigates this destructive potential.

The angels may disrupt their fellowship with the Corinthians as well. This is how appeal to Enochic tradition comes into play. So understood, the women's covering protects them from sexual advances from angels. The covering should thus be understood as signaling the woman's modesty, a strategy for her to avoid enticing male desire. If one thinks of the angels as similar to those of the Enochic Book of the Watchers, such concerns are fully warranted. This interpretation has a venerable history, found in early commentators on 1 Corinthians such as Tertullian.[48]

It is not clear, however, that an Enochic reading of 1 Corinthians 11:10 is warranted. It is not necessary to turn to the watchers myth to make sense of the passage. Paul's undisputed letters contain no unambiguous appeal to Enochic texts or traditions. First Corinthians stresses that women are to cover themselves during worship. Interaction between humans and angels in a

46. Björn Frennesson, *"In a Common Rejoicing": Liturgical Communion with Angels in Qumran*, SSU 14 (Uppsala: University of Uppsala Press, 1999).

47. Joseph A. Fitzmyer, "A Feature of Qumrân Angelology and the Angels of 1 Cor. xi.10," *NTS* 4 (1957–58): 48–58. This essay is also available, with a postscript from 1966, in his *Essays on the Semitic Background of the New Testament* (Grand Rapids: Eerdmans, 1997), 187–204. See also Henry J. Cadbury, "A Qumran Parallel to Paul," *HTR* 51 (1958): 1–2.

48. In *On the Veiling of Virgins* 7.2 he writes: "For if (it is) on account of the angels—those, to wit, whom we read of as having fallen from God and heaven on account of concupiscence after females—who can presume that it was bodies already defiled, and relics of human lust, which such angels yearned after, so as not rather to have been inflamed for virgins, whose bloom pleads an excuse for human lust likewise? For thus does Scripture withal suggest: 'And it came to pass', it says, 'when men had begun to grow more numerous upon the earth, there were withal daughters born to them; but the sons of God having descried the daughters of men, that they were fair, took to themselves wife of all whom they elected" (cf. Testament of Reuben 5:5). Cited from Lewis, "Because of the Angels," 89.

liturgical context is not an issue in 1 Enoch 6–11. In ancient Judaism, angels in general are not sexually threatening to women. In Enochic literature, this problem is restricted to a specific set of angels who went astray before the flood. They were punished and imprisoned, to await their ultimate destruction in final judgment (1 Enoch 10:4–15). If Paul had that myth in mind when he wrote to the Corinthians, those angels would have been unable to force themselves upon women.

In Watchers, the theme of male lust is important. The angels see from heaven the beautiful women and descend (1 Enoch 6:1–2). Paul does not emphasize that the head covering of women is necessary to hide female beauty from the male gaze. He compares a woman without such apparel to a female with a shaved head (1 Cor 11:5). A woman without the proper covering is, for Paul, disgraced and shamed—not a sight that will attract the sexual desire of males, angelic or human. A good analogy would not be the veiling of women in Islam and the justification for this practice in conservative circles that the veil is to curtail male lust.[49] It is not clear that 1 Corinthians 11:10 alludes to the Enochic watchers myth.[50]

Heavenly Ascension in 2 Corinthians

The interpretation of 2 Corinthians can also be enriched by comparison with Jewish apocalypticism. Second Corinthians 6:14–15, for example, attests a dualistic pairing of light and darkness, followed by one which opposes Christ and Belial. Belial is a supernatural figure of evil that appears repeatedly in Qumran texts with an apocalyptic perspective (e.g., 1QM 13:10–11; CD 5:18).[51] The combination of a Christ-Belial opposition with a light-darkness dyad suggests that Paul drew upon dualistic traditions found in the Treatise of the Two Spirits, which contrasts good and evil angelic forces, allied respectively with light and darkness (1QS 3:13–4:26).

The passage of the letter that resonates most powerfully with the Jewish apocalyptic tradition is 2 Corinthians 12:1–10.[52] The beginning of this pericope reads:

49. Such attitudes are often based on a passage of the Quran, which states that a woman should cover her beauty with garments so that it will not be seen by men, aside from her husband and male family members (24.31–32; cf. 33.59). See Leila Ahmed, *A Quiet Revolution: The Veil's Resurgence, from the Middle East to America* (New Haven: Yale University Press, 2011). I thank my colleague Adam Gaiser for these references.

50. The angels can nevertheless be understood as disruptive or even dangerous to the women of the Corinthian church. There is a long-standing Jewish tradition that being in the presence of the divine can be perilous, in particular to non-priests. Hagar, for example, expresses amazement that she has seen a heavenly being (the text is ambiguous as to whether it is God or an angel) and remains alive (Gen 16:9, 13; cf. 2 Sam 6:6–7). Standing directly before a divine presence could have easily been considered by Paul as a potentially hazardous act, for which women, whom he considers lower than men, in particular need protection. See Conzelmann, *First Corinthians*, 189.

51. Devorah Dimant, "Between Qumran Sectarian and Qumran Nonsectarian Texts: The Case of Belial and Mastema," in *History, Ideology and Bible Interpretation in the Dead Sea Scrolls*, FAT 90 (Tübingen: Mohr Siebeck, 2014), 135–51.

52. Albert Hogeterp, "The Otherworld and This World in 2 Cor 12:1–10 in Light of Early Jewish Apocalyptic Tradition," in *Other Worlds and Their Relation to This World: Early Jewish and Ancient Christian Traditions*, ed. T. Nicklas et al., JSJSup 143 (Leiden: Brill, 2010), 209–28; Christopher Rowland and Christopher R.A. Morray-Jones, *The Mystery of God: Early Jewish Mysticism and the New Testament*, CRINT 12 (Leiden: Brill, 2009), 379–408; Bockmuehl, *Revelation and Mystery*, 170–75.

> It is necessary to boast; nothing is to be gained by it, but I will go on to visions and revelations of the Lord (ὀπτασίας καὶ ἀποκαλύψεις κυρίου). I know a person in Christ who fourteen years ago was caught up to the third heaven—whether in the body or out of the body I do not know; God knows. And I know that such a person—whether in the body or out of the body I do not know; God knows—was caught up into paradise and heard things that are not to be told, that no mortal is permitted to repeat (2 Cor 12:1–4).

Paul claims that someone else had some sort of visionary experience. But it is clear that he is talking about himself (vv. 7–9). In 2 Corinthians 12:1, he uses the language of ἀποκάλυψις to signify the revelations he describes. This may refer to the "apocalypse" of Christ, some sort of vision in which he saw the resurrected Christ, that he mentions elsewhere (e.g., 1 Cor 15:8). Second Corinthians 12 may allude to a vision of the enthroned Christ in this heavenly realm. But he does not say this. Paul asserts that it is about the "third heaven" and "paradise" (more on these below), tropes that the Pauline corpus nowhere else treats in a substantive way. Paul is intentionally vague regarding the content of his vision.

The apostle twice uses the verb ἁρπάζω ("to be caught up") to describe the visionary experience (cf. Acts 8:39; 1 Thess 4:17).[53] This language suggests that he was seized and lifted to the heavenly world by angels. Paul describes a vision of heavenly ascent. This is also suggested by his elusive suggestion that he may have left his body (2 Cor 12:2–3). There is nothing about the vision that is eschatological, although elsewhere in the letter, he alludes to the dramatic event he describes in 1 Corinthians 15 (i.e., 2 Cor 5:1–5).

Second Corinthians clearly shows continuity with the apocalyptic tradition, in which visions from the heavenly world are critical. But the vision mentioned in this chapter is not simply of the sort often found in the apocalypses, in which a visionary is shown various cryptic images that are interpreted by an angel. Heavenly ascents are a major trope in one of the subtypes of the genre apocalypses distinguished by Collins—the "otherworldly journey," in which the visionary travels, often accompanied by angels, and is shown secrets about the heavenly world (e.g., 3 Baruch, Apocalypse of Abraham, 2 Enoch).[54]

The Jewish apocalypses contain several accounts of visionaries being lifted up to the heavens by angels. In 1 Enoch, this happens to Enoch repeatedly (e.g., 18:1–5; 72:1; 106:19). The beginning of the Apocalypse of Zephaniah, as preserved by Clement, describes an ascent that is similar to that of 2 Corinthians 12: "And a spirit took (ἀνέλαβέν) me and brought me up into the fifth heaven. And I saw angels who are called 'lords,' and the diadem was set upon them in the Holy Spirit and the throne of each of them was sevenfold more (brilliant) than the light of the rising sun" (*Strom.* 5.11.77.2).[55] This material supports the view that in the vision mentioned in

53. Hogeterp, "The Otherworld and This World," 217; Rowland and Morray-Jones, *Mystery of God*, 141.
54. Martha Himmelfarb, *Ascent to Heaven in Jewish and Christian Apocalypses* (New York: Oxford University Press, 1993).

2 Corinthians 12, Paul understood himself to have been seized by angels and taken to the heavenly world.

The Enochic literature is also relevant because it mingles the apocalyptic and mystical traditions.[56] Enoch is transformed by his ascent to the heavenly world. The disputed ending of the Parables of Enoch identifies Enoch as the Son of Man figure (1 Enoch 71:14). While this may be a secondary, later addition, a Jewish attempt to show that Enoch, not Jesus, is the Son of Man, the identification may be a consequence of Enoch's mystical transformation in heaven.[57] He is lifted up and placed before the Lord of Spirits (70:1). Before his presence, Enoch claims that "my flesh melted and my spirit was transformed" (71:11). Enoch's heavenly transformation is more extensive in 2 Enoch. When Enoch travels to the tenth heaven, his clothes are removed and he is given heavenly garb—an image Paul employs in 2 Corinthians 5:2—and anointed with oil (2 Enoch 21:7). Enoch realizes that he is changing: "And I looked at myself, and I had become like one of his glorious ones, and there was no observable difference" (v. 10). In 3 Enoch, the figure of Metatron, who has an exalted status in heaven, called "the Prince of the Divine Presence" and even "the Lesser Yahweh," is none other than the transformed Enoch (3 Enoch 4:3; 12:5).

Second Corinthians, like 2 Enoch and 3 Enoch, attest a combination of themes that resonate with the apocalyptic and mystical traditions of ancient Judaism.[58] This is evident not simply in Paul's claim of revelation that involves some sort of visionary glimpse of the heavenly world. The vision resonates with these Enochic texts in more specific ways. Paul states that the visionary was taken up to paradise and the third heaven (2 Cor 12:2, 4). In 2 Enoch, Enoch is shown ten heavens. Paradise, the ultimate abode of the righteous modeled after the garden of Eden, is in the third heaven.[59] In 3 Enoch, the visionary who ascends is not Enoch but Rabbi Ishmael. Enoch/Metatron is one of the rabbi's interlocutors in heaven who discloses divine knowledge to him. The goal of Ishmael's ascent is "to behold the vision of the chariot" (3 Enoch 1:1). Third Enoch not only attests and reworks traditions regarding Enoch found in older apocalyptic texts. The composition is an important witness to Merkavah mysticism, a religious tradi-

55. Gershom Scholem, *Jewish Gnosticism, Merkavah Mysticism and Talmudic Tradition* (New York: JTSA, 1960) 18–19.

56. Peter Schäfer, *Die Ursprünge der jüdischen Mystik* (Berlin: Insel Verlag, 2011), 449–50, 475; Ithamar Gruenwald, *From Apocalypticism to Gnosticism: Studies in Apocalypticism, Merkavah Mysticism and Gnosticism* (Frankfurt am. Main: Verlag Peter Lang, 1988), 142–43.

57. For this interpretation, see James C. VanderKam, "Righteous One, Messiah, Chosen One and Son of Man in 1 Enoch 37–71," in *The Messiah: Developments in Earliest Judaism and Christianity*, ed. J. H. Charlesworth (Minneapolis: Fortress Press, 1992), 169–91. Consult also Nickelsburg and VanderKam, *1 Enoch 2*, 326–32; Collins, *Apocalyptic Imagination*, 187–91.

58. So also Scholem, *Jewish Gnosticism*, 17. The fifth century *Cologne Mani Codex* likewise presents the vision of 2 Corinthians 12 as similar to the revelations of Enoch. This work, best known for its account of the early life of Mani, emphasizes Enoch and quotes material from an "Apocalypse of Enoch" that stresses that angels took him to heaven and showed him heavenly secrets. The text then immediately moves to Paul and stresses that he was likewise given revelation in the third heaven. The text appeals to both figures to argue that important apostles and prophets from the past, were recipients of revelation (58.1–62.17). See Ron Cameron, and Arthur J. Dewey, *The Cologne Mani Codex (P. Colon. inv. nr. 4780): Concerning the Origin of His Body* (Missoula: Scholars, 1979), 45–47.

59. 2 Enoch 8:1 A: "They brought me up to the third heaven. And they placed me in the midst of paradise" (cf. 9:1). The Greek Life of Adam and Eve (Apocalypse of Moses) also presents the third heaven as the location of paradise (37:5). See Hogeterp, "The Otherworld and This World," 220; Rowland and Morray-Jones, *Mystery of God*, 393–96.

tion that developed in late antiquity, according to which rabbis developed various theurgic and ecstatic techniques in order to acquire a glimpse of the "chariot," God on his heavenly throne.[60]

The exceptional claims made by Enoch in 2 Enoch and Rabbi Ishmael in 3 Enoch about what they saw in heaven helps explain why Paul is so reticent to describe what he saw in the third heaven. He asserts that the visionary saw what "no mortal is permitted to repeat" (2 Cor 12:4).[61] Such prohibitions are also found in Jewish mystical texts.[62] This reluctance speaks to the transcendent nature of the heavenly realities disclosed in the vision. Paul's reticence suggests that he considered it inappropriate to describe them, at least to the Corinthians.[63] In 1 Corinthians, he criticizes them for having a fleshly or worldly perspective (e.g., 3:1). Perhaps Paul did not think that they were ready to hear about the heavenly wonders he beheld.

Early Jewish literature contains an example of a person boasting about their affinity with the heavenly world. In one Qumran text, entitled the *Self-Glorification Hymn* (4Q491c), a person boasts of having had some sort of heavenly ascent that has changed him. He claims to be counted among the angels. He asserts in highly immodest language: "Who is comparable to me in my glory?" (l. 8). This transformative experience has also allowed him to bear sorrows and sufferings like no one else (l. 9).

The *Self-Glorification Hymn* is a good example of someone boasting about their direct interactions with the heavenly world. It is hard to take at face value Paul's claim that he is not boasting in a similar way. His indirect allusions to his incredible vision followed by his affirmation that he will not boast about it (2 Cor 12:6), conveys to his audience that his vision is very much worthy of such boasting but that Paul, the paragon of humility, chooses not to do so. Moreover, he then claims that, to avoid becoming too elated, he was given a thorn in the flesh and torments by Satan (v. 7). This suffering produces weakness and hardships, which he gladly boasts about (vv. 11–12). He, like the speaker in the *Self-Glorification Hymn*, connects his suffering to his ascent. Boasting was the context in which he brought up the vision in the first place (11:16–33; cf. 1:12; 7:14). Weakness (like foolishness) is, for Paul, not a bad thing but a sign of divine favor and affinity with the heavenly world (e.g., 1 Cor 1:25–27). Weakness and hardship thus become, paradoxically, compatible with a claim of heavenly ascent. Paul appeals to both motifs to bolster his own authority in the correspondence preserved within 2 Corinthians (e.g., 11:7; 12:11).

60. For an example of such techniques, see *Hekhalot Rabbati* (Schäfer §§204–5). Consult Rowland and Morray-Jones, *Mystery of God*, 235; Ra'anan Boustan, *From Martyr to Mystic: Rabbinic Martyrology and the Making of Merkavah Mysticism*, TSAJ 112 (Tübingen: Mohr Siebeck, 2005).

61. Contrast the Apocalypse of Paul of the Nag Hammadi library, in which Paul describes his ascent to the third heaven and then to even higher heavens, up to the seventh, recounting what he sees.

62. The famous rabbinic story about the four who entered paradise states that one is not permitted to speak about the *merkabah* with someone, unless that person is wise (*m. Ḥag* 2.1).

63. Compare the ending of the *Testament of Job*, where the daughters of Job are mystically transformed and begin to speak, but not in a language of this world but in "the angelic dialect" (48:3).

Conclusion

Collins's well-known definition of the apocalypse emphasizes that the revelation that is conveyed in a text belonging to this genre can be "temporal, insofar as it envisages eschatological salvation and spatial insofar as it involves another, supernatural world."[64] First Corinthians, with its emphasis on the *parousia*, resonates with the first point, and 2 Corinthians, and its allusions to the third heavens, with the second. Paul in these letters claims to have access to divine knowledge with regard to both history—particularly its end—and the cosmos. He lived at a time in which apocalypses were composed and the apocalyptic tradition was an important element of Judaism. There is no evidence that he wrote any apocalypses. But he nevertheless turned to this tradition to understand the death of Christ and his *parousia*. Pauline apocalypticism is not a radical transformation of Jewish apocalypticism but is, rather, in considerable continuity with it.

64. Collins, *Apocalyptic Imagination*, 5.

9

A Comparison of Paul's Letter to the Galatians with the Epistle of Enoch

James M. Scott

Introduction

In recent years, there have been several major attempts to interpret Paul's letter to the Galatians apocalyptically. Among them are J. Louis Martyn's commentary in the Anchor Bible series[1] and Martinus C. de Boer's commentary in The New Testament Library series.[2] Still more recently, N. T. Wright, in his two-volume *Paul and the Faithfulness of God*, has deplored all such efforts at an "apocalyptic" interpretation of Paul's letters.[3] Two of Wright's main critiques

1. J. Louis Martyn, *Galatians: A New Translation with Introduction and Commentary*, AB 33A (New York: Doubleday, 1997).
2. Martinus C. de Boer, *Galatians: A Commentary*, NTL (Louisville: Westminster John Knox, 2011). For the most recent commentary on the letter, see Douglas Moo, *Galatians*, BECNT (Grand Rapids: Baker Academic, 2013).
3. N. T. Wright, *Paul and the Faithfulness of God*, 2 vols., Christian Origins and the Question of God 4 (Minneapolis: Fortress Press, 2013). The rhetoric against the "apocalyptic" interpretation can become quite Pauline at points. For example, in the context of discussing his proposal that "one element in 'the problem of Galatia' may have been the social pressure of the newly burgeoning imperial ideology," and "that at least part of his polemic against 'another gospel' had to do with the 'gospel' of Caesar, then being assiduously propagated," Wright throws in yet another swipe at the "apocalyptic" interpretation: "This, obviously, would provide a radically different vision of the Galatian problem than any of the accounts that have been current in mainline scholarship. . . . And for Gala-

of the "apocalyptic" approach of Martyn and others have been: (1) their use of "apocalyptic" in a way that is unrecognizable from Jewish apocalyptic literature of the Second Temple period, and (2) their tendency to pit the "apocalyptic" interpretation against other categories of Pauline thinking (e.g., "salvation history"). To address these two perceived inadequacies, Wright espouses a covenantal approach that is not only thoroughly integrative, incorporating all sorts of categories that are generally regarded as mutually exclusive, but also more faithful to apocalypticism as it is actually found in early Jewish writings.

The purpose of the present chapter is not to enter into this debate as it has developed up to this point, pitting one abstract category (or set of categories) against another. Instead, in the limited space available to me here, I will attempt to answer a very simple, textually based question: How does Paul's letter to the Galatians compare with the Epistle of Enoch (1 Enoch 92–105)? The Epistle of Enoch (c. 170 BCE) is the last of the five Enochic books that together make up 1 Enoch, indisputably one of the most important Jewish "apocalyptic" writings of the Second Temple period. By proceeding directly to the comparison of Galatians with an actual "apocalyptic" text, we can bypass the usual, tortuous question of the definition of "apocalyptic"[4] and also avoid having to compare Galatians with whatever abstract definition of "apocalyptic" is deemed most feasible. Our argument is straightforward: If Galatians compares in some fundamental way to the "apocalyptic" Epistle of Enoch, then Galatians has a claim to being an "apocalyptic" writing as well. Admittedly, this does assume some sort of working definition of the term "apocalyptic" with regard to 1 Enoch. For this, as well as matters of text and interpretation of 1 Enoch in general, we are availing ourselves of the magisterial Hermeneia commentary on the corpus by George W. E. Nickelsburg.[5] What Nickelsburg considers to be "apocalyptic" in the Enochic corpus will form the pragmatic basis of our subsequent discussion on the comparison of the Epistle of Enoch with Galatians.

A few more words about method are in order here. First, any comparison between Galatians and the Epistle of Enoch is going to be somewhat lopsided by virtue of the relative sizes of

tians to acquire this kind of 'political' edge would sit well with the recent attempts to read the letter in terms of an 'apocalyptic' context—though, ironically, those who advocate such a thing, *wishing to make a good show in the scholarly flesh* [cf. Gal 6:12], do not themselves observe the terms of first-century 'apocalyptic' by recognizing its political meaning" (*Paul and the Faithfulness of God*, 2.1304–5 [emphasis mine]).

4. For an overview of the problem of definition, see, for example, Frederick J. Murphy, *Apocalypticism in the Bible and Its World: A Comprehensive Introduction* (Grand Rapids: Baker Academic, 2012), 1–26; David E. Aune, "Apocalyptic," in *The Westminster Dictionary of New Testament and Early Christian Literature and Rhetoric*, (Louisville: Westminster John Knox, 2003), 46–50.

5. George W. E. Nickelsburg, *1 Enoch 1: A Commentary on the Book of 1 Enoch, Chapters 1–36; 81–108*, Hermeneia (Minneapolis: Fortress Press, 2001); idem and James C. VanderKam, *1 Enoch 2: A Commentary on the Book of 1 Enoch, Chapters 37–82*, Hermeneia (Minneapolis: Fortress Press, 2012). Because of limitations of time and space, it was impossible to interact adequately with the important commentary by Loren T. Stuckenbruck, *1 Enoch 91–108*, CEJL (Berlin: de Gruyter, 2007). In any future work on the subject at hand, I would like to redress this shortcoming.

the compositions. Galatians constitutes only 2,220 words, whereas the Epistle is clearly much longer.[6]

Second, the two writings are quite distinctive in many respects, and those differences must be acknowledged and appreciated. The Epistle contains emphases that Galatians does not (e.g., the impending judgment that will deal fully and finally with the angelic rebellion that caused or contributed to human sin). By the same token, Galatians contains emphases that the Epistle does not (e.g., redemption through faith in Christ). Moreover, the Epistle is explicitly and implicitly based on the earlier parts of 1 Enoch (see further below), whereas Galatians stands alone and does not refer to any other Pauline correspondence.

Third, our goal here is primarily to compare Galatians and the Epistle of Enoch in terms of their similarities, recognizing, of course, that every comparison is also a contrast. Furthermore, any perceived similarity need not suggest a genetic relationship between the two writings; resemblance is not proof of influence. We are simply interested in exploring whether there may be an *analogy* between the two letters, and if so, how extensive that analogy may be. As is well known, Jonathan Z. Smith advocates this kind of comparative method, one that avoids the question of origins—the "genealogical argument" for dependence of one entity on another—opting instead for a more open-ended inquiry that lays entities side by side in order to explore their similarities and differences.[7] As we shall see, the application of this method to Galatians and the Epistle of Enoch will lead to new questions about each writing, and hence, to greater insight into the function and content of those writings.

The following discussion unfolds in two parts. In the first part, we compare Galatians and the Epistle of Enoch as letters, including their epistolary form, authorship, addressees, and salutation. In the second part, we compare the two writings in terms of the apocalyptic elements

6. A precise word count is impossible because of the complex text-critical situation. Cf. Nickelsburg, *1 Enoch 1*, 9–20.

7. Cf. Jonathan Z. Smith, *Drudgery Divine: On the Comparison of Early Christianities and the Religions of Late Antiquity* (Chicago: University of Chicago Press, 1990). Actually, Smith advocates a more complex method which goes beyond the practical limits of this short paper. See ibid., 51–52: "It is agreed that the statement 'x resembles y' is logically incomplete, for what is being asserted is not a question of the classification of species x and y as instances of a common genus, but rather a suppressed multi-term statement of analogy and difference capable of being properly expressed in formulations such as: 'x resembles y more than z with respect to. . . ;' or, 'x resembles y more than w resembles z with respect to. . . .' That is to say, the statement of comparison is never dyadic, but always triadic; there is always an implicit 'more than,' and there is always a 'with respect to.' [. . .] This is to say, comparison does not necessarily tell us how things 'are' (the far from lateen presupposition that lies behind the notion of the 'genealogical' with its quest for 'real' historical connections); like models and metaphors, comparison tells us how things might be conceived, how they might be 'redescribed,' in Max Black's useful term. A comparison is a disciplined exaggeration in the service of knowledge. It lifts out and strongly marks certain features within difference as being of possible intellectual significance, expressed in the rhetoric of their being 'like' in some stipulated fashion. Comparison provides the means by which *we* 're-vision' phenomena as *our* data in order to solve *our* theoretical problems." An example of such a method would be Nickelsburg, *1 Enoch 1*, 86–87: "The parallels [of the NT] with the Enochic tradition should be noted with caution. The Enochic authors posited some sort of *revealed law* as the touchstone for salvation in the judgment. Nonetheless, the NT notion parallels *1 Enoch* more closely than it does the Qumran community, where eschatological awareness did not involve a mission to the gentiles. The structural similarities between the Enochic and NT notions of eschatology and proclamation deserve closer study."

that both share, starting first and foremost with the function of the special revelation that the authors received.

Needless to say, comparing two substantial writings in terms of so many points in the course of a single chapter will require the interaction with the relevant secondary literature to be severely limited and to be confined primarily to the notes.

Comparisons between Galatians and the Epistle of Enoch as Letters

When Galatians and the Epistle of Enoch are compared as letters, we notice a number of interesting features that the two writings have in common. In the following section, we will compare the writings in terms of their epistolary form, and then, more specifically with respect to their superscriptions, adscriptions, and salutations.

Genre

Both Galatians and the Epistle of Enoch can be compared in terms of their genre as letters. Galatians is obviously a letter, and there is no dispute about that. It has, for example, the characteristic tripartite letter prescript: superscription (vv. 1–2a), adscription (v. 2b), and salutation (vv. 3–5).[8]

The epistolary character of the Epistle of Enoch (1 Enoch 92–105), however, has sometimes been questioned.[9] According to 100:6 and the subscript that appears after chapter 107 in the papyrus of these chapters, this work is designated as an ἐπιστολή or "letter." "As a whole," Nickelsburg argues, "the document imitates the genre of an epistle. . . ."[10] This will be seen in more detail as we work our way through the letter prescript.

Here, it should be noted that both Galatians and the Epistle of Enoch contain the author's self-conscious reference to his own writing as a letter. In Galatians 6:11, Paul writes, "See what large letters I make when I am writing in my own hand!" In 1 Enoch 100:6, Enoch writes, "And the wise among men will see the truth, and the sons of the earth will contemplate these words of this epistle. . . ." In 93:2, Enoch emphasizes that he himself is the one who is writing these things: " these things I say to you and I make known to you, my sons, I myself, Enoch."

8. On Galatians as a Pauline letter, see further Hans-Josef Klauck, *Ancient Letters and the New Testament: A Guide to Content and Exegesis* (Waco, TX: Baylor University Press, 2006), 311–15.
9. Cf. Klauck, *Ancient Letters*, 247–48. This is Klauck's only reference to 1 Enoch, and it is confined to a discussion of 1 Enoch 100:6. On the issue of the Epistle of Enoch as a letter, see now Lutz Doering, *Ancient Jewish Letters and the Beginnings of Christian Epistolography* (WUNT 298; Tübingen: Mohr Siebeck, 2012), 174–83, which unfortunately came to my attention too late for consideration in the present study.
10. Nickelsburg, *1 Enoch 1*, 420.

Author

The superscription of both letters names the author of the letter, and then, adds an impressive description of the author. In Galatians 1:1, Paul names himself as the author of the letter, and then goes on to describe himself as "an apostle—[sent] not from men nor by man but by Jesus Christ and God the Father, who raised him from the dead. . . ." This further description of who Paul is establishes from the outset the divine origin and agency of his apostolic commission, and thus, underscores his special authority. He will build on this foundation later in the same chapter, where he continues to lay out his apostolic credentials.

In the Epistle of Enoch, the pseudonymous author of the writing is given as Enoch: "Written by Enoch the scribe (this complete sign of wisdom) (who is) praised by all people and a leader of the whole earth. . . ." (1 Enoch 92:1). Whereas Paul describes himself as an "apostle," one who is sent by God, Enoch describes himself as a "scribe," that is, an upright man who writes "righteousness" (1 Enoch 12:4) and "truth" (15:1).[11] Enoch presents his books as life-giving wisdom (82:1–3), and the Epistle refers repeatedly to "the paths of righteousness" and "the paths of truth." This life-giving, divine wisdom was obtained when Enoch ascended to the divine throne room and toured the cosmos. Hence, as will be discussed further below, both Paul and Enoch present themselves as authors who communicate God's will.

Addressees

Both Galatians and the Epistle of Enoch are circular letters that are designed to be passed along to multiple readers in more than one location over the course of time. Paul writes his letter "to the churches of Galatia" (Gal 1:2), that is, to two or more churches—the exact number is unknown—in the large geographical region or Roman province known as "Galatia."[12] As such, Paul's letter to the Galatians is a circular letter written by their founding apostle (cf. Gal 4:13).

In a similar way, the Epistle of Enoch can be understood as a circular letter. According to 1 Enoch 92:1, Enoch writes his letter "to all my sons who dwell on the earth, and to the last generations who will observe truth and peace." According to the fictive setting of 1 Enoch, Enoch's sons are apparently located in different geographical locations, since they had to be called together by Methuselah so that Enoch their father could speak to them (91:1–2). Moreover, by the time of the "last generations," the Epistle would have been widely disseminated. In

11. Cf. Nickelsburg, *1 Enoch 1*, 65–66. Although this information comes from the Book of the Watchers (1 Enoch 1–36), the Epistle of Enoch presupposes much information from earlier parts of the Enochic corpus, including the Book of the Watchers. Cf. Nickelsburg, *1 Enoch 1*, 421–22.

12. Where these churches are located in "Galatia" and what constitutes "Galatia" for Paul are issues that we can sidestep here. For my own approach to the problem, see James M. Scott, *Paul and the Nations: The Old Testament and Jewish Background of Paul's Mission to the Nations with Special Reference to the Destination of Galatians*, WUNT 84 (Tübingen: Mohr Siebeck, 1995).

fact, Enoch looks forward to the time when "the sons of the earth will contemplate these words of this epistle" (1 Enoch 100:6), referring apparently to erring Jews and gentiles of the end time who will turn from its wicked ways through reading the Epistle.[13] Hence, the Epistle that Enoch writes must be conveyed from place to place as any circular letter would be.[14] The letter is conveyed not only horizontally across the world, but vertically through time by the faithful transmission of the Enochic community. The idea that Enoch wrote for the generations of the end time appears already in the superscriptions of the Book of the Watchers (1:1, 2–3) and the Book of Parables (37:2–3). It is probably also implied in the superscriptions of the dream visions (83:1; 85:1–2) and in the body of the Book of the Luminaries (76:14), since Methuselah, the recipient of Enoch's revelations, is to transmit them, so that they will be available in the end time (82:1–3; 91:1–3; 104:12–105:2).

Both Galatians and the Epistle of Enoch address their respective readers throughout in the second person plural. As Nickelsburg points out, this second-person direct address is a feature of 1 Enoch 92–105 that is largely lacking in the rest of the Enochic corpus.[15] Moreover, in 1 Enoch 91:18–19 and 94:1, Enoch refers to his addressees as "my children" (cf. 91:3), using the same form of direct address as Paul employs in Galatians 4:19 (τέκνα μου).

Salutation

In Galatians, the salutation is clearly identifiable: "Grace to you and peace (εἰρήνη) from God our Father and the Lord Jesus Christ" (1:3). The peace wish may reflect oriental letter form, which has been superimposed on the Greek prescript.

The situation in the Epistle of Enoch is more complicated. The typical salutation or greeting is missing in 1 Enoch 92:1. Nevertheless, as Nickelsburg suggests, "it may be hinted at in the word 'peace'" which comes at the end of the adscription in the same verse: "to all my sons who dwell on the earth, and to the last generations who will observe truth and peace."[16] Nickelsburg also takes the final reference to "peace" in the Epistle ("And you will have peace," 105:2) as "an epistolary conclusion."[17]

Thus, the Epistle of Enoch begins and ends with the word "peace." In a similar way, the word

13. Cf. Nickelsburg, *1 Enoch 1*, 502.
14. Enoch foresees the possibility that his books will be copied in the future (1 Enoch 104:11), which would facilitate the dissemination of his writings.
15. Nickelsburg, *1 Enoch 1*, 33.
16. Ibid., 420, 431.
17. Nickelsburg, *1 Enoch 1*, 535. See, however, Stuckenbruck, *1 Enoch 91–108*, 605: "Nickelsburg suggests that the pronouncement of peace on readers 'may be an epistolary conclusion.' While this is possible, the force of this pronouncement should not be lost: At last, after a number of declarations to the wicked in the *Epistle* that they will not have peace (94:6b; 98:11c, 16; 99:13; 101:3b; 102:3b; 103:8b), the writer affirms to his readers that peace will be theirs."

"peace" provides closure for Paul's letter to the Galatians (Gal 1:3; 6:16). Moreover, the very last word of both letters is "Amen" (Gal 6:18; 1 Enoch 105:2).

Conclusion

In sum, Paul and the Epistle of Enoch have a number of formal features in common as letters. Some of these are quite general, but others are more specific, and therefore, more interesting (e.g., the self-conscious reference to the author's own letter; the expanded superscription giving an impressive self-description of the author; the circular nature of the letter; the reference to the addressees as "my children"; the bracketing function of the term "peace"; the closing "Amen!"). These comparisons show that the two letters are closely analogous in certain formal respects. Are the letters also comparable with respect to the main content of their bodies? To this question, we now turn.

Comparisons between Galatians and the Epistle of Enoch in Terms of the Apocalyptic Elements They Have in Common

The central feature of both letters is the special revelation that is given to their respective authors. This special revelation has a twofold function in our letters: (1) to legitimate the authors' message, and (2) to constitute the eschatological community of the elect consisting of both Israel and the rest of humankind. The other apocalyptic elements that we will consider here either follow from this central feature of special revelation or are aspects of it.

The First Function of the Special Revelation: To Legitimate the Author's Message

First and foremost, the role of the special revelation in Galatians and the Epistle of Enoch is to legitimate their respective authors' messages. Although neither letter is formally constituted as an apocalypse, they both appeal to the claims of their respective authors to previous (visionary) revelation as the basis for the truth of the saving message that they now impart through their letters.[18]

In Galatians, this claim to previous revelatory experience is found in Galatians 1:11–12, 15–16:

18. Here, we see an inextricable relationship between revelation and truth. Martin Heidegger famously tried to argue on the basis of a dubious etymology that the original Greek concept of "truth" (ἀλήθεια < alpha-privative λανθάνω "to hide") was a form of negation: truth was an act of "dis-closure," that which is "not hidden," the revealed. For a philological critique, see Paul Friedländer, *Plato: An Introduction* (New York: Harper, 1964), 221–29.

> [11]For I want you to know, brothers, that the gospel that was proclaimed by me is not of human origin (τὸ εὐαγγέλιον τὸ εὐαγγελισθὲν ὑπ᾽ ἐμοῦ ὅτι οὐκ ἔστιν κατὰ ἄνθρωπον); [12]for I did not receive it from a human source, nor was I taught it, but I received it through a revelation of Jesus Christ (οὐδὲ γὰρ ἐγὼ παρὰ ἀνθρώπου παρέλαβον αὐτὸ οὔτε ἐδιδάχθην ἀλλὰ δι᾽ ἀποκαλύψεως Ἰησοῦ Χριστοῦ). [. . .]
>
> [15]But when God, who had set me apart from my mother's womb and called me through his grace, was pleased [16]to reveal his Son to/in me, so that I might proclaim him among the nations (ἀποκαλύψαι τὸν υἱὸν αὐτοῦ ἐν ἐμοί, ἵνα εὐαγγελίζωμαι αὐτὸν ἐν τοῖς ἔθνεσιν), I did not confer with any human being. . . .

Paul asserts that he was divinely appointed to preach the Gospel to the nations as the result of a revelation of the Son, Jesus Christ. That revelation was the origin of his Gospel message and the sole basis of his apostolic authority. The legitimacy of his apostleship and message was later recognized by James, Cephas, and John, but, as Paul emphasizes, that recognition added nothing to what he had already received independently from God himself (Gal 2:7–9).

In the Epistle of Enoch, by the same token, the claim to previous visionary revelation is explicit in the Apocalypse of Weeks (cf. 1 Enoch 93:2) and implicit in other passages (cf. 93:11–14; 98:7–8; 102:4–103:4; 104:1). In particular, Enoch's words in chapters 92–105 "assume an apocalyptic character through their appeal to the visionary material in the Book of the Watchers to which they have been attached."[19] It is by appealing to his previous visionary revelation that the putative author of the Epistle validates his message. Thus, for example, the Apocalypse of Weeks (93:2) begins with the following claim based on the revelation to Enoch:

> Concerning the sons of righteousness, and concerning the chosen of eternity, and concerning the plant of truth, these things I say to you and I make known to you, my sons, I myself, Enoch. The vision of heaven was shown to me, and from the words of the watchers and holy ones I have learned everything, and in the heavenly tablets I read everything and I have understood.

Another example is found in 103:1–2:

> And now I swear to you, the righteous, by the glory of the Great One, and by his splendid kinship and his majesty I swear to you that I know this mystery. For I have seen the writing of what must be, and I know the things that are written in them and inscribed concerning you. . . .

Similarly, we read in 104:1–2:

19. Nickelsburg, *1 Enoch 1*, 34. Thus, the Epistle of Enoch constitutes a series of addresses that are based on revelations recounted in earlier parts of 1 Enoch. According to chs. 12–16, Enoch ascended to the heavenly throne room. There he learned of the judgment of the Watchers. Subsequent chapters recount his journeys through the cosmos. The function of these journey narratives is evident in the visions that constitute their goal. Enoch sees the places of punishment (chs. 17–19; 21; 26–27), the place of the dead (ch. 22), and Jerusalem and Paradise (chs. 28–32). Then, he is shown the heavenly tablets. These contain a record of human deeds and their rewards and punishments (81:1–4). Against the background of these cosmic journeys and visions, and in light of the dream visions Enoch had received earlier (chs. 83–84; 85–90), the angels command him to compile a testimony for his children and their spiritual descendants (81:5–82:3). He does this in ch. 91 and in the Epistle. Enoch guarantees the reality of eternal blessings by referring to his own inspection of the heavenly tablets (103:1–3; cf. 81:1–4).

> I swear to you that the angels in heaven make mention of you for good before the glory of the Great One, and your names are written before the glory of the Great One, Take courage, then. . . .

Hence, in both Galatians and the Epistle, an appeal to special revelation functions to legitimate the authors' respective messages. Closely related to this authenticating function of the special revelation in each case is the *prophetic ambience* in both letters. Both the Epistle of Enoch and Paul's letter to the Galatians have a prophetic feel to them, albeit in different ways.

For readers who are familiar with the prophets, the Epistle of Enoch has what Nickelsburg has called a "prophetic ambience" because of the Epistle's extensive use of three specific forms that appear with some frequency in the biblical prophetic corpus (i.e., woes, exhortations, and descriptions of events associated with the coming judgment).[20] The Epistle of Enoch itself does not include the prophetic commissioning form,[21] but an earlier part of the Enochic corpus, to which the Epistle alludes and on which it depends, does give an account of Enoch's prophetic commission—cast in the form of a biblical call narrative—as the prophet of judgment to the sinful Watchers.[22]

In contrast, the autobiographical section of Galatians does contain a call narrative in 1:15–16, which refers to God as the one "who set me apart from my mother's womb (ἐκ κοιλίας μητρός μου) and called (καλέσας) me through his grace . . . that I might proclaim (εὐαγγελίζωμαι) him [sc. the Son of God] among the nations (ἐν τοῖς ἔθνεσιν)."[23] This evidently alludes to the commissioning of the prophet in several Old Testament texts. For example, Jeremiah describes his call in LXX Jeremiah 1:4–5:

> And the word of the Lord came to me, saying, "Before I formed you in the womb (ἐν κοιλίᾳ) I knew you, and before you came forth from [your] mother (ἐκ μήτρας), I consecrated you; I appointed you a prophet to the nations (εἰς ἔθνη)."

The difference, of course, is that Jeremiah was given a commission that was more to proclaim judgment than to announce restoration (cf. Jer 1:10), whereas Paul's commission was to proclaim the good news (εὐαγγελίζωμαι) to the nations. Another relevant text is the call of the prophet in LXX Isaiah 49:1, 6:[24]

> Hear me, O islands; pay attention, O nations (ἔθνη): . . . From my mother's womb (ἐκ κοιλίας μητρός

20. Nickelsburg, *1 Enoch 1*, 34, 416–19.
21. Cf., e.g., Isa 6:1–13; Jer 1:4–10; Ezek 1:1–3:11.
22. Cf. Nickelsburg, *1 Enoch 1*, 30.
23. Cf. Nickelsburg, *1 Enoch 1*, 246, who argues that "the accounts of the apostolic call of Saul of Tarsus [Acts 9:3–6; 22:3–11; 26:9–18] . . . have much in common with 1 Enoch 14." Cf. also Nickelsburg, *1 Enoch 1*, 30: "The form of the prophetic commissioning shapes most of the NT accounts of the post-resurrection appearances of Jesus. . . . the three accounts of Jesus' commissioning of the apostle Paul find their closest parallels in 1 Enoch 14–16." Nickelsburg notes here Johannes Munck, *Paul and the Salvation of Mankind* (London: SCM, 1959), 30–31.
24. Cf. Acts 13:47, where Paul quotes Isa 49:6 to explain why he and his companions were turning to the gentiles.

> μου) He called (ἐκάλεσεν) my name. . . . **6**And he said to me, ". . . See, I have made you a light of nations (εἰς φῶς ἐθνῶν), that you may be for salvation to the end of the earth."

Our point here is that Paul describes the revelatory experience that made him an apostle in terms of a traditional prophetic call.[25]

We have seen that the authors of our two letters make an appeal to direct divine revelation in order to authenticate their respective messages. The prophetic ambience in these letters enhances their authors' claims to being revelatory mediators.

The Second Function of the Special Revelation: To Constitute the Eschatological Community of the Elect Consisting of Israel and the Rest of Humankind

The second function of the special revelation given to the authors of Galatians and the Epistle of Enoch is to constitute the eschatological community of the elect. In both letters, salvation is open to all people, regardless of ethnicity. Indeed, there is an active mission to the nations. The key in each case is that people believe in and adhere to the revealed will of God as delivered through the revelatory mediator.

For Paul, the church is the eschatological community of the chosen constituted by revelation. Salvation is open to all people, and Paul has been commissioned to preach to the nations the message of the gospel that was revealed to him (Gal 1:12, 15–16). In the case of the Galatian churches, Paul assumes that they have received the Spirit (3:1–5) and that they are, therefore, part of the family of God (3:26–4:7, 28; 6:10). This is a direct result of the fact that the Gospel was revealed to Paul, that Paul had proclaimed the Gospel to the Galatians, and that the Galatians, in turn, had believed his message. Paul argues vehemently that these gentiles in Galatia, like those in Antioch (cf. 2:11–14), are admitted to the family of faith *as gentiles*, whereupon they assume a new identity in Christ and become heirs to the promise to Abraham. For Paul, ethnic boundaries have collapsed: there is neither Jew nor gentile; all are one in Christ (Gal 3:28). Gentiles did not need first to become Jews or observe Torah in order to make them fit for inclusion. Indeed, to attempt to do so would jeopardize their salvation in Christ (cf. 5:2–4).

In a similar way, the Enochic authors believed that they were members of the eschatological community of the chosen constituted by revelation.[26] This revelation—although it was the possession of a select group of Israel that arose in the eschaton—was to be proclaimed to "all the

25. See further Karl Olav Sandnes, *Paul—One of the Prophets? A Contribution to the Apostle's Self-Understanding*, WUNT II/43 (Tübingen: Mohr Siebeck, 1991).
26. Cf. Nickelsburg, *1 Enoch 1*, 86; idem, "Revealed Wisdom as a Criterion for Inclusion and Exclusion: From Jewish Sectarianism to Early Christianity," in *"To See Ourselves as Others See Us": Christians, Jews, "Others" in Late Antiquity*, ed. Jacob Neusner and Ernest S. Frerichs (Chico, CA: Scholars, 1985), 73–91.

sons of the earth" (1 Enoch 100:6), in the hope that they too would be saved at the end time of the final judgment. The conversion of the human race is a prominent theme in both the Enochic corpus as a whole and the Epistle of Enoch in particular. First Enoch is presented as the sacred writing of a revelation in primordial antiquity, before the division of humankind into Israel and the Gentile nations, thus giving the Enochic books an inherently universal relevance. Through a long transmission process, the writing was to be conveyed from the revelatory mediator, Enoch, through his son Methuselah, to "the generations of the world" (82:1). The Enochic corpus views two different men as pivotal in this transmission process on the way toward the universalization of the revelation, although both men occupy similar functions in that process. In the Book of the Watchers, on the one hand, the focus is on *Noah*, who receives divine revelation that teaches him "how he may preserve himself alive and escape forever" (10:3). It is Noah's seed that will be propagated: "From him a plant will be planted, and his seed will endure for all the generations of eternity" (10:4). Hence, in the eschaton, when Michael renovates the earth and eliminates evil, "the plant of righteousness and truth" will again appear and flourish (10:16–17). After this, "all the sons of men will become righteous, and all the peoples will worship" God (10:21). In the Epistle of Enoch (particularly the Apocalypse of Weeks), on the other hand, the line of transmission runs through *Abraham* and Israel, rather than through Noah. Abraham is chosen as "the plant of righteous judgment," and from him, stems Israel, "the plant of righteousness forever and ever" (93:5). Hence, in the eschaton (at the conclusion of week 7), Israel becomes the basis for a righteous remnant: "the chosen will be chosen, as witnesses of righteousness from the everlasting plant of righteousness, to whom will be given sevenfold wisdom and knowledge" (93:10). After this (in week 9), "righteous law will be revealed to all the sons of the whole earth . . . , and all humankind will look to the path of everlasting righteousness" (91:14). "Thus revelation is universalized and becomes the source of righteousness of the whole human race."[27] The rest of the Epistle of Enoch envisions a similar process of transmission of the Enochic revelation. Enoch's wisdom is written down for "the last generations who will observe truth and peace" (92:1). In the eschaton, Enoch's books will be given to "the righteous and pious and wise," and they will learn from those books "all the paths of truth," and then, instruct "the sons of the earth" (104:12–105:2). According to 100:6, "the wise among men will see the truth, and the sons of the earth will contemplate these words of this epistle, and they will recognize that their wealth cannot save when iniquity collapses."

To be sure, there is an apparent difference between Galatians and the Epistle of Enoch with respect to the kind of revelation that leads to inclusion in the eschatological community of the elect. The revelation of the gospel that commissions Paul to evangelize the nations and bring

27. Nickelsburg, *1 Enoch 1*, 53.

them into the church is based on the death and resurrection of Jesus Christ. It is this revealed message that must be believed in order for a person to be saved. In Galatians, faith in Christ necessarily leads to following the law of Christ through walking in the Spirit. In 1 Enoch, on the contrary, the revelation of wisdom through Enoch is the salvific event par excellence. It is by believing in this revealed law[28] and living in line with it that people can be included in the community of the elect, and thus, be saved at the final judgment. As we shall see, however, the similarities between the kinds of revelation in both cases are greater than it appears at first glance.

Leapfrogging the Mosaic Law

In their own distinctive ways, both Galatians and the Epistle of Enoch subvert the relevance of the Mosaic Law by appealing to an earlier, definitive revelation as the sole basis of the eschatological hope for humankind.

In the Enochic corpus as a whole, Enoch takes the place of Moses as the mediator of the definitive revelation of divine wisdom not just for Israel but for all humankind. "Thus," as Nickelsburg argues, "1 Enoch leapfrogs the Mosaic Torah and assumes for itself a prophetic authority that precedes Moses."[29] This explains the paucity of references to the Mosaic Law in 1 Enoch.[30] The fundamental premise is that wisdom originated with God and that it can be obtained only through divine revelation. "For the Enochic authors, the process of revelation occurred when the primordial seer and sage Enoch ascended to heaven, received 'wisdom,' descended, wrote it in books, and gave these books to Methuselah and his sons for transmission to the later generations (81:1–82:3; 104:12–13). Thus wisdom is both primordial and eschatological, and four of the book's five major sections refer explicitly to the eschatological transmission of this Enochic wisdom (1:2; 5:4; 37:2; 90:6; 92:1; 93:10; 100:6; 104:12–13)."[31] Hence, there was simply no room for a major role for Moses in the Enochic corpus: Standing near the very beginning (in the unsullied first "week" from creation),[32] Enoch was given the exclusive and definitive revelation, and that revelation was constitutive for the eschatological return of humankind to the origi-

28. Cf. 1 Enoch 104:13, where it is expected that future generations will not only receive the Enochic books but that "they will believe in them."

29. George W. E. Nickelsburg, "The Nature and Function of Revelation in 1 Enoch, Jubilees, and Some Qumranic Documents," in *Pseudepigraphic Perspectives: The Apocrypha and Pseudepigrapha in Light of the Dead Sea Scrolls. Proceedings of the International Symposium of the Orion Center for the Study of the Dead Sea Scrolls and Associated Literature, 12–14 January, 1997*, ed. Esther Chazon and Michael Stone, STDJ 31 (Leiden: Brill, 1999), 91–119 (101). For this concept of leapfrogging and Enoch taking Moses's place, see also idem, *1 Enoch 1*, 52–53.

30. Cf. Nickelsburg, *1 Enoch 1*, 50, 53.

31. Nickelsburg, *1 Enoch 1*, 52.

32. For the Enochic corpus, sin did not enter until after the time of Enoch, beginning with the Watchers' deeds, and the Watchers are seen as the source of all sin and evil. Cf. Nickelsburg, *1 Enoch 1*, 29, 36, 46, 47, 87, 101, 102, 167, 171, 172, 195. In contrast, Paul ascribes the origins of sin to the disobedience of Adam and Eve, the first human beings, almost immediately after the creation of the world.

nally intended will of God, and therefore, a source of righteousness for the whole human race. Nickelsburg compares the universalistic assertion that Enoch's wisdom is made available to all humanity with biblical texts such as Genesis 12:3 and some of the oracles of Second Isaiah.[33]

Paul takes a similar tack in Galatians, although it is also quite distinctive in many respects. The apostle does not appeal to a revelation supposedly given to Enoch, which in any case is not recorded in Scripture. Instead, Paul cites Scripture as witness to the divine revelation of the gospel: "The Scripture (ἡ γραφή), having foreseen that God justifies the nations on the basis of faith, proclaimed the gospel in advance (προευηγγελίσατο) to Abraham: 'In you shall all the nations be blessed' [Gen. 12:3]" (Gal 3:8). In the context of Genesis, the promise to Abraham is seen as the solution to the human plight described in the first eleven chapters, and the "nations" in Genesis 12:3 refers to the table of nations in Genesis 10. It is this gospel that God revealed to Paul as well and becomes the basis for his apostolic commission to preach the gospel to the nations (Gal 1:12, 15–16). As Paul goes on to argue in Galatians 3, the promises to Abraham, which he has identified with the revelation of his universally relevant gospel, "were spoken to Abraham and to his seed," and he identifies the seed of Abraham as Christ (Gal 3:16). This is consistent with the fact that God revealed his Son in Paul in order that he might preach the gospel among the nations (Gal 1:16). In the subsequent context, Paul relativizes the Mosaic Torah by pointing out that the Law was given much later in time:

> This is what I mean: the Law, which came four hundred thirty years later, does not invalidate a covenant previously validated by God so as to void the promise. For if the inheritance was on the basis of the Law, it would no longer be on the basis of the promise. But God has graciously given it to Abraham through the promise (Gal 3:17–18).

Moreover, Paul goes on to argue that the Mosaic Torah had an interim, time-limited function that came to the end with the advent of Christ:

> When then the Law? It was added for the sake of transgressions, until the seed [= Christ] for whom it has been promised should come, having been arranged through angels by the hand of a mediator (Gal 3:19).

What Paul has done in Galatians 3 is to deprive the Law of any ongoing validity in favor of a previously given gospel about the Son of God that Paul has (like Abraham) received and has been commissioned to preach.

If we look more closely at the Son of God who was revealed in Paul, we can add another observation that may tighten the analogy between Galatians and 1 Enoch in terms of the nature

33. Nickselsburg, *1 Enoch 1*, 54. In the same context (ibid., 53–54), Nickelsburg points to the choosing of and revelation to Abraham (Gen 12:1) as one of the models for understanding 1 Enoch's theology.

of the revelation in each case. According to Galatians 4:4–5, "When the fullness of time came, God sent forth his Son . . . in order that . . . in order that . . . (ἐξαπέστειλεν ὁ θεὸς τὸν υἱὸν αὐτοῦ . . . ἵνα . . . ἵνα . . .)." Schweizer argues that the "sending formula" in Galatians 4:4–5 can be compared to wisdom traditions, especially the sending of Wisdom in Wisdom 9:9–10:[34]

> With you is Wisdom, she who knows your works and was present when you made the world; she understands what is pleasing in your sight and what is right according to your commandments. 10Send her forth from the holy heavens (ἐξαπόστειλον αὐτὴν ἐξ ἁγίων οὐρανῶν), and from the throne of your glory send her (καὶ ἀπὸ θρόνου δόξης σου πέμψον αὐτήν), in order that (ἵνα) she may labor at my [Solomon's] side, and that I may learn what is pleasing to you.

If Schweizer is correct, then we have another possible point of comparison with the Enochic tradition. According to Nickelsburg, "1 Enoch's use of the myth of the descent of wisdom takes up an idea that is present in Proverbs 8 and interpreted in Sirach 24 and 1 Baruch 4. The last two texts see the Mosaic Torah as the real presence of heavenly wisdom. In 1 Enoch this wisdom was received by Enoch when he ascended to heaven, and it now resides in the primordial sage's written corpus."[35] Thus, the Enochic corpus repeatedly identifies wisdom with Enoch, the primordial recipient of all heavenly wisdom and its revelatory mediator on earth. Seen in this light, Paul's notion of the sending of the Son of God may mirror the wisdom tradition but does so in a way that outstrips the role both of Enoch as a revelatory mediator and of the revealed heavenly wisdom that he transmits to earth as a source of righteousness for the whole human race. For in Galatians, the incarnate Son of God himself is the *embodiment* of the divine revelation of wisdom that is universalized and becomes the source of righteousness of the whole human race; he personally performs a work of creative redemption,[36] fulfilling the expectations of Isaiah 40–55 and 65–66; and, in the analogy of 1 Enoch, the Son's work effectively undoes the deeds of the angelic "sons of God" (οἱ υἱοὶ τοῦ θεοῦ, Gen 6:2), who perpetrated evil in the world.[37] The preexistent Son of God was sent, just as preexistent Wisdom was sent. And, similar to Wis-

34. Cf. Eduard Schweizer, "Zum religionsgeschichtlichen Hintergrund der 'Sendungsformel' Gal 4,4f, Röm 8,3f, Joh 3,16f, 1 Joh 4,9," *ZNW* 57 (1966): 199–210. Cf. also Wis 9:17: "Who has known your counsel, except you have given wisdom and sent your Holy Spirit from on high (εἰ μὴ σὺ ἔδωκας σοφίαν καὶ ἔπεμψας τὸ ἅγιόν σου πνεῦμα ἀπὸ ὑψίστων)?"
35. Nickelsburg, *1 Enoch 1*, 52. Cf. also ibid., 46, 60–61, 343, 458.
36. On the concept of creative redemption, see Terence E. Fretheim, *God and World in the Old Testament: A Relational Theology of Creation* (Nashville: Abingdon, 2005), 181–98 (esp. 191–92); Bernard W. Anderson, "Exodus Typology in Second Isaiah," in *Israel's Prophetic Heritage*, ed. B. W. Anderson and W. Harrelson (New York: Harper, 1962), 177–95; Carol Stuhlmueller, *Creative Redemption in Deutero-Isaiah*, AnBib 43 (Rome: Pontifical Biblical Institute, 1970), 59–68.
37. Cf. 1 Enoch 6:1–2, which reflects the story in Gen 6:1–4 of the "sons of God" (here called "the watchers, the sons of heaven") and their intercourse with the daughters of men. Note, however, that the Epistle of Enoch seems to contradict the standard Enochic explanation for the origin of evil in the world, laying the blame instead squarely on human beings. Cf. 1 Enoch 98:4: "Thus lawlessness was not sent upon the earth; but men created it by themselves, and those who do it will come to a great curse." Nickelsburg (*1 Enoch 1*, 476) interprets the passage as denying that "certain evil is the result of divine decree or a part of the created order. To the contrary (ἀλλ', 'but'), human actions are the primary cause." On the two ways that the Enochic corpus explains the origin and presence of sin and evil on earth, see also ibid., 46, 47, 102, 347, 353, 356, 542.

dom who was present with God when he made the world (Wis 9:9), the Son is described as "the firstborn of all creation, for by him all things were created" (Col 1:15–16; cf. 1 Cor 8:6).

When we step back and take in the analogies between Galatians and 1 Enoch that we have examined so far, the sending of the Son in Galatians 4:4–5 constitutes the definitive eschatological revelation that accomplishes the recapitulation of all things in accordance with the originally intended will of God for creation. In doing so, Paul marginalizes the Mosaic Torah in much the same way that 1 Enoch does, that is, by leapfrogging—appealing to a much earlier revelation that looks forward to the eschatological restoration of the status quo ante.[38] In Galatians, the appeal to earlier revelation goes back not just to Abraham but even to the source of divine wisdom from the foundation of the world.

Marginalizing the Mosaic Torah does not, however, mean antinomianism either in 1 Enoch or in Galatians. Both writings emphasize that the proper reception of their respective revelations will result in the obedience to the universally valid law of God that is required for a positive outcome in the impending eschatological judgment (see below on the Two-Ways tradition that is prominent in both 1 Enoch and Galatians). There is, however, one big difference: Whereas 1 Enoch fails to explicate the specific laws and commandments that are the criteria of this eschatological judgment,[39] Galatians elaborates very thoroughly on this issue (cf. 5:13–6:10).

Spatial and Temporal Dualisms

In both the Epistle of Enoch and Paul's letter to the Galatians, dualisms of space (this world vs. heaven) and time (this age vs. the age to come) are important constituents of their respective worldviews. Moreover, the saving revelations of their divinely commissioned authors enable the eschatological communities constituted by those revelations both to overcome the dualisms that they have hitherto known as reality and to participate preemptively in the new spatiotemporal reality of the eschaton.

Let us turn first to the issue of *temporal dualism* in the two letters. In the Epistle of Enoch, temporal dualism is expressed as a distinction between the present evil age and the age to come, when God will eliminate evil and restore all things. This theme is expressed already in the opening verses of the Epistle (1 Enoch 92:2–5),[40] but the deterministic idea there that "the

38. Cf. Nickelsburg, *1 Enoch 1*, 61: "Extrapolations from the aforementioned considerations to the complex situation in early Christianity should be made with great caution. One striking parallel presents itself, however. The marginalization of the Mosaic Torah in 1 Enoch, the Wisdom of Solomon, and the *Mûsār lĕMēvîn* offers a precedent for the similar tendency expressed by Paul and attributed to Jesus of Nazareth in most strata of the gospel tradition. Even if the apostle's theology has been heavily influenced by the pragmatics of a mission to the gentiles and has precedent in apologetic literature like the *Letter of Aristeas* and the *Sibylline Oracles*, its expression may have been influenced by Jewish traditions like those just described."

39. Cf. Nickelsburg, *1 Enoch 1*, 28, 51, 53, 134, 156, 426.

Great Holy One has appointed days for everything" (v. 2) starts to expand the simple, present-future dualism into a much more complex and encompassing conception that reaches back to the very beginning of time and includes more incremental divisions of time in between. This more comprehensive approach continues in the immediately following Apocalypse of Weeks (93:1–10; 91:11–17), which, in summary fashion, based on Enoch's examination of the heavenly tablets and their angelic interpretation, periodizes all of history from creation[41] to the new creation. Hence, while the temporal dualism expresses the existential plight of the addressees and its need for eschatological resolution, the salvation-historical framework for that existential plight is necessarily all-encompassing, because, as we have seen, the intended addressees of the Epistle themselves span from the primordial time of Enoch all the way to the eschaton.

In Galatians, temporal dualism is expressed in a similar way, although not as elaborately. Again, right at the outset of the letter, Paul refers to "the present evil age" (*ὁ αἰών ὁ ἐνέστως πονηρός*) from which believers have already been "set free" (*ἐξέληται*) through Christ (Gal 1:4), a condition that has come about because "When the fullness of time came (*ὅτε δὲ ἦλθεν τὸ πλήρωμα τοῦ χρόνου*),[42] God sent forth his Son . . . , in order that he might redeem (*ἐξαγοράσῃ*) those under the law" (Gal 4:4–5). This suggests that, for Paul, there is an overlap of the ages: believers already participate in the age to come and enjoy some of its benefits, including "new creation" (*καινὴ κτίσις*, 6:15), even though evil (sin and death) still characterizes the present, and the full realization of the age to come—the inheritance of the kingdom of God (Gal 5:21) and "eternal life" (6:8)—still lies in the future. Moreover, the reference to "the fullness of time" implies the periodization of history,[43] a trajectory that runs from creation to new creation with a series of divinely appointed times in between (e.g., the 430 years from Abraham to the exodus and the giving of the law on Mt. Sinai in Gal 3:16 [cf. Gen 15:13–14; Exod 12:40]).

In 1 Enoch, the new creation recapitulates the original will of God for the creation. Although the term "new creation" itself occurs only once in the Enochic corpus (72:1), the concept is more widespread: "Frequent allusions to the Trito-Isaianic scenarios about a new creation and

40. 1 Enoch 92:2–5: "Let not your spirit be troubled because of the times; for the Great Holy One has appointed days for everything. (3) The righteous will arise from sleep; he will arise and walk in the paths of righteousness, and all his path and his journey (will be) in piety and everlasting mercy. (4) And (God) will be merciful to the righteous one, and to him he will give everlasting truth; and (to him) he will give authority, and he will judge in piety and in righteousness; and he will walk in everlasting light. (5) Sin will be destroyed in darkness forever; and it will not be seen from that day forever."

41. Creation is not explicitly mentioned in the Apocalypse of Weeks, but it is strongly implied by Enoch's statement, "I was born the seventh [from Adam!] in the first week [from creation]" (1 Enoch 93:3).

42. On the extensive parallels between "the fullness of time" in Gal 4:4 and 2 Baruch 13:3; 19:5; 21:8; 27:15; 29:8; 30:3; 39:7; 59:4, see George W. E. Nickelsburg, "A New Testament Reader's Guide to *2 Baruch*: Or a *2 Baruch* Reader's Guide to the New Testament," in *Fourth Ezra and Second Baruch: Reconstruction after the Fall*, ed. Matthias Henze and Gabriele Boccaccini, JSJSup 164 (Leiden: Brill, 2013), 271–93 (286).

43. The periodization of history in apocalyptic texts conveys a sense of determinism by indicating that history is measured out and under divine control. The idea of time filling up to a predetermined fixed limit is part of this concept of periodization. On the notion of "the fullness of time" and related concepts, see Rainer Stuhlmann, *Das eschatologische Maß im Neuen Testament*, FRLANT 132 (Göttingen: Vandenhoeck & Ruprecht, 1983).

a new Jerusalem color the descriptions of the new age in almost all parts of 1 Enoch (cf. 5:5–9; 10:16–22; 26:5–6; 90:28–38; 91:13–16), and even the Book of the Luminaries awaits a 'new creation' (72:1)."[44] The description of the new creation in the Animal Apocalypse (90:28–38), which may be an elaboration of that in the Apocalypse of Weeks (91:13–16), envisions the recapitulation in terms of the reunification of humankind as one people, thus restoring the status quo ante, the condition before the division into various peoples at the beginning. Just as Adam was a white bull in the beginning (85:3), so also in the end, a great white bull (the Messiah) is born (90:37), and then, all people also become white bulls (v. 38).[45] Nickelsburg suggests that "[t]he closest analogy is the two-Adams theology of the apostle Paul" (cf. Rom 5:12–21; 1 Cor 15:45–50; Phil 3:21).[46] I would like to suggest that Galatians offers an analogy as well: Paul's concept of "new creation," in which "neither circumcision nor uncircumcision is anything" (Gal 6:15), relates to his earlier statement that "There is neither Jew nor Greek, there is neither slave nor free, there is no male and female; for all of you are one in Christ Jesus" (Gal 3:28; cf. Rom 8:29).[47] In that case, the positive correspondence between *Endzeit* and *Urzeit* in terms of the originally intended will of God for creation overcomes the dualistic opposition between the present evil age and the age to come. This is accomplished through incorporation into Christ (the "image of God" and the "firstborn of all creation," according to Col 1:15), which thereby eliminates the ethnic, social, and sexual distinctions between people.[48] For instance, slavery, a form of oppression, was not part of the originally intended will of God for creation: "I swear to you, sinners, that it was not ordained <for a man> to be a slave . . ." (1 Enoch 98:4).[49] In this analogy, one wonders whether Paul's idea of "no male and female" harks back to Adam, who was originally created as a sexually undifferentiated human being (Gen 1:27; 2:7, 21–25).[50]

44. Nickelsburg, *1 Enoch 1*, 57.
45. Cf. 1 Enoch 91:14: "and all humankind will look to the path of everlasting righteousness." See also 10:21; 91:17.
46. Nickelsburg, *1 Enoch 1*, 407n17; cf. ibid., 85.
47. An advantage of citing Gal 3:28 as an analogy to the transformation of all humankind into white bulls expected by the Animal Apocalypse is that the Galatians passage explicitly includes believing Jews.
48. Cf. Eph 1:10b, the concept of the recapitulation of all things in Christ (ἀνακεφαλαιώσασθαι τὰ πάντα ἐν τῷ Χριστῷ), and Irenaeus' citation of this Pauline passage in a context that reflects the use of *1 Enoch* (*Adv. haer.* 1.10.1). Cf. James C. VanderKam, "1 Enoch, Enochic Motifs, and Enoch in Early Christian Literature," in idem and William Adler (eds.), *The Jewish Apocalyptic Heritage in Early Christianity*, CRINT 3.4 (Minneapolis: Fortress Press, 1996), 32–101 (43). On the interpretation of the notion of recapitulation in Eph 1:10b, see John McHugh, "A Reconsideration of Ephesians 1:10b in the Light of Irenaeus," in *Paul and Paulinism: Essays in Honour of C. K. Barrett*, ed. M. D. Hooker and S. G. Wilson (London SPCK, 1982), 302–9.
49. On this text, see Nickelsburg, *1 Enoch 1*, 51, 477: "Here the critique is radical: slavery was not part of the divine plan (for the use of ὁρίζω ['ordain'] and βουλή ['decree'] with reference to God's foreknowledge and foreordination, cf. Acts 2:23; 4:28). The argument is paralleled in Mark 10:2–9, where Jesus contrasts God's intention in creation with the concession made to human 'hardness of heart' in the Mosaic divorce law. The divinely created institution of marriage should not be annulled by humans."
50. Cf. Wayne A. Meeks, "Image of the Androgyne. Some Uses of a Symbol in Earliest Christianity," *HR* 13 (1974): 165–208; Alexandra R. Brown, "Creation, Gender, and Identity in (New) Cosmic Perspective: 1 Corinthians 11:2–16," in *The Unrelenting God: God's Action in Scripture. Essays in Honor of Beverly Roberts Gaventa*, ed. David J. Downs and Matthew L. Skinner (Grand Rapids, MI: Eerdmans, 2013), 172–93 (190–91). See further James L. Kugel, *Traditions of the Bible: A Guide to the Bible As It Was at the Start of the Common Era* (Cambridge, MA: Harvard University Press, 1998), 84–85; Luc Brisson, *Sexual Ambivalence: Androgyny and Hermaphroditism in Graeco-Roman Antiquity* (Berkeley: University of California Press, 2002), 73–85, 111.

The second kind of dualism found in both Galatians and the Epistle is *spatial dualism*, the mutually exclusive spheres of heaven and earth. The story of the Watchers in 1 Enoch 6–16, which the Epistle presupposes, shows that the mixing of the two spheres through the union of the heavenly Watchers and earthly women results in a series of earthly disasters that keep working their way through human history.[51] At the same time, a worthy like Enoch can play the role of a revelatory mediator for both humans and fallen angels precisely because he has access to divine revelation in the heavenly sphere (cf., e.g., 93:2), which becomes the basis for the eschatological renewal of the earthly sphere. Heaven is also the place of the heavenly bodies and cosmic elements, which, in contrast to humans on earth, faithfully follow God's commands instituted at creation, and at divine behest, they can also execute judgment on the wicked. In the Epistle of Enoch, for example, this theme occurs in 100:10–101:3 (cf. 76:5–13; Sir 39:28–31).

Spatial dualism is also found in Galatians. The heaven/earth dichotomy occurs early on in the letter, where Paul asseverates, "But even if we or an angel from heaven (καὶ ἐὰν ἡμεῖς ἢ ἄγγελος ἐξ οὐρανοῦ) should preach a gospel to you contrary to the one we did preach to you, let that person be *anathema*" (Gal 1:8). The Enochic corpus provides an interesting analogy to Paul's statement, for the rebel angels, called "the watchers of the eternal heaven" in 1 Enoch 91:15,[52] revealed pernicious knowledge to humankind, which not only had disastrous consequences for people but also resulted in the angelic revelatory mediators themselves being damned (cf. 1 Enoch 7:1; 8:1–9:11; 10:4–8, 11–13).[53] Moreover, if the story of the Watchers' revelations of pernicious knowledge provides a foil to Enoch's "true" revelation of saving knowledge,[54] then the analogy is complete: Paul could associate himself with Enoch,[55] whereas Paul's opponents, with their "different gospel," would be cast in the mold of the fallen angels.[56] There may be a par-

51. Cf., e.g., Nickelsburg, *1 Enoch 1*, 41: "The present evil age awaits the time of adjudication, deliverance, and renewal. This world is the scene of sin, violence, victimization, and pollution and is separated from the heavenly and cosmic spheres, where God's will is done. Humanity here and now is the prey of evil spirits who oppose God and are foils to the holy ones in God's heavenly entourage. Thus the Enochic authors emphasize the disastrous character of human existence by means of dualistic comparisons that are made in temporal, spatial, and ontological terms."

52. Cf. "the watchers, the sons of heaven" (1 Enoch 6:1).

53. According to Hilary of Poitiers' commentary on Ps 133:3 (*Tract. super Psal.* 132.6, CSEL 22:689), Hermon, the mountain on whose peak the Watchers descended from heaven, means "*anathema*." Cf. Nickelsburg, *1 Enoch 1*, 93: "He [Hilary] also knows that the name [Hermon] means '*anathema*' but gives no details as to why, and he adds that in the present day Gentiles venerate the mountain with profane religion and thus attest the meaning of its name, that is, their worship is *anathema*. The passage is striking because, different from all other Christian writers mentioned above, Hilary mentions the association of the watchers with the peak of Mount Hermon." Jerome has an expanded version of the same tradition, but without a reference to the meaning of Hermon. Cf. Nickelsburg, *1 Enoch 1*, 94. On the Hebrew and Aramaic wordplay for the meaning of Hermon (חרמון < חרם), see the commentary on 1 Enoch 6:6 ("And they [the Watchers] called the mountain 'Hermon' because they swore and bound one another with a curse on it") in Nickelsburg, *1 Enoch 1*, 177.

54. Cf. Nickelsburg, *1 Enoch 1*, 171, 191.

55. The analogy between Paul and Enoch may be even more extensive when the place where they received their respective revelations is considered: Enoch's heavenly journey originated from "the waters of Dan in the land of Dan, which is south of Hermon, to the west" (1 Enoch 13:7), whereas Paul received his seminal revelation on the road to Damascus, which runs along the southeast side of the mountain. See further Nickelsburg, *1 Enoch 1*, 238–47 (Excursus: Sacred Geography in 1 Enoch 6–16).

56. Galatians 3:19 is another text in which angelic mediation of revelation is mentioned, but it is not clear that Paul would want to

allel to this move in Jude.[57] The opposition between heaven and earth continues in Galatians 4:3, which states that before being redeemed, believers were "enslaved under the elements of the world" (ὑπὸ τὰ στοιχεῖα τοῦ κόσμου ἤμεθα δεδουλωμένοι). As in the Epistle of Enoch, this may refer to the cosmic elements that execute judgment on the wicked. In the Hagar-Sarah allegory (Gal 4:21–31), which reintroduces the contrast between slavery and freedom, Paul also refers to the opposition between "the present Jerusalem" (ἡ νῦν Ἰερουσαλήμ) and "the Jerusalem above" (ἡ ἄνω Ἰερουσαλήμ), where the combined spatiotemporal elements of the first member of the opposed pair are collapsed into a bare spatial element of the second member. Believers already experience the freedom associated with being the children of the promise, that is, children of Sarah, who corresponds to the Jerusalem above.

A negative assessment of the present Jerusalem—and particularly, the temple and its cult—is also found in the Epistle of Enoch, especially in the Apocalypse of Weeks, which refers to the construction and destruction of the First Temple (1 Enoch 93:7–8) but does not even mention the subsequent rebuilding of the temple.[58] The Apocalypse of Weeks does, however, expect that after the second of four judgments, an eschatological temple will be built: "the temple of the kingdom of the Great One will be built in the greatness of its glory for all generations of eternity" (91:13). According to the Animal Apocalypse, which regards the Second Temple as polluted from its very inception (89:73), the present Jerusalem will be dismantled and removed, and a new and bigger Jerusalem will be built on its site, where the whole human race, restored to its primordial condition, will dwell (90:28–36).[59] The text states that "the Lord of the sheep [= Israel] *brought*" the new Jerusalem (v. 29), presumably from heaven (cf. Rev 21:2, 10).[60]

In both the Epistle of Enoch and Paul's letter to the Galatians, the saving revelations of their divinely commissioned authors enable the eschatological communities constituted by those revelations both to overcome the dualisms that they have hitherto known as reality and to participate preemptively in the new spatiotemporal reality of the eschaton. On the one hand, the positive correspondence between *Endzeit* and *Urzeit* in terms of the originally intended will of God for creation overcomes the dualistic opposition between the present evil age and the age to come. On the other hand, the saving revelations on which both the Epistle of Enoch and Gala-

impugn the giving of the Law through angels in the same that he would the proclamation of a different gospel. For Paul, the Law is ultimately God-given. On the other hand, both the pernicious revelation given by the angelic Watchers and the revelation of the Law through the angels introduced a similar calamitous effect for human beings, from which they needed deliverance.

57. Cf. Nickelsburg, *1 Enoch 1*, 86: "In addition, the author [of Jude] knows the story of the watchers' rebellion and incarceration (Jude 6) and employs the tradition as an example of the divine punishment that will befall false teachers in the end time. The concern with false teachers is a feature of the Epistle of Enoch (see comm. on 98:4)."

58. Perhaps this is because, in accordance with 1 Enoch 12–16, "The real temple . . . is the heavenly palace of the divine King" (Nickelsburg, *1 Enoch 1*, 54).

59. The expectation of a new Jerusalem, which would be established on a renewed earth, is also found elsewhere in the Enochic corpus (e.g., 10:21–22; 25:2–6; 26:1–2; 27:1).

60. Cf. Nickelsburg, *1 Enoch 1*, 404, 405.

tians are based envisage overcoming the opposition between heaven and earth by means of earthly participation in the heavenly Jerusalem, a kind of heaven on earth or rather "on earth as in heaven."

False Teaching

Both Galatians and the Epistle of Enoch rail against false teachers, who reject the authority of their authors' revelations, pervert the truth, and lead others astray. In Galatians, Paul asserts the authenticity of his visionary revelation in the context of a polemical situation that requires him to denounce his opponents, the false teachers, and to exhort the Galatians to return to the truth of the gospel. He rebukes the Galatians for "turning to a different gospel—not that there is another gospel, but there are some who are confusing you and want to pervert the gospel of Christ" (Gal 1:6–7). Paul goes on to emphasize in 1:8–9 that his is the only gospel: "But even if we or an angel from heaven should proclaim to you a gospel contrary to what we proclaimed to you, let that one be accursed! As we have said before, so now I repeat, if anyone proclaims to you a gospel contrary to what you received, let that one be accursed!" In the course of the letter, Paul refers to "false brothers" in Jerusalem, whom he had to oppose "so that the truth of the gospel might always remain with you" (2:4–5). The conflict in Antioch shows that Paul is willing and able to defend "the truth of the gospel" against anyone, including Peter, who perverts it by requiring the Gentile believers to conform to the prescriptions of the law (2:11–14). He remonstrates against the addressees who have been taken in by the false teachers: "You foolish Galatians! Who has bewitched you?" Paul accuses the Galatians of wanting to return to pagan worship and juxtaposes this accusation to the addressees' observance of the law, suggesting that observing the law is tantamount to returning to their idolatrous past (4:8–11). Paul's opponents teach Torah observance and exclude those who do not keep the law (4:17), insisting particularly that the Galatians undergo circumcision (6:12–13). The apostle becomes vituperative about his opponents in Galatians 5:7–12: "You were running well; who prevented you from obeying the truth? Such persuasion does not come from the one who calls you. [. . .] But whoever it is that is confusing you will bear the judgment. [. . .] I wish those who unsettle you would castrate themselves!" Such rhetoric is appropriate in a situation in which the Galatians' very salvation is at stake, for to go the way of the false teachers means to fall from grace (5:2–4).

In a similar way and for similar reasons, the Epistle of Enoch inveighs against false teachers. Once again, there is a strict dichotomy between truth and error/falsehood.[61] In 98:14–99:2, for

61. Cf. Nickelsburg, *1 Enoch 1*, 51: "Strikingly, 'violence' and 'falsehood' (wrong teaching) are the two catchwords in the Apocalypse of Weeks."

example, Enoch pronounces a series of woes on these teachers for their perverting words and deeds:

> 98:14 Woe to you who annul the words of the righteous; you will have no hope of salvation.
> 15 Woe to those who write lying words and words of error; they write and lead many astray with their lies <when they hear them>. [. . .]
> 99:1 Woe to you who commit erring acts, and who for false deeds receive honor and glory; you will perish, you will have no salvation for good.
> 2 Woe to you who alter the true words and pervert the everlasting covenant and consider themselves to be without sin; they will be swallowed up in the earth.

As Nickelsburg explains, the use of cultic language in 99:1 shows that the false teachers' perverse activity is considered tantamount to idolatry.[62] It is tempting, therefore, to compare Paul's heightened rhetoric in 4:8–11, where Torah observance practiced by the Galatians (as encouraged by the false teachers) is equated with their idolatrous past. In any case, the advent of the false teachers in the end time was already revealed to antediluvian Enoch:

> And now I know this mystery, that sinners will alter and copy the words of truth, and pervert many and lie and invent great fabrications, and write books in their own names. Would that they would write all my words in truth, and neither remove nor alter these words, but write in truth all that I testify to them (1 Enoch 104:10–11).

The fact that the false teachers lead many astray is the nub of the matter for Enoch, for, just as in Galatians, the strict dichotomy between truth and falsehood determines salvation and damnation, respectively. Enoch exhorts his opponents, "Do not be deceived in your heart or lie" (μὴ πλανᾶσθε τῇ καρδίᾳ ὑμῶν μηδὲ ψεύδεσθε, 104:9), although he knows through divine revelation that they will, and that their doom is secure; Paul exhorts the Galatians, "Do not be deceived" (μὴ πλανᾶσθε), so that they can avoid corruption and gain eternal life instead (Gal 6:7–9). For Enoch, the matter of eternal destiny hinges on learning "the paths of truth" from the revelation contained in the sacred Enochic writings (1 Enoch 104:13; cf. 105:2).[63] Paul uses similar "path" imagery and emphasizes the utter seriousness of being on the right path, that is, in accordance with the gospel he has received by revelation. Thus, when Paul perceived that Peter and the Jewish Christians in Antioch "were not walking on the right path toward the truth of the gospel (οὐκ ὀρθοποδοῦσιν πρὸς τὴν ἀλήθειαν τοῦ εὐαγγελίου)" (Gal 2:14), he opposed Peter to

62. Cf. Nickelsburg, *1 Enoch 1*, 488.
63. For other passages in 1 Enoch that refer to "the path of truth," see 71:17 ("And thus there will be length of days with that son of man, and there will be peace for the righteous, and the path of truth for the righteous"); 91:4 ("Love the truth and walk in it; but do not draw near to the truth with a double heart, and do not associate with those of a double heart. But walk in righteousness, my children; and it will guide you in the paths of goodness, and righteousness will be your companion").

his face, because, in accordance with the anathema he had already pronounced on purveyors of "another gospel" (1:8–9), Peter "stood condemned" (Gal 2:11).

Obviously, then, the issue with the false teachers in both Galatians and the Epistle of Enoch relates to the two-ways tradition that is clearly evident in both letters.[64] The metaphor of the two ways or two paths was widely used in ancient ethical instruction to indicate that a life of vice or virtue was based on choice and to indicate the consequences of the way of virtue as the way of life and the way of vice as the way of death.[65] In the Epistle of Enoch, the metaphor of the two ways is a very prominent part of the exhortations (cf. 1 Enoch 92:3; 94:1–4; 99:10; 104:13; 105:2).[66] For example, 1 Enoch 99:10 reads as follows:

> Then blessed will be all who listen to the words of the wise, and learn to do the commandments of the Most High; and walk in the paths of his righteousness, and do not err with the erring; for they will be saved.

In Galatians, the two-ways tradition comes out most prominently in the opposition between the flesh and the Spirit and their respective deeds, the one leading to corruption and exclusion from inheritance of the kingdom of God and the other to eternal life (Gal 5:16–6:8).[67]

False teaching is a huge problem that both Paul and "Enoch" had to confront. Certain individuals rejected the revelatory claims of our authors, perverted the truth, and led others astray. Given the life-or-death nature of the revelatory claims, our authors fought back hard, warning readers of the false teachers' wiles and condemning the false teachers to perdition.

Persecution

Both Galatians and the Epistle of Enoch give evidence of ongoing persecution that the eschatological community of the elect experiences. Much of Jewish apocalyptic literature, including 1 Enoch (especially the Epistle), is rooted in the experience of religious persecution and social

64. On the comparison of the Pauline material in Romans and Galatians with the two-ways/two-spirits instruction in 1QS, see George W. E. Nickelsburg, "The Incarnation: Paul's Solution to the Universal Human Predicament," in *The Future of Early Christianity: Essays in Honor of Helmut Koester*, ed. Birger A. Pearson (Minneapolis: Fortress Press, 1991), 348–57; cf. Jouette Bassler, "The Faith of Christ, the Obedience of Christ, and the Spirit of Christ: Response to 'The Incarnation: Paul's Solution to the Universal Human Predicament,'" in *George W. E. Nickelsburg in Perspective: An Ongoing Dialogue of Learning*, ed. Jacob Neusner and Alan J. Avery-Peck, 2 vols., JSJSup 80, (Leiden: Brill, 2003), 2.589–612.

65. Cf. Nickelsburg, *1 Enoch 1*, 454–56 ("Excursus: The Two Ways"); David E. Aune, "Two-ways Tradition," *The Westminster Dictionary of New Testament and Early Christian Literature and Rhetoric* (Louisville: Westminster John Knox, 2003), 478.

66. Cf. Nickelsburg, *1 Enoch 1*, 50–51: "Central, especially to the paraenesis of the Epistle, is the metaphor of the two ways. . . . The commandments for right conduct and obedience to these commandments involve walking on the path of uprightness. By contrast, disobedience is construed as straying from the right path (5:4; 93:9; 99:10), walking on the path(s) of wickedness and violence, or perverting the truth (93:9; 99:2; 104:9). Within this frame of reference, the Epistle threatens punishments for wrong conduct in lengthy sets of woes that have many parallels in the prophetic corpus, but also appear in a wisdom text like Sirach." For the metaphor of the two ways in the rest of 1 Enoch, see 91:3–4, 18–19; 108:13.

67. The theme of the last judgment is more muted in Galatians (e.g., 5:10; 6:8) than it is in 1 Enoch, where it the expectation of an impending judgment occurs throughout.

oppression.[68] The Epistle of Enoch encourages the chosen in the midst of persecution. In 95:7, for example, woe is pronounced on "you sinners because you persecute the righteous; for you will be handed over and persecuted because of injustice, and their yoke will be heavy upon you."[69] "Fear not, you have suffered; for you will receive healing . . ." (96:3; cf. v. 8).[70] At the end of the seventh week, the chosen "will uproot the foundations of violence, and the structure of deceit in it, to execute judgment" (91:11). Unfortunately, it is impossible to tell whether the persecution of the chosen relates specifically to the community's marginalization of the Mosaic Torah—for the specifics of revealed law of the Enochic way are not spelled out, and the reason for the persecution of the chosen is not elaborated. We may surmise that, at least in part, the persecution is religiously motivated, because one of the key issues that Enoch emphasizes is the proper observance of times and seasons based on a solar calendar that was revealed to him (cf. esp. 1 Enoch 72–82).[71] The calendar was known to have been an especially thorny issue in early Judaism, particularly between the Temple establishment and sectarian Jewish groups—leading, in some cases, to persecution.[72]

In Galatians, we are better informed. Paul's letter makes it clear that the persecution is religiously motivated and that it pertains particularly to issues of Torah observance. Paul himself was a violent persecutor of the church before his conversion/call (Gal 1:13, 23); he does not state why he persecuted the church, but his persecuting activity evidently followed from his being a zealot for his ancestral traditions concerning the Torah (v. 14). Perhaps his use of Deuteronomy 21:23 in Galatians 3:13b gives us a clue to his former Pharisaic perspective on the

68. Cf. Nickelsburg, *1 Enoch 1*, 2, 28, 37, 40, 41, 47, 48, 62–64, 354, 355, 356, 378, 499, 556.

69. Cf. also 1 Enoch 96:5, 8; 98:4; 98:13; 99:11, 15; 100:7, 10. Nickelsburg summarizes: "Moreover, taken together, the specific references to the sinners' punishment in the woes, the vivid descriptions of the judgment, and the claims that the righteous will participate ion the judgment of the sinners suggest that the Epistle served a cathartic function for an audience that perceived itself as severely and unjustly victimized by its enemies" (*1 Enoch 1*, 429).

70. Cf. 1 Enoch 103:9–104:6.

71. Cf., e.g., 1 Enoch 82:4–8: "Blessed are the righteous who walk in the way of the righteous and have no sin like the sinners in numbering the days the sun travels in the sky through the gates, entering and emerging for thirty days with the heads of thousands of the order of the stars, with the four additional ones that divide between the four parts of the year that lead them and enter with the four days. (5) People err regarding them and do not calculate them in the numbering of the entire world because they err regarding them and people do not understand them precisely. (6) For they belong in the reckoning of the year and are indeed recorded forever; one in the first gate, one in the third gate, one in the fourth, and one in the sixth. (Thus) a year of 364 days is completed. (7) The account about it is true and its calculation is precisely recorded because the luminaries and the months, the festivals, the years, and the days he showed me, and Uriel, to whom the Lord of the entire creation gave orders for me regarding the host of heaven, breathed on me. (8) He has power in heaven over night and day to make light appear over humanity: the sun, the moon, the stars, and all the heavenly powers which revolve in their circuits."

72. A classic case in point relates to the Day of Atonement. As is well known, the Habbakuk Pesher of Qumran portrays the Wicked Priest, who is probably a high priest, as pursuing his enemies near the Dead Sea on the Day of Atonement, the holiest day of the year, the very day on which the high priest was supposed to be officiating at the solemn ceremonies in the Jerusalem temple, entering into the holy of holies on behalf of the people, and avoiding all forms of labor, including travel. The implication is that the Wicked Priest and the Qumran community followed different calendars. Cf. James C. VanderKam, *Calendars in the Dead Sea Scrolls: Measuring Time* (London: Routledge, 1998), 44–45, citing 1QpHab 11:4–8 (a commentary on Hab 2:15): "Its interpretation concerns the Wicked Priest who pursued the Teacher of Righteousness to consume him with the ferocity of his anger in the place of his banishment, in festival time, during the rest of the Day of Atonement. He paraded in front of them, to consume them and make them fall on the day of fasting, the sabbath of their rest."

crucified Christ as accursed according to the Law (and therefore, the need to root out his ardent followers).[73] In the Hagar-Sarah allegory (4:21–31), just as Ishmael "was persecuting" Isaac, "so also now" (4:29). Apparently, the Galatians are experiencing persecution, perhaps by the false teachers (who therefore represent the present Jerusalem and are the spiritual descendants of the slave woman, Hagar, and her son). In evidence that he is not proclaiming circumcision as obligatory for gentile believers, Paul asks indignantly why he is still being persecuted (5:11), although he does not mention by whom he is being persecuted or what the persecution entails. In contrast to 5:11, the false teachers are attempting to avoid persecution by proclaim circumcision as obligatory for gentile believers: "Those who want to make a good showing in the flesh are compelling you to be circumcised, only in order that they not be persecuted for the cross of Christ" (6:12).

Conclusion

In the foregoing, we have attempted to answer the question of how Paul's letter to the Galatians compares with the Epistle of Enoch (1 Enoch 92–105). To answer this question, we compared the two writings in terms of their epistolary form and the apocalyptic features they have in common, particularly the central feature of special revelation in each. Although our findings are necessarily preliminary and would require a more thoroughgoing elaboration and confirmation, we can already see that Galatians compares in some fairly fundamental and substantial ways to the "apocalyptic" Epistle of Enoch, allowing us to argue that Galatians is also an "apocalyptic" writing. Whether this means that Galatians was actually influenced by 1 Enoch is an open question for the purposes of the present study. Our goal here has been merely to ascertain whether the two writings are *analogous*, and the evidence for that possibility seems impressive. Nevertheless, when we consider the fact that the large number of specific comparisons between the two writings include similarities of *both* form *and* content, the possibility that they have a genetic relationship, whether direct or indirect, does present itself.[74] We conclude, therefore, with two questions for further consideration, which can be addressed on another occasion: (1) How likely is it that the commonalities between Galatians and the Epistle of Enoch are merely coincidental? (2) Can we invoke Occam's razor in order to argue that it is more likely that Paul was indeed influenced by the Epistle of Enoch, rather than by another epistle with many parallels in content both to Galatians and to the Epistle of Enoch?

73. In that case, Paul has modified his former perspective on the crucified Christ by stating in v. 13a that he became a curse "for us" (ὑπὲρ ἡμῶν). On this interpretation of Gal 3:13b, see further Martin Hengel, *The Pre-Christian Paul* (London: SCM Press; Philadelphia: Trinity Press International, 1991), 83–84.

74. I am grateful to Prof. George Nickelsburg for pressing me on the issue of the combined effect of form and content for my argument (personal communication, 03/06/14). He also graciously read an earlier draft of the present paper and made a number of helpful suggestions for improvement, as did my assistant, Spencer Jones. I, of course, take full responsibility for the final form.

Our comparative study breaks open new vistas for investigating Paul's letter to the Galatians. In closing, just two examples will be mentioned in brief: (1) the striking absence of the designation of "saints, holy ones" with respect to the Galatians, and (2) the meaning of the term "the Israel of God" in Galatians 6:16.

First, given the fact that both 1 Enoch in general[75] and the Epistle of Enoch in particular[76] use "holy ones" as a designation for those who constitute the eschatological community,[77] it is noteworthy that Paul does not refer to the Galatians as "saints," even though in his other letters, he often refers to the addressees as οἱ ἅγιοι.[78] The absence of this designation in Galatians may be a purposeful omission. Are the Galatians in such great danger of submitting to a "different gospel" that they are at risk of forfeiting their status as "holy ones"? As both 1 Enoch and Galatians show, it only those who believe in and act upon the special revelation of their authors who are constitutive of the eschatological community of the elect. At several points in Galatians, Paul indicates that the outcome of the situation for the Galatians' salvation seems tenuous (cf. Gal 3:4; 5:2–4, 7–12).

Second, the question of whether "the Israel of God" (ὁ Ἰσραὴλ τοῦ θεοῦ) in Galatians 6:16 should be interpreted: (a) as a designation for the church consisting of Jews and gentiles, or rather (b) as an epithet for the physical progeny of Abraham (e.g., the elect community from the historic people of Israel) is an issue that the analogy between 1 Enoch and Galatians reopens afresh. The expression "the Israel of God" is unparalleled in contemporary Jewish or Christian sources, so Paul's usage must be deduced from its context in Galatians. We are asking here whether the analogy of 1 Enoch may be helpful in ascertaining that context. For as we have seen, the eschatological community that 1 Enoch envisages includes the Gentile nations, but nothing is said there about the latter needing first to become members of the nation of Israel as

75. Cf. Nickelsburg and VanderKam, *1 Enoch 2*, 100n24: "For the expression 'the holy ones,' either by itself or in combination with 'the righteous' and/or 'the chosen,' see 38:42, 5; 39:4; 41:2; 43:4; 48:1, 7, 9; 50:1; 51:2; 58:3, 5; 62:8; 65:12." See also Paul Trebilco, "The Saints—οἱ ἅγιοι," in idem, *Self-Designations and Group Identity in the New Testament* (Cambridge: Cambridge University Press, 2012), 122–63 (125–26).

76. Cf. 1 Enoch 100:5: "He will set a guard of the holy angels over all the righteous and holy ones. . . ."

77. Cf. Nickelsburg, *1 Enoch 1*, 64: "the 108 chapters of 1 Enoch provide little explicit information about an Enochic community. Nevertheless, some textual evidence points in the direction of a community or group. Collective terms like 'the righteous, the chosen, the holy' indicate a consciousness of community, though without any indication that the community had concrete manifestations in specific places. To use a NT analogy, the terminology parallels Paul's use of 'the saints' and 'the church,' but not his reference to 'the church(es) at. . . .'"

78. Cf. Trebilco, "The Saints," 128–37 (128): "οἱ ἅγιοι is one of Paul's favorite designations for Christians. The statistics of its use are: Romans: 8; 1 Corinthians: 6; 2 Corinthians: 5; Philippians: 3; Colossians: 4; 1 Thessalonians: 1; 2 Thessalonians: 1; Philemon: 2, giving a total of thirty occurrences. The substantivized participle occurs in 1 Cor 1:2." Also absent in Galatians are the following designations for the eschatological community that are found both in *1 Enoch* and in Paul's other letters:(1) "beloved" (ἀγαπητοί): Rom 1:7; 12:19; 1 Cor 10:14; 15:58; 2 Cor 7:1; 12:19; Phil 2:12; 4:1; cf. 1 Enoch 91:3 "Hear, O sons of Enoch, every word of your father, and listen aright to the voice of my mouth; for I testify to you and speak to you, my beloved."(2) "the elect/chosen" (οἱ ἐκλεκτοί): Rom 8:33; 16:13; Col 3:12; 2 Tim 2:10; Tit 1:1; cf. 1 Enoch 1:1 ("the righteous chosen"), 3, 8; 5:6, 7, 8; 25:5; 38:2, 3, 4; 39:6, 7; 40:5; 41:2; 45:3, 5; 48:1, 9; 50:1; 51:5b; 56:6, 8; 58:1, 2, 3; 60:6 ("the elect"), 8; 61:4, 12, 13; 62:7, 8, 11, 12, 13, 15; 70:3; 92:2; 93:10.(3) "the called" (οἱ κλητοί): Rom 1:6, 7; 8:28; 1 Cor 1:2, 24.

an entry requirement. Within the Epistle of Enoch, the Apocalypse of Weeks affirms that Israel will endure “as a plant of righteousness forever and ever” (1 Enoch 93:5). Indeed, during the seventh week, “the chosen will be chosen, as witnesses of righteousness from the everlasting plant of righteousness” (93:10). In other words, an exclusive group will be chosen from within Israel. In the ninth week, the Gentiles come into the picture, but they are not incorporated into Israel; they simply follow the path of universally revealed wisdom: “After this there will arise a ninth week, in which righteous law will be revealed to all the sons of the whole earth . . . , and all humankind will look to the path of everlasting righteousness” (93:14). The eschatological status of the Gentile nations is also discussed in the Animal Apocalypse. At the time of the new creation, the Gentile nations (wild beasts) do not become Israel (sheep); rather, both Israel and the nations become white bulls (90:38), which signifies the return of humankind to its pristine condition at the creation of the world (Adam was a white bull according to 85:3). Hence, in the analogy of 1 Enoch in general and the Epistle of Enoch in particular, we would be inclined to interpret “the Israel of God” in Galatians 6:16 as referring to the physical progeny of Abraham, that is, the historic people of Israel.[79]

79. This still leaves open the question of whether ὁ Ἰσραὴλ τοῦ θεοῦ refers to the Israel designated “Israel according to the flesh” in 1 Cor 10:18 or rather to the Israel that adheres to Paul’s *κανών* as given in Gal 6:15. It seems likely that Paul is referring here to the elect community from the historic people of Israel.

10

Apocalyptic Thought in the Epistles of Colossians and Ephesians

Benjamin Wold

Most treatments of apocalyptic and Pauline letters have their point of departure in "apocalyptic eschatology."[1] In this chapter, I seek to move beyond discussions in which eschatology is the defining and overriding framework through which apocalyptic is considered. The investigation here is concerned to address an apocalyptic worldview and how it may influence the authors of Colossians and Ephesians.[2] However, with this said, such an endeavor requires at least some clarification about how I use the term "apocalyptic," which denotes here an "apocalyptic worldview." An underlying assumption about any definition of this worldview is that form, in some way, correlates to content. Since Klaus Koch suggested that the beginning of a

1. Martin C. de Boer, "Paul and Apocalyptic Eschatology," in *The Encyclopedia of Apocalypticism, Volume 1*, ed. John J. Collins (New York: Continuum, 1998), 345–83.
2. The treatment of apocalyptic in "Colossians and Ephesians" here assumes, following the *opinio communis*, that Ephesians is a product of Colossians. Moreover, Colossian's character, in broad terms, reflects "Paulinism" and the final form may be attributed to one of his followers—whether shortly after or within Paul's life time. For the sake of convenience the author is discussed here simply as "Paul." John Muddiman, *A Commentary on the Epistle to the Ephesians*, BNTC (London/New York: Continuum, 2001) makes the relationship of Ephesians and Colossians central to his commentary.

binding definition of apocalyptic starts with form,[3] we have seen developments where form is separated from content. The Society of Biblical Literature genre project that resulted in the *Semeia* 14 volume marks an important moment when apocalyptic is reduced to genre, even if John Collins comments in the introduction that "[i]f apocalypticism is assumed to be at all related to apocalypses, then the analysis of the literary genre must cast some light on the social phenomenon, even if they cannot be directly correlated."[4] When, in *Semeia* 36, the definition of apocalyptic is returned to, Adela Yarbro Collins writes that in light of ongoing discussions, apocalyptic is "intended to interpret present, earthly circumstances in light of the supernatural world and of the future, and to influence both the understanding and the behavior of the audience by means of divine authority."[5] These comments orient my perspective particularly because in Colossians and Ephesians one encounters the theme of transcendent knowledge quite regularly.

Related to revelation in these letters, authority may, at times, be seen as derived from present participation of individuals and community in another world. Adding to this, otherworldly beings—angels and demons—are part of the fabric of their apocalyptic worldview: evil is attributed to otherworldly beings and the resolution of the problem of evil comes, at least in part, from outside of this world. While revelation, otherworldly beings, and questions about evil are prominent in the presentation below, other possible characteristics of apocalyptic thought are noted, such as dualistic categories and pairings in binary opposites. Moreover, while eschatology is not the point of departure, it is by no means ignored. Future reward for the righteous and punishment for the wicked in the hereafter are present in these letters and are situated within the larger context of the ancient phenomenon of apocalypticism.

Colossians

The letter to the Colossians begins with interest in transcendent knowledge—namely, the revealing of mysteries and wisdom (Col 1:9). These hidden mysteries are revealed to the saints (1:25–26) and wisdom is the revelation of the mystery of Christ (1:28; 2:2–3). Indeed, the "mystery hidden for ages and generations" (1:26) in one textual variant reads "from angels and men," rather than "generations." Observing revelation in these verses also draws attention to a viewpoint on an elect, endtime community, community as the locus of mysteries (1:26–27), and otherworldly beings.

Several different dualistic expressions are found in Colossians. One is the dualistic pairing of

3. Klaus Koch, *The Rediscovery of Apocalyptic*, SBT 22 (London: SCM, 1972), 24.
4. John J. Collins, "Introduction: Toward the Morphology of a Genre," *Semeia* 14 (1979): 1–20 (4).
5. Adela Yarbro Collins, "Introduction: Early Christian Apocalypses," *Semeia* 36 (1986): 1–11 (7).

"light" and "darkness" and is used to depict the saints' inheritance when they are transferred from the power of darkness (1:12). The dominion of darkness and the kingdom of the Son of "light" express deliverance as being from the reign of evil and implies that an agent outside of history and humanity is responsible for present evil. This is followed up in 2:15, when God disarms the principalities and powers, and thus, triumphs over them. Another pairing is "heaven" and "earth" and this contrast (1:16; cf. 1:20) represents spatial dualities, which is a characteristic of apocalypses. Later (3:5–17), the exhortation to "put to death what is earthly" describes a type of evil impulse while "put on the new nature" describes the good. This internal duality is present in the *Treatise on the Two Spirits* (1QS 3:13–4:26) and elsewhere in the Qumran Scrolls.[6] The conflict between good and evil presented in dualistic pairings expresses a struggle of good and evil, and concludes with good prevailing, which falls within an apocalyptic framework.

In Colossians, God creates the visible and the invisible (1:15–16), making explicit the recognition of the otherworldly. The invisible is heavenly and may include otherworldly beings in the form of angels and perhaps demons (cf. 2:15).[7] Reconciling all things "whether on earth or in heaven" (1:20) implies a cosmic dimension to redemption (cf. Lord's Prayer and the *Kaddish*). Angelic beings occupy a central place in any discussion of apocalyptic thought in the epistle, and is returned to below, most notably in relationship to the "elemental spirits" (2:8) and the "worship of angels" (2:18).

Salvation is eschatological even if believers experience a new life in Christ already. Future reward is introduced in 1:5, where the Colossians have "hope laid up in heaven." That Christ is the first-born from the dead heralds resurrection for the members of the body, the church (1:18). The present reality of having been raised with Christ (3:1) is a feature of the realized eschatology of the letter, and yet, life in the present world contends with ongoing evil.[8] However, even this is immediately balanced with the future orientation of the one and only reference to the *parousia* (3:4) in Colossians.[9] The negative counterpart to reward (i.e., future "inheritance" in 3:24) concludes the letter, with the wrongdoer facing judgment and justice (3:25).

These themes—revelation of mysteries, conflict expressed with dualities, otherworldly fea-

6. Loren T. Stuckenbruck, "The Interiorization of Dualism within the Human Being in Second Temple Judasim: The Treatise on the Two Spirits (1QS III:13–IV:26) in its Tradition-Historical Context," in *Light Against Darkness: Dualism in Ancient Mediterranean Religion and the Contemporary World*, ed. Armin Lange, Eric M. Meyers, Bennie H. Reynolds, III, and Randall Styers, JAJSup 2 (Göttingen: Vandenhoeck & Ruprecht, 2011), 158.

7. A.Wesley Carr, *Angels and Principalities: The Background, Meaning and Development of the Pauline Phrase* hai archai kai hai exousiai, SNTSMS 42 (Cambridge: Cambridge University Press, 2005) challenges that there are evil powers.

8. Loren T. Stuckenbruck, "The Dead Sea Scrolls and the New Testament," *in Qumran and the Bible: Studying the Jewish and Christian Scriptures in Light of the Dead Sea Scrolls*, ed. Nóra Dávid and Armin Lange, CBET 57 (Leuven: Peters, 2010), 131–70 (145–50), discusses the "already" and "not yet" aspects of early Christian literature within the broader context of early Jewish thought and makes a convincing case that apocalyptic traditions reflect a similar scheme.

9. Unlike Ephesians, where there is no clear reference to the *parousia* (cf. possible allusions in 1:14; 4:30).

tures, future reward/punishment for individuals—introduce Colossians and are then followed through the letter. How one interprets the controversy in chapter 2 is often seen as determinative for interpreting mysteries, angelic beings, and cosmological ideas. Indeed, the "philosophy" of Paul's opponents (2:8) has long been central to any treatment of this letter and plays no less a role when considering the presence of apocalyptic worldviews here. To this topic, we now turn.

Heavenly Ascent

Colossians 2:8–23 marks out a section that has been fiercely debated. In 2:8 is our first glimpse of the Christ followers' opponents ("See to it that no one makes a prey of you by philosophy and empty deceit, according to human tradition, according to the elemental spirits of the universe [κατὰ τὰ στοιχεῖα τοῦ κόσμου], and not according to Christ"), which is followed by a review of the life that they have enjoyed in Christ.[10] The threat is that instead of believers looking to Christ as their fulfillment, they might follow an alternative in which angelic beings occupy a crucial role. Specific ways in which Christ has offered fullness of life are detailed: true circumcision (2:11), baptism (2:12), enjoyment of a new relationship to sin as defined in legal description (2:13), and also, freedom from evil personified (2:15). The opponents at Colossae call into question dietary practices and observance of Sabbath, festivals, and new moon (2:16; cf. 11Q5 27:7). In 2:18, Paul refers again to this philosophy, that they "insist on self-abasement [ταπεινοφροσύνῃ] and worship of angels [θρησκείᾳ τῶν ἀγγέλων], dwelling on visions [ἃ ἑόρακεν ἐμβατεύων]." The "elemental spirits" (στοιχεῖον τοῦ κόσμου) come into view again in 2:20 and the details of subjecting oneself to them are described by several prohibitions (2:21) and rigorous ascetic practices (2:23) that are prescribed in order to gain wisdom.

The στοιχεῖα have been convincingly translated as "elemental *spirits,*" based upon the context of 2:8–23 and the broader use of "elements" in the Greek literature of the period.[11] Spirits are also seen to control "elements" in Jewish apocalyptic thought (esp. Jubilees 2:2, Testament of Abraham 13:11; 1 Enoch 75:1). Eduard Lohse is well noted for associating these elemental spirits with the angels in 2:18 and also the cosmic powers (ἐξουσίας in 2:10, 15).[12] In Lohse's view, 2:18 depicts humanity engaged in "worship of the angels" (θρησκείᾳ τῶν ἀγγέλων) and angelic beings as recipients of worship. This practice involved making oneself subservient to them before entering into the divine "fullness" (*contra* Christ as the true fullness in 2:9–10). By relating to angels rightly, which includes an initiation by circumcision followed by ascetic practices, one

10. Unless otherwise indicated, English translations are from the NRSV.
11. See esp. D. Rusam, "Neue Belege zu den στοιχεῖα τοῦ κόσμου (Gal 4:3, 9; Kol 2:8, 20)," *ZNW* 83 (1992): 119–25; and bibliography of G. Delling, *TDNT* 7.670.
12. Eduard Lohse, *Colossians and Philemon*, Hermeneia (Philadelphia: Fortress Press, 1972), 117–18.

gains wisdom (1:9, 28; 2:3, 23; 3:16; 4:5), insight (1:9; 2:2), and knowledge (1:6, 9–10).[13] This makes sense of ἐθελοθρησκίᾳ (2:23), a term that indicates "rigorous piety" when worshiping angels. Whereas Lohse has attracted adherents to his view on the cultic veneration of angels, specifically reading angels as the object of the genitive in the phrase θρησκείᾳ τῶν ἀγγέλων, fewer have followed him when he sets this within "Gnostic" religiosity.[14]

Fred O. Francis rightly observed that in 2:18 angels could be read as the subject of the genitive (θρησκείᾳ τῶν ἀγγέλων) making them the worshippers of God.[15] For Francis, human participation in heavenly angelic worship is located within Jewish ascetic mystical piety, and the aim was "to enter heaven in order to possess themselves of salvation, a portion of the Lord."[16] Much of Francis's conclusion rests upon his assessment of the phrase ἃ ἑόρακεν ἐμβατεύων (2:18), translated "which he has seen upon entering" and refers to heavenly ascent as found in Jewish apocalyptic literature. Francis offers a number of examples of heavenly journey and participation (Ascension of Isaiah 8:17; 9:28, 33; Apocalypse of Abraham 17; Apocalypse of Zephaniah 8:3–4), and as this view has been taken up and adapted by others, a number of other parallels have been noted (1QSa 2:8–9; 1QSb 99:25–26; 1QM 7:4–6; 1QH^{a} 9:10–13; 4QShir).[17]

Despite differences in how the details are worked out, there is a growing consensus that the "philosophy" of the opponents in Colossians 2:8–23 should be situated within a Jewish context that conceives of heavenly ascent and worship with the angels. James Dunn summarizes that this is "an apocalyptic or mystical Judaism transposed to the Diaspora which has been able to make itself attractive to those sympathetic to Judaism" and that these opponents belonged to one of the Colossian synagogues. Indeed, it is difficult to deny that when food and drink are juxtaposed with Sabbath, festivals, and new moons in 2:16, this fits within inter-Jewish dynamics (cf. 1QM 2:4). In the words of Dunn, the "conflict that arises is between the synagogue and the spin put on access to heavenly worship, namely proclamation of Christ."[18]

Loren Stuckenbruck advances the topic by suggesting that the "customary alternative posed

13. James D. G. Dunn, *The Epistles to the Colossians and to Philemon*, NIGTC (Grand Rapids: Eerdmans, 1996), 27.

14. Cf. Martin Dibelius, "Die Isisweihe bei Aupleius und Verwandte Initiations-Riten," in *Botschaft und Geschichte. Gesammelte Aufsätze von Martin Dibelius* (Tübingen: J. C. B. Mohr [Paul] Siebeck, 1956), 59–64, who finds the context among mystery religions; published in English, "The Isis Initiation in Apuleius and Rleated Initiatory Rites," in *Conflict at Colossae: A Problem in the Interpretation of Early Christianity Illustrated by Selected Modern Studies, revised ed.*, ed. Fred O. Francis and Wayne Meeks, SBLSBS 4 (Missoula, MT: SBL/Scholars, 1975), 61–122.

15. Fred O. Francis, "Humility and Angelic Worship in Col. 2:18," *ST* 16 (1962): 109–34; reprinted in *Conflict at Colossae*, 163–96; idem, "The Background of EMBATEUEIN (Col 2:18) in Legal Papyri and Oracle Inscriptions," in *Conflict at Colossae*, 197–208. For similar uses of the genitive, see 4 Macc 5:7 and Josephus, *Antiquities*, 12:253.

16. Francis, "Humility," 199.

17. Thomas J. Sappington, *Revelation and Redemption at Colossae*, JSNTSup 53 (Sheffield: JSOT, 1991), 90–94; Michael Mach, *Entwicklungsstudien des jüdischen Engelglaubens in varrabbinischer Zeit*, TSAJ 34 (Tübingen: J. C. B. Mohr [Paul Siebeck], 1992), 239–40; cf. R. Yates, "'The Worship of Angels' (Col. 2:18)," *ExpTim* (1987): 12–15; Craig A. Evans, "The Colossian Mystics," *Bib* 63 (1982): 198.

18. Dunn, *Colossians*, 34; Sappington, *Revelation and Redemption*, 225 the situation at Colossae is "strongly oriented toward the ascetic-mystical piety of Jewish apocalypticism."

between a subjective and objective interpretation of τῶν ἀγγέλων is misleading."[19] That Francis has successfully demonstrated a connection between 2:8–23 and heavenly encounters is not in question; however, Stuckenbruck suggests a less literal connotation for the verb ἑόρακεν, which he contends is better understood not so much as "to see" but rather "to experience by means of seeing." For Stuckenbruck, it is unnecessary to decide whether τῶν ἀγγέλων is an objective or subjective genitive because veneration of angels and human participation in angelic worship "are found side by side in a number of early Jewish texts," and Stuckenbruck concludes that the opponents in 2:18 "are said to emphasize 'humility and worship of angels,' which they have 'experienced within a visionary medium while entering (heavenly realms).'" The reasons for a visionary context of angel veneration at Colossae may be viewed in two different ways: (1) angelic worship is exemplary and deserving of veneration, or (2) mystical ascent is dangerous and angels may be petitioned for assistance and accompaniment.[20]

Paul's polemics against his adversaries, who view participation with angelic beings as a present reality, carries implications for how he conceives of his own community sharing presently in the heavens. That is, if his opponents enjoy communion with angels in the here and now, then life in Christ is the counterpoint and the Colossian Christians already share in the glory of heaven vis-à-vis Christ (2:11; 3:1). Christopher Rowland describes the faithful enjoying an inheritance "in light" (1:12) as a reference to "communion with the angels (cf. 1QS 11.7f.)."[21] When in 3:1 the saints are said to be raised with Christ they are also exhorted to "seek the things that are above" where Christ is seated. Unlike those who follow strict ascetic practices in order to commune with angels, Christ followers need not resort to additional practices to gain access to the heavens (2:18). On account of Christ, the saints have died to the "elemental spirits" (2:20), a statement that is a rejection of regulations listed in 2:21—"do not handle, do not taste, do not touch." As Rowland explains: "It was illegitimate, therefore, for the believer to look outside his relationship with Christ for knowledge of the world above (2:19), as the very essence of divinity was to be found in his person (2:9)."[22]

Conclusions

Beyond the scope of the present chapter is a thoroughgoing assessment and adjudication of any one position on the Colossian controversy and "philosophy." Following the majority who articulate a Jewish apocalyptic, or mystical, belief in ascent and worship of angels, observa-

19. Loren T. Stuckenbruck, *Angel Veneration and Christology: A Studying in Early Judaism and in the Christology of the Apocalypse of John*, WUNT II/70 (Tübingen: Mohr Siebeck, 1995), 111–19.

20. Stuckenbruck, *Angel Veneration*, 119.

21. Christopher Rowland, "Apocalyptic Visions and the Exaltation of Christ in the Letter to the Colossians," *JSNT* 19 (1983): 73–83.

22. Rowland, "Apocalyptic Visions," 78.

tions arise in regard to Paul and his place within the phenomenon of ancient apocalypticism.[23] First, Jewish apocalypticism was a feature of religious practice among the Diaspora. As such, questions about the relationship of Paul to apocalypticism, in terms of tracing lines of influence, may be directed in like measure to his opponents. That is, many of the documents used to assess the Colossian "philosophy" are representative of Palestinian Jewish thought and just as one might pose a question about how Paul's theology is influenced or shares influences with, for instance, Qumran literature, so too his Colossian opponents. By defining Paul's opponents as "apocalyptic," it becomes more difficult to deny that similar streams of tradition orient Paul's thought. Moreover, assigning patterns of thinking to either Diaspora or Palestinian Judaism is problematized. Second, the way in which Christ's significance is described in Colossians takes shape in reaction to this "philosophy," and as such, does not reject ascent or the possibility of heavenly worship. What is unacceptable are the *means* of participating in the heavens and the *subject* of devotion. Paul's polemics could have been articulated in a more broadly sweeping condemnation of the matrices undergirding the "philosophy" (e.g., Sir 3:21–29), but he does not. This particular notion of communion with angels through Christ may be born of a response to apocalyptic and/or mystical Jewish practices in the Diaspora.

Questions about influence arise in regard to the domestic codes (the so-called *Haustafeln*) in 3:18–4:1, where family relations are the subject of teaching. However, for reasons that become clear below, this belongs to a discussion of Ephesians 5:21–6:9, where Colossians' teaching about the family are reworked.

Ephesians

Two motifs common to Colossians and Ephesians, even if different in detail, are: (1) emphasis on revelation, and (2) heavenly ascent. In relation to how knowledge is conceived, Ephesians develops ideas about revelation and emphasizes mysteries, which serves to further accentuate apocalyptic tones. How "evil" is constructed in Ephesians, and the degree to which attention is given it, is significantly more progressed than that found in Colossians. In this section, transcendent knowledge, participation in the heavenlies, and a battle against evil depicted in cosmic terms are the main topics of interest.

In Ephesians, chapters 1 and 3 are expressions related to revelation of cosmology, mysteries, and resolution of time. The fullness of time in 1:10 unites all "things in heaven and things on earth" in Christ, and this is a mystery made known through revealing wisdom and insight (1:9). Indeed, the author petitions on behalf of the saints that they be given a spirit of wisdom and revelation (1:17). By exalting Christ to God's right hand in the heavens, a type of cosmic rec-

23. This formulation begs further questions on definitions and the relationship between "apocalypticism" and "mysticism."

onciliation takes place (1:20). Christ is given authority in this age and in the time to come, but in the present Christ's place as head of the body, the church (1:22–23), and the struggle against the powers of the present darkness (6:12) have not been fully realized.

Paul's distinctive role as recipient of revelation is particularly remarkable, especially as the scope of his role broadens to the church universal to whom he is messenger and revealer of mysteries. This is found in Ephesians 3:3 where mysteries are revealed to the author who has a special role assisting others to see mysteries hidden for ages (3:4); this latter point converges with resolution of time. The present is a time of fullness, as the mysteries were not revealed to past generations but only to the apostles in the present. Revelation of wisdom and time are part of a cosmic drama which is displayed when mysteries are also made known to principalities and powers in the heavenly places (3:10).

Heavenly Ascent

Among the most difficult passages to interpret in Ephesians is 4:8–10, where imagery of mystical ascent and descent occur. How apostles came to be recipients of revelation appears to be a matter of gifts given to men (4:7–11). Gift giving, in measure to each (4:7), takes place through the heavenly ascent of Christ; he "ascended on high and led a host of captives" (4:8), and to these "captives," gifts are given. These lines have been convincingly interpreted as influenced by Moses-traditions concerning heavenly ascent at Sinai. Psalm 68:19 in later tradition comes to be associated with Moses's ascent to Sinai to receive the Torah and, while there, he takes the words of Torah "captive" (*Tg.* Ps. 68:19). Several scholars have offered details about this and how in later tradition, other gifts beside the Torah are given.[24] John Muddiman hypothesizes that the author is quoting from an early Christian hymn, an adaptation of Psalm 68, and transfers to Christ what was claimed for Moses.[25] The ascending and descending in Ephesians 4:8–10 take place in order to "fill all things" (v. 10), which is language associated with revelation. "He took captives" and "he gave the people gifts" refer to the same thing—namely, apostolic ministry.[26] The men who ascend on high as "captives" (v. 8) are given gifts, primarily apostles are recipients of revelation (3:5).

In addition to the spatial axis found in 1:10, and ascending and descending in chapter 4, access to the heavenly realm is found elsewhere in Ephesians. "In the heavenlies" (ἐν τοῖς ἐπουρανίοις) occurs five times in Ephesians (1:3; 1:20; 2:6; 3:10; 6:12) and is an expression distinctive to the epistle, without parallel even in Colossians.[27] Ephesians 2:6 describes the saints

24. E.g. W. Hall Harris III, *The Descent of Christ: Ephesians 4:7-11 and Traditional Hebrew Imagery*, AGJU 32 (Leiden: Brill, 1996), esp. 65–76.
25. Muddiman, *Ephesians*, 189; Moses mysticism may have been widespread, see Philo *Vita Mos.* 1.158; cf. 2 Cor 3:7.
26. Muddiman, *Ephesians*, 191.
27. Subject of sustained studies by Hugo Odeberg, *The View of the Universe in the Epistle to the Ephesians* (Lund, Sweden: Gleerup, 1934);

as made to sit presently with Christ in the heavenly places. That attainment to the heavens is already realized has often been met with consternation. According to Andrew Lincoln, Ephesians 1:3 refers not to "future blessings viewed as stored up in heaven," but rather is enjoyed by the saints presently. He sees this as an "apocalyptic view point" in which eschatological hope converges with "present realities in heaven."[28] Lincoln compares this with Colossians, where access to the heavenlies is through Christ, as opposed to human effort. Following on from Lincoln, Ephesians 2:6 is, in my view, a continuation of present participation in the heavens, *pace* Jeff Brannon who prefers to view it as "spiritual" experience of resurrection and discards a Jewish mystical aspect since he sees it as a "subtle and implicit polemic against a Jewish ascetic mysticism" known from Colossae.[29] Indeed, a mystical experience vis-à-vis Christ is found by others, Muddiman comments that "[i]n order to receive the spiritual blessings promised, believers need to understand themselves as mystically transported in faith and worship in the highest heavens."[30]

Mysteries

Among the Pauline epistles, Colossians and Ephesians are disproportionately interested in mysteries with seven occurrences in Ephesians (1:9; 3:3, 4, 5, 9; 5:32; 6:19) and four in Colossians (1:26, 27; 2:2; 4:3), compared with just two in Romans (11:25; 16:25) and two in 1 Corinthians (2:1; 15:51).[31] The mystery of God's will "according to his good pleasure that he set forth in Christ" (Eph 1:9; cf. Col 1:26–27) reflects an understanding of "mysteries" (רזים) similar to that found in Qumran literature where it often involves creation as well as the present and future (cf. esp. 1QpHab; 1QS; 1QH^{a}; 4QInstruction). "Mystery" in many of these scrolls relates to the divine economy and has cosmic, ethical, and eschatological dimensions. The community, as a locus of mysteries and revelation, introduces Ephesians (1:9–10). Raymond E. Brown describes these verses as "a picture of the final stages of the divine *oikonomia*: the fullness of time wherein men on earth and the angels are all subject to Christ," even if the struggle to vanquish evil forces is not yet fully realized.[32]

Andrew T. Lincoln, "A Re-Examination of 'The Heavenlies' in Ephesians," *NTS* 19 (1973): 468–83; see also idem, *Paradise Now and Not Yet: Studies in the Role of the Heavenly Dimension in Paul's Thought with Special Reference to his Eschatology*, SNTSMS 43 (Cambridge: Cambridge University Press, 1981), 140–44; and M. Jeff Brannon, *The Heavenlies in Ephesians: A Lexical, Exegetical, and Conceptual Analysis*, LNTS 447 (London: T&T Clark, 2011).

28. Lincoln, *Paradise Now*, 141–42 and cites 4 Ezra 7:14, 83; 13:18; 2 Baruch 21:12; 48:49; 52:7.
29. Brannon, *The Heavenlies*, 170–76.
30. Muddiman, *Ephesians*, 66.
31. Markus N. A. Bockmuehl, *Revelation and Mystery in Ancient Judaism and Pauline Christianity*, WUNT II/36 (Tübingen: Mohr Siebeck, 1990); J. Coppens, "'Mystery' in the Theology of St. Paul and its Parallels at Qumran," in *Paul at Qumran: Studies in New Testament Exegesis*, ed. J. Murphy-O'Connor (London: Chapman, 1968), 146.
32. Raymond E. Brown, *The Semitic Background of the Term "Mystery" in the New Testament* (Philadelphia: Fortress Press, 1968), 59.

Several other noteworthy commonalities between Qumran scrolls and Ephesians may be observed. In the *Rule of the Community* (1QS 11:3, 5), the *Maskil* plays a special role instructing the community about mysteries. So too, the author of Ephesians explains that the "mystery was made known *to me* by revelation" (Eph 3:3), and that the saints are able to "to perceive *my* understanding of the mystery of Christ" (3:4; cf. 6:19). Paul is functioning as a *Maskil* who serves as a revealer of mysteries, obtained through heavenly ascent (4:8–10). The notion that any quest for wisdom will fail unless God gives understanding undergirds ideas about mysteries at Qumran (e.g., 4Q299 8 6). In Pesher Habakkuk, periods of time come to pass as decreed by God in the "mysteries of his prudence" (1QpHab 7:8), and in Ephesians 3:5 and 3:9, sequence of time and revelation of God's mysteries, "hidden for ages," are made known. Indeed, in the *Treatise on the Two Spirit* (1QS 3:23; 4:18), mysteries relate to the present reign of evil and the time when God will destroy it. In apocalyptic thought, mysteries are already prepared in heaven so that the recipient of revelation can have knowledge of them, but they will only be revealed at the end of history (e.g. 1 Enoch 9:6; 103:2; 4 Ezra 14:15).[33]

An aspect of mystery developed in Ephesians is present participation with angelic beings in the heavenly realm, which is found in close proximity to mysteries. This is similar to the Rule of the Community at 1QS 11:5–8 and also 4QInstruction, an early second century BCE wisdom text motivated by an apocalyptic worldview. In 4QInstruction, the author does not explicitly claim to have ascended into the heavens, but he and his audience participate with angels in the present. The pursuit of mysteries in the document, closely associated with knowing good and evil (cf. 4QMysteries, 4Q299 5 2), is linked with angels who are models to be emulated and who, likely, participate with God in creating humankind. In one column of 4QInstruction (4Q418 81+81a), an exalted *Maven* partakes of the spring of the holy ones, an aspect of seeking mysteries, and is "seated" with them and honors them.

Evil

Colossians does not clearly portray a cosmic threat, but in Ephesians, we are reminded that the cosmic struggle is not yet finished and that the battle for victory awaits completion. Evil in Ephesians is constructed within a cosmological framework that includes otherworldly beings and battle against them. This is seen primarily in the conflict with the devil in 6:10–20, an allegory of Christian warfare, which recalls Isaiah 59:17 and Wisdom 5:16–23. In Isaiah and Wisdom, God is depicted as a warrior who battles earthly enemies and this tradition appears to influence the portrayal of Christ as fighting God's cosmic enemies in 1 Corinthians 15:24.[34] In Ephesians, however, a warrior God, or battling Christ, is tranformed into equipping the righteous to do

33. Lincoln, *Paradise Now*, 143.

battle with the devil themselves. The principalities and powers above and the saints below are directly at war with one another.

Parallels between Ephesians and the Qumran War Scroll have been suggested because both depict an eschatological war between the elect and otherworldly enemies. The War Scroll, by genre, is a "rule" (i.e. *Serekh*), and yet, is typically viewed as indebted to an apocalyptic worldview—in part because angelic beings feature in the struggle between good and evil. One clear difference between Ephesians and the *War Scroll* is observed by Lincoln—namely, a difference between offensive and defensive posturing.[35]

In Ephesians, the present battle is against "spiritual hosts of wickedness in the heavenly places" (6:12), and thus, we learn the sphere of the devil's authority. Moreover, in 2:2, the saints once walked in the "aeon of his world" (*αἰῶν τοῦ κόσμου*), which is a place where the "prince of the power of the air" (*ἄρχων τῆς ἐξουσίας τοῦ ἀέρος*) has dominion (cf. 1 Cor 2:6, 8; 2 Cor 4:4). If Ephesians here reflects a Jewish apocalyptic use of עולם, as both "world" and "age," then it should be understood as the present as a time when the devil is active and the future as a time of salvation (2:7, "in the coming ages"). In light of 2:2 and 6:12, questions arise as to where the devil has dominion, or, to cast some doubt on this topic, if the author should be credited with attaining to a consistency in terminology and cosmology.

Digging deeper into Paul's cosmology, he alludes to a multilayered upper world in 1 Corinthians 15:40, and indeed, levels of heaven are a feature of Jewish apocalyptic thought. The author of Ephesians is also not operating on a bi-axis model of heaven and earth, and 3:10 and 6:12 locate the realm of evil in "the lower reaches of the upper world."[36] As seen in Colossians, mystical ascent is perilous, and within Jewish apocalyptic tradition, petition for angelic protection may be made. In Ephesians, the saints ascend to the heavens through Christ, thereby eliminating, or perhaps circumnavigating (cf. 6:12), evil in the middle heavens.

In 6:12, the saints are, nonetheless, depicted as contending with "this present darkness," which precedes the description of wickedness in the heavenly places. In addition to this spatial and heavenly location of "evil" is a reference that locates it temporally: the devil is active in the here and now and the saints are exhorted to stand against his "wiles" (6:11). When the author reminds his audience that the present days are evil (5:16), this occurs in a context that describes the saints as "children of light" (5:8) who were once in darkness (cf. the binaries of light/dark, 5:6–14, in dualistic traditions from Qumran and Colossians above).

When in 6:13, we are told that an "evil day" is coming, this could relate to a general reminder

34. See Thomas Yoder Neufeld, *Put on the Armour of God: The Divine Warrior from Isaiah to Ephesians*, JSNTSup 140 (Sheffield: Sheffield Academic, 1997), 128, where he argues that Ephesians is a critical comment on 1 Corinthians.
35. Andrew T. Lincoln, *Ephesians*, WBC 42; Waco, TX: Word Books, 1990), 446.
36. Muddiman, *Ephesians*, 104.

of present evil, as in 5:16, or more likely that one should prepare for an eschatological day of evil (cf. 2 Thess 2:3; 1 Thess 5:2). Elsewhere, failure to act wisely and according to the author's instructions leads to evil, and at times, evil may be attributed to the flesh (cf. Gal 5:17; Rom 8:5–8).[37] Indeed, 2:3 describes death before being made alive in Christ with the expression "desire of our flesh" (ἐπιθυμία τῆς σαρκὸς). The present battle, though, is not against "flesh and blood" (6:12) but the attacks of the "evil one" (6:16).

Domestic Codes – "Wisdom" and "Apocalyptic"

The "mystery" of husband and wife becoming one flesh (5:31–32) indicates a deeper meaning of Genesis 2:24 ("the two shall become one flesh"), which points typologically to Christ and the church.[38] The "mystery" found here in 5:32 opens up a larger and relatively recent conversation about wisdom and apocalyptic in 4QInstruction and influences the way domestic codes are understood in Ephesians. When members of the household (husbands, wives, parents, children, slaves) are instructed in Ephesians 5:21–6:9, it was long taken as a *fait accompli* that this could be traced to influences from Hellenistic, particularly Stoic, writings.[39] Jean-Sébastian Rey and I have both offered studies on teachings about the family in 4QInstruction and Ephesians; Rey has systematically detailed themes first suggested in my work, and further helps demonstrate the significance of 4QInstruction for the study of the order of the household in Ephesians.[40] Most important is Rey's emphasis that 4QInstruction's domestic codes are closer to Ephesians than to Colossians. Similarities between Ephesians and 4QInstruction, when family members

37. The attribution of evil to the flesh has been discussed in relationship to *4QInstruction* where in 4Q416 1 line 16 is the possible expression "inclination of the flesh"; see my "'Flesh' and 'Spirit' in Qumran Sapiential Literature as the Background for the Use in Pauline Epistles," *ZNW* 106, no. 2 (2015): 262–79; cf. Jörg Frey, "Die paulinische Antithese von «Fleisch» und «Geist» und die palästinisch-jüdische Weisheitstradtion," *ZNW* 90, no. 1 (1999): 45–77; idem, "The Notion of 'Flesh' in 4QInstruction and the Background of Pauline Usage," in *Sapiential, Poetical and Liturgical Texts. Proceedings of the 3rd meeting of the International Organization for Qumran Studies, Oslo 1998*, ed. Daniel K. Falk, Florentino García Martínez, Eileen M. Schuller, STDJ 35 (Leiden: Brill, 2000), 197–226; idem, "Flesh and Spirit in the Palestinian Jewish Sapiential Tradition and in the Qumran Texts: An Inquiry into the Background of Pauline Usage," in *The Wisdom Texts from Qumran and the Development of Sapiential Thought: Studies in Wisdom at Qumran and its Relationship to Sapiential Thought in the Ancient Near East, the Hebrew Bible, Ancient Judaism and the New Testament*, ed. Charlotte Hempel, Armin Lange, and Hermann Lichtenberger, BETL 159 (Leuven: Leuven University Press, 2002), 367–404; Matthew J. Goff, "Being Fleshly or Spiritual: Anthropological Reflection and Exegesis of Genesis 1–3 in 4QInstruction and First Corinthians," in *Christian Body, Christian Self: Concepts of Early Christian Personhood*, ed. Clare K. Rothschild and Trevor W. Thompson; WUNT 284; Tübingen: Mohr Siebeck, 2011), 41–59.
38. Bockmuehl, *Revelation and Mystery*, 204.
39. See David E. Balch, *Let Wives Be Submissive: The Domestic Code in 1 Peter*, SBLMS 26 (Chico: Scholars, 1981), 21–62; Andrew T. Lincoln, "The Household Code and Wisdom Mode of Colossians," *JSNT* 74 (1999): 93–112.
40. Benjamin G. Wold, "Family Ethics in *4QInstruction* and the New Testament," *NovT* 50, no. 3 (2008): 286–300; idem, *Women, Men, and Angels: The Qumran Wisdom Document* Musar leMevin *and its Allusions to Genesis Creation Traditions*, WUNT II/201 (Tübingen: Mohr Siebeck, 2005), 237–39; Jean-Sébastian Rey, "Family Relationships in *4QInstruction* and in Eph 5:21–6:4," in *Echoes from the Caves: Qumran and the New Testament*, ed. Florentino García Martínez, STDJ 85 (Leiden: Brill, 2009), 231–55; finds these correlations: (1) Genesis 2:24 and unity of marriage (4Q416 2 iii 20; 4Q416 2 iv; Eph 5:31); (2) Genesis 2:23 two becoming one flesh (4Q416 2 iv 5–6; Eph. 5:28–30); (3) Genesis 3:16 and dominion (4Q416 iv 6–7; Eph 5:21–22); (4) instructions are rooted in mysteries (4Q416 2 iii 21; Eph 5:31–32), see esp. Exodus 20:12 when reflected on in *4QInstruction* correlates it to mystery (cf. Eph 6:1–4).

are instructed on the basis of Genesis 2–3 and Exodus 20:12, cannot be explained as the former being dependent on the latter. Rey summarizes that "the differences between Eph and Col have parallels in the text of *4QInstruction*."[41]

Rey and I both assume a verbatim reconstruction of Genesis 2:24 in 4Q416 2 iii–iv; however, the reconstruction of 4Q416 2 iv line 1 with a supplement from Genesis 2:24 would be the only extensive explicit citation of a biblical source in the document and is unconvincing. In the biblical tradition, Genesis 2:24 may be interpreted as a man leaving his "Patria potestas" and joining his wife's potestas. Lines 3–7 are concerned to instruct, *contra* Genesis 2:24, that when a daughter is given in marriage, she moves from her own household to her husband's, and that he is the one who then has rightful authority over her; if line 1 is reconstructed as a citation of Genesis 2:24, this would introduce a stark contradiction to the lines that follow. Creation of male and female undergirds both 4QInstruction's and Ephesians' teaching about members of the family; however, if there is no citation of Genesis 2:24 in 4QInstruction, and there is indeed an explicit citation of this verse in Ephesians 5:31, then this difference needs to be accounted for when suggesting common tradition.

Genesis 2–3 and the commandment to honor parents from the Decalogue (Exod 20:12) occur together in Ephesians 5:21–6:9 and *4QInstruction* when teaching about the order of the household. In Ephesians, this order is based upon a typology of Christ's relationship to the church, which is interwoven with references to Genesis 2:24 (Eph 5:28–32), Genesis 3:16 (Eph 5:21–22), and Exodus 20:12 (Eph 6:1–4). Whereas Ephesians focuses on husband and wife becoming one flesh in imitation of the single body of Christ, 4QInstruction alludes to the separation of woman from man and refers explicitly to them joining as "one flesh" (4Q416 2 iii 21, iv 4). Parents, as co-creators, have authority over their children; woman's derivation from man justifies a shift in authority from parents to husband at marriage. Whereas in Ephesians, the commandment to honor parents functions to establish the hierarchy of the household (i.e., sequentially: husband, wife, children, slaves), 4QInstruction interweaves creation with the commandment in order to provide justification for them having authority over children. In other words, in Ephesians, Genesis 2–3 and Exodus 20:12 help to justify the hierarchy of authority in a household. This contrasts with 4QInstruction, in which, although the authority of parents over children is established, questions arise as to how parental authority functions and changes when daughters are married.

The commonalities between 4QInstruction and Ephesians nonetheless shift the conversation in terms of influences on domestic codes as purely or straightforwardly derived from Hellenistic household codes. However, this is more so the case in regard to Ephesians than Colossians.

41. Rey, "Family Relationships," 254; Stuckenbruck, "The Dead Sea Scrolls and the New Testament," 165.

When Ephesians takes over Colossians' codes, it introduces a tradition of material known also by, from, or related to 4QInstruction. Because 4QInstruction offers sapiential teachings about how members of the family are to relate to one another within an apocalyptic worldview, the precise details about how Ephesians and 4QInstruction share tradition matters. Ephesians is not simply aware of allusions to the same pastiche of scriptural passages (i.e., Gen 2:23, 24; Exod 20:12), but also roots teaching in mysteries, and thus, shares apocalyptic characteristics. In Ephesians, as in *4QInstruction*, mysteries are part of cosmology and the point of departure for reflecting on everything. In the same way that *4QInstruction* is described as a sapiential document motivated by an apocalyptic worldview, so too one might say the same of Ephesians 5:21–6:9.

Conclusions

If it is fair to describe Ephesians as a type of "commentary" on Colossians, several themes related to apocalyptic are accentuated and expanded: (1) the heavenly ascent of the saints; (2) the attribution of evil to another world and otherworldly beings; and (3) mysteries are integral to cosmology and the point of departure for understanding everything.

God has raised Christ from the dead and seated him in the heavenly places (1:20) where he is far above all rule, authority, power, and dominion (1:21). The saints too were once dead and are now made to live with Christ (2:6) and have been raised with him and seated in the heavenly places (2:6). The life now experienced is not the one that was once lived in the passions of the flesh, and gentiles "in the flesh" are no longer separated from Christ because they are uncircumcised. However, the present is still a time of evil, the devil and his hosts act on earth and in heaven, and the saints are not free of their wicked intent. Ascent to the heavens plays an important role in contending with evil in Ephesians. Christ has led "captives" to heaven and gifts given there include apostleship. Apostles reveal mysteries and play a unique role offering revelation to the saints. At the same time, the heavens are not off limits to believers, who through faith, worship, and prayer (cf. 6:18) may experience mystical ascent to the highest heavens. As the community grows, on the foundation of the heavenly gifts (i.e., apostles and prophets, 2:20), they come together to form a holy temple for a dwelling place of God (2:21–22). Ascent and community as temple suggest a blurring of location, and yet, the saints' rightful place is in the heavenly realm. While one might assess Ephesians in terms of time, particularly eschatology, a shift from temporal axis to spatial axis further underscores the apocalyptic worldview that influences this author.

11

Apocalyptic Thought in Philippians

Angela Standhartinger

Although the discussion of Paul as an apocalyptic thinker has never centered on Philippians, early interpreters have noted apocalyptic imagery in this letter. For Albert Schweitzer, Philippians 1:6, 10; 2:16, 3:20–21 and 4:4–5 prove Paul's ceaseless expectation of Christ's imminent return.[1] Ernst Käsemann notes the contrast between humanity's righteousness and God's righteousness in his interpretation of δικαιοσύνη θεοῦ as apocalyptic power in Philippians 3:9.[2] J. Christiaan Beker mentions Philippians to prove the bifocal character of resurrection between the Christ-event and the *parousia* (Phil 2:16; 4:1) and "believers victory in Christ and to their lasting communion with Christ" (Phil 1:21–23).[3] Christopher Rowland finds an allusion to a temporary separation of the self from the earthly body while Paul went into God's presence in Philippians 1:23.[4] Martinus de Boer remarks that Paul uses the word ἀποκαλύπτειν in Philippians 3:15 "in connection with the communication of heavenly or divine mysteries, particularly

1. Albert Schweitzer, *Die Mystik des Apostels Paulus* (Tübingen: Mohr, 1930), 55.
2. Ernst Käsemann, "Gottesgerechtigkeit bei Paulus," in *Exegetische Versuche und Besinnungen*, 2nd ed., Vol. 2 (Göttingen: Vandenhoeck & Ruprecht, 1965), 181–93 (182). At the end of this article, he states in reference to his previous article "Die Anfänge christlicher Theologie," 82–104: "Paulus ist Apokalyptiker auch als Christ geblieben" (193).
3. J. C. Beker, *Paul the Apostle. The Triumph of God in Life and Thought* (Philadelphia: Fortress, 1980) 160; 230.
4. Christopher Rowland, *The Open Heaven. A Study in Apocalyptic in Judaism and Early Christianity* (London: SPCK, 1982), 384.

as mediated or induced by the Spirit."[5] For de Boer, Philippians 1:6 indicates the final salvation of the believers.[6]

In addition, further apocalyptic motifs can be found throughout the canonical letter. Philippians 1:1–3:1 4:1–7 is called a "letter of joy" because Paul makes continual requests to rejoice (χαίρειν κτλ.) and there are reassurances of joyful feelings on both sides: Paul's (Phil 1:4, 18; 2:2, 17; 4:1) and the community's (1:25; 2:18, 28; 3:1).[7] When Paul finally prompts the Philippians: "Rejoice in the Lord always; I shall say it again: rejoice. . . . The Lord is near" (Phil 4:4–5), the eschatological dimension of this joy becomes obvious. Despite current sufferings (cf. Phil 1:12–18, 28–30), Paul and the community participate already in the heavenly joy as God's righteous ones in their state of salvation, similar to such announcements in late prophetic and apocalyptic literature.[8] The final day is called here characteristically the "day of Christ" (ἡμέρα Χριστοῦ, Phil 1:6, 10; 2:16). It is not so much a day of judgment, as is the "day of the Lord" in 1 Corinthians 3:13; 5:5 (cf. Amos 5:18, 20; etc.), but it is a day of praise and glory for those who remain faithful.[9] "Christ's day" in Philippians will be a day of salvation similar to the way Paul quotes from LXX Isaiah 49:8 in 2 Corinthians 6:2.

Three times in Philippians 1–2, transformation caused by the heavenly world comes into view. In the hymn, Christ is proclaimed as Lord Jesus by all powers from heaven, earth, and the underworld (2:10). The scene evokes the enthronization of the Son of Man in Daniel 7:13–14 as well as the enthronization of the slaughtered lamb in Revelation 5:6–14.[10] In Philippians 1:23, Paul desires to depart and be with Christ (σὺν Χριστῷ εἶναι) and might thereby echo the apocalyptic promise of companionship with "God's elected one" or the "Lord of the Spirits" in 1 Enoch 39:4–8.[11] And when Paul challenges the community in Philippians 2:15 to become "children of God . . . in the midst of a crooked and perverse generation, in which you shine like stars in the world," he resorts to one of the most traditional apocalyptic images, the resurrection.[12]

5. Martinus C. De Boer, "Paul and Apocalyptic Eschatology," in *The Encyclopedia of Apocalypticism, Volume 1*, ed. John J. Collins (New York; London: Continuum, 2000) 345–83 (355). Paul uses the verb similarly in 1 Cor 2:10; 14:6, 26, 30; 2 Cor 12:1, 7; Gal 2:2.
6. Ibid., 372.
7. For the discussion of the fragmentation or integrity of Philippians, see Angela Standhartinger, "'Join in imitating me' (Philippians 3.17). Towards an Interpretation of Philippians 3," *NTS* 54 (2008): 417–35. The current author is of the opinion that the canonical letter was edited by the Philippians in the early second century CE out of three letters (fragments) of Paul (Phil 4:10–20; Phil 1:1–3:1 and 4:4–9 20–23 and Phil 3:2–21 [4:1–3]), which were all sent from a prison (most likely in Ephesus) within a short interval of time (perhaps only some weeks). Relating to Paul as well as to Epaphroditus, Phil 1:1–3:1 and 3:2–21 and 4:10–20 and 2:25–30 presuppose different contexts and situations. The ideal biography in Phil 3:2–21 is most likely an early farewell letter to the Philippians presumably written after receiving the death sentence mentioned in 2 Cor 1:8–9.
8. Cf. Isa 65:17–22; 1 Enoch 103:3; Jubilees 23:30; 1 Enoch 51:5; 1QS 4:7; 2 Baruch 73:2, etc.
9. Cf. "the day of our Lord Jesus" in 1 Cor 1:8 and 2 Cor 1:14.
10. Dan 7:13–14 is probably the most influential text in apocalyptic literature in the first century CE, e.g., 1 Enoch 46–69; 4 Ezra 12:50–13:56; Mark 13:24–27; Rev 1:12–18.
11. Cf. Paul Hoffmann, *Die Toten in Christus. Eine religionsgeschichtliche und exegetische Untersuchung zur paulinischen Eschatologie*, NTAbh 2 (Münster: Aschendorff, 1966), 316.
12. 1 Enoch 104:2; Daniel 12:3; Testament of Moses 10:8–9; 4 Ezra 7:97; 2 Baruch 51:10.

Finally, in Philippians 4:2–3, Paul refers to a "book of life" in which the names of three members of the community, Euodia, Syntyche, and Clement, have been written. The model of this book is not so much a charge sheet on which deeds of sinners are recorded for a final judgment (cf. Rev 20:12), but it is a citizenship list of those who belong to the heavenly realm.[13]

Apocalyptic imagery in Philippians 1–2 and 4 is only insinuated by a few images, but this imagery creates the notion that the community, although in the middle of suffering, already participates in the joy and transformation of the heavenly realm. Yet, when one considers apocalyptic thought as revelation, Philippians 3 become the most intriguing part of the letter. Here, a special revelation is explicitly promised to those who seek perfection (Phil 3:15). In the following, I will focus on this chapter.

The Context of Paul's Apocalyptic Vision in Philippians 3

Philippians 3:2 is generally understood as the beginning of a new section.[14] The addressees are abruptly commanded to be watchful through the triple use of the imperative βλέπετε.[15] The exhortation "Look at the dogs! Look at the evil workers!" serves as a backdrop for Paul's forthcoming speech. The addressees are invited to listen to this speech in the context of their own sense of affliction, loneliness, missionary competition, failure and division. Paul does not explain further. The vaguely suggestive key words provide a schematic context for the self-representation that follows.

Paul continues by modeling his own biography. First, he gives a long list of his advantages (3:5–6); however, a fundamental reevaluation of his noble birth and virtues follows: "I consider that all things are a loss because of the excellence of knowing of Christ Jesus my Lord, through whom I lost everything and I consider it all rubbish" (3:8). There is no doubt that Paul is alluding to the turning point in his life, often referred to as the Damascus Road conversion. But this is no story about the calling of a prophet of Christ (Gal 1:15–16), nor an epiphany of the resurrected one legitimizing his apostolate (1 Cor 9:1; 15:8–10), nor a journey to heaven (2 Cor 12:1–7), nor even an inner illumination (2 Cor 4:6). Neither God nor Christ makes an appearance. Paul instead uses matter-of-fact business speech. The crucial parallel to this "transvaluation of values" is the figure of the wise one in Jewish wisdom theology, especially in Sirach

13. Cf. n. 63.

14. Those who read Philippians in the canonical form detect here the last of three *exempla* (cf. 2:19–30) and "Paul's experience and life as a model to follow." (G. F. Hawthorne and R. P. Martin, *Philippians*, rev. ed., WBC 43 [Nashville: Nelson, 2004], 170.) Those who see in Philippians a collection of letter fragments mostly read Philippians 3:2–21 as a letter in its own right and call it a "Kampfbrief" (polemical letter). I opt for the latter but do not find much polemic here.

15. The traditional translation of βλέπετε τοὺς κύνας κτλ. "beware of the dogs" is not correct, as G. D. Kilpatrick, "ΒΛΕΠΕΤΕ in Philippians 3:2," in *In Memoriam Paul Kahle*, ed. Matthew Black and Georg Fohrer, BZAW 103 (Berlin: Töpelmann, 1968), 146–48, has shown. With an accusative object, βλέπετε means "see, look at, consider."

51:13–30 and Wisdom 6–9. Instead of relying on the advantages of his noble birth (cf. Wis 8:19), the wise aspire to wisdom and hope to gain through her something more valuable than all other riches.

Yet, while Lady wisdom reveals herself to those who search for her, the ideal wise one cannot hold on to wisdom; she must be sought continually.[16] The process is purposeful but remains open and unfinished. Likewise, Paul is journeying so that he "may gain Christ, and be found in him . . . to know him" (3:9). In 3:12–14, Paul becomes an athlete in a stadium who focuses solely on reaching his goal.[17] He models himself in the guise of the wise who exert themselves for Christ but who can only receive the goal, when Christ approaches. Paul is still on this journey his whole life long because he has already been grasped by Christ (3:12).

Paul's goal in this race is "the prize of the 'upward' call (τῆς ἄνω κλήσεως) of God in Christ Jesus" (3:14), yet this goal remains unattainable. At this point in Paul's speech, he transcends wisdom speech by integrating an apocalyptic motif. Wisdom comes to the one who seeks and waits at his door.[18] The wise one does not need to leave this world in search of wisdom, but Paul implies that the complete attainment of the knowledge of God occurs through the elevation of the righteous into the heavenly world. Jewish apocalyptic thought expects that the righteous ones will be elevated into the heavenly world, the above (ἄνω), in which they will recover from their earthly afflictions. Paul's imagery of a race suggests that the "the upward call of God in Christ Jesus" depicts the goal of the race, the final state and heavenly dwelling of the righteous ones, even though Paul does not explain the image further.[19]

Typically, the self-representation of the teacher of wisdom ends with an invitation to join the school of wisdom.[20] Yet, wisdom cannot be taught as an object, but the teacher of wisdom communicates his lifestyle and thus shows the way by which one can attain wisdom. Wisdom

16. Sirach 51:13–21; Wisdom 6:12–21; 8:2; 9:16–17; etc.
17. Uta Poplutz, *Athlet des Evangeliums. Eine motivgeschichtliche Studie zur Wettkampfmetaphorik bei Paulus*, Herders biblische Studien 43 (Freiburg im Breisgau: Herder, 2004), 349–73.
18. Sir 51:14, 26; 15:2–6; Wisdom 6:13–4, 16; etc.
19. For some, τὸ βραβεῖον τῆς ἄνω κλήσεως τοῦ θεοῦ (Phil 3:14) is an allusion to ancient Olympic games, in which "a herald announces the name of the victor, [. . .] and the athlete [. . .] would come to receive a palm at their hands" (cf. Hawthorne and Martin, *Philippians*, 210). Unfortunately, we have no evidence for the term being used in this context (cf. Poplutz, *Athlet*, 358–59). Others understand κλῆσις "in its customary Pauline sense of the divine calling to salvation, particularly the initial summons, while the prize is that which is announced by the call." (Peter T. O'Brien, *The Epistle to the Philippians: A Commentary on the Greek Text*, NIGTC [Grand Rapids: Eerdmans, 1991], 433). But there is no hint in 1 Cor 1:26, 7:20 or Rom 11:29 that believers will still lack something when they receive their call. There are parallels in Philo's exegesis of Exod 31:2: "On this account, those persons who are insatiable in their desire for wisdom and knowledge are said in the sacred oracles to be 'called up.'" (πρὸς γὰρ τὸ θεῖον ἄνω καλεῖσθαι θέμις τοὺς ὑπ' αὐτοῦ καταπνευσθέντας). For it is legitimate that those persons should be called up to the Deity who have been inspired by him" (*Plant.* 23–24, Translation: LCL; cf. *Her.* 69–70). But Philo speaks of a temporary ascent of the prophet's soul (not of the ascent of the body). In apocalypticism the above (ἄνω) is the heavenly space, which the righteous and wise are happy to attain. For instance Abraham is brought πρὸς τὸν ἄνω βασιλέα (Testament of Abraham A 7:7), and Enoch is raised up (ἄνω) in his heavenly journey (1 Enoch 14:8). Even though 3 Bar 4:15 was revised by some Christians, there might be a Jewish tradition behind the verse "and as through it [the vine] the human race obtained condemnation, so again through Jesus Christ the Immanuel will they receive in Him the upward calling and the entry into paradise" (ἐν αὐτῷ μέλλουσιν τὴν ἀνάκλησιν [v. l: ἄνω κλῆσιν] προσλαβεῖν, καὶ τὴν εἰς παράδεισον εἴσοδον).
20. Cf. Sir 51:23–30; Wis 6:1–21.

always remains an unexpected, inaccessible gift of God.[21] In contrast to the wisdom teachers, Paul invites not the foolish[22] but the perfect into Christ's school. And he emphasizes that God will disclose himself willingly to those who seek God's perfection: "And if you think differently about something, God will reveal this to you also" (3:15).[23] So revealing (ἀποκαλύπτειν) is an unpredictable act of God who discloses ways of thinking and understanding (φρονεῖν) to those who press on for this goal.

The aim of Paul's striving for Christ is imitation (3:17). Here, as elsewhere in antiquity imitation is a creative act.[24] "The Philippians are co-imitators, not because they perform the same task or resemble each other, but because they are engaged in the same *mimēsis*."[25] Paul and others like him have provided a pattern (τύπος), which the community is called upon to develop with its own creativity. At this point, the self-representation of the wisdom teacher has reached its culmination, and suddenly, Paul takes up a new role.

An Apocalyptic Prophecy (Phil 3:18–21)

In Philippians 3:18, Paul adopts a new mode of speech: he speaks "in tears" (κλαίων λέγω). By doing so, he takes on the part of an apocalyptic prophet.[26] The seers in Jewish apocalypses proclaim the end of the godless in the age to come,[27] and sometimes, emphasize their curse by weeping and crying. Thus, in the midst of woes against the violent and the rich, Enoch wishes:

> O that my eye were a <fountain> of water, that I might weep over you. I would pour out my tears as a cloud of water, and I would rest from the grief of my heart (1 Enoch 95:1).[28]

Paul's tears likewise express his despair.[29] The godless in this case are called "enemies of the cross." As in 3:2, Paul has no explicit criticism,[30] but rather he reveals a separation that, as in 1 Corinthians 1:18, 2 Corinthians 2:15, and Romans 9:22–23, has divided humanity in two groups, namely the lost and the saved. However, as in many apocalyptic writings, the issue is not how

21. Sirach 51:19–22; Wis 6:12–16, 7:7, 14; 8:18.
22. Invitation of the foolish: Sir 51:23–24; cf. 6:18–37; Wis 6:1–21.
23. If Paul wishes the community to share his opinion, he says: "I have confidence about you in the Lord, that you will not think otherwise" (Gal 5:10).
24. Jo-Ann A. Brant, "The Place of *mimēsis* in Paul's thought," *SR* 22 (1993): 285–300.
25. Brant, "Place", 297. In a similar vein the Thessalonians in 1 Thess 1:6–8: had already become imitators their missionaries (Paul, Silvanus, and Timothy) and of God (ὑμεῖς μιμηταὶ ἡμῶν ἐγενήθητε καὶ τοῦ κυρίου) as well as examples for all believers in Macedonia and Achaia (γενέσθαι ὑμᾶς τύπον πᾶσιν τοῖς πιστεύουσιν) because their preaching and fame had spread not only to Macedonia and Achaia but to "every place"; they thus became even more successful than their own missionaries. Cf. Brant, "Place", 290–93.
26. Of course, Enoch, Daniel, Ezra (of 4 Ezra) and Baruch (of 2 Baruch) are also sages. Cf. Collins, "The Sage in the Apocalyptic and Pseudepigraphic Literature," in *Seers, Sibyls and Sages in Hellenistic-Roman Judaism* (Leiden: Brill, 1997), 339–50.
27. Jer 8:23 (LXX 9:1); 9:10(9); 2 Baruch 35:1; 3 Baruch 1:1, 3; Jesus ben Ananias, Josephus, *B.J.* l, 6.304–9.
28. See 1 Enoch 94:8–95:2. Unless otherwise noted, translations of 1 *Enoch* are from George W. E. Nickelsburg, *1 Enoch 1: A Commentary on the Book of 1 Enoch, Chapters 1-36; 81-108*, Hermeneia (Minneapolis: Fortress Press, 2001).
29. Testament of Moses 11:1–4; 2 Baruch 5:6; 3 Baruch 1:3; Greek Apocalypse of Ezra 5:6, 9, 28.
30. Other than in Gal 5:11, 6:12–14 there is no substantial criticism besides the catchphrase "cross."

the lost might yet be saved, but how to interpret reality for those who suffer at the hands of the godless.

The characterization of the "enemies of the cross" draws on a collection of common insults: "their end is destruction, their god is the belly, and their glory is in their shame" (3:19).[31] In biblical tradition, shame (αἰσχύνη) is the result and experience of divine justice.[32] The apocalyptic seer announces humiliation for the unrighteous as compensation for the injustice done to the righteous in the here and now. For instance, Enoch laments:

> Woe to you, sinners, for your riches make you appear to be righteous, but your heart convicts you of being sinners; . . . Woe to you who devour the finest of the wheat, and drink <wine from the krater> while you tread on the lowly with your might. . . . Woe to you, mighty, who with might oppress the righteous one; for the day of your destruction will come" (1 Enoch 96:4–5, 8).

The heavenly seer curses the godless people for accumulation of unjust money, for their ignorance, and even more for suppressing and humiliating the righteous one. Their supposed honor in this world will turn to shame in the next.[33] They will be thoroughly shamed on the day of resurrection and judgment, or even already in a kind of purgatory.[34] Their limited "earthly" view on reality will prove itself as wrong. Seen from the heavenly perspective of the seer, the fate of the godless is actual destruction (ἀπώλεια), whereas the "friends of God" can hope for salvation (σωτηρία).[35] This hope, already present in wisdom literature, blossoms in apocalypticism where the seer observes the punishment of sinners on his journey to heaven, reports of them and warns future generations of them.[36] The punishment entails that, in the end, sinners will have to recognize the limitation of their "earthly" position when they see the destiny of the righteous (Wis 5:1–16). With the words "end" (τέλος), "god" (θεός), and "glory" (δόξα), Paul

31. ὁ θεὸς ἡ κοιλία call to mind an oft-quoted catchphrase of Demosthenes: "those whose measure of happiness is their belly" (τῇ γαστρὶ μετροῦντες καὶ τοῖς αἰσχίστοις τὴν εὐδαιμονίαν; *Cor.* 296; c.f. Plutarch, *Mor.* 97D; Lucian, *Patria encomia* 10; Longinus, *De sublimate* 32:2; Theon, *Progymnasmata* 107:10, Cicero, *Nat. d.* 1.113). A κοιλιόδαιμον is a parasite (Eupolis at Atheneios, *Deip.* 3.56 (100b); 3.52 (97c); Clement of Alexandria, *Paed.* 2.1.15.4; cf. also Euripides, *Kyk.* 334–35). Honor/Shame (δόξα/αἰσχύνη) is a classic opposition in the acknowledgment through peers in antiquity (Dio Chrysostom, *Rhod.* (*or.* 31)159; Plutarch, *Mor.* 822D). Aristotle's definition: "shame is a fantasy about dishonor" (περὶ ἀδοξίας φαντασία ἐστὶν ἡ αἰσχύνη; Rhetorik 2.6 1384a22) and Theophrastus, *Char.* 9:1: "Unconscionableness, to define it, is a neglect of reputation for the sake of filthy lucre" (Ἡ δὲ ἀναισχυντία ἐστὶ μέν, ὡς ὅρῳ λαβεῖν, καταφρόνησις δόξης αἰσχροῦ ἕνεκα κέρδους; Translation: J. M. Edmonds, LCL).
32. In reflection on the Exile: Ezra 8:74; Neh 9:7; Jer 31:19 (LXX 38:19); Testament of Levi 15:2. As a prophecy against enemies: Isa 19:9; 20:4; 30:3–6; etc. The righteous hope "that their enemies will clothe themselves with shame" (ἐνδύσονται αἰσχύνην); LXX Job 8:22; cf. Pss 132:18 (LXX 131:18); 35:26 (LXX 34:26); 1 Macc 1:28.
33. Cf. 1 Enoch 98:3: "Thus they will perish, together with all their possessions, and all their splendor and honor; and for dishonor and slaughter and great destitution, their spirits will be cast into the fiery furnace." Cf. Psalms of Solomon 2:31, Testament of Benjamin 10:8.
34. Daniel 12:2 TH: "And many of those who sleep in a mound of earth will be awakened, these for everlasting life and those to shame and everlasting contempt (εἰς ὀνειδισμὸν καὶ εἰς αἰσχύνην αἰώνιον). Cf. 4 Ezra 7:87; 1 Enoch 46:6; 48:8; 62:9–10; 63:11.
35. Psalms of Solomon 3:11; 9:5; 13:11; 14:9; 16:5; Wis 18:7.
36. Cf. e.g. Testament of Abraham A 11:5–12, 4 Ezra 7:78–99, 1 Enoch 91:5–10; 98:8; 104:1–7.

suggests an eschatological pseudo-perspective which amounts to a self-deception on the part of the "enemies of the cross."

For those who belong to the group around the apocalyptic seer, the description in Philippians 3:20–21 reveals to them the only true perspective, the hope they have of transformation into heavenly bodies:[37]

> For our body of citizens exists in heaven, whence we eagerly await the Lord Jesus Christ as Savior who will transform the body of our humiliation to be conformed to the body of his glory according to the power that enables him to subject everything to himself.

This passage contains a set of unusual conceptions.[38] Πολίτευμα is a term drawn out of antique political theory and practice describing "a body of citizens with political rights."[39] A person belonging to the πολίτευμα is *per definitionem* active in the politics of a given group or community, which means that this person may vote, take part in public assemblies and the public cult, and may receive, give thanks for and spend benefactions. Platonic-Stoic philosophy developed the conception of the heavenly *politeuma*. On the one hand, it portrays the heavens as the ultimate example of political order, which is to be imitated by humankind.[40] On the other hand, the heavens are also the true home of the wise from which they have come and to which they shall return after their educational sojourn on earth.[41] Philippians 3:20–21 does not, however,

37. Daniel 12:3; 1 Enoch 104:2, 4, 6; 108:11–14; etc. Apocalypticism typically opposes the fate of the wicked to that of the righteous, see 1 Enoch 103–4; 108; 1QS 3:13–4:26; 4QInstruction 416 I 1; 4 Ezra 7:78–99; and 1 Enoch 62.

38. Pauline *hapax legomena* here include πολίτευμα, σώτηρ, ταπείνωσις, ἐνέργεια. That Christ in Phil 3:21 is able "to subject everything to himself" directly contradicts what Paul says in 1 Cor 15:27–28. Therefore, some opt for a pre-Pauline Christian hymn or fragment as an ecclesiological or eschatological appendix to the Christ-hymn in 2:6–11: cf. Ernst Lohmeyer, *Die Briefe an die Philipper, an die Kolosser und an Philemon*, 2nd ed., KEK 9 (Göttingen: Vandenhoeck & Ruprecht, 1964), 156–57; J. Reumann, *Philippians*, AB 33B (New Haven/London: Yale University Press, 2008), 583–84. Some scholars find substantial parallels between Phil 3:20–21 and 2:6-11. Cf. Hawthorne and Martin, *Philippians*, 229. However, there are major theological differences in cosmological imagery (cf. Joachim Gnilka, *Der Philipperbrief*, HThKNT 10/3 [Freiburg im Breisgau: Herder, 1968] 208–9): there are no powers from the underworld or heaven in Phil 3:20–21 and there is no soteriology in 2:6–11, while God acts alone in Phil 2:9–11 and not at all (except for κατὰ τὴν ἐνέργειαν) in Phil 3:20–21. What both texts share is a negative evaluation of humankind's earthly experience, which both call humiliation (ταπεινόω/ταπείνωσις). But while it is not quite clear what happens to the body of the Godlike-being of Phil 2:6, the humiliated human body (σῶμα τῆς ταπεινώσεως) of Phil 3:21 will be transformed into a glorified (heavenly) body (σῶμα τῆς δόξης).

39. M. H. Hansen, "Polis, Politeuma and Politeia. A Note on Arist. Pol. 1287b6–14," in *From Political Architecture to Stephanus Byzantius. Sources for the Ancient Greek Polis*, ed. David Whitehead (Stuttgart: Steiner, 1994), 91–98, 94. Cf. G. Lüderitz, "What is the Politeuma?" in *Studies in Early Jewish Epigraphy*, ed. J. W. van Henten and P. W. van der Horst, AGJU 21 (Leiden: Brill, 1994), 183–225. Recently Hans Förster and Patrick Sänger, "Ist unsere Heimat im Himmel? Überlegungen zur Semantik von POLITEUMA in Phil 3,20," *Early Christianity* 5, no. 2 (2014): 149–77, as well as Peter Artzt-Grabner, "Die Stellung des Judentums in neutestamentlicher Zeit anhand der Politeuma-Papyri und anderer Texte," in *Papyrologie und Exegese. Die Auslegung des Neuen Testaments im Licht der Papyri*, ed. Jens Herzer, WUNT II/341 (Tübingen: Mohr Siebeck, 2012), 127–58, argue that *politeuma* in Phil 3:20 means citizenship. But as Kaus Aland, "Die Christen und der Staat nach Phil. 3,20," in *Paganism, judaïsme, christianisme. Mélanges offerts à Marcel Simon*, ed. M. Bernoit, et al. (Paris: de Boccard, 1978), 247–59, 240–50, argued long ago, the Latin translation of πολίτευμα is *municipatus* rather than *civitas*.

40. Cf. Dio Chrysostom, *Borysth* (*or.* 36) 22–23; 29–32. Cf. also Philo, *Spec.* 1.13–15.

41. Cf. Philo, *Conf.* 77–78: "(77) For this reason all the wise men [. . .] are represented as sojourners, for their souls are sent down from heaven upon earth as to a colony [. . .] (78) Since therefore having taken up their abode among bodies, they behold all the mortal objects of the outward senses by their means, then they subsequently return back from thence to the place from which they set out at first, looking upon the heavenly country in which they have the rights of citizens as their native land." (Translation Young). Cf. *Somn.* 1.181; *Agr.* 65.

speak of a homeward ascent for believers. On the contrary, "a body of politically active citizens" seems already to exist in heaven (ἐν οὐρανοῖς ὑπάρχει).[42] This very much calls to mind the community of the Dead Sea, which saw itself as already taking part in the heavenly assembly of angels:

> To those whom God has selected . . . he has given them an inheritance in the lot of the holy ones. He unites their assembly (סודם) to the sons of the heavens in order (to form) the council of the Community (לעצת יחד) and a foundation of the building of holiness to be an everlasting plantation throughout all future ages (1QS 11:7–9).[43]

The assembly of the angels has a cultic character, yet its description as סוד takes up political language, and thus, reflects antique conceptions of the cultic functions performed by politically elected representatives.[44]

The *politeuma* in Philippians 3:20–21 also acts politically when sending out a savior (σωτῆρ). The believers are desperately awaiting him "from there" (ἐξ οὗ).[45] Saviors are gods, men, and women, who save people or communities in times of crisis and help to improve living conditions.[46] Human saviors act by commission of the gods. The political leader Aratus, for example, is praised as a savior before the savior Gods "because to thy native city thou hast brought a sacred and heavenly reign of law."[47]

The saving act makes the human savior the agent of divine power.[48] *Politeumata* send out citizens on rescue missions, as the Athenians did with Kephisdoros,

> who has engaged honestly and incorruptibly in political life (πεπολιτευμένος) for thirty years . . . and has gone on embassies of the greatest importance for the safety (εἰς σωτηρίαν) of the cities and the countryside. . . .[49]

42. For the plural ἐν οὐρανοῖς, cf. 2 Cor 12:3. Paul uses the plural when he adopts apocalyptic traditions in 1 Thess 1:10 and 2 Cor 5:1.
43. Unless otherwise noted, translations from Florentino García Martínez and Eibert J. C. Tigchelaar, eds., *The Dead Sea Scrolls Study Edition*, 2 vols. (Leiden; Boston; Grand Rapids: Brill; Eerdmans, 1997, 1998). In the hymn of thanksgiving (1QH[a] 19:10–14), the community praises God: "[10]. . . For the sake of your glory, you have purified man from offence . . . , to become united wi[th] the sons of your truth and in the lot with [12]your holy ones, to raise the worms of the dead from the dust, to an ever[lasting] community (לסוד) and from a depraved spirit, to [your] knowledge, [13]so that he can take his place in your presence with the perpetual host and the spirits [...], to renew him with everything [14]that will exist, and with those who know in a community of jubilation"ביחד רנה))" (Sukenik 11:10–14). Cf. 1QH[a] 11:19–21 (Sukenik 3:19–21): [19]"I thank you, Lord, because you saved my life from the pit, and from the Sheol of Abaddon [20]have lifted me up to an everlasting height, so that I can walk on a boundless plain. And I know that there is hope for someone [21]you fashioned out of dust for an everlasting community (לסוד לולם)." Cf. 1QS[b] 4:24–26; 4QInstruction 418.81 4–5; etc.
44. The term סוד is already attested in the Biblical tradition as a designation of God's reign (cf. Ps 89:8). In Qumran, it is the political and cultic assembly of the heavenly ones in which the community takes part. Cf. H.-J. Fabry, Art., סוד, *ThWAT* (1989), 6:775-82.
45. Ἀπεκδέχεσθαι is a typical apocalyptic term in Paul, cf. 1 Cor 1:7; Rom 8:19, 25.
46. Cf. F. Jung, *ΣΩΤΗΡ. Studien zur Rezeption eines Hellenistischen Ehrentitels im Neuen Testament*, NTAbh 39 (Münster: Aschendorff, 2002), 154: "Retter sind Menschen [und Götter], denen es gelingt, die Lebensbedingungen anderer Menschen wesentlich zu verbessern und alles abzuwenden, was ein geregeltes Leben bedroht oder unmöglich macht." See, for example, 54–62; 112–169 and passim.
47. Plutarch, *Arat.* 14.4.
48. For more examples, cf. Jung, *ΣΩΤΗΡ*, 54–58; 84–86; etc.
49. *Hesperia* 5 (1936) 419,15 (Athens, 2nd century BCE): Translation from B. D. Meritt. Cf. Jung, *ΣΩΤΗΡ*, 149n137.

So too does the Lord Jesus Christ in Philippians 3:20 save on behalf of a *politeuma* and draw his power from Heaven.[50] But of course, who the other citizens of the heavenly *politeuma* are is not mentioned. Because the *politeuma* already acts by sending the σωτήρ, it is not very likely that only the future or exiled members, the Philippians, are in view. A *politeuma* of angels is more probably in mind, as in the case of the Dead Sea Scrolls. In any case, the σωτήρ Jesus Christ clothes the citizens to be saved with an appropriate heavenly garment that represents his body of glory.

Paul often mentions a hope for the eschatological transformation of the body.[51] Even in this case, the body is not removed but merely changes appearance.[52] The body of humiliation becomes the body of his glory. Ταπείνωσις is the humiliation and powerlessness of Israel in Egypt or of Hagar in Sarah's house.[53] The apocalyptic seer condemns: "Woe to you, mighty, who with might oppress the righteous one" (1 Enoch 96:8). But unlike other apocalyptic traditions, it is not clear in Philippians 3:21 which injustice has caused the humiliation of the righteous.

The transformation is preceded neither by a post-mortal judgment nor by a trumpet call, nor any other of the apocalyptic scenarios to which Paul alludes elsewhere.[54] There is not even mention of the resurrection which was longed for in Philippians 3:10. On the contrary, as with Philippians 2:15, the text follows the apocalyptic traditions in which only the righteous are promised an eschatological future existence among the heavenly beings and the stars and in which they are clothed with a "garment of glory."[55] In the Parables of Enoch, this happens on Judgment Day when "the kings, the governors, the high officials, and the landlords" are judged by the "The Lord of the Spirits."

> And the righteous and chosen will be saved on that day; and the faces of the sinners and the unrighteous they will henceforth not see. And the Lord of Spirits will dwell over them, and with that Son of Man they will eat, and lie down and rise up forever and ever. And the righteous and chosen will have arisen from the earth, and have ceased to cast down their faces, and have put on the garment of glory. And this will be your garment, the garment of life from the Lord of Spirits; and your gar-

50. Jung, *ΣΩΤΗΡ*, 312–3. Pace Jung, I do not see that the *politeuma* in Phil 3:20 will only be constituted in the future.
51. A verbal parallel is Rom 8:29: συμμόρφους τῆς εἰκόνος τοῦ υἱοῦ αὐτοῦ; cf. 1 Cor 15:51–54; 2 Cor 5:1–10. In 2 Cor 3:18 Paul speaks of a transformation (μεταμορφοῦσθαι) into the image of the Lord's glory (δόξα κυρίου) as a present reality.
52. *Pace* Wis 9:15; Philo, *Her.* 268 or Jubilees 23:31.
53. Deut 26:7; Gen 16:11; Luke 1:48; LXX Isa 53:8; etc.
54. Cf. e.g. 1 Cor 3:11–15; 2 Cor 5:10; Rom 14:10; 1 Thess 1:10; 4:15–18; 1 Cor 15:46–50.
55. Cf. Dan 12:2–3; 1 Enoch 104:2, 4; 4 Ezra 7:97, 125. A glorious garment first appears in the earliest text of 1QS 4:6–8: "And the reward of those who walk in it (the spirit of the sons of truth) will be healing . . . eternal enjoyment with endless life, and a crown of glory, with majestic raiment in eternal light." But see 1 Enoch 108:11. Cf. 2 Baruch 51:5, 10; Ascension of Isaiah 8:26; 9:9. These garments of glory or light honor the righteous (cf. Wis 5:14; 1 Enoch 108:11), but see also the dress of the heavenly world (2 Enoch 22:8–10), and in the following texts the dress of the first human before the fall (1QS 4:22–3; 1QH[a] 4:14–15; 2 Baruch 51:10; 3 Baruch 4:16; Apocalypse of Abraham 13:14). For Adam's original garment of light, see Apocalypse of Moses 20:24:14–15; 21:6; *Berešit Rabba* 20:12. Cf. John J. Collins, "The Otherworld in the Dead Sea Scrolls," in *Other Worlds and their Relation to this World. Early Jewish and Ancient Christian Traditions*, ed. Tobias Nicklas, et al, JSJSup 143 (Leiden: Brill, 2010), 95–116, esp. 105–9.

ments will not wear out, and your glory will not fade in the presence of the Lord of Spirits (1 Enoch 62:13–16).[56]

In Philippians, the eschatological transformation of the suffering righteous one into the heavenly figure of glory is carried out—unlike elsewhere else in Paul—not by God, but by Christ. The part he plays is comparable to the ultimate power of the "Lord of Spirits" in the Parables of Enoch.[57] This also explains why it contradicts all other traditions of LXX Psalm 8:7 in the New Testament.[58] It remains unclear whether Christ's unique divine power serves as proof of his authority or is meant as a last messianic act or as a reinstatement of the *dominum terrae* in Genesis 1:28 (cf. Philo, *Opif.* 83). But at least the quote from biblical creation stories (cf. also Ps 8:5–6) evokes the idea of the reinhabited paradise prominent in apocalyptic literature elsewhere.[59]

Conclusion

I hope to have shown that Philippians 3:18–21 contains a dense set of apocalyptic motifs. Paul frames the passage with a representation of himself as the ideal wise person. Like the sage of Sirach 51 and Wisdom 6–9, Paul is constantly on his way, but has not yet reached his goal. Paul's goal, however, is not intimacy with God's wisdom but resurrection and the upward call.[60] Here, already, he evokes apocalyptic hope and imagery. Paul is also aware that some members in the community will receive direct revelation from God (3:15). Its content he does not and cannot predict. At this point, Paul ends his self-representation as an ideal wise person and suddenly takes on the part of an apocalyptic prophet. In tears, he predicts the fate of the "enemies of the cross" and the future of his own people who shall be saved. While the enemies of the cross remain caught up in worldliness, his addressees will experience a transformation and be clothed with heavenly bodies. There exists in heaven a "body of citizens with political rights" which supports the believers by sending a savior.

Apocalyptic motifs in Philippians 3:18–21 are the crying prophet, the contrast between the unrighteous and the righteous and their respective futures, and the promise to the latter of heavenly transformation. The wrongs and the humiliation inflicted upon the righteous are however barely described. The "enemies of the cross" are not the mighty, who "with might

56. Translation from George W. E. Nickelsburg and James C. VanderKam, *1 Enoch 2: A Commentary on the Book of 1 Enoch, Chapters 37–82*, Hermeneia (Minneapolis: Fortress Press, 2012).

57. If there is any divine activity in Phil 3:21, it is the expression *κατὰ τὴν ἐνέργειαν* (according to the power); *ἐνέργεια* is the energy which radiates from the invisible deity and from which human beings can acquire knowledge of God (Philo, *Spec.* 1.47–47; Eph 1:19). Wisdom is "the spotless mirror" *τῆς τοῦ θεοῦ ἐνεργείας* (Wis 7:26).

58. Cf. 1 Cor 15:27–28; Eph 1:22.

59. E.g. 2 Baruch 51:11–14.

60. Phil 3:10, 14. Resurrection is an apocalyptic conception. Cf. e.g. Dan 12:1–3; 1 Enoch 104:2, 4; Jubilees 32:27–33; Testament of Moses 10:8–10.

oppress the righteous ones" (1 Enoch 96:8). Rather, they are those who ignore God's reality and "set their minds on earthly things" (3:19). Consequently, they remain caught up in the self-deception of worldliness. Yet, the main focus is not on the judgment of the unrighteous—at any rate, no judgment explicitly takes place here—but on the salvation of believers. The seer Paul reveals to them that they belong to a heavenly *politeuma* and are going to be saved by a savior, who will be sent by their heavenly fellow citizens in order to bring them back from exile. Therefore, their now humiliated body will be transformed into its (original) transcendent glory. With this message, the apocalyptic passage of Philippians 3:18–21 extends and confirms claims made already in Philippians 1–2 and 4. In the face of death (2 Cor 1:8; cf. Phil 2:17–18) and confronted with sad news of suffering in Philippi (Phil 2:27–29), Paul reveals what present afflictions might obscure but what is in his eyes the actual reality if one views that reality from a heavenly perspective.[61] Apocalypticism functions in Philippians as elsewhere "to interpret the present in the light of the supernatural world and of the future."[62]

But astonishingly, one question remains unanswered: Where does Paul's knowledge of transcendence actually come from? Unlike other apocalyptic seers, he does not mention any journey to heaven or any knowledge of heavenly tablets.[63] Without such a justification, Paul's promise depends solely on the experience of the transformative power of resurrection through suffering and dying with Christ crucified, an argument which can only be convincing, if the audience shares this experience. That Paul can insinuate apocalyptic imagery in the previous parts of the letter indicates that this understanding was shared by the Philippians.

61. Cf. Standhartinger, "Aus der Welt eines Gefangenen. Die Kommunikationsstruktur des Philipperbriefs im Spiegel seiner Abfassungssituation," *NovT* 55 (2013): 140–67.

62. Adela Yarbro Collins, "Introduction: Early Christian Apocalypses," *Semeia* 36 (1986): 1–11 (7).

63. In the context of *politeuma*, the "book of life" in Phil 4:3 would be a heavenly citizenship list (cf. Heb 12:23; Rev 21:27; Pilhofer, *Philippi* I.131–32; Hawthorne and Martin, *Philippians*, 243). The biblical and apocalyptic ideas of heavenly books are multifaceted (cf. Nickelsburg, *1 Enoch 1*, 478–80). There are books which contain the deeds of the righteous and sinners (cf. 1 Enoch 98:6–8; 104:2, 7–8; Jubilees 30:19–23), and others record the prayers of the righteous (1 Enoch 99:3). Enoch can read the heavenly tablets on which the future is recorded (1 Enoch 103:1–4; cf. Rev 10:8–10) and sometimes those heavenly writings are lists of those to be saved (cf. 1 Enoch 104:1). It is called "book of life" or "of the living" in LXX Ps 68:29; Jubilees 36:10; Rev 3:5; 13:9. On the concept, see Leslie Baynes, *The Heavenly Book Motif in Judeo-Christian Apocalypses 200 B.C.E–200 C.E.*, JSJSup 152 (Leiden: Brill, 2011).

12

Paul the Seer and the Apocalyptic Community at Thessalonica

John Byron

For the non-specialist, the terms "apocalypse" and "apocalyptic" are often equated with the end of the world through wanton destruction on a cataclysmic level. This is demonstrable by the number of Hollywood films whose story lines depict the collapse of society through some type of natural or human disaster. In the 1970s, this understanding of the terminology was epitomized by Francis Ford Coppola's examination of the Vietnam War era in his film *Apocalypse Now*. More recently, the obsession with a so-called Zombie Apocalypse focuses on the attempt of the few to survive the collapse of society and creation around them.

New Testament scholarship recognizes, however, that how we understand this terminology needs to be more carefully nuanced. Strictly speaking, "apocalyptic" is not a synonym for "eschatology" and is better used as a description for the "unveiling" of hidden things rather than last things.[1] While apocalyptic can include eschatology, the terminology more precisely

1. Crispin Fletcher-Louis, "Jewish Apocalyptic and Apocalypticism," in *Handbook for the Study of the Historical Jesus: The Study of Jesus*,

refers to the revelation of a new wisdom, an unseen world or an alternative perspective on the consummation of time.[2] For the recipient, it represents a new way of understanding the world around them and the trajectory of history. In Jewish and Christian literature, this new information is often revealed by an agent of God who offers it to one designated as a seer to others in his or her community. An "apocalypse," on the contrary, refers to a genre of literature that usually contains visionary (i.e., apocalyptic) material.[3]

Paul and Apocalyptic

Albert Schweitzer startled New Testament scholarship in 1930 by suggesting that Paul can only be understood correctly within the context of Jewish and Christian apocalyptic thought.[4] Similarly, Ernst Käsemann argued thirty years later that "Apocalyptic was the mother of all Christian Theology."[5] Similar approaches to Paul have been advocated by J. Louis Martyn (1967, 1985)[6], J. Christiaan Becker (1980)[7], and Christopher Rowland (1982).[8] Although Paul never wrote an "apocalypse," many scholars now recognize that Paul's theology is deeply indebted to the apocalyptic thought of his Jewish heritage.

Paul's first letter to the Thessalonians provides us with an early specimen of his apocalyptic thinking.[9] Most interpreters will identify Paul's discussion of the *parousia* and resurrection in 1 Thessalonians 4:13–17 as containing apocalyptic elements. Their attention is typically drawn here by the eschatological nature of the discussion. Many will also include Paul's discussion of the day of the Lord in 5:3–11 for the same reason. But confining Paul's apocalypticism to these two sections is too limiting. It seems to suggest that some of his theology is applicable now while the rest is waiting to be applied at some future point. Paul's purpose here, however, is not to promise the Thessalonians some future relief from their current suffering. Much of what is in this letter is a result of how Paul and the Thessalonians see the world now in light of the new revelation given to them through the death and resurrection of Jesus. To be sure, Paul's talk of the *parousia*, the resurrection, and the day of the Lord are all events yet to take place in the future. But Paul's apocalyptic language and imagery is not focused so much on the future (and thus eschatology) as it is on the present. In this letter, Paul employs an apocalyptic perspective

ed. Tom Holmén and Stanley E. Porter, Vol. 2 of *Handbook for the Study of the Historical Jesus*, ed. Tom Holmén and Stanley E. Porter (Leiden: Brill, 2011), 1569–1607 (1593).

2. Christopher Rowland, "Apocalypticism," in *The Eerdmans Dictionary of Early Judaism*, ed. John J. Collins and Daniel C. Harlow (Grand Rapids: Eerdmans, 2010), 345–48 (346).
3. John J. Collins, "Apocalypse," in *The Eerdmans Dictionary of Early Judaism* (Grand Rapids: Eerdmans, 2010), 341–45 (344).
4. Albert Schweitzer, *The Mysticism of Paul the Apostle* (New York: H. Holt and Co, 1931).
5. Ernst Käsemann, "The Beginnings of Christian Theology," in *New Testament Questions Today* (Philadelphia: Fortress Press, 1969), 102.
6. J. Louis Martyn, *Theological Issues in the Letters of Paul* (Nashville: Abingdon, 1997), 89–123.
7. J. Christiaan Becker, *Paul the Apostle: The Triumph of God in Life and Thought* (Philadelphia: Fortress Press, 1980), 135–81.
8. Christopher Rowland, *The Open Heaven: A Study of Apocalyptic in Judaism and Early Christianity* (New York: Crossroad, 1982), 374–86.
9. This assumes that 1 Thessalonians is the earliest of Paul's extant letters.

in order to explain how the future affects the present. For Paul and the Thessalonians, what is just as important as the future is how they live as a community in the present.

Consequently, this chapter focuses more broadly on 1 Thessalonians by interpreting it from the standpoint of Paul as "seer" for the Thessalonians. While Paul is certainly not claiming any specific heavenly visions here, his numerous references to the *parousia*, divine beings (Satan/angels), and the designation of the Thessalonians as sons of light demonstrate that the letter is steeped in apocalyptic thought. Paul's letter to the Thessalonians reveals to them an unseen world in which they live as an alternative community at the intersection of two ages. Paul's apocalypticism is not directed toward what *will happen* in the future, but on what *must happen now* because of the future.

Paul as Seer to the Thessalonians

Paul never wrote an apocalypse, but he does claim to have received divine revelations through visions.[10] Twice, he describes his encounter with the risen Jesus as a "revelation" (δι' ἀποκαλύψεως Ἰησοῦ Χριστοῦ, Gal 1:12) and a "vision" (ὤφθη, 1 Cor 15:8).[11] In 2 Corinthians 12:1–4, he relates a mystical experience during which he travelled to heaven (mentally or physically he is unsure), and there, saw things that he cannot describe. At one point in his ministry, he is compelled by a revelation to travel to Jerusalem and present his gospel to the leadership there (κατὰ ἀποκάλυψσιν, Gal 2:2).[12] Further reflecting this apocalyptic perspective is his designation of himself and Apollos as "stewards of the mysteries of God" (οἰκονόμους μυστηρίων θεοῦ, 1 Cor 4:1).[13] While these revelatory and visionary experiences are not a major feature of Paul's letters, his mention of them, even if only in passing, demonstrate that he considers them an important part of his religious experience. Paul's vision reports echo those found in other literary apocalypses such as Isaiah 6, Ezekiel 1, 40–48, Zechariah 1–8, Daniel 7, 1 Enoch, and Revelation.[14] Although he does not write an apocalypse in the strict understanding of the term (i.e., as a genre), the way he relates these experiences to his readers aligns him with the seers in those apocalypses.[15]

Although he does not make any claims to visions in 1 Thessalonians, the material in the letter

10. David Aune, "Understanding Jewish and Christian Apocalyptic," *Word & World* 25, no. 3 (2005): 233–45 (241).
11. While it is debated whether Paul's testimony of visions and revelations reflects his Damascus Road experience described in Acts, it is clear that Paul and his interpreters considered revelatory/mystical experiences to be an important part of his religious life.
12. James D.G. Dunn, *The Epistle to the Galatians*, BNTC (London: A & C Black, 1993), 91.
13. Christopher Rowland and Christopher R.A. Morray-Jones, *The Mystery of God: Early Jewish Mysticism and the New Testament*, CRINT 12 (Leiden: Brill, 2009), 153. For other examples of the phrase "mysteries of God" or "mysteries of the Most High," see: Joseph and Aseneth 16:14; Testament of Levi 2:10; 3 Baruch 1:6, 8; 2:6.
14. See also 1 Kgs 22:19.
15. Greg Carey, *Ultimate Things: An Introduction to Jewish and Christian Apocalyptic Literature* (St. Louis: Chalice, 2005), 128; Frederick J. Murphy, *Apocalypticism in the Bible and Its World* (Grand Rapids: Baker Academic, 2012), 310.

reflects typical elements and assumptions found in the apocalyptic. Paul reveals to the Thessalonians significant cosmological as well as eschatological information.[16] His perspective on the Thessalonians' situation "provides them with a symbolic universe in which the forces arrayed against them are seen in apocalyptic terms of the forces of Satan arrayed against God and God's righteous followers, the members of the Thessalonians congregation."[17] But Paul's purpose in using this language/imagery is not to talk about the future, but rather to remind/inform the Thessalonians of their identity in the overlapping of the ages that has begun with the resurrection of Jesus. The Thessalonian present is affected by both the past and the future. Therefore, they have become an alternative community that lives very differently from those around them. Certainly, judgment and the wrath of God are on the horizon (1:10; 2:16; 5:9), but the Thessalonians need not worry about the future since they are already part of the future age. What is most important to Paul is how they live now.

Paul's Reveled Cosmology

In 1 Thessalonians, Paul assumes that there is an unseen world and he refers to it in several ways.[18] As a group of new believers in Jesus, those recently acquainted with the God of Israel, the Thessalonians are in need of someone to introduce them to or at least make them aware of this world. The evidence available from the letter suggests that the Thessalonian audience was made up primarily of gentiles.[19] This means that, as a group, they would be unaware of the unseen world that Jewish apocalyptists such as Paul assume exists. Much of what Paul relates to them about this unseen world, therefore, constitutes a new cosmology and requires a seer to guide them. Paul fills this role as he mentions or alludes to aspects of this world in the letter.[20]

In the unseen world of Paul and the Thessalonians, Jesus is Lord and although he died, he is alive having been raised by God. But Jesus is, at the same time, hidden. He is not present in this world with the Thessalonians, but rather is located in heaven (1:10; cf. 1 Cor 1:7–8). The Thessalonians cannot see heaven, they cannot see Jesus, yet they are waiting for him to come from heaven at some point in order to rescue them from a "coming wrath." Paul, however, not only assumes the reality of this world, but directs the Thessalonians' attention towards it. In the context of their present struggles (1:6; 2:14; 3:3–4), they are encouraged not to concentrate

16. In 3:4, Paul reminds the Thessalonians of the warnings about coming opposition that the apostles had delivered while with them (cf. 2 Thess 2:5).

17. Duane Watson, "Paul's Appropriation of Apocalyptic Discourse," in *Visions and Persuasions: Rhetorical Dimensions of Apocalyptic Discourse*, ed. Greg Carey and L. Gregory Bloomquist (St. Louis: Chalice, 1999), 61–80 (63).

18. Murphy, *Apocalypticism in the Bible and Its World*, 8.

19. Abraham J. Malherbe, *The Letters to the Thessalonians*, AB 32B (New Haven: Yale University Press, 2000), 58–62.

20. It is probably safe to assume that Paul had given a fuller explanation of this hidden world when he was with them in person. Thus, what we find here is a combination of what Paul assumes they know as well as his efforts to remind them of what they know.

on what they *can* see, but that which is *hidden* from them. A world that is not accessible to them yet has been promised by their seer, Paul, to exist.

In addition to the hidden Jesus, there are other beings that exist in this unseen world. Beings who will appear when Jesus is no longer hidden, but revealed at his *parousia*. In 3:13, Paul tells the Thessalonians that the hidden Lord Jesus will strengthen them in holiness and keep them blameless before God the father until the day he appears with all of his "holy ones."[21] Moreover, when Jesus is finally revealed from heaven at the resurrection of the dead, he will be accompanied by angels who will take an active role in announcing the reappearance of Jesus (4:16). It is at this time that the unseen world will become evident to the seen world and those who have been waiting for the revelation of Jesus will see him not only for the first time, but will also be with him forever (4:17).

At the same time, the unseen world includes malevolent beings that interfere with the activities of the seen world. In Jewish apocalypticism (e.g. Jubilees, 1 Enoch, 1QM), this dualistic cosmology is fostered by the presence of demons and fallen angels who openly challenge God, commit wickedness on earth, and compel humans to imitate them.[22] In 1 Thessalonians, Paul's readers are introduced to only one evil being, Satan. In 2:18, Paul claims that he attempted to travel to Thessalonica at least twice, but Satan blocked the way. Although Paul does not explain what Satan did to hinder him, he has an acute sense that his freedom of movement was curtailed, and viewing the situation on a supernatural level, determined that Satan was interfering with the seen world.[23] A few lines later, in 3:5, Paul reveals that he was anxious for the Thessalonians lest the "tempter had somehow tempted" them and that his work be rendered in vain. While there is no discussion of any specific acts that Satan has carried out in the seen world, it is clear that in Paul's apocalyptic framework, Satan is the chief opponent of God, Paul, and the Thessalonians.[24]

Living at the Intersection of Two Realms

In addition to a dualistic cosmology, the Thessalonians must contend with the fact that they live at the intersection of two realms. They are among God's chosen (1:4), which means they

21. While some may interpret τῶν ἁγίων (holy ones) as "saints" in 1 Thess 3:13, the phrase is probably better understood as an intertextual allusion to Zech 14:5 where the phrase clearly alludes to angels. Moreover, understanding the phrase as a reference to "saints" rather than "angels" is a result of overemphasizing the eschatological nature of the letter (Gordon Fee, *The First and Second Letters to the Thessalonians*, NICNT [Grand Rapids: Eerdmans, 2009], 135–36; David Luckensmyer, *The Eschatology of First Thessalonians*, NTOA 71 [Göttingen: Vandenhoeck & Ruprecht, 2009], 229–30). It seems better to understand the reference as referring to angels which would parallel Paul's later apocalyptic imagery in 4:16.
22. Martinus C. de Boer, "Paul and Apocalyptic Eschatology," in *The Encyclopedia of Apocalypticism, Volume 1: The Origin of Apocalypticism in Judaism and Christianity*, ed. John J. Collins (New York/London: Continuum, 1998), 345–83 (358); Fletcher-Louis, "Jewish Apocalyptic and Apocalypticism," 1571.
23. Curiously, however, whatever was blocking Paul (and Silas) did not prevent Timothy from going back as we will soon see (3:2).
24. Watson, "Paul's Appropriation of Apocalyptic Discourse," 71.

stand in contrast to the "others" (λοιποί, 4:13; 5:6). There is no middle group.[25] This is demonstrated most clearly in 1:9, when Paul mentions their turn from worshipping idols to worshipping the true and living God. Here, Paul employs a typical feature of apocalyptic, the antithesis of the two realms which "emphasizes that they now share a religious and social reality very different from the one they once shared with their neighbors."[26] The Thessalonians have a different identity located outside of the typical pagan worship of their neighbors and instead with the worship of Israel's God. And as members of the new realm they are part of God's kingdom (2:12).

Paul uses kingdom/kingdom of God language in only seven passages of the undisputed letters.[27] The kingdom of God is often understood as being both a future *and* a present reality; a realm which cannot be fully entered until the *parousia*;[28] sometimes described as the "already not yet."[29] Beker argues, however, that the infrequency of Paul's kingdom language is due to the "proleptic presence of the new in the old" as probably the reason for his sparing use of the terminology as a future reality of salvation. Beker believes that Paul views "the age to come" as already present fully in Christ (Gal 4:4).[30] Beker's argument requires some nuancing, however. While Paul's apocalyptic thought certainly understands the kingdom as being a present reality, he also understands it as being fully consummated in the future at the final resurrection (cf. 5:9).[31]

But it is also incorrect to overlook the very present reality of the kingdom for believers. In 2:12, Paul reminds the Thessalonians how he and the other apostles urged them to live/walk in a way that is "worthy of God who calls you into his own kingdom and glory." Paul's purpose here is not to talk about some future reality, but to remind them that they are *already* part of God's kingdom. Emphasizing the present reality of this kingdom is Paul's reference to God's "call" (καλέω) upon them in the present tense, indicating both the present and continuing nature of the event in which they now participate.[32]

Paul further affirms their present location within the future age in 5:4–8. The Thessalonians seem to have inquired about "when" the Day of the Lord would arrive, suggesting their focus was on a future event.[33] But Paul does not direct their attention to a future time, but rather to

25. Murphy, *Apocalypticism in the Bible and Its World*, 9.
26. Watson, "Paul's Appropriation of Apocalyptic Discourse," 66.
27. 1 Thess 2:10–12; Gal 5:21; 1 Cor 4:20; 6:9–10; 15:24, 50; and Rom 14:17.
28. Charles A. Wanamaker, *The Epistles to the Thessalonians*, NIGTC (Grand Rapids: Eerdmans, 1990), 108.
29. Fee, *Thessalonians*, 83.
30. Beker, *Paul the Apostle*, 146.
31. Karl Donfried, "The Kingdom of God in Paul," in *The Kingdom of God in 20th-Century Interpretation*, ed. Wendell Willis (Peabody: Hendrickson, 1987), 175–90 (187).
32. Donfried, "The Kingdom of God in Paul," 181; Luckensmyer, *Eschatology of First Thessalonians*, 228.
33. Paul probably felt the need to address this topic because the Thessalonians had asked him to do so. The "now about times and dates" in 5:1 suggests that he is answering a question sent to him by the Thessalonians. It's possible that their concern for and con-

the present by declaring them to be "sons of light" already living in the day (5:5). Once again, this is typical apocalyptic antithesis language that creates insiders and outsiders.[34] In the Dead Sea Scrolls, "sons of light" is used to describe those who walk in perfection in God's sight and detest "the sons of darkness" (1QS 1:8–10; 3:25; 1QM 1:1–3).[35] The imagery of light and darkness to represent association with or alienation from God finds its source in the Hebrew Bible[36] and is frequently employed by Paul to designate believers as different from those outside of the community.[37] In his role as seer to the Thessalonians, Paul shifts their perspective from thinking about the future to the present. He reminds them that although their circumstances are difficult, they are no longer living in the present only, but the future as well. They are different than those around them who have not entered into the day and thus become sons of light.

The point at which these two realms intersect has its beginning at the resurrection of Jesus as evidenced by Paul's statement in 1:10 about Jesus's eventual appearance from heaven. The resurrection will be emphasized again in 4:14, where Paul sets up his discussion of Jesus's return for the dead and living believers in Christ with the conditional statement "if we believe that Jesus died and was raised." For Paul and the Thessalonians, Jesus's location in heaven and eventual return are only significant if the resurrection is in view. Paul's belief in the resurrection convinced him that the future realm had already invaded the present.[38] As Beker points out:

> Resurrection is end-time language and unintelligible apart from the apocalyptic thought world to which resurrection language belongs. Resurrection language properly belongs to the domain of the new age to come and is an inherent part of the transformation and recreation of all reality in the apocalyptic age. Thus the resurrection of Christ, the coming reign of God, and the future resurrection of the dead belong together.[39]

Paul's eschatology is not only grounded in the future, but an event in the recent past; the resurrection.[40] "Paul's apocalyptic eschatology, like that of Revelation, is thus as much a matter of a *past* eschatological event (the resurrection of Jesus, the Messiah) as of an event still to occur (the *parousia*)."[41] Jesus's resurrection inaugurates the new age and believers participate in it in the future.[42]

fusion over those who died before the resurrection may have raised some questions about timing ("Just when will these events take place and how will we know?"). The phrase τῶν χρόνων καὶ τῶν καιρῶν appears only four times in the Greek Bible (Dan 2:21; Wis 8:8; Acts 1:7; 1 Thess 5:1). All four occurrences are both eschatological and ambiguous at the same time, which is probably purposeful. On the one hand, the phrase acknowledges the certainty that these events will happen. At the same time, however, it underlines the reality that only God knows the precise nature and timing of these events.

34. Wanamaker, *Thessalonians*, 181.
35. Watson, "Paul's Appropriation of Apocalyptic Discourse," 76.
36. Pss 27:1; 74:20; 82:5; 112:4; Isa 2:5; 9:2; 60:19–20; Prov 4:18–19.
37. Rom 13:12; 2 Cor 4:6; 6:14; 11:14; Col 1:12–13.
38. Aune, "Understanding Jewish and Christian Apocalyptic," 242.
39. Beker, *Paul the Apostle*, 152.
40. Martyn, *Theological Issues*, 121.
41. de Boer, "Paul and Apocalyptic Eschatology," 355.

The Present Impacted by the Future

In some ways, the present probably did not look all that different from the past for the Thessalonians. They were still living in the same city and were, presumably, working the same jobs and living with their same families. On the contrary, one aspect that probably did look different was the level of opposition they were receiving from their neighbors as a result of their decision to follow a Jewish messiah (1:6; 2:14; 3:3–4). In this way, the Thessalonians were acutely aware of how the past was influencing their present.

Paul acknowledges how they are being affected by their past and present suffering and is worried that it might cause them to waver (3:5). But he also does not dwell on the future, at least not as a way to make them forget the present. Instead, he focuses on how the future impacts the present.[43] Paul reveals to them how the future is already a reality. And the "now" is wrapped up in the future event of Jesus's *parousia*.

Five times in this letter, Paul refers to the future return of Jesus (1:10; 2:19; 3:13; 4:15; 5:23). Each time Paul refers to this future event, he links the Thessalonians to it, whether it is their rescue from God's wrath (1:10; cf. 5:9), or their preservation in holiness (3:13; 5:23). The result is that the Thessalonians no longer have an identity that merely focuses on the past or present, but one that is impacted by the future on the present.[44] As Foster notes: "For Paul, the Thessalonian believers have an apocalyptic identity that is inextricably linked to the coming of the Lord Jesus."[45] The present identity of the Christian community is revealed in the future *parousia*. The Thessalonians can only fully understand their present in the light of the resurrection of Jesus in the past and his *parousia* in the future.[46] Moreover, their corporate identity is only disclosed through the *parousia*.[47]

An Alternative Community

While the Thessalonians still live in the present, they are, nonetheless, different. Their awareness of an unseen world, their living at the intersection of two ages and their identity in the *parousia* transforms them into an alternative community. Paul makes this clear in 4:13–5:11, where he establishes a dualistic apocalyptic worldview by dividing all of humanity into two

42. Carey, *Ultimate Things*, 133.
43. This is similar to other Jewish apocalypses, like the Animal Apocalypse in 1 Enoch 83–90, where human are affected by that past and whose actions have both present and future consequences (George W. E. Nickelsburg, *1 Enoch 1: A commentary on the Book of Enoch Chapters 1–36, 81–108* [Minneapolis: Fortress Press, 2001], 38).
44. Luckensmyer, *Eschatology of First Thessalonians*, 227–28.
45. Paul Foster, "The Eschatology of the Thessalonian Correspondence: An Exercise in Pastoral Pedagogy and Constructive Theology," *JSPL* 1, no. 1 (2010): 57–82 (69).
46. Wanamaker, *Thessalonians*, 230.
47. Foster, "Eschatology of the Thessalonian Correspondence," 69.

groups. On the one side are the Thessalonian believers, and on the other, the rest of humanity who has no hope of rescue from God's coming wrath or life beyond death (4:13; 5:6, 9; cf. 1:10; 2:16).[48]

Similar to the Qumran community, the Thessalonians are designated by Paul as "sons of light" and (the unattested elsewhere) "sons of day." These monikers place them in contradistinction to the "sons of darkness" or "sons of night" (although Paul never specifically uses these phrases), and thus, create a boundary between them and everyone else (5:5). Unlike those around them, they are waiting for the day of the Lord and their destiny as a community includes a positive experience with the events of the day of the Lord.[49]

The first indication that the Thessalonians represent an alternative community is found in 1:10, when Paul reminds them of their response to the gospel message: "you turned to God from idols to serve the living and true God, and to wait for his Son from heaven, whom he raised from the dead—Jesus, who rescues us from the wrath that is coming." As Meeks notes, the apocalyptic elements are rather clear here. There is a duality in cosmology (heaven/earth), a duality in time (this age/the coming age), but there is also a duality of worship (idols/living God).[50] As worshippers of the living and true God, the Thessalonians stand in contrast to those who participate in false/idol worship.[51] The decision to worship God excludes the Thessalonians, therefore, from worshipping Dionysus, Roma, Serapis, or any of the other gods that were a part of Thessalonica's vibrant religious atmosphere.[52] Paul's revelation of Jesus Christ to them caused them to separate from those other gods and those who worship them. This means that those who are *not* part of the community of Thessalonian believers are *not* children of the day and are, therefore, children of the night. Whatever familial, ethnic, or civic kinship ties may have linked them together previously is now dissolved as a result of the apocalyptic community established by Paul in Thessalonica. They are not like those whom Paul describes later as drunk and asleep (5:7).

At the same time, the Thessalonians are not merely some local, separatist group, but part of a larger cosmic community. In 1 Thessalonians, Paul twice commends them for becoming

48. Watson, "Paul's Appropriation of Apocalyptic Discourse," 73.

49. Ibid., 76.

50. Wayne A. Meeks, "Social Functions of Apocalyptic Language," in *Apocalypticism in the Mediterranean World and the Near East*, ed. David Hellholm, 2nd ed. (Tubingen: J. C. B. Mohr [Paul Siebeck], 1989), 687–705 (690).

51. Talk of turning to the "true and living God" (1:9) is common Jewish conversion language. In the LXX "turning to God' is often used to refer to repentance (Deut 30:2; 1 Sam 7:3; 1 Kgs 8:33; Isa 6:10; Jer 24:7; Joel 2:12–14; Zech 1:3; Sir 5:7; 17:25). But outside of the LXX, it is used to refer to gentile conversion. The apocryphal book of Tobit, for instance, talks about turning to fear God truly rather than idols (14:6). In the Jewish romance novella Joseph and Aseneth, Joseph marries an Egyptian woman who in her conversion speech "turns" and confesses her belief in the "true God" of the Hebrews (11:10–11). Jewish polemics against idolatry considered idols as the direct opposite of "living" (Isa 44:9–20; Wis 13–15; Philo, *Decal.* 52–81; *Spec. Laws* 1.13–31).

52. Charles Edson, "Cults of Thessalonica," *HTR* (1948): 158–81; Karl P. Donfried, *Paul, Thessalonica, and Early Christianity* (Grand Rapids: Eerdmans, 2002), 25–29.

imitators in the midst of great suffering. In 1:6, he notes that "you became imitators of us and the Lord, receiving the word in much tribulation with the joy of the Holy Spirit."[53] Later, in 2:14, he makes a similar claim: "For you became imitators of the churches of God in Judea in Christ Jesus, because you suffered the same things by your fellow countrymen and them by the Jews."[54] In both cases, Paul's statements affirm that although the Thessalonians' experience of opposition and hostility may isolate them from their family and fellow citizens, it also creates a cosmic solidarity. First, their experience of suffering places them in solidarity with the risen Lord Jesus for whom they are waiting to be revealed from heaven and rescue them from both God's wrath and the experience of death (1:10; 4:16–17). Second, it connects them to the apostles who themselves have suffered in conjunction with the gospel message (2:2; 3:7). Lastly, it links them to other Christian communities that they have never seen, specifically the churches in Judea (2:14). In other words, the experience of both the power of the gospel (1:5) and the hostility that often accompanies it is not a localized event but a worldwide one, which can only be comprehended fully at the eschatological *parousia* of the Lord (1:10; 4:15). Moreover, as Meeks points out, the hostilities they have experienced are, in Paul's opinion, "part of a comprehensive pattern of God's activity in and for the world."[55]

Community Behavior

An important aspect of being this alternative community is that it not only believes and worships differently, but also behaves differently. As an alternative community, the Thessalonians' behavior in the present is impacted by the future. At times, readers of 1 Thessalonians can be distracted by the presence of apocalyptic eschatology in the letter. The promise of a future age inaugurated by the *parousia* and the day of the Lord can lead to the assumption that what Paul is doing here is describing that future age. But in reality, apocalypses rarely devote much time to describing the future age. As Rowland and Morray-Jones note: "While apocalypses may devote much attention to the progress of history leading up to the new age, there is an evident reluctance to speculate about its character."[56] A careful reading of 1 Thessalonians reveals that the principle is the same in this letter. Paul has very little to say about the day of the Lord and more about how the Thessalonians should live in preparation for the day. "The link between eschatological expectation and the call to faithfulness in the present characterizes Pauline apocalyptic exhortation."[57]

53. Translation mine.
54. Translation mine.
55. Meeks, "Social Functions of Apocalyptic Language," 692.
56. Rowland and Morray-Jones, *Mystery of God*, 17.
57. Carey, *Ultimate Things*, 137.

As children of the day, the expectation of Jesus's imminent *parousia* brings about morally appropriate behavior. At times, the apocalyptic eschatology of 1 Thessalonians is read with a threat of judgment in view. In other words, this is the future fate of nonbelievers at the day of the Lord. But as both Fee and Foster point out, this is a rather minor theme in this letter.[58] Apart from a passing statement about them grieving without hope (4:13) and being surprised by the day of the Lord (5:2–3), Paul has very little to say about the fate of the unbeliever in 1 Thessalonians. Instead, he spends much more time focusing on how believers should live in the run up to the day of the Lord. In 4:4–8 and 5:4–11, Paul lays out how it is they should live. In particular, they are to avoid sexual immorality and live in a state of sobriety[59] and watchfulness.[60] And both sets of instructions are given in contrast to those around them. In 4:5, they are not to act out "with lustful passion, like the Gentiles who do not know God." In 5:6–7, it is the "others" (λοιποί), not the Thessalonian children of light, who sleep and get drunk at night.[61]

There is, to be sure, a threat of judgment in this letter. But it is not as strongly stated as one might expect, and again, it is not focused on the unbeliever, but rather believers.[62] In 4:6–8, Paul warns his readers that anyone who exploits his brother in the area of sexual immorality is in danger of incurring the Lord's vengeance and has rejected the Holy Spirit. But again, the main theme of Paul's statements here is not to talk about what might or will happen in the future. The apocalyptic imagery of the Lord as "avenger" serves not to threaten so much as it does to reinforce the uniqueness and solidarity in the community.[63] The same can also be said for Paul's words in 5:4–5. The apocalyptic context of his exhortation enhances the community boundaries that make them distinct.[64] Similar to the Qumran community (1QS 5:1, 7–8), as children of light, the Thessalonians constitute a separate community. And as such, the appropriate behavior internally would be observed by outsiders as what make them distinct (4:9–12).

An Unbroken Community

In 4:13–18, Paul addresses what may be the most significant challenge to the community. Some

58. Fee, *Thessalonians*, 185; Foster, "Eschatology of the Thessalonian Correspondence," 9.

59. The verb translated as "sober" is *νήφω* which is used elsewhere in the New Testament for the idea of being "aware," "well-balanced," and "self-controlled" (2 Tim 4:5; 1 Pet 1:13; 4:7; 5:8). The association with drunkenness is figurative not literal.

60. The sleep he has in mind here is not the "sleep of death" that he discusses in 4:13–15 and 5:10. His exhortation for them to be "awake" (5:6) could also be translated as "watchful" or "alert" and understood in an eschatological sense as it is in Matt 24:42, Mark 13:34–37, Luke 12:37 and Rev 3:2. Therefore, those whom Paul describes as "asleep" or "drunk" are those who are unaware of their surroundings and what is happening. They are just the kind of people who will be surprised when the thief comes at night (5:2, 4). Paul's ultimate point here is that the Thessalonians are *not* like this at all since they are children of the day.

61. Luckensmeyer, *Eschatology of First Thessalonians*, 312.

62. The wrath of God (similar language) is mentioned five times in this letter (1:10; 2:16; 4:6; 5:1–3; 5:9), but Paul never elaborates on it. Rather, while Paul acknowledges that it will occur at some point in the future, his main focus is that the Thessalonians have nothing to fear.

63. Meeks, "Social Functions of Apocalyptic Language,"693.

64. Carey, *Ultimate Things*, 139.

members of the community have died[65] and there appears to be a level of confusion as to the status of the dead in conjunction with the future *parousia*.[66] In a passage steeped in apocalyptic language and imagery similar to that of Daniel 7:13 and Mark 13:26, Paul provides the reason for Thessalonian hope (4:13). Those who are still living need not grieve like the others (λοιποί). With one short stroke of his pen, Paul links the fate of the dead and the living together through the resurrection (the past) and the return (the future) of Jesus (4:14). As members of this apocalyptic community with knowledge of the unseen world, the Thessalonians need not fear death because they have believed in the revelation of Jesus that was given to them by Paul. Death has no power over them ultimately, whether in this age or the next. The destiny of both the living and the dead are inextricably entwined with the resurrection and *parousia* of the Lord Jesus.

One way to read 4:13–18 is with the conclusion that Paul promises a solution to the problem of death by providing a positive view of the future. But while the Thessalonians certainly have good reason to be optimistic about the future, Paul is doing something more nuanced here than simply talking about the future age. The problem that he is addressing is the fear that death can somehow permanently separate the members of the community from one another. As Meeks state, however:

> It is not the problem of death as a universal phenomenon that is addressed here, but just the power of death to shatter the unique bonds of intimate new community. By using the apocalyptic scenario of the return (παρουσία) of Jesus, Paul declares that the community of Christians crosses even the boundary of death, "that we, the living, who survive until the Parousia of the Lord, will certainly not precede those who have died" (4:15). Then we the living, the survivors *together with them* will be caught up in clouds to meet the Lord . . . and thus we shall always be with the Lord (4:17).[67]

Thus, the cosmic connection and identity that the Thessalonians have with the Lord (1:10), the apostles, and the believers in Judea (2:14) extends even further to include those who have already died. The same apocalyptic language and imagery that serves to separate the community from those on the outside also serves to expand the boundaries by including those who are no longer alive.[68] "Paul's central purpose here is not to clarify the existential quality of the intermediate state, but to emphasize that the fidelity of dead believers is not undone by death."[69] Probably the most important thing Paul has to say to this community is not just that it has distinct identity and cosmic solidarity with the Lord and other believers. Rather, it is that

65. It is not clear how many have died nor does Paul give any clue as to when and how they may have died. It is possible that the opposition they were facing led to a few deaths, but this is not clear from what Paul writes here.

66. Gerbern S. Oegema, *Apocalyptic Interpretation of the Bible: Apocalypticism and Biblical Interpretation in Early Judaism, the Apostle Paul, the Historical Jesus, and their Reception History*, JCTC 13 (London: Continuum T & T Clark, 2012), 126.

67. Meeks, "Social Functions of Apocalyptic Language," 695.

68. Carey, *Ultimate Things*, 139.

69. Foster, "Eschatology of the Thessalonian Correspondence," 8.

the experience of death cannot destroy the community since their cosmic identity expands to include them.

Paul's reference to the dead believers here as "the dead in Christ" (4:16) further emphasizes that they are not at a disadvantage. For Paul, it's not a matter of either being alive or dead that identifies them as part of the community. Rather, their cosmic identity is based on their identity with the risen Lord—an identity that will be fully revealed with the second revelation of Jesus from heaven (4:16).[70] The future *parousia* of Jesus binds all members of the community together (living and dead) in the same way as his resurrection in the past. Just as Jesus's resurrection in the past provided them a cosmic identity with him, so too their own resurrection at his coming will seal that identity. Jesus will no longer be hidden from them (1:10). Rather, they will be together, all of them, with him, forever (4:17).

It's at this point in the letter that Paul's apocalyptic thought shifts in a slight but important way from his Jewish heritage. Jewish apocalypticism sometimes stressed the virtue of being among those who lived until the end of time when the resurrection would occur. Those who looked toward a future, eschatological hope *and* lived to experience it were considered to be among the blessed (Dan 12:12–13; 4 Ezra 6:18–28; 7:27–28; Psalms of Solomon 17:44; Sibylline Oracles 3:367–80). Thus, the statement in 4 Ezra 13:24: "Understand then that those who are left are more blessed than those who have died."[71] The conclusion among some Jewish apocalyptists was that the living had an advantage over the dead even though both were considered to be blessed (4 Ezra 13:16–20). Paul, however, does not view the situation the same way. His promise to the Thessalonians that "we who are alive, those remaining until the coming of the Lord, will by no means precede those who have fallen asleep"[72] undermines the notion that those who survive to the end are somehow more blessed than those who have already died.[73] In Paul's apocalyptic schema, both the dead and the living will be "caught up together" (4:17). Just as death cannot separate the apocalyptic community from one another, it also cannot disadvantage one over the other.

Conclusion

In his letter to the Thessalonians, Paul assumes the role of seer to the nascent community he founded in Thessalonica. Between the time Paul left this community and wrote this letter to them, they had begun to experience some level of opposition from those in the city who do not share their faith. Paul uses this occasion as an opportunity to remind them that they are a dif-

70. Luckensmeyer, *Eschatology of First Thessalonians*, 246.
71. Translation by Bruce M. Metzger, "*The Fourth Book of Ezra*," *OTP* 1:552.
72. Translation mine.
73. Earl J. Richard, *First and Second Thessalonians*, Sacra Pagina 11 (Collegeville, MN: Liturgical, 1995), 242.

ferent from those around them and he does this through the use of apocalyptic language and imagery.

Paul's letter allows us to observe the dual cosmology that both he and his readers assume exists. Both Paul and the Thessalonians have placed their faith and hope in the Lord Jesus who is hidden from them in an unseen realm. They are waiting for the day when Jesus will return and be revealed to them fully. They are waiting for the day when the hidden world will fully intersect with the seen world. In the meantime, the hidden world sometimes interferes with the seen world through the actions of malevolent beings. Paul's reference to the activity of "the tempter" demonstrates that he considers the chief opponent of himself, the Thessalonians and God to be not local unbelievers, but Satan.

Modern readers of 1 Thessalonians commonly gravitate toward the eschatology of the letter. They typically understand Paul's language here as promising the Thessalonians relief from their oppressors. But Paul's apocalyptic language/imagery in 1 Thessalonians is more widespread than 4:13–17 and 5:1–10. Although eschatology is certainly present in the letter, Paul does not employ it as a way to promise the Thessalonians some future paradise. Nor is Paul promising divine retribution against those who persecute them.[74] Rather, he is reminding them of their location at the intersection of the ages and is calling them to be different because of their new identity. How they live/behave now is influenced by a future event, the *parousia* of Jesus.

Paul's ultimate purpose in this letter is not to redirect their attention to the future, but to remind them of how the future impacts their present. They are not like the "others," but rather as sons of light and sons of the day they represent an alternative community. As members of a new community, they have a cosmic connection, not only with the apostles and other believers, but also with the Lord. Consequently, they are expected to live and behave in ways that are in contrast from those around them.

Finally, and perhaps most importantly, their identity as a community is not undone by death. The cosmic connection and identity that they have with the Lord and other believers extends to include even those who have already died. The same apocalyptic language and imagery that separates them from those around them at the same time expands the boundaries by including those who are no longer alive.

74. But see 2 Thess 1:5–10.

13

Apocalypticism in the Pastoral Epistles

Mark Harding

Introduction

The origins of apocalypticism as a worldview and of the apocalypses which articulate that worldview have been the subject of much recent debate. No account does full justice to the richness and complexity of the phenomena which encounters us in the apocalypses. But perhaps one can endorse, as a starting point, the recent emphasis on apocalypse as a genre of revelatory literature in which divine secrets are disclosed.[1] This is preferable to the older convention that the Jewish and early Christian apocalypses gave expression to distinctively expressed and unprecedented ideas associated with the imminent catastrophic ending of history, the overthrow of the existing order, and the establishment of the age to come through divine intervention.[2]

1. See especially Christopher Rowland, *The Open Heaven: A Study of Apocalyptic in Judaism and Early Christianity* (London: SPCK, 1982).
2. As in Rudolf Bultmann, *Theology of the New Testament*, trans. Kendrick Grobel, 2 vols. (New York: Charles Scribner's Sons, 1951, 1955), 1:4–6. W. Bousset, *Die Religion des Judentums* (Tübingen: Mohr [Siebeck], 1926), 242–86, only surveys the apocalypses from the point of view of eschatology and dualism. Note also Ernst Käsemann's article, "The Beginnings of Christian Theology," originally published in *ZTK* 57 (1960), in which he reduces "primitive Christian apocalyptic" to "the expectation of an imminent parousia." See his *New Testament Questions of Today* (Philadelphia: Fortress Press, 1979), 109n1.

Apocalypticism articulates a worldview which professes dependence on the revelation of divine secrets, without prejudging the nature of the subject matter of those secrets, and which cannot be attained except through divine disclosure and the opening of the heavens.[3] Within Second Temple Judaism, the seer Daniel and the Righteous Teacher of the Dead Sea Scrolls are two to whom access to divine secrets is disclosed.[4] But this worldview is by no means encountered within Judaism only, but is a phenomenon now widely recognized in broadly contemporaneous and contiguous cultures of the Eastern Mediterranean, Persia, Egypt, Greece, and Rome, and expressed in mantic utterances and dream visions.[5]

This chapter will focus largely on the Pastoral Epistles, considered both in their own right and as part of the Pauline corpus. These letters are not, by any means, apocalypses, but they do pose for us the question of the extent to which we can legitimately speak of the presence in the NT *outside of the apocalypses* of an apocalyptic worldview which we are denoting by the term "apocalypticism."[6]

Apocalypticism in the New Testament

There is, of course, an apocalypse among the books of the NT canon. But it would be a mistake to restrict the presence of apocalypticism in the NT to that book. The transcendent world of apocalyptic vision—of heavenly realities and the age to come—in which God's will is perfectly done is announced as standing at the very gates; eschatological conditions are already being manifested. The eschatological hour is dawning. Jesus, Paul and other early foundational figures address their hearers in the conviction that they are imparting revealed truths which place all hearers of the gospel in crisis—whether to hear and obey the news and be found acceptable to God or to ignore it and be forever lost.[7] Such disclosures create insider/outsider

3. The term "apocalypse" is derived from the Greek ἀποκάλυψις denoting an uncovering or an unveiling of what lies hidden. Christopher Rowland's basic contention is sound. The definition of an "apocalypse" must arise from the mode of discourse that the genre and related literature articulate—that of direct and authoritative revelation of divine secrets. See his *Open Heaven*, 14.
4. Note the use of רז, secret, in Dan 2:18, 19, 27, 28, 29, 30, 47, and 4:9. True insights into the scriptural deposit have been disclosed to the Righteous Teacher. The most singular passage from the scrolls in this regard is 1QpHab 7:4–5. Here, it is claimed that the Teacher possesses insight into "all the mysteries" (רזים)—secrets that were not even revealed to the prophets. Those privileged to be taught by the Teacher are in possession of knowledge, of truth no less, which leads assuredly to salvation. See also Martin Hengel, *Judaism and Hellenism*, trans. John Bowden, 2 vols. (Philadelphia: Fortress Press, 1974), 1:202–3; A. Lange, "Interpretation als Offenbarung: zum Verhältnis von Schriftauslegung und Offenbarung in apokalyptischer und nicht-apokalyptischer Literatur," in *Wisdom and Apocalypticism in the Dead Sea Scrolls and the Biblical Tradition*, ed. F. García Martínez, BETL 168 (Leuven: Leuven University Press, 2003), 17–33 (esp. 18–22).
5. See, for example, the surveys by Francis T. Fallon ("The Gnostic Apocalypses"), Harold W. Attridge ("Greek and Latin Apocalypses"), and John J. Collins ("Persian Apocalypses") in *Semeia* 14 (1979); D. Hellholm, ed., *Apocalypticism in the Mediterranean World and the Near East: Proceedings of the International Colloquium on Apocalypticism, Uppsala, August 12–17, 1979* (Tübingen: Mohr [Siebeck], 1983).
6. Note the definition of "apocalypticism" in P. D. Hanson, "Apocalypse, Genre" and "Apocalypticism" in *The Interpreter's Dictionary of the Bible: Supplementary Volume*, ed. Keith Crim, et al (Nashville: Abingdon, 1976), 28–34.
7. See R. Bultmann, *Theology of the New Testament*, 1:6–11. Hope and warning go together, as do salvation and catastrophe in Käsemann, "The Beginnings of Christian Theology," 97 and 105, respectively.

boundaries, depending on the stance one takes with respect to commitment to the truths the founders impart.[8] It is with justification, therefore, that we can affirm the view that the NT is imbued with an apocalyptic worldview.

In the Gospels, the presentations of the ministry of Jesus assume its nature as one in which divine secrets are revealed. The three Synoptic Gospels present the baptism of Jesus as an occasion when the heavens are opened and the Spirit descends on Jesus, thus investing and empowering that ministry, from its beginning, with divine, revelatory authority.[9] In Mark 4:11, the Evangelist contrasts the revelation of the secret (τὸ μυστήριον) (cf. Matt 13:11, but note the plural τὰ μυστήρια in Luke 8:10) of the Kingdom of God to the disciples with the obscurity and opaqueness of parabolic discourse—"but to those outside (τοῖς ἔξω) everything is in parables."[10] The Fourth Gospel presents Jesus as the revealer from Heaven in whom the glory of God is fully, finally, and exclusively disclosed, whose words are truth, and for whose followers (those who believe), the eschatological realities of salvation and everlasting life are bestowed in the present. Fully consistent with the apocalypticism of the Fourth Gospel is the pericope Matthew 11:25–27 in which Jesus gives thanks to God that the matters which are the subject of the discourse commencing at 11:2 have been hidden from the wise but have now been revealed ("you have revealed," ἀπεκάλυψας, v. 25) to "babes," presumably the disciples. Those who receive these disclosures are in possession of secrets not attainable by any other means but only through the mediation of Jesus.

The Apostle Paul as an Apocalypticist

That Paul the Apostle espoused an apocalyptic worldview is widely recognized.[11] In Paul's own words, the gospel he preaches came to him not by human mediation but directly from God, "by apocalypse" (δι' ἀποκαλύψεως, Gal 1:12, cf. 1:16).[12] On the basis of these verses, J. Christiaan Beker proposes that the core of Paul's thought is "apocalyptic," and that the apocalypse of

8. G. W. E. Nickelsburg, "Revealed Wisdom as a Criterion for Inclusion and Exclusion: From Jewish Sectarianism to Early Christianity," in *"To See Ourselves as Others See Us": Christians, Jews, and "Others" in Late Antiquity*, ed. J. Neusner and Ernest S. Frerichs (Chico: Scholars, 1985), 73–91.

9. Matt 3:16; Mark 1:10; Luke 3:21; cf. John 1:51 and the opening of the heavens. See also Daniel M. Gurtner, "Interpreting Apocalyptic Symbolism," *BBR* 22, no. 4 (2012), 525–45. N. T. Wright argues that the Gospel of Mark functions as an apocalypse. See his *The New Testament and the People of God: Christian Origins and the Question of God, Volume 1* (London: SPCK, 1992), 395.

10. Joel Marcus, *The Mystery of the Kingdom of God*, SBLDS 90 (Atlanta: Scholars, 1986), 96, 98, observes that the parables, specifically the Parable of the Sower, have an "apocalyptic function"—they are revelatory discourses, "instruments of revelation," to insiders. Cf. Amos N. Wilder, *Early Christian Rhetoric: The Language of the Gospel* (London: SCM, 1964), 80.

11. J. Christiaan Beker is the champion of this view. See his *Paul the Apostle: The Triumph of God in Life and Thought* (Philadelphia: Fortress Press, 1980) and several subsequent works written more popularly. Note also J. Louis Martyn, "Apocalyptic Antinomies in Paul's Letter to the Galatians," *NTS* 31 (1985), 410–24 and his *Galatians*, AB 33A (New York: Doubleday, 1997), 97–105, 148–68; Alan F. Segal, *Paul the Convert* (New Haven: Yale University Press, 1990); J. D. G. Dunn, *The Theology of Paul the Apostle* (Grand Rapids: Eerdmans, 1998), 47, 179–81; Douglas A. Campbell, *The Deliverance of God: An Apocalyptic Rereading of Justification in Paul* (Grand Rapids: Eerdmans, 2009), 188–92. However, see Rowland, *Open Heaven*, 374–86, where the discussion of Paul and apocalyptic in early Christianity is devoted to a study of Paul's visionary experiences not to his eschatology.

which he speaks in Galatians radically confirmed his already well-formed apocalyptic worldview. Beker argues that apocalyptic theology revolves around three central ideas—historical dualism, universal cosmic expectation, and the imminent end of the world—and that apocalyptic theology, now confirmed by the revelation of Christ as resurrected Lord, accords Paul's thought with coherence out of which he flexibly and dialogically addresses and engages the contingent situations of the communities to which he writes.[13] Whether Beker is correct in surmising that Paul's encounter with the risen Christ on the Damascus Road confirmed an already formed apocalyptic worldview is not at issue here. But we can argue that Beker does not do full justice to the diverse content that we encounter in the apocalypses. The apocalyptic worldview of the apostle cannot be limited to his eschatological expectation.

In 2 Corinthians 12:1, Paul speaks obliquely about having received visions and revelations of the Lord (ὀπτασίαι καὶ ἀποκαλύψεις), relating one vision in which he was caught up into the "third heaven" (v. 2). He has seen Christ (1 Cor 9:1; 15:8). He imparts or refers to "mysteries," secrets, in his letters.[14] The term μυστήριον occurs eight times (sg. 5x; pl. 3x) in the undisputed corpus. In the singular, μυστήριον can refer to the gospel message, once hidden, now divinely revealed (Rom 16:25; 1 Cor 2:1, 7; cf. Col 1:27; Eph 3:9; cf. 1 Tim 3:16). Paul uses μυστήριον of the revelation—the medium of the revelation is not specified—that, though some believers have died and some will remain at the *parousia*, all will be changed (1 Cor 15:51) and of the hardening that has come on part of Israel (Rom 11:25). He speaks of himself and his colleagues Apollos and Cephas as "stewards of the mysteries of Christ" (οἰκονόμοι μυστήριων θεοῦ, 1 Cor 4:1).[15] Paul imparts mysteries, secrets revealed by God no less. The visions and revelations which he experienced, and insights now imparted, invest his discourse with incontrovertible authority and persuasive power. We will say more about Paul's rhetoric below.

Paul's apocalypticism, narrowly defined as it is in Beker's work, must appear in a diminished light when it comes to interpreting the disputed letters Ephesians, Colossians, and the three Pastoral Epistles.[16] In the first two letters, Christology eclipses the focus on the triumph of God in the undisputed letters (though see Col 3:4); in Ephesians, the language of resurrec-

12. See Käsemann, "Primitive Christian Apocalyptic," in *New Testament Questions of Today* (Philadelphia: Fortress Press, 1979), 131: "Paul's apostolic self-consciousness is only comprehensible on the basis of his apocalyptic."

13. *Paul the Apostle*, 136. For a critique of Beker, see R. Barry Matlock, *Unveiling the Apocalyptic Paul: Paul's Interpreters and the Rhetoric of Criticism*, JSNTSup 127 (Sheffield: Sheffield Academic, 1996), 147–49, 299–304. Note also Käsemann, "The Beginnings of Christian Theology," 103, where he argues that for Paul and John, preaching has "revelational character as being the word of the exalted Lord" and 98 where he contends, "Paraenesis in the post-Easter community was founded primarily on apocalyptic."

14. See 1 Cor 2:1–7; cf. Dan 2:27–30; 1QpHab 7:4–5. Note the excellent surveys of Raymond E. Brown, *The Semitic Background of the Term "Mystery" in the New Testament*, FBBS 21 (Philadelphia: Fortress Press, 1968); Markus N. A. Bockmuehl, *Revelation and Mystery in Ancient Judaism and Pauline Christianity*, WUNT II/36 (Tübingen: Mohr Siebeck, 1990).

15. Μυστήρια also appears at 1 Cor 13:2 and 14:2.

16. I include my own brief treatment of Ephesians and Colossians in this negative judgment. See my "Disputed and Undisputed Letters of Paul," in *The Pauline Canon*, ed. Stanley E. Porter (Leiden; Boston: Brill, 2004), 127–68 (156–59).

tion—always a part of the future for believers in the undisputed corpus—is now an aspect of present life for believers (Eph 2:6). In all five letters, the imminence of the *parousia* has receded into the more distant future.[17] While these characteristics are undeniably present in the letters, Beker's reading overlooks the palpable appeal to revelation which marks them as affirming an apocalyptic worldview because Beker has limited Paul's apocalypticism to his eschatological outlook. On the contrary, the pseudonymous authors of the disputed letters actualize Paul the apocalypticist—the Paul who appeals to the content of the mysteries which have been disclosed by God himself. In assuming Paul's persona, and writing with his authority, they articulated his apocalyptic worldview, so much of the essence of the apostle's identity, for a new day. As we have seen, Paul's ministry and message derive from an apocalypse, a revelation (Gal 1:12, 16), and were sustained by further visions and revelations. I contend below that Paul's apocalypticism constituted a fundamental aspect of the apostle which the authors of the disputed letters, including the Pastor (the author of the Pastoral Epistles), mediated.[18]

We see evidence of Paul's apocalypticism in Ephesians and Colossians preeminently in the use of the term *μυστήριον* (mystery, secret). It occurs ten times in these letters—four in Colossians (1:26, 27; 2:2; 4:3) and six in Ephesians (1:9; 3:3, 4, 9; 5:32; 6:19). In Colossians, the writer appeals to the mystery, once hidden, but now made manifest, which is revealed to be "Christ in you, the hope of glory" (1:27). The usage of *μυστήριον* in Ephesians has different content. The secret, *τὸ μυστήριον*, the once hidden truth, that has now been made known by revelation (*κατὰ ἀποκάλυψιν*, 3:3) to Paul and revealed (*ἀπεκαλύφθη*, 3:5) to the apostles and prophets is that the Gentiles are fellow heirs (with Jewish believers) of the promises of Christ Jesus. This is the mystery of the gospel that Paul is commissioned to disclose, to make known (*γνωρίσαι τὸ μυστήριον*, 6:19). The author of Ephesians also uses *μυστήριον* of his unique exegetical insight. He perceives an intimation of the oneness of Christ and the church in Genesis 2:24, where it says that husband and wife become one flesh. This disclosure of hidden meaning now revealed calls to mind Paul's similar claims in Romans 11:25 and 1 Corinthians 15:51, and also recalls the Righteous Teacher's claim to be the mediator of "mysteries" (רזים) in the Habakkuk Pesher (1QpHab 7:4–5). Admittedly, there are divergences between the content of the mysteries revealed in Ephesians and Colossians and those about which Paul speaks in the undisputed letters. But the authors of Ephesians and Colossians have brought to speech, or actualized, an essential and defining characteristic of the Pauline tradition—namely, that secrets, mysteries, were revealed to Paul which he communicated to his addressees by way of his preaching when present and

17. See Beker, *Heirs of Paul: Paul's Legacy in the New Testament and in the Church Today* (Minneapolis: Fortress Press, 1991), 44 (the Pastoral Epistles), 72 (Ephesians), 90 (Ephesians, Colossians).

18. Note the perceptive comment on the phenomenon of pseudonymity in the NT by Wilder, *Early Christian Rhetoric*, 41: "The unknown writer felt that he was a voice of the shared tradition and revelation. . . ."

by his letters when absent. The apocalyptic eschatology that is articulated in the undisputed letters might not be present in Ephesians and Colossians (as Beker and others affirm), but the apocalyptic worldview of the apostle certainly is.[19]

Apocalypticism in the Pastoral Epistles

It has been customary to argue that Paul's apocalypticism, as it is articulated in the undisputed letters, is eclipsed in the Pastoral Epistles and gives way to "catholicizing" tendencies related to the consolidation of church order (community protection),[20] or that the apostle Paul's apocalypticism recedes in favor of the need to define how believers might conduct themselves in the world for generations to come.[21] The Pastoral Epistles, it is claimed, are no longer imbued with the sharply delineated dualism, cosmic expectation and imminence that might be traced in the undisputed letters, and which have often been thought to be the defining marks of Paul's apocalyptic worldview. We have already had cause above to revise negative assessments of the presence of apocalypticism in Ephesians and Colossians, and to underscore the prominence of the discourse of divine disclosure, of "mystery," in those two letters, even if we remain doubtful that the apostle actually penned them. What shall we say about the Pastoral Epistles?

The Pastoral Epistles and Apocalyptic Eschatology

To a far greater extent than in Colossians and Ephesians, a number of the themes customarily associated with apocalyptic eschatology do appear in the Pastoral Epistles. There is a strong sense of the accountability of believers—leaders and their opponents especially—in the light of the certainty of the judgment to come in which there will be vindication and salvation for the faithful but disaster for the unfaithful (e.g. 1 Tim 4:8; 5:24; 2 Tim 1:12, 18; 4:1, 8, 14; Titus 2:13; cf. Rom 5:9; 1 Cor 3:13–15; 1 Thess 1:10). On this score, there is an unambiguous continuity between the undisputed letters and the Pastoral Epistles.

First Timothy 3:16 celebrates the transformation of the world as a direct consequence of the Christ-event. The Pastoral Epistles are redolent of the overlapping of the "two ages."[22] The

19. See Joseph Coppens, "'Mystery' in the Theology of Saint Paul and its Parallels at Qumran," repr. in *Paul and the Dead Sea Scrolls*, ed. J. Murphy-O'Connor and James H. Charlesworth (New York: Crossroad, 1990), 132–58.

20. See Margaret Y. MacDonald, *The Pauline Churches: A Socio-Historical Study of Institutionalization in the Pauline and Deutero-Pauline Writings*, SNTSMS 60 (Cambridge; Cambridge University Press, 1988), 159–234.

21. Beker, *Heirs of Paul*, 44. Note the extended comment by Martin Dibelius and Hans Conzelmann, *The Pastoral Epistles* (Philadelphia: Fortress Press, 1972), 39–41, on "good Christian citizenship" (bürgerliches Christentum). A succession of scholars has disputed the commentators' modest claims. The exhortation of 2 Tim 2:2 assumes the passing of the tradition from Timothy to his successors and from them to the next generation.

22. Note the incidence of the phrase ὁ νῦν αἰών, the present age, in 1 Tim 6:17; 2 Tim 4:10; Titus 2:12. The certainty of the "age to come" is assumed throughout the Pastoral Epistles. In the context of the three passages cited above, see especially 1 Tim 6:14; 2 Tim 4:8; Titus 2:13 in which the Pastor uses the term ἐπιφάνεια of the future appearing of Christ.

age to come, the age in which creation will be transformed according to some scenarios anticipated in the apocalypses and related literature, is already breaking into the present.[23] This passage testifies to the triumph of the Christ of history, who is none other than the exalted, vindicated and glorified Lord. His authority is already being publicly and openly acknowledged on earth as in heaven (ἀγγέλοις . . . ἐν ἔθνεσιν). The use of a succession of passive aorists here (ἐφανερώθη, ἐδικαιώθη, ὤφθη, ἐκηρύχθη, ἐπιστεύθη, ἀνελήμφθη) emphatically and decisively underscores the completed, indeed triumphant, nature of the events celebrated.[24] The Lord has been enthroned.[25] The church waits in expectation for the exalted Christ to sweep up believers into his lordship.[26] Moreover, the concisely summarized account of the Christ-event in 1 Timothy 3:16 is presented as the great "mystery of our religion" (μέγα ἐστὶν τὸ τῆς εὐσεβείας μυστήριον). In other words, the content of the faith has been disclosed; it is a divine revelation. The reference to "mystery" and revelation is neatly underscored by the phrase "he [Christ] was manifested," ἐφανερώθη,[27] in the first line of the hymn. We shall return below to the Pastoral Epistles' use of the language of mystery and revelation.

However, there is no imminent expectation of the *parousia* at the same level of intensity as the undisputed letters,[28] though the proposition that Christ will return in glory is confidently affirmed (1 Tim 6:14–15) and these are the "last days" (1 Tim 4:1; 2 Tim 3:1). In 2 Tim 2:18, the author castigates Hymenaeus and Philetus for teaching that the resurrection is a past event, and therefore, a present reality. The teaching of these two has more in common with Ephesians 2:6, which proclaims that God has already raised believers and seated them with Christ in the heavenly places (συνήγειρεν καὶ συνεκάθισεν ἐν τοῖς ἐπουρανίοις) and with the enthusiasts in Corinth.[29] The perspective of the Pastoral Epistles, and more specifically, with respect to the condemnation of the view referred to in 2 Timothy 2:18, is that the resurrection is a future hope for believers. Here, the author is closer to the apostle Paul for whom discourse about the resurrection confirmed the expectation that just as Christ had been raised, so now-dead believers will also be raised from the dead at his return (see 1 Cor 15:20, 23; Rom 6:5, 8; 1 Thess 4:14). Paul does not allow talk of the resurrection as a present reality or experience of believers.[30]

23. Rev 21:1–22:5; 1 Enoch 91; 2 Baruch 73; Testament of Levi 18; and Jubilees 23:27–31.
24. Käsemann, "Primitive Christian Apocalyptic," 127.
25. Dibelius and Conzelmann, *Pastoral Epistles*, 63.
26. Norbert Brox, *Die Pastoralbriefe* (Regensburg: Pustet, 1969), 161.
27. In the Pauline corpus, φανερόω is a synonym of ἀποκαλύπτω. See *TDNT* 9:4–5 where the authors (Bultmann and Lührmann) note the use of these two verbs in parallel contexts in 1:17 (ἀποκαλύπτω) and Rom 3:21 (φανερόω) and in Eph 3:5 (ἀποκαλύπτω) and Col 1:26 (φανερόω). See also Markus Barth, *Ephesians 1-3*, AB 34 (Garden City: Doubleday, 1974), 351.
28. See 1 Cor 7:29; 15:51; Rom 13:11–13; 1 Thess 4:17.
29. Philip H. Towner, "Gnosis and Realized Eschatology in Ephesus (of the Pastoral Epistles) and the Corinthian Enthusiasm," *JSNT* 31 (1987), 95–124 on the links between the proponents of realized eschatology encountered in 1 Corinthians and the false teaching condemned in the Pastoral Epistles.
30. See Mark Harding, "Kyrios Christos: Johannine and Pauline Perspectives on the Christ-Event," in *Paul and the Gospels: Christologies, Conflicts and Convergences*, ed. Michael F. Bird and Joel Willitts, LNTS 411 (London: T. & T. Clark, 2011), 169–96 (191–94). Käsemann

The Pastoral Epistles and Divine Disclosure

"Mystery" (μυστήριον)

The use of the term *μυστήριον* (Heb: רז) in the book of Daniel, certain of the Dead Sea Scrolls (such as the Habakkuk Pesher), and the NT to denote divine secrets, once hidden but now revealed, is integral to the discourse of the apocalypses and to the apocalyptic worldview. In the Pastoral Epistles, we encounter the term in 1 Timothy 3:9 and in 3:16, a passage briefly discussed above. At 3:9, the writer speaks of the "mystery of faith," by which he refers to the content of the Christian faith, what is believed (*fides quae creditur*).[31] The usage is, of course, somewhat different to what we encounter of the *μυστήριον* spoken about in Colossians and Ephesians and in the undisputed Pauline corpus, but this need not detain us. The significant matter is the appeal to a verity disclosed by apocalypse. The content of the faith has been divinely revealed.[32] It cannot be a matter of debate and conjecture. The confession of that faith by believers, summarized in 1 Timothy 3:16, bears the guarantee of God himself whose secret it is, but which is now revealed exclusively through the teaching of the apostle and safeguarded by his delegates and their successors.[33]

The faith, the content of revelation, has profound implications for the Christian life.[34] Good servants, such as Timothy, hold the mystery of faith with a good conscience.[35] The mystery has unavoidable ethical connotations, vitally important when combating the errors of the false teachers and drawing distinctions between faithfulness to the Pauline "deposit" (παραθήκη) and the traducing of that deposit by the false teachers.[36]

The Language of Epiphany and Manifestation

The use of the language of epiphany (ἐπιφάνεια, φανερόω) in the Pastoral Epistles is a much-observed phenomenon. In his still influential study of the vocabulary of the Pastoral Epistles, P. N. Harrison argued that the Pastor adopts this language, which is unique to the Pastoral Epistles

("Primitive Christian Apocalyptic," 125) contends that "resurrection now" is the slogan of the false teachers (see 2 Tim 2:18) and that Hellenism understood the Christian faith as a mystery religion (citing Eph 2:5; 5:14; Col 2:12–13 as evidence).

31. See I. H. Marshall, *A Critical and Exegetical Commentary on the Pastoral Epistles*, ICC (Edinburgh: T&T Clark, 1999), 490–91.
32. Brox, *Pastoralbriefe*, 153.
33. Brox, *Pastoralbriefe*, 159: "Der Inhalt des Evangeliums ist 'Geheimnis,' sofern es Offenbarung von sonst Unzugängenlichem ist (vgl. Kol 1,26f.)."
34. R. F. Collins, *1 & 2 Timothy and Titus*, NTL (Louisville: Westminster John Knox, 2002), 88 (citing Helmut Krämer).
35. Collins, *1 & 2 Timothy and Titus*, 88.
36. I understand παραθήκη in the Pastoral Epistles (see 1 Tim 6:20 [τὴν παραθήκην φύλαξον]; 2 Tim 1:12, 14) to denote the Pauline tradition, the Pauline heritage, "now conceived as something immutable," normative, entrusted to Paul's delegates to be protected and transmitted without diminution. See my *What Are They Saying About the Pastoral Epistles?* (Mahwah: Paulist, 2001), 29; Michael Wolter, *Die Pastoralbriefe als Paulustradition*, FRLANT 146 (Göttingen: Vandenhoek & Ruprecht, 1988), 118–19.

when compared to the genuine Pauline letters, because it was part of the early second-century milieu in which the Pastoral Epistles were written.[37] Whereas the apostle spoke of the return or the coming of Christ, his *παρουσία*, the pastor speaks about his epiphany, his *ἐπιφάνεια*.[38] Thus, the appearance of epiphany language in the Pastoral Epistles is a marker of their non-Pauline authorship and of their provenance in a post-Pauline era. The concept is also broader than the Pauline *παρουσία* because it is used to denote the divine epiphany that is the incarnation of Christ as well as his appearing as judge.

When used in a religious sense, as it is in the Pastoral Epistles, an epiphany is a divine manifestation with emphasis on the splendor of that appearance. The term has a long history in Greek literature to denote events, in a cultic setting as well as in the events of history, in which the gods reveal themselves and "appear," the term passing into the emperor cult of his birthday, his accession, or of a visit he might pay.[39] With justification, therefore, scholars contend that *ἐπιφάνεια* and *ἀποκάλυψις* are broadly synonymous with respect to the concept of divine disclosure.[40]

The language of epiphany only appears on four occasions in the NT outside the Pastoral Epistles, three of which refer to divine manifestation.[41] This leaves seven instances of the language in the Pastorals.[42] The use of *ἐπιφάνεια* in 1 Timothy 6:14; 2 Timothy 4:1, 8; and Titus 2:13 clearly refers to the end-time appearance of the Lord as judge. In 2 Timothy 1:10; Titus 2:11 and 3:4 the manifestation of the Lord Jesus Christ refers to the incarnation, as does 1 Timothy 3:16, where the passive form of the verb *φανερόω* is used to denote the historical event of the revelation of Christ as past event. Insofar as the *ἐπιφάνεια* of Christ frames the first and second coming, the whole of the Christ-event discloses saving significance.[43] Moreover, according to Titus 2:11, the

37. See P. N. Harrison, *The Problem of the Pastoral Epistles* (Oxford: Oxford University Press, 1921), 7, 29, noting second century Christian parallels to the Pastoral Epistles' use of ἐπιφάνεια for the return of Christ where Paul had used παρουσία (*2 Clem.* 12:1; 17:4; and in Justin, *Apol.* 14.3; 40.1; *Dial.* 22.3). Harrison's conclusions are vigorously contested by defenders of the Pauline authorship of the Pastoral Epistles. See, e.g., William D. Mounce, *The Pastoral Epistles*, WBC (Nashville: Thomas Nelson, 2000), xcix–cxviii.

38. Note the phrase ἐπιφάνεια τῆς παρουσίας, the "appearance (or manifestation) of his coming," in 2 Thess 2:8. This letter (often listed among the disputed letters of Paul), I contend, is pseudonymous. But note the perceptive comments on the polemical anti-imperial use of ἐπιφάνεια in this passage in James R. Harrison, *Paul and the Imperial Authorities in Thessalonica and Rome: A Study in the Conflict of Ideology*, WUNT 273 (Tübingen: Mohr Siebeck, 2011), 86–90. Harrison connects the passage with the ἐπιφάνεια that is the accession of Caligula in the imperial propaganda with Paul's contention that the real saving epiphany is the imminent coming (παρουσία) of Christ.

39. See *TDNT* 9:8–9; MM 250; Harrison, *Paul and the Imperial Authorities*, 86–90. For the use of ἐπιφάνεια in the Pastoral Epistles, see more particularly R. F. Collins, "From παρουσία to ἐπιφάνεια: The Transformation of a Pauline Motif," in *Unity and Diversity in the Gospels and Paul: Essays in Honor of Frank J. Matera*, ed. C. W. Skinner and K. R. Iverson, ECL 7 (Atlanta: Society of Biblical Literature, 2012), 273–99.

40. See B. S. Easton, *The Pastoral Epistles* (London: SCM, 1948), 171–72, for the "apocalyptic force" of ἐπιφαίνω in Titus 2:11 and 3:4.

41. These three passages are 2 Thess 2:8 of the manifestation of his coming (ἡ ἐπιφάνεια τῆς παρουσίας αὐτοῦ), Luke 1:79 of the dawning of the day to give light (ἐπιφᾶναι) on those dwelling in darkness and the shadow of death, and Acts 2:20 (citing LXX Joel 3:5) which celebrates the dawning of the great and manifest (ἐπιφανῆς) day of the Lord. The fourth occurrence is at Acts 27:20 of the sun and stars not appearing (ἐπιφαινόντων) for many days.

42. Ἐπιφάνεια: 1 Tim 6:14; 2 Tim 1:10; 4:1, 8; Titus 2:13; ἐπιφαίνω: Titus 2:11; 3:4.

43. There is close link between the epiphany and salvation. See 2 Tim 1:8–10; Titus 2:11; 3:4.

ἐπιφάνεια of Christ has present significance with respect to the manner of life beneficiaries of the manifestation must now live. The apostle's message infallibly delineates the shape of that life commitment. That message also participates in the divine epiphany, as Jouette Bassler has persuasively argued, and contributes to the presentation of the absolute authority of the apostle, his example, and his teaching.[44] Tellingly, the Pastor writes in Titus 1:2–3 of the hope of eternal life which God manifested (i.e., revealed) in his word through the message (ἐφανέρωσεν . . . τὸν λὸγον αὐτοῦ ἐν κηρύγματι, v3) with which Paul has been entrusted.[45] Closely related to Titus 1:3 is 2 Timothy 1:10–11 which speaks of God's purpose and grace that "has been manifested (φανερωθεῖσαν) through the appearing (διὰ τῆς ἐπιφανείας) of our Savior Jesus Christ . . . who brought life and immortality to light (φωτίσαντος) through the gospel." The preaching of Paul is thus a divine disclosure. Indeed, the whole Pauline deposit, the παραθήκη, brought to speech in the Pastoral Epistles bears revelatory significance. It arises out of the divine disclosure to which the life and ongoing ministry of Paul continues to bear witness through his delegates Timothy and Titus. Adherence to the teaching that is contained in the deposit guarantees salvation. It is the sole basis for hope. Outside of the community that bears faithful witness to Paul and his delegates, no salvation can be forthcoming.

The Pastoral Epistles and "Apocalyptic Rhetoric"

The letters[46] range over a variety of topics, not just the duties of deacons, elders, and the bishop. In the name of Paul, the Pastor assumes supreme authority to address and command, to warn, rebuke, to vilify, and to publicly delegate these functions to the apostle's successors, thus leaving the readers in no doubt as to the commitment they are required to make and to maintain in the face of competing claims on their loyalty.[47] This is particularly apparent in 2 Timothy. This letter functions as Paul's testament.[48] The testament is a mode of exhortatory discourse that carries a double authority not only because of its indissoluble anchoring in the apostle's

44. Jouette Bassler, "A Plethora of Epiphanies: Christology in the Pastoral Epistles," *PSB* 17 (1996), 310–25. Bassler has correctly identified the use of ἐπιφάνεια in the Pastoral Epistles as language denoting the revelation "of a reality about God" (313).

45. Brox, *Pastoralbriefe*, 281: "Gottes Offenbaren ist im Wort der apostolischen und kirchlichen Verkündigung präsent, angeboten, aktualisiert." For the strong sense of Paul's divine calling, see 1 Tim 1:1, 12; 2 Tim 1:11; Titus 1:3.

46. For "apocalyptic rhetoric," see Adela Yarbro Collins, *Crisis and Catharsis: The Power of the Apocalypse* (Philadelphia: Westminster Press, 1984); Nickelsburg, "Revealed Wisdom," 73–91; Elisabeth Schüssler Fiorenza, "The Followers of the Lamb: Visionary Rhetoric and Social-Political Structures," *Semeia* 36 (1986): 123–46 (esp. 129–42); Stephenson Humphries-Brooks, "Apocalyptic Paraenesis in Matthew 6.19–34," in *Apocalyptic and the New Testament: Essays in Honour of J. Louis Martyn*, ed. Marion L. Soards and Joel Marcus, JSNTSup 24 (Sheffield: JSOT, 1989), 95–112; Brent Nongbri, "A Touch of Condemnation in a Word of Exhortation: Apocalyptic Language and Graeco-Roman Rhetoric in Hebrews 6:4–12," *NovT* 45, no. 3 (2003): 265–79; Michael Wolter, "Apokalyptik als Redeform im Neuen Testament," *NTS* 51 (2005): 171–91.

47. The three Pastoral Epistles must not be classed as private letters as they have full public intent as indicated by the plural final greetings in each. See M. Harding, "The Pastoral Epistles," in *All Things to All Cultures: Paul among Jews, Greeks, and Romans*, ed. M. Harding and Alanna Nobbs (Grand Rapids: Eerdmans, 2013), 328–52 (332–33).

48. Séan Charles Martin, *Pauli Testamentum: 2 Timothy and the Last Words of Moses*, TGST 18 (Rome: Gregorian University, 1997).

divinely-bestowed ministry but also because that ministry is now being furthered in the midst of abandonment and hardship, and in the face of certain death—the death of a martyr.

My initial research on the Pastoral Epistles examined the way in which Greco-Roman rhetorical conventions are utilized by the Pastor to present a persuasive portrait of the apostle. In doing so, the Pastor attempted to preserve the Pauline identity of the churches addressed in the letters and to deflect loyalty from competing actualizations of the Pauline tradition by the false teachers.[49] I argued that the Pastor presents the addressees with a powerful evocation of the apostle as the paradigm *par excellence* of piety and leadership. The three letters render Paul, though physically absent, present. Letters were understood as surrogates for the writer. In Paul's case, his letters conveyed his apostolic presence, the apostolic *parousia*. Through that mediated presence, he could address his readers as though actually present. The letters extended Paul's pastoral care, his psychagogy, of the churches and furthered his apostolic ministry.

But my presentation of the rhetoric of the Pastoral Epistles can now be enhanced by the acknowledgement that in actualizing the apostolic presence of the now departed Paul, the Pastor also gave speech to Paul whose ministry and message was set in train by an apocalypse (Gal 1:12, 16). He could title himself (and his colleagues, as we saw above) as "custodians of the mysteries of God" (1 Cor 4:1). To him, further mysteries were revealed periodically and, in turn, imparted to the believers. This helps to explain the compelling mandate of the apostle both in the letters he authored (or dictated) and in the letters written in his name. Revelation bestows authority.

Truth claims in the Pauline corpus are predicated on the unique access the apostle has to the "mystery of faith." This confidence of the apostle, which in the undisputed letters is generated by the apocalypse to which he refers in Galatians 1:12, 16, has been actualized by the Pastor out of the tradition, perhaps through access to the ten-letter deposit.[50] This extends to the message of the Paul brought to speech in the Pastoral Epistles, as we saw above in our discussion of Titus 1:3. The Pastor can adopt, in full continuity with Galatians 1:12, 16, the language of apocalypse when he says that God manifested (ἐφανέρωσεν) to him the message of the hope of eternal life.

It is for this reason that the language of truth (ἀλήθεια) is frequently invoked in the Pastoral Epistles. In 1 Timothy 2:7, Paul speaks "the truth"; he is a teacher of the Gentiles "in faith and truth," appointed by God. Those who "know the truth" (1 Tim 4:3) will recognize marriage and food (not abstinence) as God's gifts to be received with thanksgiving. Timothy is to strive to be an approved workman "rightly handling the word of truth" (2 Tim 2:15). His opponents, once

49. Mark Harding, *Tradition and Rhetoric in the Pastoral Epistles*, StBibLit 3 (New York: Peter Lang, 1998).
50. Harrison, *Problem*, 8; A. E. Barnett, *Paul Becomes a Literary Influence* (Chicago: Chicago University Press, 1941), 251, 277.

corrected, may yet repent and come to "know the truth" (2 Tim 2:25). In the greeting of the letter to Titus (1:1), the apostle describes his apostleship as the means "to further the faith of God's elect and their knowledge of the truth"—the fourth time in the letters the phrase "knowledge of the truth" has occurred (see also 1 Tim 2:4; cf. 4:3; 2 Tim 2:25; 3:7). Sound teaching (1 Tim 6:3; 2 Tim 1:13; 4:3; Titus 2:1), another frequently invoked theme of the Pastoral Epistles, is synonymous with teaching that accords with the truth.[51]

By contrast, every impulse and characteristic of the opponents underscores their falsehood. The Pastor cultivates aversion to them for the sake of those disposed to hear him. The false teachers are repeatedly and roundly vilified in the letters because their teaching and moral disposition does not accord with the sound teaching of Paul and his delegates. The whole tenor of the opponents' lives and their teaching is characterized by a willful and culpable rejection of the truth (2 Tim 3:8). Some of the faithful, so the Spirit says, will depart from the faith by giving heed to liars (1 Tim 4:1–2). Hymenaeus and Philetus have "swerved from the truth" (2 Tim 2:18) by teaching that the resurrection is a past event. Those who do not discriminate between the delegates of the apostle on the one hand and the false teachers on the other will never come to a "knowledge of the truth" (2 Tim 3:7); they listen to anybody. The time is coming when people will turn away from "listening to the truth" (2 Tim 4:4). Lacking soundness, the effect of false teaching is gangrenous (2 Tim 2:17). The Pastor evokes the Paul who could consign to the judgment and vindication of God those who, like Alexander the Coppersmith, have wronged him (2 Tim 4:14, 16; cf. 1 Cor 5:3–5).[52] Rejecting conscience leads to shipwreck (1 Tim 1:19). Falling away from Paul and the sound teaching he endorses is evidence that the last days have arrived (1 Tim 4:1; 2 Tim 3:1–9). Any other teaching is unsound and depraved by definition (1 Tim 6:3–5). Salvation, eternal life no less, depends on conformity to the teaching of Paul revealed and disclosed to him by God, and now vouchsafed to his delegates as settled tradition.[53]

Writing of the Paul encountered in the undisputed corpus, Ernst Käsemann aptly wrote that "[H]is decrees are sacrosanct and cannot be questioned. But only understanding love can really fulfil them. . . ."[54] On the contrary, Käsemann proceeds to argue, in the Pastoral Epistles "Paul's role has been almost reduced to that of a man who, in virtue of his authority, establishes order within the community and sets up a new system of ecclesiastical law." What is missing in this neat contrast is the perception that the authority wielded by the Paul of the Pastoral Epistles is

51. See J. Murphy-O'Connor, "Truth: Paul and Qumran," repr. in *Paul and the Dead Sea Scrolls*, ed. Murphy-O'Connor and Charlesworth, 179–230, esp. 213–30.

52. Käsemann, "Sentences of Holy Law," *New Testament Questions of Today* (Philadelphia: Fortress Press, 1979), 76.

53. Wolter, *Pastoralbriefe*, 91, 95, 130. The Pastoral Epistles embody the apostle's presence and his claim to be the guarantor of the addressees' eschatological salvation. See Harding, *What Are They Saying?* 36. Brox, *Pastoralbriefe*, 159–61, comments on the emphasis on knowing the truth in the Pastoral Epistles.

54. Käsemann, "Sentences of Holy Law," 75.

consistent with the authority of the Paul of the undisputed letters and of his message brought to speech in them. Moreover, that authority springs from divine disclosure, the mystery that is the revealed faith, and from the manifestation of the hope of eternal life in the message Paul preaches. That authority is now extended to those (and only those) whom he nominates as his delegates and those faithful men whom they, in turn, appoint as their successors (see 2 Tim 2:2). In the language of the Pastoral Epistles, the ground of the apostle's authority is the epiphany of Christ and the moral and credal implications—vouchsafed uniquely to Paul and then to those he commissions—that are in accord with that revelation and to which his message infallibly and exclusively bears witness. The epiphany that is the Christ-event and its significance is a matter of ongoing moment. Rightly understood and correctly employed, the revelation assumes nothing less than saving significance for the addressees of the Pastoral Epistles.

Conclusion

It is my belief that the Pastoral Epistles were written in Ephesus in about 100 CE to defend a particular expression of the Pauline heritage against competing actualizations. I subscribe to Michael Goulder's contention that the context of the letters is best explained by the activity of Jewish-Christian visionaries in the Ephesian church.[55] Goulder explains the statements in 1 Timothy 1:4 and elsewhere in the Pastoral Epistles concerning the danger of myths and endless genealogies as a reference to Jewish speculation, encountered as early as Philo, about the process by which an impassible God created the universe.

About a generation later, we encounter two fully-formed expressions of the Pauline tradition in the form of the writings attributed to the Gnostic Valentinus (and works inspired by him) and the teaching of Marcion. Valentinus (c. 100–175 CE), we are told, traced his interpretation of Paul to his teacher Theudas, who claimed to have been taught by the apostle.[56] Marcion (fl. 140 CE), as is well known, regarded Paul as the apostle and teacher of the church *par excellence*.[57] But the teachings of Valentinus and Marcion, as far as they can be reconstructed, sit uneasily with the outline of the Pauline heritage defended in the Pastoral Epistles. Valentinus and Marcion taught asceticism with respect to food, drink and marriage—views which were condemned by the Pastor in 1 Timothy 4:1–5 and 5:23.[58] They allowed a prominent place for women.[59] The

55. Michael Goulder, "The Pastor's Wolves: Jewish Christian Visionaries Behind the Pastoral Epistles," *NovT* 38 (1996), 242–56. These visionaries are also encountered in the post-Pauline Col 2:16–18 and possibly earlier in the church in Corinth.

56. See Clement of Alexandria, *Stromata* 7.17. Irenaeus claims that the esoteric teaching of the Valentinians should be traced not to Paul but to the Samaritan sorcerer Simon Magus (Irenaeus, *Adversus haereses* 1.22; 23.1–3). The oral tradition taught by the Valentinians claims to be "Paul's own secret wisdom," so Elaine Pagels, *The Gnostic Paul: Gnostic Exegesis of the Pauline Letters* (Philadelphia: Fortress Press, 1975), 4, citing Irenaeus, *Haer.* 3.2.1.

57. There is much value in F. C. Baur, *Die sogennanten Pastoralbriefe des Apostel Paulus* (Stuttgart and Tübingen: J. G. Gotta'schen Verlagshandlung, 1835). Baur argues that the Pastoral Epistles were written to counteract Marcion, arguing that Marcion's work *The Antitheses* is mentioned by name in 1 Tim 6:20.

Pastor's views on that subject are well known (see 1 Tim 2:9–15). The Pastor condemned the incipient Gnosticism that he encountered[60] and singles out for particular mention the view advocated by Hymenaeus and Philetus that the resurrection has already passed (2 Tim 2:18). Valentinus taught a gnostic system.[61] For him, the resurrection was a present reality.[62] The Pastoral Epistles were not part of Marcion's canon, and are rarely encountered in the writings of the mid-second-century gnostics.[63] In the last twenty years of the second century, Irenaeus and Tertullian vigorously defend the Pauline authorship of the Pastoral Epistles and enlist the Paul of the closed thirteen-letter deposit in their struggle to secure an anti-gnostic vision of the Pauline heritage in the face of a pro-gnostic interpretation.[64] The Pastoral Epistles were well-suited to this use since they had emanated from an earlier period in which their author, defending an interpretation of Paul against false teachers, vilified teachings which were continuous with those of the heretics condemned by Irenaeus and Tertullian. The fact that the letters also broadly affirm Greco-Roman values that keep women and slaves in their place and endorse conventional morality among the necessary attainments for leaders (all godly householders) certainly assisted the eclipse of competing expressions of the Pauline heritage and the accommodation of the church with much that was socially acceptable.

We have argued that the Pastor invokes Paul the apocalypticist—the receiver and mediator of mysteries and divinely imparted epiphanies. The Pastor does not promulgate new visions and lately disclosed mysteries. He chose to incorporate Paul the apocalypticist into his actualization of Pauline tradition, and to speak of a closed, immutable and sufficient deposit (παραθήκη) which allowed no further supplementation. The successful rhetoric of the letters lies, in large part, in the use made by the Pastor of the classic rhetorical strategies, including the use of the testament in 2 Timothy. But we can now conclude that there is a compelling appeal on the part of the Pastor to the full, perfect and sufficient deposit, the παραθήκη, in which the

58. On Marcion, see Baur, *Pastoralbriefe*, 18–19, 24, 25. On the Gnostics, see Irenaeus, *Haer.* 1.24.2 (food, drink, marriage); Tertullian, *De praescriptione haereticorum*, 33 (Marcion and Apelles); Clement of Alexandria, *Strom.*, 3.6 (heretics in general). See also Kurt Rudolph, *Gnosis: The Nature and History of Gnosticism* (San Francisco: Harper and Row, 1987), 257–63.

59. For women in Marcion's communities, see the passages discussed in Harding, *Tradition and Rhetoric*, 10, 56n18. For the prominence of women in Gnosticism, see Rudoph, *Gnosis*, 211–12, cf. 270–72. It is worth noting here the thesis of Dennis R. MacDonald, *The Legend and the Apostle: The Battle for Paul in Story and Canon* (Philadelphia: Westminster, 1983). MacDonald argues that *The Acts of Paul (and Thecla)* preserve the memory of Paul as a supporter of the ministry of women and a counter-cultural preacher, a view that the Pastoral Epistles seek to counter.

60. 1 Tim 1:4: "myths and endless genealogies"; 6:20 (cf. 2 Tim 4:4; Titus 1:14): "Avoid the contradictions (ἀντιθέσεις; antitheses) of what is falsely called knowledge" (γνῶσις). Marcion wrote a book called the Antitheses, but it is unlikely the book is referred to in 1 Tim 6:20 given the likely date of the Pastoral Epistles to about AD 100 (unless this verse is a later explicitly anti-Marcionite addition to the text of 1 Tim).

61. As reported in Irenaeus, *Haer.* 1.11.1.

62. See *Treatise on Resurrection* (attributed to the school of Valentinus), 49:13.

63. For Marcion and the Pastoral Epistles see Harding, "Pastoral Epistles," 328. For Valentinus's indebtedness to the Apostle and the role of the Pastoral Epistles among the Gnostics, see Pagels, *Gnostic Paul*, 163, 166nn41–42.

64. See Pagels, *Gnostic Paul*, 5. Cf. Walter Bauer, *Orthodoxy and Heresy in Earliest Christianity* (Philadelphia: Fortress Press, 1971), 221–28.

"mystery" vouchsafed to Paul and the unique epiphanic disclosure of the Christ-event in its past, present and future manifestations is exclusively encapsulated such that any addition to it by false teachers is a profound betrayal of the Pauline heritage.

PART III

Hebrews, the Catholic Epistles, and Revelation

14

Heavenly Revelation in the Epistle to the Hebrews

Eric F. Mason

Introduction

With apologies to the author of the Epistle to the Hebrews, one might say that scholars have long investigated many and various connections between Hebrews and Jewish apocalyptic traditions. This has especially been the case with Hebrews' discussion of the heavenly and earthly sanctuaries in chapters 8–10, usually in conjunction with considerations of whether and/or how the author has melded apocalyptic eschatological notions and the concept of a heavenly sanctuary with ideas from Middle Platonic thought. Similarly, interpreters have argued that the book's presentation of Jesus as the heavenly high priest who offers his sacrifice in the heavenly sanctuary and then takes his seat beside God's heavenly throne demonstrates the influence of Jewish apocalyptic thought. The discussion of Melchizedek, particularly in Hebrews 7, also invites comparison with Jewish apocalyptic traditions in which he is a heavenly, angelic figure. The climactic call to commitment in Hebrews 12, with its vivid, contrasting descriptions of the terrifying Mount Sinai and the idyllic Mount Zion, evokes rich apocalyptic imagery. Finally, some scholars have argued recently that exhortations in the book such as those calling the recipients to approach the "throne of grace" concern more than just prayer and worship but rather an invitation to (or even reports of) mystical experiences.[1]

While naturally there is much disagreement over the details, most scholars of Hebrews today would find at least *some* influence of apocalyptic thought on the author of the New Testament book. But many scholars of apocalypticism find something else more central to apocalyptic thought than the eschatological and cosmological elements mentioned above. Most notably, Christopher Rowland protests the trend to associate apocalypticism chiefly with eschatological concerns, and instead, argues that the essence of apocalyptic lies with the idea of heavenly revelation. He writes, "Apocalyptic seems essentially to be about the revelation of the divine mysteries through visions or some other form of immediate disclosure of heavenly truths."[2] Rowland notes that both the contents and modes of revelation may vary from text to text, but he adds, "Heavenly ascents, dream-visions, with or without interpretations, and angelic or divine pronouncements are all typical ways of communicating the divine will and the mysteries of the heavenly world."[3]

I propose that one may find something like this kind of heavenly revelation in Hebrews, utilized rhetorically in God's statements about the Son and the angels in Hebrews 1.[4] This kind of idea is implicit in several publications by Scott D. Mackie on Hebrews' call for the audience to approach God's throne in a way consistent with mysticism, but he does not develop the discussion of Hebrews 1 as apocalyptic revelation in the manner I seek to do here.[5] More recently, Jody A. Barnard has argued extensively for links between apocalypticism and Hebrews and suggests that Hebrews might even reflect the author's own mystical experiences. My arguments for apocalyptic elements in Hebrews correspond with his at certain points, but I do not seek to engage his mysticism proposal.[6] I should also comment here on the phrase "apocalyptic revela-

1. It is not feasible to present a full bibliographic treatment here, but I have addressed some of these issues previously in Eric F. Mason, "Cosmology, Messianism, and Melchizedek: Apocalyptic Jewish Traditions and Hebrews," in *Reading the Epistle to the Hebrews: A Resource for Students*, ed. Eric F. Mason and Kevin B. McCruden, RBS 66 (Atlanta: Society of Biblical Literature, 2011), 53–76. See notes 5 and 6 below on mysticism.

2. Christopher Rowland, *The Open Heaven: A Study of Apocalyptic in Judaism and Early Christianity* (New York: Crossroad, 1982), 70.

3. Rowland, *Open Heaven*, 72.

4. Compare the discussion of this material as an example of "quasi-prosopographic exegesis" in Amy L. B. Peeler, *You Are My Son: The Family of God in the Epistle to the Hebrews*, LNTS 486 (London: Bloomsbury T&T Clark, 2014), 29–37. A key difference in our positions is that I ground this rhetorical use of the quotations in apocalyptic revelation.

5. See especially Scott D. Mackie, *Eschatology and Exhortation in the Epistle to the Hebrews*, WUNT II/223 (Tübingen: Mohr Siebeck, 2007) and three subsequent journal articles: "Heavenly Sanctuary Mysticism in the Epistle to the Hebrews," *JTS* 62 (2011): 77–117; "Ancient Jewish Mystical Motifs in Hebrews' Theology of Access and Entry Exhortations," *NTS* 58 (2011): 88–104; and "Early Christian Eschatological Experience in the Warnings and Exhortations of the Epistle to the Hebrews," *TynBul* 63 (2012): 93–114.

6. Jody A. Barnard, *The Mysticism of Hebrews: Exploring the Role of Jewish Apocalyptic Mysticism in the Epistle to the Hebrews*, WUNT II/331 (Tübingen: Mohr Siebeck, 2012). I drafted my thesis before reading Barnard's monograph. We agree significantly on the presence of apocalyptic motifs in Hebrews 1, but for different reasons. Whereas I argue here that the author uses a modified form of apocalyptic revelation in a rhetorical manner in order to add authority to the statements about the Son in Hebrews 1, Barnard connects the discussion here to the author's own mystical experiences (281). He further suggests that the book may have been written by a leader of a community accustomed to mystical access to the celestial sanctuary in order to provide "a kind of guide to heavenly ascent and transformation" during a time when he was absent from the group (283–84). Barnard's approach differs from both

tion." Admittedly, this language might seem redundant, but I use it simply to denote information that is made known in an apocalyptic context, as distinct from other kinds of revelation and other motifs of apocalyptic literature.

Divine Speech in Hebrews

Discussions of the role of God in the book of Hebrews quite naturally give significant attention to the presentation of God as one who speaks in the book. Peter T. O'Brien notes that "the author of Hebrews emphatically stresses that God is the speaking God," and he affirms William L. Lane's (perhaps overstated) assertion that "the central theme of Hebrews is the importance of listening to the voice of God in Scripture and in the act of Christian preaching."[7] Harold W. Attridge writes, "Hebrews . . . operates with the conceit that readers and hearers of Scripture can listen to God speaking, first to the Son and ultimately to all God's children. In this conceit, the character of God and of his scriptural speech provides the raw material for both reflection and parenesis."[8]

God "speaks" in Hebrews in a variety of ways.[9] The author begins the book with a subtle comparison of God's revelatory activity in the past and present. Attridge's translation of Hebrews 1:1–2 captures well the continuity yet difference intended by the author in these opening words: "Having spoken of old in multiple forms and multiple fashions to the fathers through the prophets, in these final days God has spoken to us through a Son."[10] This is an extremely fitting introductory statement for a book in which God's words are so prominent. Numerous interpreters have noted the contrasting language in this statement: "long ago" and (the apocalyptically-tinged) "these last days"; to the "ancestors" (literally "fathers") and to "us"; and through the prophets and through a Son.[11] The prophetic revelation is said to come through

my argument and that of Mackie by putting major emphasis on priestly motifs already in Hebrews 1, whereas Mackie and I focus chiefly on Sonship themes in this chapter.

7. Peter T. O'Brien, "God as the Speaking God: 'Theology' in the Letter to the Hebrews," in *Understanding the Times: New Testament Studies in the 21st Century*, ed. Andreas J. Kostenberger and Robert W. Yarbrough (Wheaton, IL: Crossway, 2011), 196–206, esp. 197; William L. Lane, *Hebrews 1-8*, WBC 47A (Dallas: Word, 1991), cxxvii.

8. Harold W. Attridge, "God in Hebrews: Urging Children to Heavenly Glory," in *The Forgotten God: Perspectives in Biblical Theology: Essays in Honor of Paul J. Achtemeier on the Occasion of His Seventy-fifth Birthday*, ed. A. Andrew Das and Frank J. Matera (Louisville: Westminster John Knox, 2002), 197–209, esp. 203–4. See additional examples and bibliography in Peeler, *You Are My Son*, 2–3n5.

9. See the list of occurrences compiled in O'Brien, "God as the Speaking God," 197. O'Brien's list is broader than the survey here; I address only places in which God is presented specifically as a speaker. For example, one reads that "God added his testimony" through various phenomena in 2:4, but no words of God are recorded.

10. Harold W. Attridge, *The Epistle to the Hebrews: A Commentary on the Epistle to the Hebrews*, Hermeneia (Philadelphia: Fortress, 1989), 35. Attridge's rendering more accurately reflects the Greek construction than those of the RSV, NRSV, and NIV, which insert the word "but" and imply more discontinuity than is present in the Greek. On issues of contrast and continuity in Heb 1:1–2, see Jonathan I. Griffiths, *Hebrews and Divine Speech*, LNTS 507 (London: Bloomsbury T&T Clark, 2014), 37–42.

11. The commencement of the "last days" in conjunction with the Son is not a problem for an apocalyptic perspective. As John J. Collins notes, "The primary difference between Christian and Jewish apocalypticism in the first century CE is that the Christians believed that the messiah had already come and that the firstfruits of the resurrection had taken place." See Collins, *The Apocalyptic Imagination: An Introduction to Jewish Apocalyptic Literature*, 2nd ed. (Grand Rapids: Eerdmans, 1998), 268. Similarly, M. C. De Boer notes that

"many and various ways," but no corresponding phrase appears for the revelation through the Son. Nevertheless, interpreters usually propose that something like "final," "complete," or "unitary" is implied because of emphases elsewhere in the book on the once-for-all nature of Jesus's sacrifice or the comments about the necessity for many Levitical priests in contrast to the one Son.

Either way, God speaks. Yet, when one encounters statements explicitly presented as the words of God elsewhere in the book, these are in the form of Scripture quotations, that is, words spoken long ago through the prophets (including the prophetic David in the Psalms, as widely understood by ancient interpreters) but now placed directly in the mouth of God.[12] In contrast, one finds only indirect references elsewhere to God "speaking" through Jesus (one example of which might be 2:1–4; see below). Of course, the *idea* of God "speaking" need not be limited to specific scriptural utterances (cf. 4:12–13), and one might say that God's speech through the Son is "embodied" revelation.

Regardless, this statement provides an ideal introduction to the affirmations that follow about the Son in Hebrews 1:2–4. He is appointed heir of all things, through him God created the worlds (αἰῶνας), he is the reflection (or radiance) of God's glory and the exact imprint of God's very being, he sustains all things by his powerful word, he made purification for sins, he sat down at God's right hand, and he has become as much superior to angels as his inherited name is superior to theirs.[13] Mention of angels provides a fluid transition to 1:5–14, where God speaks through a series of Scripture quotations recast to demonstrate the superiority of the Son over the angels, who ultimately are identified as ministering spirits in the divine service deployed to act for the sake of humanity (1:14).

The setting for these proclamations by God is the heavenly context, and the occasion seems

"the crucified Christ whom God raised from the dead is Paul's criterion for the appropriation of Jewish apocalyptic-eschatological categories; the latter serve the former, not vice versa." See his "Paul and Apocalyptic Eschatology," in *The Encyclopedia of Apocalypticism*, ed. John J. Collins, Vol. 1, The Origins of Apocalypticism in Judaism and Christianity (New York: Continuum, 2000), 345–83, esp. 367–68.

12. Compare the observation of Martin Karrer about the speech of Jesus in Hebrews: "Evidently, the Jesus of Hebrews ignores the utterances of the Jesus delivered in the Synoptic, Johannine and other Jesus traditions. Instead, he speaks in words of Israel's Scripture." See Martin Karrer, "LXX Psalm 39:7–10 in Hebrews 10:5–7," in *Psalms and Hebrews: Studies in Reception*, ed. Dirk J. Human and Gert Jacobus Steyn, LHBOTS 527 (London: T&T Clark, 2010), 126–46, esp. 126–27. On David as a prophet, see especially 11QPsa [11Q5] 27:2–11 (the non-canonical psalm "David's Compositions"). Note the differing evaluations of David as prophet in Peter W. Flint, "David," in *Encyclopedia of the Dead Sea Scrolls*, ed. Lawrence H. Schiffman and James C. VanderKam, 2 vols. (Oxford: Oxford University Press, 2000), 1:178–80; and Kenneth E. Pomykala, "David," in *The Eerdmans Dictionary of Early Judaism*, ed. John J. Collins and Daniel C. Harlow (Grand Rapids: Eerdmans, 2010), 517–19.

13. About the superior name, Christopher Rowland comments, "His exaltation is closely linked with his inheritance of 'a more excellent name' (1:4). Mere possession of the divine name is no guarantee of superiority, however, for the angel Jaoel in the Apocalypse of Abraham shared the divine name, as also did Metatron." See Christopher Rowland and Christopher R. A. Morray-Jones, *The Mystery of God: Early Jewish Mysticism and the New Testament*, CRINT 12 (Leiden: Brill, 2009), 168–69. Here, however, the point of the assertion definitely is that superiority is signified by possession of the special name, and Rowland's observation does not acknowledge that "Son" may instead be the name bestowed. This seems to be affirmed in the two biblical citations (of Ps 2:7 and 2 Sam 7:14) that immediately follow this statement in Heb 1:5, and compare the importance of the status of "Son" in Heb 3:1–6.

to be Jesus's entrance into God's heavenly throne room after completing his self-sacrificial priestly mission. This understanding hinges on the interpretation of language in the transition statement in 1:6, "when he brings [or introduces] the firstborn into the world [οἰκουμένη]." Οἰκουμένη normally was used to refer to the inhabited, terrestrial world or more specifically to the Greek or Roman worlds, and in light of the former, some interpreters argue that the occasion for God's statement here best refers either to the inauguration of Jesus's ministry on earth or else to his parousia. (This divergence concerns how to understand πάλιν, "again," in this context, which is best understood as referencing God's next statement, the quotation in 1:6, instead of the Son's second entrance.) Others argue that οἰκουμένη has a heavenly or eschatological meaning. The word appears only once more in Hebrews at 2:5, where the author writes that "it is not to angels that God subjected the world to come [τὴν οἰκουμένην τὴν μέλλουσαν]" (NRSV), that is, the heavenly, eschatological world that awaits faithful humanity. Some interpreters argue that the meaning here must differ from that of 1:6 because the author specifies in 2:5 that this world is "coming." Others argue that the author has used οἰκουμένη in the same sense both places and note that he uses κόσμος in 10:5 when Christ "comes into the world" and is obedient to God's will in his earthly ministry. It seems best to opt for a heavenly meaning of "world" in both 1:6 and 2:5. Thus, one finds in 1:6 a statement about the Son's entrance into the heavenly world at his exaltation, in conjunction with his self-sacrifice in the heavenly sanctuary upon completion of his earthly mission, when he is enthroned by God as narrated in 1:3.[14]

Scholars express differing opinions on how the author has organized the quotations in this section, but most recognize some sort of alternation and pairing of comments to or about the Son and to the angels. Most (but not all) of the quotations are drawn from the Psalms, particularly royal psalms that lend themselves well to such usage because they already present God addressing another figure. The Davidic messianic import of this divine speech is highlighted by the fact that the first two quotations in Hebrews 1:5 are from Psalm 2:7 ("You are my Son; today I have begotten you") and 2 Samuel 7:14 ("I will be his Father, and he will be my Son") while the last in Hebrews 1:13 is from Psalm 110 (LXX 109):1 ("Sit at my right hand until I make your enemies a footstool for your feet"). Still other texts originally were addressed to or about God but now are recast to speak of the Son, such that the Son now is called "God" as in the quotation of Psalm 45:6–7 in Hebrews 1:8–9. Quotations are sometimes cast negatively toward angels, by which I mean the author denies that God made certain proclamations to them that instead describe the Son. Two with differing sorts of introductions do, however, specify things about angels. In 1:6, God's angels are called to worship the Son when he enters the world.[15] In 1:7, the

14. See the thorough discussion of οἰκουμένη in David M. Moffitt, *Atonement and the Logic of Resurrection in the Epistle to the Hebrews*, NovTSup 141 (Leiden: Brill, 2011), 53–69, with which I concur.

Son is said to have dominion over the angels, making them winds and flames of fire (from Ps 104 [LXX 103]:4).[16] Language from the latter statement recurs in the author's summary statement about the role of angels in 1:14, that they are spirits intended for divine service for the sake of humanity.

Two major things dominate chapter 2—the book's first warning to the recipients to maintain their faithfulness in verses 1-4, and the book's first explanation of Jesus's solidarity with humanity in verses 5-18. In 2:1-4, the author exhorts his audience with a *qal wa-homer* argument comparing the penalties for transgressing the law ("declared through angels") with the dangers of neglecting "so great a salvation." The latter concerns the gospel message that was "declared at first through the Lord," that is, Jesus in this context, and the author adds that God confirmed this message for the community of the author and recipients with spiritual phenomena and experiences. (I mention this here as a possible way one might discern God speaking through the Son in Hebrews, as the comparison here of the law and message of Jesus offers a potential parallel to the book's opening statement about God's speech through the prophets and the Son.) The discussion in 2:5–18 builds on a quotation of Psalm 8:4–6, curiously credited to "someone" who testified "somewhere." God is not presented as the speaker, and in fact, the words of the psalm actually address God, here and in its original context. As such, this is one of the few quotations of Scripture in the book that is not placed in the mouth of God, Jesus, or the Holy Spirit (cf. 10:37–38; 12:5–6; 13:6; and texts quoted when discussing events of Hebrew history). Yet, in the subsequent discussion of this quotation, God's intentions for Jesus and the means by which God brings salvation for humanity through him are explained. Jesus is credited with words of Scripture when he responds to God in 2:12–13 with the language of Psalm 22:22 and Isaiah 8:17–18 to affirm his solidarity with humanity. Because this appears in the midst of a discussion of Jesus's humanness and his task to redeem humanity by means of his suffering, it seems that these words are intended by the author as "spoken" or embodied in his earthly ministry rather than a response in heavenly dialogue with God.[17]

15. The identification of the text cited in Heb 1:6 is problematic, with suggestions including Ps 97:7 (LXX 96:7) or Deut 32:43 (in the LXX or 4QDeut$_q$, but not the MT). See, for example, the discussion in Craig R. Koester, *Hebrews*, AB 36 (New York: Doubleday, 2001), 193.
16. Paul Ellingworth argues that God speaks here about his own dominion over the angels (as in the original context of Ps 104 [LXX 103]:4), not that of the Son. See *The Epistle to the Hebrews*, NIGTC (Grand Rapids: Eerdmans, 1993), 120.
17. My approach here differs from that of numerous other interpreters who understand these words of Jesus as a response to God's statements in the Scripture quotations in 1:5–14. See, for example, Attridge, "God in Hebrews," 203–5; Mackie, *Eschatology*, 216–20; and Peeler, *You Are My Son*, 30–31, 85. Space here does not allow a detailed response to their readings, but one might note that even though God's words about the Son appear in Hebrews 1 and Jesus's words about his solidarity with humanity appear in Hebrews 2, in the conceptual narrative of the book Jesus's words predate those of God if Jesus is understood as speaking in his incarnation and God at Jesus's exaltation, as I have suggested. Both Mackie and Barnard (*Mysticism*, 244)—for different purposes—emphasize the change of pronouns from second person (in Ps 2:7) to third person (2 Sam 7:14) in God's speech via quotations in Heb 1:5. Mackie argues that the shift implies that God addresses the worshiping community that is repeatedly called in the book to enter the heavenly sanctuary, whereas Barnard understands the angels as the audience and links the language shift to the subsequent charge for them to acknowledge this Son. One should note, however, that both quotations preserve the pronouns of the source texts in the LXX.

After the brief comments in 3:1–6 comparing Moses, who is faithful *in* God's house with Jesus, who is faithful *over* God's house, the author turns in 3:7–4:13 to present the negative example of the wilderness generation. They were unable to enter "rest" in Canaan due to unbelief, and thus they serve as a forceful reminder to the audience of Hebrews that they must remain faithful to the end in order to enter God's rest. The passage opens with a quotation of Psalm 95 (LXX 94):7–11, here attributed to the Holy Spirit. Later, in Hebrews 4:3, as the quotation is unpacked, God is credited as speaker of the final line of the quotation, "As in my anger I swore, 'They shall not enter my rest.'" Also, the discussion in Hebrews assumes that God is the active party all along in this discussion. This passage (along with a few others in the book) raises the vexing issue of what (τὸ) πνεῦμα (τὸ) ἅγιον is in Hebrews, and it anticipates a similar situation later in the book (10:15–17) in which a portion of a biblical quotation first attributed to God may later be ascribed to the Holy Spirit (a sequence that works opposite of what one finds here in chs. 3–4).[18] Alternately, one might explain the attribution to God in Hebrews 4:3 as simply an acknowledgement that God is the speaker of those words on a literary level from the perspective of the psalmist. Perhaps that is preferable in light of something else one encounters just four verses later—the opening exhortation of the Psalm 95 quotation is now attributed to David (4:7). Admittedly, the psalmist is identified as the person through whom *God* speaks (and this makes it very likely that God also is the speaking "he" referenced in the next verse). Also, this introduction of David into the discussion is conducive for the author's argument: he now draws on the assumed biblical chronology to "date" (for lack of a better term) the words of David as later than both the statement in Genesis 2:2 that God rested on the seventh day and the eventual conquest of Canaan under the leadership of Joshua. As such, this allows for an exhortation to enter God's rest even after the entrance into Canaan and points to the more profound nature of that "rest" that still remains. All of this reveals something else that is very important for discerning how the author of Hebrews deals with these particular words of the Holy Spirit and of God—they are indeed texts which one can exegete and which have human conduits, even if they ultimately are understood as divine words. The section concludes in 4:12–13 with a reflection on the penetrating nature of the "word of God."

God's speech is very prominent in the next section of the book, 4:14–5:10, which is the first of two passages in Hebrews that explain how Jesus may be priest. Here, the author explains how Jesus functions as a priest by utilizing a *favorable* comparison to priests of the Aaronic (i.e., Levitical) order in terms of the priest's experience of human weakness that engenders compassion for others, his duty to offer sacrifices for others, and his accession to the priestly office

18. The author of Hebrews is inconsistent in his use of the article with πνεῦμα ἅγιον, leaving open the possibility that he sometimes may speak of something other than *the* Holy Spirit. While interpreters should take care not to read later Trinitarian formulations back into earlier texts, the article is indeed present in both 3:7 and 10:15.

only by divine appointment. The key element for our survey is that Jesus is appointed to this priesthood by means of the first of the book's several citations of Psalm 110 (LXX 109):4. This appointment is said to parallel the way God installed Aaron as the first high priest by means of a call. God is clearly implied to be the speaker, literally "the one who said to him" (5:5), who thus installs Jesus in his priesthood "according to the order of Melchizedek." This is facilitated by an explicit appeal to the words of God in 1:5–14. There, the first and last quotations placed in the mouth of God are Psalm 2:7 and Psalm 110 (LXX 109):1, both of which are cast to identify Jesus as the exalted Son. Here, one now finds Psalm 2:7 paired directly with Psalm 110:4, making it explicit that the Son addressed in Hebrews 1 is indeed the same figure now appointed as priest.

One next hears the voice of God in Hebrews 6:13–20, where the author quotes God's promise to bless Abraham and builds on this to stress the absolute certainty of God's trustworthiness to "the heirs of the promise." This is a recollection of God's dealing with Abraham in the past, so we need not dwell on it for the purposes of this study except to note that it is the second of three passages in Hebrews to present God as "swearing" (ὀμνύω). This language appeared earlier in the discussion of Psalm 95 and the wilderness generation (quotations in 3:11 [Holy Spirit] and 4:3; elaboration in 3:18), and now in 6:13, God swears a promise to Abraham.

The author then moves in Hebrews 7 to his second section in which he legitimates Jesus's priestly office. Earlier in chapter 5, Jesus's priestly identity was modeled positively on the biblical (Levitical) priesthood that began with Aaron, including Jesus's appointment by means of Psalm 110:4, but here in chapter 7, the author *contrasts* Jesus and the Levitical priests and explains why it is important that Jesus's priesthood is instead like that of Melchizedek. In 7:1–10, the author reflects on the identity and nature of Melchizedek and playfully explains how Abraham's descendant Levi acknowledged Melchizedek's superiority. Then, the author turns to identify Jesus with Melchizedek, and while doing so, he reasserts in 7:21 that God appointed Jesus to this priesthood by means of the language of Psalm 110:4 (cf. 7:17, which implicitly refers to God's words), this time quoted in a different form than had yet appeared. Previous quotations of Psalm 110:4 in Hebrews always began with the assertion "You are a priest forever," but this time, the author includes introductory language from the psalm itself and thus provides the third "swearing" discussion in the book: "The Lord has sworn [ὤμοσεν κύριος] and will not change his mind, 'You are a priest forever.'" God had sworn judgment on the unfaithful wilderness generation in 3:7–4:13, then a promise of blessing to Abraham in Hebrews 6. Now, the author exploits the idea of God's oath in Hebrews 7. In Hebrews 5, Jesus was appointed by God to the priesthood as Aaron had been, but in Hebrews 7, Jesus's installation by oath marks his priesthood as superior to that of the Levites, who now are said to enter their service by genealogy instead (7:20–22).

This comparison of Jesus with Levitical priests in Hebrews 7 sets the stage for further comparisons of the old and new covenants, the earthly and heavenly sanctuaries, the sacrifices of Levitical priests and Jesus, and so on, that dominate Hebrews 8–10. The author recalls God's command to Moses to craft the tabernacle according to the pattern revealed on the mountain (Heb 8:5; cf. Exod 25:40 and 25:9), but the more significant speech of God occurs a few verses later when God is attributed the words of Jeremiah 31 (LXX 38):31–34 in Hebrews 8:8–12. (In the Greek, the speaker of the quotation is not specified beyond the "he" of the third-person verb, but context clarifies that this is God.) This new covenant language drives much of the subsequent discussion, and part of the quotation recurs in 10:15–17, where it is credited to the Holy Spirit.[19] Much is said about Jesus's sacrifice in the heavenly sanctuary in this section of the book, and naturally, one would locate God in heaven when he utters the words of Jeremiah 31, but one does not get the sense that the spatial location for this quotation itself is significant. Elsewhere in the section, Christ also speaks Scripture, as his obedience to God's will in his earthly mission in the *κόσμος* is explained by means of LXX Psalm 40:6–8. Later, in Hebrews 10, God is identified as the one who will judge the disobedient (Deut 32:35–36 in Heb 10:30) and who expects faithfulness from his people (Isa 26:20 LXX and Hab 2:3–4 in Heb 10:37–38). These two passages—especially the latter—seem more like reminders of God's declarations in the past (i.e., in Scripture) than words uttered by God as a character in the narrative world of Hebrews.

In Hebrews 11, the author affirms creation "by the word of God [ῥήματι θεοῦ]" (11:3; cf. 1:2, 10 on creation, and τῷ ῥήματι τῆς δυνάμεως αὐτοῦ in 1:3) before he considers God's communication with several faithful figures of Israel's past. Two features here should be noted. First, the only explicit language attributed to God concerns his promise in Hebrews 11:18 (quoting Gen 21:12) that Abraham's descendants will come through Isaac. Here too, the quotation appears to be a reminder of a statement in Scripture rather than divine discourse in the context of Hebrews itself. Second, it is interesting that the stories recounted in this list emphasize accounts from the Hebrew Scriptures in which God speaks directly with the faithful figure rather than through the "angel of the Lord" or other angelic envoys. Examples include God warning Noah to build the ark in 11:7; God calling Abraham to migrate in 11:8; fulfillment of God's promise to Abraham about innumerable descendants in 11:12; and God's call for Abraham to sacrifice Isaac in 11:17–18. Genesis accounts concerning the promise of childbearing despite

19. So, for example, Attridge, *Hebrews*, 281; Koester, *Hebrews*, 441; and Ellingworth, *Hebrews*, 512. Mackie ("Heavenly Sanctuary," 86–87) disagrees, arguing that the witness of the Holy Spirit concerns the believer's experience of "the new covenant's promised benefits," while the Jeremiah quotation is credited to the *κύριος* who speaks within the quotation in Heb 10:16. Mackie follows Steven Motyer, "The Temple in Hebrews: Is It There?" in *Heaven on Earth: The Temple in Biblical Theology*, ed. T. Desmond Alexander and Simon Gathercole (Carlisle, PA: Paternoster, 2004), 177–89, esp. 186.

Sarah's age vary, sometimes with and without mediators, and the Joshua 6 account of the fall of Jericho, mentioned in brief summary in Hebrews 11:30, does include an encounter between Joshua and an angel. Barnard highlights the fact that Enoch, so prominent in apocalyptic speculation, also appears in this recital.[20]

The discussion in Hebrews 12 of God's fatherly discipline includes language from Proverbs 3:11–12 (in Heb 12:5–6), but this is presented as a reminder of an "exhortation," and thus seems to function essentially as a Scripture quotation recalled by the author of Hebrews. Later in the chapter in 12:25, the author reminds the audience not to ignore "the one who is speaking," which some have identified as Jesus but probably instead should be understood as God.[21] The speaker is credited with the promise to shake earth and heaven from Haggai 2:6. This, too, points to God rather than Jesus as speaker. The language appears just after the vivid contrast of Mount Sinai and Mount Zion in Hebrews 12:18–24 and may imply that the words are spoken from heaven. They have an eschatological tinge, as the faithful are offered a kingdom that cannot be shaken (Heb 12:28). The comments are reminiscent of the reflection on the nature of God's word in Hebrews 4:12–13. The final statement attributed to God in the book is a citation of Joshua 1:5 in Hebrews 13:5, but here too, the passage seems to be more a reminder of God's statement in the past rather than a new divine utterance.

This survey has demonstrated that God typically "speaks" words of Scripture in Hebrews, but this can be presented by the author in differing ways. Sometimes, one reads *that* God speaks, and sometimes, one reads *what* God speaks. What God said in the biblical past may be recalled, as can what God said to Jesus and the angels, or what God says openly to those who will hear the words of this homily. God's words may present the opportunity for the author to undertake sustained exegetical argumentation, or they may function as utterances that need little or no additional elaboration.

God's Revelatory Speech in Hebrews 1:5–14

In the midst of all this, God's address to the Son and the angels in 1:5–14 stands out as distinctive, as is widely acknowledged. Occasionally, one finds composite quotations drawing on multiple biblical texts elsewhere in Hebrews, but this section provides the only example of an extended collection of quotations. This is the most striking section in which quotations appear without further elaboration, strung together gracefully with sparse transition statements.[22] Indeed, this collection of quotations certainly has not lacked for scholarly investiga-

20. Barnard, *Mysticism*, 260–62.
21. Attridge, *Hebrews*, 379.
22. Cf. Peeler's comments on Hebrews' lack of use of the introductory formulae attached to some of these quotations in their original

tion on numerous levels: How do the wordings of the quotations compare to those of the LXX, the Hebrew of the Masoretic Text and other textual traditions preserved at Qumran, or even the Odes of Solomon? Did the author of Hebrews compile this collection for his own purposes, or did he find them gathered in a *testimonia* collection that was already circulating among early Christians? If the author is responsible for their collection, how faithful has he been to their original contexts? If he found them already assembled, what was the original purpose of the list? The last line of 1:4 asserts the superiority of the Son and his name to the angels, which provides the natural transition into this catena, but are there other thematic relationships between the affirmations of 1:1–4 and the citations of 1:5–14 that extend beyond this comparison? Does the author have pastoral and theological concerns about how the recipients presently understand angels or the Son in relation to angels, or is this detailed comparison chiefly necessary to set the stage for various things the author wishes to argue in chapter 2?[23]

All of these issues are very important, but in the midst of such discussions, something else very distinctive about these particular quotations can easily be overlooked. David deSilva notes that "the OT texts become the author's window into this unseen rite, the session of the Son at God's right hand as God's vice-regent."[24] This certainly is correct in terms of the author's creative means of description. But perhaps Lane better captures the *effect* of this section: "The seven quotations are presented as a succession of words spoken by God to the Son, which the Church on earth is permitted to overhear."[25] Though Lane does not develop this idea further, his description of these quotations as words "that the Church on earth is permitted to overhear" is very apt.

After the opening declaration in Hebrews 1 that God has spoken through the prophets and now a Son, everything in the rest of the chapter—both the affirmations about the Son and the quotations in the mouth of God—essentially is a disclosure of heavenly information. The affirmations about the Son in 1:2–4 provide essential information for one to understand the true nature and identity of the Son. One cannot understand the message of the remainder of the book (including the priesthood of this Son) without knowing the things stated here about the Son, but this is heavenly information that can only be known by humanity if it is revealed in some way. Admittedly the things disclosed here are mentioned only in brief summary. Mackie has argued that this was intentional so that the audience members would use their imaginations to fill out the setting or envision themselves as present.[26]

contexts: "he had to 'decrease the quotation level' by not repeating their introductions to God's speech. . . . Hebrews silences the human medium in these texts and allows the audience to hear God speaking directly" (*You Are My Son*, 32–33).

23. Space does not allow for bibliography here, but these issues are routinely addressed in critical commentaries.
24. David A. deSilva, *Perseverance in Gratitude: A Socio-Rhetorical Commentary on the Epistle "to the Hebrews"* (Grand Rapids: Eerdmans, 2000), 97.
25. Lane, *Hebrews 1–8*, 32.

In addition, it is very significant that the things disclosed here are among the same kinds of things often emphasized in revelatory accounts in Jewish apocalyptic literature. Numerous Second Temple period texts include disclosures of heavenly details of God's enthronement in heaven, hierarchies of angels, and figures with honorific names. Likewise, in Hebrews, things such as the Son's status as God's heir, his enthronement, his relationship with angels, and his great name can only be known by those privy to heavenly insight. Similarly, the nature of God's glory is a frequent topic of apocalyptic revelation. As such, the statement that the Son shares God's glory and bears the "stamp" (RSV) or "imprint" (NRSV) of God's very being can only be confirmed by those to whom such has been revealed. Finally, a very common apocalyptic revelatory theme concerns the inability of humans to comprehend how God created the world and how the physical universe continues to function. Likewise, no human can know the details of God's creative activity and oversight of the world—here with stress on the Son's participation in creation and subsequent dominion—without such secrets being disclosed. Disclosure of cultic or priestly matters is common in apocalyptic revelatory texts, and the Son is said to have made purification for sins. (Indeed, it is no accident that one section of Hebrews most commonly discussed in relation to apocalypticism is chs. 8–10, where Jesus's sacrifice in the heavenly sanctuary is discussed most fully.) Admittedly, here in Hebrews 1:2–4, one does not find the *detailed* descriptions of these matters that are standard in texts with apocalyptic revelatory discussions, but it is striking that the *kinds* of things affirmed here about the Son match quite closely with the *kinds* of things very often addressed in apocalyptic revelatory texts.[27]

One also finds a strong resonance with apocalyptic revelatory materials in the quotations of Hebrews 1:5–14. The affirmations of 1:2–4 have corresponded with the topics of heavenly revelation in other texts, and the themes of the individual quotations likely do as well. I agree with those scholars of Hebrews who find significant parallels between the themes of the affirmations of 1:2–4 and the contents of the biblical quotations.[28] Thus, the quotations simultaneously do three things: they illustrate and confirm the affirmations, subtly affirm the divine and Davidic

26. Mackie, "Heavenly Sanctuary Mysticism," 105.

27. Several of these motifs already appear in the Book of the Watchers (1 Enoch 1–36), including God's enthronement and glory, multiplicities of angels, and descriptions of elements of the created world. Detailed discussion of the workings of the physical world (created by God) are found in the Astronomical Book (1 Enoch 72–82), and in the Similitudes (1 Enoch 37–71) Enoch sees a heavenly figure variously called the "Chosen [or Elect] One," "Son of Man," "Messiah," and "Righteous and Chosen One." Levi's priesthood is confirmed with heavenly visions in the Aramaic Levi Document and the much later Testament of Levi (in Testaments of the Twelve Patriarchs). See the relevant articles on these texts in *The Eerdmans Dictionary of Early Judaism*. See also Carol A. Newsom, "The Rhetoric of Jewish Apocalyptic Literature," in *The Oxford Handbook of Apocalyptic Literature*, ed. John J. Collins (Oxford: Oxford University Press, 2014), 201–17; and the classic study by Michael E. Stone, "Lists of Revealed Things in the Apocalyptic Literature," in *Magnalia Dei: The Mighty Acts of God: Essays on the Bible and Archaeology in Memory of G. Ernest Wright*, ed. Frank Moore Cross, Werner E. Lemke, and Patrick D. Miller, Jr. (Garden City, NY: Doubleday, 1976), 414–52.

28. My understanding of the thematic relationship between the affirmations of 1:1–4 and the quotations in 1:5–14 is strongly influenced by the analysis of John P. Meier, published in two articles as "Structure and Theology in Heb 1,1–14," *Bib* 66 (1985): 168–89; and "Symmetry and Theology in the Old Testament Citations of Heb 1,5–14," *Bib* 66 (1985): 504–33.

messianic identities of the Son, and advance the comparison of the Son and angels in preparation for the subsequent warning about drifting into unfaithfulness and the discussion of Jesus's solidarity with humanity in chapter 2. But, of course, the key issue for the present discussion is that now one encounters language that is presented as the direct proclamation of God in a way that resembles apocalyptic revelation.[29] The twist is that in Hebrews, God's words are the words of Scripture, whereas apocalyptic revelation usually interprets, supplements, or otherwise goes *beyond* what already is recognized as authoritative written revelation.[30]

That important observation need not, however, rule out the correspondences of these words of God with apocalyptic revelation. Barnard properly notes that modern interpreters of Hebrews likely are more concerned about the sources of these words than the ancient audience would have been, since they would have experienced the text through oral reading and would not have been distracted by things such as notations for biblical quotations in the margins of our modern critical editions.[31] Alternately, one might expect the use of Scripture quotations since Scripture, not esoteric revelation, would be the normal "stuff" from which a homily such as Hebrews should be constructed. Early Christians certainly would have recognized much of this language as coming from Scripture, but the author has recontextualized these words as utterances of God directed to the Son and the angels within the heavenly abode. Indeed, this recontextualization is very much a revelatory reinterpretation as the words of Scripture are imbued with *new* meaning as they now are *re*-presented in the mouth of God. These quotations from ancient Scripture now become God's words in the heavenly sanctuary that are made available to the audience of Hebrews. As such, they take on special significance and power as God's own direct utterances in heaven that now *are revealed* and *themselves reveal* the true identity and nature of the Son.

All of this takes on even greater significance when one recalls what comes immediately after this contrast of the angels and the Son: the warning passage that compares the consequences of transgression of the "message declared by angels" and neglecting "such a great salvation," that is, the message of the Son. Thus, by the time the author reaches Hebrews 2:4, he has done four very important things: he has prioritized God's speech through the Son over God's speech through the prophets, reported God's words exalting the Son over the angels, declared more

29. Compare 2 Enoch 24–36, where God speaks directly to Enoch in an apocalyptic revelatory context (here about creation) rather than through an angelic mediator.

30. Commenting on the book of Revelation, William Adler notes the following: "Numerous allusions to and phrases from the Old Testament permeate the work, but like other apocalypses, it does not seek confirmation through direct quotations from the biblical text." Following Hans von Campenhausen, he adds that "only in the Apocalypse of Peter does the principle of not citing biblical texts 'start to become blurred.'" See William Adler, "Introduction," in *The Jewish Apocalyptic Heritage in Early Christianity*, ed. James C. VanderKam and William Adler, CRINT 3.4 (Assen: Van Gorcum, 1996), 1–31, esp. 20; and Hans von Campenhausen, *The Formation of the Christian Bible* (Philadelphia: Fortress, 1972), 218.

31. Barnard, *Mysticism*, 234.

dire consequences for disobedience to the message of the Son than even to the law (the "message declared by angels"), and reminded his audience that God confirmed the message of the Son which they had received from those who knew him. Thus, God affirms the Son's message on earth as he has exalted the Son in heaven.

Again, Scripture is the means by which God proclaims the superiority of the Son. When these words are put directly in the mouth of God by the author of Hebrews in the heavenly court, they are now deemed to surpass even the earlier revelation of these same words. This certainly is not the norm for apocalyptic revelations in the broader Jewish and early Christian context. Instead, while allusions to Scripture can be very common in revelatory material, the authority of the revealed message is grounded in the experience of its divine disclosure, not biblical authorization.[32] According to my reading, the author of Hebrews does not claim a visionary experience, but he does claim to report God's very words from heaven.[33] What matters most and what ultimately is most real is their utterance in heaven itself—God has made his definitive declaration in heaven, and the real identity of the Son is revealed. That sort of theme is also present elsewhere in Hebrews. The next time God addresses the Son directly in the book (Heb 5:5–6), the Son is appointed to be the priest who, we subsequently learn, outranks all who have come before him and who serves in the real sanctuary in heaven.

Conclusion

I have proposed that one may consider the language of Hebrews 1:2–4 and especially God's words in 1:5–14 in light of heavenly revelations in Jewish apocalyptic literature. The mechanics of this revelation certainly differ from what one normally finds in the apocalyptic tradition—there is no description of a vision, nor is there an angelic spokesman or heavenly tour guide—yet, there clearly is the disclosure of heavenly things that could not otherwise be known to humans. If we indeed have an example of apocalyptic revelation here, perhaps there is no journey of ascent so as not to compete with the author's "faith as journey" motif that is so prominent later in the Hebrews. Perhaps a more explicit revelatory framework is lacking in Hebrews because of the nature of this text itself—it is written to exhort its audience toward faithfulness, and the focus is on what may be known of Jesus to this end and the

32. Michael E. Stone, "Apocalyptic Literature," in *Jewish Writings of the Second Temple Period*, ed. Michael E. Stone, CRINT 2.2 (Assen: Van Gorcum, 1984), 383–441, esp. 428–29 (cf. 390–91).

33. Note the different assessment by Barnard, though he also recognizes the role of rhetoric in the passage (*Mysticism of Hebrews*, 220): "Heb 1:5–13 . . . is neither an apocalypse nor an account of mystical experience, but there is an implicit claim to knowledge of heavenly realities, which points to the role of mystical experience, and the motifs that are engaged point to mystical concerns. . . . [The passage] (like so much of Hebrews) represents the intersection of experience, reflection and rhetoric. . . . [It] is the result of an ultimately unrecoverable combination of mystical experiences of the risen Jesus, interpreted within a matrix of Jewish apocalyptic mysticism, expressed with the vocabulary of the Jewish Scriptures, for the purpose of rousing a discouraged audience to remember and reinvigorate their devotion to, and experience of, the risen Jesus."

proper response to this on behalf of the audience.[34] Or perhaps the author thought emphasis on his own ecstatic experiences (if such occurred) might detract from or muddle the communal emphasis evident elsewhere throughout the text. Ultimately, what matters most is that the author can reveal the heavenly words of God. The power of the message is strengthened when God's own heavenly testimony and validation—re-presenting Scripture in the very mouth of God—can be used to explain and affirm the identity and mission of the Son who is also the great heavenly high priest.

34. Compare the language on the function of an apocalypse that Adela Yarbro Collins suggested should be added to the definition of the genre drafted in *Semeia* 14 (1979): "intended to interpret present, earthly circumstances in light of the supernatural world and of the future, and to influence both the understanding and the behavior of the audience by means of divine authority." See Adela Yarbro Collins, "Introduction," *Semeia* 36 (1986): 1–11, esp. 7. I am indebted to Benjamin Reynolds for this observation. Note also David Aune's discussion of the threefold function of apocalypses (written especially with Revelation in view): "they legitimate the message through the appeal to transcendent authority by the author (i.e., it is from God), they create a literary surrogate of the author's revelatory experience for readers or hearers (i.e., God speaks to the modern reader just as he spoke to John), and they motivate the recipients to modify their views and behaviors in conformity with transcendent perspectives (i.e., they demand changed behavior)." See his chapters titled "Understanding Jewish and Christian Apocalyptic" (1–12, esp. 2) and "The Apocalypse of John and the Problem of Genre" (39–65; reprinted from *Semeia* 36) in David E. Aune, *Apocalypticism, Prophecy, and Magic in Early Christianity*, WUNT 199 (Tübingen: Mohr Siebeck, 2006).

15

James and Apocalyptic Wisdom

Mariam Kamell Kovalishyn

When one looks at definitions of "apocalyptic" literature, such as given by John J. Collins and the Society of Biblical Literature genre project in 1979, James does not fit.[1] In fact, there is very little about James that would lead one to tag it with the label "apocalyptic" on an initial reading. There is no visionary experience, no "otherworldly" mediator, no "divine authority" who helps to interpret the supernatural world for the author to gain perspective on earthly events. In James, we have no sense of a journey to an otherworldly realm where true reality is unveiled for the reader. Instead, we have practical wisdom for life in *this* world. Although Aune observes that "apocalypses can be broadly characterized as *protest literature*,"[2] other than the feisty start to chapter 5, the subsequent text counsels *endurance*—at surface, the acceptance of the status quo, anything but a protest. James is, in many ways, anything but apocalyptic, whether in form or content.

There are two threads, however, that should be considered before we rule out James in a discussion of apocalyptic literature. First, wisdom may function as an intermediary between

1. See Frederick J. Murphy, *Apocalypticism in the Bible and Its World* (Grand Rapids: Baker, 2012), 6.
2. David E. Aune, *Apocalypticism, Prophecy, and Magic in Early Christianity: Collected Essays* (Grand Rapids: Baker Academic, 2008), 3.

God and his people, teaching them how to live according to God's ways and revealed by God to those who ask for it. Second, the text appears to divide the audience between the righteous and the wicked, the peaceful and the violent, the wise and the fools, the merciful and the unmerciful. Accompanying that dualism is the very imminent sense of God's judgment, which will formalize these two categories with reward or punishment. While not arguing that James is an apocalypse, it has unquestionably been influenced by the apocalyptic worldview. We may find a surprising parallel in the Epistle of Enoch, part of the undisputedly apocalyptic text 1 Enoch, which is mainly "moral teaching which has an eschatological emphasis."[3]

It is worth considering the breadth of scope for the term "apocalyptic." For instance, John J. Collins observes that at times, the apocalyptic "worldview could also come to expression in other genres, that were not directly reports of visions or otherworldly journeys."[4] This may be exemplified in the development of the themes of wisdom and judgment in James. Likewise, characteristics given by Klaus Koch of apocalyptic eschatology, particularly the "acute expectation of the fulfillment of divine promises" (see Jas 2:12 and its μέλλοντες κρίνεσθαι; 5:9 and its ὁ κριτὴς πρὸ τῶν θυρῶν ἕστηκεν) and "salvation proceeding from God" (see Jas 2:12–13; 4:11–12 and its one lawgiver; 5:11–12) resonate strongly with this epistle.[5] Because of the widespread influence of the apocalyptic worldview on the literature of the Hellenistic period, it is legitimate to discuss the *worldview* as it affected the writing of the Epistle of James and New Testament wisdom, and indeed, we find it is not amiss.[6]

Wisdom as an Otherworldly Mediator

Let us first examine the role that Wisdom plays in this epistle. There are places in James where σοφία takes on a bit of a personified character, much like she is first presented in Proverbs 1–8. The first glimpse we catch of σοφία is in James 1:5, referencing to the need to ask for wisdom before moving to discuss faith. However, the role it plays there is potentially more than the simple verse reference may suggest. In context, verse 5 stands at the end of the progression of verses 2–4, which are, in many ways, the goal of all wisdom literature: a life lived "mature and

3. Michael E. Stone, "Apocalyptic Literature," in *Jewish Writings of the Second Temple Period: Apocrypha, Pseudepigrapha, Qumran, Sectarian Writings, Philo, Josephus*, ed. Michael E. Stone, CRINT 2 (Assen: Van Gorcum; Philadelphia: Fortress Press, 1984), 405. Patrick Hartin, *James*, SP 14 (Collegeville, MN: Liturgical, 2003), 252–54, sees very close parallels between James and the Epistle of Enoch.
4. John J. Collins, "From Prophecy to Apocalypticism: The Expectation of the End," in *The Continuum History of Apocalypticism*, ed. Bernard McGinn, John J. Collins, and Stephen J. Stein (New York and London: Continuum, 2003), 85.
5. As listed in Stone, "Apocalyptic," 393. He cites Klaus Koch, *The Rediscovery of Apocalyptic* (London: SCM, 1972), 28–33, for a summary of the features that characterize "apocalypticism."
6. Stone, "Apocalyptic," 388, supports that there are similarities, but warns the influence probably does not run the other way. "Some lines of connection may be discerned between the apocalypses and the wisdom literature. The sapiential character of the stories in Daniel has been emphasized and implications drawn from the utilization of a wisdom figure like Daniel as the pseudepigraphic author of an epistle. Von Rad's claim that the origin of apocalyptic is in Wisdom alone, however, seems extreme" (referencing Gerhard von Rad, *Theologie Des Alten Testaments, Band II* [Munich: Chr. Kaiser, 1960], 319ff).

complete, lacking in nothing." Immediately after setting that goal, the author continues with, "*but if* you lack wisdom" (1:5), wherein the clear implication is that one cannot attain to the goal without wisdom. This, of course, is not controversial, for even when Wisdom first appears in Proverbs 1:20–33, she makes it clear that those who reject her will fail to be able to please God. Dale Allison observes that "a link between 'wisdom' and 'perfection' was probably traditional. . . . wisdom enables one to endure patiently, which in turn leads to a 'perfected work.'"[7] However, this reality sets up the contrast between the righteous and wicked, as we will see below. Instead of wisdom for life and rewards solely in the here-and-now, James's wisdom has both present and eschatological implications.

Wisdom is only possessed by those who αἰτείτω παρὰ τοῦ διδόντος θεοῦ ("ask the giving God"). This way of posing of the question already shows influence of the apocalyptic genre, wherein the visionary would plead for God's revelation, and in response to their fervency, a vision would be granted. In the apocalyptic approach, the supplicant must already be on the path of holiness as they approach (think of the fasting and purification described in 4 Ezra 5). This development in wisdom literature has been foreshadowed in Sirach and the Wisdom of Solomon (see Sir 39:5; Wis 8:21, 16:28).[8] In James, wisdom is given to the one who already seeks to have the correct perspective on trials (although wisdom enhances their ability to understand this perspective), and commits to asking God to give it to them (πίστις).[9] One cannot expect to receive from a God one does not believe gives.

We should read the rest of chapter one in light of the necessity of wisdom for maturity. If one cannot be τέλειοι καὶ ὁλόκληροι (1:4) without wisdom, and if, as some have suggested, 1:4 is a possible thesis for the letter,[10] then chapter 1 continues the introduction by expanding the meaning of wisdom's τέλος. Dan McCartney notes that "the maturing of the believer [in 1:4] is simply becoming what God intends that a human being should be. In other words, to be mature is to be what Jesus was as a perfect human being, a goal both prescribed and made possible for believers of Jesus" (cf. Matt 5:48).[11] In James, wisdom is the key mediator necessary for this

7. Dale C. Allison, *A Critical and Exegetical Commentary on the Epistle of James*, ICC (New York: Bloomsbury T&T Clark, 2013), 156.
8. M. Gilbert ("Wisdom Literature," in *Jewish Writings of the Second Temple Period: Apocrypha, Pseudepigrapha, Qumran, Sectarian Writings, Philo, Josephus*, ed. Michael E. Stone, CRINT 2 [Assen: Van Gorcum; Philadelphia: Fortress Press, 1984], 294) observes that in Sirach, "the relation between wisdom and the one who seeks it [is love]. . . . Perseverance and tenacity are required. . . . He must also be a man of prayer. From morning on, he turns to the Lord and entreats him (39:5; see Isa 50:4–5; Wis 16:28). This will make him pleasing to God." Likewise, in the Wisdom of Solomon, "Wisdom is to be had only by begging it of God, [so the author] decides to compose his prayer."
9. πίστις here is not a vending-machine coin by which one can manipulate God into giving a person whatever one asks. It is necessary that one not doubt God's character as "the giving God," who gives to his people the wisdom they need to endure the trials they face.
10. See, for instance, Luke L. Cheung, *The Genre, Composition and Hermeneutics of the Epistle of James* (Milton Keynes/Waynesboro, GA: Paternoster, 2003), 67, who calls all of 1:2–27 "the 'programme of perfection' with the author stating his overarching concern right at the beginning of the work."
11. Dan McCartney, *James*, BECNT (Grand Rapids: Baker, 2009), 87.

transformation, and only by the generous gift of wisdom acting as an otherworldly mediator does a person come to know and follow in the path that leads to perfection. Wisdom in some ways, then, functions much as the intermediary does in more "traditional" apocalyptic texts.

It is worth noting that already in the epistle, we have hints of eschatological judgment, as Allison concludes, citing "Klein, who shows that elsewhere in early Christian literature, ἔργον and ἔργον τέλειον refer to a person's lifework as judged by God."[12] Peter Davids adds that we can see "a pattern of eschatological perfection in James."[13] He finds support from Mussner, who enthusiastically states "Der ‚Perfecktionismus' des Jak ist ein eschatologischer!"[14] These few introductory verses introduce the theme of eschatological perfection, of becoming τέλειον, which presumes a judgment issued by God. And in order to attain this perfect state, one requires the mediation of wisdom, who comes from God.

The next use of σοφία/σοφός language occurs in 3:13–18. Prior to this, however, we have a hint of wisdom language in 1:17, where wisdom may be the ultimate "good gift" coming down from heaven. This connection is supported by the three uses of ἄνωθεν in James. The word first appears in 1:17 in connection with the "good gifts", while in 3:15, 17, the adverb is paired with wisdom (3:17, ἄνωθεν σοφία).[15] The author emphasizes wisdom's *place of origin*, namely, sent from God as an intermediary to reveal his will and his character.[16] The Epistle of James seeks to train people into exhibiting very character of God through its ethical teaching,[17] but it is God who empowers this transformation through the gift of wisdom, which both reveals his character *and* enables people to live accordingly. The description of wisdom as "coming down from above" (ἡ δὲ ἄνωθεν σοφία) reminds us of wisdom's source and abode. With that in mind, this whole section of 3:13–17 almost echoes 1 Enoch 42:1–3:

> Wisdom did not find a place where she might dwell, so her dwelling was in the heavens. Wisdom went forth to dwell among the sons of men, but she did not find a dwelling. Wisdom returned to her place, and sat down in the midst of the angels. Iniquity went forth from her chambers, those whom she did not seek she found, and she dwelt among them like rain in a desert and dew in a thirsty land.[18]

Whereas wisdom was not made welcome in the people of the land, and so resides in heaven (cf.

12. Allison, *James*, 154.
13. Peter H. Davids, *James*, NIGNT (Grand Rapids: Eerdmans, 1982), 70.
14. Franz Mußner, *Der Jakobusbrief*, HThKNT 13 (Freiberg: Herder, 1964), 67. See Allison, *James*, 154: "One concurs then with Mußner, 67: James 1.2–4 should be set against the background of eschatological reward. The perfection for which one strives in the present will be realized in the end."
15. Indeed, note the remarkable parallel description of the gifts ἄνωθέν . . . καταβαῖνον in 1:17, and of wisdom ἄνωθέν κατερχομένη in 3:15.
16. Cf. Ben Sira, of which Gilbert, "Wisdom Literature," 293, notes, ""Man's wisdom comes from God and not from man himself. But wisdom, which is not a purely human quality, abides in God."
17. See Mariam J. Kamell, "The Implications of Grace for the Ethics of James," *Biblica* 92 (2011): 274–87.
18. Translation from George W. E. Nickelsburg and and James C. VanderKam, *1 Enoch: The Hermeneia Translation* (Minneapolis: Fortress Press, 2012).

ἄνωθεν in Jas, 3:13, 17), iniquity made itself at home on earth (cf. Jas 3:15, the false "wisdom" that is ἐπίγειος, ψυχική, δαιμονιώδης). In 1 Enoch 42, a personified Wisdom sets out to "dwell" among humans. She provides a different sort of Mediator than a typical apocalyptic guide who comes from heaven for brief intervals to instruct a single visionary; Wisdom, rather, sought to dwell among those whom she would instruct, but she is denied a place. And in her place, instead, people find a guide in "iniquity," who guides people along an alternative "wisdom," much like the "earthly" and "unspiritual wisdom" of James 3:15 misguides people to live according to its false path.[19] The story briefly told in 1 Enoch 42:1–2 could well have found exposition in James 3:13–17, where the two guides of life and their sources are laid forth.

Wisdom's heavenly origin can be seen in the description of her nature in 3:17: πρῶτον μὲν ἁγνή ἐστιν, ἔπειτα εἰρηνική, ἐπιεικής, εὐπειθής, μεστὴ ἐλέους καὶ καρπῶν ἀγαθῶν, ἀδιάκριτος, ἀνυπόκριτος.[20] Dibelius was uncertain why purity was highlighted as the first of the list,[21] but most other scholars agree with Ropes that the other adjectives "stand over against ἁγνή, the quality from which they all proceed."[22] Intriguingly, the other text from wisdom literature noted for having an eschatological direction to wisdom, the Wisdom of Solomon, also focuses on purity. Gilbert observes, "Wisdom's purity is absolute, it penetrates all things and only seeks to do good. To justify these attributions, the author shows how wisdom is a reflection, a mirror, a perfect image of God."[23] Emphasis on wisdom's purity appears most in correlation with calls to maturity and perfection in light of eschatological judgment.

Wisdom comes from God, and only that which comes from God can be called wisdom, illustrated in the brilliant way the author never once names the anti-wisdom of James 3:14–15. He fails to provide a noun, forcing the reader to fill in the gap.[24] Wisdom trains people in her fruit (3:18), and many of those listed traits, whether chosen simply for alliterative affect or not, summarize the desired traits throughout James, and even wisdom literature more broadly: non-hypocritical (speaking and acting with honesty and transparency), peace-making, non-judgmental, and of course, full of good works and mercy. Wisdom is the ultimate mediator between God and his people, so strong that Kirk argues that "Wisdom plays exactly the same

19. Leo G. Perdue, *Wisdom and Creation* (Eugene, OR: Wipf & Stock, 2009), 315, notes the parallel between 1 Enoch 42:1–2 and Wisdom 14, particularly regarding the "failure to understand and recognize the power and knowledge of God in matters of providence" due to the outworking of idolatry (cf. "false wisdom" and "iniquity" in James and 1 Enoch respectively).

20. Cf. the list of twenty-one of Wisdom's attributes in Wis 7:22–23. Given that apocalypticism tends to prioritize numbers and symbols, the observation of Richard Bauckham, *James: Wisdom of James, Disciple of Jesus the Sage* (London: Routledge, 1999), 73, is particularly relevant: "Seven is the number of perfection or completeness, which is also why the 'wisdom from above' is summed up in seven attributes in 3:17."

21. "The priority given to 'pure' (ἁγνή) does not fit well with the train of thought": M. Dibelius, *James: A Commentary on the Epistle of James*, trans. Michael A. Williams, Hermeneia (Philadelphia: Fortress, 1976), 152.

22. J. H. Ropes, *A Critical and Exegetical Commentary on the Epistle of St. James*, ICC (Edinburgh: T. & T. Clark, 1916), 250.

23. Gilbert, "Wisdom," 303.

24. Jas 3:15: *οὐκ ἔστιν αὕτη ἡ σοφία ἄνωθεν κατερχομένη.*

part as Paul's 'fruit of the Spirit,'"[25] and Hartin observes in a more nuanced manner that "both wisdom and the spirit are divine in origin; and both wisdom and the spirit produce effects in the life of the believer."[26]

While this is not the place to argue the nuances of the overlap between wisdom and the Holy Spirit in James, it is worth noting it and recalling the personification of Wisdom as was begun from Proverbs onward. With Gilbert, then, we ask, "How is this personification of wisdom to be understood? This is related to the broader question of intermediaries between God and the world."[27] While it is impossible—and impractical—to make σοφία in James function identically to the intermediaries in traditional apocalyptic literature, it is significant that James very clearly highlights that one *cannot* understand God's will and ways without his wisdom, which comes only from his presence.[28] Rowland notes, the knowledge that is gained "is not the product of human observation,"[29] but in contrast to traditional apocalyptic paradigms, neither is it brought by an otherworldly mediator who returns to heaven immediately after the message is imparted. In contrast, Σοφία is given "from above" with every intention of remaining among the people she instructs. Σοφία alone, however, teaches God's way of perfection, and she is given to those who pray and seek her, as introduced right at the start of the epistle.

The Merciful, Endurance, and the Eschaton

One other key element that should be at the forefront of any comparison of James with typical apocalyptic themes is that of the future judgment. Very often, both wisdom and apocalyptic literature divide their audience into two groups: the righteous and the wicked, categorized by various key group identity markers, a division made in preparation of the coming (imminent) judgment. James, as well, sees the people in these polar dichotomies. Whether it is the humble versus the arrogant rich, those who endure versus those who give way to temptation, or the merciful versus those who refuse to show mercy, they each should be able to recognize themselves and their coming fates dependent upon their actions. The path of wisdom, of course, is to choose the correct actions, particularly those of mercy. The need to act with mercy depends on

25. J. Andrew Kirk, "The Meaning of Wisdom in James: Examination of a Hypothesis," *NTS* 16, no. 1 (1969): 24–38 (27).

26. Hartin, *James*, 103–4.

27. Gilbert, "Wisdom Literature," 287. He continues, "This figure of Wisdom is a purely literary personification according to some, which is a minimalistic view. Others have spoken of a hypostasis, a vague notion, while yet others speak of a personification of the order of the world, the source of which is in God. Finally, others speak of the presence of God in the world and among men" (287–88).

28. Todd C. Penner, *The Epistle of James and Eschatology: Re-reading an Ancient Christian Letter*, JSNTSup 121 (Sheffield: Sheffield Academic, 1996), 223n1, argues "that if one takes the eschatological framework of James seriously, then this wisdom also takes on an eschatological orientation, as it becomes the criterion for the purification of the community which is a prerequisite for blessing at the time of judgment. The closest parallel to James's understanding of wisdom is that found in 1 Enoch 1–5."

29. Christopher Rowland and Christopher R. A. Morray-Jones, *The Mystery of God: Early Jewish Mysticism and the New Testament*, CRINT 12 (Leiden: Brill, 2009), 18.

recognizing the eschatological perspective of James's wisdom, a perspective that follows very closely on Jesus's teaching, particularly as represented in Matthew.[30] As Richard Hays observes,

> in Matthew, eschatology becomes a powerful *warrant* for moral behavior. The motivation for obedience to God is repeatedly grounded in the rewards and punishments that await everyone at the final judgment. . . . God's ultimate judgment of all will be based upon *concrete works of love and mercy*, in accordance with the teachings of Jesus. Confessional orthodoxy counts for nothing unless it is accompanied by obedience to the will of God. The kingdom of God is characterized by compassionate outreach to the weak and needy.[31]

Jesus emphasizes how people were to live in their communities. As one receives mercy, so one acts with mercy. This is perhaps the strongest connection between the teachings in James and those of Jesus in Matthew.

The crucial text to consider here is James 2:12–13, an elusive saying concluding a difficult section. Is James teaching full Torah-obedience in 2:8-11, and if not, what else can he mean with his argument in 2:10 about being accountable for the whole?[32] This is not the place to analyze those arguments, but rather to identify 2:12–13 as the compact hinge between the arguments against partiality in 2:1–11 and for merciful actions in 2:14–26. Of crucial importance in this chapter (and book), 2:12–13 provides the proper eschatological understanding of how judgment works.

First, the author presents judgment as a certain reality that each person will face. In chapter 2, judgment is predicted, and when read with the damning indictment of the prideful rich in 5:1–6, the picture becomes clear of a judgment that includes every person. More startling, perhaps, the judgment appears to be based upon how one acts, whether in mercy and justice for the poor, or in arrogance and oppression of the less fortunate.[33] It should be noted that faith in God has already been stressed as essential, and one might quote the author of Hebrews that "without faith it is impossible to please God" (11:6). In James, one cannot obtain wisdom without faith, and therefore cannot please God. Faith places a person into a receptive position regarding God's will, trusting that God's will for his people is for their good.[34] However, to fail

30. See, particularly, Matt 6:14–15; 7:1–2; 25:31–46.

31. Richard B. Hays, *The Moral Vision of the New Testament: Community, Cross, New Creation* (San Francisco: HarperSanFrancisco, 1996), 106, 109, emphasis original. He adds, "It would not be correct to say that these stories provide only *warrants* for obedience to God; they also define significant ethical *norms* having to do primarily with just and merciful treatment of others and with responsible use of property. . . . The parable of the sheep and the goats, with its powerful portrayal of care for the needy as the basic criterion for God's eschatological judgment of human deeds, has had a powerful impact on the church's imagination; the story reinforces Matthew's earlier emphasis on mercy as the hallmark of the kingdom of God" (107).

32. See, for instance, Allison, *James*, on 4:10–14; Sophie Laws, *A Commentary on the Epistle of James*, BNTC (London: A. & C. Black, 1980), 111–12, both of whom point to the clearly Jewish background of this method of argumentation. For further nuanced discussion, see Cheung, *Genre*, 121–24.

33. Scot McKnight (*The Letter of James*, NICNT [Grand Rapids, Mich.: Eerdmans, 2011], 219) observes, "The final judgment for James, as for Jesus (e.g., Matt 12:36; 16:27; 25:31–46) and Paul (1 Cor 3:10–15; 2 Cor 5:1–10), will be established on the basis of both what the messianic community says (Jas 1:19, 26; 3:1–12; 4:11–16; 5:12) and what it does (1:27; 2;1–26; 4:1–10; 5:1–6)."

to live according to God's wisdom brings one under judgment. Wisdom, as mediator of God's will for how His people should live, teaches that one must live a life of active mercy and hospitality (ch. 2), with generous and humble speech (chs. 3–4), and endure even in situations of oppression (ch. 5). Appropriately enough, then, the warning in 2:12 begins with οὕτως λαλεῖτε καὶ οὕτως ποιεῖτε, "so *speak* and so *act*." Allison notes that this phrase "underlines the comprehensive scope of his statement."[35] How one speaks (cf. particularly 3:1–4:12) and how one acts (cf. particularly 1:22–2:26) are of vital importance. While culminating the argument against favoritism, it also "foreshadows the emphasis of the next section, verses 14–26, where words without deeds are empty."[36]

Second, in James, as in apocalyptic thought, the coming judgment provides a source of hope for the oppressed.[37] The most obvious place is in 5:1–6, a rhetorical tour de force where the "language and style are reminiscent of the prophets. . . . aimed at the hearers/readers rather than the rich themselves, who act as a foil for the message James is communicating."[38] By providing a public announcement of the punishment coming to those who are oppressing them, James provides a strong incentive toward faithfulness despite the oppression. Better to suffer here and be vindicated, than have "fattened your hearts in a day of slaughter" (5:5). The vivid warning of judgment reminds the reader of scenes from the Epistle of Enoch, for instance in 1 Enoch 98:6–16, where the sinners are warned that their deeds have been seen and recorded (98:6–8; cf. Jas 5:4), and that "[all things have been made ready] for you for the day of destruction" (ὅ[τι ἠτοίμασται] ὑμῖν εἰς ἡμέραν ἀπωλείας, 98:10; cf. Jas 5:5), and so on.[39] The warnings in James 5 are as equally dire and vivid as those given in the epistle or in other apocalyptic texts, such as Revelation, where judgment is carried out on those who chose to oppress the poor. Aune observes that the popularity of one medieval history of philosophy, "based in part on the Revelation of John, was a response to conflicts between the poor and the rich, the worldly and the spiritual, which tested the church of his day."[40] The threat of future judgment provides hope in the present to those who suffer.

Apocalyptic literature, in imaging the protest by the oppressed,[41] refuses to allow the *current*

34. So, for instance, D. Edmond Hiebert, *The Epistle of James: Tests of a Living Faith* (Chicago: Moody, 1979), organized his commentary around the various tests of faith, seeing that as the central theme of James.
35. Allison, *James*, 417.
36. Ibid.
37. Rowland and Morray-Jones, *Mystery of God*, 16, observe, "The detailed demonstration of divine foreknowledge of human plight and of the divine plan for human history could enable a beleaguered religious group to have confidence in its traditional affirmations and hopes. The reader thereby sees the totality of human history from the divine perspective, so ensuring that the inevitable preoccupation with the present plight does not detract from belief in God's saving purposes."
38. Hartin, *James*, 226, 235.
39. Pedrito U. Maynard-Reid, *Poverty and Wealth in James* (Maryknoll, NY: Orbis, 1987; repr. Eugene, OR: Wipf & Stock, 2004), 96: "The apocalyptic threat of judgment upon the rich in James recalls even more strikingly the intertestamental apocalyptic ideas. One cannot fail to observe the striking resemblance in language and thought between James and Ethiopian Enoch."
40. Aune, *Apocalypticism*, 10–11. Joachim of Fiore, ca. 1132–1202 CE.

social order to stand.[42] Murphy, in distinguishing sapiential from apocalyptic literature, notes, "While apocalypticism focuses on eschatology and cosmological knowledge, wisdom more frequently concerns itself with the everyday life of an ordinary person or of a member of the upper class."[43] It is intriguing that, while concerned with "the everyday life," James shows none of the elitism that lurks in Ben Sira.[44] Instead, Murphy concludes for James that "The basic apocalyptic worldview is taken for granted."[45] Those who proudly depend on their wealth while failing to remember that all of life is a gift from God and that they will be held accountable, they will face devastating judgment (Jas 4:13–5:6).[46]

This revealed reality, however, brings comfort to those who struggle to make sense of the oppression they are forced to endure. Of this challenge and comfort, Gilbert writes of the Wisdom of Solomon what could be written of any apocalypse:

> the life of the faithful is itself a paradox. Good men are suffering, they are childless instead of being blessed with children, dying in the prime of youth instead of aging with dignity—such paradoxes! Confronted with this sort of situation—which perpetually recurs—the author affirms that God created the world for life, that man was made as an incorruptible being and that the just will enjoy immortality with God, while the ungodly, by refusing all thought of an afterlife, make a pact with death, spiritual death, a pact which will come into effect at the time of God's "visitation", at the end of this earthly life.[47]

In James, three groups find encouragement: the desperately poor (the πτωχός), shamed in the assembly (2:1–4) and ignored in their need (2:14–16); the oppressed, hauled to court (2:6) or wages withheld (5:3–4); and the humble (the ταπεινός), who recognize their place before God and are consistently promised that they will be raised from their place of humiliation (1:9; 4:6–7). Each of these groups finds in the text that *they* are on the side of right (2:5).

With the comfort of certain judgment for the oppressors comes the possibility of endurance. The theme of endurance frames the epistle, from its essential role in attaining the state of

41. Aune, *Apocalypticism*, 3: "apocalypses can be broadly characterized as *protest literature*. That is, they typically represent the perspective of an oppressed minority."

42. N. T. Wright, in his vast *Paul and the Faithfulness of God* (Minneapolis: Fortress, 2013) appears to want to limit "apocalyptic" to the political/social realm, such as in his sections dealing with Paul, the Gospel, and Rome (e.g., chs. 5, 12), but he is absolutely correct that the Gospel has significant implications for our social order: "If what is coming to birth in the God-given new day is a world of love and justice, then it behooves followers of Jesus to live by, and in accordance with, that love and justice in the present, so as to be ready for the day when it comes" (1303–4).

43. Murphy, *Apocalypticism*, 20.

44. E.g., Sir 38:24: "The wisdom of the scribe depends on the opportunity of leisure, only the one who has little business can become wise."

45. Murphy, *Apocalyptic*, 373.

46. See Mariam J. Kamell, "The Economics of Humility: The Rich and the Humble in James," in *Engaging Economics: New Testament Scenarios and Early Christian Reception*, ed. Bruce W. Longenecker and Kelly Leibengood. Grand Rapids: Eerdmans, 2009): "Ultimately, humility or humiliation will come to every person, whether rich or poor. The question is whether one chooses to humble oneself (4:10) or be humbled (1:10)" (175).

47. Gilbert, "Wisdom," 309.

becoming τέλειοι καὶ ὁλόκληροι in 1:3–4 and the eschatological blessing of 1:12, to its return to prominence in the conclusion of 5:7–11. Endurance in James is motivated entirely by the perspective offered by the Mediator Wisdom. In chapter 1, one can endure because one has the end in sight, both currently in terms of attaining the goal of "perfection" (1:4), or eschatologically as seen in 1:12, when those who endure because of their love of God discover λήμψεται τὸν στέφανον τῆς ζωῆς. In the latter, all the pieces of this promise should be kept together. In 1:12 and 2:5, we have startling promises made in both instances "to those who love him" (τοῖς ἀγαπῶσιν αὐτόν). These verses are not carte blanche promises simply to those who endure or who lack possessions, but to the ones described as *loving him*, God makes dramatic promises of vindication. And so they can endure, because they know "he who promised is faithful" (Heb 10:23; cf. Jas 1:5–8, 17–18), and that life will be their reward (cf. Gilbert's observation about Wisdom of Solomon above; 1 Enoch 104:1–5).

The examples of endurance given in chapter 5, however, teach us what James means by ὑπομονή and μακροθυμία.[48] While often people categorize endurance as a passive virtue, a simple "waiting" for the situation to change, in traditional wisdom style, James gives two models to emulate. First are "the prophets who spoke in the name of the Lord." Many of these suffered greatly in the course of their faithfulness to God's call. But often, they suffered *because* of the message they were given to speak, and yet, speak they did. They spoke against oppression and abuse of the poor, against the idolatry of wealth, against a social order that turned a blind eye to the widows and orphans in their midst. The prophets *spoke* the word of God faithfully into a hostile situation, and because of that, they had to *endure* the hostile world's response. They are not a model of passive suffering, but of active boldness pronouncing a different reality from the one we see.[49] Likewise, for all that the Testament of Job paints Job as patiently and quietly suffering without grumble, the canonical Job complains verbosely about the injustice of his situation.[50] But, Job complains *to* God, pronouncing his faith in God's justice with every sentence. He raises his complaints to heaven, and eventually, heaven responds. Neither of these models teaches us that endurance simply is to grit one's teeth and be passive. But both models *are* marked by their faith in God, that crucial character from James 1:6–8, dependent on Wisdom to reveal the heavenly perspective on reality.

48. Contra Hartin, *James*, 248, who sees the ὑπομονή word-group as capturing "the nuance of passively enduring something," it appears the two terms are nearly interchangeable in James. Cf. McKnight, *James*, 405: "There is one major weakness to this view: James seems to use the terms synonymously in our paragraph." So also McCartney, *James*, 243; Allison, *James*, 696–97.

49. Elsa Tamez, *The Scandalous Message of James: Faith Without Works is Dead* (New York: Crossroad, 2002), 31, calls this a "militant patience." She is frustrated with scholars like Davids (*James*, 181), who posits that "Patience, not resistance, is the virtue of the poor," and who thus fail to develop a nuanced understanding of what patience/endurance might entail in James. Cf. Walter Brueggemann, *The Prophetic Imagination*, 2nd ed. (Minneapolis: Fortress Press, 2001).

50. It may be our desire to find a "passive" model of endurance that sends scholars to find the background to this exemplar in Testament of Job, rather than seeing how the Job does illustrate faithful endurance.

Finally, the future judgment is anticipated to come at any moment. All through the epistle, the language hints at this. The rich will "wither away" in the midst of their busy life (1:10); the repetition of the word "dead" through 2:14–26; the tongue as a "deadly poison" (3:8); the warning of coming judgment by the one "who is able to save and to destroy" (4:12); the warning that life is "a mist that appears for a little while and then vanishes" (4:14); the rant against the wealthy in 5:1–6, warned that they are in the day of slaughter. But in two places, the eschatological imminence is most emphatic—in 2:12 and 5:8–9.

First, we return to the crux verses of 2:12–13, wherein the audience is warned to speak and act as ones for whom judgment is imminent (μέλλοντες). Judgment day is nigh for all, and will be based on how one has lived, most notably in relation to mercy. In the elusive *lex talionis* of 2:13a,[51] the author warns the audience that they will face a "merciless" judgment if they themselves have failed to show mercy—in context, to the poor in their congregations. But, κατακαυχᾶται ἔλεος κρίσεως (2:13b)! Is it human mercy that "boasts" over God's judgment and frees the defendant, or is it God's mercy that triumphs upon seeing itself reflected in human mercy? Either way, this is a triumphant promise to balance the warning in the first half, but it serves as a reminder that the hearers *must* be merciful and not show favoritism *now*, because if the judgment is imminent, how they act now will be the grounds for that judgment.

Then, in 5:8–9, we are told that ἡ παρουσία τοῦ κυρίου ἤγγικεν and ὁ κριτὴς πρὸ τῶν θυρῶν ἕστηκεν. With yet another imperative, James commands, μακροθυμήσατε! The inspiration to follow arises from the confidence of the imminence of the end. Indeed, as Mußner concludes, "Auch seine Ethik kennt eine eschatologische Motivation,"[52] or, as Hartin describes, "the eschatological dimension acts as the motivation behind all the wisdom admonitions. This motivation envisages either judgment or salvation."[53] The *parousia* appears to refer to "the arrival of Messiah Jesus in judgment," as "reinforced by the next verse."[54] This language is nearly universally understood to be eschatological, referring to the coming of the Lord in final judgment. Thus, Knowling concludes, "This nearness of the Judge should prevent the brethren from anticipating His judgment of their complaints against their neighbours, and so taking upon themselves the office of judge, as was the case with the friends of Job."[55] Knowling's interpretation neatly

51. Allison (*James*, 420), notes that this is "the obverse of the eschatological *lex talionis*, in Mt 5.7," but suggests Matt 18:21–35; 25:31–46 as equally good parallels, as well as 1 Enoch 27:3–7; Sir 28.1, 4; Testament of Zebulun 5:3; 8:1, etc., from the Jewish tradition.

52. As Mußner, *Jakobusbrief*, 210, argues against those who posit the epistle is a late writing and lacks eschatological urgency: "Die Ethik des Jak-Briefes findet also ihre Motive weithin in der Eschatologie und nicht etwa in einer ‚naturalichen' Vollendungslehre wie die stoische Ethik, und dies trotz mancher ‚Parallelen' zu deren ethischen Forderungen. . . . Die Eschatologie unseres Briefes steht sogar in großer Nähe zu jener Jesu (genau wie die Ethik). . . . Und auch sein ‚Existenzverständnis' ist weithin bestimmt durch seine eschatologische Verkündigung."

53. Hartin, *James*, 251.

54. McCartney, *James*, 241.

55. R. J. Knowling, *The Epistle of St. James* (London: Methuen & Co. Ltd, 1922), 131. He adds, "The language here has a striking parallel in *Apocalypse of Baruch*, xlvii. 39: 'for the judge will come, and will not tarry.'"

ties the warnings against complaining against one another in 5:9 with that of slandering one another and consequent warning of judgment in 4:11.

These warnings of the judge's imminence in 5:9–10 are paired with the description of God from Exodus 34:6, when the Lord passed before Moses and declared his name as "a God merciful and gracious, slow to anger, and abounding in steadfast love and faithfulness." In James, judgment is always paired with mercy: 2:12–13; 4:11–12; 5:1–11, 19–20, because that is God's character.[56] For that reason, God's people, his first fruit (1:18), are also expected to act with mercy. Having received God's wisdom (1:5), his every good gift (1:17), and his word implanted in them (1:21), there is no excuse for failure to act in accordance with his love for the poor and oppressed. For this reason, judgment is forewarned in 2:12 for those who choose not to act mercifully. God is judge, but he is merciful, and will judge his people according to whether they have lived mercifully as well.

One must note, however, before leaving the issue of the imminent judgment, that James does not portray a strictly present-future paradigm. While apocalyptic literature does indeed often present an otherworldly judgment (see again, Epistle of Enoch), judgment does not exist solely on a future timeframe. Perhaps the clearest contrast that exemplifies how James blends future and present as well as heavenly and earthly comes in the two beatitudes of chapter 1. In James 1:12, the promise is clearly future: "Blessed is anyone who endures temptation. Such a one has stood the test and will receive the crown of life that the Lord has promised to those who love him." There is fairly strong agreement that the "crown of life" is an epexegetical genitive, better translated the "crown which is life," so life is the prize won at the end of endurance's journey. In this, we find the continuance of divine revelation: "The mystery of the reign of God is that the one who endures to the end will be saved."[57] A few verses later, however, the second beatitude presents the reward for obedience not as future and elsewhere, but very much in the here and now. James 1:25 promises, "But those who look into the perfect law, the law of liberty, and persevere, being not hearers who forget but doers who act—*they will be blessed in their doing* (*οὗτος μακάριος ἐν τῇ ποιήσει αὐτοῦ ἔσται*)." Faithfulness and obedience to God's law breaks down the wall between the kingdom of heaven and earth, and the eschatological blessing is proleptically found *in the actual doing*. As his people act in accordance with the Wisdom and Law of the kingdom, so they find themselves living in the blessings of the kingdom *now*.[58]

56. Cf. the historic recognition of this balance in James as shown in David B. Gowler, *James through the Centuries* (Chichester: Wiley Blackwell, 2014), 279–87.
57. Rowland and Morray-Jones, *Mystery of God*, 22.
58. Thereby fulfilling the prayer of Matt. 6:10: "Your kingdom come; your will be done; on earth as it is in heaven."

Conclusion

Throughout the book, the apocalyptic mindset permeates the Epistle of James. Although Gilbert concludes that "the Epistle of James has the appearance of a sapiential book, staying close to everyday life, and mainly addressed to Christians coming from the Jewish diaspora,"[59] that assumption must be challenged. Accordingly, Murphy concludes that James fits well within the apocalyptic tradition,[60] while Hartin argues that "Eschatology is an essential feature of this letter. It is the very air James and his hearers/readers inhale."[61] Indeed, Bauckham witnesses that "God's eschatological action, in judgment or vindication, is the criterion for judging right or wrong acts," which was "not at all foreign to the wisdom tradition, but James focuses on it to the exclusion of other features of that tradition."[62] The eschatological worldview interplays with current communal concerns, and this makes the epistle harder to categorize than one might initially suspect. Thus, we find we must ask, as Burkes did of Wisdom of Solomon:

> How then is the book to be understood? The present exercise suggests that neither "wisdom" nor "apocalypticism," as the terms are usually employed, is a sufficient description of the whole. The book seems to be sapiential in form (a series of reflections by the ranking wise man of Jewish tradition, rather than a visionary experience mediated by a supernatural being) but bridges the sapiential and apocalyptic worldviews. One way to approach such a text might be to reconsider the common notion that a literary form entails a particular worldview.[63]

While I would not wish to go so far as Penner's conclusion, his observation that "the sapiential content of James thus takes on the nuance of eschatological wisdom provided to the community which awaits the impending judgment of God" is on target.[64] Wisdom literature had always emphasized God's justice, but the location (temporal and physical) of that enactment carries a tension between the present revelation and the role of that revelation in the life of the community.

James highlights the necessity of wisdom, for no one can reach the intended goal of becoming τέλος without it. Wisdom is given by God to those who pray and seek him, comes down from his heavenly abode, and reveals God's ways to God's people. It seems accurate to understand wisdom as the necessary teacher and empowerer so that humans may be able to understand

59. Gilbert, "Wisdom," 320.

60. Murphy (*Apocalyptic*, 373): "James's basic standpoint for the poor and against the rich echoes the teaching of Jesus as well as the teaching of many Jewish and Christian apocalypses. James displays belief in demons (2:19), hell (3:6), judgment (2:13), the devil (4:7), and Christ's parousia (5:7)."

61. Hartin, *James*, 252.

62. Bauckham, *James*, 98.

63. Shannon Burkes, "Wisdom and Apocalypticism in the Wisdom of Solomon," *HTR* 95, no. 1 (2002): 21–44 (44).

64. Penner, *James and Eschatology*, 223. Examples of "traditional" wisdom literature from the era (e.g., Pseudo-Phocylides) stand out as unusual, thus highlighting how widespread the crossbreeding of wisdom and apocalyptic had become.

the way of pleasing God. As a result, wisdom becomes the necessary intermediary that teaches the correct perspective on trials, on wealth, on oppression, on endurance, on faithfulness, and on judgment and mercy. The necessity for obtaining wisdom and for acting accordingly gains momentum from the warnings of death and judgment that permeate the text (1:9–11, 12–15; 2:8–13; 3:6–9; 4:1–12, 13–17; 5:1–6, 7–12, 19–20). Indeed, there may be no theme more prominent than that of the coming judgment. As Wachob observes, however, "life in this world receives its significance from the eschatological future, but the eschatological future of those who hold Jesus' faith is determined by their present behavior. . . . Apocalyptic topics, just like wisdom and prophetic texts, are configured by James for this argumentative purpose."[65] And in the end, although we cannot minimize the influence of the eschatological worldview on the text of James, James stands as an exemplar of what we might call "apocalyptic wisdom," where the apocalyptic worldview has permeated the thinking of this early Christian sage and imbued all his practical advice with a new eschatological urgency and a renewed role for Wisdom.

65. Wesley Hiram Wachob, "The Apocalyptic Intertexture of the Epistle of James," in *The Intertexture of Apocalyptic Discourse in the New Testament*, ed. Duane F. Watson, SymS 14 (Atlanta: Society of Biblical Literature, 2002), 185.

16

Apocalypse and the Epistles of 1, 2 Peter and Jude

Chad Pierce

The more general meaning of "apocalypse" is the revelation of something that has previously been hidden—from the Greek words ἀπό ("from") and καλύπτω ("hidden"). Not surprisingly, the genre of apocalyptic literature often reveals previously hidden heavenly secrets, or at least divine secrets, to a specific group of human recipients.[1] Within 1–2 Peter and Jude, evidence of Jewish apocalyptic thought may be found in various aspects of these epistles. Each epistle reports revelation given from God about secret knowledge, mentions supernatural beings and realms, and looks forward to a consummation of time in which God's revelation will be disclosed. In addition, 1 Peter, 2 Peter, and Jude each utilize apocalyptic characteristics in order to either comfort faithful followers or encourage the proper behavior of their readers in the here and now.

1. For a general discussion of apocalypticism in early Jewish and Christian literature, see John J. Collins, *The Apocalyptic Imagination: An Introduction to Jewish Apocalyptic Literature*, 2nd ed. (Grand Rapids: Eerdmans, 1998); Lorenzo DiTommaso, "Apocalypses and Apocalypticism in Antiquity," *CurBR* 5 (2007): 235–86, 367–432; Christopher Rowland, *The Open Heaven: A Study of Apocalyptic in Judaism and Early Christianity* (New York: Crossroad, 1982).

1 Peter

While 1 Peter does not contain every aspect of traditional apocalypses, it does stress the revelation of secret knowledge.[2] First Peter includes elements of both realized and future revelations and affirms that Christ's work has already brought about something unique. The incarnation of Christ into the world, as well as its benefits, is a secret itself which has been revealed to 1 Peter's readers. And yet, the epistle also envisions and reveals secrets regarding the consummation of time, including the restoration of the faithful as well as the judgment of the wicked.[3] This work will engage 1 Peter's use of apocalyptic elements to discuss the epistle's understanding of the revealed consummation of time, which includes both present and future implications for its readers. Included in this discussion will be the author's use of the word "glory" as well as the depictions of angels. Particular emphasis will be placed on 1 Peter 3:18–22, which it will be argued serves as the fulcrum of 1 Peter's revelation.

Revealed and Future Consummation

First Peter employs the words "reveal" (ἀποκαλύπτω, 1:5, 12; 5:1) and "revelation" (ἀποκάλυπσις, 1:7, 13; 4:13). The epistle articulates the coming of Christ as a fulfillment of a revelation. Christ's incarnation, death, resurrection, and ascension—or at least the supposed effects of those events—are revelation of God's plan to save humanity, or at least, a chosen group of people. First Peter 1:10–12 describes that the Spirit of Christ revealed to the prophets of the Hebrew Bible the secrets of the sufferings of Christ and his subsequent glory. Chapter 1:19–20 states that Jesus was destined before the foundation of the world, but "he was revealed at the end of ages for your sake."[4] It is interesting to note here the use of the aorist passive participle (φανερωθέντον) with "at the end of ages." In some way, the end of ages has either already happened with the coming of Christ, or the author understands the epistle's audience to be living in the end of the ages now that Christ's fulfillment of the prophets has been revealed. Therefore, it is at least possible that for 1 Peter, Christ's first coming was a revelatory event disclosed to the prophets for the sake of its original readers.

2. It should be noted that John Elliott says that, in contrast to Paul and the book of Revelation, 1 Peter "makes no claim to be passing on any privileged revelation." However, further discussion makes it appear that 1 Peter is in fact concerned with the dispensing of privileged information. See John Elliott, *1 Peter: A New Translation with Introduction and Commentary*, AB 37b (New York: Doubleday, 2000), 112.

3. While 1 Peter does indicate that it is revealing a secret knowledge, it does not use the formal term "mystery" (*raz*) as is used in some Pauline works as well as the Dead Sea Scrolls. See Raymond E. Brown, *The Semitic Background of the Term "Mystery" in the New Testament*, FBBS 21 (Philadelphia: Fortress Press, 1968).

4. The mention of Christ being "chosen before the foundation of the world" is similar in language and purpose to the description of the son of man from the Book of Parables. First Enoch 48:3–4 states that the son of man was chosen even before the creation of the stars in heaven. Similarly, verse 6 says that the son of man was chosen before the world was created.

While there is definitely a realized eschatological component in 1 Peter, a future eschatology is also present, since the followers of Jesus await a future reward. Conversely, a future punishment of evil is also assured for those who are not followers. In 1 Peter 1:4, the recipients of the letter are informed that there is an "inheritance waiting in heaven for you." Within the same thought cluster, the author expands the description of this reward as a "salvation ready to be revealed in the last time" (1 Pet 1:5). Verse 13 of this chapter articulates that its readers are to set their hope on the grace they will receive when Jesus is revealed (ἐλπίσατε ἐπὶ τὴν φερομένην ὑμῖν χάριν ἐν ἀποκαλύψει Ἰησοῦ Χριστοῦ). First Peter 5:7 further postulates that "the end of all things is near." Finally, as encouragement for their endurance of present suffering, the readers are encouraged with the hope that they will receive "the crown of glory that never fades away."

The revealed consummation of time in 1 Peter also includes instances of future judgment. In 1 Peter 2:12, the author encourages his readers to act honorably among the gentiles so that these nonbelievers will see their honorable deeds "when God comes to judge." Similarly, 1 Peter 4:5 says that those who commit evil "will have to give an accounting to him who stands ready to judge the living and the dead." Thus, part of 1 Peter's revelation is assurance of both reward for the righteous and judgment for the wicked.

The Apocalyptic Use of "Glory"

Another aspect of revelation used in Jewish apocalyptic thought found in 1 Peter is the use of the word "glory." John Collins articulates that one of the characteristics of apocalypticism is the use of the catchword "glory."[5] While the use of this word in and of itself is not a guarantee of the epistle's place in the genre of apocalypse or even within apocalypticism, the placement of δόξα throughout 1 Peter does further solidify the author's use of apocalyptic elements. The epistle exhibits a few general references to God or Christ being glorified or receiving glory in the epistle. First Peter 4:11 articulates that the readers must speak and act so that God is glorified. In 1 Peter 2:12, the readers are to conduct themselves in such a way that even the gentiles glorify God when he comes to judge.[6] It should be noted here that the glorifying of God is paired with eschatological judgment.

The word δόξα is often used in 1 Peter in reference to God or Christ. Regarding Christ, the glory he receives is often juxtaposed with his suffering. The opening verses of 1 Peter contend that the prophets of the Hebrew Bible testified both to the sufferings of Christ as well as to his

5. Klaus Koch, *The Rediscovery of Apocalyptic*, trans. Margaret Kohl, SBT 2:22 (London: SCM Press, 1972), 28–32, as cited by Collins, *Apocalyptic Imagination*, 12.
6. See also 1 Pet 4:16, in which the readers are called to glorify God because they bear God's name.

subsequent glory (1:11). Similarly, in 1 Peter 1:21, God has raised Jesus from the dead and "given him glory." In both of these cases, the δόξα that Christ has received appears to have already been given to him by God, presumably at his resurrection.

Many references to glory in 1 Peter involve Christ's future revelation. In these instances, δόξα is combined with the word ἀποκαλύπτω, implying that "glory" is something which will be revealed from heaven at some important future time. In 1 Peter 1:7, the author encourages his readers to endure times of trial so that their faith "may result in praise and glory when Jesus Christ is revealed." Similarly, 1 Peter 4:13 encourages readers to share presently in Christ's sufferings because they will "shout for joy when Christ's glory is revealed."[7] In both of these instances, the glory is Christ's, presumably referring to his *parousia*. Thus, 1 Peter assumes an eschatological event in which Christ's glory will be revealed to his people.

However, glory is also given to the people of God. First Peter 4:14 describes the spirit of glory that rests upon God's people. Likewise, in 1 Peter 5:1, the author describes himself as an elder, who will share in the glory to be revealed,[8] and in 5:4, in what appears to be an eschatological reward, the faithful will receive the crown of glory that will never fade away when the chief shepherd appears. Finally, 1 Peter 5:10 concludes the epistle by saying that the God of all grace has called the readers into his eternal glory.

Thus, it is evident, that 1 Peter utilizes the idea of glory both in the more generic sense of a special revelation as well as more specific reference to a future consummation. This revelation is often paired with the coming of Christ or a future eternal reward for the faithful.

The Apocalyptic Use of Angels in 1 Peter

The apocalyptic nature of 1 Peter 1:10–12 is furthered by the mentions of angels. Collins and others have demonstrated that one of the characteristics of the apocalyptic genre is the use of angelic mediators.[9] These beings serve as a buffer between the divine and humanity. It appears that 1 Peter is familiar with the use of angels in this manner, and yet expands upon it. First Peter 1:12 states that the revelation of Christ is something into which "even angels long to look." Here, the author is possibly suggesting that his revelation from the Holy Spirit is better than most apocalypses. First Peter's revelation comes directly from God. It is so secretive or special that the usual mediators are not needed and even appear to be jealous of the recipients

7. In some ascent apocalypses, the seer envisions the divine seated on a throne. For example, 1 Enoch 14:20 describes God on a throne and refers to the being as "the Great Glory."
8. In this instance, the author of the epistle describes his future glorification. This appears to be similar to the exaltation of seers in early Jewish and Christian literature (2 Enoch 22:1–24:1 and Testament of Levi 2:10–11). The exaltation of all of the Christian community in 1 Peter will be discussed briefly below.
9. Collins, *Apocalyptic Imagination*, 18.

who have received it. Either they are unable to grasp the revelation or have not been given permission to look into it. Additionally, this direct revelation could be similar to the elevation of the seer over the angels in some early Jewish literature. One example is 2 Enoch 22:10–24:4, in which Enoch, the seer, is told that God had not even revealed these secrets to his angels. For 1 Peter, it is not simply the author who is elevated, but rather it appears that the Christian community as a whole is elevated due the receipt of a revelation.[10]

Revelation and Suffering in 1 Peter

The need for a second or complete revelation within the framework of 1 Peter's apocalypticism is necessitated by the perceived suffering or marginalization of its audience. The author of 1 Peter employs a "Christ-Christian parallel" model that focuses on suffering and vindication. Christ suffered for sin, and yet was vindicated by God through his resurrection. Similarly, the readers of 1 Peter are currently suffering for their faith. First Peter is written, at least in part, to provide a new apocalypse (revelation) that would provide hope for future reward in the midst of present perceived despair. Therefore, a new revelation, or rather, a continuation or fulfillment of the revelation is needed to give the readers hope of a future reward.

The reality of suffering and hope of reward is present from the outset of the letter. In 1 Peter 1:3–7, the readers are promised an imperishable inheritance in heaven and are being protected by God for a coming salvation. Verse 6 suggests that the promise of these rewards is meant to help the readers who are suffering various trials "for a little while," and 3:7 suggests that these trials are a test to determine whether or not the faith of the readers is indeed genuine. Readers have previously been encouraged to act honorably among the gentiles even though they are being maligned by them (2:12).

The Christ-Christian parallel regarding present suffering and future glory is most apparent in 1 Peter 3:14–15, which encourages the readers not to fear anything even though they are currently suffering for doing good. Similarly, 3:16–17 instructs Christians to keep their commitment to God even in the midst of abuse for their good conduct for Christ. First Peter 3:18–22 proceeds to elucidate this Christ-Christian parallel both in that what Christ has done allows Christians to suffer with assurance as well as serving as an example for Christians to follow. Therefore, it is important to look carefully at these verses to understand better the nature of 1 Peter's eschatology.

10. For further discussion, see Andrei Orlov, *The Enoch-Metatron* Tradition, TSAJ 107 (Tübingen: Mohr Siebeck, 2005), 162–64.

1 Peter 3:18–22 and the Revelation of 1 Peter

First Peter 3:18–22 is a confusing passage that has produced a variety of scholarly opinions. The passage reads as follows:

> [18]For Christ also suffered for sins once for all, the righteous for the unrighteous, in order to bring you to God. He was put to death in the flesh, but made alive in the spirit, [19]in which also he went and made a proclamation to the spirits in prison, [20]who in former times did not obey, when God waited patiently in the days of Noah, during the building of the ark, in which a few, that is, eight persons, were saved through water. [21]And baptism, which this prefigured, now saves you—not as a removal of dirt from the body, but as an appeal to God for a good conscience, through the resurrection of Jesus Christ, [22]who has gone into heaven and is at the right hand of God, with angels, authorities, and powers made subject to him (NRSV).

While the exact details or outcomes vary, current consensus views this passage within the broader fallen angel and giant traditions of early Jewish and Christian literature (1 Enoch 6–11; etc.). While it is beyond the scope of this work to provide an in-depth exegesis of 1 Peter 3:18–22, a more detailed examination of these verses is beneficial insofar as it helps to understand better the apocalyptic nature of 1 Peter.[11]

The use of various fallen angel, giant, and evil spirit traditions is prevalent in early Jewish and Christian literature.[12] Both apocalyptic and non-apocalyptic works demonstrate that they are not only familiar with various forms of these stories but continue to adapt them to their respective purposes. In order to understand this passage, a brief discussion is needed to understand the identity of the spirits, the timing of Christ's proclamation of his message, and the content of his proclamation. Answering these questions will aid in understanding 1 Peter's apocalyptic eschatology.

As has been noted by Bo Reicke, William Joseph Dalton, John Elliott, and others, the connection between 1 Peter and 1 Enoch, as well as other early Jewish and Christian literature, makes angelic recipients of Christ's proclamation the most probable choice.[13] These traditions exist in

11. For a detailed discussion of this passage, see Bo Reicke, *The Disobedient Spirits and Christian Baptism* (New York: AMS, 1946); William Joseph Dalton, S.J., *Christ's Proclamation to the Spirits: A Study of 1 Peter 3:18–4:6*, AnBib 23 (Rome: Pontifical Biblical Institute, 1965); and Chad T. Pierce, *Spirits and the Proclamation of Christ: 1 Peter 3:18–22 in Light of Sin and Punishment Traditions in Early Jewish and Christian Literature*, WUNT II/305 (Tübingen: Mohr Siebeck, 2011).
12. For a non-exhaustive list of examples of these traditions, see 1 Enoch (1–36; 37–71; 85–90; 94–105); The Book of Giants; Jubilees; Apocalypse of Abraham; 4QInstruction (1Q26, 4Q415–418, 423); Book of Mysteries (1Q27, 4Q299–301); 4QPesher on the Periods (4Q180–181); 4QSongs of the Sage (4Q510–511); Tobit; Ben Sira; Wisdom of Solomon; Sibylline Oracles; Philo; 2 Enoch; Testament of the Twelve Patriarchs. For a detailed discussion of these traditions in Early Jewish and Christian literature, see Loren T. Stuckenbruck, *The Myth of Rebellious Angels: Studies in Second Temple Judaism and New Testament Texts*, WUNT 335 (Tübingen: Mohr Siebeck, 2014); Archie Wright, *The Origin of Evil Spirits: The Reception of Genesis 6.1–4 in Early Jewish Literature*, 2nd ed., WUNT II/198 (Tübingen: Mohr Siebeck, 2013); Angela Kim Harris, Kelley Coblentz Bautch and John Endres, eds., *The Watchers in Jewish and Christian Traditions* (Minneapolis: Fortress Press, 2014), and Pierce, *Spirits and the Proclamation of Christ*.
13. 1 Enoch 19:1 at least includes the possibility that the angels continue to lead humanity astray, although it is arguable their offspring giants are in view.

such multiple and conflated forms that it is best to understand 1 Peter drawing from a shared tradition, rather than from 1 Enoch in particular. Therefore, the spirits in 1 Peter might better be understood simply as cosmic beings, including fallen angels, the spirits of the giants, and other evil spirits. Using the tradition of the fallen angels found in the Book of the Watchers, the writer of 1 Peter, like other early Jewish and Christian writers, recast those myths to cohere with his understanding of what cosmic realities were responsible for the suffering experienced by the righteous.

It is apparent from early Jewish and Christian literature that fallen angels were still understood as causing distress for the righteous. The majority of angelic punishment traditions indicate that these beings are imprisoned, or, at times, even destroyed for their illicit union or improper instruction.[14] Yet, there are a few examples that depict further evil caused by these beings. Most common, the illicit union between the angels and human women resulted in the birth of the giants whose emanations continue to lead humanity astray.[15] Thus, the angels through their wickedness, were the original cause of the present evil.

Additionally, many examples can be found in early Jewish and Christian literature in which evil spirits, occasionally emanating from the giants, continue to torment humans (1 Enoch 15:8–12). The literature from Qumran also portrays evil spirits, often under the direction of Belial, as encouraging sin upon the earth. At times, the spirits of the giants are in view but references to these spirits are often contained in lists that include a variety of evil spirits. Thus, it appears that there exists in Qumran literature evil spirits not associated with the giants.[16]

The NT contains numerous examples of evil spirits indwelling humans and causing them to sin. These cosmic evil forces are known as δαιμόνιον ("demon"), a term which appears over sixty times throughout the NT. The phrase πνεῦμα ἀκάθαρτον ("unclean spirit") is also used frequently. Other descriptors include πνεύματα πονερότερα ("evil spirit," Matt 12:45; Luke 7:21; 8:2; 11:26; Acts 19:12–16) and πνεῦμα δαιμονίου ("demonic spirit," Luke 4:33). The word πνεῦμα ("spirit") without any modifier may also refer to evil spirits (Matt 8:16; Luke 9:39; 10:20). These demons or spirits can be the cause of physical affliction (Matt 8:28; 9:32; 12:22; 17:15; Mark 5:1–5; 9:25; Luke 9:39). In other instances, humans are merely possessed by an evil demon or demons (Mark 5:1–20; Acts 16:16–18).

Therefore, it is apparent that traditions existed in which both fallen angels and evil spirits lead humanity astray and cause harm to humans. It would seem then in the setting of 1 Peter that fallen angels and evil spirits would need to be subjugated or defeated by Christ in order to

14. 1 Enoch 10:4–8, 11–15; 14:1–7; 18–19; 21:7–10; 88:1; Jubilees 5:6, 10.
15. For additional examples of spirits leading humanity astray, see Jubilees 7:26–28; 19:1–14; 11:4–5; 12:20; 15:26; 19:28; Tobit 3:15; 6:3–9; 8:3.
16. 4Q510 frg. 1 5 (possibly) and 4Q511 frg. 35 7; 4Q511 frg. 1 3; frg 43 6; 4Q444 frg. 1 2, 4, 8; 11Q11 frg 4 *i* 7, 9; *ii* 3; and *iv* 7–12, frg. 4 v 6; CD MS A 12:2, 3; 1QS 3:20–25.

comfort those who were experiencing marginalization. Thus, rather than attempting to determine whether the imprisoned spirits from 1 Peter 3:19 are angels or evil spirits, it seems more prudent, and better cohering with the message of the epistle, that Christ's proclamation to the spirits in prison is the proclamation of a message of victory over all the cosmic forces of evil. Drawing from a common tradition of the fallen angel myth, the writer of 1 Peter, in a manner similar to Jewish apocalyptic texts, has recast these myths to assure all of his readers that Jesus has achieved victory over the spiritual cause of their affliction.

Christ's proclamation to spiritual and human agents of evil also coheres better with the statement in 1 Peter 3:22 that Christ "is at the right hand of God, having gone into heaven, angels, authorities, and powers having been made subject to him" (ὅς ἐστιν ἐν δεξιᾷ τοῦ θεοῦ πορευθεὶς εἰς οὐρανόν ὑποταγέντων αὐτῷ ἀγγέλων καὶ ἐξουσιῶν καὶ δυνάμεων). Numerous people have linked 3:22 with 3:19. Dalton has detailed a number of scholars who suggest that, taken together, these verses include some sort of early Christian hymn or creed.[17] While Christ did not overthrow the Roman Empire through his death and resurrection, he did defeat evil kingdoms through his obedient suffering so that the Empire's ultimate power was taken away. If Jesus has subjugated the cosmic powers of evil, he has achieved victory over their human representatives as well.

People in the first century CE, including the recipients of the Petrine epistle, understood angels, spirits, and human beings as active forces of evil in the world and responsible for the leading astray of and the cause of suffering for the righteous. Furthermore, a general shift appears to occur in the literature in which sins, punishments, and even the identities of cosmic beings are placed onto humans.[18] At other times, the distinction between cosmic and earthly sinners is so blurred they cannot be distinguished.[19] It may be that the author of 1 Peter 3:18–22 has purposely left the recipients of Christ's message vague so as to include all forms of evil beings. The spirits in prison would thus represent all the forces of evil which Christ has now subjugated and defeated.

Therefore, a number of factors all point to Christ's proclamation being made to evil in all of its forms on the occasion of his ascent and exaltation at the right hand of God in heaven. Grammatical considerations such as the use of ἐν ᾧ and πορεύομαι as well as the cosmology of the places of punishment for evil beings in Hellenistic Jewish and Christian literature suggest such

17. For a discussion on the hymnic qualities of these verses, see Dalton, *Christ's Proclamation*, 109–19.

18. This shift is most evident within 1 Enoch in which sins and punishments that had been previously associated with cosmic evil figures in the Book of the Watchers are recast and attributed to humans. More specifically, sins and punishments of cosmic figures are now associated with the kings and the mighty of the earth. For a more detailed discussion of this shift, see Dalton, *Christ's Proclamation*, 69–101.

19. While this shift occurs in a variety of places in early Jewish and Christian literature, it is most evident in the Parables of Enoch (1 Enoch 37–71). For specific examples, see 1 Enoch 45:5–6; 53:2; 54:1–3; 56:2–4.

a reading.[20] Additionally, the use of traditions similar to those found with the Enochic Son of Man regarding christological judgment and announcements also support this interpretation. There is no reason to view Christ's "going" in 3:19 to be read apart from his "going" and exaltation in 3:22. Furthermore, a message of victory on the occasion of Christ's glorified state corresponds better with the overall message and purpose of this passage within the letter as a whole.

This overall purpose of 1 Peter is to comfort a marginalized and persecuted church and to exhort its readers to remain steadfast in their faith despite their present circumstances. The content, the recipients, and the occasion of Christ's proclamation to the spirits in prison must all work toward the overall message of the letter. Christ's pronouncement of his subjugation of evil entities offers hope to the epistle's audience that the powers of evil have, in some way, been curtailed. The focus is on Christ's suffering and ultimate vindication as an example of the recipients' suffering and their assurance of reward even in the midst of present hostilities. Therefore, it seems that a message of victory over and subjugation of evil best fits with the purpose of 1 Peter.

The whole message of the letter, as noted by Dalton, can be found in 1 Peter 5:12, which reads, "This is the true grace of God; stand fast in it."[21] The readers are being encouraged to stand firm in their faith in the midst of growing opposition. Christ's message is both one of victory and exhortation. On the one hand, the readers are to take comfort because Christ has achieved victory over evil. On the other hand, this victory takes place over cosmic forces of evil, and throughout much of early Jewish and Christian literature, these cosmic forces are viewed as the ultimate source of evil. At his death, resurrection, and ascension, Christ has subjected all evil forces under his command. While their final defeat is assured, it has not yet taken place. Thus, evil in all of its forms still exists in the world, but it does so now in a defeated state as it awaits final judgment. This waiting period coincides with the many different examples within the literature in which evil beings, whether angelic or giant, are allowed to exist in a defeated state.[22]

Therefore, the victory that Christ achieved through his death, resurrection, and ascension assures believers that they have the ability to resist the cosmic forces of evil. However, as noted above, there was a strong link between these spiritual forces and their human counterparts. The Petrine Christians were most immediately faced with human marginalization and persecution at the hands of evil humans, even if spiritual powers were ultimately behind them.[23]

20. For examples of imprisoned or punishment occurring in the heavenly realm, see 2 Enoch 7, 18; 3 Baruch 2:2–7; Asc. Isa. 3:13–4:2; 7:9–12; 9:6–18; 10:7–11:33.

21. Dalton, *Christ's Proclamation*, 187.

22. 1 Enoch 15; Book of Giants at 4Q531 frg. 14 2; Jubilees 10:11. See also 1 Pet 5:8–9.

23. The notion of spiritual forces working through human agents can be found in 1 Cor 2:6–9; 2 Cor 6:15; Eph 2:2. See also Rev 13:1–18 in which the devil specifically empowers the Roman Empire.

Christ's victory over evil does not assure the recipients of the letter that their persecution would end. In fact, the opposite message appears to be insinuated. But, the marginalization and persecution of the Petrine audience should not be understood as their defeat. Rather, Christ's victory assured the readers that human agents of evil would never be able to ultimately harm God's people.[24]

Not only did Christ's victory assure 1 Peter's audience of the final victory of Christ, and thus themselves, the letter also calls Christians to follow Christ in suffering, with 1 Peter 3:18–22 offering them hope as they join with Christ in his suffering. The Petrine community is often called to remain constant in their faith and to trust and hope in God (1:3, 5, 7, 9, 13, 21; 3:10–12, 15; 5:5–7, 10). They are told to live within the Roman Empire, even honoring the emperor (2:13–17), because that was the example given to them by Christ (2:21–25). In 1 Peter 3:8–17, the writer calls for Christians to suffer for doing right. Thus, chapters 2 and 3 alternate in delineating the call to remain faithful in suffering and to follow the example of Jesus's own suffering. First Peter 3:18–22 serves to offer followers of Christ their ultimate hope as they imitate Christ even in the midst of suffering. Because Christ suffered to the point of death (1 Pet 3:18), God vindicated him through his resurrection and ascension (3:19–22). This is meant to assure the believers that if they suffer as Christ suffered, they will ultimately be vindicated and exalted as Christ was exalted (1 Pet 5:9–11).[25]

It is apparent then that Christ's proclamation over evil in all of its forms was revealed in order to assure the believers that a new cosmological reality had occurred because Christ is now at the right hand of God and has subjected all evil powers. First Peter 3:22 declares that "rulers and powers" have now been made subject to Christ. Evil, both human and cosmic, now exists in a defeated state and awaits a final destruction.[26] A similar idea is found in 2 Baruch in which a messianic figure is revealed as inaugurating the eschatological era. This is followed by a second state in which the heavenly messiah has dominion over the earth and the defeat of powerful rulers.[27]

Thus, according to 1 Peter, the new cosmological reality brought about by Christ's defeat of evil as highlighted in 1 Peter 3:22 supports further the timing of Christ's proclamation as the occasion of his ascension. The overall message of 1 Peter was not only to remind its readers of Christ's death, but it also served to give them hope because of his resurrection and ascension. Just as Christ's suffering served as an example for their own suffering, so Christ's resurrection and ascension assures the readers of their own resurrection and exaltation (5:4, 11). A message

24. Reicke, *Disobedient Spirits*, 200–201.

25. For further discussion on the parallels of Christ and Christian suffering, see Elliott, *1 Peter*, 107–8.

26. Daniel 7 describes the destruction of the fourth beast, a human kingdom, by God who sits on a throne. Similar traditions are further developed in 1 Enoch 46:2–3; 61:8; 62:2; 69:29; 4 Ezra 7:26; 12:32; 13:26, 52; 4Q174 1 I 7–8; 11Q13 2 13.

27. 2 Baruch 39:7–40:1.

during the *triduum mortis*, when Christ was "dead," that potentially offered salvation to those who had committed evil during their earthly lives would not provide the ultimate message of victory and hope needed by a marginalized community. Rather, 1 Peter utilizes this proclamation to reveal the mystery of his defeat of evil and the new cosmological reality his death and resurrection brought about despite the readers' present struggles.

Therefore, it is evident that 1 Peter 3:18–22 serves as a fulcrum for the apocalyptic elements of the epistle. In it, as well as in the work as a whole, the author utilizes apocalyptic elements in its disclosure of the consummation of time (present and future), glory, and angelic traditions. Overall, Jesus is himself the apocalyptic revelation. His death and resurrection have defeated evil in all of its forms, and he serves as an example of a hidden message that has now been revealed. This apocalyptic message is one of future reward for Christ's followers who are currently experiencing some form of marginalization, and it is meant to provide hopeful encouragement in the midst of suffering since they will receive salvation and glory when it is revealed in the last time (1:5; 5:1).

First Peter contains a number of apocalyptic elements that include both the revelation found in the person of Christ as well as the hope for a revelation of the consummation of time. Both of these are used by the epistle to give comfort and hope to a marginalized people. First Peter reveals that Christ serves both as the example of how to live in the midst of suffering but also provides a hope that eventually, the world will be restored to the way God had intended.

Jude

The epistle of Jude is generally considered a "catholic letter" composed in Greek dating from the mid-to-late first century CE.[28] The letter was written to instruct a church or group of churches who were being led astray by the author's theological opponents. While the opponents saw themselves as part of and participated in the church community (v. 12), the author of the epistle clearly disagrees. Richard Bauckham understands these opponents as antinomians who were abusing their newfound freedom in Christ.[29] Jörg Frey, on the contrary, argues that the opponents of Jude, similar to those of Colossians, did not respect celestial beings. In response, the author of Jude composed his epistle to contradict his opponents by utilizing sto-

28. The date of Jude is dependent upon whether or not one argues for authorship by Jude, the brother of Jesus, or if the work is written pseudonymously, which would indicate a date after his death. For those arguing that the historical Jude composed the letter, it is difficult to pinpoint a date of composition since it remains unclear when Jude died. For a discussion on the potential date of Jude, see Richard Bauckham, *Jude, 2 Peter*, WBC 50 (Waco: Word, 1983), 13–16. The majority of NT scholarship, represented by Jörg Frey, in his article "The Epistle of Jude Between Judaism and Hellenism," *The Catholic Epistles and Apostolic Tradition*, ed. K. Niebuhr and R. Wall (Waco: Baylor University Press, 2009), 309–29, argues that Jude is best understood as written pseudonymously in the late first century CE.

29. Bauckham, *Jude, 2 Peter*, 11–13.

ries from Jewish tradition that highlight the role and power of the angelic realm.[30] Differentiating between these two understandings of Jude's opponents is beyond the scope of this work; however, common to both of them, and the most probable description of these false teachers, is the opponents' rejection of celestial and earthly authority. The desired result of the letter would be to convince the teachers to maintain a proper respect for the celestial realm, to follow the law of Christ, and thus, to live an acceptable life before God.

When Jewish apocalyptic thought is understood to include the revelation of previously hidden things, Jude clearly shows evidence of apocalyptic revelation, yet what is most distinctive concerning this epistle is that the revelation the readers receive is an old revelation. Rather than new cosmic epiphanies, Jude's audience is encouraged, often through Hebrew Bible narratives and the use of traditional apocalyptic imagery, such as good and evil angels, to continue in the revelation that has been received through earlier tradition. Therefore, the purpose of this section will be to understand how Jude utilizes the more general understanding of apocalypse or revelations to encourage his readers to proper behavior.

Revealed Knowledge concerning the Angelic Realm

Regardless of whether or not Jude's opponents are primarily antinomians or disrespectful to angelic beings, the epistle of Jude places emphasis on the "right sort" of knowledge. Unlike the Book of the Watchers (1 Enoch 1–36), Jude does not make use of the Watcher tradition to explain the origin of evil, but rather to instill proper behavior among the readers. Therefore, human punishment can be intertwined with previous traditions associated with cosmic beings. One of the primary charges leveled against the false teachers is that they defile the flesh and reject authority. In evidence of revealed knowledge, the false teachers "slander the glorious ones" (δόξας δὲ βλασφημοῦσιν, v. 8) and "slander whatever they do not understand" (v. 10). The use of the verb slander (βλασφημέω) in Jude 8 and 10 and the noun (βλασφημία) in verse 9 to describe the archangel Michael's refusal to "slander" the devil suggests that the slander referenced in these verses refers to the slandering of angelic beings by the false teachers.

Jude encourages its readers to continue a godly life, as opposed to the one suggested by his opponents, by including three examples of God's judgment against his beings who disobey his commands. In verses 6–7, Jude begins by including a narrative of the Israelites from the Exodus who were punished in the wilderness. The third example references the inhabitants of Sodom and Gomorrah who "indulged in sexual immorality and pursued unnatural lust" (NRSV) from Genesis 19.[31] In the second example, Jude provides further evidence of his use of reve-

30. Frey, "Epistle of Jude," 309–29.

lation from otherworldly realms. Jude 6 records "the angels, too, who did not keep their own position, but abandoned their proper home, he has kept in eternal chains in the nether darkness, until the judgment of the great day" (ἀγγέλους τε τοὺς μὴ τηρήσαντας τὴν ἑαυτῶν ἀρχὴν ἀλλ' ἀπολιπόντας τὸ ἴδιον οἰκητήριον εἰς κρίσιν μεγάλης ἡμέρας δεσμοῖς ἀϊδίοις ὑπὸ ζόφον τετήρηκεν).[32] This example draws on Genesis 6:1–4, but it reflects the tradition found in the Book of the Watchers and throughout the Enoch tradition. This should not be that surprising since Jude 14–15 cites 1 Enoch 1:9 (more on that below). The themes of Watcher tradition in Jude 6 are: the abandoning of heaven (1 Enoch 12:4; 15:3); the great Day of Judgment (1 Enoch 10:6; 84:4; 94:9; 98:10; 99:15; 104:5); combination of chains and imprisonment (1 Enoch 54:7); and the association of binding and darkness (1 Enoch 10:4, 12).

More specifically, Jude 6 recounts the fall of *Shemiḥaza* and his companions first recorded in 1 Enoch 6:1–6.[33] The accusations of not keeping their own positions and abandoning their proper home are reminiscent of 1 Enoch 15:1–7, which also charges the watchers with abandoning their proper dwelling in heaven. Both of these articulate the sin and potential punishment for beings who reject God's order and/or law. The punishment of binding these angels in chains in darkness awaiting a final judgment appears to be drawn from 1 Enoch 10:1–8. This imprisonment, like 1 Enoch 10:12–14, is temporary as the prisoners will apparently meet a different fate on a great Day of Judgment.

Furthermore, Jude likens the false teachers to the fallen angels suggesting that they will meet a similar fate. Jude 13 references the wandering stars that will be cast into darkness. This appears to be drawn from 1 Enoch 80:6; 88:1, 3. Like the stars from 1 Enoch, the false teachers will experience punishment of darkness. Furthermore, Jude 23 describes those who stop another member from following the teachings of the opponents as saving others by "snatching them from the fire" (ἐκ πυρὸς ἁρπάζοντες), which indicates a fiery punishment after death.[34]

31. It should be noted that this example (Sodom and Gomorrah) could also be read as referencing inappropriate relationship between humans (the citizens of Sodom) and angels (Lot's guests) similar to the example from Gen 6:1–4.

32. 2 Pet 2:4 uses this example as well. However, in 2 Peter, the angels are imprisoned by being cast into Tartarus. As noted above, this links the punishment story with the mythic Titans who were compared to the giants mentioned in Gen 6:1–4 (*Ant.* 1.73; Sir 16:7). However, the angels are called titans in Jdt 16:6 and Sibylline Oracles 2:231).

33. The link between Jude 6 and the Enochic tradition is solidified by the reference to the "prophet" and the loose quotation of 1 Enoch 1:9 found in Jude 14 as well as the punishment of wandering stars in darkness from 1 Enoch 80:6; 88:1, 3. For a discussion on Jude's use of 1 Enoch 1:9, see Bauckham, *Jude, 2 Peter*, 94–96, in which he argues that Jude was familiar with the Greek version but appears to have made his own translation from the Aramaic. Bauckham also contends that the epistle stems from a Judeo-Christian context in Palestine. However, Frey, in "Epistle of Jude," 324–29, has convincingly argued that despite utilizing Jewish or Judeo-Christian elements, the language of Jude, as well as its connections to James, suggests that the epistle fits somewhere between the letters of James and 2 Peter. Thus, Jude should be understood "as a specific product of the encounter between Judaism and Hellenism." Furthermore, on pages 20–21, Frey contends that it is possible that Jude is dependent upon a Greek version of 1 Enoch rather than the Aramaic.

34. A similar example is found in Jude 7, which states "Likewise, Sodom and Gomorrah and the surrounding cities, which, in the same manner as they, indulged in sexual immorality and pursued unnatural lust, serve as an example by undergoing a punishment of eternal fire" (NRSV). While this story from Genesis 19 is often associated with homosexuality, the context both in Genesis as well as in Jude make it clear that an inappropriate relationship between humans and celestial beings are in view.

In addition to references to evil angels, the epistle of Jude incorporates good heavenly beings as well. Jude 14–15 indicates that the punishment of evil humanity will be carried out by Jesus (the Lord) with ten thousand of his holy ones. This reference to 1 Enoch 1:9 appears to be a gloss in which Jude applies the coming of God in 1 Enoch with Christ. Jesus is accompanied by a heavenly army to condemn and punish all ungodly humanity. Jude has adapted 1 Enoch 1:9 "to the new historicized situation in view of his eschatological purpose and his Christological understandings."[35]

As briefly noted above, Jude also utilizes an early Jewish tradition of the archangel Michael in his argument with the Devil over Moses's body. Jude 9 is based upon or at least shares a tradition with a story from the Assumption of Moses.[36] It is also noteworthy that Jude assumes the existence of celestial good and evil and uses their existence to rebuke the false teachers for their lack of belief in, or at least, respect for cosmic beings.

Therefore, Jude utilizes this shared cosmological understanding for a few basic reasons. First, the epistle denounces the false teachers for their slandering of the celestial beings. Second, it uses these myths to encourage his readers to live acceptably before God. Finally, Jude warns the audience of the judgment that will happen if they do not.

Jude and the Consummation of Time

While Jude is clearly concerned with the celestial realm, it is also evident that the epistle also contains apocalyptic elements regarding the consummation of time. This manifests itself both in eternal life for the righteous (those who follow the teachings outlined in Jude) as well as in judgment for those who chose to follow the false teachers. Jude 15 states that the Lord is coming to "execute judgment on all." Verse 21 encourages the righteous by pointing to the hope found in the mercy of Christ that "leads to eternal life" (προσδεχόμενοι τὸ ἔλεος τοῦ κυρίου ἡμῶν Ἰησοῦ Χριστοῦ εἰς ζωὴν αἰώνιον). Verse 23 encourages the audience to save individuals by "snatching them from the fire," (σῴζετε ἐκ πυρὸς ἁρπάζοντες), which would imply a salvation from some punishment in the afterlife. The opening verse of Jude indicates that the letter is written to those who are "kept safe for Jesus Christ" (Ἰησοῦ Χριστῷ τετηρημένοις). This at least implies a potential future punishment for those apart from Christ. Finally, the closing benediction of the letter (v. 24) describes God who allows the faithful to stand before God without blemish in the presence of God's glory. The use of the word "glory" here itself points to the apocalyptic nature of Jude.[37]

35. Carroll D. Osburn, "The Christological Use of 1 Enoch i. 9 in Jude 14, 15," *NTS* 23 (1976–77): 334–41.
36. For a discussion on the *Testament of Moses*, see J. Priest, "The Testament of Moses," *OTP* (Peabody: Hendrickson, 2010), 2:319–34.
37. See Koch, *Rediscovery of Apocalyptic*, 28–33, and Collins, *Apocalyptic Imagination*, 12. According to Collins, as noted above in the discussion of 1 Peter, the use of the word "glory is itself an apocalyptic trait."

In addition to descriptions of a positive afterlife, Jude also describes a final punishment. Jude 7, which utilizes the Sodom and Gomorrah tradition, described above, articulates that these sinners described in Genesis 19 serve as an example for those who will undergo a "punishment of eternal fire" (δεῖγμα πυρὸς αἰωνίου δίκη ὑπέχουσαι). As noted above, both Jude 14–15 and 23 also anticipate a final judgment in which some will be judged, convicted, and punished for their actions.

Jude and Revelation of Tradition

While the term "apocalypse" often conjures up ideas of innovative or otherworldly instruction, Jude reminds readers that revelation has already occurred to those in the past, and that revelation still holds value. In fact, Jude uses tradition to stifle to new teachings brought about by the false teachers. These false teachings, although Jude never explicitly states this, must at least be apocalyptic in nature since they are new teachings about God's plan. Jude's argument is not based upon new revelation, but rather on revelation that has already occurred and is known. This use of traditional imagery, according to John Collins, is one of the characteristics of the apocalyptic genre.[38]

In response to the false teachers' lack of respect for celestial beings or antinomian tendencies, Jude responds with tradition, citing both stories from the Hebrew Bible and early Jewish tradition. Verse 5 articulates that Jude's argument is based upon what God had done in the past. Jude's plea to his readers is based on a reminder of God's previous judgments against sinners. The references to familiar narratives from Israel's past including the exodus, the fallen angels from Genesis 6:1–4, Sodom and Gomorrah, Cain, the dispute over Moses's body, Balaam, and Korah, demonstrate the previous revelation of God's judgment against those who were previously disobedient. These narratives, including the citation of 1 Enoch 1:9 in Jude 14–16 reminds readers of a familiar or recognizable revelation and not a new revelation.

Therefore, it is evident that Jude utilizes apocalyptic tradition to counter a new revelation put forth by the false teachers. Jude does so in order to remind his readers of what they have already heard and believed to encourage his readers to live a godly life by both following Christ's law and having respect for the celestial realm.

2 Peter

Similar to Jude, the author of 2 Peter writes his epistle in order to encourage his readers to turn away from the teachings of his theological opponents. The majority of current scholar-

38. Collins, *Apocalyptic Imagination*, 18–19.

ship understands 2 Peter to be a pseudepigraphical work written around the turn of the era, although the dating of the epistle remains elusive.[39] It is also widely held that the work is literarily dependent upon the epistle of Jude.[40] Some scholars, such as Bauckham, contend that this epistle coheres with the genre of "testament" found in early Jewish and Christian literature. Namely, (1) the author of the letter or hero—in this case, "Peter"—knows that his death is near (2 Pet 1:14), and (2) he wishes that his teachings are remembered after his death (1:12).[41] Second Peter, like Jude, is written to counteract false teachers. In this case, however, the false teachers appear to be influenced by gnostic theology.[42] This letter is written to oppose these teachers and to keep the readers from following their false teachings.

Similar to 1 Peter and Jude, 2 Peter utilizes apocalyptic elements in an hortatory function in order to both condemn his opponents and urge his readers to live godly lives. The apocalyptic elements of the letter include the use of otherworldly beings and realms, dualism, judgment, as well as the concepts of the "Day of the Lord" or judgment and deliverance with regard to an "age to come." As with Jude, 2 Peter does not rely on mystical visions or dream journeys for its apocalyptic elements. Rather, 2 Peter continues to reinforce previous revelations for the contemporary audience.

Otherworldly Beings and Realms

Second Peter assumes the existence of otherworldly beings and realms. Given the lack of exposition about angels or other beings, it appears that the author understands his readers to be familiar with them as well. Second Peter 2:4 references the fallen angels from Genesis 6:1–4 as understood by the Book of the Watchers and other early Jewish and Christian literature. Additionally, 2 Peter 2:10–12 recounts how the false teachers are willing to slander the "glorious ones" while not even the angels dare to do that. Both of these examples draw from 2 Peter's dependence upon Jude (Jude 6, 8–9). Yet, the author does not have the need to explain these examples in further detail, which points to an assumed familiarity.[43]

In addition to otherworldly beings, 2 Peter also references otherworldly realms. Regarding the underworld, 2 Peter 2:4 mentions how the sinful angels will be cast down into *tartarus*, often translated "hell" as in the NRSV, and kept in chains in the deepest darkness until the final judg-

39. Bauckham, *Jude, 2 Peter*, 157–61.

40. For a discussion of the literary dependence on Jude by 2 Peter, see Peter Davids, *The Letters of 2 Peter and Jude*, Pillar (Grand Rapids: Eerdmans, 2006), 140–43.

41. Bauckham, *Jude, 2 Peter*, 194. For other examples of testaments, see 2 Baruch 78–86 and Josephus' *Ant.* 4.309–19.

42. See Bart Ehrman, *The New Testament: a Historical Introduction to the Early Christian Writings*, 4th ed. (New York: Oxford University Press, 2008), 466.

43. The syntax of 2 Pet 2:12 is difficult and has led to a number of readings. For a discussion of the possibilities, see Bauckham, *Jude, 2 Peter*, 259–64.

ment. The combination of binding with chains and placed in darkness for a temporary period until a final judgment is reminiscent of the punishment of Asael and Shemiḥaza as recorded in 1 Enoch 10.[44] These examples of punishment for fallen angels are meant to warn the readers of what will await them if they too disobey God. Second Peter 2:17 articulates that the "deepest darkness" has been reserved for the false teachers. In addition to places of punishment, 2 Peter 3:7–13 looks toward the coming destruction of the current world and the creation of new heavens and a new earth. Previous examples of destruction of creation are used such as the flood and Sodom and Gomorrah (2 Pet 2:4–6) in an *Endzeit wird Urzeit* manner in which these primordial events foreshadow the future destruction and recreation of the cosmos.[45]

Judgment and the Day of the Lord

The "Day of the Lord" and judgment is one of the principle themes of the letter. In 2 Peter, the opponents' apparent lack of belief in the second coming of Christ, or possibly, even an afterlife altogether, is what prompted this testament. While the false teachers might articulate that there is no judgment of the wicked or reward for the righteous, 2 Peter utilizes earlier revelatory traditions to remind his readers of previous punishments recorded in Scripture. As has been mentioned above, these examples are meant to encourage his readers to proper behavior.

Second Peter 3:10 records that "the day of the Lord will come like a thief, and then the heavens will pass away with a loud noise, and the elements will be dissolved with fire, and the earth and everything that is done in it will be disclosed" (NRSV). Similarly 3:7 argues that even the present heaven and earth have been reserved for fire. As noted above, 2 Peter utilizes previous examples of God's punishment in order to serve as "proof" that God does punish evil. Like the fallen angels, the unrighteous are kept under punishment until the "day of judgment" (2:9).

The author's apocalyptic orientation (3:7–13) and the opponents' denial of final judgment (2:9; 3:4) seem to prompt an apology that makes up the core of the letter. For 2 Peter, the eschaton is ushered in with the coming of Christ, and is a time when the earth will be destroyed by fire (3:12). The heavens will be set ablaze and pass away with a loud noise. Elements and earthly entities will be dissolved with fire (3:10–11).[46]

Those who deny the *parousia* the triumphal return of Christ or the visitation of God are trou-

44. For more discussion on the use of angelic beings in 2 Peter, see Eric F. Mason, "Biblical and Nonbiblical Traditions in Jude and 2 Peter: Sources, Usage, and the Question of Canon," in *Reading 1–2 Peter and Jude: A Resource for Students*, ed. Eric F. Mason and Troy Martin, RBS 66 (Atlanta: Society of Biblical Literature, 2014), 181–200. For a discussion of *tartarus*, see Bauckham, *Jude, 2 Peter*, 53, 248, 249; Jerome Neyrey, *2 Peter and Jude*, AB 37C (New York: Doubleday, 1993), 198.

45. See also Sir 16:7–10; CD 2:17–3:12, 3 Macc 2:4–7; Testament of Naphtali 3:4–5; and m. Sanh. 10:3. For more on the use of this technique, see D. F. Watson, *Invention, Arrangement, and Style: Rhetorical Criticism of Jude and 2 Peter*, SBLDS 104 (Atlanta: Scholars, 1988), 188; Bauckham, *Jude, 2 Peter*, 46–47; Neyrey, *2 Peter and Jude*, 59.

46. For Hellenistic and Roman ideas on primal forces or elements and creation, see Pheme Perkins, *First and Second Peter, James, and Jude*, Interpretation (Louisville: John Knox, 1995), 190–192, and Bauckham, *Jude, 2 Peter*, 303.

bling for the author of the epistle (3:1–13). The false teachers, or scoffers, suggest there is no precedent for the second coming or of one age ending and the beginning of a new (3:4). Second Peter uses the flood as an example of worldwide punishment (3:5–7).[47] The author of the epistle uses apocalyptic examples, which will be discussed below, to strengthen the argument.

The author of the epistle envisions the presence of scoffers regarding the *parousia* as evidence itself that the end is at hand (3:3). In contrast to the false teachers' claims, 2 Peter 3:8–10 assures the readers that the day of judgment will, in fact, come. More than that, 2 Peter hints that the readers are living in the last days. Yet no specific timetable for the imminent return of Christ is given, but the author utilizes Psalm 90:4 and states that with the Lord, "a day is like a thousand years, and a thousand years like a day" (2 Pet 3:8, NRSV). Rather than seeing the delay in the *parousia* as evidence that it will not occur at all, 2 Peter argues that God is waiting out of mercy, so that more have the opportunity to repent (3:9).

Deliverance and the Age to Come

Second Peter gives two pictures when, in earlier biblical history, God intervened to save God's people. God preserved Noah and his family when he destroyed the earth with the flood (2:5). God also intervened to rescue Lot, the righteous, from the destruction of Sodom and Gomorrah. These examples are included to assure readers that just as God has saved righteous individuals in the past, God will continue to rescue the godly from trials while the unrighteous are held for punishment (2:9).

Second Peter reveals God's final or ultimate deliverance for the righteous by revealing not only the destruction of the wicked but in the creation of a new and eternal home for the righteous. Second Peter 3:13 records that upon the destruction of the cosmos, God will create a new heavens and new earth as a home for the righteous. As has been the case throughout this letter, the apocalyptic inclusion here is meant to condemn the unrighteous and to encourage the epistle's readers to correct behavior.

The Continuation of God's Revelation

Second Peter does not include dream visions or angelic tours of heaven. Instead, the author of the epistle appeals to apocalyptic traditions rather than relying upon direct revelation from God.[48] While 2 Peter presents direct revelation from Christ, the epistle often encourages his

47. Second Peter 3:5–7 along with verse 13, according to Bauckham, *Jude, 2 Peter*, 326, describes the destruction of the earth and it renewal at the flood as a type for the destruction and recreation of the world.

48. Watson, *Invention, Arrangement, and Style*, 212, argues that 2 Peter is borrowing materials to support his understanding of the *parousia* and is less immersed in apocalyptic understanding than Jude.

readers to remember what they have already been taught. The author reminds them and refreshes their memories regarding the truth that has been revealed (1:12–13). The false teachers are, in fact, the ones who used to follow the teachings of Christ, but have traded their traditions for "bombastic nonsense" (2:18). "They have escaped the defilements of the world through the knowledge of our Lord and Savior . . . but they are entangled in them and overpowered" (2:20). They are worse off than if they had never known truth (2:21).

Second Peter does say that correct knowledge comes from God. In 2 Peter 1:3, the author writes that "His divine power has given us everything needed for life and godliness, through the knowledge of him who called us by his own glory and goodness." Furthermore, the author of the epistle imagines his teachings as being a continuation of the revelatory experience previously given to the Hebrew prophets. Second Peter 1:19 states that "we have the prophetic message more fully confirmed" (NRSV), and in 1:27, that the prophets spoke from God through the Holy Spirit. Second Peter 3:2 also contends that the false teachers should remember "the words spoken in the past by the holy prophets, and the commandment of the Lord and Savior spoken through your apostles" (NRSV). Again, the author of 2 Peter, who claims to be the apostle Peter (1:1), contends that the apostles have received a direct revelation from God similar to the prophets. Thus, the author claims that he is providing a more perfect prophetic revelation from God. This apocalyptic revelation is intended to give credibility to the author's claims as a way of encouraging proper behavior in the present.

Conclusion

Therefore, it is evident that 1 Peter, Jude, and 2 Peter each utilize apocalyptic elements in their own unique ways for their own unique purposes. Whether it is to give hope to a church facing marginalization such as 1 Peter or combating false teachers in Jude and 2 Peter, the apocalyptic characteristics are used to influence present thought and behavior. Revelations concerning otherworldly beings and realms and the consummation of time are of use to each of the authors in as much as the revelations are relevant in urging readers to live in such a way as to be faithful to God's plan.

17

Demonology and Eschatology in the Oppositional Language of the Johannine Epistles and Jewish Apocalyptic Texts

Bennie H. Reynolds, III

Jewish apocalypticism was not a single or unified movement during Hellenistic times, even if groups and individuals with apocalyptic ideologies shared obvious similarities.[1] It also appears that expressions of apocalypticism can be found across a wide spectrum of socio-religious locations within Hellenistic Judaism.[2] The reach of apocalypticism was at least as wide within early

1. John J. Collins, "Pseudepigraphy and Group Formation in Second Temple Judaism," in *Pseudepigraphic Perspectives: The Apocrypha and Pseudepigrapha in Light of the Dead Sea Scrolls*, ed. Esther G. Chazon and Michael E. Stone, STDJ 31 (Leiden: Brill, 1999), 43–58.
2. For example, Patrick Tiller finds evidence that those responsible for some apocalypses were members of large social groups, some of which might have held privileged social offices. Tiller, "The Sociological Context of the Dream Visions of Daniel and 1 Enoch," in *Enoch and Qumran Origins: New Light on a Forgotten Connection*, ed. Gabriele Boccaccini (Grand Rapids: Eerdmans, 2005), 23–26. See also Stephen Cook, *Prophecy and Apocalypticism: The Postexilic Social Setting* (Minneapolis: Fortress Press, 1995), who investigates developments primarily before the Hellenistic Period. Texts such as *Serek haYaḥad* indicate that apocalypticism can also be found in smaller and perhaps more marginalized socio-religious scenarios in Hellenistic times. Bennie H. Reynolds III has suggested that the language of apocalypses may point to a variety of large and small apocalyptic groups. Reynolds, *Between Symbolism and Realism: The Use of Symbolic and Non-Symbolic Language in Ancient Jewish Apocalypses 333–63 B.C.E.*, JAJSup 8 (Vandenhoeck & Ruprecht: 2011). Anathea Portier-Young explores the ways that apocalypses function as resistance literature and finds several distinct plans for resistance against Seleucid tyranny. Portier-Young, *Apocalypse Against Empire: Theologies of Resistance in Early Judaism* (Grand Rapids: Eerdmans, 2011).

Christian groups. Since the 1970s, especially, scholars have called attention to the ways in which the earliest Christian literature presents Jesus an apocalyptic figure.[3] Significant topics of scholarly discussions are now: how, when, and in what specific ways did early Christians appropriate, emulate, or transform Jewish apocalyptic traditions. The Johannine Epistles (1–3 John) offer a particularly interesting test case for asking and answering these types of questions. They present us with several windows into a second- or third-generation community of early Christians as they struggled and competed to define the theological identity of their movement. In this chapter, I focus on the way in which demonology and eschatology are expressed in the oppositional language of 1–3 John and suggest that the best way to understand this combination of features is by reference to Jewish apocalyptic texts from Hellenistic times.

1–3 John

Scholars disagree about the authorship of the Johannine Epistles. Many now hold that 2–3 John were written by the same person. A significant number also believe that the same writer produced 1 John. It is my view that the same writer most likely produced all three documents, or at least that the writer of 2–3 John had a copy of 1 John and used it extensively in producing 2–3 John.[4] The language used in all three letters is similar and one finds several verbatim collocations shared between the documents. Some have pointed out, and importantly so, that while 2–3 John are both typical Greek letters, 1 John is not. This point is important for interpreting the documents, though it may not be critical for determining their authorship.

The Johannine Epistles have been designated traditionally as general or "Catholic" epistles. In other words, unlike Paul's "occasional" epistles, these documents express a more universal theology. This view is almost certainly wrong. Already in the fourth century CE, Eusebius seemed to doubt this description, referring to them as the "so-called" (λεγομένων) Catholics (*Ecclesiastical History* 2.23.25). In fact, the letters seem to address a very specific problem: a split within the Johannine community. Many scholars now locate that controversy in competing christologies. Some members of the community apparently held that Jesus's divinity prevented him from taking human form, even if he appeared to do that (i.e., "docetism"). Others in the

3. Bart D. Ehrman, *Jesus: Apocalyptic Prophet of the New Millennium* (Oxford: Oxford University Press, 1999); John P. Meier, *The Roots of the Problem and Person*, Vol. 1 of *Jesus: A Marginal Jew: Rethinking the Historical Jesus* (New York: Doubleday, 1991); Geza Vermes, *Jesus the Jew: A Historian's Reading of the Gospels* (London: Collins, 1973). Also earlier, Albert Schweitzer, *The Quest of the Historical Jesus: A Critical Study of Its Progress from Reimarus to Wrede* (New York: Macmillan, 1978; German 1906).

4. For more thorough articulations of the view that the same writer penned all three documents, see Raymond Brown, *The Epistles of John*, AB 30 (New York: Doubleday, 1992), 14–19; Bart Ehrman, *The New Testament: A Historical Introduction to the Early Christian Writings*, 3rd ed. (Oxford: Oxford University Press, 2004), 176–78. Georg Strecker finds that 2-3 John were produced first and by the same writer. First John and the Gospel of John were then subsequently produced by the Johannine community independently of 2–3 John. Georg Strecker, *The Johannine Letters*, trans. Linda M. Maloney, Hermeneia (Minneapolis: Fortress Press, 1996). Judith Lieu finds no evidence that 1 John is dependent on the Gospel, but does find it likely that 2 John is derivative from 1 John and perhaps even from 3 John. Lieu, *I, II, III John*, NTL (Louisville, Westminster John Knox, 2008), 6–9, 17–18.

community, those responsible for 1–3 John, emphasized Jesus's humanity and the waywardness of those who fail to recognize it: "By this you know the Spirit of God: every spirit that confesses that Jesus Christ has come in the flesh is from God, and every spirit that does not confess Jesus is not from God" (1 John 4:2).

Several features within 1 John reflect an apocalyptic worldview.[5] One finds significant interest in the *ἐσχάτη ὥρα* "last hour" (2:18) and *τῇ ἡμέρᾳ τῆς κρίσεως* "the day of judgment" (4:17). According to the text, the present world is corrupt and will pass away, but those who know the truth will be rewarded with eternal life (2:13–23). Lee Quinby's description of apocalypticism as a "regime of truth" seems to apply well to the arguments presented in 1 John.[6] Quinby finds that "The discourse of apocalypse has rules and conventions for establishing meaning, designating the true from the false, empowering certain speakers and writers and disqualifying others."[7] First John takes considerable pains not only to distinguish truth from falsehood but to suggest the final, cosmic implications of affiliations with either side. In doing so, the text validates some and repudiates others within its intra-community struggle.

In addition, one also finds the use of terms such as *ἀντίχριστος* "antichrist."[8] Indeed, the term "antichrist" is one of the ways in which the text seems to link explicitly its community conflicts within the larger cosmic drama of the coming apocalypse. For 1 John, an antichrist is anyone who denies that Christ came in the flesh. And it is within this regime of truth (the juxtaposition of those who possess the correct Christology and those who do not) that 1 John separates those bound for destruction and those bound for eternal life.

One can find similar regimes of truth in ancient Jewish apocalypses and apocalyptic texts. In this chapter, I compare the relationship between rhetoric and worldview in the Johannine Epistles and several Jewish texts from Hellenistic times. I attempt to show how the widespread use of a particular rhetorical technique (the use of binary oppositions) expresses an apocalyptic worldview as it is intertwined with demonology and eschatology to present each text's unique regime of truth.

Binary Oppositions in 1–3 John

One of the most prominent features of 1–3 John from a literary and rhetorical perspective is its continual use of oppositional pairs. For example, light is contrasted with darkness and the

5. For a succinct discussion of apocalyptic features within 1–3 John, see Frederick J. Murphy, *Apocalypticism in the Bible and Its World: A Comprehensive Introduction* (Grand Rapids: Baker Academic, 2012), 373–77. For an exhaustive discussion of the features we associate with apocalyptic thought more generally, see John J. Collins, ed., *The Oxford Handbook of Apocalyptic Literature* (Oxford: Oxford University Press, 2014). See also John J. Collins, *Apocalypticism in the Dead Sea Scrolls* (London/New York: Routledge, 1997).
6. Lee Quinby, *Anti-Apocalypse: Exercises in Genealogical Criticism* (Minneapolis: University of Minnesota Press, 1994), xv–xix.
7. Quinby, *Anti-Apocalypse*, xv.
8. Cf. 1 John 2:18, 22; 4:3; 2 John 1:7.

children of God are contrasted with the children of the Devil. This rhetorical device is most pronounced in 1 John, though perhaps only because 1 John is considerably longer than 2 or 3 John. The opposing pairs within the texts have long been singled out for analysis, though not always for the same reasons. Most prominently, Rudolf Bultmann used the many antithetic couplets within 1 and 2 John to posit an original literary source that most likely derived from a non-Christian gnostic setting, a setting that he conceived of in light of later Mandaean literature.[9] One must agree with Raymond Brown that whatever one thinks of source criticism, a feature so imposing within one or two small texts demands a critical, literary explanation.[10] And in this regard, Bultmann's theory is both logical and impressive. More recent discoveries, however, provide a better context for understanding the many antithetical statements. The Dead Sea Scrolls, and especially some large scrolls from Cave 1, use similar literary devices to express a similar worldview. Indeed, the similarities between 1–3 John and the scrolls from Cave 1 have attracted considerable attention.[11] But scholarship of the 1950s and 1960s probably erred in its eagerness to find direct literary parallels between Johannine literature (especially the Fourth Gospel) and Qumran literature (especially the so-called *Treatise on the Two Spirits*) as well as in their assumption that texts such as *Serek haYaḥad* were representative of "Qumran" thought or even Essene thought more generally.[12] I think it is important to say, however, that earlier generations of scholars often moved us forward even in their failures (and given that most scholars' access to the Dead Sea Scrolls was severely limited in the 1950s and 1960s, it is hardly surprising that they overestimated the significance of certain large scrolls from Cave

9. Rudolf Bultmann, "Analyse des ersten Johannesbriefes," in *Festgabe für Adolf Jülicher zum 70. Geburtstag* (Tübingen: Mohr, 1927), 138–58; "Die kirchliche Redaktion des ersten Johannesbriefes," in *In Memorium Ernst Lohmeyer*, ed. W. Schmauch (Stuttgart: Evangelisches Verlagswerk, 1951), 189–201. A similar though less refined proposal had already been made by E. von Dobschütz, "Johannine Studien, I" *ZNW* 8 (1907): 1–8. For a succinct history of the source theories for 1 John, see Brown, *Epistles of John*, 36–46.

10. Brown, *Epistles of John*, 37.

11. Cf. Raymond Brown, "The Qumran Scrolls and the Johannine Gospel and Epistles," *CBQ* 17 (1955): 403–19, 559–74; reprinted in Krister Stendahl, ed., *The Scrolls and the New Testament* (New York: Harper, 1957), 183–207, and Raymond Brown, *New Testament Essays* (Milwaukee: Bruce, 1965), 138–73. James Charlesworth, "A Critical Comparison of the Dualism in 1QS 3:13–4:26 and the 'Dualism' Contained in the Gospel of John," *NTS* 15 (1968–69): 389–418; reprinted in James Charlesworth, ed., *John and the Dead Sea Scrolls* (New York: Crossroad, 1990), 76–101; *idem* "The Dead Sea Scrolls and the Gospel According to John," in *Exploring the Gospel of John: In Honor of D. Moody Smith*, ed., R. A. Culpepper and C. C. Black (Louisville: Westminster John Knox, 1996), 65–87; *idem* "The Priority of the Gospel of John? Reflections on the Essenes and the First Edition of John," in *Für und Wider die Priorität des Johannesevangeliums*, ed., Peter L. Hofrichter, TTS 9 (Hildesheim: Olms, 2002), 73–114.

12. For critical responses, see Richard Bauckham, "Qumran and the Fourth Gospel: Is there a Connection?" in *The Scrolls and the Scriptures: Qumran Fifty Years After*, ed., Stanley E. Porter and Craig A. Evans, JSPSup 26, RILP 3 (Sheffield: Sheffield Academic, 1997), 267–79; *idem* "The Qumran Community and the Gospel of John," in *The Dead Sea Scrolls Fifty Years After Their Discovery: Proceedings of the Jerusalem Congress, July 20-25, 1997*, ed., Lawrence H. Schiffman, Emmanuel Tov, and James C. VanderKam (Jerusalem: Israel Exploration Society, 2000), 105–15; David E. Aune, "Dualism in the Fourth Gospel and Dead Sea Scrolls: A Reassessment of the Problem," in *Neotestamentica et Philonica: Studies in Honor of Peter Borgen*, ed., D. E. Aune, T. Seland, and J. H. Ulrichsen NovTSup 106 (Leiden: Brill, 2003), 281–303; Jörg Frey, "Die Bedeutung der Qumranfünde fur das Verständnis des Neuen Testaments," in *Qumran—Die Schriftrollen vom Toten Meer: Vorträge des St. Galler Qumran-Symposiums vom 2./3. Juli 1999*, ed. M. Fieger, K. Schmid, P. Schwagmeier, NTOA 47 (Freiburg: Universitätsverlag; Göttingen: Vandenhoeck & Ruprecht, 2001), 129–208; and especially, "Recent Perspectives on Johannine Dualism and Its Background," in *Text, Thought and Practice in Qumran and Early Christianity*, ed. R. A. Clements and D. R. Schwartz, STDJ 84 (Leiden: Brill, 2009), 127–61.

1 for understanding the entire corpus). My goals for this chapter are more modest: I hope to highlight the Jewish and apocalyptic character of the rhetoric found in 1–3 John.[13] Below, I list examples of binary oppositions from 1–3 John:

1 John

1:5 light vs. darkness	2:9 light vs. darkness	3:7–8 righteous vs. children of the devil
1:6 lie vs. true	2:10–11 light vs. darkness	3:10 children of God vs. children of the devil
1:6–7 darkness vs. light	2:15–16 love of the father vs. those who love the world	3:14 those who love vs. those who abide in death
1:8–9 truth vs. liar	2:18 antichrist, antichrists	4:1–4 spirit of God vs. spirit of antichrist
2:4–5 liar vs. truly	2:19 those who went out vs. those who remain (those who belong and do not belong)	4:6 spirit of truth vs. spirit of error
2:7 new commandment vs. old commandment	2:21 truth vs. lie	4:19–20 love vs. hate
2:8 darkness vs. true light	2:23 those who deny the Son vs. those who confess the Son	5:10 those who believe in the son of God vs. those who do not believe in God (concerning the Son)
	2:23 those who deny the Son vs. those who confess the Son	5:18–19 God vs. the evil one (x2)

2 John

1:5 new commandment vs. commandment from the beginning

1:7 deceivers and antichrists (interacting with 1 John?)

1:7 those who abide in the teaching of Christ vs. those who do not abide in the teaching of Christ

3 John

1:3–4 walk in the truth (interacting with 1 John?)

1:11 evil vs. good

1:11 from God vs. has not seen God

Dualism as *Topos* in Religious Studies

Not every use of binary oppositions reflects what historians of religion mean by the term "dual-

13. Here, I adapt the language of Jörg Frey, "Recent Perspectives on Johannine Dualism and Its Background," 156.

ism." Thus, a few words about the concept of dualism are in order. It is important to emphasize upfront that dualism is a scholarly construct. It is not possible to determine empirically if a certain text or group is "truly" dualistic. Instead, dualism is a trope or theory that allows scholars to make useful kinds of comparisons between data sets.[14] It provides a critical lens through which to organize and view our evidence. And if Jonathan Z. Smith is correct that our most basic and important scholarly tool in the study of religion is comparison,[15] then categories such as dualism are indispensable.

Dualism resists an unambiguous definition.[16] In general, scholars use the word to indicate a situation within any given domain where there are two basic or fundamental categories or types of things. Very often, these two categories are represented as irreducible.[17] Within the field of Religious Studies, it has become customary to distinguish between different types of dualism. For example, ethical dualism might name the distinction between good and evil or righteousness and wickedness, whereas cosmological dualism might name the distinction between supernatural forces in the universe, such as the Zoroastrian conceptions of Ahura Mazda and Angra Mainyu. In the end, this chapter will problematize these various dualisms by presenting examples that seem simultaneously to cut across several different varieties of dualism. So I suggest that dualism may actually name a flexible trope within which other features of a text can interact. Devorah Dimant has recently expressed similar sentiments about categories of dualism, pleading that scholars allow for "the multifaceted single dualistic system" within their reconstructions of ancient Jewish thought.[18] Nevertheless, I am happy to stipulate that most of the scholars that use lots of subcategories of dualism understand that those subcategories are tools for describing cultural and intellectual artifacts, not empirical distinctions,

14. For a nice description of how theories function in the study of religions, see Bradley Herling, *A Beginner's Guide to the Study of Religion* (London/New York: Continuum, 2007), 23–46.

15. Cf. Jonathan Z. Smith, "On Comparison," in *Drudgery Divine: On the Comparison of Early Christianities and the Religions of Late Antiquity* (Chicago: University of Chicago Press, 1990), 36–53. See also, "The Devil in Mr. Jones," in *Imagining Religion: From Babylon to Jonestown* (Chicago: University of Chicago Press, 1982), 102–20; "When the Chips Are Down," in *Relating Religion: Essays in the Study of Religion* (Chicago: University of Chicago Press, 2004), 1–60, esp. 19–25. See also David M. Freidenreich, "Comparisons Compared: A Methodological Survey of Comparisons of Religion from 'A Magic Dwells' to *A Magic Still Dwells*," *Method and Theory in the Study of Religion* 16 (2004): 80–101. Bruce Lincoln, "Theses on Comparison," in *Gods and Demons, Priests and Scholars: Critical Explorations in the History of Religions* (Chicago: University of Chicago Press, 2012), 121–30.

16. Cf. the discussion in Ugo Bianchi, "Dualism," in *Encyclopedia of Religion*, ed. Mircea Eliade and Charles J. Adams, 2nd ed. (New York: Macmillan, 1987), 4:2504–17.

17. Cf. Howard Robinson, "Dualism," in *The Stanford Encyclopedia of Philosophy* (Winter 2012 Edition), ed. Edward N. Zalta, http://plato.stanford.edu/archives/win2012/entries/dualism/.

18. Devorah Dimant, "The Demonic Realm in Qumran Sectarian Literature," in *Gut und Böse in Mensch und Welt: Philosophische und religiöse Konzeptionen vom Alten Orient bis zum frühen Islam*, ed. Heinz-Günther Nesselrath und Florian Wilk, ORA 10 (Tübingen: Mohr Siebeck, 2013), 103–17 (104). See also Loren Stuckenbruck, "The Interiorization of Dualism within the Human Being in Second Temple Judaism: The Treatise of the Two Spirits (IQS III:13–IV: 26) in its Tradition Historical Context," in *Light Against Darkness: Dualism in Ancient Mediterranean Religion and the Contemporary World*, ed. Armin Lange; et al, JAJSup 2 (Göttingen: Vandenhoeck & Ruprecht, 2011), 145–68 (145–47).

and certainly not distinctions the ancients would have been likely to make on their own. To put it another way, I think most recognize that these are etic—not emic—categories.[19]

In addition to various categories of dualism, scholars sometimes also distinguish between the levels of intensity or comprehensiveness of dualism in a given data set. For example, one might describe *Serek haYaḥad*'s juxtaposition of God and Belial (e.g., 1QS 1–2) as a moderate or limited dualism since the text ultimately imagines that relationship within a monotheistic framework (the powers of God and Belial might be opposite, but they are not equal and irreducible—the relationship must also be hierarchical). Indeed, because each of the texts discussed in this chapter seems to maintain an array of terms that can be interchanged easily within various binary oppositions, we always find a sort of flexible dualism. But the way in which the texts make use of binary oppositions and connect them with other quintessentially apocalyptic tropes seems to indicate that "dualism," as a critical theory, can be helpful for understanding the patterns of thought at work in the texts. Indeed, in her description of apocalyptic rhetoric, Carol Newsom has characterized dualism as a "signature trope."[20] While this chapter is not devoted to dualism *per se*, it might be able to add some clarity to what we mean we when describe an apocalypse or apocalyptic text as "dualistic." Newsom sees dualism as tool used by apocalyptic writers to manifest their obsession with order: "Most cultures use various forms of binary classification to structure reality. Binary thinking is a radical simplification of reality that rhetorically emphasizes clarity at the expense of nuance and ambiguity."[21] Where Newsom sees this strategy most clearly and regularly within Jewish apocalyptic texts is in the realm of moral order, but she also notes that it provides a language to describe evolving Jewish beliefs about the constituents of the cosmos: "Although traditions about demonic spirits and adversarial angels were part of Israelite culture before the development of apocalyptic literature, dualism organizes this material to develop etiologies of evil (e.g., the fallen watchers of 1 Enoch 6–16 and the evil spirits that come from the slain giants) and to construct an angelic or demonic opponent for God, variously known as Mastema ("malice"), Belial ("worthlessness"), Satan ("adversary"), or Melkiresha ("king of evil")."[22] We will have the opportunity to observe binary constructions in 1–3 John that accomplish some of these purposes and which may better illustrate what we mean by apocalyptic dualism. It is important to note, however, that each text under consideration in this chapter also makes unique interchanges and substitutions within its binary system. And these interchanges blur the lines between traditional categories of "dualism" (e.g., ethical vs. cosmic dualism). If we begin with the assumption that apocalyptic dualism is multifaceted and

19. Cf. Stuckenbruck, "Interiorization of Dualism," 145–47.
20. Carol Newsom, "The Rhetoric of Jewish Apocalyptic Literature," in *The Oxford Handbook of Apocalyptic Literature*, ed. John J. Collins (Oxford: Oxford University Press, 2014), 201–17 (213).
21. Ibid., 213.
22. Ibid., 214.

not fixed into clearly defined categories, then I suggest that we might benefit from viewing "apocalyptic dualism" as a trope in which a range of binary thinking is used to express a distinctive concern for order, particularly in demonological and eschatological contexts,[23] oftentimes providing theological resources for navigating real or imagined contemporary conflicts.

Possible Jewish Backgrounds for Johannine Binary Oppositions

The oldest Christian texts are heavily indebted to Jewish Scripture.[24] So it would be reasonable to start a search for the Jewish backgrounds of 1–3 John's language in the texts of the Hebrew Bible. Certainly, one can find the regular use of opposing categories in the Hebrew Bible. For example, in the wisdom literature, one finds contrasts such as the one between the wise one and the fool: "Fools (אֱוִיל) think their own way is right, but the wise (חָכָם) listen to advice" (Prov 12:15).[25] Throughout Hebrew biblical texts, one finds a contrast between both righteousness/wickedness and sacred/profane. The oppositions remain most formulaic in wisdom texts: "The wicked (רָשָׁע) covet the proceeds of wickedness, but the root of the righteous (צַדִּיקִים) bears fruit" (Prov 12:12). But these categorical oppositions are also found in prophetic texts, liturgical texts, and even narrative texts in the Pentateuch.[26] Aside from the Book of Daniel, however, the oppositional pairs used in the Hebrew Bible do not function to express an apocalyptic worldview. And most historians of religion would not prefer to see them as examples of "dualism." So while these texts undoubtedly form part of the cultural encyclopedia used by the writers of 1–3 John (directly or indirectly), other sources may provide better help for understanding the specifically Jewish and apocalyptic character of 1–3 John.

Comparing Epistles and Scrolls

There are twenty-nine examples of binary oppositions in 1–3 John, more if we were to count all the cases of implied oppositions. It is neither possible nor necessary to perform a detailed analysis of each pair in this chapter. Since several of the pairs represent the same or similar oppositions, we can analyze a representative example in light of the oppositional language that we find in early Jewish apocalypses and apocalyptic texts. For this chapter, I investigate the

23. Within texts that describe otherworldly journeys, we would need to add "geographical" to our list features that help define the binary oppositions of apocalypses in a distinctly "apocalyptic" way.

24. Cf. D. A. Carson and H. G. M. Williamson, *It is Written: Scripture Citing Scripture* (Cambridge: Cambridge University Press, 1988), chs. 11–19; E. E. Ellis, "Biblical Interpretation in the New Testament Church," in *Mikra: Text, Translation, Reading and Interpretation of the Hebrew Bible in Ancient Judaism and Early Christianity*, ed. M. J. Mulder, CRINT 2.1 (Philadelphia: Fortress Press, 1988), 691–725.

25. There are numerous other examples and often the dualism expressed is more complex than mere juxtapositions. See Matthew Goff, "Looking for Sapiential Wisdom at Qumran," in *Dualism in Qumran*, ed. Géza G. Xeravits, LSTS 76 (London: T&T Clark, 2010), 20–38, esp. 25–29.

26. A representative sample of the expressed opposition between righteousness/wickedness can be found in Gen 18:23, 2 Sam 4:11, Ps 7:9, Ezek 18:24, Hab 1:4, and Mal 3:18.

opposition presented between truth and lie since it is one of the most often invoked. I suggest that this comparison illuminates the apocalyptic milieu out of which several distinct Jewish and Christians examples derived—each with its own regime of truth often rooted in immediate and local circumstances. The scope of this chapter is limited, so I begin with some programmatic statements and assumptions that should contextualize my comparisons.

1. I find no evidence of any direct, literary relationship between 1–3 John and any other Jewish text. In other words, the Johannine Epistles are products of their environment, but do not appear to be responses to or appropriations of any specific Jewish document.[27] The benefit of this situation is that we can observe how different apocalyptically minded groups used similar techniques to deal with different localized problems. Thus, while we do not learn much in terms of genealogies, we might learn about how apocalypticism grew and functioned organically.
2. Jewish apocalyptic texts from the Hellenistic period probably provide the best basis for understanding the apocalypticism within 1–3 John, but this does not mean that other traditions, even later ones, are irrelevant. For example, Georg Strecker has called attention to the use of "light vs. darkness" language in, for example, the *Corpus Hermeticum* and the Nag Hammadi library.[28] While it would be impossible that 1–3 John could have been directly influenced by texts in those collections, no one imagines that the dualistic ideas and worldviews inherent in those texts simply popped into existence in the second or third centuries CE.
3. The evidence from Qumran is complex. It is still not uncommon for all the writings from Qumran to be treated as a unified corpus. Some, especially non-specialists, even seem to regard them all as Essene texts. Several decades of diligent research have shown that many (virtually all!) of the documents have complicated literary histories. Many of the documents (or, parts thereof) were produced before the existence of the sect that came to own them. Early Enochic texts such as the Book of the Watchers provide obvious examples of this. But even sectarian texts such as *Serek haYaḥad* ("Community Rule")

27. It is possible that direct relationships exist between the Johannine texts themselves. See n. 4. As Jörg Frey has pointed out, earlier generations of scholars used linguistic parallels to find direct links between Johannine literature and Qumran texts. These studies were reasonable exercises in their time, but direct links between 1–3 John and Qumran simply cannot be demonstrated. See Jörg Frey, "Recent Perspectives on Johannine Dualism and Its Background," 127–61.
28. Strecker, *Johannine Letters*, 26–28.

provide evidence.[29] In many ways, this complexity is fortunate since it gives us a much broader spectrum of data about Second Temple Judaism.

4. While the oldest roots of the genre apocalypse perhaps run deepest within prophecy, the writers of apocalypses continued to interact and form matrices with other genres, such as wisdom literature, throughout the Hellenistic Period. So when one attempts to undertake a comparative study of the apocalyptic worldviews maintained by ancient Jewish and Christian writers, the question of origins may not be of greatest significance.

Truth vs. Lie

It is not difficult to find contrasts between truth and lies in literature across times and cultures.[30] It is a ubiquitous contrast. But several features of the oppositions reflected in 1–3 John's regime of truth are unique to apocalyptic thought and are best understood in light of Jewish apocalyptic texts from the Hellenistic Period. Early in 1 John 1, one encounters several juxtapositions of truth and lies within an exposition of the community's esoteric knowledge:

> God is light and in him there is no darkness at all. If we say that we have fellowship with him while we are walking in darkness, we lie and do not do what is true; but if we walk in the light as he himself is in the light, we have fellowship with one another, and the blood of Jesus his Son cleanses us from all sin (1 John 1:5–7).

The text then continues to use the trope of truth vs. lie to describe orthodoxy within the community's esoteric set of beliefs (cf 1 John 1:8; 2:4–5, 8, etc.). With each exposition, the stakes of the juxtaposition between truth and lie appear to rise. For example, in 1 John 2:22, the "liar" is explicitly described as ὁ ἀντίχριστος "the antichrist." In chapter 2, the expression "antichrist" can refer to any human, but the text implies a far broader significance for the role in chapter 4 when the writer juxtaposes the τὸ τοῦ ἀντιχρίστου "spirit of the antichrist" with the τὸ πνεῦμα τοῦ θεοῦ "spirit of God" (1 John 4:2–3). And it is within the context of this more cosmologically oriented juxtaposition that we see the truth vs. lie trope take on extra significance. The text does not limit its use of the truth vs. lie trope to humans and/or ethical affairs. Indeed, the contrast between truth and error presented in 1 John 4:6 is not even limited to earth. Instead, the text presents a worldview in which figures and events on earth are mirrored in an other-

29. Among others, see the various opinions of J. Murphy-O'Connor, "Le genèse littéraire de la Règle de la Communauté," *RB* 76 (1969): 528–49; Armin Lange, *Weisheit und Prädestination: Weisheitliche Urordnung und Prädestination in den Textfunden von Qumran*, STDJ 18 (Leiden: Brill, 1995), 126–27; Sarianna Metso, *The Textual Development of the Qumran Community Rule*, STDJ 21 (Leiden: Brill, 1997), 151–55. Charlotte Hempel, "The *Treatise on the Two Spirits* and the Literary History of the Rule of the Community," in *Dualism in Qumran*, ed. Géza G. Xeravits, LSTS 76 (London: T&T Clark, 2010), 102–20.

30. While the invocation of truth remains constant in our comparisons, it is juxtaposed with several different terms that share semantic overlap with "lie."

worldly realm. In this way, the text demonstrates an angel/demonology that is not present in the truth/lie contrasts one might find, for example, in the wisdom literature from the Hebrew Bible (or in classical literature or Nietzsche or Sartre or Mark Twain, etc.). In other words, I think it is in constructions like these that we might see the distinctive features of apocalyptic thought developed in Jewish writings during the Hellenistic Period.

For the writer of 1 John, the cosmos is filled with trans-worldly spirits. Some of the spirits are affiliated with God. Other spirits are associated with the rivals of God. First John 4:1–6 provides explicit criteria for discerning these spirits. The most important criterion is the confession that "Jesus Christ has come in the flesh" (1 John 4:2). This criterion helps the Johannine community discern who among them is led by the spirit of God and who is led by the spirit of God's enemies. The writer concludes the section, "From this we know the spirit of truth (τὸ πνεῦμα τῆς ἀληθείας) and the spirit of error (τὸ πνεῦμα τῆς πλάνης)" (1 John 4:6b) and suggests that this distinction will function to separate humans for eternal reward and eternal punishment on τῇ ἡμέρᾳ τῆς κρίσεως, "the day of judgment" (1 John 4:17). In other words, the text invests a contemporary conflict with cosmic and eternal significance and in doing so, variously authorizes and invalidates actors within that conflict. The text produces what Quinby calls an apocalyptic "regime of truth."[31] What seems to connect this regime of truth to those found in Jewish apocalyptic texts is the combination of eschatological and demonological concerns within a binary framework.

Before moving to a direct comparison between the truth/lie oppositions in 1–3 John and Jewish parallel texts, it is important to call attention to the way in which the "binary" oppositions of 1–3 John often interchange their constituent elements. In other words, while the texts often present a certain opposition as binary or irreducible, they often proceed to interchange the constituent features of the opposition with other terms and expressions that might seems to undermine the comparison. For example, in 1 John 2 and 3, τὰ τέκνα τοῦ διαβόλου "the children of the devil" are explicitly juxtaposed with *both* δίκαιός "the righteous" and τὰ τέκνα τοῦ θεοῦ "the children of God." Moreover, the "children of the devil" are linked with the ψεύστης "liar[s]" (who do not love) and the τοῦ πονηροῦ "evil one" (who hates). For modern thinkers, this flexibility might seem to violate rules of binary logic or at least of consistency. It appears not to have been a major issue for the ancient writers. Indeed, within the logic of the texts, this interchangeability appears to function as an important rhetorical tool for variously authorizing and invalidating participants within theological conflicts. In other words, the use of binary oppositions in Jewish apocalypses is mostly about creating patterns of order—often at the expense of nuance and subtlety.[32]

31. Quinby, *Anti-Apocalypse*, xv–xix.

Truth vs. Lie in Jewish Apocalyptic Texts

One of the oldest examples with which we might compare the opposition of truth and lie/error in 1 John is an Aramaic text from Qumran called 4QVisions of Amram^{a-f}. While the text was found at Qumran, it predates the settlement of the Qumran community. Linguistic and paleographic considerations place it in the second century BCE.[33] It was almost certainly not a text that Essenes (Qumran or otherwise) produced, though it may have been influenced by other pre-Essene texts found at Qumran, such as the Enochic literature.[34] The text may serve as an early forerunner of the "literary testament" genre,[35] which has significant overlaps with the apocalypse genre.[36] In the text, the patriarch Amram narrates a vision in which two transworldly beings (demi-gods) vie for his allegiance. According to the demi-gods, all humans are ruled by one of the two spirits: "We have received] control and control all the sons of Adam. They said to me: Which of us do you [choose?" (4Q544 1:11–12). Under the authority of the demi-gods, one group of humans is referred to alternatively as בני נהורא "sons of light," בני צדקתא "sons of righteousness," and בני קשט "sons of truth." The other group of humans is described as both the בני חשוכא "sons of darkness" and the בני שקר "sons of lie" (4Q548 1:1–16).

One can find immediately several similarities between the worldview expressed in this text and the worldview presented in 1–3 John. First, the text uses its demonology to extend the concepts of truth and lie beyond the earthly realm. The sons of truth and the sons of lie participate within a cosmic drama through their allegiance to a demi-god that functions in both the earthly and heavenly realms. In light of the fact that the demi-god who rules the sons of light claims to have three names (4Q544 3:1), it seems reasonable that those names might correspond to the three names given to his human followers in the text (i.e., the "spirit of light," the "spirit of righteousness," and the "spirit of truth"). In other words, one assumes that the ethical categories used to describe the humans are personified to describe the demi-God. And one assumes a mirror image explanation for the names of the other demi-god (i.e., "spirit of lie").

32. Cf. Carol Newsom, "Rhetoric of Jewish Apocalyptic Literature," 213.
33. See Michael Stone, "Amram," in *Encyclopedia of the Dead Sea Scrolls*, ed. Lawrence H. Schiffman and James C. VanderKam, 2 vols. (Oxford: Oxford University Press, 2000), 1:23–24. Others prefer a date quite early in the second century or possibly even in the late third century. Cf. J. Frey, "Apocalyptic Dualism," 277; J. T. Milik preferred a date in the early second century BCE in "4Q Visions de 'Amram et une citation d'Origène," *RB* 79 (1972): 77–97.
34. For one of the most recent and sophisticated views of the relationship between the scrolls found at Qumran and the Jewish groups presumed to have collected and/or written them, see John J. Collins, *Beyond the Qumran Community: The Sectarian Movement of the Dead Sea Scrolls* (Grand Rapids: Eerdmans, 2010). For the possible connection between *Visions of Amram* and Enochic texts, see Stephen Hultgren, *From the Damascus Document to the Covenant of the Community: Literary, Historical, and Theological Studies in the Dead Sea Scrolls*, STDJ 66 (Leiden: Brill, 2007), 323–25.
35. Jörg Frey, "On the Origins of the Genre of the 'Literary Testament': Farewell Discourses in the Qumran Library and their relevance for the history of the genre," in *Qumranica Aramaica. The Aramaic Texts from Qumran*, ed. K. Berthelot and D. Stoekl Ben Ezra (Leiden: Brill, 2010), 345–75.
36. Cf. John J. Collins, *The Apocalyptic Imagination: An Introduction to Jewish Apocalyptic Literature*, 2nd ed. (Grand Rapids: Eerdmans, 1998), 127–44.

Another important consideration in the way that *Visions of Amram* divides both heaven and earth into two groups is the fate ordained for each group: the sons of truth will go to the light and eternal happiness while the sons of lie will go to death and annihilation (4Q548 1:12–14). Although the text is fragmentary, it appears to imply that the primary distinction between the groups and the catalyst of their fates is (right) knowledge (4Q548 1:11–12). Thus, we find that *Visions of Amram* uses its binary oppositions to express its demonology and eschatology in such a way that emphasizes the utility of esoteric knowledge. Finally, we should note that in the same way that 1–3 John appears sometimes to "mix and match" elements within its oppositional pairs, *Visions of Amram* seems to present a multifaceted (interchangeable) series of oppositions.[37]

Another illuminating comparison might be made with the exegetical text referred to as 4QCatena[a] (4Q177=4QMidrEschat[b]).[38] This thematic commentary collects and interprets several "biblical"[39] texts in order to elucidate the last days, the final period before God's final judgment of the world.[40] In light of its distinctive terminology and date, many scholars consider the text a product of the Qumran community.[41] Like 1–3 John and *Visions of Amram*, 4QCatena[a] claims there is a cosmic conflict between light and darkness. And like them, it divides all humans into two camps: children of light [and children of darkness].[42] Like 1–3 John, the text seems to describe a theological conflict within (or, at least related to) the community that produced it. Moreover, it presents a regime of truth that helps readers or hearers understand how to navigate the conflict. The text's interpretation of Hosea 5:8 indicates that the conflict revolves around the acceptance or rejection of certain Scriptures: "'Sound the horn in Gibeah,' The horn is the book [of the law . . . the trum]pet of alarm is the book of the Second Law which all the men of his council have spurned and they have spoken revolt against him" (4Q177 3:13b–14). The text distinguishes between those who accept and those who spurn the "Second Law." The ultimate significance of this conflict becomes clear in the text's interpretation of Psalm 6. Therein, the exegete contrasts the fates of those associated with the רוח אמת "spirit of truth" and the מלאך אמתו "angel of his truth" against the fate of those associated with Belial (and probably

37. Moreover, the demi-gods explicitly claim to have multiple names, see *4QVisions of Amram*[b] 3:1–2.

38. 4Q177 appears to derive from the second half of the first century BCE. See George Brooke, "Catena" in *EDSS* 1:121–22.

39. The notion of a Bible at Qumran is anachronistic. Cf. James Bowley and John Reeves, "Rethinking the Concept of 'Bible': Some Theses and Proposals," *Hen* 25 (2003): 3–18; Armin Lange and Karin Finsterbusch, eds., *What is Bible?* (Leuven: Peeters, 2012).

40. See e.g., 4Q177 2:14–15, 3:7–8, 4:7, 14–16.

41. The handwriting of the text fits within the early Herodian period. The text was probably written in the second half of the first century BCE. See John Strugnell, "Notes en Marge du Volume V des 'Discoveries in the Judaean Desert of Jordan,'" *RevQ* 7 (1970): 163–276 (236). The most detailed and comprehensive work on this text has been produced by Annette Steudel: *Der Midrasch zur Eschatologie aus der Qumrangemeinde (4QMidrEschata,b): Materielle Rekonstruktion, Textbestand, Gatttung und traditionsgeschichtliche Einordnung des durch 4Q174 ("Florilegium") und 4Q177 ("Catena*[a]*") repräsentierten Werkes aus den Qumranfunden*, STDJ 13 (Leiden: Brill, 1994).

42. Only the children of light are mentioned explicitly, but the division of the fates of humans into two categories is unmistakable.

also the רוחו]ת בליעל "the spirit[s of Belial]"). Those that cling to the Law will suffer in the near term, but they will quickly be rescued by God. On the contrary, Belial and all his lot will be finished forever (4Q177 4:7–16).

The opposition represented here is another example of an imperfect (or, flexible) contrast—several expressions, which are not necessarily synonymous, are interchanged with one another in the text. This characteristic of the text is similar to what one finds in 1–3 John. But one must also call attention to the fact that the oppositional pairs in 4QCatena[a] are not a precise match for the ones we find in 1 John. In this case, the "spirit of truth" is contrasted with Belial instead of the spirit of error or the spirit of deceit. Lest this incompatibility be overemphasized, one should note, of course, that in texts such as the Testament of Benjamin, Beliar is also referred to as the "spirit of deceit" (6:1). Moreover, one of the features that make the Qumran sectarian version of these oppositions unique is their juxtaposition of Belial with "truth." For example, in *Milḥamah* 13:11–12, the lot of Belial is contrasted with the גורל אמתכה "lot of your [God's] truth." Similar examples are found in 1QS (see below).

It is also important to note that on a rhetorical/structural level, all of the texts compared in this chapter nurture imperfect, interchangeable parallels in the same ways, perhaps presenting what Dimant refers to as a "multifaceted single dualistic system."[43] 4QCatena[a] presents a contrast between God and Belial (a head-demon comparable to Satan in the New Testament or Mastemah in Jubilees), a contrast between the spirit of truth (or, spirit of God) and the spirit of Belial, and a contrast between the children of light and the children of darkness. These terms are sometimes interchanged for one another (possibly but not necessarily implying equivalence). Nevertheless, while each opposition can be expressed in several alternative versions, 4QCatena[a] envisions a fundamental conflict that extends to all levels of the universe: between humans, between demi-gods (demons), and even in some sense with the cosmic superpower (God). This worldview is similar to 1–3 John not only in terms of its structure, but also in terms of the way the writer(s) attempt to wield this binary worldview as a way to settle inter- and/or intra-group theological disputes that have become pressing concerns at the advent of the end of days.[44] In other words, these conflicts and oppositions are about establishing order.

Another text with which one might compare 1–3 John in order to illuminate the apocalyptic regime of truth presented in the Johannine Epistles is the *Serek haYaḥad* (*Community Rule*) found at Qumran. 1QS 3:13–4:26 (*Treatise on the Two Spirits*) presents a unique anthropology. It utilizes some of the same terms and ideas one finds in 1 John, but wields them to promote an even more distinctive worldview. According to the *Treatise*, two spirits control humanity: רוחות האמת "the

43. Dimant, "The Demonic Realm in Qumran Sectarian Literature," 104.
44. Like 1 John, 4QCatena[a] is focused significantly on אחרית הימים "the last days" and דור הא]חרון "the last generation" (cf. 4QCatena[a] 9).

spirit of truth" and רוחות העול "the spirit of wickedness/deceit" (1QS 3:18–19). In this regard, the text is similar to both 1 John 4 and the *Visions of Amram*. The *Treatise* constructs an opposition between truth and deceit that not only extends to both human and otherworldly realms, but that connects the two realms in present circumstances and future judgment. The *Treatise* also contains significant differences. In 1 John and *Visions of Amram*, humans appear to be ruled by one spirit exclusively. Moreover, it appears that humans have the ability to choose their affiliation with otherworldly figures. In the *Treatise*, however, each human is influenced by *both* the spirit of truth and the spirit of deceit and humans seem to have more limited personal agency (1QS 3:18–19). Thus, 1 John seems to maintain a worldview closer to *Visions of Amram* since humans can both discern spirits and choose between them when equipped with right knowledge.

Like 1 John, the *Treatise* constructs a diagnostic for understanding one's place among the righteous and the wicked and this diagnostic has clear eschatological implications. But the diagnostic is not as simple a procedure in the *Treatise*. Even those with a majority portion of the spirit of truth stray and are misled by the Angel of Darkness (1QS 3:21–24). Nevertheless, the *Treatise* constructs a regime of truth in which special knowledge remains available to a few. God will use truth to refine the lot of truth and purify them. Recognizing God's work of purification is a clear sign that one is ruled by the spirit of truth: "In this way the upright will understand knowledge of the Most High, and the wisdom of the sons of heaven will teach those of perfect behavior. For these are those selected by God for an everlasting covenant and to them shall belong all the glory of Adam" (1QS 4:22–23). The sons of truth, who walk in the spirit of truth, will gain "eternal enjoyment with endless life, and a crown of glory with majestic raiment in eternal light" (1QS 3:7–8). By contrast, those who walk in the spirit of deceit will suffer "eternal damnation for the scorching wrath of the God of revenge, for permanent error and shame without end with the humiliation of destruction by the fire of the dark regions" (1QS 4:12–13).

Another comparison might be made between 1–3 John and the Testament of Judah.[45] Like 1 John, the Testament of Judah makes a contrast between truth and lie/error. And like 1 John, this opposition is framed within larger demonological and eschatological contexts. The patriarch implores his audience, "Understand, my children, that two spirits await an opportunity with humanity: the spirit of truth and the spirit of error. In between is the conscience of the mind which inclines as it will" (Testament of Judah 20:1–2).[46] The writer's personification of

45. Dating the *Testaments of the Twelve Patriarchs* is complicated. There is little doubt that the Greek text as it exists is a Christian text. Aramaic fragments from Qumran, possibly including a small piece of *Testament of Judah*, demonstrate beyond doubt that the text has Jewish origins and must have existed in some (perhaps considerably more limited) form no later than the second century BCE. See Robert Kugler, "Twelve Patriarchs, Testaments of the," in *Encyclopedia of the Dead Sea Scrolls*, ed. Lawrence H. Schiffman and James C. VanderKam, 2 vols. (Oxford: Oxford University Press, 2000), 2:952.

46. Translation from Howard Clark Kee, "Testament of the Twelve Patriarchs," *OTP* 1:800.

truth and error as demons links the dualism of truth and error on earth with the larger cosmic struggle between those forces in otherworldly realms. And the patriarch makes clear that the implications of one's affiliations are of permanent significance. The spirit of error, said to belong to Beliar (cf. also Testament of Benjamin 6:1), "will be thrown into eternal fire" (Testament of Judah 25:3).[47] Alternatively, the sons of truth, who walk in the light of the spirit of truth, will walk in both the first and final decrees of God (Testament of Judah 24:3–5). The text emphasizes human agency in a way that places it much closer to 1 John or the *Visions of Amram* than the *Treatise on the Two Spirits.* Affiliation with the spirit of truth and the spirit of error is chosen by the human conscience. But there are also differences that should be noted. For example, unlike 1 John and 4QCatena[a], the Testament of Judah does not seem to marshal its regime of truth in order to contextualize or adjudicate an immediate contemporary conflict.

What About the Literary Apocalypses?

Thus far, I have compared 1–3 John with Jewish texts that can be described as "apocalyptic" but which are not literary apocalypses. In one sense, it is fitting since none of the letters in 1–3 are apocalypses and do not share the generic form of an apocalypse. Moreover, the texts I have surveyed each provide compellingly close linguistic and literary parallels to examine. But it is also beneficial to ask if we can find this phenomenon within the literary apocalypses themselves. From a formal perspective, one does not find parallels that are as impressive. But certainly, one does find examples binary logic used to create patterns of order. Moreover, one can observe that those binary patterns are disproportionately concerned with eschatology and demonology. Finally, one can observe that these combinations of features tend to variously authorize and de-legitimize actors within the contemporary social world of the writers. For example, the figure of Daniel is described several times as pursuing or receiving "the truth" through visions.[48] The truth Daniel experiences in his visions reflects an implicit contrast with the "lie" of the mundane world as it is experienced by most people. In other words, the course of history seems to reveal that the righteous are marginalized, oppressed, and helpless. But the course of history revealed to Daniel through his visions communicates a different reality: suffering is temporary and God is masterminding a plan (behind the scenes) that will result in

47. Kee, "Twelve Patriarchs," *OTP* 1:802.

48. For example, after Daniel experiences a dream vision in ch. 7, he asks to know the "truth" (יציב) about it (7:16). In Dan 8:26, the angel Gabriel declares the vision he reveals to Daniel to be true: "The vision of the evenings and the mornings that has been told is true (אמת). As for you, seal up the vision, for it refers to many days from now." The narrator of Daniel 10–12 authorizes Daniel's vision as "true" in 10:1: "In the third year of King Cyrus of Persia a word was revealed to Daniel, who was named Belteshazzar. The word was true (אמת), and it concerned a great conflict." The angelic mediator in Daniel 10 also declares to Daniel that he has been charged to reveal to Daniel what is in the "Book of truth" (כתב אמת). Finally, the same angel announces in Dan 11:2 that, "Now I will announce the truth (אמת) to you."

the exaltation of the righteous and the punishment of the wicked. This binary fate of humans is described explicitly in Daniel 12:2: "Many of those who sleep in the dust of the earth shall awake, some to everlasting life, and some to shame and everlasting contempt."

We can also find useful comparisons in the Epistle of Enoch (1 Enoch 92–105). The Epistle makes regular contrasts between the righteous and sinners as well as the wise and the foolish. Sinners are repeatedly grouped with liars and with the rich. The types of contrasts found in the Epistle are similar to the contrasts one finds in the biblical Wisdom literature, though there are at least two important differences. The Epistle of Enoch is squarely focused on eschatological concerns. Moreover, the world in which the contrasts are animated is not merely a mortal world, but a world inhabited by and influenced by otherworldly beings. Contrasts between truth and lie in the Epistle are concentrated most heavily in the conclusion, a point that serves to emphasize their importance. The writer exhorts the reader not to, "err in your hearts or lie, or alter the words of truth, or falsify the words of the Holy One, or give praise to your errors" (1 Enoch 104:9). The writer goes on to explain that, "It is not to righteousness that all your lies and all your error lead, but to great sin." Exhortations such as these might at first seem little different than what one might find in the Book of Proverbs, but they are, in fact, quite different. The writer explains their meaning through two esoteric "mysteries" (1 Enoch 104:10–13). Understanding binary oppositions in the Wisdom texts of the Bible is represented as a simple process for anyone who pays attention to the ethical world around them: "Does not wisdom call, and does not understanding raise her voice? On the heights, beside the way, at the crossroads she takes her stand; beside the gates in front of the town, at the entrance of the portals she cries out" (Prov 8:1–3). On the contrary, the writer of the Epistle claims to understand them by means of revelation (1 Enoch 93:2). The binary opposition of truth and lie found in the Epistle can also be distinguished from examples found in biblical Wisdom texts on the basis of the Epistle of Enoch's eschatology. The righteous, who know the truth, even those that have died, will live and become the companions of the host of heaven (1 Enoch 104:6), while the sinners will be judged by God and punished for all eternity (1 Enoch 103:7–8). In biblical Wisdom texts, punishment and reward are never eschatological. Thus, the Epistle provides another example of how the truth vs. lie opposition can be used to animate an apocalyptic worldview when it is contextualized within larger eschatological and demonological concerns.

Conclusions

Umberto Eco has suggested that:

> To organize a text, its author has to rely upon a series of codes that assign given contents to the expressions he uses. To make his text communicative, the author has to assume that the ensemble of

> codes he relies upon is the same as that shared by his possible reader. The author has thus to foresee a model of the possible reader (hereafter Model Reader) supposedly able to deal interpretatively with the expressions in the same way as the author deals with them.[49]

If Eco is correct, then the rhetoric of the oppositional pairs of 1–3 John should, at least theoretically, be illuminated by comparative evidence. Indeed, critical biblical scholars have proceeded under this assumption for more than two hundred years.

A number of features within the Johannine Epistles, and especially 1 John, serve to indicate that their writer had an apocalyptic worldview that was a product of developments seen most clearly in Jewish texts from Hellenistic times. I have chosen to focus on a feature of the texts that is, from a rhetorical perspective, more imposing than any other: their binary oppositions. Indeed, I am only the most recent in a long line of scholars whose attention has been captured by the rhetoric of 1–3 John. In the middle of the twentieth century, scholars exploited the newly discovered Dead Sea Scrolls in this endeavor and reached daring conclusions, especially concerning the relationship between the Johannine literature and the *Treatise on the Two Spirits*. More than six decades of research on the scrolls has raised serious questions about the relationships between these texts.

My goal in this chapter has been more modest. I claim that the Jewish, apocalyptic character of 1–3 John—and especially 1 John—can be illuminated by comparing their binary oppositions with similar examples found in Jewish texts from Hellenistic times. I focused on the opposition between truth and lie/error as found in 1 John and I compared it with texts that use the same or similar terminology to construct their own apocalyptic regimes of truth. First John, *Visions of Amram*, 4QCatena^{a}, *Treatise on the Two Spirits*, and Testament of Judah all personify the same or similar ethical categories in a way that connects the actions of humans with otherworldly realities in a cosmic drama whose imminent conclusion forever separates both worldly and otherworldly actors for eternal judgment and reward. In a slightly less formal way, one can observe the same phenomenon within literary apocalypses such as Daniel 7, 8, 10–12 and the Epistle of Enoch.

Binary oppositions are perhaps ubiquitous in world literature. But they take on a distinctively Jewish and apocalyptic character through their interaction with demonological and eschatological concepts in texts from Hellenistic times. In several cases, the regimes of truth produced by these oppositions serve to provide intellectual or theological resources for use in local, contemporary conflicts. I have attempted to show that the examples one finds in 1–3 John are best understood within the Jewish and apocalyptic thought-world that produced *Visions of*

49. Umberto Eco, *The Role of the Reader: Explorations in the Semiotics of Texts* (Bloomington: Indiana University Press, 1979), 7.

Amram, 4QCatena[a], *Treatise on the Two Spirits*, and Testament of Judah, the Book of Daniel, and the Epistle of Enoch.

18

The Book of Revelation as a Disclosure of Wisdom

Loren T. Stuckenbruck

Introduction

It is not often that, in the first instance, the Apocalypse of John is thought to have been concerned with the disclosure of wisdom. After all, in the history of its reception, so much attention has been given to the work as a book about eschatology, that is, about events to occur as history draws to a close.[1] To be sure, there is plenty in the text for such an emphasis on future time, whether imminent or ultimate. No less than four times does the book summarily declare that therein things "to take place" are being disclosed (1:1, 19; 4:1; 22:6), and in two of these that frame the book (1:1; 22:6), the work claims to reveal what is to happen "soon" (ἐν τάχει). In addition, it is hard to escape the impression that for the author, the three series of sevenfold depic-

1. Despite the recognition that the book is not simply concerned with "predicting future events," the attention it gives to eschatology has largely remained a *sine qua non* in the history of interpretation. This is amply illustrated, for example, in the collection and discussion of art and images exhibited at the Museum Pfalzgalerie Kaiserslautern, Germany, dating from 810 through to 2014, published in eds. Heinz Höfchen and Christoph Zuschlag, *Apocalypse Now! Visionen von Schrecken und Hoffnung in der Kunst vom Mittelalter bis heute* (Kaiserslautern; Berlin: MPK Museum Pfalzgalerie Kaiserslautern / Deutscher Kunstverlag, 2014). For a balanced overview that focuses on its reception from the early patristic era through to the early post-Reformation period, see eds. Ian Boxall and Richard Tresley, *The Book of Revelation and Its Interpreters: Short Studies and an Annotated Bibliography* (Lanham, Maryland: Rowman & Littlefield, 2016), especially the essay by Christopher Rowland on "The Reception of Revelation: An Overview," 1–25.

tions of divine judgment are concerned with imminently forthcoming episodes: The breaking of the seals (6:1–17; 8:2), the blowing of the trumpets (8:6–9:20; 11:15–19), and the pouring out of bowls of wrath (15:5–16:21) each herald, with increasing intensity and specificity, how the wicked, who are *ipso facto* considered allied to the Roman empire in its embodiment of Satanic power, shall be held to account. Even intervening and subsequent announcements of judgment not found among these series are concerned with the future, whether they are envisioned as punishment of the wicked (14:6–13, 14–20; 18:1–24; 20:11–15), as reward of the righteous (20:4–6), or as an open embattled conflict (19:11–21; 20:7–10) that will result in the triumph of God and the creation of a new world order (21:1–22:5).

Nevertheless, to assume that the book of Revelation is simply or even primarily concerned with the future, whether in whole or in part, is misleading. Of course, statements about future events—whether these are anticipated through the writer's denunciations of Rome and of those who are unfaithful, or alternatively, contemplate reward for the righteous—are made with remarkable confidence throughout the work. If, however, we inquire into *the basis* for such confidence, many scholars would agree that the events anticipated in the text are not simply the result of prognostication or even prediction. They are, instead, the function of an epistemology, and so, reflect a way of construing the world that is shaped by what has been revealed. With this in mind, we may ask what it is that, according to the author, is being revealed in the book? In answering this question, one can begin with Revelation 1:1, which forms part of the work's self-introduction: "The unveiling (ἀποκάλυψις) of Jesus Christ, which God gave him to show his servants things that must (δεῖ) take place soon; and he made (it) known, having sent (a message) through his angel to his servant, John."[2] Whether one decides that the unveiling (or revelation) is *about* Jesus, who will ultimately be presented as the Lamb (5:6), or *by* Jesus Christ, who is presented in a mediatory role (cf. 4:1, 22:6), it is the writer's Christology, through which a fundamental understanding of God in the book is conveyed and out of which the worldview of the text unfolds.

The Apocalypse was not, however, a composition intended to disclose knowledge unidirectionally. The writer, who calls himself John (1:1, 4, 9; 22:8), does not merely present a divine perspective on the world in a way that expects the audience to respond with passive acceptance. Despite his uncompromising, perhaps even one-sided views on what faithfulness to God should entail among the recipient churches in Asia Minor, John's book also *seeks to persuade*.[3] In

2. The translation is my own. Unless otherwise indicated, English citations of the text below follow the NRSV.
3. In this respect, see especially the important monograph-length treatments by Martin Karrer, *Die Johannesoffenbarung als Brief. Studien zu ihrem literarischen, historischen und theologischen Ort*, FRLANT 140 (Göttingen: Vandenhoeck & Ruprecht, 1986); David DeSilva, *Seeing Things John's Way: The Rhetoric of the Book of Revelation* (Louisville: Westminster John Knox Press, 2009; and Robyn J. Whitaker, *Ekphrasis, Vision, and Persuasion in the Book of Revelation*, WUNT II/410 (Tübingen: Mohr Siebeck, 2015). See further the contributions in eds. Stefan Alkier, Thomas Hieke, and Tobias Nicklas, *Poetik und Intertextualität der Johannesapokalypse*, WUNT 346 (Tübingen:

other words, the writer adopts a communicative strategy that assumes operative interactivity on the part of the audience by providing a heavy dose of symbols that can be perceived through visionary, auditory, emotional, and cognitive experience and imagination. Thus what is given to John to see, hear, feel, and know is not his alone, but assumes a process of "actualization" among an ideal audience.[4] Significantly, as will be discussed below, it is within such a framework that the writer's reference to "wisdom" in both 13:18 and 17:9 (discussed below) may be understood.

Wisdom in Revelation 5:12 and 7:12

If we restrict ourselves at first to the use and function of σοφία ("wisdom") in the Apocalypse as a whole, it becomes possible to offer several observations. The term occurs four times, of which the first two instances in chapters 5 and 7 may be distinguished from the second pair (on which see section C below). Wisdom first occurs among a list of attributes ascribed to "the Lamb," the most important designation in the book for Jesus,[5] when he is acclaimed by "many angels" numbering to a myriad myriads and thousand thousands around the divine throne, as well as by the four living creatures and the twenty-four elders (5:12). Wisdom is given as the third of seven attributes of which the Lamb, as "slaughtered" (5:6, 9, 12), is proclaimed to be worthy. The text presents these in the following sequence: power, wealth, wisdom, might, honor, glory, and blessing. Interestingly, the acclamation that immediately follows in 5:13—this time, it is spoken by all creatures in heaven and on earth, under the earth, and in the sea—is directed both to the one seated on the throne and to the Lamb, and the attributes, which this time are fourfold, do not include wisdom and are limited to the last four elements just ascribed to the Lamb: blessing, honor, glory, and might. While this simple observation provides no warrant to suppose that the three additional attributes in 5:12 do not carry over to the divine throne (cf. on 7:12 below), the declaration that the Lamb is additionally worthy of power, wealth and wisdom in 5:12 reflects the author's conviction that the Lamb, who is imaged as slaughtered (5:6, 9, 12) and who in the end is functionally and inextricably linked to the divine throne (cf. 22:3–4), represents a crucial redefinition of meaning. *False notions of power, wealth and wisdom are close at hand*, and it is through Jesus as the Lamb that a contrast to these is painted in

Mohr Siebeck, 2015) by Robyn J. Whitaker, "The Poetics of Ekphrasis: Vivid Description and Rhetoric in the Apocalypse," 227–40, and Annette Weissenrieder, Bilder zum Sehen – Bilder zum Hören? Über die Grenzen von visuellem Bild und Sprache als Ekphrasis in Apk 17," 241–68.

4. See David E. Aune, "The Apocalypse of John and the Problem of Genre," *Semeia* 36 (1986): 65–96 (here 89).
5. The title ἀρνίον occurs 27 times in relation to Jesus, and once in the Fourth Gospel (John 21:15) in which the synonym ἀμνός is otherwise used (1:29, 36; cf. also Acts 8:32; 1 Pet 1:19).

the strongest possible terms. It is through the Lamb that one may discern true power (closely linked to the lexeme "to conquer"),[6] true wealth,[7] and true wisdom; these features, bound up with the Lamb, not only call conventional associations into question, they are also deployed to turn them on their head.[8] As such it is not so much the image of the Lamb "as slaughtered" (5:6, 12; 13:8) that marks the reversal of expectations—the image itself, in light of Passover tradition, is not in itself surprising—as it is the powerlessness, vulnerability, and challenge it represents. The Lamb's suffering does not offer a soteriology of redemption and liberation that relieves followers from suffering themselves; rather, it is through participation in such suffering that the promises given to those who are faithful become most realizable.[9]

As in chapter 5, the next mention of "wisdom" occurs within an acclamation of worship (7:12). It takes its place among seven divine attributes that are declared by "all angels standing around the throne along with the elders and the four living creatures" (7:11). In contrast to chapter 5, the focus of worship centers more explicitly on God; however, in the description of worship just prior to this text, the Lamb is closely associated with the position of God's throne (7:9, human worshipers stand "before the throne and before the Lamb"; cf. 7:17, according to which the Lamb is "in the midst of the throne"), and a great multitude attributes "salvation" both to God who is enthroned "and to the Lamb" (7:10). In connection with the present discussion, this passage allows for two observations. First, what is specifically proclaimed to be God's in 7:12 is, by extension, also being ascribed to the Lamb. With small adjustment in vocabulary (the substitution of "wealth" with "thanksgiving") and the sequential rearrangement of elements, the content of the declaration in 7:12 corresponds largely to the picture an audience will already have encountered in chapter 5. Second, one may note what the text specifies regarding those who worship. In 7:9–10, those who offer praise before the throne and the Lamb are described in universalizing terms; "robed in white," they consist of people from all parts of the inhabited world (every tribe, people, and language). When they proclaim that "salvation belongs to *our* God, who is seated on the throne, and to the Lamb" (7:10), they are also claiming it for themselves. Real salvation is for all, and coming from God (who alone in the book is "the

6. Much has been written about the reversal of power in the book. For a discussion of power and conquering as a matter of spiritual *discernment*, see esp. Loren L. Johns, *The Lamb Christology of the Apocalypse of John*, WUNT II/167 (Tübingen: Mohr Siebeck, 2003), 175–80.

7. Cf. the different, yet complementary in-depth discussions by Robert M. Royalty, *The Streets of Heaven: The Ideology of Wealth in the Apocalypse of John* (Macon: Mercer University Press, 1998) and Mark D. Mathews, *Riches, Poverty, and the Faithful: Perspectives on Wealth in the Second Temple Period and the Apocalypse of John*, SNTSMS 154 (Cambridge: Cambridge University Press, 2013).

8. Hence the importance of the adjective "true" (ἀληθινός) throughout the Apocalypse (3:7, 14; 6:10; 15:3; 16:7; 19:2, 9, 11; 21:5; 22:6) to describe what is authentic, as opposed to that which is "false" (cf. the vocabulary linked to ψευδ- lexeme: "liar" in 2:2, 21:9; "to lie" in 3:9; "falsehood" in 14:5, 21:27, 22:15; and "false prophet" in 16:13, 19:20, 20:10).

9. Thus, the notion of Jesus's death as substitutionary or vicarious or as suffering *for others* does not do justice to the challenge the Christology of Revelation represents: readers and hearers of the book are not only given to recognize the comprehensive significance of Jesus's death, the image of him as a Lamb also invites them to become participants in that suffering.

almighty"; 1:8; 4:8; 11:17; 15:3; 16:7, 11; 19:6, 15; 21:22), has a far-reaching and comprehensive embrace; it stands in sharp contrast with another reality, to which other ideologies—whether imperial or economic—lay claim.[10] The acclamation of God by the great multitude in verse 10 is reinforced in verse 12 through the series of divine attributes proclaimed by all the angels, the elders, and four living creatures: blessing, glory, wisdom, thanksgiving, honor, power, and might. On the one hand, "power" and "might," which conclude the list, draw attention to God's incontestable control of cosmic affairs, while the elements of "glory" and "honor" single out God's unique position in the cosmic hierarchy, and "blessing" and "thanksgiving" denote the (effective) means by which this is acknowledged. What "wisdom" might refer to in any particular sense is difficult to determine, though the inference that it has to do with the *divine perception of reality* is not far afield. If so, then the text not only holds that God alone has insight into the world order, but also, in the form of the acclamation, it *subordinates any other form of insight or wisdom to God*, with whom *alone* it authentically resides (cf. Wis 9:4,10). The attribution of wisdom is not simply a matter of registering a characteristic that singles God out as unique and other; ascribing wisdom to God has social consequences due to the rejection of other available means and forms of insight. However, as yet in the narrative of the book, no formal petition is made that such wisdom be granted or passed on to those who worship God.

Wisdom in Revelation 13:18 and 17:9

The following two uses of "wisdom" in 13:18 and 17:9, however, challenge the audience to gain insight. In a text near the center of the book, the writer states, "Here is wisdom (ἡ σοφία): let anyone who has a mind[11] (ὁ ἔχων νοῦν) calculate the number of the beast, for it is the number of a person. Its number is six hundred sixty-six" (13:18). While this statement has played a disproportionate role in the interpretation of Revelation down the centuries, an understanding of how "wisdom" functions in the text is enhanced by a brief look at the context. The announcement of wisdom comes in the middle of a section, spanning from 11:19–15:4,[12] flanked on either end by a sevenfold series of trumpet blasts (8:1–9:21, 11:15–18) and bowls of wrath (15:5–16:21), respectively, both of which herald and depict events associated with divine judgment. In the present section, which consists of a series of unnumbered visions, the author paints a mythological picture of a conflict between two beasts representing the socio-economic and political

10. Among the many discussions of Roman imperial ideologies that provide some context for the Apocalypse of John, see the excellent summary by DeSilva, *Seeing Things John's Way*, 37–48.

11. *Contra* the NRSV: "anyone with understanding."

12. On the beginning of this section at 11:19 instead of 12:1, see esp. David E. Aune, *Revelation*, WBC 52A-C (Nashville: Nelson, 1997–98), 2:664–65; Craig R. Koester, *Revelation*, AB 38A (New Haven: Yale University Press, 2014), 524.

power of Rome, on the one hand, and the "saints" (13:7) and those refusing to worship the (second) beast (13:15), on the other. For the latter, the result of non-complicity with the activities of the beast's image is deemed to be death, so that the very existence of the people of God in the described order of things is under threat. While in chapter 13, it is the two beasts representing Roman rule that lie behind the threat, the ultimate source thereof is represented in chapter 12 as a dragon, who is unequivocally identified as "the devil, Satan, and the deceiver of the whole world" (12:9). Thus, when the text announces wisdom and couples it with the calculation of a number, the knowledge to be unlocked not only identifies who the second beast is but also places that beast's activities within a wider mythological framework: the myth of beginnings.

13:18: Behind Calculating the Number of the Second Beast

Comprehended within the context of chapters 12 and 13, the wisdom announced at the end of chapter 13 may be of several sorts. The first and perhaps more obvious aspect of this wisdom, which stands in close relation to having a "mind," is straightforward: it is assumed as something given to or attainable by those for whom the writing is intended; an ideal audience is, as a whole, expected to figure out the identification to which the number points. As a commodity of knowledge, however, it can technically be acquired by anyone, whether or not they belong to those who reject the beast. In other words, in and of itself the identification of the number "six hundred sixty-six" with Nero is not as such a matter of *divine disclosure*. Indeed, the text offers not only the possibility of arriving at the emperor's name and title through Hebrew letters[13] but also through a Hebrew transcription of the Greek nominative form of "beast," θηρίον (so for תריון).[14]

Second, it is not clear that the significance of the wisdom to which the text refers is entirely comprehended by the double decoding of the beast's name. Written into the acclamations of the Lamb and God in 5:12 and 7:12, respectively, σοφία may be thought to reflect a kind of insight or *revealed perspective that, if indeed revealed, has an impact on the way one lives*. In other words, the acclamations of the Lamb and of God, with all the attributes ascribed to them, are acts of worship. Indeed, in 7:11, the text introduces the expression of heavenly praise as fol-

13. The number 666 through the addition of numerical equivalents letters is possible through a defective spelling of "Nero Caesar" (קסר נרון, i.e. without י between the first two letters in the title: נ twice 50 = 100, ר twice 200 = 400, ס = 60, ק = 100, ו = 6), as found in an Aramaic document of debt found at Murabbaʿat dated to the second year of Nero's reign; cf. the text Klaus Beyer, *Die aramäischen Texte vom Toten Meer* (Göttingen: Vandenhoeck & Ruprecht, 1984), 306–7 (no. 18, line 1).

14. ת = 400, ר = 200, י = 10, ו = 6, נ = 50. For still the best discussion of this *isopsephism* for two different words and the larger context of such calculations in Revelation and the ancient world, see Richard Bauckham, "Nero and the Beast," in idem, *The Climax of Prophecy: Studies on the Book of Revelation* (London: T & T Clark, 1993), 384–452 (here 389–91). As with the Hebrew transcription of Nero's name, the leaving out of one letter *n* to correspond to the genitive form (θηρίου), results in the text-critical variant of "616."

lows: "And all the angels stood around the throne and around the elders and the four living creatures, and they fell on their faces before the throne and worshiped God (ἐπὶ τὰ πρόσωπα αὐτῶν καὶ προσεκύνησαν τῷ θεῷ)." If we return to the scene in chapter 13, it is precisely the act of *worship* that functions as a determinative criterion for religious identity; those who refuse to worship the image of the beast (v. 15, ὅσοι ἐὰν μὴ προσκυνήσωσιν τῇ εἰκόνι τοῦ θηρίου)—these are the very ones whose understanding is appealed to in verse 18—are under threat, and closely aligned to this, are excluded from participating in commercial buying and selling (v. 17).[15] "*Here* (ὧδε) is wisdom" does not simply introduce the following calculation, but may very well link what follows to the consequences for the faithful of the true worship just described, that is, to their refusal to have anything to do with the second beast and the image it has erected. The decoding of the number thus takes on an exhortatory function *if* what precedes in verses 15–17 marks out what loyalty to God means; in a world of stark contrasts between one kind of loyalty and another, the identification of 666 with Nero boldly underscores the audience's awareness of a system with which there can be no effective or reasonable negotiation. The number is not merely one to decode, but also, as becomes clear within the text to follow, one to *conquer* (15:2, those with harps in their hands have "conquered the beast and its image and the number of its name").

Third, we note that the mention of wisdom in 13:18 occurs at a midpoint within a new section in the Apocalypse (11:19–15:4) that, as mentioned above, follows the cycle of seven trumpets (8:6–11:18) and precedes the cycle of seven plagues (15:5–16:21). The placement of the announcement of "wisdom" as immanent is strategic. It concludes the mythical vision of powers that threaten the faithful (embodied by the dragon, the first and second beasts), and precedes the counter-vision of 144,000 faithful standing with the Lamb on Mount Zion (14:1–5). The contrasting visions of threat, on the one hand, and of unhindered worship, on the other, reveal the exclusionary, non-overlapping contours of the conflict. Those who recognize and can calculate the number of the beast, whose mark (χάραγμα) accords a wide range of humanity a free hand of participation in the economy and protection (vv. 16–17; cf. further 14:9,11; 16:2; 19:20; 20:4), are to position themselves with the Lamb, identified by both his and his Father's

15. To be sure, the images of marking bodies through stigmatization or tattoo, whether to link slaves with a temple or to identify members of a cult, draws on a plausibility structure of practices well known in the Mediterranean world (Egypt, Syria, and mystery cults); cf. the evidence reviewed by Thomas Witulski, *Die Johannesoffenbarung und der Kaiser Hadrian*, FRLANT 221 (Göttingen: Vandenhoeck & Ruprecht, 2007), 143–237 (esp. 166–78) and Franz Tóth, *Das Tier, sein Bild und der falsche Prophet: Untersuchungen zum zeitgeschichtlichen Hintergrund von Johannesoffenbarung 13 unter Einbeziehung des antiken Orakelwesens*, BTS 126 (Neukirchen-Vluyn: Neukirchener, 2012), 134–54. Nevertheless, as Tóth also recognizes, it should not be assumed that the text reflects descriptively back on a persecution already underway and experienced by its hearers and readers; instead, it projects onto the world unnuanced consequences the follow from the categorical worship to which it calls; cf. Leonard L. Thompson, "A Sociological Analysis of Tribulation in the Apocalypse of John," *Semeia* 36 (1986): 147–174; Bauckham, *Climax of Prophecy*, 447; Loren T. Stuckenbruck, "The Book of Revelation," in *Eerdmans Commentary on the Bible*, eds. James D. G. Dunn and John W. Rogerson (Grand Rapids: Eerdmans, 2003), 1535–72 (1556).

name (ὄνομα)[16] and are given to learn a new song that is exclusively theirs to sing (14:1–3). While "wisdom" may involve insight into the oppositional spheres of existence for the beast's adherents and those who follow the Lamb, its position at the end of chapters 12 and 13 may signify more. The visions convey insight into the nature of the dragon and the two beasts' activities. From the very beginning, the dragon is portrayed as posing a threat to the woman who bears a child (12:1–5); after a brief period of temporary protection for the woman and child (v. 6), the dragon "wages war" against them (12:17; cf. verse 13)—a conflict that extends, through the two beasts, until the end of chapter 13.[17] The insight, however, that the text offers relates to the initial outcome of the conflict, as described in 12:7–9, and the immediately following proclamation from heaven (vv. 10–13). By the time the situation of conflict threatens the well-being of believers (13:7), the dragon and its minions have indeed already been involved in a celestial war (12:7–9). This event is not simply a "battle" that marks out one phase in a prolonged struggle, but rather is one that *from the outset* determines, and indeed, defines the status of "the great dragon." Significantly, the dragon is also called "the ancient serpent," "the devil", and "Satan, who deceives (pres. ptc. ὁ πλανῶν) the whole world." In other words, the beasts' activities go back to a power, which has *already been defeated*.[18] This power, in all its symbolic and numerical representation, can be readily identified as one who, in the present, foments deceit.

When, precisely, has the defeat of Satan already taken place? Some interpreters think the text refers to an eschatological event that, as yet, lies in the author and the audience's future.[19] For instance, Jan Dochhorn, by focusing narrowly on tradition history in relation to Satan (or the devil) as a single figure, has insisted that there is no evidence prior to the John's Apocalypse that refers to or describes a defeat of the devil in the past. Rather, if one follows the lead of parallel texts such as the *War Scroll* (1QM 17:5–8, the eschatological war between the "sons of light" led by the archangel Michael against the "sons of darkness" led by Belial) and John 12:31 ("now the ruler of this world *will* be cast out"), such a victory should be considered eschatological. Such a case is, however, overstated; an interpretation of Luke 10:18, in which Jesus is made to say "I saw Satan fall like lightning," is by no means a clear-cut reference to the future. In addition, this interpretation presupposes a clear line of demarcation between past defeats of evil of groups of angels (such as the rebellious "sons of God" in the Book of Watchers at 1 Enoch 6–16,

16. The author seems careful not to refer to the Lamb and God in the plural. With the possible exception of a mention of "their wrath" in 6:17, the text, when mentioning the Lamb and God together, retains language in the singular, whether it be "name" (3:12; 14:1) or pronouns (22:3–4; cf. 1:1); as more indirect indications of this, see also the acclamations in 5:13 and 7:10.

17. The argument here assumes, despite the complex history of religions and mythological backgrounds behind the dragon, the beasts, and the woman and child, a certain literary cohesion in the overall sequence of visions in chapters 12 and 13 remains unmistakable.

18. On the notion of the prior defeat of evil in Second Temple apocalyptic literature, see Loren T. Stuckenbruck, *The Myth of Rebellious Angels: Studies in Second Temple Judaism and in the New Testament*, WUNT 335 (Tübingen: Mohr Siebeck, 2014), esp. chs. 1 (pp. 1–35), 9 (161–86), and 12 (240–56).

19. Cf. Jan Dochhorn, *Schriftgelehrte Prophetie: Der eschatologische Teufelsfall in Apc Joh 12 und seine Bedeutung für das Verständnis der Johannesoffenbarung*, WUNT 268 (Tübingen: Mohr Siebeck, 2010), 254–85; see further Aune, *Revelation*, 2:692–93.

in which Michael, at the time of the Flood, is involved in carrying out the punishment against their leader Shemihazah and his minions; cf. 10:11–13), on the one hand, and of any defeat of a primary figure representing evil, on the other. David Aune, who likewise regards the event as eschatological,[20] has dismissed any influence of the fallen angels tradition on the grounds that they were not *cast out* or forcibly removed from heaven (cf. ἐβλήθη in Rev 12:10, 11), but rather *left* heaven on their own volition (1 Enoch 6:1–5). It should be noted, however, that in 12:12, the resumé of what has happened is described in the active voice: "the devil has come down (κατέβη) to you." Significantly, this interchange of passive verbs with an active one in Revelation is similarly found in the Animal Apocalypse, which clearly stands under the influence of the angelic rebellious myth of the Book of Watchers. Although the lead star (equivalent to Shemihazah in the Book of Watchers) *fell from heaven* (*wadqa 'em-samāy*; 1 Enoch 86:1), those "many stars" coming after him are said not only to have come down (*waredu*), but also to have been *thrown down* from heaven (86:3).[21]

An unnecessary precision, that opts for one or another alternative, distracts from the unequivocal conviction that the devil and his forces have undergo a decisive defeat, and *as such*, have nevertheless gone about wielding power against God's people. Although a background in the fallen angels' tradition in the primordial past cannot be dismissed, it is not this event from the primordial past that is determinative for the defeat of the dragon. Critical is the heavenly proclamation in Revelation 12:11: "they (the faithful) have conquered him (the devil) by the blood of the Lamb and by the word of their testimony." It is tempting to regard this defeat of the devil as not having happened until Jesus's death "on the cross" (11:9 refers to the crucifixion of Jesus, but only in passing).[22] However, for the writer, what happened in Jesus's death carries with it an all-encompassing reality that did not so much begin with the crucifixion as it reached back to reflect something that had been inaugurated by God "at the foundation of the world," when not only the Lamb is in a slaughtered state but also when it has been determined whose names would and would not be inscribed in the book of life (cf. 13:8; further 17:8).[23]

20. See the previous note.

21. Similarly, 1 Enoch 88:1 refers to the lead star as having fallen, followed by a description of how one of the archangels bound him hand and foot and threw him into the abyss, as also happens to the other stars (88:3).

22. So e.g. Jürgen Roloff, *Die Offenbarung des Johannes*, 3rd ed., ZBK (Zurich: Theologischer Verlag Zürich, 2001), 134 and 138; Brian K. Blount, *Revelation: A Commentary*, NTL (Louisville: Westminster John Knox, 2009), 252; Koester, *Revelation*, 575.

23. Following the wording in 17:8, which, without mentioning the Lamb, refers to those whose names are not written in the book of life from the foundation of the world (ἀπὸ καταβολῆς κόσμου), many interpreters render 13:8 with the same emphasis (so most modern translations): "everyone whose name has not been written from the foundation of the world in the book of life of the Lamb that was slaughtered" (so the NRSV). The Greek text, however, reads more straightforwardly as follows: "everyone whose name has not been written in the book of life of the Lamb that was slaughtered from the foundation of the world," thus presenting the Lamb's sacrifice as primordial reality (cf. 1 Pet 1:20–21). Regarding the meaning as problematic, Ulrich B. Müller, *Die Offenbarung des Johannes*, 2nd ed., ÖTK 19 (Gütersloh: Echter, 1995), 252 and Aune, *Revelation*, 2:747, prefer a solution that regards the phrase "of the Lamb that was slaughtered" as an interpolator's intrusion rather than a statement attributable to the original writer. However, even if one follows the NRSV translation, there remains the implication that the recording and non-recording of names in the book of life, even in primordial time, depends on how people line up in relation to the slaughtered Lamb; in this sense, Ernst Lohmeyer,

These alternative backgrounds are not mutually exclusive; indeed, the author of Revelation is capable of conflating traditions to construct an interactive world of meaning within the text.[24] In this particular case, the crucial dawn of "salvation and power and the kingdom of God and of his Messiah" (Rev 12:10) has been generated by the Lamb's blood (i.e. his death, sacrificially understood). The new reality that has come into being is modeled on a prior one. According to the older Jewish apocalyptic tradition, a formative perspective is lent to the present on the basis of a defeat of Satan that excludes evil from the heavenly sphere.[25] Though images from this prior defeat, which happened at the time of the Flood, can still be identified in 12:7–9, language of triumph is ultimately absorbed into a christological framework. The advent of Jesus (12:1–5) and its culmination in his death, resurrection and ascent (12:11; cf. the reference to the son's being taken away to God and God's throne in verse 5b) become the new foci around which that defeat is defined. At the same time, the new context is not simply a matter of reassigning a primordial defeat of Satan to the more recent past; even the recent past, Jesus's death, is but the outworking of a reality that existed in primordial time as well.

Aside from the knowledge of Jesus's death and its principled significance, it is not clear whether the text of chapters 12 and 13 presupposes the audience's ability to identify with precision each of the several traditions upon which the author, in conflated form, draws. They will, however, have been in no doubt that the ominous and imminently life-threatening activities of the two beasts are under divine control, even if it initially seems to be ironic. More than this, the assertion of God's rule over the precarious situation is not teleological, that is, a matter of simply expressing confidence that the beasts' defeat will take place; rather, that defeat has already been inscribed in cosmic reality through Jesus's slaughter as the Lamb and the casting out of Satan and his angels from heaven.

Die Offenbarung des Johannes, 3rd ed., HNT 16 (Tübingen: Mohr Siebeck, 1953), 112, could describe the phrase as "doppeldeutig." See further the remarks on the syntax 13:8 and its relation to 17:8 by Robert H. Mounce, *The Book of Revelation*, NICNT 17 (Grand Rapids: Eerdmans, 1977), 256; Gregory K. Beale, *The Book of Revelation: A Commentary on the Greek Text*, NIGTC (Grand Rapids: Eerdmans, 1999), 702–3; and Edmundo F. Lupieri, *A Commentary on the Apocalypse of John* (Grand Rapids: Eerdmans, 2006), 208. The inference to be drawn from reading the Lamb's slaughter in relation to primordial time is not insignificant. What happened in the death by crucifixion of Jesus in recent time does not mark a shift in the perception of reality. The slaughtered Lamb is not only cast into and presented within the realm of myth, it is projected back into aforetime and, as such, expresses something that is woven into the fabric of the cosmos itself. Primordial, then, is not only Jesus's death, but also the conquering that goes with it and that determines those whose names are recorded and not recorded in the book of life.

24. On this in relation to Rev 12, see esp. Adela Yarbro Collins, *The Combat Myth in the Book of Revelation* (Eugene: Wipf & Stock, 2001, repr. Missoula, MT: Scholars, 1976), esp. 57–100; further, see Leonard L. Thompson, *The Book of Revelation: Apocalypse and Empire* (New York: Oxford University Press, 1990), 38; Stuckenbruck, *The Myth of Rebellious Angels*, 303–4.

25. Cf. Loren T. Stuckenbruck, "Some Reflections on Apocalyptic Thought and Time in Literature from the Second Temple Period," in *Paul and the Apocalyptic Imagination*, eds. Ben C. Blackwell, John K. Goodrich, and Jason Maston (Minneapolis: Fortress Press, 2016), 137–55.

17:9: Behind the Vision of the Whore of Babylon and the Seven Heads

It remains to consider the fourth occurrence of "wisdom" in the Apocalypse at 17:9. Revelation 17:9–14 reads:

> 9Here is[26] a mind that has wisdom (ὧδε ὁ νοῦς ὁ ἔχων σοφίαν): the seven heads are seven mountains on which the woman is seated; also, they are seven kings, 10of whom five have fallen, one is living, and the other has not yet come; and when he comes, he must remain only a little while. 11As for the beast that was and is not, it is an eighth but it belongs to the seven, and it goes to destruction. 12And the ten horns that you saw are ten kings who have not yet received a kingdom, but they are to receive authority as kings for one hour, together with the beast. 13These are united in yielding their power and authority to the beast; 14they will make war on the Lamb, and the Lamb will conquer them, for he is Lord of lords and King of kings, and those with him are called chosen and faithful.

Here, my comment shall focus less on the identification of the kings to which the text refers. Instead, with respect to verse 9, it initially bears noting what seems to be a close linguistic parallel to 13:18, with the mention of "here" and the combination of "wisdom" and "mind." Although both passages link having a "mind" with wisdom, it is not clear that they are to be taken as one and the same. I have suggested above that "wisdom" in 13:18 not only denotes the ability to calculate the number of the beast but also involves: (a) a perception that this beast is but a defeated power, and therefore, (b) the confidence to resist any strictures the beast might impose, even to the point of death. Wisdom, in other words, embraces more than what even the discerning mind can more immediately carry out. Analogous to 13:18, the wisdom in 17:9 includes the possession of knowledge regarding the identity of the beast, which the interpreting angel in 17:11 describes as the eighth king. However, with 13:18 in view, the relationship between the terms "mind" and "wisdom" in 17:9 seems even closer; whereas the text in 13:18 refers to one who "has a mind," here, the writer refers to "the mind that has wisdom," that is, "wisdom" functions as the essential qualifier for a mind that functions in its ideal state.

The differences of symbolism between chapters 12–13 and 17 aside, the temporal focus of 17 marks a shift. Whereas the sequence of events in the episodes of chapters 12 and 13 takes its point of departure in the primordial and recent past, in which the Lamb is presented as already victorious over Satan, chapter 17 focuses on the future conflict in which the Lamb *shall* defeat the ten kings allied with the (second) beast. Although the immediate reason for the Lamb's victory lies is the designation "Lord of lords and King of kings," (17:14, introduced with causal ὅτι; cf. also 19:16 in the context of the eschatological battle), it is a title that ultimately comes to

26. NRSV has "This calls for."

him by virtue of his conquering death and the ensuing defeat of the dragon. Therefore, within the narrative flow of the Apocalypse, the vision of the whore of Babylon, of the kings associated with her and of the beast (17:12–13) does not stand on its own. The sapiential confidence in the Lamb's future victory, in which "the chosen and faithful" ones will share, emerges from the sapiential perception that has also located this victory in the past.

A further observation suggests that the "wisdom" mentioned in chapter 17 is not exhausted by the identification of the seven heads (v. 9) and ten horns (v. 12). The decoding of these symbols is preceded by a process of discernment in which the seer has been corrected from entertaining a false perception of the whore of Babylon. Although the interpreting angel informs the seer that the vision he will be given of the whore concerns her "judgment" (v. 1, τὸ κρίμα) and although he sees her "drunk with the blood of the saints and the blood of the witnesses to Jesus" (v. 6a), he nevertheless marvels at her appearance (ἐθαύμασα ἰδὼν αὐτὴν θαῦμα μέγα, "Seeing, I admired her with great wonder," verse 6b). This response (as in the seer's reaction to the interpreting angel in 19:10 and 22:8–9[27]) is misguided; far too much, it resembles the response to the beast by the inhabitants of the earth immediately thereafter: "seeing the beast, they will admire it" (v. 8: θαυμασθήσονται . . . βλεπόντων τὸ θηρίον). Before proceeding to explain the meaning of the vision, the angel wastes no time by reprimanding the seer with the question, "Why do you show (her) admiration (διὰ τί ἐθαύμασας)?"[28] This correction of the seer,[29] which is absent in chapters 12 and 13, serves to add a dimension to the wisdom mentioned in 17:9. If we remember that the book was to be read aloud (Rev 1:3) and therefore to be *heard* (1:3; cf. 2:7, 11, 17, 29; 3:6, 13, 20, 22; 13:9; 22:17, 18), then what the seer presents as having learned through the vision is to be pondered and absorbed by the book's recipients, as indicated in the words, "Here is the mind that has wisdom."[30] The understanding that accompanies wisdom, then, points to a deeper, contrastive reality than what the vision of the whore may lead one to think.

Conclusion

The above overview of "wisdom" in the Apocalypse demonstrates that, although the term occurs only four times, its significance is interwoven with the message of the book as a whole. To proclaim wisdom among the features of the Lamb (5:12) and of God (7:12) is to locate the

27. On which, see Loren T. Stuckenbruck, *Angel Veneration and Christology*, WUNT II/70 (Tübingen: Mohr Siebeck, 1995) and "An Angelic Refusal of Worship: The Tradition and Its Function in the Apocalypse of John," in *SBL Seminar Papers 1994*, ed. Eugene Lovelace (Atlanta: Scholars, 1994), 679–96.
28. Translations here and immediately below are my own.
29. On the impropriety of the seer's response, see Whitaker, *Ekphrasis, Vision, and Persuasion*, 203–7.
30. As indicated above, the mention of wisdom in 13:18 likewise presupposes a direct interactive participation of the audience with the vision of the beast.

true perception of things in a faith-based reality that contrasts with the world that the recipients of the revelation are presumed to experience. This reality expresses itself in a worship and devotion that does not falter when confronted by a system thoroughly caught up in a web of deception. Where, then, is wisdom? It is "here" (13:18; 17:9), when recipients of the vision are able to identify the beast (13:18), its fraudulent lure to unhindered participation in economic life (13:16–17), and its status as a force whose time is marked and that, despite the power it wields, has already been defeated (12:7–12). Wisdom is also at work in the wake of the correction of a misperception to which even the seer himself is subject (17:6–7, 9).

Wisdom in the Apocalypse is, thus, an affirmation and perspective not bound up with or ultimately dependent on a series of in-breaking or forthcoming eschatological events. It is, rather, a kind of knowing that is revealed through the messages and visions of the book, and in that it covers primordial as well as eschatological time, embraces reality as a whole.

Finally, *σοφία* belies a world of communication that an audience is called to inhabit. Whereas visions and messages have been revealed through a complex hierarchy of mediators, the book assumes a process of active discernment on the part of the audience of "the prophecy of this book" (22:7, 10, 18; cf. 1:3 and 22:19). The need to exercise discernment is partly modeled by John who, although he gives a first person account of what he sees and hears through the work, has to be taught what is means (5:4–5; 7:13–17), even if through initial ignorance or misperception (5:4–5; 7:13–14; 19:10; 22:8–9). While the recipients participate in the revelatory experiences of the seer as the work is read in their presence, it falls to them, apart from John, to engage on their own in activities of discernment through identification and dissociation. Hence, each of the messages to the seven churches concludes with the identical exhortation: "Let anyone who has an ear listen to what the Spirit is saying to the churches" (2:6, 11, 17, 29; 3:6, 13, 22). The wisdom of the Apocalypse is thus not only a matter of discerning "the true nature of the situation, but also of heeding the prophetic *demand* for an appropriate response."[31]

31. Richard Bauckham, "Approaching the Apocalypse," in *Decide for Peace: Evangelicals and the Bomb*, ed. Dana Mills-Powell (Basingstoke: Marshall Pickering, 1986), 88–98 (here 94); cf. Johns, *The Lamb Christology of the Apocalypse of John*, 91.

Contributors

Leslie Baynes is associate professor of New Testament and Second Temple Judaism at Missouri State University in Springfield, Missouri. She is the author of *The Heavenly Book Motif in Judeo-Christian Apocalypses, 200 BCE–200 CE* (2012) and "The Parables of Enoch and Luke's Parable of the Rich Man and Lazarus," in *Enoch and the Synoptic Gospels: Reminiscences, Allusions, Intertextuality*, eds. Loren T. Stuckenbruck and Gabriele Boccaccini (2016).

Kristian A. Bendoraitis teaches at Spring Arbor University and has written *Behold They Came and Served Him: A Compositional Analysis of Angels in Matthew* (2015) and co-edited, with Nijay K. Gupta, *Matthew and Mark Across Perspectives: Essays in Honour of Stephen C. Barton and William R. Telford* (2016).

John Byron is professor of New Testament at Ashland Theological Seminary. His publications include *Recent Research on Paul and Slavery* (2008), *Cain and Abel in Text and Tradition* (2011), and a commentary on *1 & 2 Thessalonians* (2014).

Kindalee Pfremmer De Long is associate professor of religion at Pepperdine University and the author of *Surprised by God: Praise Responses in the Narrative of Luke-Acts* (2009), "Ask a Woman: Childbearing and Ezra's Transformation in 4 Ezra" (*Journal for the Study of the Pseudepigrapha*, 2012), and a chapter on Tobit in *The Wiley-Blackwell Companion to Old Testament Apocrypha and Pseudepigrapha* (forthcoming).

Matthew Goff is a professor of Hebrew Bible and Second Temple Judaism in the Department of Religion at Florida State University. His most recent book is *4QInstruction: A Commentary* (2013). He is also author of *Discerning Wisdom: An Introduction to the Sapiential Literature of the Dead Sea Scrolls* (2007).

Mark Harding was Dean and CEO of the Australian College of Theology from 1996 to 2016. He is an honorary associate of Macquarie University and the author of *What Are They Saying About the Pastoral Epistles* (2001) and *Tradition and Rhetoric in the Pastoral Epistles* (1998).

Karina Martin Hogan is associate professor of Old Testament and ancient Judaism at Fordham University. She is the author of *Theologies in Conflict in 4 Ezra: Wisdom Debate and Apocalyptic Solution* (2008) and co-editor of *The "Other" in Second Temple Judaism: Essays in Honor of John J. Collins* (2011) and *Pedagogy in Ancient Judaism and Early Christianity* (forthcoming).

Mariam Kamell Kovalishyn is assistant professor at Regent College in British Columbia. She has focused her research on the epistle of James, including her doctoral thesis and numerous articles in books and journals. She is also the co-author of the *Zondervan Exegetical Commentary on James* with Craig Blomberg.

Grant Macaskill holds the Kirby Laing Chair of New Testament Exegesis at the University of Aberdeen. He is the author of *Union with Christ in the New Testament* (2013), *The Slavonic Texts of 2 Enoch* (2013), and *Revealed Wisdom and Inaugurated Eschatology in Ancient Judaism and Early Christianity* (2007).

Eric F. Mason holds the Julius R. Mantey Chair of Biblical Studies at Judson University, Elgin, Illinois. He is the author of *'You Are a Priest Forever': Second Temple Jewish Messianism and the Priestly Christology of the Epistle to the Hebrews* (2008; reprinted, 2014) and editor (with Kevin B. McCruden) of *Reading the Epistle to the Hebrews: A Resource for Students* (2011).

Chad Pierce is the senior pastor at Faith Christian Reformed Church in Holland, Michigan, and part-time instructor at Western Theological Seminary. His previous publications include *Spirits and the Proclamation of Christ: 1 Peter 3:18–22 in Light of Sin and Punishment Traditions in Early Jewish and Christian Literature* (2011) and works on apotropaic prayers and Jewish apocalyptic traditions in the New Testament.

Benjamin E. Reynolds is associate professor of New Testament at Tyndale University College, Toronto, Ontario. He is the author of *The Apocalyptic Son of Man in the Gospel of John* (2008) and "The Otherworldly Mediators in *4 Ezra* and *2 Baruch*: A Comparison with Angelic Mediators in Ascent Apocalypses and in Daniel, Zechariah, and Ezekiel," in *Fourth Ezra and Second Baruch: Reconstruction after the Fall*, eds. Matthias Henze and Gabriele Boccaccini (2013).

Bennie H. Reynolds III is assistant director of assessment at the Medical University of South Carolina. He is the author of the monograph *Between Symbolism and Realism: The Use of Symbolic and Non-Symbolic Language in Ancient Jewish Apocalypses 333–63 B.C.E.* (2011) and the forthcoming essay "A Dwelling Place of Demons: Apocalypticism and the Dead Sea Scrolls" (*ISBL Vienna Volume in Honor of John J. Collins*, 2017).

Christopher Rowland is Dean Ireland Professor of the Exegesis of Holy Scripture Emeritus at the University of Oxford. He has a longstanding interest in apocalypticism and its history in Christianity. His book on William Blake's use of the Bible (*Blake and the Bible*, 2011) includes a discussion of Blake's apocalyptic interests. His book on radical prophecy is forthcoming.

James M. Scott is professor of religious studies at Trinity Western University in Langley, British Columbia. He is the author of several books bearing on the subject of the present volume, including *Paul and the Nations: The Old Testament and Jewish Background of Paul's Mission to the Nations with Special Reference to the Destination of Galatians* (1995) and *One Earth as in Heaven: The Restoration of Sacred Time and Sacred Space in the Book of Jubilees* (2005).

Angela Standhartinger is professor of New Testament studies at the Philipps-University Marburg, Germany. Her most recent publications include: "Letter from Prison as Hidden Transcript: What it tells us about the people at Philippi," in *The People beside Paul. The Philippian Assembly and History from Below*, ed. Joseph A. Marchal (2015) and "Eintracht in Philippi. Zugleich ein Beitrag zur Funktion von Phil 2,6-11 im Kontext," in *Paulus: Werk und Wirkung. Festschrift für Andreas Lindemann zum 70. Geburtstag*, eds. Paul-Gerhard Klumbies and David S. du Toit (2013).

Loren T. Stuckenbruck is professor of New Testament (with emphasis on Second Temple Judaism) at the Ludwig-Maximilians-Universität München. He is the author of *Angel Veneration and Christology* (1995), *The Book of Giants from Qumran* (1997), *1 Enoch 91-108* (2007); *The Myth of Rebellious Angels* (2014), and the co-editor and author of numerous books and articles.

Benjamin Wold is assistant professor in early Judaism and Christianity at Trinity College Dublin, Ireland. His academic articles have focused on the Dead Sea Scrolls, wisdom and apocalyptic literature, and conceptualizations of evil. He has published *Women, Men and Angels* (2005), *Evil, the Devil, and Demons* (2016), and *4QInstruction: Divisions and Hierarchies* (forthcoming).

Index of Subjects and Key Terms

angel(s), 2, 3, 6–10, 12, 16, 17–20, 23, 26–30, 31, 33, 34–35, 37–51, 68–69, 74, 79–99, 102–3, 105–7, 111–16, 120–28, 134, 135, 148–49, 152, 159, 170, 172, 173, 177–78, 180, 183, 187–91, 200n19, 201, 205, 210, 212, 217n76, 220–25, 227–29, 240, 241, 247, 249, 278, 280–82, 285–90, 296, 308, 310–15, 317–24, 333, 337, 339, 341, 342n48, 348–51, 353–58
angelology, 10, 33, 37nn41, 38n45, 187n47
angelomorphology, 16, 32, 110–11, 135
*angelus interpres,*16, 17, 19, 22, 29, 30, 82, 85, 103n100, 177–78, 180, 181
antichrist, 114n17, 329, 331, 336

Baruch, 8, 16, 17–19, 21, 111, 116, 122–23, 126, 237n26
beast, 3, 183, 218, 316n26, 351–54, 356–59

christology, 22, 63, 75, 173, 262, 329, 348, 350n9
creation/created order, 8, 10, 19, 105, 112, 157–59, 161–62, 166, 174, 176, 179, 180–81, 186, 204, 206n37, 207–11, 215n71, 218, 227, 231, 242, 265, 285, 288, 289n29, 308n4, 323, 348

Daniel, 3, 7, 21, 24, 44, 61, 75, 83, 85, 98, 115, 120–21, 124, 126, 179, 260, 294n6, 342
demon/ology, 12, 17, 22, 23, 33, 61n21, 62–63, 64, 69, 79, 85, 89–90, 93, 104–7, 220, 221, 249, 305n60, 313, 327–45
dualism/dual cosmology, 5, 33, 36, 111n11, 156, 176, 207–8, 210–11, 258, 259n2, 262, 264, 294, 322, 331–34
dualism, spatial, 207–12, 221
dualism, temporal, 207–12, 229, 232

eschatology/eschatological, 1–6, 7n48, 9–12, 23, 26, 29, 32–36, 39, 41–44, 47n90, 48n92, 50, 50n106, 51, 53–54, 56–57, 59, 61, 68, 72–75, 77, 79, 81, 82, 83, 86, 87n46, 88–90, 94, 96, 98, 105–7, 109–10, 128, 132–35, 138, 150–53, 155–57, 160–61, 163–67, 169–74, 176–78, 182–85, 192, 195, 199, 202–4, 207–8, 210–11, 217–18, 219–21, 227, 229–30, 232, 234, 239, 241–42, 245–46, 248–49, 251, 254–55, 257–58, 259n2, 260–64, 270n53, 277–78, 281, 286, 294–99, 301–6, 309–12, 320, 328–29, 334, 337, 339, 341–44, 347, 354–55, 357, 359
Elijah *redivivus,* 68
Enoch, 4, 7–8, 16, 19–21, 25–26, 44, 70–71, 83–84,

91, 98, 111, 115–16, 121–23, 126–27, 189–91, 196–198, 200–206, 208, 210, 213, 215, 236n19, 237–38, 243n63, 286, 288n27, 289n29
epiphany, 11, 16, 24, 30, 136, 232205, 266–68, 271
evil, 3, 11, 27, 61–63, 71, 81, 85–86, 89–90, 93, 105, 107, 113–14, 166–68, 176–77, 180, 182, 188, 203, 204n32, 206–11, 220–22, 225, 227–35, 249, 309, 312–18, 320, 323, 331–33, 354–56
evil spirit, 60–62, 63, 71, 86, 105n104, 210n51, 312–14, 333
ex eventu prophecy, 73
Ezekiel, 16, 84, 98, 115–16, 120, 135–36
Ezra, 7–8, 17–19, 44, 111, 160–61, 167–69, 237n26

fallen angel, 12, 17, 38n46, 210, 249, 312–14, 319, 321, 322–23, 355

glory, 10, 12, 23–28, 37, 41–44, 47–48, 58–59, 68–70, 79, 83–97, 100, 102–4, 107, 111, 115–20, 127, 134, 138–40, 142, 157, 160, 169–74, 179, 185–86, 191, 200–201, 206, 211, 213, 224, 234, 238–43, 250, 261, 263, 265, 280, 288, 308–11, 317, 320, 325, 341, 349, 351
gnostic, 65, 110, 118, 125, 135, 148, 223, 271–72, 322, 330

heavenly books, 22, 30, 243n63
heavenly figure/being, 16, 20, 26, 38, 59, 69, 70, 75, 80, 82n10, 85–86, 91–92, 111–13, 127, 134, 184, 188n50, 241–42, 288n27, 320
human messenger, 82n10

John, 3, 16, 22, 24, 30, 39n56, 56–57, 68, 71, 82, 84, 100, 102, 112, 113, 116, 125, 200, 262n13, 348–49, 359

judgment, 1–3, 10, 27, 36n33, 39–43, 46, 50–51, 66, 92, 119, 123, 142, 157–59, 161, 164–70, 172–74, 176, 180, 183–84, 188, 195, 201, 203, 204, 207, 210–12, 214n67, 215, 221, 234–35, 238, 241, 243, 248, 255, 264, 270, 284, 294, 296–301, 303–6, 308–9, 315, 318–24, 329, 337, 339, 341, 344, 348, 351, 358

Levi, 8, 16, 25–26, 98n84, 115–16, 123, 126, 284, 288n27

messiah/messianism, 2–3, 20, 23–25, 36n30, 43, 47n91, 63, 72–74, 82, 85, 86n35, 90, 104, 107, 118, 137, 140, 142, 150–51, 162, 177, 183–86, 209, 251–52, 279n11, 288n27, 303, 316, 356
mystery, 9, 11, 18, 20, 65–66, 69, 121, 123, 127, 138–39, 141–42, 150, 177, 179–81, 200, 213, 220, 223n14, 225, 227–28, 230, 263–66, 269, 271, 273, 304, 308n3, 317, 353n15
mystic/ism, 5, 96–98, 115, 131–40, 148–51, 190–91, 223–27, 229, 232, 247, 278, 290n33, 322

parable, 9–10, 17–20, 23–24, 30, 40–42, 49, 54, 63–67, 124–25, 160, 261, 299n31
parousia, 1, 11, 35, 39, 75, 156–57, 160, 163, 171, 173, 175–76, 181–85, 192, 221, 233, 246–47, 249–52, 254–58, 259n2, 262–63, 265, 269, 281, 303, 305, 310, 323–24
prophet/prophecy, seer, 2, 3, 5n29, 7, 11–12, 16, 18, 22, 37, 38n47, 56–59, 67–68, 72–73, 82, 84–86, 90, 94n77, 98, 101–3, 106, 115–16, 119, 121, 123, 125, 127, 134, 136, 138–39, 141–42, 148, 150–52, 179, 180, 190n58, 201, 204, 232, 235, 236n19, 237–39, 241–43, 245–49, 251, 257, 260, 263, 279–80, 282, 287, 289, 300, 302,

308–9, 310n7, 311, 319n33, 325, 336, 350n8, 358–59

resurrection, 2, 10–11, 23–24, 26n44, 28–29, 44, 48–50, 60, 63, 71, 81, 90–93, 96n81, 103–4, 106–7, 110n6, 114, 117, 126, 138, 152, 155–57, 163–68, 171–74, 177–78, 181–85, 201, 204, 221, 227, 233–34, 238, 241–43, 246, 248–52, 256–57, 265, 266n30, 270, 272, 279n11, 308, 310–12, 314–17, 356

sapiential books, 232, 294n6, 305
sapiential tradition, 180–81, 305, 306n37
Satan, 17, 22–23, 38n44, 40n62, 60–62, 64, 79–80, 85, 89n57, 90, 97, 99–100, 102–7, 113, 141, 162n33, 191, 247–49, 258, 333, 340, 348, 352, 354, 356–57
secret(s), heavenly/divine, 4, 17–18, 20–21, 38, 50, 58, 79, 138, 189, 190n58, 259–63, 266, 288, 307, 310–11
Son of God, 16–17, 30, 45, 47, 54n1, 59, 63, 67, 71, 74–77, 116, 118, 201, 205–6, 331
Son of Man, 3, 10, 16, 24, 27, 30, 35, 39–44, 46, 47n90, 48n97, 50–51, 59, 70–71, 73–76, 95, 99, 101, 103, 112–13, 118, 141, 183–84, 190, 213n63, 234, 241, 288n27, 308n4, 315
spiritual/spirituality, 7, 33, 45, 57–64, 106, 147, 151, 178, 181, 227, 282, 312–15, 331, 336–42
Sibylline Oracles, 40n58, 98n84, 207n38, 257, 312n12, 319n32

theophany, 16n6, 30, 42n68, 69–70
Thomas, 40n57
transfiguration, 10, 16n6, 23–25, 28–30, 37n40, 41, 54, 67–70, 76, 85, 91–93, 99–104

vision/ary, 3, 10, 12, 16, 17, 19, 22–23, 26, 28–30, 34, 36, 38, 40, 44, 45n84, 58, 60n19, 68, 79–85, 88, 91, 92n66, 93, 96, 97–107, 110, 112, 115–28, 132–40, 142–43, 149–50, 152, 177–78, 180–81, 189–91, 193n3, 198–200, 203, 208–9, 212, 222, 224, 246–47, 260, 261n11, 262–63, 271–72, 278, 288n27, 290, 293–95, 297, 305, 322, 324, 338, 342n48, 349, 351, 353–54, 358–59

wisdom/σοφία, 7–9, 11–12, 19, 21, 23, 28, 54, 57, 59, 62–67, 72, 74, 76–77, 97, 104, 110, 133–34, 138–40, 142–44, 148, 158, 172, 176, 179, 181, 197, 203–7, 218, 220, 222–23, 225–26, 228, 230, 235–38, 246, 271n56, 293–306, 334, 336–37, 341, 347, 349–54, 357–59

Index of Modern Authors

Adams, Edward, 8n56, 75n68
Adler, William, 21n23, 209n48, 289n30
Ahmed, Leila, 188n49
Aland, K., 239n39
Alkier, Stefan, 348n3
Allison, Dale C., 2n6, 40n57, 45n84, 46nn86–87, 47n90, 49n101, 295, 296, 299n32, 300, 302n48, 303n51
Anderson, Bernard W., 206n36
Argall, Randal A., 7
Arida, Robert M., 20n19, 23n29
Artzt-Grabner, Peter, 239n39
Ashton, John, 110, 112nn12,15, 113n16, 117–19, 123, 127, 132
Attridge, Harold W., 260n5, 279, 282n17, 285n19, 286n21
Aune, David E., 5n33, 36n36, 194n4, 214n65, 247n10, 251n38, 291n34, 293, 300, 301n41, 330n12, 349n4, 351n12, 354n19, 355

Balch, David E., 230n39
Barnard, Jody A., 278, 282n17, 286, 289, 290n33
Barnett, A. E., 269n50
Barrett, C. K., 117n34, 125, 209n48
Bassler, Jouette, 214n64, 268
Bauckham, Richard, 163, 164, 297n20, 305, 317, 319n33, 322, 323nn44–46, 324n47, 330n12, 352n14, 353n15, 359n31
Bauer, Walter, 119n48, 272n64
Baur, F. C., 271n57, 272n58
Baynes, Leslie, 10, 22n28, 243n63
Beale, Gregory K., 15n1, 65n34, 356n23
Beker, J. Christiaan, 132, 156, 164n41, 166n45, 175nn1–2, 176, 233, 250, 251, 261–64
Bergmann, Claudia D., 163n36
Best, Ernest, 46n86
Beyer, H. W., 46n87
Beyerle, Stefan, 32n8, 38n50, 44n77, 45n80
Bianchi, Ugo, 332n16
Blackwell, Ben C., 2n15, 356n25
Blount, Brian K., 355n22
Boccaccini, Gabriele, 16n7, 24n35, 28n47, 208n42, 327n2
Bock, Darrell L., 59n14, 82n9, 86n33, 97n83, 118n41
Bockmuehl, Markus N. A., 21n24, 23, 134n10, 179n16, 188n52, 227n31, 230n38, 262n14
Bousset, Wilhelm, 37n42, 38n43, 259n2
Boustan, Ra'anan, 191n60
Bovon, Fran?ois, 84n22, 86n34

Bowker, J., 135–36
Bowley, James, 339n39
Box, G. H., 17n9
Boxall, Ian, 347n1
Brannon, M. Jeff, 227
Brant, Jo-Ann A., 237nn24–25
Brooke, George, 339n38
Brown, Raymond E., 17n11, 20nn20–21, 39n52, 45n81, 116n30, 179, 227, 262n14, 308n3, 328n4, 330
Brox, Norbert, 265n26, 266n32, 268n45, 270n53
Bruce, F. F., 99n91
Brueggemann, Walter, 302n49
Bühner, J.-A., 112n14, 124n73
Bultmann, Rudolf, 24n38, 28n48, 41n66, 109n2, 110, 114, 117, 118, 125, 126n82, 176, 259n2, 260n7, 265n27, 330
Burkes, Shannon, 305
Burkett, Delbert, 39n55
Burridge, Richard, 54n2
Byrne, Brendan, 158n16, 161n28, 164n41, 170n58, 171nn60,62, 173n64

Cadbury, Henry J., 187n47
Cameron, R., 133n8, 190n58
Campbell, Douglas A., 2n12, 261n11
Campenhausen, Hans von, 289n30
Caragounis, Chrys C., 41n66
Carey, Greg, 247n15, 248n17, 252n42, 254n57, 255n64, 256n68
Carr, A. Wesley, 221n7
Carson, D. A., 65n34, 334n24
Casey, Maurice, 183n35
Cassem, N. H., 114n20,
Cedrenus, Georgius, 83n15,
Charles, R. H., 123
Charlesworth, James H., 16n7, 17n9, 59n14, 61n26, 116n28, 118n41, 190n57, 264n19, 270n51, 330n11
Cheung, Luke L., 295n10, 299n32
Chilton, Bruce, 62n28, 65n35
Clivaz, Claire, 80n1
Coblentz Bautch, Kelley, 8n55, 111n10, 186n43, 312n12
Collins, John J., 1n5, 2n10, 5n28, 6, 16nn3–4, 24n35, 26nn44–45, 30n57, 32nn2,4–8, 33nn9,12, 34n15, 37n36, 38, 45n80, 75n67, 85n24, 110–11, 126nn81–82, 135n12, 176n5, 177–78, 183nn33–34, 184n38, 189, 190n57, 192, 219n1, 220, 234n5, 237n26, 241n55, 246nn2–3, 249n22, 260n5, 279n11, 280n12, 288n27, 293–94, 307n1, 309–10, 320n37, 321, 327n1, 328n3, 329n5, 333n20, 338nn34,36
Collins, R. F., 266nn34–35, 267n39
Como, D., 146n33
Conzelmann, Hans, 79, 178n15, 182n29, 188n50, 264n21, 265n25
Cook, Stephen, 327n2
Coppens, Joseph, 227n31, 264n19
Crossan, John Dominic, 2n7

Dalton, William Joseph, 312, 314–15
Danker, Frederick William, 119n48
Davids, Peter H., 296, 302n49, 322n40
Davidson, Maxwell J., 83n13, 84n20
Davies, W. D., 40n57, 45n84, 46n86–87, 47n90, 146
de Boer, Martinus C., 2nn10,13, 8n53, 176, 182n32, 193, 219n1, 233–34, 249n22, 251n41, 279n11
de Jonge, M., 61n25

De Long, Kindalee Pfremmer, 10, 87nn45–46, 88n49, 89nn52,55, 90n58
de Villiers, Pieter G. R., 91n62
DeBuhn, Jason, 186n43
deSilva, David A., 287, 348n3, 351n10
Dewey, A. J., 133n8, 190n58
Dibelius, Martin, 24n38, 223n14, 264n21, 265n25, 297
Dimant, Devorah, 188n51, 332, 340
DiTommaso, Lorenzo, 2n14, 4n26, 5, 6n36, 32nn2,8, 177n10, 307n1
Dochhorn, Jan, 354
Dodd, C. H., 28n49, 124–25
Dodson, Joseph R., 161
Doering, Lutz, 157n12, 196n9
Donfried, Karl P., 250nn31–32, 253n52
Drury, John, 18nn12–13
Dunn, James D. G., 2n10, 136n18, 156n5, 223, 247n12, 261n11, 353n15

Easton, B. S., 267n40
Eco, Umberto, 343–44
Edson, Charles, 253n52
Ehrman, Bart D., 2n6, 80n1, 322n42, 328nn3–4
Eichrodt, Walther, 44n78
Ellingworth, Paul, 282n16, 285n19
Elliott, John, 308n2, 312, 316n25
Ellis, E. E., 334n24
Endres, John, 186n43, 312n12
Evans, Craig A., 223n17, 330n12
Eynikel, Erik, 119n48

Fabry, H.-J., 240n44
Fallon, Francis T., 260n5
Fee, Gordon, 249n21, 250n29, 255
Fitzmyer, Joseph A., 93n69, 157, 164n40, 168n50, 170nn53,58, 173nn64–65, 187
Fletcher-Louis, Crispin, 6n36, 7n41, 170, 245n1, 249n22
Flint, Peter W., 280n12
Förster, Hans, 239n39
Fossum, J. E., 90n60, 134n10
Foster, Paul, 252, 255, 256n69
Francis, Fred O., 134n9, 223–24
Freidenreich, David M., 332n15
Frennesson, Björn, 187n46
Fretheim, Terence E., 206n36
Frey, Jörg, 2n9, 110n6, 182n28, 230n37, 317–18, 319n33, 330n12, 331n13, 335n27, 338nn33,35
Friedländer, Paul, 199n18
Friedrich, Gerhard, 42n68, 46n87

Garrett, Susan R., 81nn3,5, 89n57
Gathercole, Simon, 86n35, 285n19
Gaventa, Beverly Roberts, 2n12, 209n50
Gerhardsson, Birger, 46n86
Gibson, Jeffrey B., 46n87
Gieschen, Charles A., 30n60, 44n78
Gilbert, M., 295n8, 296n16, 297–98, 301–2, 305
Gladd, Benjamin, 179n18
Gnilka, Joachim, 239n38
Goff, Matthew J., 180nn21–23, 181n25, 182n27, 230n37, 334n25
Gooder, Paula R., 138n24
Goodrich, John K., 2n15, 356n25
Goulder, Michael, 271
Gowler, David B., 304n56
Grabbe, Lester L., 5n29
Gressmann, Hugo, 37n42
Griffith-Jones, Robin, 58n13, 76

Griffiths, Jonathan I., 279n10
Grindheim, Sigurd, 181n24
Grossman, Maxine, 67n45
Gundry, Robert H., 40n57, 41n65, 46n86
Gunkel, Hermann, 157n12
Gurtner, Daniel M., 33n13, 36–37, 48nn93,95, 261n9

Haenchen, Ernst, 124n73
Hagner, Donald A., 31n1, 34n16, 35–36, 40n57, 41n65, 47nn89–91, 50n105
Hahne, Harry A., 157n13, 158n14, 161n28, 162n33
Hall, David D., 141n26
Halperin, David J., 131n2
Hamid-Khani, Saeed, 117–18
Hannah, Darrell D., 30n59, 37n41, 38nn46,49, 49n99
Hanneken, Todd R., 6n36
Hansen, M. H., 239n39
Hanson, P. D., 260n6
Harding, Mark, 265n30, 268n47, 269n49, 270n53, 272nn59,63
Hare, Douglas R. A., 47n90
Harrington, Daniel J., 40n57, 47n90
Harris, Angela Kim, 312n12
Harrison, James R., 267n38
Harrison, P. N., 266–67, 269n50
Hartin, Patrick, 294n3, 298, 300n38, 302n48, 303, 305
Hauspie, Katrin, 119n48
Hawthorne, G. F., 235n14, 236n19, 239n38, 243n63
Hays, Richard B., 43n73, 299
Hedley, Douglas, 149
Hedrick, Charles, 18n13
Heidegger, Martin, 199n18
Heil, John Paul, 16n6, 29n51, 91n61
Hempel, Charlotte, 230n37, 336n29
Hengel, Martin, 216n73, 260n4
Henze, Matthias, 3nn18,20, 20n18, 28n47, 159n25, 166n46, 184n39, 185nn40–41, 208n42
Herling, Bradley, 332n14
Hermaniuk, Maxime, 20
Hiebert, D. Edmond, 300n34
Hieke, Thomas, 348n3
Hill, David, 41n65
Hills, Julian Victor, 104n101
Himmelfarb, Martha, 8nn50,54,56, 58n12, 115n22, 189n54
Höfchen, Heinz, 347n1
Hoffmann, Paul, 234n11
Hogan, Karina Martin, 4n21, 161nn30,32
Hogeterp, Albert., 188n52, 189n53, 190n59
Hooker, Morna D., 41n66, 209n48
Hultgren, Stephen, 182n27, 338n34
Humphries-Brooks, Stephenson, 268n46
Hurtado, Larry W., 38n43

Jassen, Alex P., 7n47
Jeremias, J., 66
Jewett, Robert, 157n10, 159n22, 161, 164n41, 165n43, 168n47
Johns, Loren L., 350n6, 359n31
Johnson, Luke Timothy, 94n77
Johnson, Timothy Jay, 6n36
Jülicher, Adolf, 23, 330n9
Jung, F., 240nn46,48,49, 241n50

Kamell, Mariam J., 296n17, 201n46
Kanagaraj, Jey J., 116n29

Karrer, Martin, 280n12, 348n3
Käsemann, Ernst, 1, 2n5, 9, 109n1, 132, 155–56, 159nn22–23, 163n37, 165nn43–44, 176, 233, 246, 259n2, 260n7, 262nn12–13, 265nn24,30, 270
Keck, Leander E., 176n6
Kee, Howard Clark, 24, 158n19, 341n46, 342n47
Kelber, Werner H., 20n19, 24
Kilpatrick, G. D., 235n15
Kim, Seyoon, 137n21
Kirk, J. Andrew, 297, 298n25
Klauck, Hans-Josef, 145n31, 196nn8–9
Klein, Hans, 82n7, 89n56, 296
Klink III, Edward W., 111n11, 115n20
Knibb, Michael A., 7n46, 8n49, 121n58
Knowling, R. J., 303
Knox, J., 133n6, 146
Koch, Klaus, 5, 109n2, 219–20, 294, 309n5, 320n37
Koester, Craig R., 117n36, 282n15, 285n19, 351n12, 355n22
Kovacs, Judith L., 114n18
Kugler, Robert, 341n45
Kuhn, Harold Barnes, 37n41, 38n45
Kulik, Alexander, 116n26, 122n66
Kupp, David D., 44, 48n98

Lane, William L., 279, 287
Lang, Amy Schrager, 141n26
Lange, Armin, 221nn6,8, 230n37, 260n4, 332n18, 336n29, 339n39
Laws, Sophie, 299n32
Lee, Dorothy, 16n5
Lee, Simon S., 25nn40–41, 29n53
Lemke, W. E., 4n26, 134n11, 288n27
Leonhardt-Balzer, Jutta, 113–14
Lewis, Scott M., 186nn43,45, 187n48
Lied, Liv Ingebord, 21n25, 28n47
Lieu, Judith, 328n4
Lincoln, Andrew T., 124n72, 152n43, 227, 228n33, 229, 230n39
Lincoln, Bruce, 332n15
Lohmeyer, Ernst, 239n38, 330n9, 355n23
Lohse, Eduard, 222–23
Longenecker, Bruce W., 136n18, 159n22, 168n48, 301n46
Lucas, Alec J., 158n18
Luckensmyer, David, 249n21, 250n32, 252n44
Lüderitz, G., 239n39
Lührmann, 265n27
Luz, Ulrich, 39n55, 41n65, 42nn66,67, 44n79, 50, 136–37

Macaskill, Grant, 135n14, 151n41
MacCulloch, Diarmaid, 152n42
MacDonald, Dennis R., 272n59
MacDonald, Margaret Y., 264n20
Mackie, Scott D., 278, 282n17, 285n19, 287–88
Maddox, Robert, 41n66
Malherbe, Abraham J., 248n19
Manson, T. W., 66n42
Marcus, Joel, 26n43, 29, 34n18, 60n19, 65–66, 176n5, 261n10, 268n46
Marguerat, Daniel, 41n63
Marshall, I. H., 266n31
Martin, Dale, 156n3
Martin, R. P. 235n14, 236n19, 239n38, 243n63
Martin, Séan Charles, 268n48
Martínez, Florentio García, 67n45, 230nn37,40, 240n43, 260n4
Martyn, J. Louis, 2n12, 34n18, 112n15, 132–33,

175n1, 176n5, 193–94, 246, 251n40, 261n11, 268n46
Mason, Eric F., 278n1, 323n44
Maston, Jason, 2n15, 356n25
Mathews, Mark D., 350n7
Matlock, R. Barry, 175n1, 262n13
Maynard-Reid, Pedrito U., 300n39
Mayordomo, Moisés, 145n31
McCartney, Dan, 295, 302n48, 303n54
McCruden, Kevin B., 278n1
McGinn, B., 135, 176n5, 294n4
McKnight, Scot, 299n33, 302n48
Meadowcroft, T. J., 158n52
Meeks, Wayne A., 134n9, 209n50, 223n14, 253–54, 255n63, 256
Meier, John P., 258n28, 328n3
Meritt, B. D., 240n49
Metso, Sarianna, 336n29
Michaels, J. Ramsey, 124n72
Milik, Józef T., 177n9, 338n33
Miller, John B. F., 102n95
Miller, P. D., 4n26, 134n11, 288n27
Miller, R. D., 29n53
Mitchell, Margaret, 143
Moffitt, David M., 281n14
Moloney, Francis J., 118n41
Moore, Carey A., 95
Morray-Jones, Christopher R. A., 4n22, 5n29, 56n6, 69nn52,54,55, 88, 110n6, 115n21, 116n29, 118n42, 134nn9–10, 138n23, 139n25, 144n30, 150n40, 152n43, 188n52, 189nn53, 190n59, 191n60, 247n13, 254, 280n13, 298n29, 300n37, 304n57
Morris, Leon, 47n90
Motyer, Steven, 285n19
Moule, C. F. D., 133n6, 146, 151n41
Mounce, Robert H., 356n23
Mounce, William D., 267n37
Muddiman, John, 219n2, 226–27, 229n36
Mullen, E. Theodore, 38n44
Müller, Hans-Peter, 7n43
Müller, Ulrich B., 3n17, 255n23
Murphy, Frederick J., 1, 5nn32,34 32nn2–3, 33n13, 37nn36,41, 109n2, 194n4, 247n15, 248n18, 250n25, 293n1, 301, 305, 329n5
Murphy-O'Connor, J., 227n31, 264n19, 270n51, 336n29
Muβner, Franz, 296n14, 303

Najman, Hindy, 126n82
Neufeld, Thomas Yoder, 229n34
Newsom, Carol A., 6n36, 67n45, 69n51, 87n42, 88n50, 89n53, 288n27, 333
Nickelsburg, G. W. E., 4nn24,27, 19n16, 20n21, 21n22, 24n37, 25n41, 69n53, 85n27, 88n49, 95n79, 115n24, 121nn56,59, 122, 158n20, 179n20, 183n34, 190n57, 194–98, 200n19, 201–17, 237n28, 242n56, 243n63, 252n43, 261n8, 268n46, 296n18
Nicklas, Tobias, 33n8, 48nn93,96, 49n99, 82n7, 188n52, 241n55, 348n3
Nolland, John, 46n86, 82n7, 87n44, 88, 92n66
Nongbri, Brent, 268n46

O'Brien, Peter T., 236n19, 279
Odeberg, Hugo, 116n28, 125, 226n27
Oegema, Gerbern S., 256n66
Olav, Karl, 202n25
Olyan, Saul M., 45n79
Orlov, Andrei, 17n10, 116n25, 126n81, 311n10

Osburn, Caroll D., 320n35

Pagels, Elaine, 271n56, 272nn63
Parsons, Mikeal Carl, 93n69, 94n75
Patte, Daniel, 47n90
Peeler, Amy L. B., 278n4, 279n8, 282n17, 286n22
Penner, Todd C., 298n28, 305
Pennington, Jonathan T., 8n56, 51n107, 111n11
Pentiuc, Eugen J., 28n48
Perdue, Leo G., 297n19
Perkins, Pheme, 323n46
Pesch, Rudolf, 72n60
Petersen, David L., 55n4
Pierce, Chad T., 312nn11–12
Pierce, Madison N., 112n14
Plunkett, Mark A., 80n1
Pomykala, Kenneth E., 280n12
Poplutz, Uta, 236nn17,19
Portier-Young, Anathea, 327n2
Priest, J., 320n36

Quinby, Lee, 329, 337

Räisänen, Heiki, 63n32
Reed, Annette Yoshiko, 17n10
Reeves, John, 339n39
Reicke, Bo, 312, 316n24
Reumann, J., 24n36, 239n38
Rey, Jean-Sébastin, 156n9, 176n4, 230–31
Reynolds III, Bennie H., 6n36, 221n6, 327n2
Reynolds, Benjamin E., 22n27, 33n13, 112nn13–14, 291n34
Richard, Earl J., 257n73
Ridderbos, Herman, 116–17, 124–25
Robinson, Howard, 332n17
Robinson, Theodore, 47n90
Roloff, Jürgen, 355n22
Ropes, J. H., 297
Rosen-Zvi, Ishay, 163n39
Rowe, Robert D., 59n15, 60n16
Rowland, Christopher, 4–5, 33–34, 37nn36,41, 38n46,47, 45n79,82, 56, 69, 88, 102n96, 103, 109n2, 110n6, 114n17, 115, 116n29, 118n42, 119n47, 134nn9,10, 137n22, 138n23, 139n25, 143n28, 144n30, 146n33,148n37, 150n40, 152n43, 178n12, 188n52, 189n53, 190n59, 191n60, 224, 233, 246–47, 254, 259n1, 260n3, 261n11, 278, 280, 298, 300n37, 304n57, 307n1, 347n1
Royalty, Robert M., 350n7
Rubinkiewicz, R., 17n9
Rudolph, Kurt, 272n58
Rusam, D., 222n11
Russell, D. S., 38nn42,46

Sabourin, Leopold, 31n1, 35–36, 47n91
Sanders, E. P., 131–32, 151, 156n5
Sänger, Patrick, 239n39
Sappington, Thomas J., 223n17
Schäfer, Peter, 132, 190n56, 191n60
Schmithals, W., 60n18
Scholem, Gershom, 131, 133, 134n10, 146n32, 190nn55,58
Schüle, Andreas , 18n13, 19n15
Schweitzer, Albert, 2, 132, 135–36, 146n32, 151n41, 155, 233, 246, 328n3
Schweizer, Eduard, 206
Scott, James M., 197n12
Segal, Alan F., 132, 261n11
Setzer, Claudia, 24n37

Senior, Donald, 47n90
Shantz, Colleen, 137, 150n40
Shively, Elizabeth, 60n20, 61
Sim, David C., 36, 40n57, 43n71, 50n106
Smith, Jonathan Z., 7n43, 195, 332
Snodgrass, Klyne, 42n69, 66–67
Sprinkle, Preston, 158n15, 169n52, 170nn57–58, 171nn59,61, 173n65
Squires, John T., 81n6, 87n46
Standhartinger, Angela, 234n7, 243n61
Stein, Robert H., 28n49, 29n55
Steudel, Annette, 339n41
Stone, Michael E., 3n18, 4nn25–26, 5n34, 6, 7nn40,42, 8, 19n14, 61n25, 134, 158n17, 159n25, 160n27, 184n37, 204n29, 288n27, 290n32, 294nn3,5,6, 295n8, 327n1, 338n33
Strawbridge, Jennifer R., 141n27
Strecker, Georg, 328n4, 335
Stroumsa, G., 134n10
Strugnell, John, 339n41
Stuckenbruck, Loren T., 2n11, 3n19, 30n58, 40nn58,61, 48n95, 114, 122, 152–53, 156nn7,9, 176, 186nn43–44, 194n5, 198n17, 221nn6,8, 223–24, 231n41, 312n12, 332n18, 333n19, 353n15, 354n18, 356nn24–25, 358n27
Stuhlmann, Rainer, 208n43
Stuhlmueller, Carol, 206n36
Sullivan, Kevin P., 91n63
Suter, David, 19n15
Sysling, Harry, 164n42

Tamez, Elsa, 302n49
Tannehill, Robert C., 93
Taubes, J., 146
Taylor, Richard A., 91n64
Thiselton, A. C., 148n37
Thomas, Samuel I., 18n11
Thompson, Leonard L., 353n15, 356n24
Thyen, Hartwig, 124n72
Tigchelaar, Eibert, 55n3, 62, 240n43
Tilborg, Sjef Van, 117n40
Tiller, Patrick, 327n2
Tomson, Peter J., 149
Tooman, William, 55n3
Towner, Philip H., 265n29
Trebilco, Paul, 217nn75,78
Tresley, Richard, 347n1
Tuschling, R. M. M., 44n78
Tóth, Franz, 353n15

Urbach, E. E., 131–32

VanderKam, James C., 4nn24,27, 16n7, 19n16, 21n23, 81n4, 83n14, 85n25, 121nn56,59, 122, 190n57, 194n5, 209n48, 215n72, 217n75, 242n56, 280n12, 289n30, 296n18, 330n12, 338n33, 341n45
Vermes, Geza, 328n3
Vielhauer, Paul, 1, 109n1
Vollenwieder, Samuel, 185n39
von Dobschütz, E., 330n9
von Lips, Hermann, 181n24
von Rad, Gerhard, 7n43, 38n42, 44n78, 294n6
Von Wahlde, Urban C., 124n73

Wachob, Wesley Hiram, 306
Waldron, Jeremy, 147n36
Wanamaker, Charles A., 250n28, 251n34, 252n46
Waters, Sr., Kenneth L., 48n93

Watson, Duane F., 248n17, 249n24, 250n26, 251n35, 253n48, 306n65, 323n45, 324n48
Watts, Rikki, 57n7, 65n34, 68n47
Weissenrieder, Annette, 349n3
Westermann, Claus, 162n34
Whitaker, Robyn J., 348n3, 358n29
Wilder, Amos N., 19n15, 20n17, 261n10, 263n18
Williams, Catrin H., 109n2, 114n17, 117n33, 119n47, 121n53
Williamson, H. G. M., 334n24
Wills, Lawrence M., 7n43, 21n26
Wintermute, O. S., 61n26
Witherington III, Ben, 93n71, 95n80
Witulski, Thomas, 353n15
Wold, Benjamin G., 230n40
Wolter, Michael, 266n36, 268n46, 270n53
Wrede, Wilhelm, 2n8, 24n39, 63, 328n3
Wright, Archie, 61n21, 62n28, 312n12
Wright, Benjamin G., 7n43, 21n26
Wright, N. T., 75, 193–94, 261n9, 301n42

Yarbro Collins, Adela, 1n5, 6n35, 8n52, 8n57, 17n8, 18n13, 20n18, 24n35, 28n49, 54n1, 57, 58n9, 60n17, 62n29, 63nn31,32, 66n41, 70, 72nn59,63, 73n64, 109n2, 184n36, 220, 243n62, 268n46, 291n34, 356n24

Zuschlag, Christoph, 347n1